Withdrawn

THE DETROIT PISTONS
Four Decades of Motor City Memories

by
Steve Addy

Sports Publishing Inc.
a division of Sagamore Publishing

©1997 Steve Addy

Interior design and layout: Michelle R. Dressen
Editor: Susan M. McKinney
Cover and color section design: Deborah M. Bellaire

ISBN: 1-57167-144-7
Library of Congress catalog card number: 97-80343

Printed in the United States.

www.sagamorepub.com

This book is sincerely dedicated to
Tom and Gail Addy, who taught me to love words;
to absent friends Shelby Strother and Corky Meinecke;
and to everyone who reads the sports section first.

Table of Contents

ACKNOWLEDGMENTS

Because this is my first book, there is a temptation to thank everybody who has ever helped me, in case I never get another chance. When you're a 34-year-old sportswriter and you've never been envious of someone else's job, it means you have a lot of people to thank.

Space and foggy memory prevent acknowledging everyone, but I want to express my sincere gratitude to those who helped this book become a reality and to others who gave me the wherewithal to write it.

First and foremost, thanks to the Detroit Pistons organization, especially Palace Sports and Entertainment President Thomas S. Wilson, and Vice President of Public Relations Matt Dobek and their respective staffs. Wilson provided unfailing support and agreed to license the book, but never once attempted to sanitize its contents or make it an "in-house" publication; such courage and integrity are indeed rare. Dobek and his staff were professional and cooperative from the start and invaluable in helping me do research and gather photos. For this, thanks to media relations director Bill Wickett and assistants Sue Emerick and Brian Bierley. The latter was especially helpful with the appendices. Elsewhere in the organization, thanks to John Ciszewski, Dan Hauser, Ron Campbell, Lou Korpas, Steve Moreland, Judy Romero, Nancy Bontumasi, Michelle Yaros and Steve Stuckey. Also, thanks to former Pistons PR directors George Maskin, Brian Hitsky and Bill Kriefeldt, whose work helped simplify the research.

I also wish to thank the talented staff at Sagamore Publishing. My undying gratitude to Mike Pearson, who phoned me in February 1997 and said, "How would you like to write a Pistons book for us?" My thanks to him for showing me how to do it. I am indebted to Peter Bannon for his counsel, and to Michelle Dressen, Susan McKinney and Deborah Bellaire for their design and editing skills and Bret Kroencke for his diligent marketing.

Many thanks to Allen Einstein, whose marvelous photography appears throughout the book. Thanks to Morrie Moorawnick for the use of his old photo collection and Joe Abramson for his sharp memory. Special thanks to Joe Dumars for writing the foreword and to Pistons players and coaches, past and present, even those who vowed never to speak to me again. Also, thanks to *The Oakland Press* for use of its microfilm, which contains the excellent work of past beat writers Jere Craig, Jack O'Connell, Mark Skaer and Keith Langlois. *The Flint Journal* was also generous in allowing me access to its archives.

Now, some personal thanks. To my parents, Tom and Gail Addy, who taught me to read the newspaper by age four; to my brothers, Mike, John and Chuck, and sister Mary, who indulge my absences to do the job I love; to Bessie Boucher, for bragging about me to her friends; and to Colleen (Weston) Rebock, my most cherished friend, for reasons she understands better than anyone. For their friendship and encouragement over the years, I also thank Mark and Dana Newton (and Samantha and Ryan, whom I adore as my own), Rex Gurniak, Brent Lavanway, George Pushies, Danielle Brownfield, Shelley Vollmar, Mike Arkush, Ken Wensel, Pam Bunka, Joe Falls, Dean Howe, Dave Poniers, Bill Khan, Brendan Savage, Don Beil and Jeannie Roberts.

— Steve Addy
September 15, 1997

By Joe Dumars

Joe Dumars — Piston for life. Photo by Allen Einstein.

When the Detroit Pistons picked me 18th in the 1985 NBA draft, some of their fans probably reacted with one word: either "Who?" or "Why?" Not only because the Pistons had passed on local favorite Sam Vincent, the high-scoring Michigan State standout, but because they already had three fantastic guards—Isiah Thomas, Vinnie Johnson and John Long.

I, too, was asking, "Why?" and "Where?" I knew Detroit was loaded at guard. I also knew Detroit gets cold in the winter. Being a Louisiana kid raised on Cajun delicacies, it wasn't easy picturing myself in a strange northern city, wearing a winter coat six months of the year. I arrived with high hopes, but my expectations were somewhat down the scale.

But after playing 12 seasons with the Pistons, Detroit is my home. My original uncertainty off the court disappeared years ago, largely due to the amazing hospitality I was shown from Day 1. On the court, I quickly realized this team had a promising future. That growth process was not fast or painless, but it paid off richly with two NBA championships and memories that will live forever.

This book is a catalog of those memories.

In these pages, longtime NBA reporter Steve Addy has pulled together four decades of Detroit Pistons basketball to present a team history of unprecedented completeness. It is a book to be savored, a year-by-year account of a franchise that arrived from Fort Wayne in 1957 and had to establish pro basketball in a city that hadn't previously embraced it. It was a long and sometimes frustrating climb, but we know how it ends; the banners in the Palace rafters are the visible reminders. Now, as we move toward a new millenium, Grant Hill makes us confident that more banners will one day be hung.

In that spirit, this is an encyclopedia of fun. If you want a diagram of an illegal defense or a detailed translation of the salary cap, you won't find them here. If you're seeking a rehash of brief "controversies" that don't hold up in the historical context, you won't find that either. You'll find thousands of facts and figures, stars and stats, Bad Boys and great players. You'll find games you remember and names you forgot. All told, you'll find an entertaining, easy-to-read history of your favorite team, and mine. I'm proud and honored to be a part of it.

A Message from the Palace Sports and Entertainment President

Dear Readers,

Let me be the first to thank you for remembering the first 40 years of Detroit Pistons Basketball in this book. As the Pistons begin their 41st NBA season in Detroit, I myself am beginning my 21st season with the club and some of the memories I have, both as an employee and as a fan, seem to define different periods in life. We all have those precious few memories that make time stand still; maybe your wedding day, the birth of a child, important moments in history and yes, certain sporting events.

I know most of the people reading this book remember Vinnie Johnson's game-winning shot in Game Five of the 1990 NBA Finals as if it happened yesterday. For Detroiters, that moment was no different than Kirk Gibson's home run versus the San Diego Padres as the Detroit Tigers won the 1984 World Series, or the night Isiah Thomas scored 16 points in 94 seconds for the Pistons versus the New York Knicks in the 1984 NBA Playoffs. Each of those events is indelibly etched in our minds. One mention of a specific moment and we instantly remember how old we were, where we were watching the game, what we were doing and the people with whom we shared that moment.

The memories of those events do not just begin and end with one individual, they dominate an entire community's focus. Everyone, whether the most ardent basketball follower or the most casual sports observer, becomes a "fan" of the local team in the truest sense of the word during the postseason. The team, once referred to by its fans as "them," becomes "us." Meet a stranger on the street and talk quickly turns to the championship team. Detroit in particular is one of America's great sporting communities, because its people, our fans, have such a passion for their champions. Field a winning team and nothing else seems to matter to Detroiters.

Sporting events are magic, maybe more than any other form of entertainment, because they possess that wonderful power to make time stand still in our minds. And that magical, powerful event can happen at any time. Nobody knew that Wilt Chamberlain was going to score 100 points for the Philadelphia Warriors versus the New York Knicks on March 2, 1962, but after it happened, it became an event that helped frame our lives. It became a reference point on the timeline of life for people in the 1960s.

I think this retrospective of Detroit Pistons Basketball by Steve Addy of *The Oakland Press* will rekindle those same types of memories for Pistons fans everywhere. Sweet memories of "BINGO" ringing out through Cobo Arena as Dave Bing would swish a 20-foot jumper. Classical memories of Bob Lanier clashing in the paint versus Kareem Abdul-Jabaar. Muggy memories of huge crowds on springtime evenings during the postseason at the Pontiac Silverdome. Painful memories of Isiah spraining his right ankle in Game Six of the 1988 NBA Finals versus the Los Angeles Lakers. Joyful memories of our NBA World Championship victory parades marching up Woodward Avenue from Hart Plaza to The Palace of Auburn Hills.

Memories...some were sorrowful, but many more were gleeful, and now as I reflect back on those memories I can not help but look into the future, when Grant Hill holds that trophy high above his head as he rides up Three Championship Drive...

Sincerely,

Tom Wilson
President

"ZOLLNER'S PISTONS"
THE FORT WAYNE YEARS

Pistons founder and owner Fred Zollner — "The Z" — added the Pistons to Detroit's sports landscape in 1957. Photo from Morrie Moorawnick collection.

Former referee Charlie Eckman coached Fort Wayne to two straight NBA Finals, then was the Pistons' first coach in Detroit. Photo from Morrie Moorawnick collection.

On February 14, 1957, when Fort Wayne piston magnate Fred Zollner signed an agreement to relocate his basketball team to Detroit, where much of his business was transacted, the decision wasn't without risk.

After all, he didn't have a bad thing going in Fort Wayne. His Pistons—the nickname was a holdover from the industrial league days—had won two straight division crowns, losing the NBA Finals both years, and had developed a devoted corps of fans over 16 seasons.

"We were big in Fort Wayne," Pistons star George Yardley would later say. "We were held up as heroes."

In addition, Zollner's team was heading to a city where pro basketball had largely failed. Detroit's first National Basketball League entry, the Eagles, won the 1941 World Tournament at Chicago, but soon disbanded because of World War II. Of Detroit's three subsequent teams in the NBL and the Basketball Association of America (BAA), two folded after only one season and the third left town in midseason.

But realizing a need to better compete with thriving teams in Boston, New York and Philadelphia, Zollner knew the Pistons couldn't last much longer in Fort Wayne. Louisville and Milwaukee were briefly considered, but Detroit, with a vast blue-collar population, was the natural landing spot. It also didn't hurt that Detroit was sports-crazy over the NHL Red Wings and NFL Lions, both in their heyday.

So on March 19, 1957, when Fort Wayne hosted the Minneapolis Lakers at Allen County War Memorial Coliseum, its home court since 1952, the lame-duck Pistons played their final game in their original incarnation. They were beaten 110-108 in Game 2 of the Western Semifinals, losing the series 2-0 to halt their two-year streak of NBA Finals appearances. There would be no fairy-tale finish for Zollner's Fort Wayne Pistons.

But what an era it had been. Through much of the '40s, Fort Wayne had been the magnetic center of the pro basketball world.

Having joined in 1941, the Pistons quickly became the NBL's top team, racking up a 101-32 record on their way to four straight division titles ('43-46), two playoff titles ('44-45) and three straight 16-team World Tournament championships ('44-46).

The Pistons' first star, unquestionably, was 5-11 pepperpot guard Bob McDermott, their leading scorer each of their first five seasons, with a high of 20.3 in '44-45, their best season (25-5). A New York-bred high-school dropout, McDermott was famous for his long-range two-hand set shot as well as his ferocious temper. In '45, after he helped the Pistons rally from an 0-2 deficit to beat Sheboygan in the best-of-five finals, NBL coaches voted McDermott as the best pro basketball player in history.

But McDermott was dealt to the Chicago Gears in '46 after he brawled with teammate Milo Komenich on a losing Eastern road trip. The Pistons—Fort Wayne or Detroit—didn't win another championship for 43 years.

In 1948, the Pistons and three NBL teams were absorbed into the BAA, and the two leagues merged a year later. Their new conglomeration was dubbed the National Basketball Association.

Success was slower coming to Fort Wayne in the NBA. In the first five seasons, despite three over-.500 records, the Pistons finished no higher than third and never got past the second playoff round. But at least they traveled in style, flying around on Zollner's DC-3, called "The Flying Z." Fort Wayne players were the envy of their contemporaries.

And they made history, too. On November 22, 1950, the Pistons defeated the host Minneapolis Lakers 19-18 in the lowest-scoring NBA game ever. It was a leading impetus for the addition of the 24-second shot clock, the rule change that surely saved the NBA from failure.

Then in 1954, the Pistons became the first (and only) pro sports team to hire a referee as coach. Zollner hired veteran NBA ref Charlie Eckman on a whim, more or less, but the move ushered in the last great era of Fort Wayne basketball. Eckman, acid-tongued, glib and driven, was a good fit. He had never coached, but his refereeing experience made him a natural.

"I have been booed by the best fans in the world," he told the Pistons' booster club upon his introduction. "I hope you were among them."

Sparked by scoring king Larry Foust (17.0 ppg), playmaker Andy Phillip (7.7 apg) and George Yardley, who had joined in '53, the Pistons won the Western Division with a 43-29 mark in Eckman's first season. They lost to the Syracuse Nationals in the seven-game Finals, blowing a 17-point first-half lead in Game 7 and losing 92-91 on a George King free throw.

The Pistons got back to the Finals in '56, but were beaten 4-1 by Paul Arizin and the Philadelphia Warriors. In '57, having acquired guard Gene Shue, Fort Wayne tied for its third straight division crown. But the impending move to Detroit, announced on a heartbreaking Valentine's Day, had cost the club much of its support. Only 2,212 fans witnessed the final game, the playoff loss to Minneapolis on March 19.

There were no guarantees that the Pistons would draw better at their new home base.

Detroit had essentially ignored pro basketball. The Eagles, coached by former Original Celtics star "Dutch" Dehnert, created a brief sensation in two NBL seasons (1939-41), winning the '41 World Tournament. They beat the Oshkosh All-Stars 39-37 in the finals after upsetting the best all-black clubs of the day, the New York Rens and Harlem Globetrotters.

But the Eagles broke up because of the war, and three postwar teams could not pick up their fallen standard. Detroit had two teams in 1946-47, the NBL's Gems and BAA's Falcons, the latter housed at Olympia and operated by the Norris family of Red Wings fame. The Gems went 4-40, finished last and folded. Stan Miasek was third in the BAA in scoring at 14.9 points per game, but the Falcons went only 20-40 and closed shop. In 1948-49, the Detroit Vagabond Kings, one final NBL team, lived up to their name by moving to Dayton at midseason, nursing a 2-17 record.

The void lasted for eight years before Zollner decided that his Pistons could fill it. Coach Eckman and six players—Yardley, Shue, Chuck Noble, Bob Houbregs, Bill Kenville and Bill Thieben—migrated 150 miles north to the Motor City, hoping to finally sell the locals on pro basketball.

In his introductory address to Detroit fans, Zollner wrote: "All season long, Major League Basketball will be presented. This is a clean, rugged sport, played by superbly developed athletes of intelligence. I hope that you'll enjoy seeing these great stars playing under the modern rules (in the) ideal playing conditions at Olympia Stadium."

Thus begins the colorful history of the Detroit Pistons.

FORT WAYNE PISTONS
Yearly Records
NATIONAL BASKETBALL LEAGUE (NBL)

Season	Record	Finish	Playoffs
1941-42	15-9	2nd	y-3-3
1942-43	17-6	1st	y-3-3
1943-44	18-4	1st	xz-5-0
1944-45	25-5	1st	xz-3-2
1945-46	26-8	1st Eastern	z-1-3
1946-47	25-19	2nd Eastern	4-4
1947-48	40-20	3rd Eastern	1-3
NBL TOTAL	**166-71**		**20-18**

BASKETBALL ASSN. of AMERICA (BAA)

Season	Record	Finish	Playoffs
1948-49	22-38	5th Western	DNQ

NATIONAL BASKETBALL ASSN. (NBA)

Season	Record	Finish	Playoffs
1949-50	40-28	3rd Central	2-2
1950-51	32-36	3rd Western	1-2
1951-52	29-37	4th Western	0-2
1952-53	36-33	3rd Western	4-4
1953-54	40-32	3rd Western	0-4
1954-55	43-29	1st Western	y-6-5
1955-56	37-35	1st Western	y-4-6
1956-57	34-38	1st Western	0-2
NBA TOTAL	**313-306**		**17-27**
OVERALL	**479-377**		**37-45**

x-won championship series
y-lost championship series
z-won World Tournament

Detroit NBL Entries
Yearly Records
DETROIT EAGLES

Season	Record	Finish	Playoffs
1939-40	Records unavailable		
1940-41	z-Records unavailable		

z-won World Tournament

DETROIT GEMS

Season	Record	Finish	Playoffs
1946-47	4-40	6th Western	DNQ

DETROIT VAGABOND KINGS

Season	Record	Finish	Playoffs
1948-49	2-17	6th Western	—

(Moved to Dayton in midseason)

Detroit BAA Entry
Yearly Record
DETROIT FALCONS

Season	Record	Finish	Playoffs
1946-47	20-40	4th Western	DNQ

1957 1958

TIME CAPSULE

October 4, 1957:
The Soviet Union launches Sputnik I, the first Earth satellite.

December 29, 1957:
The Detroit Lions win their fourth NFL championship, defeating the Cleveland Browns, 59-14, at Tiger Stadium.

March 25, 1958:
Sugar Ray Robinson beats Carmen Basilio, regaining the world middleweight boxing title for an unprecedented fifth time.

SEASON SNAPSHOT

Most Points
x-George Yardley (2,001, 27.8 avg.)

Most Rebounds
Walter Dukes (954, 13.3 avg.)

Most Assists
Dick McGuire (454, 6.6 avg.)

Most Minutes
George Yardley (2,843, 39.5 avg.)

Field-Goal Percentage
George Yardley (41.3%)

Free-Throw Percentage
Gene Shue (84.4%)

Team Offense Average
105.3 (7,585 in 72 games)

Team Defense Average
107.7 (7,754 in 72 games)

All-NBA Team
George Yardley, F (First Team)

Pistons in All-Star Game
George Yardley, F; Gene Shue, G; Dick McGuire, G

x-led league

1957-58

FINAL STANDINGS

Western Division	W	L	Pct.	GB
St. Louis	41	31	.569	—
PISTONS	**33**	**39**	**.458**	**8**
Cincinnati	33	39	.458	8
Minneapolis	19	53	.264	22

Eastern Division Winner—Boston

PLAYOFF RESULTS

Western Semifinals: Pistons d. Cincinnati, 2-0
Western Finals: St. Louis d. Pistons, 4-1

PISTONS PLAYOFF LEADERS

Scoring: George Yardley (23.4 avg.)
Rebounding: Walter Dukes (13.9)
Assists: Dick McGuire (5.7)

NBA CHAMPION

St. Louis Hawks

1957-58
SEASON IN REVIEW

Professional basketball came to the Motor City—permanently—in the fall of 1957 when Fred Zollner's relocated Pistons took up residence in Olympia Stadium, the old red barn on Grand River. Their first star, hands down, was jump-shooting forward George Yardley, who pumped in 2,001 points to become the first NBA player to top 2,000 and break the league record held by another great George (Mikan). "The Bird," as Yardley was known, was named to the All-NBA first team and joined two teammates in the All-Star Game: point guard Dick McGuire, the longtime New York Knicks star, and shooting guard Gene Shue. The maiden season didn't go quite so smoothly for the team. Off to a 9-16 start on December 19, holdover coach Charley Eckman was forced to resign, less than three years after guiding Fort Wayne within one point of the 1955 NBA title. Under new coach Ephraim "Red" Rocha, the Pistons went 24-23 for a 33-39 record and a second-place tie with Cincinnati. Having won a playoff coin flip to gain the home-court edge in the best-of-three Western semifinals, Detroit swept Cincy 2-0, then moved on to the division finals against St. Louis. The teams had split their season series 6-6, but All-NBA forward Bob Pettit and the eventual champion Hawks were too much in the playoffs, taking the series 4-1 as Detroit gained only a Game 3 win at St. Louis.

George Yardley's NBA scoring title highlighted the Pistons' first season in Detroit. Photo from Morrie Moorawnick collection.

October 23, 1957

Less a society event than a curiosity for 10,965 fans at the Olympia, the Pistons' first game in their Detroit incarnation—a 105-94 loss to the star-laden Boston Celtics—actually spanned two days, October 23 and 24. The game didn't end until after midnight because it was the second half of a double-header. The St. Louis Hawks and New York Knicks played in the 7:30 opener and then Detroit squared off with Boston, beginning a rivalry that would create some of the most magnificent moments in Pistons history. On this unseasonably warm night, though, it was the savvy Celtics who emerged with the first win. Behind Bill Sharman (24 points), Bill Russell (15) and Frank Ramsey (15), Boston took command

Pistons' Harry Gallatin (10) shields the ball from Boston's Andy Phillip while Detroit gunner Gene Shue (21) roams free. Photo from Morrie Moorawnick collection.

early against the nervous upstart Pistons. Detroit was keyed by George Yardley with 20 points and 7-foot center Walter Dukes with 19, but the Pistons couldn't contain a balanced Celtics nucleus that would go on to win eight straight NBA titles and 10 of 11 from 1959-69. As if to add further insult, the fans and players got rained on much of the night due to condensation that dripped steadily from the ceiling. In the '80s, the Pistons would experience the same problem at the Pontiac Silverdome.

WHAT A NIGHT!

Premier Piston

George "The Bird" Yardley

Jump-shot pioneer George Yardley, a 1996 Basketball Hall of Fame inductee. Photo from Morrie Moorawnick collection.

Even by 1957 standards, George Yardley looked more like an insurance salesman than a pro basketball player. Balding at age 30, slightly built, Stanford-educated and a summer employee in missile research, there was little outward indication that Yardley was one of the top players of his era. But don't let appearances deceive. He was a star, a jump-shot pioneer who became the first NBA player with 2,000 points in a season and a 1996 inductee into the Basketball Hall of Fame. Yardley came to Detroit as one of six holdovers from Fort Wayne, where he starred for four seasons. In 1956-57 at Fort Wayne, his 21.5-point average ranked fifth in the NBA and included a team-record 40 against Minneapolis and 23 in one quarter against Rochester. "I've been around basketball just about all my life and I've yet to see a jump shot better than Yardley's," coach Charley Eckman said. But not even Eckman could have envisioned the amazing season his team captain put together in 1957-58. Yardley was unstoppable. After setting the team record with 52 points against Syracuse on February 4, he went on a scoring tear unlike any in team history before or since. In a nine-game stretch from February 18 to March 6, Yardley had games of 49, 48, 44, 43, and 41 points. His 49 points at Minneapolis broke Geroge Mikan's season scoring record of 1,932. Needing 25 points in the season finale to reach 2,000, Yardley foiled the Syracuse Nats' triple-teaming tactics and attained the goal on his final basket, giving him 2,001. He also led the NBA in free throws made (655), free throws attempted (808), and nicknames—he was known variously as the Bird, Yardbird, California Comet, and Bones. But Yardley's career as a Piston ended unceremoniously on February 7, 1959, when the slumping shooter was dealt to Syracuse for Eddie Conlin after a spat with owner Fred Zollner. In his return game against Detroit on February 22, he scored 33 to lead the Nats to a 139-108 victory. Even as an ex-Piston, George Yardley was a basketball star, despite all appearances to the contrary.

AT A GLANCE

GEORGE YARDLEY

FULL NAME:
George Harry Yardley III
BORN:
November 3, 1928; Los Angeles, California
POSITION, HEIGHT, WEIGHT:
Forward, 6-foot-5, 190 pounds
COLLEGE:
Stanford
TENURE WITH PISTONS:
Detroit 1957-58 – 1958-59
Also: Fort Wayne 1953-57
BEST SEASON WITH PISTONS:
1957-58, 72 GP, 27.8 ppg, 10.7 rpg
TOTALS WITH PISTONS:
Regular season: 118 GP, 25.1 ppg, 9.3 rpg
Playoffs: 7 GP, 23.4 ppg, 10.3 rpg
HONORS:
Basketball Hall of Fame, 1996
All-Star Game: 1957-58, 1958-59
All-NBA Team: 1957-58

PISTON LIST

George Yardley's Highest-Scoring Games as a Piston

- **52 points**
  February 4, 1958 vs. Syracuse
- **51 points**
  January 15, 1958 at Boston
- **49 points**
  March 6, 1958 at Minneapolis
- **48 points**
  December 26, 1957 at St. Louis
  February 18, 1958 vs. Syracuse
- **44 points**
  January 23, 1958 at Minneapolis
  February 25, 1958 vs. St. Louis
- **43 points**
  February 19, 1958 at Minneapolis
- **41 points**
  October 26, 1957 vs. Philadelphia
  February 27, 1958 vs. Minneapolis

CHANGING FACES

CHARLEY ECKMAN, the referee-turned-coach, had guided the Fort Wayne Pistons to three straight division crowns and a 114-102 record. But he didn't last long once the franchise moved to Detroit. With the Pistons off to a 9-16 start, including an attendance-draining 3-8 home record, owner Fred Zollner sought Eckman's resignation and replaced him with Hawaiian-born Ephraim "Red" Rocha, a 1956-57 Piston who had never coached; the team he took over wasn't exactly bereft. The Pistons had beefed up considerably in the summer, swinging a trade with the Knicks to add veteran greats Harry Gallatin, Dick McGuire, Nat "Sweetwater" Clifton and Dick Atha. The cost was Detroit's first-round draftee in 1957 (Charlie Tyra) and its first-round pick in '58. The longest-lasting acquisition, though, was 7-foot center Walter Dukes, a former Harlem Globetrotter who came to the Pistons from Minneapolis on September 12 for Larry Foust. Dukes would play six seasons in Detroit and retire in 1963 as the team's all-time rebounding king with 4,986.

Red Rocha took over as coach only 25 games into the 1957-58 season. Photo from Morrie Moorawnick collection.

The VILLAIN

Bob Pettit and Cliff Hagan

The St. Louis Hawks, sparked by Cliff Hagan (16), confounded Harry Gallatin (10) and the Pistons in the 1958 playoffs. Photo from Morrie Moorawnick collection.

The Pistons allowed opposing stars to scored 30 or more points nine times in their opening season in Detroit, and this St. Louis Hawks pair accounted for five of them, including a 40-point night for each. Bob Pettit, the 6-9 All-Star forward, averaged 23.8 points in the 12-game season series against Detroit. He scored 40 on January 18 at St. Louis, helping to cover for Cliff Hagan's absence in a 105-103 Hawks victory. Pettit supplied 36 points on December 17 as St. Louis beat the Pistons 106-99 in a neutral-site game at New York. Hagan, in his second year after a terrific career at Kentucky, averaged 21.5 points against Detroit. The 6-4 swingman scored 40 in the teams' first meeting of the season, St. Louis' 115-100 home victory November 23. He had 32 and 34, respectively, in the final two meetings on February 22 and 25, though the Pistons won both to earn a split in the season series. The St. Louis twosome was just as unstoppable in the playoffs, in which they blasted Detroit 4-1 in the Western finals en route to an NBA title. Hagan averaged 27.7 in the playoffs, Pettit 24.2.

Game Results

1957-58 REGULAR SEASON

Date	Opponent	Result	Record
10-23	BOSTON	L, 94-105	0-1
10-26	PHILADELPHIA	L, 100-112	0-2
10-30	at Minneapolis	W, 115-96	1-2
11-3	at Cincinnati	W, 94-88	2-2
11-5	n-Boston	L, 105-111	2-3
11-12	NEW YORK	W, 109-107	3-3
11-15	MINNEAPOLIS	L, 104-112	3-4
11-16	at New York	W, 109-105	4-4
11-17	at Philadelphia	W, 95-91	5-4
11-19	n-Cincinnati	L, 75-92	5-5
11-21	BOSTON	L, 90-112	5-6
11-23	at St. Louis	L, 110-115	5-7
11-26	n-Minneapolis	W, 109-91	6-7
11-27	ST. LOUIS	L, 110-121	6-8
11-29	at Cincinnati	L, 96-99 (OT)	6-9
11-30	CINCINNATI	W, 100-96	7-9
12-1	at New York	L, 102-109	7-10
12-3	BOSTON	L, 113-124	7-11
12-5	n-Cincinnati	L, 99-109	7-12
12-6	at Syracuse	L, 91-118	7-13
12-7	CINCINNATI	W, 109-105	8-13
12-10	PHILADELPHIA	W, 97-100	8-14
12-12	at Philadelphia	W, 101-96	9-14
12-15	NEW YORK	L, 109-116	9-15
12-17	n-St. Louis	L, 99-106	9-16
12-21	CINCINNATI	W, 112-101	10-16
12-22	at Syracuse	L, 93-119	10-17
12-25	MINNEAPOLIS	L, 104-106	10-18
12-26	at St. Louis	W, 110-106	11-18
12-27	at New York	L, 120-125	11-19
12-28	SYRACUSE	W, 117-111	12-19
12-31	at Cincinnati	L, 96-130	12-20
1-4	PHILADELPHIA	W, 81-78	13-20
1-5	at St. Louis	L, 93-95	13-21
1-7	n-Cincinnati	L, 99-114	13-22
1-8	SYRACUSE	W, 109-107	14-22
1-10	n-Minneapolis	L, 114-124	14-23
1-11	MINNEAPOLIS	W, 129-102	15-23
1-12	at Syracuse	L, 109-135	15-24
1-15	at Boston	L, 113-131	15-25
1-16	at Philadelphia	W, 113-108	16-25
1-17	CINCINNATI	W, 115-94	17-25
1-18	at St. Louis	L, 103-105	17-26
1-19	at Minneapolis	L, 111-118	17-27
1-22	NEW YORK	L, 92-115	17-28
1-23	at Minneapolis	L, 125-128 (OT)	17-29
1-25	ST. LOUIS	W, 105-98	18-29
1-26	at Cincinnati	L, 103-107	18-30
1-27	PHILADELPHIA	W, 115-93	19-30
1-30	n-Syracuse	W, 87-83	20-30
1-31	n-New York	W, 119-105	21-30
2-1	n-Philadelphia	L, 86-106	21-31
2-2	at Boston	L, 115-119	21-32
2-4	SYRACUSE	W, 118-113	22-32
2-7	n-St. Louis	W, 125-107	23-32
2-9	NEW YORK	L, 98-100	23-33
2-11	at Philadelphia	L, 98-115	23-34
2-12	ST. LOUIS	L, 105-122	23-35
2-14	at Boston	W, 111-109	24-35
2-15	MINNEAPOLIS	L, 110-111	24-36
2-16	at St. Louis	W, 100-98	25-36
2-18	SYRACUSE	W, 120-98	26-36
2-19	at Minneapolis	W, 117-115 (OT)	27-36
2-21	at Cincinnati	W, 109-107	28-36
2-22	ST. LOUIS	W, 98-96	29-36
2-25	n-St. Louis	W, 114-113 (OT)	30-36
2-26	BOSTON	L, 99-106	30-37
2-27	n-Minneapolis	W, 112-109	31-37
3-1	at New York	W, 103-101	32-37
3-6	at Minneapolis	W, 112-109	33-37
3-8	at Boston	L, 103-108	33-38
3-9	at Syracuse	L, 90-111	33-39

PLAYOFFS

Western Semifinals—(Best-of-Three)

3-15	CINCINNATI	W, 100-83	1-0
3-16	at Cincinnati	W, 124-104	2-0

Western Finals—(Best-of-Seven)

3-19	at St. Louis	L, 111-114	0-1
3-22	ST. LOUIS	L, 96-99	0-2
3-23	at St. Louis	W, 109-89	1-2
3-25	ST. LOUIS	L, 101-145	1-3
3-27	at St. Louis	L, 96-120	1-4

(Home games in ALL CAPS; n-neutral site)

1958 1959

TIME CAPSULE

October 9, 1958:
The New York Yankees score four runs in the eighth inning of the seventh game and beat the Milwaukee Braves 6-2 to win the World Series.

January 3, 1959:
President Dwight Eisenhower proclaims Alaska the 49th state.

February 3, 1959:
Rock and roll stars Buddy Holly, Richie Valens and J.P. "The Big Bopper" Richardson die in an airplane crash.

SEASON SNAPSHOT

Most Points
Gene Shue (1,266, 17.6 avg.)

Most Rebounds
Walter Dukes (958, 13.3 avg.)

Most Assists
Dick McGuire (443, 6.2 avg.)

Most Minutes
George Yardley (2,745, 38.1 avg.)

Field-Goal Percentage
Shellie McMillon (43.9%)

Free-Throw Percentage
Gene Shue (80.3%)

Team Offense Average
105.1 (7,565 in 72 games)

Team Defense Average
106.6 (7,676 in 72 games)

Pistons in All-Star Game
George Yardley, F; Gene Shue, G; Dick McGuire, G

FINAL STANDINGS

Western Division	W	L	Pct.	GB
St. Louis	49	23	.681	—
Minneapolis	33	39	.458	16
PISTONS	**28**	**44**	**.389**	**21**
Cincinnati	19	53	.264	30

Eastern Division Winner—Boston

PLAYOFF RESULTS

Western Semifinals: Minneapolis d. Pistons, 2-1

PISTONS PLAYOFF LEADERS

Scoring: Gene Shue (27.7 avg.)
Rebounding: Walter Dukes (13.3)
Assists: Dick McGuire (6.3)

NBA CHAMPION

Boston Celtics

1958-59
SEASON IN REVIEW

What honeymoon? After reaching the Western Finals in their premiere season in Detroit, the Pistons' second season became a soap opera with two lead characters: scoring champ George Yardley and club owner Fred Zollner. When the show finally closed, Yardley was an ex-Piston, having been shipped to the Syracuse Nats for Ed Conlin, and the Pistons sagged to a 28-44 record. Zollner had grown disenchanted with the oft-injured Yardley, feeling he was not giving full effort, and the relationship grew testier when Yardley broke his hand January 25 at Boston. That injury came in the midst of a nine-game skid that dropped the Pistons to 19-30 and out of contention. Yardley never again played for Detroit. He demanded a trade and threatened retirement, and GM Nick Kerbawy found a taker for his $25,000 contract. On February 12, the Yardley-for-Conlin deal was made and the Detroit Pistons' first star was gone. Before and after the trade, there were few team highlights. Gene Shue led them in points with 17.6 per game (45 in a rare win over Boston), Dick McGuire's 443 assists were second in the NBA and Walter Dukes' 958 rebounds were sixth. On February 4, Phil Jordon (14.3 ppg) made a 25-foot hook to end the second OT and nip Philadelphia 119-117. The January 23 NBA All-Star game at Detroit drew a crowd of 10,541. The Pistons' average gate was far less, a scant 3,978.

On a happier day, George Yardley (left) and coach Red Rocha (center) accept a welcome from Detroit Mayor Louis Miriani. Photo from Morrie Moorawnick collection.

November 9, 1958

WHAT A NIGHT!

Any victory over Boston was something to be savored. Few clubs knew that better than the Pistons, who fashioned a 1-8 record vs. the Celtics in 1957-58 and then repeated it in '58-59. At least they captured their victory quicker in the latter, though, riding Gene Shue's 45 points to a record-setting 136-133 home win on national TV. The Pistons' 79 points in the first half were then an NBA record, as were the game's 269 points. The 136 points were also a Pistons record. The victory seemed well in hand after the third quarter when Shue's eight straight points gave Detroit a 109-92 lead. But Bill Russell led Boston on a late 13-0 spurt that made the Pistons hang on. Shue was amazing, scoring the second-most points by any NBA guard to that point, trailing the 47 by New York's Carl Braun in 1947. With his 14 baskets and 17 free throws, Shue became the first Piston besides Yardley to top the 40-point mark. Yardley helped the win with 28 points and Phil Jordon supplied 18. For the Celtics, Russell had 32, Tommy Heinsohn 23 and Bill Sharman 22. It wasn't just the Pistons' only win over Boston in '58-59, but also their only TV win in five tries. They lost on the tube to Syracuse three times and also to Minneapolis.

Gene Shue, a holdover from the Fort Wayne era, became Detroit's first high-scoring guard. Photo from Morrie Moorawnick collection.

Premier Piston

"Tricky Dick" McGuire

Dick McGuire's crisp passing directed the Pistons' offense. Photo from Morrie Moorawnick collection.

If the debate is over '50s playmakers, the conversation usually begins and ends with two names: Bob Cousy and Dick McGuire. Most will choose the flashier Cousy, truth be told, but there are old-timers who will tell you McGuire was every bit Cousy's equal. "Tricky Dick," a speedy 6-foot point guard from St. John's, played his first eight seasons with the New York Knicks and topped the NBA in assists (386) as a rookie in 1949-50. Over the next nine years, McGuire was second in assists four times and fourth three times. He dealt a career-high 542 in 1954-55 and finished second to Cousy's 557. They would place 1-2 twice more, but only after McGuire came to the Pistons before the 1957-58 season. As then-coach Charlie Eckman said, "We stole him." The Pistons traded two No. 1 draft picks to the Knicks for McGuire, Harry Gallatin and two others. McGuire, making George Yardley his leading beneficiary, was an immediate hit as the Pistons' floor leader; he was an unflappable quarterback on the fast break. His 454 assists in '57-58 (second to Cousy's 463) played a major role in Yardley claiming the NBA scoring title with a then-record 2,001 points. McGuire wasn't a high scorer, but had his best career point total (655, 9.2 ppg) with Detroit in '58-59. The soft-spoken McGuire was also among the league's cleanest players, setting a record with 361 straight games without fouling out. His terrific 11-year career was rewarded in 1993 with his induction to the Basketball Hall of Fame. But his place in Pistons lore is not solely as a player. On December 28, 1959, McGuire became player-coach and put in three more seasons as coach after retiring as a player in 1960. His best season was '61-62, when the Pistons went 37-43 and lost to the Lakers in six games in the Western Finals.

AT A GLANCE

DICK McGUIRE

FULL NAME:
Richard Joseph McGuire
BORN:
January 25, 1926; Huntington, N.Y.
POSITION, HEIGHT, WEIGHT:
Guard, 6-foot-0, 180 pounds
COLLEGE:
St. John's
ACQUIRED:
April 3, 1957, from New York (trade)

TENURE WITH PISTONS:
Player: 1957-58 – 1959-60
Coach: 1959-60 – 1962-63
Also played: New York 1949-57
Also coached: New York 1965-68
BEST SEASON WITH PISTONS:
Player: 1958-59, 71 GP, 9.2 ppg, 6.2 apg
Coach: 1961-62, 80 GP, 37-43 (.463)
PLAYING TOTALS WITH PISTONS:
Regular season: 208 GP, 8.1 ppg, 6.0 apg
Playoffs: 12 GP, 10.4 ppg, 5.7 apg
COACHING TOTALS
WITH PISTONS:
Regular season: 280 GP, 122-158 (.436)
Playoffs: 21 GP, 8-13 (.381)
HONORS:
Basketball Hall of Fame, 1993
All-Star Game (7): New York 1950-51,
1951-52, 1953-54, 1954-55, 1955-56;
Detroit 1957-58, 1958-59
All-NBA Team: Second Team 1950-51
NBA Assist Champion: 1950-51

PISTON LIST

Highest Individual Scoring Totals vs. Pistons

73 points
- David Thompson, Denver, April 9, 1978

61 points—
- x-Michael Jordan, Chicago, March 4, 1987

59 points—
- x-Wilt Chamberlain, San Francisco, February 11, 1964
- Michael Jordan, Chicago, April 3, 1988

58 points
- Wilt Chamberlain, at Philadelphia, January 25, 1960
- Wilt Chamberlain, at Philadelphia, November 4, 1961
- Wilt Chamberlain, Philadelphia, November 8, 1961
- Wilt Chamberlain, at San Francisco, January 24, 1963

57 points
- Elgin Baylor, L.A. Lakers, February 16, 1961
  Bob Pettit, St. Louis, February 18, 1961
x-overtime game

CHANGING FACES

EDDIE CONLIN just couldn't win. The 26-year-old forward did not ask to be traded for George Yardley. The Fordham grad was having a fine career with Syracuse when he was sent to Detroit in a straight-up deal for the disruptive Yardley on February 12. Though Conlin was coming off his best pro year—15.0 points and 7.3 boards with the Nationals—he wasn't able to repeat that success for the Pistons. Conlin averaged 11.3 points and 5.1 rebounds in 85 games for Detroit through 1960, but the locals didn't let him forget he was the dividend of the Yardley swap. That was magnified February 22 when the Pistons and Nats faced off for the first time since the trade; Yardley outscored Conlin 33-14. The Pistons' most vital addition of '58 was the purchase of veteran forward Earl Lloyd (and role-playing Dick Farley) from Syracuse before the season. Lloyd would become a key figure in club history. His spot in league annals was already secure—on October 31, 1950, he became the first African-American to play in the NBA.

Eddie Conlin was known for his driving layups and 30-foot shooting range. Photo from Morrie Moorawnick collection.

The VILLAIN

Elgin Baylor

The Lakers' Elgin Baylor averaged 24.9 points and 15.0 rebounds in 70 games en route to the 1958-59 Rookie of the Year award.

Veteran sports columnist Jim Murray once referred to Elgin Baylor as, "the only man to look dignified in short pants." To the Pistons in 1958-59, the rookie forward of the Minneapolis Lakers was not only dignified, he was dominant. In 12 regular-season games vs. Detroit, Baylor scored 286 points for a 23.8 average, helping the Lakers win the season series, 8-4. The 6-foot-5 gunner from Seattle scored 26 points December 18 to push the Lakers to a 113-104 home win over Detroit, then 23, 27, 17, 29 and 18 in five victories over the Pistons spanning January 30 to March 6. Oddly, three of Baylor's highest-scoring performances—39, 30 and 28—came in Detroit victories. He got 39 on March 11 in the Pistons' 123-118 win in the season finale, a prelude to the clubs' first-round playoff. Baylor, voted NBA Rookie of the Year, keyed the Lakers' 2-1 series victory with a 27.0 average. It was an occurrence that would become a trend; Detroit was eliminated by Baylor and Co. for the next three years, too.

Game Results

1958-59 REGULAR SEASON

Date	Opponent	Result	Record
10-19	at Syracuse	L, 94-103	0-1
10-23	at St. Louis	L, 103-104	0-2
10-25	ST. LOUIS	W, 117-112	1-2
10-26	at Minneapolis	L, 100-108	1-3
10-31	CINCINNATI	W, 120-113	2-3
11-1	at Boston	L, 98-112	2-4
11-2	at Philadelphia	W, 107-91	3-4
11-7	NEW YORK	L, 101-115	3-5
11-9	BOSTON	W, 136-133	4-5
11-13	n-Minneapolis	W, 119-110	5-5
11-14	SYRACUSE	L, 109-111	5-6
11-15	at St. Louis	L, 91-102	5-7
11-18	n-Boston	L, 102-115	5-8
11-22	CINCINNATI	W, 103-86	6-8
11-23	at Minneapolis	W, 124-109	7-8
11-25	MINNEAPOLIS	W, 90-98	7-9
11-26	at Cincinnati	W, 112-95	8-9
11-28	SYRACUSE	W, 101-93	9-9
11-29	at Boston	L, 96-110	9-10
12-2	PHILADELPHIA	W, 95-91	10-10
12-5	NEW YORK	L, 108-110	10-11
12-6	at New York	W, 99-92	11-11
12-10	n-St. Louis	W, 89-82	12-11
12-11	n-St. Louis	W, 107-101	13-11
12-12	PHILADELPHIA	W, 97-95	14-11
12-14	SYRACUSE	L, 95-101	14-12
12-17	BOSTON	L, 95-102	14-13
12-18	at Minneapolis	L, 104-113	14-14
12-20	ST. LOUIS	L, 104-111	14-15
12-25	n-Minneapolis	W, 98-97 (OT)	15-15
12-26	CINCINNATI	W, 131-91	16-15
12-30	at New York	L, 90-93	16-16
1-2	n-Cincinnati	L, 104-111	16-17
1-3	NEW YORK	L, 102-106	16-18
1-4	at Syracuse	L, 94-118	16-19
1-6	at Philadelphia	W, 107-105	17-19
1-9	BOSTON	L, 90-103	17-20
1-10	at Cincinnati	W, 101-69	18-20
1-11	at St. Louis	L, 100-111	18-21
1-13	n-Cincinnati	W, 112-92	19-21
1-14	ST. LOUIS	L, 108-114	19-22
1-17	PHILADELPHIA	L, 104-106	19-23
1-18	at Cincinnati	L, 88-107	19-24
1-21	at Philadelphia	L, 105-112	19-25
1-24	at New York	L, 118-122 (OT)	19-26
1-25	at Boston	L, 118-119	19-27
1-26	at Philadelphia	L, 98-102	19-28
1-27	SYRACUSE	L, 107-121	19-29
1-30	n-Minneapolis	L, 86-88	19-30
1-31	CINCINNATI	W, 103-88	20-30
2-1	at St. Louis	L, 96-130	20-31
2-4	PHILADELPHIA	W, 119-118 (2OT)	21-31
2-6	n-Syracuse	L, 103-122	21-32
2-8	MINNEAPOLIS	L, 103-115	21-33
2-9	at Cincinnati	W, 122-97	22-33
2-11	at Syracuse	W, 118-114 (OT)	23-33
2-13	NEW YORK	W, 96-90	24-33
2-15	at Boston	L, 94-120	24-34
2-17	MINNEAPOLIS	L, 90-97	24-35
2-18	at Minneapolis	L, 95-105	24-36
2-20	BOSTON	L, 106-111 (OT)	24-37
2-21	n-New York	W, 114-101	25-37
2-22	at Syracuse	L, 108-139	25-38
2-25	ST. LOUIS	L, 100-104	25-39
2-26	at Cincinnati	L, 101-106	25-40
3-1	CINCINNATI	W, 117-101	26-40
3-3	n-Philadelphia	L, 107-116	26-41
3-4	ST. LOUIS	W, 127-97	27-41
3-6	MINNEAPOLIS	L, 98-99	27-42
3-7	at St. Louis	L, 128-137	27-43
3-8	at New York	L, 120-127	27-44
3-11	at Minneapolis	W, 123-118	28-44

PLAYOFFS

Western Semifinals—(Best-of-Three)

3-14	at Minneapolis	L, 89-92	0-1
3-15	MINNEAPOLIS	W, 117-103	1-1
3-17	at Minneapolis	L, 102-129	1-2

(Home games in CAPS; n-neutral site)

11

1959 1960

TIME CAPSULE

September 15, 1959:
Soviet Premier Nikita Khrushchev arrives in the U.S. for meetings with President Dwight Eisenhower.

January 4, 1960:
The United Steel Workers and the nation's steel companies agree on a wage increase to settle a six-month strike.

June 20, 1960:
Floyd Patterson knocks out Ingemar Johansson, becoming the first boxer ever to regain the heavyweight championship.

SEASON SNAPSHOT

Most Points
Gene Shue (1,712, 22.8 avg.)

Most Rebounds
Walter Dukes (883, 13.4 avg.)

Most Assists
Dick McGuire (358, 5.3 avg.)

Most Minutes
x-Gene Shue (3,338, 44.5 avg.)

Field-Goal Percentage
Bailey Howell (45.6%)

Free-Throw Percentage
Gene Shue (87.2%)

Team Offense Average
111.6 (8,367 in 75 games)

Team Defense Average
115.0 (8,624 in 75 games)

NBA All-Stars
Gene Shue, G (First Team)

Pistons in All-Star Game
Gene Shue, G; Walter Dukes, C; Chuck Noble, G

x-led league

1959-60

FINAL STANDINGS

Western Division	W	L	Pct.	GB
St. Louis	46	29	.613	—
PISTONS	**30**	**45**	**.400**	**16**
Minneapolis	25	50	.333	21
Cincinnati	19	56	.253	27

Eastern Division Winner—Boston

PLAYOFF RESULTS

Western Semifinals: Minneapolis d. Pistons, 2-0

PISTONS PLAYOFF LEADERS

Scoring: Walter Dukes and Gene Shue (24.0 avg.)
Rebounding: Walter Dukes (16.5)
Assists: Chuck Noble (6.5)

NBA CHAMPION

Boston Celtics

1959-60
SEASON IN REVIEW

Three seasons, three coaches, three sub-.500 finishes. Not the sort of pattern a new club wants to follow when it's trying to build a fan base. But that was the Pistons' bottom line in '59-60, as they staggered to a 30-45 record and a two-game exit in the playoffs, thanks to the Lakers for a second straight year. They even had to play their playoff opener at Grosse Pointe High School because Olympia was unavilable; they lost in the last minute. The Pistons received little help from an overwhelming schedule, it should be noted. After a 2-2 start, they played 12 games in 15 days, including an eight-day span in which they went 1-6 and did not play two straight games in the same town. There were two more rugged stretches in which they played a combined 16 games in 20 days (6-10), but coach Red Rocha didn't get to see it. With the Pistons off to a 13-21 start December 28, he was fired and relieved by Dick McGuire as player-coach. The club responded, going 11-5 from January 13-February 9, but ran out of gas. The season foreshadowed better days, though. Bailey Howell, Detroit's first-round draft pick out of Mississippi State, averaged 17.8 points and 10.5 rebounds. Team points leader Gene Shue (22.8 ppg) made the All-NBA first team, tying for the league lead in minutes, and was an All-Star along with Walter Dukes (13.4 rpg) and Chuck Noble (11.3 ppg).

At his first practice as player-coach, Dick McGuire (left) gathers with (L-R) Chuck Noble, Billy Kenville, trainer Stan Kenworthy and Eddie Conlin. Photo from Morrie Moorawnick collection.

WHAT A NIGHT!

February 9, 1960

A 7-foot-1, 275-pound nightmare arrived in the NBA in 1959-60, able and willing to torment opponents at his own leisure. His name was Wilt Chamberlain, the former Kansas all-American, who immediately made a contender of the Philadelphia Warriors. The Pistons had a solid big man, 7-foot center Walter Dukes, but even he was sorely overmatched by the wunderkind, who became the first rookie to earn the league MVP award. On February 9 at Olympia, Chamberlain victimized the Pistons for 41 points, giving him 2,134 for the season to break the NBA record. The record had been 2,001 by Detroit's George Yardley in 1958, then 2,105 by St. Louis' Bob Pettit in '59. Chamberlain would stretch the record to 2,707 by the end of his rookie season, then 3,033 in '61 and—no misprint—4,029 in '62. In eight games vs. Detroit in his first year, Chamberlain scored 36, 41, 44, 44, 58, 41, 23 and 41 for a 41.0 average and 6-2 record. But one of the Pistons' victories, 122-113, came on The Stilt's record-breaking night. Detroit's 31-22 third quarter made the difference. Gene Shue had 30 points to spark the win over his former team (Philly had drafted him in 1954), while Bailey Howell scored 29 and Dukes 20.

Walter Dukes, Detroit's 7-footer, had the unenviable task of guarding Warriors center Wilt Chamberlain. Photo from Morrie Moorawnick collection.

Gene Shue

Hot-shot guard Gene Shue played in the All-Star Game all five seasons with Detroit. Photo from Morrie Moorawnick collection.

Years before Pistons announcers began to elongate "Joe Duuuu-mars!," they reserved their screaming for Gene Shue. A 6-foot-2 Maryland-bred gunner—easily Detroit's finest guard pre-Dave Bing—Shue would hit a jumper or weave through defenders for a layup. The P.A. man would open his microphone and boom the plaudit "Twoooo for Shuuuuue!" throughout Olympia or Cobo Arena. For five years in Detroit, he kept the announcers hoarse; Shue led the Pistons in scoring twice and finished second in his other three seasons. When the Pistons shipped him to the Knicks on August 29, 1962 after a tiff with management—getting little in return—Shue left as their career leader in most offensive categories. Even excluding his year with Fort Wayne ('56-57), he led the Pistons in points (7,247), assists (1,693), field goals made (2,667), free throws made (1,913) and minutes (14,920). Durability was a Shue specialty. In 1959-60, when he made the All-NBA first team, he played 11 complete games and tied for the NBA lead with 3,338 minutes, including 58 in a double-OT game and 53 in two single-OT games. There wasn't much Shue didn't do that year, averaging a career-best 22.8 points (sixth in the NBA) and 5.5 rebounds (third among guards) while playing superb defense. On November 24, 1959, he scored 43 points against Cincinnati, two shy of his career-high against the Celtics a year before. After being dealt in '62 for 6-foot-10 Darrall Imhoff, Shue ended his 10-season playing career with one each for New York and Baltimore. He became Baltimore's head coach in '66, starting a 22-year sideline career that led to Finals berths in '71 (Baltimore) and '77 (Philadelphia). Count the berths: "Twoooo for Shuuuuue!"

AT A GLANCE

GENE SHUE

FULL NAME:
Eugene William Shue
BORN:
December 18, 1931; Baltimore
POSITION, HEIGHT, WEIGHT:
Guard, 6-foot-2, 175 pounds
COLLEGE:
Maryland

ACQUIRED:
By Fort Wayne, April 30, 1956, from New York (trade)
TENURE WITH PISTONS:
Detroit 1957-58 – 1961-62
Also: Fort Wayne 1956-57
BEST SEASON WITH PISTONS:
1960-61, 78 GP, 22.6 ppg, 4.3 rpg, 6.8 apg
TOTALS WITH PISTONS:
Regular season: 368 GP, 19.7 ppg, 4.8 rpg, 4.6 apg
Playoffs: 27 GP, 19.1 ppg, 4.2 rpg, 4.4 apg
HONORS:
All-Star Game (5): 1957-58, 1958-59, 1959-60, 1960-61, 1961-62
All-NBA Team: First Team 1959-60; Second Team 1960-61
NBA Coach of the Year: 1968-69 (Baltimore), 1981-82 (Washington)

PISTON LIST

Most Field Goal Attempts (Season)

- Dave Bing, 1,893, 1967-68
- Dave Bing, 1,710, 1970-71
- Bob Lanier, 1,690, 1971-72
- Bob Lanier, 1,654, 1972-73
- George Yardley, 1,624, 1957-58
- Dave Bing, 1,594, 1968-69
- Gene Shue, 1,545, 1960-61
- Dave Bing, 1,545, 1972-73
- Isiah Thomas, 1,537, 1982-83
- Dave Bing, 1,522, 1966-67
- Gene Shue, 1,501, 1959-60
- Bob Lanier, 1,483, 1973-74
- Joe Dumars, 1,454, 1992-93
- Don Ohl, 1,450, 1962-63

CHANGING FACES

THE PISTONS' first two drafts in Detroit didn't produce much—besides sixth-round forward Shellie McMillon in '59—but they came away from the '60 derby with a new star and two solid role players. Picking fourth overall (second in the first non-territorial round), Detroit got 6-foot-7 forward Bailey Howell, who would have five marvelous Pistons seasons en route to a Hall of Fame career. Rebounder Gary Alcorn was drafted in the third round and Michigan guard George Lee, a Detroit-area native, in the fourth. Alcorn averaged 4.8 rebounds in his only Pistons season; Lee waited a year before his two-season stint with Detroit and was a solid contributor in the '61 playoffs before being shipped to San Francisco in '62. Another vital acquisition was Archie Dees, a 6-foot-8 forward who responded with his finest NBA season: 9.7 points and 5.4 rebounds in 73 games. The Pistons got Dees from Cincinnati, trading Phil Jordon, who'd had his best season in '58-59 with a 14.3-point average.

Archie Dees was the Pistons' No. 1 substitute at forward and center in '59-60. Photo from Morrie Moorawnick collection.

Take a Bow

Chuck Noble

Chuck Noble earned his first and only All-Star berth in 1959-60. Photo from Morrie Moorawnick collection.

The NBA didn't institute a Most Improved Player award until 1986, but Chuck Noble would've won it in 1959-60. He was widely regarded as the player who made the greatest strides, capturing a berth in the All-Star Game at Philadelphia. He went scoreless in his 11-minute stint, but had one rebound and three assists. A 6-foot-4 guard out of Louisville, Noble was essentially a defensive specialist, but averaged a career-high 11.2 points and 4.6 assists in '59-60. He took over as the Pistons' playmaker late in the season after player-coach Dick McGuire began to concentrate mostly on coaching. A broken rib sidelined Noble for the last nine games and also slowed him in the two playoff games. In fact, injuries hindered Noble much of his 411-game NBA career, spent totally with the Pistons. He joined Fort Wayne in '55-56, averaging 9.5 points as the Pistons lost in the NBA Finals. When the club moved north in '57, Noble brought along his keen one-hand set shot, defensive tenacity and a nickname: "Flash."

Game Results

1959-60 REGULAR SEASON

Date	Opponent	Result	Record
10-18	at Minneapolis	W, 106-105	1-0
10-24	at Cincinnati	L, 103-108	1-1
10-28	SYRACUSE	W, 117-102	2-1
10-31	at Philadelphia	L, 112-120	2-2
11-4	NEW YORK	L, 101-107	2-3
11-6	at Minneapolis	W, 118-113 (2OT)	3-3
11-7	MINNEAPOLIS	L, 111-113 (OT)	3-4
11-8	at Syracuse	L, 107-118	3-5
11-10	n-Boston	L, 109-128	3-6
11-11	PHILADELPHIA	L, 105-119	3-7
11-12	n-Minneapolis	W, 107-93	4-7
11-14	CINCINNATI	W, 111-103	5-7
11-15	at New York	W, 103-94	6-7
11-17	BOSTON	L, 129-132 (2OT)	6-8
11-18	at Cincinnati	W, 110-93	7-8
11-20	at Minneapolis	L, 85-105	7-9
11-21	at St. Louis	W, 109-107	8-9
11-22	NEW YORK	W, 115-104	9-9
11-24	n-Cincinnati	W, 104-91	10-9
11-25	ST. LOUIS	L, 97-104	10-10
11-28	at Boston	L, 110-136	10-11
12-4	MINNEAPOLIS	W, 120-101	11-11
12-5	at New York	L, 108-124	11-12
12-6	at Philadelphia	L, 116-118	11-13
12-9	n-Cincinnati	L, 119-129	11-14
12-10	n-St. Louis	L, 111-129	11-15
12-13	NEW YORK	W, 147-129	12-15
12-16	ST. LOUIS	L, 106-107	12-16
12-19	SYRACUSE	W, 120-112	13-16
12-20	at St. Louis	L, 86-102	13-17
12-22	BOSTON	L, 104-136	13-18
12-25	at Cincinnati	L, 103-121	13-19
12-26	MINNEAPOLIS	L, 105-108	13-20
12-27	at Minneapolis	L, 109-119	13-21
12-30	n-New York	L, 109-124	13-22
1-1	ST. LOUIS	W, 119-107	14-22
1-2	at St. Louis	L, 113-114	14-23
1-3	CINCINNATI	W, 114-112	15-23
1-5	at New York	L, 110-121	15-24
1-7	n-Philadelphia	L, 105-120	15-25
1-8	at Syracuse	L, 107-118	15-26
1-9	BOSTON	L, 103-126	15-27
1-10	at Syracuse	L, 103-108	15-28
1-13	at New York	W, 114-113	16-28
1-16	at Minneapolis	W, 105-98	17-28
1-17	CINCINNATI	W, 115-110	18-28
1-24	PHILADELPHIA	W, 130-110	19-28
1-25	at Philadelphia	L, 117-127	19-29
1-26	n-Syracuse	W, 121-114	20-29
1-27	SYRACUSE	L, 108-144	20-30
1-29	at St. Louis	L, 125-130 (OT)	20-31
1-30	ST. LOUIS	W, 117-107	21-31
1-31	at Boston	L, 128-146	21-32
2-3	CINCINNATI	W, 117-105	22-32
2-4	at Cincinnati	W, 121-102	23-32
2-6	MINNEAPOLIS	W, 116-101	24-32
2-7	at Minneapolis	L, 102-104	24-33
2-9	PHILADELPHIA	W, 122-113	25-33
2-10	at Boston	L, 121-153	25-34
2-12	at Cincinnati	L, 101-133	25-35
2-13	MINNEAPOLIS	L, 117-123 (OT)	25-36
2-16	ST. LOUIS	L, 104-111	25-37
2-19	BOSTON	L, 116-136	25-38
2-20	at Cincinnati	L, 107-110	25-39
2-21	at Syracuse	L, 120-122	25-40
2-24	SYRACUSE	W, 128-110	26-40
2-25	at Boston	L, 107-121	26-41
2-27	at St. Louis	W, 116-114	27-41
2-28	PHILADELPHIA	L, 111-113	27-42
3-1	n-Cincinnati	W, 108-106	28-42
3-2	ST. LOUIS	W, 116-100	29-42
3-3	at Philadelphia	L, 101-110	29-43
3-6	at New York	L, 112-120	29-44
3-8	at St. Louis	L, 101-122	29-45
3-9	Minneapolis	W, 117-116	30-45

PLAYOFFS

Western Semifinals—(Best-of-Three)

Date	Opponent	Result	Record
3-12	MINNEAPOLIS	L, 112-113	0-1
3-13	at Minneapolis	L, 99-114	0-2

(Home games in CAPS; n-neutral site)

15

1960 🏀 1961

TIME CAPSULE

October 13, 1960:
Bill Mazeroski of Pittsburgh slams a game-winning home run against the New York Yankees, giving the Pirates the World Series championship.

November 8, 1960:
John F. Kennedy is elected president of the United States in a narrow victory over Richard M. Nixon.

May 5, 1961:
Alan Shepard makes a successful flight aboard the Project Mercury capsule Freedom Seven, becoming the first American in space.

SEASON SNAPSHOT

Most Points
Bailey Howell (1,815, 23.6 avg.)

Most Rebounds
Bailey Howell (1,111, 14.4 avg.)

Most Assists
Gene Shue (530, 6.8 avg.)

Most Minutes
Gene Shue (3,361, 43.1 avg.)

Field-Goal Percentage
Bailey Howell (46.9%)

Free-Throw Percentage
Gene Shue (85.6%)

Team Offense Average
118.6 (9,370 in 79 games)

Team Defense Average
121.0 (9,558 in 79 games)

NBA All-Stars
Gene Shue, G (Second Team)

Pistons in All-Star Game
Gene Shue, G; Walter Dukes, C; Bailey Howell, F

1960-61

FINAL STANDINGS

Western Division	W	L	Pct.	GB
St. Louis	51	28	.646	—
Los Angeles	36	43	.456	15
PISTONS	**34**	**45**	**.430**	**17**
Cincinnati	33	46	.418	18

Eastern Division Winner—Boston

PLAYOFF RESULTS

Western Semifinals: Los Angeles d. Pistons, 3-2

PISTONS PLAYOFF LEADERS

Scoring: Bob Ferry (20.2 avg.)
Rebounding: Walter Dukes (9.8)
Assists: Gene Shue and Bailey Howell (4.4)

NBA CHAMPION

Boston Celtics

1960-61
SEASON IN REVIEW

If you believed the hype, the Pistons were ready for a breakthrough in 1960-61. Three weeks after the previous season, April 16, they'd made two vital acquisitions, getting center-forward Bob Ferry from St. Louis (for Eddie Conlin) and wiry shooting guard Don Ohl from Philadelphia. In training camp, GM Nick Kerbawy said, "We feel Ferry, Bailey Howell and (top draftee) Jackie Moreland will give us one of the youngest and most promising front lines in NBA history." In NBA history? Time would tell, but '60-61 wasn't much different from the prior three seasons. Despite a strong home record (21-10) in their final season at Olympia Stadium, the Pistons were conversely lousy on the road (13-35) and finished 34-45, a game out of the Western cellar. The home-road pattern held in the playoffs; Detroit won two at home vs. the transplanted Lakers, but lost all three at Los Angeles to suffer a third straight first-round knockout. Howell had a superb year, averaging a club-leading 23.6 points and 14.4 boards. He grabbed 32 rebounds November 5 vs. Philly, then a club record, and had 43 points and 30 boards November 25 vs. the Lakers. Gene Shue (22.6 ppg) made All-NBA second team, and Walter Dukes (1,028 boards) joined him and Howell as All-Stars. Lowlights? L.A.'s Elgin Baylor scored 57 points vs. Detroit on February 16, as did St. Louis' Bob Pettit two days later.

Forward Shellie McMillon from Bradley averaged 8.5 points in four seasons with the Pistons. Photo from Morrie Moorawnick collection.

WHAT A NIGHT!

March 18, 1961

More than a year earlier, the Pistons had decided to move up the road to Cobo Arena in '61-62, so they knew they would have to wave goodbye to Olympia Stadium sooner or later. When they played their last game at Olympia on March 18, 1961, the Pistons didn't know it was the last one, though they must have had a strong inkling. In the first playoff round vs. the Lakers, Los Angeles had won Games 1 and 2 at home, moving Detroit within a loss of elimination from the best-of-five series. The Pistons had to hold serve twice at home or their season was over—as well as their four-year stay at Olympia. On Friday night, March 17, they gained a 124-113 win to keep the series going and then nudged the Lakers again 123-114 on Saturday afternoon for a 2-2 deadlock. Gene Shue's 29 points led the latter win, while Bob Ferry scored 24 and Don Ohl 20 to help Detroit overcome 42 by Lakers star Elgin Baylor. The clubs immediately flew to L.A. for Sunday's Game 5 to complete a bicoastal three-day, three-game marathon that's unheard of nowadays. With a spot in the Western Finals at stake, the Pistons were eliminated handily 137-120, making them 0-6 at L.A. for the season. Game 4 had indeed been their Olympia finale.

Rookie small forward George Lee averaged 15.6 points in the '60-61 playoffs. Photo from Morrie Moorawnick collection.

Premier Piston

Bailey Howell

Bailey Howell took over as the Pistons' newest star in 1960-61. Photo from Morrie Moorawnick collection.

Squeaky wheels do not have a monopoly on grease. When Bailey Howell—mild-mannered, modest Bailey Howell—was elected to the Naismith Basketball Hall of Fame in 1997, the theory was proven. Howell figured he had the statistics and championships to merit his selection, but had never made any noise about it. In fact, he said he'd rather be passed up with deserving credentials than to get in without deserving it. There is no doubt Howell deserved his enshrinement with the game's greatest of all-time. After his All-American career at Mississippi State, where he averaged 27.1 points and 17.1 rebounds in 75 games over three seasons, Howell was drafted in the first round by Detroit in 1959. Thus began an excellent 12-year pro career in which the aggressive 6-foot-7 forward averaged 18.7 points, including 21.1 over five seasons with the Pistons. If not for Wilt Chamberlain, Howell almost surely would have been NBA Rookie of the Year in '59-60, setting Pistons rookie records with 1,332 points and 790 rebounds. Howell's next season would be his best from a statistical standpoint, as he racked up career highs of 1,815 points and 1,111 rebounds. That season would also produce his career single-game bests of 43 points and 32 rebounds and the first of his six berths in the All-Star Game. But stardom couldn't hide Howell's disappointment over the Pistons' lack of team success and he was finally dealt to Baltimore (with four teammates) June 18, 1964, exiting as Detroit's career point leader with 8,182. The Bullets gave Howell a major career break in '66, swapping him to Boston where he starred on the Celtics' NBA championship teams of '68 and '69, averaging 19.8 and 19.7 points, respectively.

AT A GLANCE

BAILEY HOWELL

FULL NAME:
Bailey E. Howell
BORN:
January 20, 1937; Starkville, Mississippi
POSITION, HEIGHT, WEIGHT:
Forward, 6-foot-7, 220 pounds
COLLEGE:
Mississippi State
ACQUIRED:
Drafted, first round, 1959 (2nd overall)

TENURE WITH PISTONS:
1959-60 — 1963-64
Also: Baltimore 1964-66, Boston 1966-70, Philadelphia 1970-71
BEST SEASON WITH PISTONS:
1960-61, 77 GP, 23.6 ppg, 14.4 rpg
TOTALS WITH PISTONS:
Regular season: 387 GP, 21.1 ppg, 11.8 rpg
Playoffs: 21 GP, 17.2 ppg, 9.6 rpg
HONORS:
Basketball Hall of Fame, 1997
All-Star Game (6): 1960-61, 1961-62, 1962-63, 1963-64 (Detroit); 1965-66 (Baltimore); 1966-67 (Boston)
All-NBA Team: Second Team 1962-63 (Detroit)

PISTON LIST

Bailey Howell's Career Highs With Pistons

Points (Game)
- 43, vs. L.A. Lakers, November 25, 1960
Points (Season)
- 1,815 (23.6), 1960-61
Rebounds (Game)
- 32, vs. Philadelphia, November 5, 1960
Rebounds (Season)
- 1,111 (14.4), 1960-61
Assists (Season)
- 232, 1962-63
Field Goal % (Season)
- .516, 1962-63
Free Throw % (Season)
- .809, 1963-64
Minutes (Season)
- 2,971, 1962-63

CHANGING FACES

THE PISTONS added six new players in '60-61, but the general manager who acquired them didn't last the season. Nick Kerbawy, the former GM of the Detroit Lions, had been hired in the summer of '58 to soup up the roster. His track record was mixed, the highlights being his acquisition of Bob Ferry and Don Ohl in the '60 off-season. But when Pistons owner Fred Zollner learned Kerbawy hadn't fully severed his ties to the Lions, he fired the GM in January, citing conflicts of interest. Kerbawy filed a $5.5 million libel suit and finally settled for $250,000 after four years of wrangling. Other than Ohl and Ferry, who would star for four years in Detroit, the Pistons signed '59 draftee George Lee and '60 picks Jackie Moreland (fourth overall choice), Ron Johnson (second round) and Willie Jones (fifth). A 6-foot-7 forward from Louisiana Tech, Moreland would play five seasons for Detroit and three for New Orleans of the ABA, but died in 1971 at age 33.

General manager Nick Kerbawy, fired in '60-61, had formerly been the Lions' GM.

The VILLAIN — Boston Celtics

Bill Russell, rebounder and defender extraordinaire, was always a thorn in the Pistons' side.

Beating Boston has never been any team's habit, especially in the late '50s and early '60s. In their first four years in Detroit, the Pistons had a 4-33 record against the Celtics, then in the midst of 11 NBA titles in 13 seasons. Boston's '60-61 cast featured eight Hall of Famers—coach Red Auerbach, Bill Russell, Bob Cousy, Tommy Heinsohn, Sam Jones, K.C. Jones, Frank Ramsey and Bill Sharman. Detroit went 2-8 vs. the Celtics that season, escaping by one (in overtime) and three points, including a team-record 106 rebounds in the November 15 OT win. The Celtics' victories included a 150-106 rout December 24 in which they set the NBA record with 109 rebounds, a mark that remains along with the Pistons'. In the clubs' final meeting March 9, Detroit trailed 118-116 with four seconds to go when Walter Dukes called a timeout the Pistons did not have, resulting in a technical foul. Ramsey made the free throw, expanding the Celtics' lead to three and making moot Gene Shue's layup at the buzzer.

Game Results

1960-61 REGULAR SEASON

Date	Opponent	Result	Record
10-22	at Boston	L, 116-118	0-1
10-26	CINCINNATI	W, 131-117	1-1
10-29	NEW YORK	W, 115-110	2-1
11-2	ST. LOUIS	L, 117-132	2-2
11-4	at Philadelphia	L, 121-136	2-3
11-5	n-Philadelphia	L, 123-130	2-4
11-9	at St. Louis	L, 120-126	2-5
11-12	CINCINNATI	W, 116-112	3-5
11-13	at Cincinnati	W, 125-113	4-5
11-15	n-Boston	W, 115-114 (OT)	5-5
11-16	PHILADELPHIA	W, 119-118	6-5
11-17	n-St. Louis	L, 105-112	6-6
11-19	at Los Angeles	L, 122-130	6-7
11-20	at Los Angeles	L, 131-135	6-8
11-23	SYRACUSE	W, 122-115	7-8
11-25	LOS ANGELES	L, 128-141 (OT)	7-9
11-26	n-New York	L, 119-127	7-10
11-29	at New York	L, 107-118	7-11
11-30	BOSTON	L, 110-125	7-12
12-4	at Cincinnati	W, 116-115	8-12
12-6	at St. Louis	L, 110-146	8-13
12-7	ST. LOUIS	W, 113-83	9-13
12-10	SYRACUSE	L, 107-117	9-14
12-13	at Philadelphia	L, 108-110	9-15
12-14	at Philadelphia	W, 134-126	10-15
12-16	NEW YORK	L, 104-108	10-16
12-19	n-Los Angeles	L, 103-107	10-17
12-20	n-Los Angeles	W, 97-94	11-17
12-24	at Boston	L, 106-150	11-18
12-25	at Cincinnati	L, 119-126	11-19
12-26	CINCINNATI	W, 137-132	12-19
12-29	ST. LOUIS	W, 112-89	13-19
12-30	n-Syracuse	W, 121-112	14-19
1-1	LOS ANGELES	W, 116-105	15-19
1-2	n-Los Angeles	L, 113-123	15-20
1-3	n-Philadelphia	L, 125-128 (OT)	15-21
1-5	n-New York	L, 102-104	15-22
1-6	BOSTON	L, 102-108	15-23
1-8	at Syracuse	L, 115-138	15-24
1-10	n-Boston	L, 98-118	15-25
1-11	CINCINNATI	L, 126-122	16-25
1-12	n-Cincinnati	W, 124-112	17-25
1-14	at St. Louis	L, 113-135	17-26
1-15	ST. LOUIS	W, 137-122	18-26
1-18	at Cincinnati	W, 144-128	19-26
1-20	NEW YORK	W, 132-128	20-26
1-21	n-Cincinnati	W, 130-106	21-26
1-22	PHILADELPHIA	W, 136-128	22-26
1-24	at Cincinnati	W, 106-104	23-26
1-25	CINCINNATI	W, 138-125	24-26
1-27	at Boston	L, 111-140	24-27
1-29	at Los Angeles	L, 113-137	24-28
1-30	at Los Angeles	L, 116-117	24-29
1-31	n-Los Angeles	W, 121-112	25-29
2-1	n-St. Louis	L, 131-137	25-30
2-3	SYRACUSE	W, 121-118	26-30
2-4	n-Syracuse	W, 111-104	27-30
2-5	LOS ANGELES	L, 120-125	27-31
2-7	at New York	L, 120-131	27-32
2-8	PHILADELPHIA	W, 125-123	28-32
2-10	Boston	W, 137-134	29-32
2-11	n-Syracuse	L, 111-141	29-33
2-12	at Syracuse	L, 122-148	29-34
2-14	at St. Louis	L, 134-135	29-35
2-16	LOS ANGELES	L, 106-129	29-36
2-17	n-Syracuse	L, 113-115	29-37
2-18	ST. LOUIS	L, 138-141	29-38
2-21	n-Syracuse	L, 118-123	29-39
2-22	NEW YORK	W, 123-117	30-39
2-23	at Philadelphia	L, 121-129	30-40
2-26	BOSTON	L, 99-113	30-41
3-1	at Cincinnati	L, 122-137	30-42
3-3	n-New York	W, 129-112	31-42
3-4	at St. Louis	L, 102-104	31-43
3-5	ST. LOUIS	L, 122-127	31-44
3-8	LOS ANGELES	W, 120-102	32-44
3-9	n-Boston	L, 118-119	32-45
3-10	n-Philadelphia	W, 120-103	33-45
3-12	at New York	W, 120-106	34-45

PLAYOFFS

Western Semifinals—(Best-of-Five)

Date	Opponent	Result	Record
3-14	at Los Angeles	L, 102-120	0-1
3-15	at Los Angeles	L, 118-127	0-2
3-17	LOS ANGELES	W, 124-113	1-2
3-18	LOS ANGELES	W, 123-114	2-2
3-19	at Los Angeles	L, 120-137	2-3

(Home games in CAPS; n-neutral site)

1961 1962

TIME CAPSULE

October 1, 1961:
Roger Maris of the New York Yankees slugs his 61st home run, breaking Babe Ruth's single-season record.

February 20, 1962:
Astronaut John Glenn becomes the first American to orbit the Earth, circling the globe three times aboard Friendship 7.

August 5, 1962:
Movie star Marilyn Monroe, 36, dies in her Los Angeles bungalow of an apparent overdose of sleeping pills.

SEASON SNAPSHOT

Most Points
Bailey Howell (1,576, 19.9 avg.)

Most Rebounds
Bailey Howell (996, 12.6 avg.)

Most Assists
Gene Shue (465, 5.8 avg.)

Most Minutes
Gene Shue (3,143, 39.3 avg.)

Field-Goal Percentage
Bailey Howell (46.4%)

Free-Throw Percentage
Gene Shue (81.0%)

Team Offense Average
115.4 (9,234 in 80 games)

Team Defense Average
117.1 (9,369 in 80 games)

Pistons in All-Star Game
Bailey Howell, F; Gene Shue, G

FINAL STANDINGS

Western Division	W	L	Pct.	GB
Los Angeles	54	26	.675	—
Cincinnati	43	37	.538	11
PISTONS	**37**	**43**	**.463**	**17**
St. Louis	29	51	.363	25
Chicago	18	62	.225	36

Eastern Division Winner—Boston

PLAYOFF RESULTS

Western Semifinals: Pistons d. Cincinnati, 3-1
Western Finals: Los Angeles d. Pistons, 4-2

PISTONS PLAYOFF LEADERS

Scoring: Don Ohl (20.5 avg.)
Rebounding: Ray Scott (14.5)
Assists: Gene Shue (4.9)

NBA CHAMPION

Boston Celtics

1961-62
SEASON IN REVIEW

The Pistons got close enough to sniff the NBA Finals for the first time in '61-62, but they couldn't fight the Army. If not for the cooperation of the U.S. Army, which granted a special playoff leave to Pfc. Elgin Baylor of the L.A. Lakers, the Pistons could have slipped into the championship. Alas, they were turned aside by the Lakers, 4-2, in the Western Finals as Baylor averaged 35.4 points on leave from the Army. In the first of their 17 seasons at Cobo Arena (then Convention Arena), the Pistons hadn't been viewed as a postseason threat. Though they had a solid nucleus keyed by All-Star Bailey Howell, their scoring and rebounding leader, the Pistons lost nine of their final 13 games to finish 37-43. They were even worse at the start, going 1-6 and twice being victimized for 58 points by Wilt Chamberlain. But in between, Detroit was 32-28, including a 9-2 streak that immediately preceded its bad finish. In the first round, the Pistons nudged St. Louis, 3-1, sparked by Don Ohl (23.8 ppg) and rookie Ray Scott (34 points in Game 1, 26 rebounds in Game 3). In the Western Finals, the Lakers nabbed a 3-0 lead, but Bailey Howell and Johnny Egan fueled two straight Detroit wins. Despite erasing a 24-point deficit to gain a 117-117 tie with 21 seconds left, the Pistons lost Game 6 and the series. It was the closest they'd get to the NBA Finals until 1987.

Rookie Ray Scott gave the Pistons a frontcourt boost in '61-62, and he was even better in the playoffs.

WHAT A NIGHT!

March 20, 1962

Only once in Pistons history had they won a playoff series, romping at Cincinnati to clinch a best-of-three series in '57-58 in their first year in Detroit. So, here they were again in '62, heading to Cincinnati with a 2-1 lead in a best-of-five first-round series. One more win would send the Pistons to the Western Division Finals vs. Los Angeles. In Games 1-3, Detroit's balanced offense had confounded the Royals, who banked on Oscar Robertson for much of their attack. So far, Ray Scott (34 points), Bailey Howell (28, 27), Gene Shue (25) and Don Ohl (24) had taken turns sparking the Pistons. Ohl's number came up again in Game 4. Playing all 48 minutes, the 6-foot-3 guard had 33 points, including Detroit's final basket, in a 112-111 clinching win at Cincinnati Gardens. The Pistons controlled the game most of the way, but had to rebuff a Royals rally. Cincinnati's Jack Twyman scored with 1:01 left, cutting Detroit's lead to 110-108, but Ohl came back with a jumper, restoring the four-point margin. That allowed the Pistons to withstand a free throw by Robertson and a moot layup by Twyman with two seconds left. Shue scored 21 and Howell 20. The Royals were led by Robertson's 32 and Twyman's 22.

Don Ohl's last-minute basket provided the winning margin as Detroit clinched its first-round playoff against Cincinnati.

Premier Piston

Walter "Waldo" Dukes

Until Wilt Chamberlain arrived in 1959, Walter Dukes of the Pistons was the NBA's only 7-footer.

If Bill Laimbeer really thinks the referees had it in for him, he should examine Walter Dukes' lifetime stats. Laimbeer was a referee's darling compared to Dukes, the lanky 7-footer who patrolled the middle for the Pistons' first six years in Detroit (1957-63). For the first five seasons after he was acquired from Minneapolis in '57, Dukes led the Pistons in fouls, committing at least 300 every year and leading the NBA the first two seasons (311, 332). He was the first of only three NBA players who have committed 300 for five straight seasons; the others are ex-Piston James Edwards ('78-82) and Elvin Hayes ('77-81). There is no debate as to whether Dukes was a hack; he was, leading the NBA in foul-outs four times ('59-62), averaging 19.5 per year. In his defense, however, he rarely got a night off from guarding the NBA's great big men, players who held more sway with the referees. Grappling Bill Russell nine times a year was no picnic; ditto for Wilt Chamberlain and Walt Bellamy. Dukes usually held his own as a rebounder, averaging 956 a season from 1957-61, good for four consecutive top-eight finishes among the league leaders. Until Bob Lanier got 33 boards vs. Seattle in '72, Dukes shared the Pistons record with Bailey Howell at 32; Dukes got his on December 13, 1959 vs. the Knicks, the team that drafted him in '53 after a two-time All-American career at Seton Hall. Dukes played in two All-Star games ('60, '61), grabbing a team-high 15 rebounds in the first. Having played two seasons with the Harlem Globetrotters and one apiece with New York and Minneapolis, he came to Detroit in '57 for Larry Foust. He was cut just prior to the '63-64 season, retiring as the Pistons' all-time rebound king with 4,986.

AT A GLANCE

WALTER DUKES

FULL NAME:
Walter F. Dukes
BORN:
June 23, 1930; New York
POSITION, HEIGHT, WEIGHT:
Center, 7-foot-0, 220 pounds
COLLEGE:
Seton Hall '53
ACQUIRED:
1957, trade from Minneapolis
TENURE WITH PISTONS:
1957-58 — 1962-63
Also: New York 1955-56, Minneapolis 1956-57
BEST SEASON WITH PISTONS:
1959-60, 66 GP, 15.2 ppg, 13.4 rpg
TOTALS WITH PISTONS:
Regular season: 422 GP, 10.9 ppg, 11.8 rpg
Playoffs: 30 GP, 12.6 ppg, 11.9 rpg
HONORS:
All-Star Game: 1959-60, 1960-61

PISTON LIST

Pistons Records From Olympia Era (Still unbroken)

INDIVIDUAL/GAME
- Rebounds (half): 21, Bailey Howell, 11-25-60
- FTs made: 20, George Yardley, 12-26-57; Walter Dukes, 1-19-61
- FTs attempted: 24, Yardley, 12-26-57; Dukes, 1-19-61

INDIVIDUAL/SEASON
- Scoring average: 27.8, Yardley, 1957-58
- FTs made: 655, Yardley, 1960-61
- FTs attempted: 808, Yardley, 1960-61
- Disqualifications: 22, Dukes, 1958-59

TEAM/GAME
- Rebounds: 106, Boston, 11-15-60
- Rebounds (qt.): 38, St. Louis, 12-7-60
- FGs attempted: 142, Boston, 11-17-59

CHANGING FACES

THE PISTONS helped themselves most through the '61 draft, choosing to preserve their nucleus during the season. The team made only one trade, peddling forward Shellie McMillon's rights to St. Louis on December 1. He was a sometimes-starter, known as a solid rebounder for standing 6-foot-5. In 215 games from '58-61, McMillon averaged 8.5 points and 5.9 boards, with season highs of 10.1 and 6.2 in '60-61. Prior to the season, Detroit picked two comple-mentary players in the draft—6-foot-9 forward Ray Scott and 6-foot guard Johnny Egan. Scott's huge impact in the playoffs—17.3 points, 14.5 re-bounds—capped his rookie season and he would go on to a 10-year Pistons career, the last four as coach ('72-76).

Johnny Egan's three seasons with Detroit began his much-traveled NBA career.

Barely a week before being picked 12th overall, Egan led Providence to victory in the National Invitation Tournament (the NIT meant a lot then). He played for seven clubs in 11 NBA seasons, culminating with Houston in '72, and also coached the Rockets to a 129-152 record from 1973-76.

Take a Bow

Olympia Stadium

Olympia Stadium served as the Pistons' arena from 1957-61, but they were the building's No. 2 tenant behind the successful Red Wings.

The Pistons moved out of their starter home in '61-62, saying goodbye to venerable Olympia Stadium in favor of 10,939-seat Convention Arena on the banks of the Detroit River. The struggling club moved because the rent was cheap—the per-game levy fell from $2,500 to $600—but also because it had grown tired of being the second tenant at Olympia, where Gordie Howe and the Red Wings ruled. The Pistons were better than .500 at Olympia over their four seasons, going 57-52 (.523), but they were at the Wings' mercy over scheduling. The hockey team got the prime dates, often forcing the Pistons to play at the University of Detroit and, in one embarrassing instance, Grosse Pointe High School. The Pistons' Olympia era was marked by some terrific individual play, espe-cially by the likes of George Yardley, Gene Shue and Bailey Howell, but little team success. By 1997, more than a dozen club records remained from the Olympia era—such unbreakables as the Pistons' 106 rebounds vs. Boston on November 15, 1960 and Walter Dukes' 22 foul-outs in '58-59.

Game Results
1961-62
REGULAR SEASON

Date	Opponent	Result	Record
10-21	at Boston	L, 102-127	0-1
10-25	L.A. LAKERS	L, 116-120	0-2
10-27	at L.A. Lakers	L, 118-128	0-3
10-28	at L.A. Lakers	L, 126-135	0-4
11-1	NEW YORK	W, 111-95	1-4
11-4	at Philadelphia	L, 132-135	1-5
11-8	PHILADELPHIA	L, 128-132	1-6
11-9	n-Boston	W, 116-110	2-6
11-10	at New York	W, 124-118	3-6
11-11	at St. Louis	L, 119-132	3-7
11-15	ST. LOUIS	W, 127-122	4-7
11-18	CHICAGO	W, 119-112	5-7
11-19	n-Cincinnati	L, 112-128	5-8
11-21	n-L.A. Lakers	W, 108-102	6-8
11-24	n-St. Louis	W, 142-135	7-8
11-25	L.A. LAKERS	W, 104-103	8-8
11-26	BOSTON	L, 101-107	8-9
11-28	n-Boston	L, 108-116	8-10
12-1	at St. Louis	L, 116-119	8-11
12-2	ST. LOUIS	W, 118-109	9-11
12-6	NEW YORK	W, 133-97	10-11
12-8	n-Chicago	W, 133-107	11-11
12-9	L.A. LAKERS	L, 107-114	11-12
12-12	n-Philadelphia	L, 109-132	11-13
12-14	at Cincinnati	W, 107-103	12-13
12-16	CINCINNATI	L, 110-121	12-14
12-17	n-L.A. Lakers	L, 116-122	12-15
12-19	n-Syracuse	L, 111-124	12-16
12-20	PHILADELPHIA	L, 102-117	12-17
12-23	n-Cincinnati	W, 134-125	13-17
12-25	n-Chicago	L, 97-118	13-18
12-26	n-Chicago	L, 101-108	13-19
12-27	CHICAGO	W, 121-93	14-19
12-29	at Cincinnati	W, 131-116	15-19
12-30	at Syracuse	L, 108-109	15-20
1-1	ST. LOUIS	L, 139-145	15-21
1-2	at New York	L, 104-110	15-22
1-3	BOSTON	W, 112-103	16-22
1-5	n-Syracuse	W, 138-135 (OT)	17-22
1-6	n-New York	L, 111-115	17-23
1-9	n-St. Louis	W, 122-113	18-23
1-10	PHILADELPHIA	L, 110-113	18-24
1-12	at Chicago	W, 102-99	19-24
1-13	CINCINNATI	L, 112-119	19-25
1-14	n-L.A. Lakers	W, 118-108	20-25
1-17	BOSTON	L, 116-126	20-26
1-19	n-Philadelphia	L, 125-136	20-27
1-20	at Philadelphia	L, 107-123	20-28
1-21	at Boston	W, 124-120	21-28
1-22	n-Cincinnati	L, 106-115	21-29
1-24	SYRACUSE	W, 111-102	22-29
1-25	n-Syracuse	W, 101-100	23-29
1-27	NEW YORK	W, 115-107	24-29
1-28	at St. Louis	L, 97-110	24-30
1-31	L.A. LAKERS	L, 122-123 (OT)	24-31
2-2	at Chicago	L, 96-112	24-32
2-3	n-Chicago	W, 116-109	25-32
2-4	ST. LOUIS	W, 121-113	26-32
2-6	at Cincinnati	W, 119-118	27-32
2-7	CINCINNATI	W, 113-107	28-32
2-11	at Syracuse	L, 116-132	28-33
2-14	PHILADELPHIA	W, 119-110	29-33
2-16	L.A. LAKERS	W, 127-121	30-33
2-17	at Cincinnati	W, 123-118	31-33
2-18	ST. LOUIS	W, 119-112	32-33
2-20	at New York	L, 103-110	32-34
2-21	at St. Louis	W, 126-123	33-34
2-23	CINCINNATI	L, 120-134	33-35
2-25	at L.A. Lakers	L, 99-128	33-36
2-27	at L.A. Lakers	L, 100-107	33-37
2-28	n-New York	L, 109-119	33-38
3-2	n-Cincinnati	L, 112-120	33-39
3-3	SYRACUSE	L, 114-128	33-40
3-4	n-Chicago	W, 133-116	34-40
3-7	n-New York	W, 119-112	35-40
3-9	BOSTON	L, 111-130	35-41
3-10	at Syracuse	L, 111-128	35-42
3-11	at St. Louis	L, 123-126	35-43
3-12	n-Chicago	W, 121-116	36-43
3-14	SYRACUSE	W, 105-102	37-43

PLAYOFFS

Western Semifinals—(Best-of-Five)

3-16	CINCINNATI	W, 123-122	1-0
3-17	at Cincinnati	L, 107-129	1-1
3-18	CINCINNATI	W, 118-107	2-1
3-20	at Cincinnati	W, 112-111	3-1

Western Finals—(Best-of-Seven)

3-24	at L.A. Lakers	L, 108-132	0-1
3-25	at L.A. Lakers	L, 112-127	0-2
3-27	L.A. LAKERS	L, 106-111	0-3
3-29	L.A. LAKERS	W, 118-117	1-3
3-31	at L.A. Lakers	W, 132-125	2-3
4-3	L.A. LAKERS	L, 117-123	2-4

(Home games in ALL CAPS; n-neutral site)

DAVE DeBUSSCHERE

When Detroit's favorite son, Dave DeBusschere, was traded to the New York Knicks in 1968 and helped them win two NBA championships in the next five years, it verified what had been widely presumed. For his six-plus years as a Piston, he had been a good player hidden on a bad team.

Sadly, that is DeBusschere's legacy with the Pistons: what might have been. He joined them in 1962 as a born-and-reared Eastsider—a legend from Austin Catholic High School and the University of Detroit. For 440 games he put his heart into making the Pistons a successful team, even assuming the coaching duties for 222 regrettable games from 1964-67.

But it was never enough. Constant upheaval—wasted drafts, ill-fated coaching moves, underperforming talent—limited Detroit to 10 playoff games during DeBusschere's tenure. By comparison, he played in 86 with New York. He was chosen to three All-Star games with Detroit and four

with the Knicks. He made six All-Defensive squads, all with the Knicks, though his first berth was in '68-69, which he began with the Pistons.

The bottom line was glorious, though, as "Big Dave" was picked to the Basketball Hall of Fame in 1982 and chosen to the NBA's 50-player All-Time team in 1996. He is now a New York commercial real estate exec.

From his days as a schoolboy hero, it was apparent DeBusschere would be successful at whatever he tried. His size (6-foot-6, 235 pounds) and strength made him a star in basketball and baseball at both Austin High and the University of Detroit. He led Austin to the state prep basketball championship, beating Chet Walker's Benton Harbor team. He helped U-D qualify for three straight NCAA tournaments. As a right-handed pitcher he was the subject of a '62 bidding war between the Detroit Tigers and the Chicago White Sox, won by the latter for

AT A GLANCE

DAVE DeBUSSCHERE

FULL NAME:
David Albert DeBusschere
BORN:
October 16, 1940; Detroit
POSITION, HEIGHT, WEIGHT:
Forward, 6-foot-6, 235 pounds
COLLEGE:
Detroit '62
ACQUIRED:
1962, Pistons' No. 1 draft pick (territorial)
TENURE WITH PISTONS:
Player: 1962-63—December 19, 1968
Coach: November 9, 1964—March 7, 1967
Also played: New York, December 19, 1968—1972-73

BEST SEASON WITH PISTONS:
Player: 1967-68, 80 GP, 17.9 ppg, 13.5 rpg
Coach: 1964-65, 69 GP, 29-40 (.420)
PLAYING TOTALS WITH PISTONS:
Regular season: 440 GP, 7,096 pts. (16.1), 4,947 reb. (11.2)
Playoffs: 10 GP, 196 pts. (19.6), 160 reb. (16.0)
COACHING TOTALS WITH PISTONS:
Regular season: 222 GP, 79-143 (.356)
HONORS:
Basketball Hall of Fame, 1982
Top 50 Players of All-Time, 1996
No. 22 retired by Knicks, 1981
NBA All-Rookie Team, 1962-63
All-NBA Team: Second Team 1968-69 (Detroit-New York)
NBA All-Defensive Team (6): 1968-69 (Detroit-New York), 1969-70, 1970-71, 1971-72, 1972-73, 1973-74
All-Star Game (7): Detroit 1965-66, 1966-67, 1967-68; New York 1969-70, 1970-71, 1971-72, 1972-73

PISTON LIST

DeBusschere's Season Highs with Detroit and New York

	Pistons	Knicks
• Points	1,435 ('68)	1,282 ('74)
• Pts. Avg.	18.2 ('67)	18.1 ('74)
• Rebounds	1,081 ('68)	901 (twice)
• Reb. Avg.	13.5 ('68)	11.3 ('72)
• Assists	253 ('65)	291 ('72)
• Games	80 (twice)	81 ('71)
• Minutes	3,125 ('68)	3,072 ('72)
• FG%	.447 ('69)	.461 ('74)
• FT%	.723 ('69)	.756 ('74)

$65,000 mainly because it would also allow him to pursue pro basketball (the Tigers would not).

DeBusschere's Pistons career also began in '62 as they drafted him in the territorial round, becoming the first such pick in team history. (Bill Buntin would be the other in '65, the last territorial season). Playing in all 80 games, DeBusschere immediately proved deserving of his status, averaging 12.7 points and 8.7 rebounds to make the All-Rookie team. He was even better in the playoffs against St. Louis, averaging 20.0 points and 15.8 rebounds, including 26 boards in one game. A broken foot limited him to 15 games in '63-64, but he came back the next season to become the franchise's lynchpin in a most historical manner.

Not since 1914 when 23-year-old Roger Peckinpaugh managed the New York Highlanders, precursors of the Yankees, had someone so young been named coach of a pro sports team. But on November 9, 1964, with the Pistons having lost six straight games and nine of 11 under coach Charley Wolf, the club turned to its 24-year-old star; new GM Don Wattrick convinced DeBusschere to become Detroit's player-coach. Before or since, the NBA has never had a younger coach, a distinction that brings DeBusschere no real satisfaction because of his 79-143 coaching record through 1967.

"It was a big mistake," he later conceded. "I wasn't mature enough. It hurt me as a player, thinking about what we could do on the floor."

If it stunted his development, it did not show in his statistics. During DeBusschere's three years as player-coach, he averaged 17.1 points and 11.5 boards. He scored a career-high 41 points on January 12, 1966 against Philadelphia, using a sweet left-handed jumper to hit 19 baskets. Later that season, his aggressive style led to a career-best 27-rebound game.

In the meantime, DeBusschere had finally given up on baseball. He was 0-0 with the White Sox in '62 and 3-4 in '63, but lingered in the minors much of his career until quitting in '66 to concentrate on basketball. He had a minor-league mark of 40-21 with 395 strikeouts in 512 innings.

Late in the '66-67 season, it was time for DeBusschere to give up one more of his hats, agreeing to pass the coaching baton to former Pistons guard Donnis Butcher, his assistant; the change occurred March 7 with eight games left. In the All-Star Game two months earlier, DeBusschere had 22 points off the bench in 25 minutes to key a West win; that was a vast improvement over his 1-for-14 performance in the '66 classic.

Though DeBusschere would build his finest Detroit season in '67-68—17.9 ppg, 13.5 rpg—and the addition of Dave Bing in '66 had eased some of his leadership burden, it was apparent that a master stroke would be needed to make the Pistons anything resembling a serious contender. As it turned out, the supposed master stroke was to trade DeBusschere. On December 19, 1968, with DeBusschere only 39 rebounds behind Walter Dukes' Pistons career record, coach Paul Seymour shipped him to New York for well-traveled center Walt Bellamy and guard Howie Komives. It was not a good trade for Detroit—Bellamy would be dealt away in barely a year—but it was the career break DeBusschere had long coveted. The Knicks were a team with title aspirations and a lineup to match.

It didn't take long for DeBusschere to make it in the Big Apple. Though he had split '68-69 between Detroit and New York, he was named to the All-NBA second team with 16.3 points and 11.7 boards. Then everything came together for the Knicks in '69-70 as they finally reached the NBA summit, beating the L.A. Lakers in seven terrifically contentious Finals games. DeBusschere started all 19 postseason games, his 11.6 rebounds ranking second on the team to Willis Reed's 13.8. Though Reed is widely applauded, deservedly so, for overcoming a knee injury to fuel New York in the Finals, it is just as universally under-stood that the acquisition of DeBusschere the year before had put the Knicks' lineup over the top. His team-high 10.5 rebounds in the '73 playoffs helped New York to another title, again over the Lakers. In the regular season, his 10.2 rebounds led the team and his 16.3 points ranked second to Walt Frazier.

DeBusschere could've hung on as a player for two or three more years, but retired after averaging 18.1 points and 10.7 rebounds in '73-74. His post-retirement was just as busy, though. He signed as GM of the ABA's New York (later New Jersey) Nets, then was drafted as commissioner of the ABA in '75 to expedite a complicated merger with the NBA. He went back to the Knicks in 1982 as GM, a four-year stint highlighted when he drafted Patrick Ewing in '85 after New York won the first lottery. From beginning to end, Dave DeBusschere's luck was a lot better in New York.

Dave DeBusschere's Regular-Season Statistics with Detroit

SEASON	G	MIN	FGM	FGA	PCT	FTM	FTA	PCT	REB	AST	PF	DQ	PTS	PPG
1962-63	80	2352	406	944	.430	206	287	.718	694	207	247	2	1018	12.7
1963-64	15	304	52	133	.391	25	43	.581	105	23	32	1	129	8.6
1964-65	79	2769	508	1196	.425	306	437	.700	874	253	242	5	1322	16.7
1965-66	79	2696	524	1284	.408	249	378	.659	916	209	252	5	1297	16.4
1966-67	78	2897	531	1278	.415	361	512	.705	924	216	297	7	1423	18.2
1967-68	80	3125	573	1295	.442	289	435	.664	1081	181	304	3	1435	17.9
1968-69	29	1092	189	423	.447	94	130	.723	353	63	111	1	472	16.3
TOTALS	440	15235	2783	6553	.425	1530	2222	.689	4947	1152	1317	24	7096	16.1

1962 🏀 1963

TIME CAPSULE

October 1, 1962:
James Meredith, escorted by U.S. marshals, becomes the first black to attend classes at the University of Mississippi. Two men are killed in the ensuing mob violence.

October 22, 1963:
President John F. Kennedy addresses the nation on television regarding the Cuban missile crisis, leading to the dismantling of the missile bases by the Soviet Union 11 days later.

August 28, 1963:
Dr. Martin Luther King Jr. presents his "I Have a Dream" speech to a crowd of 200,000 at the Lincoln Memorial in Washington, D.C.; he had "tested" the speech previously in Detroit.

SEASON SNAPSHOT

Most Points
Bailey Howell (1,793, 22.7 avg.)

Most Rebounds
Bailey Howell (910, 11.5 avg.)

Most Assists
Don Ohl (325, 4.1 avg.)

Most Minutes
Bailey Howell (2,971, 37.6 avg.)

Field-Goal Percentage
Bailey Howell (51.6%)

Free-Throw Percentage
Bailey Howell (79.8%)

Team Offense Average
113.9 (9,112 in 80 games)

Team Defense Average
117.6 (9,408 in 80 games)

NBA All-Stars
Bailey Howell, F (Second Team)

Pistons in All-Star Game
Bailey Howell, F; Don Ohl, G

1962-63

FINAL STANDINGS

Western Division	W	L	Pct.	GB
Los Angeles	53	27	.663	—
St. Louis	48	32	.600	5
PISTONS	**34**	**46**	**.425**	**19**
San Francisco	31	49	.388	22
Chicago	25	55	.313	28

Eastern Division Winner—Boston

PLAYOFF RESULTS

Western Semifinals: St. Louis d. Pistons, 3-1

PISTONS PLAYOFF LEADERS

Scoring: Don Ohl (21.3 avg.)
Rebounding: Dave DeBusschere (15.8)
Assists: Don Ohl (4.8)

NBA CHAMPION

Boston Celtics

1962-63
SEASON IN REVIEW

The Pistons expected to take the next step in '62-63, having advanced to the second round the previous spring. Their illusions lasted less than a month, as they lost their first seven games, 10 of 11 and 16 of 19. By November 27, they were 3-16, giving up roughly 121 points a game and coach Dick McGuire was squarely on the hot seat. Gene Shue had been traded to New York for defensive big man Darrall Imhoff and the Pistons were not able to replace his 19-point average and court savvy. It would require a speedy revival to keep the team from collapsing, and it was provided by Bailey Howell, Don Ohl, Ray Scott, Bob Ferry and a 6-foot-6 wunderkind from the University of Detroit, Dave DeBusschere. From their low point, the Pistons went 31-30 to finish 34-46 and make the Western playoffs, where they lost 3-1 to St. Louis. Howell was strong on both ends with a team-leading 22.7 points (sixth in the league) and 11.5 rebounds—good for an All-NBA second-team berth. Fellow All-Star Ohl scored at a 19.3 clip and territorial draftee DeBusschere showed fast development (12.7 ppg, 8.7 rpg). He really emerged in the playoffs, averaging 20.0 and 15.8. Defense was the Pistons' bugaboo; opponents averaged 117.6 points and surpassed 140 five times. Syracuse's 162 points on February 8 remained the Pistons' opponent record until 1983.

Bailey Howell led the Pistons in almost every statistical category en route to All-NBA second team.

WHAT A NIGHT!

February 12-13, 1963

In the modern NBA, teams usually aren't scheduled to play on back-to-back nights if it involves more than a three-hour plane ride. Clubs were not so lucky in the 1960s when scheduling rules didn't exist. In '63, for example, the Pistons played four straight nights out West from January 21-24, then had to fly back to Chicago to play the fifth night. So it was not shocking when the Pistons and San Francisco Warriors had a home-and-home series less than a month later, on February 12-13. The games were not throwaways, either, because the teams were still battling for the third and final Western playoff spot. On Tuesday the 12th at Detroit, a record house of 11,028 showed up at Cobo to see the Pistons beat the Warriors, 120-115. Detroit blew an 11-point second-half edge, but Bailey Howell scored eight points in a row to restore the lead and the Pistons hung on. Bob Ferry made eight straight shots among 29 points and Don Ohl scored 24, helping offset Wilt Chamberlain's customary 46 (with 32 rebounds). After flying overnight to San Francisco, the clubs went overtime on the 13th with Detroit winning 134-132. Ohl scored 32, Howell 28 and Ferry 22, while Chamberlain led everyone with 51. The sweep put the Pistons 2½ games ahead of the Warriors, leading to an eventual playoff bid.

Bob Ferry was a force in a two-game sweep of San Francisco that was crucial to Detroit's playoff hopes.

Premier Piston

Don Ohl

Don Ohl played in five All-Star games, three of them after being traded by Detroit in 1964.

Don Ohl did not need to be discovered. He merely needed the Pistons to bring him out of the shadows. When they did so in 1960, signing the 24-year-old out of an Illinois semi-pro league, Ohl did the rest. A 6-foot-3 shooting guard, Ohl built an exceptional 10-year career in which he was a five-time All-Star and annual inhabitant of the scoring leaders. In his four Detroit seasons, a tenure that ended in '64 with a misguided trade, Ohl averaged 16.7 points as the Pistons' No. 1 perimeter threat. Perhaps forgotten over the decades but highly respected by his contemporaries, Ohl had the sort of skill that could have made him the Pistons' all-time scoring king. As it was, he ranked third with 5,137 when he was sent to the Baltimore Bullets in a massive eight-player swap on June 18, 1964, a one-sided deal that badly went against the Pistons. Ohl made the All-Star game twice with the Pistons and three times with Baltimore, then finished out his career with the Hawks (St. Louis and Atlanta) in '70. He scored his career-high 43 points with Detroit on January 23, 1963 against the Lakers, then compiled 41 two months later vs. San Francisco. Those totals were part of his best Pistons season, '62-63, in which he scored a career-high 1,547 points, good for 10th in the league. From '61-62 on, he ranked 21st, 10th, 22nd, 10th and 12th in consecutive years. None of it might have happened had the Pistons not spotted Ohl with the Peoria Cats of the semi-pro NIBL. Ohl had been an All-Big Ten guard at Illinois, ranking third in conference scoring at 21.1 in '58. He was drafted in the fifth round by Philadelphia, but went to Peoria instead for two years of seasoning. The Pistons bought his rights in '60, some of the best money they ever spent.

AT A GLANCE

DON OHL

FULL NAME:
Donald Jay Ohl
BORN:
April 18, 1936; Edwardsville, Illinois
POSITION, HEIGHT, WEIGHT:
Guard, 6-foot-3, 190 pounds
COLLEGE:
Illinois '58
ACQUIRED:
1960, purchased from Philadelphia
TENURE WITH PISTONS:
1960-61 — 1963-64
Also: Peoria (NIBL) 1958-60, Baltimore 1964-68, Atlanta 1968-70
BEST SEASON WITH PISTONS:
1962-63, 80 GP, 19.3 ppg, 4.1 apg
TOTALS WITH PISTONS:
Regular season: 307 GP, 16.7 ppg, 3.4 apg
Playoffs: 17 GP, 18.4 ppg, 3.4 apg
HONORS:
All-Star Game: Detroit 1962-63, 1963-64; Baltimore 1964-65, 1965-66, 1966-67

PISTON LIST

Pistons Who Became NBA Head Coaches

(Record thru '96-97)

- Donnis Butcher (52-60, .464)
- M.L. Carr (48-116, .293)
- Dave DeBusschere (79-143, .356)
- Terry Dischinger (0-2, .000)
- Johnny Egan (129-152, .459)
- Chris Ford (255-237, .518)
- Harry Gallatin (136-120, .531)
- Bob Lanier (12-25, .324)
- George Lee (63-71, .470)
- Earl Lloyd (22-55, .286)
- Kevin Loughery (474-662, .417)
- Sidney Lowe (33-102, .244)
- Dick McGuire (161-215, .428)
- Ray Scott (147-134, .523)
- Gene Shue (784-861, .477)
- Larry Staverman (58-74, .439)
- Rod Thorn (15-15, .500)
- Darrell Walker (30-52, .366)

CHANGING FACES

THE '62-63 PISTONS: cradle of coaches and GMs. They traded two future NBA coaches before the season, Gene Shue (to New York) and George Lee (to San Francisco), but got two more in the draft, Dave DeBusschere and Kevin Loughery. Three others on the roster—Johnny Egan, Ray Scott and Bob Ferry—were also future coaches or general managers. DeBusschere and Scott went on to coach the Pistons and DeBusschere was also GM of the Knicks. Loughery and Egan became coaches and Ferry was a longtime GM with Washington. Combined, the four coaches-to-be wound up with a 829-1091 record, mostly Loughery's 474-662 with six clubs. Shue, who had a 784-861 mark in 22 seasons, was traded to the Knicks on August 29, ending a six-year Pistons career that began in Fort Wayne. In return the Pistons got 6-foot-10 Darrall Imhoff, early in an unremarkable 12-year career. Loughery was picked in the second round (13th) and averaged 6.4 points. In the fourth round, Detroit picked 7-foot center Reggie Harding, a local non-collegian, but didn't sign him until '64.

Kevin Loughery fashioned an 11-year NBA career, but played only 58 games with Detroit over two seasons.

The VILLAIN

Wilt Chamberlain

Wilt Chamberlain dominated the NBA in the early '60s, and the Pistons were among his most frequent victims.

Go ahead and try to convince the Pistons that Wilt Chamberlain had a "down" year in 1962-63 when the Philadelphia Warriors moved across the country to San Francisco. Technically speaking, Stilt's scoring and rebounding averages decreased that season, but only because he had an amazing '61-62 with 50.4 points, an NBA record, and 25.7 rebounds. He followed that with averages of 44.8 points and 24.3 boards in his first season at San Francisco, and the Pistons were his main victims. Out of 36 games with 46 points or more, Chamberlain did it to the Pistons 10 times in 12 meetings. In order, he compiled 56 (overtime), 50 (with 41 rebounds), 49, 51, 52, 37, 58, 48, 46 (32 boards), 51 (OT), 35, 51 (OT). Though Detroit won the last two OT games, Chamberlain forced both of them into the extra session with last-second baskets in regulation. He scored 58 points January 24 in a neutral-site clash at Bakersfield, California, matching his previous high against the Pistons, but he would beat that total on February 11, 1964 with 59 in an overtime victory at Detroit.

Game Results
1962-63
REGULAR SEASON

Date	Opponent	Result	Record
10-16	n-L.A. Lakers	L, 106-122	0-1
10-20	at St. Louis	L, 111-120	0-2
10-23	at San Francisco	L, 113-140	0-3
10-26	at San Francisco	L, 131-132 (OT)	0-4
10-27	at L.A. Lakers	L, 118-134	0-5
10-31	BOSTON	L, 100-115	0-6
11-3	at Boston	L, 114-125	0-7
11-8	CINCINNATI	W, 116-114	1-7
11-10	at Cincinnati	L, 124-135	1-8
11-11	at St. Louis	L, 100-117	1-9
11-13	n-Cincinnati	L, 109-127	1-10
11-14	SAN FRANCISCO	W, 123-115	2-10
11-17	n-New York	W, 121-113 (OT)	3-10
11-18	L.A. LAKERS	L, 98-116	3-11
11-21	SYRACUSE	L, 120-122	3-12
11-22	at St. Louis	L, 91-106	3-13
11-23	ST. LOUIS	L, 93-121	3-14
11-24	at Chicago	L, 103-124	3-15
11-27	n-Boston	L, 115-125	3-16
11-28	NEW YORK	W, 143-101	4-16
12-1	n-New York	W, 117-115	5-16
12-4	n-Syracuse	W, 130-129	6-16
12-5	BOSTON	L, 93-106	6-17
12-7	SAN FRANCISCO	W, 123-116	7-17
12-8	at New York	L, 78-87	7-18
12-9	n-St. Louis	W, 123-119	8-18
12-10	n-Chicago	W, 109-100	9-18
12-12	NEW YORK	W, 115-106	10-18
12-13	n-Boston	L, 93-103	10-19
12-15	ST. LOUIS	L, 94-112	10-20
12-16	n-Chicago	L, 106-110	10-21
12-18	n-Chicago	L, 110-113	10-22
12-19	CHICAGO	W, 115-113	11-22
12-21	SAN FRANCISCO	L, 113-122	11-23
12-22	n-Chicago	W, 122-110	12-23
12-25	at Cincinnati	L, 120-131	12-24
12-26	at Chicago	W, 123-116	13-24
12-30	L.A. LAKERS	L, 130-135	13-25
1-2	Cincinnati	W, 138-118	14-25
1-4	n-St. Louis	L, 100-121	14-26
1-5	ST. LOUIS	W, 92-90	15-26
1-6	at New York	W, 103-102	16-26
1-8	n-New York	W, 109-93	17-26
1-9	L.A. LAKERS	L, 115-123	17-27
1-11	CHICAGO	W, 116-112	18-27
1-12	n-Syracuse	W, 146-115	19-27
1-13	at Syracuse	L, 114-148	19-28
1-21	at L.A. Lakers	L, 94-124	19-29
1-22	at San Francisco	W, 115-107	20-29
1-23	at L.A. Lakers	L, 119-123	20-30
1-24	n-San Francisco	L, 114-138	20-31
1-25	at Chicago	W, 113-111	21-31
1-31	n-L.A. Lakers	L, 122-127	21-32
2-1	L.A. LAKERS	L, 109-119	21-33
2-3	at Boston	L, 128-137	21-34
2-5	n-St. Louis	L, 105-120	21-35
2-6	SAN FRANCISCO	L, 116-117	21-36
2-8	SYRACUSE	L, 135-162	21-37
2-10	at St. Louis	W, 102-95	22-37
2-12	SAN FRANCISCO	W, 120-115	23-37
2-13	at San Francisco	W, 134-132 (OT)	24-37
2-14	at L.A. Lakers	L, 111-128	24-38
2-16	CINCINNATI	L, 99-110	24-39
2-17	at Syracuse	L, 124-143	24-40
2-19	at New York	W, 121-112	25-40
2-20	BOSTON	L, 113-117	25-41
2-22	SYRACUSE	W, 126-117	26-41
2-23	at Cincinnati	W, 105-102	27-41
2-24	n-Cincinnati	W, 119-110	28-41
2-25	n-L.A. Lakers	L, 107-113	28-42
2-28	CHICAGO	W, 112-104	29-42
3-1	n-St. Louis	W, 115-113	30-42
3-2	at Syracuse	L, 128-152	30-43
3-3	SYRACUSE	L, 123-127	30-44
3-5	n-San Francisco	W, 111-102	31-44
3-7	BOSTON	L, 104-115	31-45
3-8	n-San Francisco	W, 131-123 (OT)	32-45
3-10	L.A. LAKERS	W, 124-116	33-45
3-13	NEW YORK	W, 112-89	34-45
3-17	at St. Louis	L, 105-119	34-46

PLAYOFFS
Western Semifinals—(Best-of-Seven)

Date	Opponent	Result	Record
3-20	at St. Louis	L, 99-118	0-1
3-22	at St. Louis	L, 108-122	0-2
3-24	ST. LOUIS	W, 107-103	1-2
3-26	ST. LOUIS	L, 100-104	1-3

(Home games in ALL CAPS; n-neutral site)

1963 1964

TIME CAPSULE

November 22, 1963:
President John F. Kennedy is assassinated as his motorcade drives through downtown Dallas; Lyndon B. Johnson sworn in as 36th president.

February 7, 1964:
The Beatles arrive in New York for the first of two appearances on The Ed Sullivan Show; millions tune in.

February 25, 1964:
Challenger Cassius Clay (later Muhammad Ali) defeats Sonny Liston for the world heavyweight boxing title.

July 2, 1964:
The Civil Rights Act of 1964 is signed by President Johnson.

SEASON SNAPSHOT

Most Points
Bailey Howell (1,666, 21.6 avg.)

Most Rebounds
Ray Scott (1,078, 13.5 avg.)

Most Assists
Ray Scott (244, 4.1 avg.)

Most Minutes
Ray Scott (2,964, 37.1 avg.)

Field-Goal Percentage
Bailey Howell (47.2%)

Free-Throw Percentage
Bailey Howell (80.9%)

Team Offense Average
107.8 (8,620 in 80 games)

Team Defense Average
115.5 (9,238 in 80 games)

Pistons in All-Star Game
Bailey Howell, F; Don Ohl, G

1963-64

FINAL STANDINGS

Western Division	W	L	Pct.	GB
San Francisco	48	32	.600	—
St. Louis	46	34	.575	2
Los Angeles	42	38	.525	6
Baltimore	31	49	.388	17
PISTONS	**23**	**57**	**.288**	**25**

Eastern Division Winner—Boston

PLAYOFF RESULTS

Pistons Did Not Qualify

PISTONS PLAYOFF LEADERS

NBA CHAMPION

Boston Celtics

1963-64
SEASON IN REVIEW

As bad as the Pistons had usually been since coming from Fort Wayne, they had always managed to nose into the playoffs—until '63-64. They had not finished last—until '63-64. And they hadn't lost faith in a new coach so fast—until '63-64. All of that happened as the Pistons wound up with a 23-57 record, their worst to date, 25 games out of first. The bottom fell out early. Idling with a 4-6 record November 15, the Pistons lost 10 of their next 11 and 30 of 37 to tumble to a hopeless 11-36 mark by January 26. It only got worse, as players began to grumble about new coach Charley Wolf, successor to the self-fired Dick McGuire. Injuries did not help matters, as an ankle fracture limited Dave DeBusschere to only 15 games and Bailey Howell (finger) and Don Ohl (ankle sprain) also needed sideline time. Only three times all season did the Pistons gain back-to-back victories, while the losing side included two seven-game streaks, two five-gamers and two four-gamers. The few positives: Howell (21.7 ppg) and Ohl (17.3 ppg) were named to the All-Star Game, and Ray Scott had his best season with 17.6 ppg and a team-leading 13.5 boards. But a sense of foreboding hung heavy late in the season; the battle lines were drawn between the players and Wolf. Something had to give. It soon did, and the results would be disastrous.

Charley Wolf succeeded Dick McGuire as Pistons coach, but injuries and player dissatisfaction marred his first season.

WHAT A NIGHT!

February 24, 1964

Like most pro teams, the Pistons and Celtics stood aside to mourn the late president, John F. Kennedy, who was assassinated November 22, 1963 in Dallas. Instead of playing as scheduled two days later, the clubs agreed on February 24 as a makeup date. It became one of Detroit's biggest wins all season because of a player who wasn't even with the team in November. Rookie 7-footer Reggie Harding had 23 points and 19 rebounds as Detroit came back to beat the first-place Celtics 115-113, halting a 12-game losing skid in the rivalry. Boston scored the game's first 14 points, 11 by Tom Heinsohn, but Harding outplayed Bill Russell to fuel Detroit's comeback. Harding hadn't joined the club until January 20 because of a gun charge that led to an NBA suspension. He soon showed why the center-needy Pistons signed him directly out of Detroit Eastern High. He led them in rebounds with 906 in '64-65, the best of his three seasons with the Pistons, and averaged nearly 21 points over a 22-game span that season. Finally weary of Harding's lengthening rap sheet, the Pistons traded him to Chicago in '67. One well-worn tale had Harding robbing a store in his own neighborhood—a pistol-wielding 7-footer, a nylon stocking covering his face. "Don't do this, Reggie," the store owner says. "That ain't me, man," came the reply. On September 2, 1972, Harding was shot dead on a Detroit street.

Reggie Harding's promising career, and life, flamed out quickly in Detroit.

Fred "The Z" Zollner

Fred Zollner brought pro basketball to Detroit and made sure it stayed there.

By the time the Pistons won their back-to-back NBA championships in 1989 and '90, Fred Zollner's name was seldom heard in Detroit anymore. He hadn't owned the club since 1974 and it hadn't been very successful under his stewardship, winning only two playoff series in 17 seasons in the Motor City. To the majority of Pistons fans, old or new, Zollner played no more a role in the titles than Harvey Marlatt, Erwin Mueller, "Dancing Gus" or some other bit player from the Cobo Arena era. Maybe that's just how it goes in sports. "What have you done for us lately?" is the accepted credo, fairly or not. But that does a terrible disservice to Fred Zollner.

If not for "The Z," as he was known, there would be no Detroit Pistons. And quite possibly, there would be no National Basketball Association. Zollner was there from the start, with wise counsel, unflagging support and financial generosity. When various franchises were struggling to meet their payrolls in the upstart league, it was often Zollner who stepped in with rescue loans. He did it because he strongly believed that pro basketball could succeed as a major sport. It was a vision formed long before the Pistons came to Detroit in 1957.

Zollner was an industrialist in Fort Wayne, Indiana, a manufacturer of alloy pistons for automobiles, tractors and warplanes. Zollner Machine Works—later Zollner Corp.—was a longtime sponsor of amateur sports teams in Fort Wayne for employees and youths alike, mainly baseball, and basketball. In '41, the Fort Wayne "Zollner Pistons" entered the old National Basketball League and dominated the war years. They captured two NBL titles ('44, '45), reached the finals two others years ('42, '43) and also won three straight so-called World Tournaments ('44-46). The NBA was formed in 1948 and the Zollner Pistons were charter members of the 12-team league. Throughout the '50s, Zollner fielded solid clubs, losing in the championship final in '55 and '56.

Finally, with attendance stagnating in Fort Wayne and the league eyeing larger markets, it came time for Zollner's Pistons to relocate. The Z felt Detroit was a natural. "I feel a club can do better in a metropolitan area of two million people than an area of 200,000," he said regretfully. But even in the early days in Detroit, Zollner was pressured by the NBA and other team owners to move again. They thought Detroit was not big-league enough, as its poor attendance numbers indicated, but Zollner resisted every solicitation. The Pistons, for all their faults—their mediocre seasons, crowds of 4,000 and, yes, often misguided management—would remain in Detroit.

When Zollner finally decided in '69 to sell his club, potential buyers had to fit his criteria—the club couldn't be moved out of Michigan. Zollner got such assurances from William Davidson and his bidding group in 1974 and sold the team, getting $8.1 million. Having retired to Florida full-time, Zollner died in 1982 at age 81. He never got the championship he deserved, but he made sure that when the Pistons did win it, Detroit would be their home city.

CHANGING FACES

DICK MCGUIRE decided he'd had enough. He'd been the Pistons' coach for almost four seasons, but they won only one playoff series in his tenure. After the 1962-63 season, McGuire didn't wait to get fired; he chose to step down on his own accord, taking with him a 122-158 record (.436). His replacement was Charley Wolf, a former Cincinnati Reds farmhand, a cerebral coach, a stickler for conditioning. He'd just been fired by the Cincinnati Royals after a three-year stay, though he had gotten them to the '63 Eastern Finals. Wolf wasn't the only new Piston in '63-64. They added 6-foot-4 shooting guard Eddie Miles out of Seattle with the fifth draft pick. He was called "The Man with the Golden Arm" because of his sharp

Eddie Miles was a high scorer in college, but averaged only 5.4 points as a Pistons rookie.

shooting, but his rookie season was nagged by a foot injury that needed off-season surgery. Before the season, the Pistons waived their career rebounding king Walter Dukes. During the season, they got Donnis Butcher and Bob Duffy from the Knicks for Johnny Egan and traded Kevin Loughery to Baltimore for Larry Staverman.

Take a Bow

Donnis Butcher

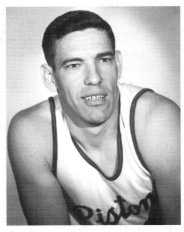

Donnis Butcher was a hard-nosed guard for three seasons, then the Pistons' head coach for parts of three more.

Every basketball team needs good soldiers, guys who'll get after loose balls without regard for a skinned knee, guys who will play hurt. Donnis Butcher was such a player, a sturdily built 6-foot-3 defensive guard. He came to the Pistons on December 16, 1963 when Detroit dealt Johnny Egan to the Knicks for Butcher and Bob Duffy. Thus began a six-year association with the Pistons that would see Butcher rise all the way to head coach, pushing them to a 40-42 record in '67-68 for their best season ever (to that point). From the last eight games of '66-67 through the first 22 of '68-69, Butcher had a 52-60 coaching mark, a .464 percentage that was then tops on Detroit's career list. It was a longshot that Butcher played in the NBA at all. Having prepped in his native Kentucky at tiny Pikeville College, where his brother Paul was coach, Butcher was drafted in 1961 in the seventh round by New York. The 60th overall pick not only made it through the roster cuts, he forged a five-year playing career, averaging 6.1 points and just as many floorburns.

Game Results

1963-64 REGULAR SEASON

Date	Opponent	Result	Record
10-16	PHILADELPHIA	L, 115-117	0-1
10-19	at Philadelphia	W, 124-121	1-1
10-23	L.A. LAKERS	L, 116-124	1-2
10-26	at St. Louis	L, 103-127	1-3
10-30	BOSTON	L, 102-108	1-4
11-2	at Boston	L, 109-117	1-5
11-6	PHILADELPHIA	W, 119-101	2-5
11-9	at Cincinnati	L, 109-118	2-6
11-11	n-L.A. Lakers	W, 116-109	3-6
11-15	at San Francisco	W, 101-98	4-6
11-16	at L.A. Lakers	L, 95-115	4-7
11-17	at San Francisco	L, 96-120	4-8
11-19	n-Cincinnati	L, 102-127	4-9
11-20	CINCINNATI	W, 124-118	5-9
11-23	at New York	L, 99-108	5-10
11-27	ST. LOUIS	L, 105-113	5-11
11-28	at St. Louis	L, 101-118	5-12
11-29	L.A. LAKERS	L, 111-127	5-13
11-30	n-Baltimore	L, 101-120	5-14
12-1	n-Philadelphia	L, 121-132	5-15
12-4	NEW YORK	L, 119-120	5-16
12-6	ST. LOUIS	W, 112-108 (OT)	6-16
12-11	CINCINNATI	L, 107-127	6-17
12-14	at St. Louis	L, 92-104	6-18
12-17	at New York	W, 107-103	7-18
12-18	BALTIMORE	L, 107-124	7-19
12-21	ST. LOUIS	L, 91-100	7-20
12-26	at Baltimore	L, 108-110	7-21
12-27	n-Philadelphia	L, 107-119	7-22
12-29	n-L.A. Lakers	L, 128-140	7-23
12-30	n-San Francisco	W, 114-112 (OT)	8-23
1-2	n-Cincinnati	L, 111-112	8-24
1-5	at St. Louis	L, 99-116	8-25
1-8	BALTIMORE	L, 99-106	8-26
1-9	n-Baltimore	W, 125-115	9-26
1-11	ST. LOUIS	L, 107-112	9-27
1-12	at Cincinnati	L, 88-120	9-28
1-15	SAN FRANCISCO	L, 79-89	9-29
1-16	n-New York	L, 116-124	9-30
1-17	n-New York	W, 101-99	10-30
1-18	BOSTON	L, 115-121	10-31
1-20	at L.A. Lakers	W, 118-107	11-31
1-21	at San Francisco	L, 88-100	11-32
1-22	at L.A. Lakers	L, 101-110	11-33
1-23	at San Francisco	L, 93-125	11-34
1-25	ST. LOUIS	L, 98-107	11-35
1-26	at St. Louis	L, 104-106	11-36
1-28	L.A. LAKERS	W, 93-92	12-36
1-30	SAN FRANCISCO	W, 109-100	13-36
2-1	at Baltimore	W, 112-111	14-36
2-4	at San Francisco	L, 79-118	14-37
2-5	at L.A. Lakers	L, 85-111	14-38
2-6	n-San Francisco	L, 97-104	14-39
2-7	at L.A. Lakers	W, 111-103	15-39
2-9	at Cincinnati	L, 107-135	15-40
2-11	SAN FRANCISCO	L, 118-128 (OT)	15-41
2-12	n-Cincinnati	L, 121-147	15-42
2-14	at Philadelphia	L, 123-130	15-43
2-15	at Baltimore	L, 122-124	15-44
2-16	BALTIMORE	L, 99-111	15-45
2-18	n-San Francisco	L, 98-108	15-46
2-19	n-L.A. Lakers	W, 116-115	16-46
2-20	L.A. LAKERS	L, 101-106	16-47
2-22	NEW YORK	L, 119-125 (OT)	16-48
2-23	at Baltimore	L, 104-129	16-49
2-24	BOSTON	W, 115-113	17-49
2-26	PHILADELPHIA	L, 122-130	17-50
2-28	n-New York	W, 112-110	18-50
2-29	n-Boston	L, 108-115	18-51
3-1	SAN FRANCISCO	L, 86-100	18-52
3-5	n-Baltimore	W, 125-120	19-52
3-7	BOSTON	L, 94-112	19-53
3-8	at Boston	L, 118-128	19-54
3-10	CINCINNATI	W, 114-103	20-54
3-12	n-Boston	L, 120-140	20-55
3-13	n-Philadelphia	W, 133-122	21-55
3-14	NEW YORK	W, 126-124	22-55
3-15	at New York	L, 125-139	22-56
3-17	at St. Louis	L, 99-115	22-57
3-18	ST. LOUIS	W, 126-96	23-57

(Home games in ALL CAPS; n-neutral site)

1964 🏀 DETROIT PISTONS BASKETBALL CLUB 1965

TIME CAPSULE

September 27, 1964:
The Warren Commission reports that Lee Harvey Oswald acted alone in the assassination of President Kennedy and no conspiracy existed; the findings are immediately questioned.

March 8, 1965:
The first U.S. combat forces land in South Vietnam to guard the U.S. Air Force base at Da Nang.

June 5, 1965:
Astronaut Edward White successfully completes a 20-minute walk in space, the first by an American.

SEASON SNAPSHOT

Most Points
Terry Dischinger (1,456, 18.2 avg.)

Most Rebounds
Reggie Harding (906, 11.6 avg.)

Most Assists
Dave DeBusschere (253, 3.2 avg.)

Most Minutes
Dave DeBusschere (2,769, 35.1 avg.)

Field-Goal Percentage
Terry Dischinger (49.3%)

Free-Throw Percentage
Terry Dischinger (75.5%)

Team Offense Average
108.5 (8,681 in 80 games)

Team Defense Average
111.9 (8,954 in 80 games)

Pistons in All-Star Game
Terry Dischinger, F

1964-65

FINAL STANDINGS

Western Division	W	L	Pct.	GB
Los Angeles	49	31	.613	—
St. Louis	45	35	.563	4
Baltimore	37	43	.463	12
PISTONS	**31**	**49**	**.388**	**18**
San Francisco	17	63	.213	32

Eastern Division Winner—Boston

PLAYOFF RESULTS

Pistons Did Not Qualify

PISTONS PLAYOFF LEADERS

NBA CHAMPION

Boston Celtics

1964-65
SEASON IN REVIEW

It was a season of major change for the Pistons, little of it good. They made a terrible trade that cost them for many years to come. They fired another coach, then experimented with a 24-year-old player-coach. And they hired a general manager to clean up the mess, but he would be dead inside a year. All in all, a dreadful year. It started on June 9 when coach Charley Wolf dealt No. 1 scorer Bailey Howell (21.6 ppg), Don Ohl (17.3), Bob Ferry (10.6), Les Hunter and Wali Jones to Baltimore. In return, the Pistons got only scoring forward Terry Dischinger and guards Rod Thorn and Don Kojis. Dischinger would lead Detroit in scoring (18.2) to start a yeomanlike six-season stay, but it was small return for the better part of the Pistons' nucleus. After the club got off 2-9, Don Wattrick, whose basketball background was limited to broadcasting, was promoted to GM in November. "My job is to find out why the team isn't winning," he said. "I feel the fault lies with the coach and I intend to replace him." And he did, canning Wolf and naming Dave DeBusschere player-coach on November 10. It helped briefly as the Pistons won four of five, but the club staggered to a 31-49 finish, losing its final eight. DeBusschere was viewed as the interim coach, but retained the job until late in '66-67. Sadly, Wattrick died of a heart attack in October, 1965, unable to see his job through.

Forward Terry Dischinger was one of the few rewards for the Pistons in their dreadful trade of 1964.

November 10, 1964

It was a coming-out party and reunion all in one. When the Pistons and Baltimore Bullets visited Convention Hall in Philadelphia for a neutral-site battle, it was Dave DeBusschere's debut as Detroit's player-coach, as well as a reunion after the teams' major swap in June. Baltimore got the better of the trade, but Detroit won the game, 119-117, thanks to the heroics of Rod Thorn and DeBusschere. Thorn, who came to Detroit from Baltimore in the eight-player blockbuster, broke a 115-115 tie with 57 seconds to go, then hit two clinching free throws. His 27 points led the Pistons. "I just wanted to make my roomie look good," Thorn said about DeBusschere. One day prior, DeBusschere became Detroit's player-coach after the firing of Charley Wolf. At 24 years old, merely one month into his third NBA season, DeBusschere took over a team nursing a six-game skid. "Man, I sure loved that sound," he said of the final horn. "It's good to win. I think everybody was trying extra hard, and not only because of me. We were in a losing streak and we wanted to end it." DeBusschere's 26 points helped the cause. Baltimore was fueled by ex-Pistons Don Ohl (32 points) and Bailey Howell (18) and future Piston Walt Bellamy (33).

WHAT A NIGHT!

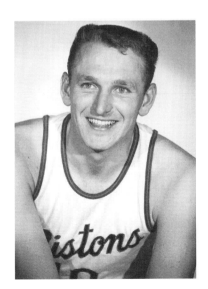

Guard Rod Thorn, the Pistons' perceived enemy during the Bad Boy era, played two solid seasons for Detroit from 1964-66.

Premier Piston

Terry Dischinger

Terry Dischinger, a former ROTC student, became a dentist after his retirement in 1973.

Terry Dischinger gave the Pistons everything he had from 1964 to '72, but unfortunately the U.S. Army took the rest. Maybe it's not comparable to Ted Williams losing valuable years to the Korean War, but Dischinger had to leave the Pistons for two years at the peak of his career in 1965. When he was discharged in the summer of '67 after two years in Hawaii as a second lieutenant, Dischinger said confidently, "I feel I'm a better player than when I left two years ago." But that wasn't the case. The 6-foot-7 forward still possessed abundant skills, as shown by his career-high 39-point game in '68, but couldn't regain the form that earned him NBA Rookie of the Year honors with the Chicago Zephyrs in '62-63. When Dischinger came to Detroit in '64, arriving from Baltimore in the clubs' eight-player swap, he was still in his prime. He became the Pistons' top scorer with 18.2 points, exhibiting the consistency and fast-break skill that made him a three-time all-America selection for Purdue. Of his six post-Army seasons—five with the Pistons—his best was '70-71 when he averaged 11.8 points. Through the end of his career in '73 after being traded for Portland for his last season, Dischinger maintained his great shooting percentage. He led the Pistons five times in six years and was fourth in NBA history at 50.6 upon retiring, trailing some fast company: Kareem Abdul-Jabbar, Wilt Chamberlain and Walt Bellamy. He also made three All-Star teams, including his rookie season when his 25.5 scoring average in 57 games ranked sixth in the league. Pondering retirement in '72 to start his dentistry career, Dischinger was traded to Portland in a three-team swap that brought 76ers guard Fred Foster to Detroit.

AT A GLANCE

TERRY DISCHINGER

FULL NAME:
Terry Gilbert Dischinger

BORN:
November 21, 1940; Terre Haute, Indiana

POSITION, HEIGHT, WEIGHT:
Forward, 6-foot-7, 200 pounds

COLLEGE:
Purdue '62

ACQUIRED:
1964, trade from Baltimore

TENURE WITH PISTONS:
Player: 1964-65; 1967-72
Coach: Nov. 1-8, 1971
Also played: Chicago 1962-63, Baltimore 1963-64, Portland 1972-73

BEST SEASON WITH PISTONS:
1964-65, 80 GP, 18.2 ppg, 6.0 rpg

PLAYING TOTALS WITH PISTONS:
Regular season: 456 GP, 12.1 ppg, 5.1 rpg
Playoffs: 6 GP, 9.3 ppg, 4.8 rpg

COACHING TOTALS WITH PISTONS:
Regular season: 2 GP, 0-2 (.000)

HONORS:
NBA Rookie of the Year, 1962-63 (Chicago)
NBA All-Rookie Team, 1962-63 (Chicago)
All-Star Game (3): 1962-63 (Chicago), 1963-64 (Baltimore); 1964-65 (Detroit)
U.S. Olympic Team, 1960

PISTON LIST

Longest Winning Streaks (Within Same Season)

13 games
- January 23-February 21, 1990

12 games
- February 25-March 20, 1990

11 games
- December 26, 1990-January 17, 1991

10 games
- February 12-28, 1986
- December 1-26, 1987
- November 13-30, 1990

Nine games
- October 14-28, 1970
- March 1-17, 1989

Eight games
- January 11-29, 1985
- November 4-18, 1988
- March 21-April 2, 1989

CHANGING FACES

JUST LIKE THAT, they were gone, three important pieces of the Pistons' lineup: Bailey Howell, Don Ohl and Bob Ferry. All three of them, in their own way, had been critical of coach Charley Wolf. Even mild-mannered Howell, then the Pistons' all-time scoring leader, had gone public with concerns about the club's future. In one fell swoop, the threesome was sent to Baltimore along with two of Detroit's drafted rookies, second-rounder Les Hunter and third-rounder Wali Jones. The Pistons got back three veterans, making it a historical eight-player trade. Until '96-97, it was the most populous swap in NBA history; it was beaten by a nine-player deal between Dallas and New Jersey, the principals being Shawn Bradley (to Dallas) and Jim Jackson (to New Jersey). Having traded two of their selections, the Pistons got little quick help in the '64 draft. In the first round, after originally trolling for a center, Wolf spent the No. 4 pick on 6-foot-5 forward Joe "Pogo" Caldwell from Arizona State.

Joe "Pogo" Caldwell caught Charley Wolf's fancy at the 1964 Olympic Trials.

Take a Bow

Bob Ferry

Bob Ferry's emergence with the Pistons occurred in the '60-61 playoffs when he averaged 20.2 points and 12.6 rebounds.

Sometimes, the best trade is the one you don't make. Any NBA general manager learns that lesson sooner or later. GM-to-be Bob Ferry learned it first-hand with the Pistons in '64, because he was part of one of the worst NBA trades ever. He went from Detroit to Baltimore in the clubs' eight-player swap that tore out the heart of the Pistons' lineup. He put the lesson to great use from 1973-90 as the Washington Bullets' GM, a career that produced an NBA championship (1978) and two Executive of the Year awards by *The Sporting News* (1979, '82). Ferry began his NBA career in '59 as a territorial draftee by the Hawks after starring at St. Louis University. He was dealt to Detroit for Ed Conlin in '60 and put in four solid seasons, averaging 12.3 points and 6.3 rebounds. He was even better in the postseason, averaging 13.8 and 7.7, respectively. As GM at Washington, he engineered several trades with the Pistons, the biggest being the Dave Bing-Kevin Porter swap in '75. He also sent Rick Mahorn to Detroit in '85. Ferry's son Danny is a seven-year NBA veteran.

Game Results

1964-65 REGULAR SEASON

Date	Opponent	Result	Record
10-16	at Philadelphia	L, 113-125	0-1
10-17	at Boston	L, 81-112	0-2
10-21	SAN FRANCISCO	W, 108-104	1-2
10-22	n-Boston	L, 102-104	1-3
10-24	at New York	W, 118-108 (OT)	2-3
10-25	n-New York	L, 95-108	2-4
10-30	BOSTON	L, 90-106	2-5
10-31	at St. Louis	L, 99-107	2-6
11-1	at Cincinnati	L, 101-114	2-7
11-4	BALTIMORE	L, 108-121	2-8
11-7	at Boston	L, 113-130	2-9
11-10	n-Baltimore	W, 119-117	3-9
11-12	SAN FRANCISCO	W, 121-99	4-9
11-15	L.A. LAKERS	L, 105-111	4-10
11-18	PHILADELPHIA	W, 124-111	5-10
11-20	at Baltimore	W, 106-105	6-10
11-21	at St. Louis	L, 94-100	6-11
11-22	at San Francisco	W, 99-97	7-11
11-25	at L.A. Lakers	L, 117-130	7-12
11-27	at L.A. Lakers	L, 111-117	7-13
11-28	PHILADELPHIA	L, 93-101	7-14
12-1	n-Cincinnati	L, 107-129	7-15
12-2	CINCINNATI	W, 125-115	8-15
12-4	at Philadelphia	L, 106-119	8-16
12-5	NEW YORK	W, 111-100	9-16
12-8	at New York	W, 102-100	10-16
12-9	CINCINNATI	L, 114-122	10-17
12-11	at San Francisco	W, 104-100	11-17
12-12	at San Francisco	L, 107-124	11-18
12-13	at L.A. Lakers	L, 115-116	11-19
12-15	at L.A. Lakers	W, 131-116	12-19
12-16	L.A. LAKERS	L, 120-126 (OT)	12-20
12-18	ST. LOUIS	W, 114-108	13-20
12-19	at Baltimore	L, 99-104	13-21
12-25	n-Boston	L, 106-118	13-22
12-27	n-Boston	L, 106-112	13-23
12-28	n-New York	W, 123-117	14-23
12-30	ST. LOUIS	L, 120-125	14-24
1-2	BOSTON	L, 89-101	14-25
1-5	n-St. Louis	L, 108-109	14-26
1-6	BALTIMORE	L, 121-129	14-27
1-7	at Baltimore	L, 105-110	14-28
1-9	at New York	W, 118-115	15-28
1-10	at Cincinnati	L, 114-140	15-29
1-11	n-L.A. Lakers	W, 128-127	16-29
1-14	L.A. LAKERS	L, 100-104	16-30
1-18	n-Philadelphia	L, 95-109	16-31
1-19	n-Philadelphia	W, 103-97	17-31
1-20	CINCINNATI	L, 90-102	17-32
1-22	n-Philadelphia	L, 103-109 (OT)	17-33
1-23	at Cincinnati	W, 105-102	18-33
1-26	n-Philadelphia	W, 107-105	19-33
1-27	BALTIMORE	W, 122-108	20-33
1-29	n-New York	L, 99-106	20-34
1-30	ST. LOUIS	W, 121-97	21-34
1-31	at St. Louis	W, 110-107	22-34
2-2	n-L.A. LAKERS	W, 121-118	23-34
2-3	SAN FRANCISCO	W, 111-106	24-34
2-5	NEW YORK	L, 112-118 (OT)	24-35
2-6	at New York	L, 106-109	24-36
2-7	BALTIMORE	W, 119-112	25-36
2-10	BOSTON	L, 106-117	25-37
2-11	n-Cincinnati	L, 109-130	25-38
2-13	at Baltimore	L, 107-123	25-39
2-16	at San Francisco	W, 114-106	26-39
2-18	n-San Francisco	W, 107-106	27-39
2-20	ST. LOUIS	L, 98-110	27-40
2-21	at St. Louis	L, 107-112	27-41
2-24	PHILADELPHIA	W, 106-104	28-41
2-27	CINCINNATI	W, 117-115	29-41
3-1	n-Cincinnati	W, 130-110	30-41
3-3	SAN FRANCISCO	W, 110-107	31-41
3-4	n-San Francisco	L, 110-115	31-42
3-6	NEW YORK	L, 93-96	31-43
3-7	at Baltimore	L, 105-111	31-44
3-10	BOSTON	L, 106-124	31-45
3-11	n-Boston	L, 100-112	31-46
3-13	at Philadelphia	L, 116-131	31-47
3-16	L.A. LAKERS	W, 99-100	31-48
3-20	at St. Louis	L, 98-107	31-49

(Home games in ALL CAPS; n-neutral site)

1965 1966
DETROIT PISTONS BASKETBALL CLUB
NATIONAL BASKETBALL ASSN.

TIME CAPSULE

November 9, 1965:
Millions of people in the Northeast are affected by a massive power blackout lasting 13 hours.

January 31, 1966:
President Johnson announces that U.S. pilots resumed bombing raids on North Vietnam, a 38-day hiatus having failed to further peace negotiations.

June 8, 1966:
The National and American football leagues merge, effective in 1970, setting up a Super Bowl game between the league champions.

SEASON SNAPSHOT

Most Points
Eddie Miles (1,566, 19.6 avg.)

Most Rebounds
Dave DeBusschere (916, 11.6 avg.)

Most Assists
Ray Scott (238, 3.0 avg.)

Most Minutes
Eddie Miles (2,788, 34.9 avg.)

Field-Goal Percentage
Eddie Miles (44.7%)

Free-Throw Percentage
Ray Scott (74.3%)

Team Offense Average
110.3 (8,827 in 80 games)

Team Defense Average
117.2 (9,373 in 80 games)

Pistons in All-Star Game
Eddie Miles, G; Dave DeBusschere, F

1965-66

FINAL STANDINGS

Western Division	W	L	Pct.	GB
Los Angeles	45	35	.563	—
Baltimore	38	42	.475	7
St. Louis	36	44	.450	9
San Francisco	35	45	.438	10
PISTONS	**22**	**58**	**.275**	**23**

Eastern Division Winner—Philadelphia

PLAYOFF RESULTS

Pistons Did Not Qualify

PISTONS PLAYOFF LEADERS

NBA CHAMPION

Boston Celtics

1965-66
SEASON IN REVIEW

The Pistons had experienced some poor seasons in Detroit, but '65-66 was their worst so far, falling to 22-58 and tumbling into the Western cellar, 13 games behind the next-closest team. It shouldn't have been a surprise. The Pistons still hadn't recovered from the ill-fated June '64 trade that cost them Bailey Howell, Don Ohl and Bob Ferry. They also lost '64-65 scoring leader Terry Dischinger to a two-year Army hitch and rebounding leader Reggie Harding to a suspension for criminal activity. The sudden lack of depth placed too heavy a burden on Eddie Miles, Ray Scott and player-coach Dave DeBusschere. The season fell apart all too quickly, with a nine-game losing skid in November and eight-gamer in December leading to a 10-29 record by January 6. In that span they were only 4-21 away from Cobo. A brief 8-10 "hot streak" around midseason merely set the stage for another pratfall in the final 23 games—4-19. The only silver lining—as it often was for the '60s Pistons—was that they'd have a chance at the top draft pick in the spring, which everyone agreed would be Michigan all-American Cazzie Russell. The Pistons put two players in the All-Star Game: Miles and DeBusschere. Miles had his best season, averaging 19.6 points to assume Dischinger's club scoring title, and DeBusschere supplied his usual 16.4 points and 11.6 rebounds.

Player-coach Dave DeBusschere talks strategy with assistant coach Earl Lloyd (left) on November 5, 1965 against Cincinnati.

November 3, 1965

When Wilt Chamberlain scores "only" 32 points and you're glad, it has to mean you won the game. "I thought we did a really good job on Wilt," Detroit player-coach Dave DeBusschere remarked. "I think we made him work for anything he got." His comments came after a 110-100 Pistons victory over the Philadelphia 76ers at Cobo Arena. DeBusschere's relief was genuine, because only 12 days earlier at Philadelphia, Chamberlain had dominated Detroit for 53 points in a 120-103 76ers win—his 18th 50-point performance vs. the Pistons in seven seasons. When the Sixers came to Cobo, DeBusschere had two defenders follow Stilt anywhere he went. Much of the game, the task was handled by rookies Bill Buntin and Joe Strawder, and Chamberlain endured a six-minute scoring drought in both halves. His cold spells enabled the Pistons to lead most of the way and hold on for the victory despite a late 12-1 spurt by Philadelphia. Ed Miles' 27 points keyed Detroit, which improved to 4-5. Joe Caldwell hit for 21 and rookie Tom Van Arsdale supplied 19. For the 76ers, Hal Greer scored 21 and Chet Walker from Benton Harbor added 20.

Rookie forward Bill Buntin from Michigan played a key defensive role against Wilt Chamberlain in an early-season Pistons victory.

Premier Piston

Ray Scott

As a player and coach, Ray Scott's career with the Pistons lasted 10 divergent seasons.

Pistons history is full of triumph and strife, but few principals got a first-hand look at both extremes like Ray Scott, the last of six former Pistons players who also coached the team. As a player, he saw mostly strife from a team standpoint in his six seasons (1961-67), but from a personal angle, Scott had a strong career. Then as coach from 1972-76, he became NBA Coach of the Year in '74, only to be fired just two years later in the middle of a practice session. Truly one extreme to another. A 6-9 forward with a line-drive jumper and terrific rebounding skills, Scott averaged 16 points and 10.7 boards in 421 games with Detroit. In retrospect, it's a surprise he never made the All-Star game, especially in '63-64 when he averaged 17.6 points and a team-high 13.5 rebounds. He scored a career-high 39 points on December 1, 1964 vs. Cincinnati. Scott came to Detroit in 1961 as the No. 4 draft pick, but had already been playing professionally for three years with Allentown of the Eastern League; he had left Portland U. in '59 and had to kill time in the Eastern League until his graduating class became draft-eligible in '61. His Detroit playing career lasted until he was dealt to Baltimore on January 16, 1967. But Scott returned to the club in 1972 as chief scout and assistant coach under Earl Lloyd and then became head coach two months later when Lloyd was fired October 28. It would become the best tenure of any Pistons coach prior to Chuck Daly. Including a team-best 52-30 mark in '73-74, which resulted in Scott's Coach of the Year award, the only one in Pistons history, he had a 147-134 career record. He got fired in 1976, the deed occurring at practice, but he left as the first coach in club history with a winning record.

AT A GLANCE

RAY SCOTT

FULL NAME:
John Raymond Scott
BORN:
July 15, 1938; Philadelphia
POSITION, HEIGHT, WEIGHT:
Forward, 6-foot-9, 215 pounds
COLLEGE:
Portland University

ACQUIRED:
Drafted, first round, 1961 (4th overall)
TENURE WITH PISTONS:
Player: 1961-62 — January 16, 1967
Coach: October 28, 1972 — January 26, 1976
Also played: Baltimore 1967-70, Virginia (ABA) 1970-72
BEST SEASON WITH PISTONS:
Player: 1963-64, 80 GP, 17.6 ppg, 13.5 rpg
Coach: 1973-74, 82 GP, 52-30 (.634)
PLAYING TOTALS WITH PISTONS:
Regular season: 421 GP, 16.0 ppg, 10.7 rpg
Playoffs: 14 GP, 16.9 ppg, 13.8 rpg
COACHING TOTALS WITH PISTONS:
Regular season: 281 GP, 147-134 (.523)
Playoffs: 10 GP, 4-6 (.400)
HONORS:
NBA Coach of the Year, 1973-74

PISTON LIST

Pistons Who Attended College in Michigan

Detroit (Nine)
- Dennis Boyd, Earl Cureton, Dave DeBusschere, Terry Duerod, Bill Ebben, John Long, Dorie Murrey, Terry Thomas, Terry Tyler

Michigan (Seven)
- Wayman Britt, Bill Buntin, Rickey Green, Alan Hardy, Phil Hubbard, George Lee, Terry Mills

Central Michigan (Four)
- Ben Kelso, James McElroy, Ben Poquette, Dan Roundfield

Michigan State (Four)
- Lindsay Hairston, Greg Kelser, Mike Peplowski, Ralph Simpson

Eastern Michigan (Three)
- Grant Long, Harvey Marlatt, Charles Thomas

Western Michigan (One)
- Walker D. Russell

CHANGING FACES

OH, WHAT MIGHT'VE BEEN! The Pistons could have selected Willis Reed in the first round of the 1964 draft, but coach Charley Wolf had taken a flier on a high-jumping forward from Arizona State, Joe "Pogo" Caldwell. While Reed went on to a Hall of Fame career with the Knicks, Caldwell washed out with the Pistons in less than two disappointing seasons. On December 28, 1965, he was traded to the St. Louis Hawks. It was the teams' second deal in the same week; on December 24, Detroit traded Rod Thorn to the Hawks for John Tresvant and Charles Vaughn. In the '65 draft, the Pistons emerged with Bill Buntin as the final territorial pick in club history. He lasted but one season because of weight problems and died of a heart ailment during a pickup game May 9, 1968. Detroit also drafted Tom Van Arsdale out of Indiana, where he starred with brother Dick, and two-sport star Ron Reed from Notre Dame. Van Arsdale stayed for two-plus seasons (11.4 ppg) until February 1, 1968 when he and Tresvant went to Cincinnati for Happy Hairston.

Tom Van Arsdale averaged 15.3 points with six NBA teams in 12 seasons.

Take a Bow

Ron Reed

Pistons forward Ron Reed was a two-sport athlete nearly two decades before Bo Jackson and Deion Sanders.

When Ron Reed came to the Pistons in 1965, Dave DeBusschere was almost done pitching for the Chicago White Sox. The right-hander went 0-0 in '62 and 3-4 in '63, then languished in the minors until quitting in '66. But Reed, also a 6-foot-6 righty, was just getting started when the Pistons drafted him in the fourth round in '65. The Notre Dame graduate stayed with the Pistons for two seasons and averaged 8.1 points and 6.5 boards, but also spent some of each off-season with the Atlanta Braves, going 2-2. Finally, realizing it was time to get serious about his career, Reed quit the NBA in '67 after going to the SuperSonics in the expansion draft. It was a wise decision. He immediately entered Atlanta's rotation in '68 and was 11-10 with a 3.35 earned run average. He followed in '69 with his finest season, going 18-10, 3.47. En route to a 146-140 record in 19 seasons with four clubs, Reed had seven 10-win seasons. His eight years with the Philadelphia Phillies (1976-83) produced a World Series title in 1980 and Series loss in '83.

Game Results

1965-66 REGULAR SEASON

Date	Opponent	Result	Record
10-16	at New York	L, 103-111	0-1
10-20	NEW YORK	W, 116-103	1-1
10-23	at Philadelphia	L, 103-120	1-2
10-26	BALTIMORE	L, 98-117	1-3
10-27	at Baltimore	W, 108-107	2-3
10-29	BOSTON	W, 108-106	3-3
10-30	at St. Louis	L, 95-122	3-4
10-31	at Cincinnati	L, 107-113	3-5
11-3	PHILADELPHIA	W, 110-100	4-5
11-5	CINCINNATI	L, 114-120	4-6
11-6	at San Francisco	L, 100-110	4-7
11-9	at San Francisco	L, 102-107	4-8
11-10	at L.A. Lakers	L, 125-133	4-9
11-12	SAN FRANCISCO	L, 102-103	4-10
11-13	at Boston	L, 93-122	4-11
11-16	at New York	L, 95-120	4-12
11-19	NEW YORK	L, 109-116	4-13
11-20	at St. Louis	L, 101-110	4-14
11-23	n-Cincinnati	W, 118-115	5-14
11-24	BALTIMORE	W, 130-124	6-14
11-26	n-Boston	L, 114-134	6-15
11-28	L.A. LAKERS	L, 110-128	6-16
12-1	ST. LOUIS	L, 101-110	6-17
12-4	BALTIMORE	W, 130-119	7-17
12-8	SAN FRANCISCO	W, 115-113	8-17
12-10	at Philadelphia	W, 116-114	9-17
12-14	n-Baltimore	L, 129-142	9-18
12-17	BOSTON	L, 112-114	9-19
12-18	at Baltimore	L, 114-143	9-20
12-22	n-San Francisco	L, 104-114	9-21
12-23	at L.A. Lakers	L, 112-122	9-22
12-25	at L.A. Lakers	L, 106-115	9-23
12-28	n-San Francisco	L, 107-120	9-24
12-29	PHILADELPHIA	L, 112-113	9-25
12-30	n-L.A. Lakers	W, 117-114	10-25
1-1	at Baltimore	L, 112-116	10-26
1-2	n-San Francisco	L, 113-136	10-27
1-5	n-Cincinnati	L, 103-117	10-28
1-6	n-Cincinnati	L, 97-109	10-29
1-7	ST. LOUIS	W, 137-97	11-29
1-9	L.A. LAKERS	L, 98-111	11-30
1-12	PHILADELPHIA	W, 129-111	12-30
1-15	BALTIMORE	W, 122-117	13-30
1-16	at Cincinnati	L, 106-108	13-31
1-18	n-Boston	W, 116-115	14-31
1-19	n-Philadelphia	L, 93-110	14-32
1-20	n-St. Louis	L, 92-103	14-33
1-21	ST. LOUIS	W, 117-108	15-33
1-25	at New York	L, 100-115	15-34
1-26	L.A. LAKERS	L, 110-126	15-35
1-27	n-Boston	L, 112-131	15-36
1-28	at Boston	W, 108-105	16-36
1-30	at Philadelphia	L, 98-117	16-37
2-1	n-Boston	L, 81-100	16-38
2-2	BOSTON	W, 99-93	17-38
2-4	NEW YORK	L, 113-115	17-39
2-7	n-Cincinnati	W, 124-118	18-39
2-8	n-San Francisco	L, 103-113	18-40
2-9	PHILADELPHIA	L, 91-108	18-41
2-11	n-New York	L, 107-122	18-42
2-12	at Cincinnati	L, 116-143	18-43
2-14	n-Philadelphia	L, 123-149	18-44
2-15	at Baltimore	L, 105-114	18-45
2-18	NEW YORK	W, 120-118	19-45
2-20	CINCINNATI	L, 129-133	19-46
2-22	n-Philadelphia	L, 112-122	19-47
2-23	n-New York	L, 98-100	19-48
2-26	L.A. LAKERS	L, 118-131	19-49
2-27	at St. Louis	L, 114-125	19-50
2-28	n-St. Louis	L, 103-108	19-51
3-1	n-Baltimore	W, 122-110	20-51
3-2	SAN FRANCISCO	W, 131-118	21-51
3-4	n-New York	L, 119-121	21-52
3-6	CINCINNATI	L, 125-137	21-53
3-11	at L.A. Lakers	W, 116-114	22-53
3-13	n-San Francisco	L, 119-121	22-54
3-15	at L.A. Lakers	L, 108-135	22-55
3-17	BOSTON	L, 103-128	22-56
3-19	at St. Louis	L, 112-115	22-57
3-20	ST. LOUIS	L, 117-121	22-58

(Home games in ALL CAPS; n-neutral site)

DAVE BING

Funny how things work out.

The day Dave Bing arrived in Detroit in 1966, advertised as the city's basketball savior, local fans would not have voted him dog catcher, let alone endorsed him as the Pistons' new Pied Piper.

Twenty-five years later, they wanted to make him mayor of Detroit—not some cutesy honorary title, but the real mayor, if only he'd run.

That was the kind of effect Bing had on Detroit in his nine seasons as the Pistons' high-scoring point guard and in his post-basketball career as head of the country's leading minority-owned steel company.

Solid as steel, that was Bing. He exploded on to the NBA scene after a star-studded career at Syracuse, becoming Rookie of the Year in 1966-67 and NBA scoring champ in his second season. For more than a decade Bing thrived as one of the league's top stars, a status confirmed by his 1990 induction into the Naismith Basketball Hall of Fame and his 1996 selection as one of the NBA's Top 50 Players of All-Time.

Along the way Bing was picked to three All-NBA teams and seven All-Star games (one with Washington, being named MVP); he scored 15,235 points for the Pistons, including 54 against Chicago in 1971 to set the team record; and he eclipsed many other records, some still standing.

All this by a speedy, reed-thin 6-foot-3 guard with a dependable 18-foot jumper, agile ballhandling skills and the guts to take the big shot, skills finely honed on the playgrounds of Washington D.C.

It goes without saying that no other Piston will wear No. 21 again. On March 18, 1983, the number Bing wore with dignity through good times and bad—team-wise, the latter was prevalent —became the first ever retired by the Pistons. It hangs majestically in the Palace rafters.

No one, least of all Bing, could've envisioned all of that in 1966 when he showed up in Detroit essentially as an unwanted consolation prize—the Pistons' lovely parting gift for losing a coin flip with the New York Knicks on May 11, the morning of the NBA draft.

The coin flip, at the Plaza Hotel in New York, was to determine which of the NBA's cellar-dwellers—Detroit in the West and New York in the East—would get the No. 1 draft choice and the right to select Michigan consensus All-American Cazzie Russell. The loser would pick second.

AT A GLANCE

DAVE BING

FULL NAME:
David Bing
BORN:
November 29, 1943; Washington, D.C.
POSITION, HEIGHT, WEIGHT:
Guard, 6-foot-3, 185 pounds
COLLEGE:
Syracuse, '66
ACQUIRED:
1966, Pistons' No. 1 draft pick (2nd overall)

TENURE WITH PISTONS:
1966-67 — 1974-75
Also: Washington 1975-77, Boston 1977-78
BEST SEASON WITH PISTONS:
1967-68, 79 GP, 27.1 ppg, 6.4 apg
TOTALS WITH PISTONS:
Regular season: 675 GP, 15,235 pts.
   (22.6), 2,828 ast. (4.2)
Playoffs: 16 GP, 319 pts. (19.9), 100 ast.
   (6.3)
HONORS:
Basketball Hall of Fame, 1990
Top 50 Players of All-Time, 1996
NBA Rookie of the Year, 1966-67
All-NBA Team: First Team 1967-68, 1970-71; Second Team 1973-74
All-Star Game (7): 1967-68, 1968-69, 1970-71, 1972-73, 1973-74, 1974-75, 1975-76 (Washington)
All-Star MVP: 1975-76 (Washington)
NBA Scoring Champion: 1967-68

PISTON LIST

Dave Bing's Highest-Scoring Games as a Piston

- **54 points**
  February 21, 1971 vs. Chicago
- **49 points**
  March 9, 1971 vs. Phoenix
- **47 points**
  March 8, 1967 vs. Baltimore
- **45 points**
  March 17, 1968 at Los Angeles
- **44 points**
  February 6, 1970 at Baltimore
- **43 points**
  December 13, 1967 vs. New York
- **42 points**
  November 3, 1967 at Baltimore
  March 6, 1970 vs. Milwaukee
  February 16, 1973 at Philadelphia
- **41 points**
  January 31, 1968 at Baltimore

Detroit's player-coach Dave DeBusschere, age 25, called tails. NBA commissioner J. Walter Kennedy tossed a $20 gold piece and it nestled into the lush carpeting ... heads.

The Knicks took Russell, magnetic NBA-star-to-be, and Detroit, going to Plan B, settled on Bing, All-American at Syracuse, the NCAA's fifth-leading scorer at 28.4 points per game. But still, a little runt guard.

A Detroit newspaper bannered this headline: "Sorry, Pistons—Knicks Draft Cazzie." And DeBusschere could barely cloak his disappointment: "Bing was the best player in the country available to us." (DeBusschere would later be Russell's teammate during the Knicks' glory years.)

Bing signed for $15,000 and a $500 bonus, and drove his wife and two daughters to Detroit to face an uncertain future.

"I wasn't real happy when I first came to Detroit," he later admitted.

But an odd thing happened when Bing got on the hardcourt. He excelled immediately, bombing accurately from the perimeter, taking opponents off the dribble for layups and delivering deft passes to teammates. His game had no shortcomings, no holes. On March 8, he scored 47 points vs. Baltimore to set a team rookie mark that would last 15 years. The city was falling in love with its consolation prize. When Bing hit a shot, the Cobo Arena P.A. man would shout "Bingo!" as the scoreboard flashed the same message. Indeed, Cazzie who?

Bing's booty for his debut season was handsome. He was selected NBA Rookie of the Year, edging St. Louis' Lou Hudson and New York's Russell. He joined them on the All-Rookie team. He led the Pistons in scoring at 20.0 points a game, becoming the first Detroit rookie to do so (the feat would be repeated by Grant Hill, also Rookie of the Year, in 1994-95).

But Bing's rookie exploits were a mere prelude to his amazing 1967-68 season. A hint came on opening night October 17 when he scored 35 points, sitting out the fourth quarter, in a home win over Cincinnati and Oscar

Robertson. Then he scored 43 at Baltimore on November 3, and 40 on November 15 in a win over Wilt Chamberlain and defending NBA champ Philadelphia.

Seemingly no one could shut down Bing and the points kept coming. He got 43 vs. New York, 41 at Baltimore and 45 at Los Angeles. The season ended with Bing becoming the first (and only) Piston to lead the NBA in scoring, compiling 2,142 points for a 27.1 average to beat Elgin Baylor, Chamberlain and Earl Monroe.

Bing averaged 28.2 points against Boston in the 1968 playoffs, including 44 in Game 6 (with a team-record 37 in the second half), but couldn't stop the Pistons from losing the series 4-2. That was the beginning of what would be an unfortunate pattern in Bing's NBA career—his teams were never a playoff success. In Game 7 vs. Chicago in 1974, his last-second inbounds pass was tipped away by Dennis Awtrey, letting the Bulls win the game 96-94 and the series 4-3.

Individually, Bing's career settled into an All-Star pattern. He led the Pistons in points his first five seasons, scoring a club-record 2,213 in 1970-71 when he was third in the MVP voting. He scored 54 points February 21, 1971 vs. Chicago, topping George Yardley's Pistons-record 52 from 1957. Kelly Tripucka would gain the No. 1 spot with 56 points in 1983, but Bing's 22 field goals that night remain a club record.

Bing was honored in 1974 with the fifth Maurice Stokes Award, given in memory of the late Cincinnati Royals standout whose career and life were cut short by encephalitis. Bing was cited because he overcame a career-threatening eye injury two seasons prior, stemming from an inadvertent poke to his right eye by the Lakers' Happy Hairston. Bing required six hours of surgery to repair a partially detached retina.

"I went 12 hours without sight," he said. "My wife and a friend had to lead me around by the hand."

The injury caused Bing to miss 37 games

in 1971-72 and his eyesight never fully recovered. He began to wear one contact lens during games, but still had to identify teammates largely by size and uniform color.

There were other injuries along the way—two broken thumbs, broken cheekbone, all manner of bumps and bruises—but Bing remained one of the Pistons' most durable players. Aside from the eye injury, he played all but four games over his final five seasons in Detroit.

He had intended to become the first long-term Piston to start and end his career with Detroit, but it was not to be. He held out to renegotiate his contract in 1974, but the front office wouldn't budge and the whole episode soured relations on both sides.

Finally, after 691 games with the Pistons but only 16 in the playoffs, Bing was traded to Washington before the 1975-76 season. On August 28, he was dealt (with a first-round pick) for point guard Kevin Porter, the NBA's reigning assist king. When Bing left, he led the Pistons in almost every career stat, including scoring and assists, though his totals have all been topped.

Bing retired in 1978 after two seasons with Washington and one with the Celtics, and for a while he wanted to be the Pistons' coach in 1979. He interviewed to be Dick Vitale's replacement, but nothing came of it.

So Bing entered private business in Detroit and excelled there just as he had on the court. Steadily, Bing Steel became a thriving company and has evolved into the Bing Group, a collection of five automotive-related companies with more than $130 million in annual sales. Eighty percent of his 600 employees are African-American, and Bing's business skills are lauded throughout the corporate community, locally and nationally.

In the early '90s, some Detroit business and political leaders tried to enlist Bing to run for mayor, but he declined. The requests are likely to arise again, though. Detroit's love affair with Dave Bing is not likely to wither anytime soon.

Dave Bing's Regular-Season Statistics With Detroit

SEASON	G	MIN	FGM	FGA	PCT	FTM	FTA	PCT	O-RB	D-RB	TOT	AST	PF	DQ	STL	BLK	PTS	PPG	HI
1966-67	80	2762	664	1522	.436	273	370	.738	—	—	359	330	217	2	—	—	1601	20.0	47
1967-68	79	3209	835	1893	.441	472	668	.707	—	—	373	509	254	2	—	—	2142	27.1	45
1968-69	77	3039	678	1594	.425	444	623	.713	—	—	382	546	256	3	—	—	1800	23.4	39
1969-70	70	2334	575	1295	.444	454	580	.783	—	—	299	418	196	0	—	—	1604	22.9	42
1970-71	82	3065	799	1710	.467	615	772	.797	—	—	364	408	228	4	—	—	2213	27.0	54
1971-72	45	1936	369	891	.414	278	354	.785	—	—	186	317	138	3	—	—	1016	22.6	37
1972-73	82	3361	692	1545	.448	456	560	.814	—	—	298	637	229	1	—	—	1840	22.4	42
1973-74	81	3124	582	1336	.436	356	438	.813	108	173	281	555	216	1	109	17	1520	18.8	33
1974-75	79	3222	578	1333	.434	343	424	.809	86	200	286	610	222	3	116	26	1499	19.0	32
TOTALS	675	26052	5772	13119	.440	3691	4789	.771	(194)	(373)	2828	4330	1956	19	(225)	(43)	15235	22.6	54

()-total doesn't reflect entire career due to NBA statistical changes

1966 1967

DETROIT PISTONS BASKETBALL CLUB NATIONAL BASKETBALL ASSN

TIME CAPSULE

November 11, 1966:
The last mission of the Gemini space program is launched as astronauts Jim Lovell and "Buzz" Aldrin successfully rendezvous with an Agena target vehicle.

January 15, 1967:
Coached by legendary Vince Lombardi, the Green Bay Packers beat the Kansas City Chiefs 35-10 in the first Super Bowl.

July 23, 1967:
The worst race riot in U.S. history erupts in Detroit, resulting in the deaths of 43 people.

SEASON SNAPSHOT

Most Points
Dave Bing (1,601, 20.0 avg.)

Most Rebounds
Dave DeBusschere (924, 11.8 avg.)

Most Assists
Dave Bing (330, 4.1 avg.)

Most Minutes
Dave DeBusschere (2,897, 37.1 avg.)

Field-Goal Percentage
Reggie Harding (44.9%)

Free-Throw Percentage
Tom Van Arsdale (78.4%)

Team Offense Average
111.3 (9,015 in 81 games)

Team Defense Average
116.6 (9,443 in 81 games)

NBA Rookie of the Year
Dave Bing

Pistons in All-Star Game
Dave DeBusschere, F

1966-67

FINAL STANDINGS

Western Division	W	L	Pct.	GB
San Francisco	44	37	.543	—
St. Louis	39	42	.481	5
Los Angeles	36	45	.444	8
Chicago	33	48	.407	11
PISTONS	**30**	**51**	**.370**	**14**

Eastern Division Winner—Philadelphia

PLAYOFF RESULTS

Pistons Did Not Qualify

PISTONS PLAYOFF LEADERS

NBA CHAMPION

Philadelphia 76ers

1966-67
SEASON IN REVIEW

Like the Pistons would feel in 1981 when Isiah Thomas showed up and again in '94 when Grant Hill arrived, that was the kind of lift Dave Bing brought to a moribund franchise in '66. Though the Pistons could not get out of the Western cellar, they boosted their win total by eight (30-51) and Bing's Rookie of the Year season heralded a new era of basketball in Detroit. The Pistons had their heart set on Michigan star Cazzie Russell in the draft, but lost the coin flip to New York, leaving Bing as Detroit's consolation prize. What a piece of luck. Bing, the high-scoring Syracuse guard, was an immediate sensation, averaging exactly 20 points to lead the Pistons, including a team rookie record 47 vs. Baltimore on March 8. Bing's rapid development was a diversion from the Pistons' false-start season. Despite a 56-point loss to the Lakers (144-88) as part of a 1-7 slide, the Pistons battled back to 13-13, then sank like a rock with six losses. They'd have five losing skids of four or more, including five in a row to end the season. By then player-coach Dave DeBusschere was just a player and Donnis Butcher was head coach. The switch occurred March 7, capping DeBusschere's 79-143 career record. Despite the distraction, he again led the club in rebounding (11.8) and was second in scoring (18.2).

Dave Bing's Hall-of-Fame career had a roaring start in '66-67 with a 47-point game and Rookie of the Year award.

WHAT A NIGHT!

November 23, 1966

In the old days, the Pistons rarely drew big crowds to Cobo unless the opponent was especially intriguing, and that custom was never truer than on November 23, 1966. A near-packed house of 10,086 was in attendance, but it was principally because of somebody from the other side, Knicks rookie Cazzie Russell, the two-time Michigan all-American guard. Detroit fans were there to dream about what might've been. Six months earlier, New York had won the draft-day coin flip over the Pistons for the No. 1 pick, selecting Russell, the local hero, and leaving Dave Bing for Detroit with the second pick. This was Russell's first game at Cobo with the Knicks, but Bing and Co. would have the last laugh. With Bing outscoring Russell 18-10 and outrebounding him 6-0, the Pistons got past the Knicks 118-110. Detroit player-coach Dave DeBusschere, later Russell's teammate, said, "You can't compare those guys on the basis of just one game." But that game was a fairly accurate foreshadowing of their NBA careers. Each playing 12 seasons, Bing outscored Russell by almost 6,000 points (18,327-12,377). But Russell would gain the championship (New York, 1970) that eluded Bing.

When Dave Bing made a great play, the scoreboard would flash "Bingo!" and the P.A. announcer would scream it as well.

Premier Piston

Eddie Miles

Perimeter artist Eddie Miles, the Man with the Golden Nickname, spent 6½ productive seasons with the Pistons.

The Pistons spent their 1963 No. 1 draft pick (fifth overall) on a long-distance shooter from Seattle University, Eddie Miles, who had been the NCAA's seventh-best scorer (25.8 ppg) as a senior. But despite his lofty draft status, Miles was slightly worried after averaging only 5.4 points in an abbreviated rookie year. "I sweated it out for a while," Miles said. "I was afraid they were going to cut me." Luckily for both parties, they didn't, because it was the start of a productive seven-year association. Miles remained with the Pistons until '69-70, exiting via trade as their all-time leader in games played and field goals made and attempted. He was also second in career scoring (7,419) behind Bailey Howell (8,182). Before Dave Bing began to monopolize Detroit's annual point leadership, Miles was the Pistons' leader in 1965-66, averaging 19.6 and beginning a three-year stretch in which he averaged 18.5 over 237 games. He also made a big splash in his lone All-Star Game, scoring a West-leading 17 points off the bench in '65-66. Among his other career highlights, Miles tallied a 21-point quarter vs. the SuperSonics on March 12, 1968, topping his 19-pointer vs. Baltimore on January 7, 1967. With his textbook perimeter shooting form, Miles lived up to his unique nickname: "The Man with the Golden Arm." In tribute to Miles' outside accuracy, the Seattle U. sports information man borrowed the phrase from the 1955 Frank Sinatra film of the same name and it stuck. "That guy had a wild imagination," Miles said. An avid reader and a summer auditor with a Detroit grocery chain, Miles became an ex-Piston on February 1, 1970; five months before his 30th birthday, he was dealt to Baltimore for Bob Quick and a draft choice.

AT A GLANCE

EDDIE MILES

FULL NAME:
Edward Miles Jr.
BORN:
July 5, 1940; Little Rock, Arkansas
POSITION, HEIGHT, WEIGHT:
Guard, 6-foot-4, 195 pounds
COLLEGE:
Seattle, '63
ACQUIRED:
Drafted, first round, 1963 (5th overall)
TENURE WITH PISTONS:
1963-64 — Feb. 1, 1970
Also: Baltimore 1970-71, New York 1971-72
BEST SEASON WITH PISTONS:
1965-66, 80 GP, 19.2 ppg, 3.8 rpg
TOTALS WITH PISTONS:
Regular season: 497 GP, 14.9 ppg, 3.4 rpg
Playoffs: 6 GP, 14.5 ppg, 3.7 rpg
HONORS:
All-Star Game (1): 1965-66

PISTON LIST

Most Foul-Outs in a Season

- 22, x-Walter Dukes, 1958-59
- 20, x-Walter Dukes, 1959-60
- 20, x-Walter Dukes, 1961-62
- 19, x-Joe Strawder, 1966-67
- 18, x-Joe Strawder, 1967-68
- 17, Walter Dukes, 1957-58
- 16, x-Walter Dukes, 1960-61
- 15, Earl Lloyd, 1958-59
- 15, John Tresvant, 1967-68
- 14, Phil Hubbard, 1980-81
- 13, Bailey Howell, 1959-60
- 13, Leon Douglas, 1978-79
- 12, Joe Holup, 1958-59

x-led league

CHANGING FACES

AS DAVE DEBUSSCHERE later would say, "It was a big mistake." Sure, it made for nifty trivia that, at age 24, he had become the youngest coach in NBA history. But he was embarrassed by his three seasons as player-coach of the Pistons, a misguided experiment that ended March 7, 1967. Stuck in the cellar with eight games left in the season, the Pistons had to make a move for the future. They got DeBusschere to give up the job, allowing assistant Donnis Butcher to take over. Butcher, who played for Detroit from 1963-66, had also been the team's top scout. "I've always wanted to coach in the NBA," he said. Two months previous, the Pistons sent Ray Scott to the Baltimore Bullets in a three-team trade

Two Hall-of-Famers: Detroit's Dave DeBusschere, in his coaching garb, poses with coat-and-tied Philadelphia 76ers coach Dolph Schayes.

that was supposed to bring them two-way forward Rudy LaRusso from the Lakers. But LaRusso, author of a 50-point game in 1962, refused to come to the Pistons, saying he'd sooner retire. He never relented and Detroit finally was awarded the Lakers' 1967 first-round pick. They wound up wasting it on two-year bust Sonny Dove, a forward from St. John's.

Take a Bow

Joe Strawder

Joe Strawder's three-year NBA career was filled with fouls, though he twice averaged 10 or more rebounds.

Big Joe Strawder's NBA career wasn't long, but it was distinctive. The 6-10, 230 lb. center lasted three seasons, all with the Pistons from 1965-68, and averaged 9.9 rebounds over 231 games. He was Detroit's second-leading rebounder behind Dave DeBusschere all three seasons, averaging 10.4 in '65-66, then 10.0 and 9.4 thereafter. But Strawder is in the NBA record book for a less flattering reason: no other player committed 300 or more personal fouls each year of his career, as he did with 305, 344 (NBA high) and 312. Twenty-two other players have topped 300 in three straight years or more, but also had at least one NBA season under 300. Strawder was the second of three Pistons who led the league in fouls—Walter Dukes did it twice, in the franchise's first two years in Detroit, and Otis Thorpe did it with 300 in '95-96. Strawder also led the league in foul-outs with 19 in '66-67 and 18 the following year. But again, his career was not all "foul." His 26 rebounds vs. the Lakers were Detroit's game high for '67-68, as were his 24 vs. Boston in '66-67.

Game Results

1966-67 REGULAR SEASON

Date	Opponent	Result	Record
10-15	at Cincinnati	L, 99-103	0-1
10-18	CINCINNATI	W, 114-112	1-1
10-20	ST. LOUIS	L, 105-113	1-2
10-21	at San Francisco	L, 119-136	1-3
10-23	n-San Francisco	W, 119-110	2-3
10-28	n-Chicago	W, 129-117	3-3
10-29	BALTIMORE	W, 103-97	4-3
10-30	n-L.A. Lakers	W, 124-121	5-3
11-4	CINCINNATI	L, 115-120	5-4
11-5	at New York	L, 104-115	5-5
11-8	n-Philadelphia	L, 100-118	5-6
11-10	at L.A. Lakers	W, 133-132 (OT)	6-6
11-12	at L.A. Lakers	L, 88-144	6-7
11-13	at San Francisco	L, 96-135	6-8
11-14	at San Francisco	L, 104-115	6-9
11-16	ST. LOUIS	L, 101-104	6-10
11-17	n-New York	W, 123-108	7-10
11-18	L.A. LAKERS	W, 121-118	8-10
11-19	at St. Louis	L, 87-105	8-11
11-23	NEW YORK	W, 118-100	9-11
11-25	BOSTON	W, 107-105	10-11
11-26	at Philadelphia	L, 123-131	10-12
11-29	n-Boston	W, 104-100	11-12
11-30	PHILADELPHIA	L, 119-128	11-13
12-2	at Boston	W, 119-116	12-13
12-3	CHICAGO	W, 104-98	13-13
12-6	n-Boston	L, 111-130	13-14
12-7	NEW YORK	L, 116-118	13-15
12-14	n-Chicago	L, 87-93	13-16
12-16	BALTIMORE	L, 113-121	13-17
12-17	n-Philadelphia	L, 105-120	13-18
12-20	n-Boston	L, 113-116 (OT)	13-19
12-23	at Chicago	W, 103-102	14-19
12-25	at Baltimore	W, 129-127 (OT)	15-19
12-26	NEW YORK	L, 109-114	15-20
12-27	at Cincinnati	L, 123-131	15-21
12-30	n-Philadelphia	L, 113-137	15-22
1-2	n-St. Louis	L, 120-112	15-23
1-3	n-Baltimore	W, 117-100	16-23
1-4	at Baltimore	W, 132-126 (2OT)	17-23
1-6	CHICAGO	L, 126-135	17-24
1-8	at St. Louis	L, 115-117	17-25
1-13	n-Baltimore	W, 119-118	18-25
1-14	SAN FRANCISCO	L, 121-136	18-26
1-15	L.A. LAKERS	L, 116-127	18-27
1-18	PHILADELPHIA	L, 105-113	18-28
1-20	at Chicago	L, 124-125 (OT)	18-29
1-21	at Cincinnati	L, 108-122	18-30
1-24	at Chicago	W, 108-95	19-30
1-25	BOSTON	L, 105-112	19-31
1-26	n-Cincinnati	W, 118-110	20-31
1-27	at Boston	L, 106-112	20-32
1-31	n-San Francisco	L, 106-108	20-33
2-1	NEW YORK	W, 104-101	21-33
2-3	n-New York	L, 111-124	21-34
2-4	at New York	L, 101-102	21-35
2-5	ST. LOUIS	W, 114-104	22-35
2-7	at Chicago	W, 98-90	23-35
2-10	at Cincinnati	L, 104-133	23-36
2-11	CINCINNATI	L, 117-132	23-37
2-12	SAN FRANCISCO	W, 134-127	24-37
2-15	PHILADELPHIA	L, 121-127	24-38
2-16	n-Cincinnati	L, 110-122	24-39
2-18	n-Baltimore	W, 118-113	25-39
2-19	BALTIMORE	L, 104-131	25-40
2-21	at St. Louis	W, 112-109	26-40
2-24	L.A. LAKERS	W, 102-101	27-40
2-27	n-St. Louis	L, 94-105	27-41
2-28	n-L.A. Lakers	L, 117-119	27-42
3-1	NEW YORK	W, 118-101	28-42
3-3	n-Philadelphia	L, 103-129	28-43
3-5	at Philadelphia	L, 106-131	28-44
3-6	n-Boston	L, 103-127	28-45
3-8	BALTIMORE	W, 120-113	29-45
3-10	at L.A. Lakers	L, 103-118	29-46
3-12	at L.A. Lakers	W, 120-104	30-46
3-13	at San Francisco	L, 109-135	30-47
3-15	CHICAGO	L, 91-98	30-48
3-16	BOSTON	L, 109-132	30-49
3-18	at St. Louis	L, 99-102	30-50
3-19	SAN FRANCISCO	L, 127-135	30-51

(Home games in ALL CAPS; n-neutral site)

1967 1968

DETROIT PISTONS BASKETBALL CLUB
NATIONAL BASKETBALL ASSN.

TIME CAPSULE

October 2, 1967:
Thurgood Marshall is sworn in as the United States' first black Supreme Court justice.

April 4, 1968:
Dr. Martin Luther King Jr. is assassinated by a sniper at the Lorraine Motel in Memphis, Tennessee, setting off a week of rioting in urban ghettos.

June 5, 1968:
President candidate Robert F. Kennedy is fatally shot in Los Angeles, moments after delivering a speech to acknowledge his victory in the California primary.

SEASON SNAPSHOT

Most Points
x-Dave Bing (2,142, 27.1 avg.)

Most Rebounds
Dave DeBusschere (1,081, 13.5 avg.)

Most Assists
Dave Bing (509, 6.4 avg.)

Most Minutes
Dave Bing (3,209, 40.6 avg.)

Field-Goal Percentage
Len Chappell (51.4%)

Free-Throw Percentage
Jimmy Walker (76.6%)

Team Offense Average
118.6 (9,725 in 82 games)

Team Defense Average
120.6 (9,889 in 82 games)

NBA All-Stars
Dave Bing, G (First Team)

Pistons in All-Star Game
Dave Bing, G; Dave DeBusschere, F

x-led league

1967-68

FINAL STANDINGS

Eastern Division	W	L	Pct.	GB
Philadelphia	62	20	.756	—
Boston	54	28	.659	8
New York	43	39	.524	19
PISTONS	**40**	**42**	**.488**	**22**
Cincinnati	39	43	.476	23
Baltimore	36	46	.439	26

Western Division Winner—St. Louis

PLAYOFF RESULTS

Eastern Semifinals: Boston d. Pistons, 4-2

PISTONS PLAYOFF LEADERS

Scoring: Dave Bing (28.2 avg.)
Rebounding: Dave DeBusschere (16.2)
Assists: Dave Bing (4.8)

NBA CHAMPION

Boston Celtics

1967-68
SEASON IN REVIEW

When the Pistons won 18 of their first 30 games, they seemed well on their way to the team's first winning season since it arrived in Detroit. They had a new star, Dave Bing, who would compile five 40-point games en route to the NBA scoring title in his second season. His 2,142 points, then a club record, made him the second Piston to lead the NBA, a whole decade after George Yardley did it. One of Bing's 40-point games was in a key 123-120 win over the 76ers. But despite Bing's efforts, and those of fellow All-Star Dave DeBusschere, who led the team in rebounds, and Terry Dischinger, who resumed his NBA career after his Army hitch, the Pistons slumped badly in midseason. From December 12 through March 2, they went 13-28, with a 5-21 mark away from home. One of the road defeats was a 131-121 loss on February 2 when the Sixers' Wilt Chamberlain earned the first and only 20-20-20 triple-double in league history—22 points, 25 rebounds and 21 assists. But the Pistons, to their credit, made a late charge for their first playoff berth in five years. They won nine of their final 11 contests to finish 40-42, their best record ever. In the Eastern Semifinals, they played Boston in the playoffs for the first time, losing 4-2 despite winning Game 3 at Boston 109-98 for a 2-1 lead. They then lost the next three games, despite Bing's 44 points in Game 6 at home.

The 1967-68 Pistons: (seated, from left) Dave Bing, Tom Van Arsdale, GM Ed Coil, coach Donnis Butcher, Jimmy Walker and Eddie Miles; (standing) trainer Bud Shockro, Dave DeBusschere, John Tresvant, Len Chappell, Joe Strawder, George Patterson and Terry Dischinger.

WHAT A NIGHT!

March 27, 1968

The Pistons were not used to success at the Boston Garden. From 1957 to 1968, their record on the storied parquet was nothing short of lousy, 5-25, and then they'd been beaten again 123-116 in Game 1 of the 1968 Eastern Semifinals. But this Pistons team refused to take on a "here we go again" posture. It got back on its feet with a 126-116 win in Game 2 at home, then returned to Boston and gained one of the biggest victories to that point in team history. Fueled by Dave Bing's 27 points and rookie Jimmy Walker's 22 off the bench, the Pistons took control with a 33-15 third quarter and halted the feared Celtics 109-98. "Our guys played the hardest I've seen them play all year," Pistons coach Donnis Butcher said in the happy locker room. Walker cemented the win, scoring 14 points in the fourth quarter in relief of Eddie Miles. But the Pistons' performance in the third period made the difference as they outrebounded the Celtics 24-13 and hassled them into 5-of-24 shooting. Boston player-coach Bill Russell was held to six points in 48 minutes. The Pistons' happiness did not last, as they'd drop the next three games and the series. It would be 20 seasons before they again won a playoff game at Boston.

Dave Bing scores on a driving shot, while Terry Dischinger (43) awaits the rebound.

Premier Piston

Jimmy Walker

Jimmy Walker (left) poses with team owner Fred Zollner (right) after signing his rookie contract.

Jimmy Walker was born to be a Celtic. He grew up in Roxbury, Massachusetts, in the shadow of Boston Garden. In his childhood, he revered the dynasty of the '60s Celtics, closely watching favorites Sam Jones and Bill Russell. Then he became a college All-American at nearby Providence, averaging a nation-leading 30.4 points as a senior and 25.2 for his 81-game career. But Boston never had a chance at Walker; only the NBA's bottom-feeders were able to draft high enough to pick a player of his stature. Unlike the 1966 draft, when Detroit lost a coin flip for the No. 1 pick and got Dave Bing at No. 2, the Pistons won the flip over Baltimore in '67. They made Walker, a 6-foot-3 guard, the team's first-ever No. 1 overall draft pick, while the Bullets selected Earl Monroe, the eventual Rookie of the Year. Though Walker's five Pistons seasons were ultimately disappointing, he had two 20-point years for them and was seventh on their career points list (6,262) when he was traded in 1972; he also ranked third in assists (1,278). A good passer, trusty free-throw shooter (82.9 percent career) and solid outside gunner, Walker had his finest Pistons season in 1971-72 when he claimed his second and last All-Star berth. Though his 21.3-point average was third on the Pistons behind Bob Lanier and Dave Bing, Walker's career-record 44 points against Portland on December 7, 1971 were Detroit's season high. In four games against the Trail Blazers that year, he averaged 38.0 points. He was dealt to Houston for Stu Lantz after the season, then was traded to Kansas City-Omaha in 1973, spending his final two-plus seasons there and leading them in scoring in '73-74. Walker is the father of NBA player Jalen Rose, the former Michigan star.

AT A GLANCE

JIMMY WALKER

FULL NAME:
James Walker
BORN:
April 8, 1944; Amherst, Virginia
POSITION, HEIGHT, WEIGHT:
Guard, 6-foot-3, 205 pounds
COLLEGE:
Providence '67
ACQUIRED:
1967, Pistons' No. 1 draft pick (1st overall)
TENURE WITH PISTONS:
Detroit 1967-68 — 1971-72
Also: Houston 1972-73, Kansas City-Omaha 1973-76
BEST SEASON WITH PISTONS:
1971-72, 78 GP, 21.3 ppg, 4.0 apg
TOTALS WITH PISTONS:
Regular season: 388 GP, 16.1 ppg, 3.3 apg
Playoffs: 6 GP, 12.7 ppg, 1.5 apg
HONORS:
All-Star Game (2): 1969-70, 1971-72

PISTON LIST

How Dave Bing Scored vs. 1967-68 Opponents

- **vs. Baltimore**
  8 games, 258 pts., 32.3 avg.
- **vs. Boston**
  8 games, 199 pts., 24.9 avg.
- **vs. Chicago**
  6 games, 184 pts., 30.7 avg.
- **vs. Cincinnati**
  8 games, 240 pts., 30.0 avg.
- **vs. L.A. Lakers**
  7 games, 168 pts., 24.0 avg.
- **vs. New York**
  8 games, 177 pts., 22.1 avg.
- **vs. Philadelphia**
  8 games, 195 pts., 24.4 avg.
- **vs. St. Louis**
  7 games, 181 pts., 25.9 avg.
- **vs. San Diego**
  7 games, 183 pts., 26.1 avg.
- **vs. San Francisco**
  5 games, 150 pts., 30.0 avg.
- **vs. Seattle**
  7 games, 207 pts., 29.6 avg.

CHANGING FACES

EN ROUTE to their first playoff berth since 1963, the Pistons bolstered their '67-68 lineup with one major trade and two smaller deals. The big prize was 6-foot-7 forward Harold "Happy" Hairston, who was acquired from Cincinnati on February 1 with 6-foot-10 center Jim Fox. The trade cost the Pistons two dependable players they'd had for three seasons apiece, Tom Van Arsdale and John Tresvant, but Hairston quickly became a vital part of Detroit's attack, averaging 18.8 points and 10 boards in the last 26 games of the season. His scoring average fell to 11.7 in the playoffs, but Hairston wound up averaging 17.3 points in parts of three seasons in Detroit. Tresvant had averaged 10.6 points and Van Arsdale 10.2 in their Pistons stints. Detroit's other acquisitions came before the season.

Happy Hairston

After drafting Jimmy Walker No. 1 overall, the Pistons used the fourth pick on St. John's forward Lloyd "Sonny" Dove, but he washed out after only two NBA seasons spanning 57 games. Detroit also dealt a draft pick to Cincinnati for veteran forward Len Chappell, who averaged 10 points in his only Pistons season, and traded troubled center Reggie Harding to the Bulls for a draft pick.

Take a Bow

Dave Bing

Dave Bing accepts yet another plaque.

The NBA had been in business since 1946 and only once had a guard led the league in scoring: Max Zaslofsky of the Chicago Stags in 1947-48 by averaging 21 points in a 48-game schedule. Twenty years passed before it happened again, and Detroit's Dave Bing was the man. He scored 2,142 in '67-68 to claim the title over Elgin Baylor (2,002), Wilt Chamberlain (1,992) and Earl Monroe (1,992). It was the second straight NBA scoring title by a second-year player; San Francisco's Rick Barry had won in '67. "After being Rookie of the Year, I knew I could play well in the league," Bing said. "But I didn't have a goal to lead the league in scoring, because Oscar Robertson, Jerry West, Elgin Baylor and Wilt Chamberlain were at the top of their games still. It just happened that the team I was on and the talent I had allowed me to score a lot of points." It also allowed the Pistons' star to quickly boost his salary. He earned $15,000 as a rookie, $37,500 in '67-68 and was doubled to $75,000 the next season.

Game Results
1967-68
REGULAR SEASON

Date	Opponent	Result	Record
10-17	CINCINNATI	W, 131-108	1-0
10-21	at Philadelphia	L, 111-116	1-1
10-24	n-Philadelphia	L, 102-124	1-2
10-25	CHICAGO	W, 107-99	2-2
10-27	BOSTON	L, 109-129	2-3
10-28	at New York	W, 111-98	3-3
11-1	SAN FRANCISCO	L, 132-137	3-4
11-3	at Baltimore	W, 115-113	4-4
11-4	BALTIMORE	W, 127-118	5-4
11-8	NEW YORK	W, 110-108	6-4
11-9	n-Seattle	W, 119-118	7-4
11-10	ST. LOUIS	L, 140-143 (OT)	7-5
11-14	n-St. Louis	W, 124-107	8-5
11-15	PHILADELPHIA	W, 123-120	9-5
11-18	at Chicago	L, 130-132	9-6
11-19	at Seattle	L, 130-132 (OT)	9-7
11-20	at Seattle	W, 120-118	10-7
11-21	at San Francisco	L, 98-124	10-8
11-23	at Los Angeles	L, 120-132	10-9
11-24	SAN DIEGO	W, 130-122	11-9
11-25	at Cincinnati	W, 133-123	12-9
11-28	at Boston	L, 111-118	12-10
11-29	LOS ANGELES	W, 127-123	13-10
12-2	BOSTON	W, 112-107	14-10
12-5	n-San Diego	W, 111-110	15-10
12-6	CHICAGO	W, 135-121	16-10
12-8	LOS ANGELES	L, 103-115	16-11
12-9	at New York	W, 124-121	17-11
12-12	at Baltimore	L, 117-140	17-12
12-13	NEW YORK	W, 129-117	18-12
12-15	n-Cincinnati	L, 130-147	18-13
12-16	CINCINNATI	L, 110-122	18-14
12-17	at Seattle	W, 140-122	19-14
12-18	at San Francisco	L, 109-113	19-15
12-20	at San Francisco	L, 109-113	19-16
12-22	at Los Angeles	L, 105-133	19-17
12-23	at San Diego	W, 123-119	20-17
12-26	ST. LOUIS	W, 127-110	21-17
12-29	n-St. Louis	L, 111-122	21-18
12-30	n-Philadelphia	L, 107-122	21-19
1-2	n-Baltimore	W, 114-112	22-19
1-5	CINCINNATI	W, 142-141 (OT)	23-19
1-6	at New York	L, 101-118	23-20
1-9	n-San Francisco	W, 118-102	24-20
1-10	at San Diego	L, 118-122	24-21
1-12	at Boston	L, 126-148	24-22
1-13	PHILADELPHIA	L, 106-115	24-23
1-17	SAN FRANCISCO	W, 117-109	25-23
1-19	SEATTLE	W, 133-119	26-23
1-20	at Cincinnati	L, 120-128	26-24
1-21	NEW YORK	L, 103-115	26-25
1-25	PHILADELPHIA	L, 108-123	26-26
1-27	LOS ANGELES	W, 125-119	27-26
1-30	n-Cincinnati	L, 101-121	27-27
1-31	at Baltimore	L, 108-113	27-28
2-2	at Philadelphia	L, 121-131	27-29
2-4	BALTIMORE	W, 117-115	28-29
2-6	n-San Diego	W, 120-93	29-29
2-8	at Chicago	L, 110-131	29-30
2-9	at Boston	L, 100-107	29-31
2-10	BALTIMORE	L, 109-114	29-32
2-13	BOSTON	L, 115-127	29-33
2-14	n-Boston	L, 96-118	29-34
2-18	SAN FRANCISCO	W, 123-104	30-34
2-20	n-Chicago	L, 121-124	30-35
2-22	n-St. Louis	L, 128-151	30-36
2-23	at Philadelphia	L, 117-138	30-37
2-24	at Baltimore	L, 132-140	30-38
2-25	NEW YORK	L, 115-124	30-39
3-1	ST. LOUIS	W, 131-121	31-39
3-2	at New York	L, 107-133	31-40
3-3	CHICAGO	W, 134-123	32-40
3-5	at Chicago	W, 121-119	33-40
3-6	SAN DIEGO	W, 140-118	34-40
3-8	at Cincinnati	W, 129-118	35-40
3-10	at St. Louis	W, 133-121	36-40
3-12	SEATTLE	W, 139-123	37-40
3-15	at San Francisco	W, 122-118	38-40
3-16	at Los Angeles	L, 108-135	38-41
3-17	at Los Angeles	L, 116-120	38-42
3-18	at Seattle	W, 88-82	39-42
3-20	at Boston	W, 125-116	40-42

PLAYOFFS
Eastern Semifinals—(Best-of-Seven)

3-24	at Boston	L, 116-123	0-1
3-25	BOSTON	W, 126-116	1-1
3-27	at Boston	W, 109-98	2-1
3-28	BOSTON	L, 110-135	2-2
3-31	at Boston	L, 96-110	2-3
4-1	BOSTON	L, 103-111	2-4

(Home games in ALL CAPS; n-neutral site)

PISTONS/CELTICS RIVALRY

In 1957 at Olympia, Pistons center Walter Dukes (23) challenges Boston's Bill Russell (6) on the opening tip, while Gene Shue (21) stands ready.

Spanning 269 games over 40 seasons, the Pistons' contentious series with the Boston Celtics—unlike no other rivalry—has been the source of Detroit's most cherished victories and most excruciating losses.

It's not a surprise that the Celtics have won seven of every 10 games in the rivalry. After all, Boston had a 63-8 record against Detroit from 1957-65, owns eight season sweeps to the Pistons' one (1996-97) and won 21 straight meetings at the Boston Garden from 1982-88.

Yet, let's ponder this trivia question: How many teams own a winning playoff record vs. the Celtics (five-game minimum)? Answer: One. Your Pistons have an 18-16 edge in the postseason, winning nine of the last 11 meetings with Boston from 1988-91.

And there's this poser: Which team owns the record for points scored vs. the Celtics in both a regular-season game and a playoff game? Yup, you guessed it. Led by Kevin Porter's 30 points, Detroit pounded Boston 160-117 on March 9, 1979 at the Silverdome to set the regular-season mark. No Celtics opponent, before or since,

AT A GLANCE

PISTONS-CELTICS

PISTONS' SERIES RECORD:
Regular Season: 65-170 (Home 39-71, Road 22-74, Neutral 4-25)
Playoffs: 18-16 (Home 12-5, Road 6-11)

TEAM RECORDS (Regular Season)
BEST SEASON:
Pistons: 4-0, 1996-97
Celtics: 10-0, 1964-65

HIGHEST POINT TOTAL:
Pistons: 160, March 9, 1979
Celtics: 153, February 10, 1960
HIGHEST COMBINED SCORE:
Pistons 160, Celtics 117 (277), March 9, 1979
BIGGEST WIN MARGIN:
Pistons: 43 (160-117), March 9, 1979
Celtics: 44 (150-106), December 24, 1960
MOST REBOUNDS:
Pistons: 106, November 15, 1960
Celtics: 109, December 24, 1960 (NBA Record)

INDIVIDUAL RECORDS (Regular Season)
MOST POINTS:
Pistons: 51, George Yardley, January 15, 1958
Celtics: 56, Kevin McHale, March 3, 1985

MOST REBOUNDS:
Pistons: 25, tie, Dennis Rodman, March 20, 1992, and Earl Williams, January 23, 1976

PLAYERS WHO PLAYED FOR BOTH TEAMS (14)
Marvin Barnes, Dave Bing, M.L. Carr, Terry Duerod, Chris Ford, Rickey Green, Gerald Henderson, Bailey Howell, Bob McAdoo, Rich Niemann, Curtis Rowe, Earl Tatum, David Thirdkill, Earl Williams.

scored more points or made more field goals (69) in a game. The Pistons' 145-119 win in Game 4 of the Eastern finals in 1987 set the playoff record for a Boston opponent.

In 1960, both clubs victimized each other for their team single-game rebound records, both still on the books 37 years later. The Pistons got 106 rebounds Nov. 15 while nipping Boston, 115-114, in OT in a neutral-site game at New York. Barely more than a month later, the Celtics set the NBA record with 109 rebounds in a 150-106 win over the Pistons.

Those records and others have been exiled to footnote status over the years, however. They have been obscured by the national magnitude and throbbing intensity of 28 Pistons-Celtics postseason games (over five series) from 1985-91. With the likely exception of the Celtics-Lakers, no other '80s postseason rivalry created more memorable moments.

Like in Game 4 of the Eastern semifinals in '85, when Vinnie Johnson scored 22 of his 34 points in the fourth quarter at Joe Louis Arena and sparked the Pistons' 102-99 comeback win. He made 10-of-11 shots in the quarter. Celtics guard Danny Ainge said afterward, "Vinnie Johnson is The Microwave. He heated up in a hurry," and the nickname stuck.

Then, in the '88 Eastern finals, there was Isiah Thomas scoring 35 in Game 1 to fuel the Pistons' 104-96 victory, their first in Boston since December 19, 1982, and scoring 35 again in Game 5 to rally the Pistons to a 102-99 OT win. That set up their Game 6 clincher at the Silverdome.

As special as those memories are for Detroit fans, the signature play in the Celtics rivalry was the most crushing in Pistons history and one of the most outstanding plays in NBA history. Detroit was five seconds away from taking a 3-2 lead in the 1987 Eastern finals, holding a 107-106 lead in Game 5 at Boston. But with Isiah inbounding in the Pistons' end, Larry Bird bolted in front of his pass to Bill Laimbeer and stole it. In one motion, Bird pivoted on the left baseline and passed to a cutting Dennis Johnson, who made the layup for a 108-107 lead. Game over.

"I'll be seeing that play in my nightmares forever," longtime Pistons general manager Jack McCloskey said.

Bird's heartbreaking steal-and-dish became the pivotal play in one of the most competitive playoff series ever, in which the home team won every game. The flames had been stoked earlier in Game 5 when Boston center Robert Parish, tiring of Laimbeer's aggressive defense, punched him thrice from behind as they tussled for a rebound. In Game 6 back at Pontiac, the Pistons bravely tossed aside their Game 5 disappointment, claiming a 113-105 win to tie the series 3-3. But at Boston Garden, on a sweltering Saturday, the Celtics finally prevailed, 117-114, in Game 7.

A lot of the Pistons' trouble with the Celtics has been self-inflicted. In 1979, they traded two No. 1 draft choices to Boston for Bob McAdoo, five years removed from his MVP season in Buffalo. The injury-plagued star washed out in Detroit after less than two seasons, but the Celtics parlayed the two No. 1 picks into a June 9, 1980 trade for Parish (with Golden State) and the drafting of Kevin McHale only a day later. It's one of the most lopsided deals ever, one that helped Boston form the NBA's best front line of the '80s. The Pistons, meanwhile, would have to wait for Isiah to arrive in 1981 to begin digging out.

They eventually did so, resulting in some of the greatest memories in team history.

Pistons' seasons against Celtics

REGULAR SEASON

SEASON	HOME	AWAY	NEUTRAL	TOTAL
1957-58	0-4	1-3	0-1	1-8
1958-59	1-3	0-4	0-1	1-8
1959-60	0-4	0-2	0-3	0-9
1960-61	1-3	0-3	1-2	2-8
1961-62	1-3	1-1	1-1	3-5
1962-63	0-4	0-2	0-2	0-8
1963-64	1-3	0-2	0-2	1-7
1964-65	0-4	0-2	0-4	0-10
1965-66	2-2	1-1	1-3	4-6
1966-67	1-2	1-1	1-3	3-6
1967-68	1-2	1-3	0-1	2-6
1968-69	0-3	1-2	—	1-5
1969-70	2-1	1-2	0-1	3-4
1970-71	1-2	2-0	—	3-2
1971-72	0-2	0-3	—	0-5
1972-73	0-2	1-1	—	1-3
1973-74	1-1	0-1	0-1	1-3
1974-75	0-2	1-1	—	1-3
1975-76	0-2	0-2	—	0-4
1976-77	1-1	1-1	—	2-2
1977-78	2-0	1-1	—	3-1
1978-79	1-1	1-1	—	2-2
1979-80	0-3	0-3	—	0-6
1980-81	0-3	1-1	—	1-4
1981-82	0-3	0-3	—	0-6
1982-83	1-2	2-1	—	3-3
1983-84	2-1	0-3	—	2-4
1984-85	2-1	0-3	—	2-4
1985-86	1-1	0-3	—	1-4
1986-87	2-1	0-2	—	2-3
1987-88	3-0	0-3	—	3-3
1988-89	2-0	1-1	—	3-1
1989-90	2-0	0-2	—	2-2
1990-91	2-0	0-2	—	2-2
1991-92	0-2	0-2	—	0-4
1992-93	2-0	1-1	—	3-1
1993-94	0-2	1-1	—	1-3
1994-95	1-1	0-2	—	1-3
1995-96	1-0	0-2	—	1-2
1996-97	2-0	2-0	—	4-0
TOTAL	**39-71**	**22-74**	**4-25**	**65-170**

PLAYOFFS

SEASON	HOME	AWAY	TOTAL
1967-68	1-2	1-2	2-4
1984-85	2-1	0-3	2-4
1986-87	3-0	0-4	3-4
1987-88	2-1	2-1	4-2
1988-89	2-0	1-0	3-0
1990-91	2-1	2-1	4-2
TOTAL	**12-5**	**6-11**	**18-16**

1968 1969

DETROIT PISTONS BASKETBALL CLUB NATIONAL BASKETBALL ASSN.

TIME CAPSULE

October 10, 1968:
The Detroit Tigers, rallying from a 3-1 series deficit, beat the St. Louis Cardinals in Game 7 to win the World Series for the first time since 1945.

November 5, 1968:
Republican Richard M. Nixon wins the presidential election, beating Democrat Hubert H. Humphrey by only 500,000 votes.

July 16, 1969:
U.S. space capsule Apollo 11 lands on the moon at 4:17 p.m. EDT; Neil Armstrong becomes the first person to set foot on the lunar surface.

SEASON SNAPSHOT

Most Points
Dave Bing (1,800, 23.4 avg.)

Most Rebounds
Happy Hairston (959, 13.5 avg.)

Most Assists
Dave Bing (546, 7.1 avg.)

Most Minutes
Dave Bing (3,039, 39.5 avg.)

Field-Goal Percentage
Terry Dischinger (51.5%)

Free-Throw Percentage
Jimmy Walker (79.5%)

Team Offense Average
114.1 (9,359 in 82 games)

Team Defense Average
117.3 (9,618 in 82 games)

NBA All-Stars
Dave DeBusschere, F (Second Team)

Pistons in All-Star Game
Dave Bing, G

1968-69

FINAL STANDINGS

Eastern Division	W	L	Pct.	GB
Baltimore	57	25	.695	—
Philadelphia	55	27	.671	2
New York	54	28	.659	3
Boston	48	34	.585	9
Cincinnati	41	41	.500	16
PISTONS	**32**	**50**	**.390**	**25**
Milwaukee	27	55	.329	30

Western Division Winner—Los Angeles

PLAYOFF RESULTS

Pistons Did Not Qualify

PISTONS PLAYOFF LEADERS

NBA CHAMPION

Boston Celtics

1968-69
SEASON IN REVIEW

The Pistons dropped all illusions in 1968-69. They'd come closer than ever to .500 the year before (40-42), but it's as if they finally realized how far they were from true contention; all bets were off. Firing coach Donnis Butcher on December 2 wasn't a radical idea—they did that by rote— but the December 19 trade of native Detroiter Dave DeBusschere was a shock. Tired of DeBusschere's alleged sulking, new coach Paul Seymour traded the forward to New York for 6-11 center Walt Bellamy and guard Howie Komives. "I know we gave up a lot, but the name of the game is winning ... and we weren't winning," Seymour said. DeBusschere, liberated after six-plus seasons in Detroit, said, "It is not the end of the world. I knew the Pistons would have to do something to start winning." Trouble was, they didn't win. They were 11-18 at the time of the trade and stumbled to a 32-50 record; their 8-22 skid from January 25-March 16 was a killer. Dave Bing had his typical season, averaging 23.4 points and also setting Detroit's then-single-game assist record October 31 with 19 at Milwaukee. Bellamy averaged 18.8 points in 53 games. On March 11 the Lakers' Wilt Chamberlain shot 14-of-14 vs. Detroit, the fourth-most ever without a miss. In the season finale, the Pistons pounded Chicago 158-114 to top their scoring record, since broken. In New York, DeBusschere made the All-NBA second team.

Walt Bellamy played for five franchises over his 14-year NBA career. The Pistons were his third club.

WHAT A NIGHT!

February 4, 1969

A time would come in the '80s when crowds of more than 40,000 were common for the Pistons. From 1985-88, they drew at least that many to the Silverdome 10 times, including a record 61,983 on January 29, 1988 vs. Boston. But until one special Tuesday night at the Houston Astrodome in 1969, NBA crowds like that didn't exist. A year earlier on January 20, 1968, 52,693 had gathered there to see No. 2-ranked Houston nudge No. 1 UCLA 71-69 in the first regular-season NCAA game ever aired on national TV. On February 4, 1969, the NBA invaded the Astrodome for a double-header: the Pistons vs. the Cincinnati Royals

and Boston vs. San Diego. Enlarged by a national sporting goods convention in Houston, a record crowd of 41,163 saw the Pistons lose to Cinci 125-114. Detroit led much of the way, but couldn't hold on. The Royals went ahead for good with 57 seconds left in the third quarter, taking a 93-91 lead on a basket by ex-Piston Tom Van Arsdale, who'd been dealt to Cincinnati a year before. Royals star Oscar Robertson tallied 37 points and 10 assists, while Jerry Lucas seized 26 rebounds. Dave Bing scored 29 and Walt Bellamy 19 for the Pistons, who would fare better in later games before 40,000-plus (7-4 total).

Premier Piston

Otto Moore

Despite a few promising seasons, Otto Moore wasn't the franchise center the Piston had been hoping for.

As long as Detroit fans could recall—back to the era of Walter Dukes, Bob Ferry and Joe Caldwell—the Pistons had sought a franchise center. Not just someone to occasionally hold down the fort, but a big man who could dominate games and dilute the ridiculous mismatches against the NBA's great centers, like Wilt Chamberlain and Bill Russell. By drafting 6-11 Otto Moore out of Pan American with the sixth overall pick in '68, the Pistons thought they finally filled that void. They felt so confident, in fact, they dealt their best veteran big man, Dave DeBusschere, to the Knicks only three months into Moore's NBA career. In retrospect, it was a failed project; though highly touted in college, where Moore broke the career point and rebound records of Lucious Jackson, he was simply too light (210) and wiry to grapple big centers. The Pistons recognized that after only two seasons, compelling them to pick burly Bob Lanier in '70. But taken on his own terms, Moore wasn't a total bust with the Pistons. In three full seasons, he led them in rebounds twice—with 900 in '69-70 and 700 in '70-71, nudging rookie Lanier in the latter season. Moore became a dependable starter in '69-70, moving into the lineup on January 2 and averaging 15.5 points and 15 rebounds in the final 44 games. In that span, he set his Detroit career highs of 27 points and 28 boards; his big rebound game came March 17 vs. DeBusschere and the Knicks. Moore left Detroit under strange circumstances after '70-71 when he was dealt to Phoenix for Mel Counts. But before going to the Suns, he signed with the Virginia Squires in the ABA. After he reported to Phoenix, inexplicably, the Suns got to keep Counts while the Moore-ABA litigation dragged on.

AT A GLANCE

OTTO MOORE

FULL NAME:
Otto George Moore
BORN:
August 27, 1946; Miami
POSITION, HEIGHT, WEIGHT:
Center, 6-foot-11, 205 pounds
COLLEGE:
Pan American '68
ACQUIRED:
Drafted, first round, 1968 (6th overall)
TENURE WITH PISTONS:
Detroit 1968-69 — 1970-71; '74
BEST SEASON WITH PISTONS:
1969-70, 81 GP, 11.9 ppg, 11.1 rpg
TOTALS WITH PISTONS:
Regular season: 239 GP, 9.5 ppg, 8.9 rpg
Playoffs: None

PISTON LIST

Most Free Throws Made in a Game (With Attempts)

20
- George Yardley (24), 12-26-57
- Walter Dukes (24), 1-19-61
- Kelly Tripucka (22), 1-29-83

19
- Bailey Howell (21), 11-25-60
- Adrian Dantley (22), 11-21-87

18
- Joe Dumars (19), 3-2-90
- Adrian Dantley (20), 11-7-87
- Adrian Dantley (19), 12-2-88

17
- 8 times by 5 players

16
- 8 times by 6 players

15
- 18 times by 10 players

CHANGING FACES

WHEN DAVE DEBUSSCHERE
walked off the court at Cobo Arena on
December 20, the fans rose and gave
their hero a lusty ovation. But he
wasn't wearing a Pistons uniform
anymore. He was in Knicks blue,
having been traded to New York one
day before. It was rather poetic that
the clubs' first game after their big
trade was against each other at
Detroit and DeBusschere starred in
the Knicks' 135-87 win, still their
widest victory margin vs. the Pistons.
"I really appreciated that,"
DeBusschere said of the cheers. "It
was a funny feeling." He had 21
points and 15 rebounds, team-highs.
"He played great," Pistons coach Paul
Seymour said. "He didn't look like the
guy who played eight games for me."
Detroit's trade booty was Walt
Bellamy and point man Howie

From University of Detroit to the Pistons, Dave DeBusschere had spent his entire career in the Motor City until going to the Knicks.

Komives. "(Komives) gets the ball moving. Not moving the ball has been one of
our problems," Seymour said. As for Bellamy, by playing 35 games for the
Knicks and then 53 for Detroit, he had the longest regular season for any
player in NBA history, 88 games, compared to the usual 82.

Take a Bow
Edwin E. Coil

Ed Coil, an accountant by trade, served as Pistons general manager for a decade.

It had never been popular to be in the Pistons' front office, but it was especially unpopular in '68. Trading Dave DeBusschere had not endeared club management to fans devoted to the hometown star. But Edwin Coil, the Pistons' general manager from 1966-75, had merely done what the boss wanted. He was not a "basketball man," having been an accountant with the Zollner Corp. in Fort Wayne, but Coil lent stability to the team when he took over as full-time GM in '66. The Pistons' front office still hadn't recovered from the death of previous GM Don Wattrick in October 1965, and Coil put the club on a financial path that helped it withstand years of poor attendance. "It (was) the last thing I ever dreamed would happen to me, to become general manager of a major league team," said Coil, a native of Willshire, Ohio. "People wondered about my basketball background, but I had been very close to the team and the league." When the Pistons' new ownership group took control in '74, Coil was the only management member held over.

Game Results

1968-69 REGULAR SEASON

Date	Opponent	Result	Record
10-14	at Baltimore	L, 116-124	0-1
10-18	BOSTON	L, 88-106	0-2
10-19	at Cincinnati	L, 115-127	0-3
10-23	L.A. LAKERS	W, 117-110	1-3
10-25	PHILADELPHIA	W, 132-122	2-3
10-30	at Boston	W, 119-117	3-3
10-31	at Milwaukee	L, 118-134	3-4
11-2	NEW YORK	W, 112-104	4-4
11-6	SEATTLE	W, 127-118	5-4
11-8	SAN FRANCISCO	W, 122-118 (OT)	6-4
11-10	at Phoenix	L, 128-130 (OT)	6-5
11-13	at San Diego	L, 120-122	6-6
11-14	n-Phoenix	W, 111-109	7-6
11-15	at San Francisco	L, 105-133	7-7
11-16	at Seattle	L, 119-123	7-8
11-19	CINCINNATI	W, 121-107	8-8
11-21	ATLANTA	L, 121-129	8-9
11-23	BALTIMORE	L, 127-128	8-10
11-26	n-San Diego	W, 134-120	9-10
11-27	PHOENIX	W, 125-111	10-10
11-29	n-Cincinnati	L, 112-122	10-11
11-30	at New York	L, 108-120	10-12
12-4	BALTIMORE	L, 106-112	10-13
12-6	at Boston	L, 106-108	10-14
12-7	at Philadelphia	L, 106-140	10-15
12-10	at Chicago	L, 83-100	10-16
12-11	BOSTON	L, 106-108	10-17
12-14	PHOENIX	L, 118-123	10-18
12-18	SAN DIEGO	W, 124-112	11-18
12-20	NEW YORK	L, 87-135	11-19
12-21	at Atlanta	L, 110-120	11-20
12-25	at Milwaukee	W, 119-113	12-20
12-26	L.A. LAKERS	L, 94-95	12-21
12-28	SAN FRANCISCO	W, 131-102	13-21
12-29	at L.A. Lakers	L, 108-111	13-22
12-31	at L.A. Lakers	W, 127-107	14-22
1-3	ATLANTA	L, 106-128	14-23
1-4	at New York	L, 103-111	14-24
1-5	at Philadelphia	L, 119-126	14-25
1-7	PHILADELPHIA	W, 117-114	15-25
1-8	at Boston	L, 104-113	15-26
1-10	at Atlanta	L, 101-104	15-27
1-11	CINCINNATI	W, 118-115	16-27
1-12	at Cincinnati	W, 113-111	17-27
1-17	MILWAUKEE	W, 123-108	18-27
1-19	CHICAGO	W, 120-111	19-27
1-20	n-Milwaukee	L, 101-102	19-28
1-22	L.A. LAKERS	W, 116-115	20-28
1-24	NEW YORK	W, 107-106	21-28
1-25	at Philadelphia	L, 106-124	21-29
1-27	at Baltimore	L, 106-126	21-30
1-29	SAN FRANCISCO	L, 126-133	21-31
1-30	n-Seattle	W, 144-118	22-31
1-31	at Chicago	W, 103-102	23-31
2-1	at Atlanta	L, 99-119	23-32
2-2	BALTIMORE	L, 106-128	23-33
2-4	n-Cincinnati	L, 114-125	23-34
2-5	CHICAGO	L, 108-120	23-35
2-8	SAN DIEGO	W, 123-119 (OT)	24-35
2-12	BOSTON	L, 106-113	24-36
2-13	CHICAGO	L, 101-120	24-37
2-14	PHOENIX	W, 128-123	25-37
2-16	at Seattle	L, 119-127	25-38
2-18	at San Francisco	L, 114-121	25-39
2-19	at Seattle	W, 131-124	26-39
2-20	ATLANTA	L, 87-97	26-40
2-22	MILWAUKEE	L, 107-108	26-41
2-24	at Baltimore	L, 119-123	26-42
2-27	n-Philadelphia	W, 126-123	27-42
2-28	BALTIMORE	L, 116-134	27-43
3-2	PHILADELPHIA	L, 112-126	27-44
3-4	at New York	L, 99-102	27-45
3-5	NEW YORK	W, 128-120	28-45
3-7	CINCINNATI	W, 114-105	29-45
3-9	MILWAUKEE	L, 121-126	29-46
3-11	at L.A. Lakers	L, 121-126	29-47
3-13	at San Diego	L, 105-120	29-48
3-14	at San Francisco	L, 110-114	29-49
3-16	at San Diego	L, 111-120	29-50
3-17	at Phoenix	W, 119-95	30-50
3-21	SEATTLE	W, 110-104	31-50
3-23	CHICAGO	W, 158-114	32-50

(Home games in CAPS; n-neutral site)

1969 DETROIT PISTONS BASKETBALL CLUB 1970

TIME CAPSULE

August 15, 1969:
The Woodstock Music and Art Fair begins at Bethel, N.Y., drawing an estimated crowd of a half-million people.

March 18, 1970:
The first major U.S. postal workers' strike begins.

April 29, 1970:
U.S. and South Vietnamese troops invade Cambodia.

May 4, 1970:
Four students at Kent State University are killed by National Guard troops during an antiwar demonstration.

SEASON SNAPSHOT

Most Points
Dave Bing (1,604, 22.9 avg.)

Most Rebounds
Otto Moore (900, 11.2 avg.)

Most Assists
Dave Bing (418, 6.0 avg.)

Most Minutes
Jimmy Walker (2,869, 35.4 avg.)

Field-Goal Percentage
Terry Dischinger (52.6%)

Free-Throw Percentage
McCoy McLemore (82.1%)

Team Offense Average
112.8 (9,246 in 82 games)

Team Defense Average
116.1 (9,518 in 82 games)

Pistons in All-Star Game
Jimmy Walker, G

FINAL STANDINGS

Eastern Division	W	L	Pct.	GB
New York	60	22	.732	—
Milwaukee	56	26	.683	4
Baltimore	50	32	.610	10
Philadelphia	42	40	.512	18
Cincinnati	36	46	.439	24
Boston	34	48	.415	26
PISTONS	**31**	**51**	**.378**	**29**

Western Division Winner—Atlanta

PLAYOFF RESULTS

Pistons Did Not Qualify

PISTONS PLAYOFF LEADERS

NBA CHAMPION

New York Knicks

58

1969-70
SEASON IN REVIEW

The Pistons finally went and got themselves a coach with a good track record in the NBA: Bill "Butch" van Breda Kolff, who had just guided the Lakers to two straight NBA Finals berths, both losses to Boston. But the 1969-70 Pistons didn't have Lakers-like talent—far from it—and they stumbled to a 31-51 record in their first year under coach VBK. Despite showing promise with a competitive 7-9 road mark through December 9, Dave Bing, first-time All-Star Jimmy Walker and Co. could not continue their early pace, going 3-16 on the road thereafter. A 1-11 overall skid from December 12 to January 3 dropped the Pistons to 13-27 and they never recovered. VBK tried to tweak the roster, trading Happy Hairston for rebounder Bill Hewitt in November, then dealing Walt Bellamy and Eddie Miles on February 1 in seperate swaps, but nothing could pull Detroit out of its freefall. The only consolation was that finishing last in the Eastern Division gave the Pistons a coin-flip opportunity for the No. 1 draft pick; winning the flip would bring Detroit franchise center Bob Lanier next season. Again, Bing led the team in scoring for the fourth straight season with 22.9 per game, and Walker had a breakout season with 20.8 ppg. There was little help in the draft; first-round forward Terry Driscoll signed in Italy and fourth-rounder Steve Mix missed most of the season on military duty.

Dave Bing and erstwhile Piston Dave DeBusschere of the Knicks battle for a loose ball at Cobo Arena.

November 29, 1969

The Pistons' season went downhill so badly after mid-December, they had to reach all the way back to Game 21 for their highlight. When they played the New York Knicks at famed Madison Square Garden on November 29, the Pistons had just lost to Philadelphia to begin an eight-game 11-day road trip that would take them from one coast to the other. Without the injured Dave Bing, the odds of the Pistons beating New York were lousy; the Knicks were now among the favorites to win the NBA championship, having rounded out their nucleus the previous December by trading for Detroit's Dave DeBusschere. They had also pounded the Pistons by 24 in the teams' first meeting of the season. But things were different this time. The Pistons refused to let the host Knicks run away, trailing only 78-75 going into the fourth quarter. Then, to the surprise of everybody, the Pistons blew right past the Knicks in the fourth quarter, outscoring them 35-20 behind guard Jimmy Walker and rolling to a 110-98 victory. Walker, finally fulfilling his lofty potential, scored 27 points and Eddie Miles 24 for Detroit. The Knicks, the eventual league champs, got 26 by Willis Reed, 24 by Walt Frazier and 17 by Bill Bradley—Hall-of-Famers all.

WHAT A NIGHT!

Jimmy Walker sparked the Pistons' biggest victory of the season with 27 points off the bench.

Premier Piston

Bill "Butch" van Breda Kolff

Coach Bill van Breda Kolff couldn't repeat his Lakers success with the Pistons.

It takes a man of strong will to leave the penthouse and volunteer for the outhouse. Or it takes somebody crazy enough to believe he can make it work. Coach Bill "Butch" van Breda Kolff was such a man. Princeton-educated (sort of; he flunked out twice) and Marine-hardened, van Breda Kolff had guided the star-studded L.A. Lakers to the NBA Finals in 1968 and '69, losing to dynastic Boston in six games the first time and seven games in the rematch. But while the Lakers had come within two points of being world champions, van Breda Kolff (aka VBK) had quickly grown weary of high-maintenance center Wilt Chamberlain. He quit the Lakers a week after the '69 Finals, thrilled to escape with his sanity despite a two-year record of 107-57. VBK wasn't unemployed for long, though; he was snapped up in two days by Fred Zollner, who made him the Pistons' eighth coach in 13 years. Though they didn't make the playoffs in VBK's two-plus seasons, he deserves high praise for leading them to the first over-.500 record in team history, 45-37 in 1970-71 behind steady Dave Bing and rookie Bob Lanier. But VBK's combustible ways did not sit well with all players and their insolence similarly angered him. Finally, just hours after Doug Barkley quit as coach of the Red Wings, van Breda Kolff quit the Pistons on November 1, 1971, merely 10 games into his third season. He exited with an 82-92 record, a .471 percentage that was No. 1 among all Pistons coaches to that point. He would serve later stints at Phoenix and New Orleans, but VBK might be best remembered for having coached Bill Bradley at Princeton. He guided the Tigers to a third-place finish in the 1965 NCAA tournament, part of a five-year span in which Princeton won four Ivy League championships.

AT A GLANCE

BILL van BREDA KOLFF

FULL NAME:
Willem Hendrik van Breda Kolff
BORN:
October 28, 1922; New York
COLLEGE:
Princeton, New York University
NBA COACHING TENURE:
Detroit 1969-70 — November 1, 1971
Also: L.A. Lakers 1967-69, Phoenix 1972-73, New Orleans 1974-76
NBA COACHING RECORD:
Regular season: 266-253 (.513)
Detroit 82-92 (.471), L.A. Lakers 107-57 (.652), Phoenix 3-4 (.429), New Orleans 74-100 (.425)
Playoffs: 21-12 (Lakers)
BEST SEASON WITH PISTONS:
1970-71: 45-37 (.549)

PISTON LIST

Worst Home Record in 82-Game Season

- **10-31**, 1993-94
- **13-28**, 1979-80
- **14-27**, 1980-81
- **16-25**, 1971-72
- **22-19**, 1978-79
- **22-19**, 1994-95
- **23-18**, 1981-82
- **23-18**, 1982-83
- **24-17**, 1970-71
- **24-17**, 1975-76
- **24-17**, 1977-78

CHANGING FACES

WALT BELLAMY had worn out his welcome before. Through his first eight NBA seasons, he had averaged 23 points and been traded three times. So it wasn't surprising that he quickly moved into coach VBK's doghouse in Detroit, especially since his scoring average had sagged to 10.0 a game. The Pistons were so eager to get rid of him, they basically took nothing in return February 1, 1970 when they traded the 6-foot-11 center to Atlanta in a three-team deal. The trade brought 6-foot-4 rookie John Arthurs to Detroit, but he didn't play a game for them. VBK made another bad trade that day, sending guard Eddie Miles to the Baltimore Bullets for 6-foot-5 Bob Quick and a draft pick. Miles had averaged 14.9 points in six-plus Pistons seasons; Quick would contribute little in two-plus seasons. The Pistons' most productive trades came in November when they picked up bespectacled center Erwin Mueller from Seattle for a draft pick; he would average 10.3 points in '69-70. Then they got rebounding ace Bill Hewitt from the Lakers for Happy Hairston, who had also steamed VBK.

Center Erwin Mueller played parts of four seasons with the Pistons, averaging 6.7 points over 189 games.

The VILLAIN
Lew Alcindor

Lew Alcindor—later Kareem Abdul-Jabbar—was an immediate hit against the Pistons and the rest of the NBA.

The Pistons got the NBA's first look at Lew Alcindor and its last look at Kareem Abdul-Jabbar. When the three-time UCLA all-American made his long-anticipated NBA debut on Saturday, October 18, 1969, the Pistons were the opposition. Alcindor, a 7-foot-2 center, was successful from the start, racking up 29 points, 12 rebounds and three blocked shots to spark the host Milwaukee Bucks to a 119-110 victory over Detroit. The game was not just the start of an amazing Rookie of the Year season in which he led the NBA in scoring (28.8 ppg), it began a 20-year career in which the renamed Abdul-Jabbar became the league's all-time scoring leader (38,387) and a six-time MVP. In seven games against the Pistons in 1969-70, Alcindor averaged 31.4 points, though his 46 points on February 24 came in Detroit's only win over the Bucks. In 1989, Abdul-Jabbar's final NBA game was also vs. the Pistons. Limiting him to seven points, Detroit beat the Lakers 105-97 to cap its 4-0 sweep in the NBA Finals. As he exited in the final minute, the Pistons joined the packed Forum in a standing ovation for the retiring legend.

Game Results

1969-70 REGULAR SEASON

Date	Opponent	Result	Record
10-18	at Milwaukee	L, 110-119	0-1
10-21	BOSTON	W, 98-97	1-1
10-24	NEW YORK	L, 92-116	1-2
10-25	at Atlanta	W, 125-104	2-2
10-28	BALTIMORE	L, 110-125	2-3
10-30	MILWAUKEE	L, 81-102	2-4
11-1	SAN DIEGO	W, 130-113	3-4
11-4	SEATTLE	L, 102-118	3-5
11-7	PHILADELPHIA	W, 134-128 (2OT)	4-5
11-8	at Milwaukee	L, 96-100	4-6
11-9	at Phoenix	L, 129-140	4-7
11-11	at L.A. Lakers	W, 110-102	5-7
11-12	at San Diego	L, 119-132	5-8
11-13	at Seattle	L, 113-117	5-9
11-15	at Cincinnati	W, 105-104	6-9
11-18	L.A. LAKERS	L, 114-125	6-10
11-21	ATLANTA	L, 106-118	6-11
11-25	n-Chicago	W, 104-103	7-11
11-26	CHICAGO	L, 109-129	7-12
11-28	at Philadelphia	L, 91-110	7-13
11-29	at New York	W, 110-98	8-13
12-2	at San Francisco	L, 109-116	8-14
12-3	at San Francisco	W, 106-102	9-14
12-5	at L.A. Lakers	L, 109-128	9-15
12-7	at Phoenix	W, 118-113	10-15
12-8	at San Diego	W, 111-102	11-15
12-9	at Seattle	L, 104-109	11-16
12-11	CINCINNATI	W, 119-116 (OT)	12-16
12-12	at Philadelphia	L, 111-125	12-17
12-13	SAN FRANCISCO	L, 97-104	12-18
12-16	n-Boston	L, 98-117	12-19
12-17	SAN DIEGO	L, 107-114	12-20
12-19	at Baltimore	L, 105-108	12-21
12-20	PHOENIX	W, 114-113	13-21
12-25	at New York	L, 111-112	13-22
12-26	MILWAUKEE	L, 101-114	13-23
12-29	CINCINNATI	L, 103-110	13-24
12-31	at Boston	L, 121-124	13-25
1-2	BOSTON	L, 92-110	13-26
1-3	at Phoenix	L, 109-114	13-27
1-4	n-Seattle	W, 116-110	14-27
1-5	at San Francisco	L, 102-118	14-28
1-7	n-Baltimore	L, 116-121	14-29
1-10	SEATTLE	W, 129-128	15-29
1-12	n-Atlanta	W, 113-110	16-29
1-13	SAN FRANCISCO	W, 115-102	17-29
1-14	at Boston	L, 116-120	17-30
1-16	NEW YORK	L, 102-104	17-31
1-18	L.A. LAKERS	W, 106-100	18-31
1-22	n-Baltimore	L, 115-119	18-32
1-23	at Boston	W, 109-105 (OT)	19-32
1-24	CHICAGO	W, 128-122	20-32
1-25	at Chicago	L, 111-120	20-33
1-29	at New York	L, 106-127	20-34
1-30	BALTIMORE	W, 129-117	21-34
1-31	at Cincinnati	L, 115-117	21-35
2-1	NEW YORK	L, 111-117	21-36
2-2	n-Atlanta	L, 121-125	21-37
2-4	L.A. LAKERS	W, 125-109	22-37
2-6	at Baltimore	L, 148-153 (2OT)	22-38
2-7	SEATTLE	W, 113-109	23-38
2-10	CINCINNATI	L, 115-117	23-39
2-11	n-Cincinnati	L, 113-124	23-40
2-13	PHOENIX	W, 132-120	24-40
2-15	CHICAGO	W, 126-119	25-40
2-19	n-Philadelphia	L, 114-133	25-41
2-20	at Baltimore	W, 122-119	26-41
2-21	PHILADELPHIA	L, 110-112	26-42
2-22	at Atlanta	W, 116-114	27-42
2-24	MILWAUKEE	W, 136-111	28-42
2-25	at Philadelphia	L, 105-122	28-43
2-26	PHOENIX	L, 123-131	28-44
2-27	at Milwaukee	L, 113-131	28-45
3-1	SAN FRANCISCO	W, 116-99	29-45
3-6	MILWAUKEE	L, 118-121	29-46
3-7	SAN DIEGO	W, 134-126	30-46
3-10	BOSTON	W, 115-112	31-46
3-14	at Chicago	L, 96-111	31-47
3-17	NEW YORK	L, 106-122	31-48
3-19	at San Diego	L, 118-132	31-49
3-20	at L.A. Lakers	L, 111-117	31-50
3-21	ATLANTA	L, 126-130	31-51

(Home games in CAPS; n-neutral site)

BOB "DOBBER" LANIER

All of the glowing statistics in the world couldn't buy Bob Lanier what he wanted most in his 14-year NBA career: a championship ring. Nothing meant more to the Pistons' 6-foot-11 center than to be recognized as a champion in the literal sense as well as the figurative.

Throughout the 1970s, Lanier reigned as one of the NBA's leading low-post players, a smooth-shooting lefty who led Detroit in scoring eight straight seasons, made seven All-Star Games in that span and rewrote the team record book before he was traded to Milwaukee in 1980.

In '91, basketball's heirarchy recognized "Dobber" for his outstanding career, electing him to the Hall of Fame—a much-deserved honor for a player who overcame balky knees to average 20.1 points and 10.1 points in 959 NBA games. No Piston had more 40-point games than Lanier (20).

But, well, there's always a "but" when Lanier's career is the subject. Though the blame can hardly be placed completely on his shoulders, the Pistons never advanced past the conference semifinals in Lanier's nine full seasons with the team. Detroit got to the playoffs four times with Lanier (1974-77), but

lasted only one round three times. A seven-game loss to Chicago in '74 and a six-game loss to Golden State in '76, both thrilling conference semis, were as close as his Pistons would come to postseason success. Nevertheless, Lanier was his usual dominant self, averaging 25.6 points and 13.8 boards in 22 playoff games. Those stats were better than his Detroit regular-season career averages of 22.7 and 11.8—still club records almost two decades after he was traded.

In fact, when the Pistons finally honored Lanier's long-standing trade request on February 4, 1980, shipping him to the Milwaukee Bucks for center Kent Benson and a No. 1 draft pick, it gave him the opportunity to stamp himself as a player who could foster team success. Lanier immediately made the Bucks better, helping them earn 20 victories in their final 26 games to win the Midwest Division. In his four full seasons with them, all as a starter, the Bucks went 226-112 and won four straight Central Divisions ('81-84). Though they twice lost in the Eastern Finals to the eventual world champions—Philadelphia in '83, Boston in '84—Lanier was a contributor all the way; in 45 Bucks playoff games, he averaged 15.1 points and 7.6 rebounds. When he retired

AT A GLANCE

BOB LANIER

FULL NAME:
Robert Jerry Lanier Jr.
BORN:
September 10, 1948; Buffalo, New York
POSITION, HEIGHT, WEIGHT:
Center, 6-foot-11, 265 pounds
COLLEGE:
St. Bonaventure, '70
ACQUIRED:
1970, Pistons' No. 1 draft pick (1st overall)

TENURE WITH PISTONS:
1970-71—February 4, 1980
Also: Milwaukee February 4, 1980—1983-84
BEST SEASON WITH PISTONS:
1972-73, 81 GP, 23.8 ppg, 14.9 rpg, 3.2 apg
TOTALS WITH PISTONS:
Regular season: 681 GP, 15,488 pts. (22.7), 8,063 reb. (11.8), 2,256 ast. (3.3)
Playoffs: 22 GP, 564 pts. (25.6), 303 reb. (13.8), 76 ast. (3.5)
NBA COACHING RECORD:
Golden State, 1994-95: 12-25 (.324)
HONORS:
Basketball Hall of Fame, 1991
All-Star Game (8): Detroit 1971-72, 1972-73, 1973-74, 1974-75, 1976-77, 1977-78, 1978-79; Milwaukee 1981-82
All-Star MVP (1): 1973-74
NBA All-Rookie Team: 1970-71
Kennedy Citizenship Award, 1977-78

PISTON LIST

Bob Lanier's Highest-Scoring Games as a Piston

- **48 points**
  November 28, 1972 vs. Portland
- **45 points**
  February 15, 1974 at Buffalo
  November 10, 1974 vs. Buffalo
- **44 points**
  October 19, 1971 at Portland
- **43 points**
  January 11, 1975 at Atlanta
- **42 points**
  January 11, 1972 vs. L.A. Lakers
  February 1, 1972 at New York
  March 7, 1972 vs. Phoenix
  November 4, 1972 at Houston
  February 25, 1973 vs. Houston
- **41 points**
  Four occasions
- **40 points**
  Six occasions

September 24, 1984, only two weeks past his 36th birthday, Lanier had become a hero in Milwaukee, where he continues to live. His No. 16 was retired there December 6, 1984.

In fact, when the Pistons finally retired Lanier's number January 9, 1993, he joined only five other players to be similarly honored by two teams: Julius Erving, Kareem Abdul-Jabbar, Wilt Chamberlain, Oscar Robertson and Nate Thurmond.

To most NBA fans, however, Lanier will always be a Piston. Having won the predraft coin flip over San Diego for the No. 1 overall pick in 1970, Detroit selected Lanier after his two-time All-American career at St. Bonaventure in which he averaged 27.5 points and 15.7 rebounds. It was not an automatic pick, though, because on draft day Lanier was lying in a Buffalo hospital after having right knee surgery; he'd injured the knee the previous week in the NCAA tournament. Though the Pistons needed a big man, Lanier's condition briefly tempted them to opt for LSU scoring guard Pete Maravich. Finally, Detroit coach Butch Van Breda Kolff made the call—Lanier it was. He got a five-year contract worth $1.2 million, salaries having escalated because of bidding wars with the rival ABA.

Lanier's knee recovered in plenty of time for him to debut on schedule and he became an immediate hit, finally giving the Pistons a dependable inside threat to go with Dave Bing's perimeter wizardry, though Lanier would develop into an excellent outside shooter over time. He averaged only 24.6 minutes in his first season, but his 15.7 points ranked third on the team and included 40 points March 19 vs. his hometown Buffalo Braves; it was then the most points ever by a Pistons center. He also averaged 8.1 boards en route to a berth on the '70-71 All-Rookie team.

Though Lanier would never again play all 82 games in a season, as he had as a rookie, it wasn't until much later—1975—that injuries began costing him games in multiples. Over his first five seasons, he missed only 10

games and racked up statistics that quickly moved him into the upper echelon of NBA pivotmen. Including his career-best 2,056 points (25.7) in '71-72 and 1,205 rebounds (14.9) in '72-73, Lanier averaged 22.3 points and 12.5 boards over his first five seasons (400 games). He scored 48 points on November 28, 1972 against Portland (the Blazers' coach: Jack McCloskey) for the highest-scoring game of his career. One month later, December 22 vs. Seattle, Lanier had a career-high 33 rebounds to break the Pistons record of 32 by Walter Dukes and Bailey Howell. It would be almost 20 years until Lanier's mark was topped by Dennis Rodman, who grabbed 34 vs. Indiana on March 3, 1992, though Worm needed overtime.

From his second season to his ninth, Lanier made annual appearances in the All-Star Game with one exception (1976). His best showing was in the 1974 game at Seattle, capturing MVP honors after he came off the bench to tally a game-high 24 points (11-of-15 shots) and 10 rebounds in 26 minutes. He helped the West win 134-123. He had another double-double in the West's win in 1977 (17 points, 10 boards), and then scored 10 in 1979 when Detroit hosted at the Silverdome. Lanier was celebrated by the home fans with a rousing ovation, calling it one of the highlights of his career.

Lanier's individual glory continued unabated. He was third in the NBA MVP balloting in 1974, placed in the league top 10 in scoring six times in his first eight seasons and became the Pistons' career rebounding king April 2, 1975, passing Dukes' 4,986. But no matter how much Lanier and Bing did, the Pistons could never get past the conference semis in the playoffs. Even their 52-30 club of '73-74 was stonewalled by the Bulls in the first round, albeit a terrific series in which Game 7 at Chicago was decided in the final seconds 96-94.

Worse yet, injuries began to afflict Lanier. He broke his left shoulder on January 3, 1976,

keeping him out of eight straight games, and he sat out 10 more either with a spine ailment or tendinitis in both elbows. Then on March 4, 1977, he broke his right hand against the Celtics and had to miss 15 games. Though he'd returned to the All-Star Game after a year absence, the injury robbed him of serious MVP consideration; he wound up averaging 25.3 points (sixth in the NBA) and 11.6 rebounds. In 1978, it was left knee surgery that shelved him for the season's last 12 games.

Feeling his career mortality creeping—and seeing that the rebuilding Pistons were several years from contention—Lanier started seeking a trade after the arrival of coach Dick Vitale in '78-79. It didn't help that he was limited to 53 games due to another knee operation and a jammed toe, and that he and Vitale feuded after the coach reportedly criticized him to management for malingering. Finally, after McCloskey became GM on December 11, 1979, the Pistons started to field serious offers for Lanier. Potential trades were scuttled after he fractured his left hand December 26 against Indiana, but that would turn out to be his last game in a Detroit uniform. Luckily, he'd passed Bing as the Pistons' career scoring leader earlier in the month, topping Bing's 15,235 and finishing with 15,488.

Stats like that ticketed Lanier for the Hall of Fame, and his four-plus seasons in Milwaukee merely solidified that status. But he was already going to the Hall anyway. Well, at least his sneakers were.

Yes, the sneakers—a popular bit of Lanier trivia, but one of his least favorite topics after all these years. Lanier was long said to have worn specially made size 22D Converses, a tale put out by the shoe company. A nice, harmless little story, right? "Except it wasn't true," said Jerry Dziedzic, the club's former longtime equipment manager. "I have a pair of Bob's basketball shoes at my house and they're 20s. And he wore an 18½ (dress) shoe. I hate to spoil the fable, but that's the truth."

Bob Lanier's Regular-Season Statistics with Detroit

SEASON	G	GS	MIN	FGM	FGA	PCT	FTM	FTA	PCT	O-RB	D-RB	TOT	AST	PF	DQ	STL	TO	BLK	PTS	PPG	HI
1971-72	80	—	3092	834	1690	.493	388	505	.768	—	—	1132	248	297	6	—	—	—	2056	25.7	44
1972-73	81	—	3150	810	1654	.490	307	397	.773	—	—	1205	260	278	4	—	—	—	1927	23.8	48
1973-74	81	—	3047	748	1483	.504	326	409	.797	269	805	1074	343	273	7	10	—	247	1822	22.5	45
1974-75	76	—	2987	731	1433	.510	361	450	.802	225	689	914	350	237	1	75	—	172	1823	24.0	45
1975-76	64	—	2363	541	1017	.532	284	370	.768	217	529	746	217	203	2	79	—	86	1366	21.3	41
1976-77	64	—	2446	678	1269	.534	260	318	.818	200	545	745	214	174	0	70	—	126	1616	25.3	40
1977-78	63	63	2311	622	1159	.537	298	386	.772	197	518	715	216	185	2	82	225	93	1542	24.5	41
1978-79	53	53	1835	489	950	.515	275	367	.749	164	330	494	140	181	5	20	175	75	1253	23.6	38
1979-80	37	37	1392	319	584	.546	164	210	.781	108	265	373	122	130	2	38	113	60	802	21.7	34
TOTALS	681	(153)	24640	6276	12347	.508	2936	3788	.775	(1380)	(3681)	8063	2256	2230	33	(504)	(513)	(859)	15488	22.7	48

3-point FGs: 1979-80, 0-5 (.000). TOTALS, 0-5 (.000).
()-total doesn't reflect entire career due to NBA statistical changes

1970 1971

DETROIT PISTONS BASKETBALL CLUB NATIONAL BASKETBALL ASSN

TIME CAPSULE

November 8, 1970:
Tom Dempsey of the New Orleans Saints kicks an NFL-record 63-yard field goal.

December 23, 1970:
The World Trade Center is completed in New York, becoming the world's largest building.

January 25, 1971:
Charles Manson and three of his followers are convicted of the 1969 murders of actress Sharon Tate and six others in Southern California.

SEASON SNAPSHOT

Most Points
Dave Bing (2,213, 27.0 avg.)

Most Rebounds
Otto Moore (700, 8.5 avg.)

Most Assists
Dave Bing (408, 5.0 avg.)

Most Minutes
Dave Bing (3,065, 37.4 avg.)

Field-Goal Percentage
Terry Dischinger (53.5%)

Free-Throw Percentage
Jimmy Walker (83.1%)

Team Offense Average
110.1 (9,029 in 82 games)

Team Defense Average
110.9 (9,090 in 82 games)

NBA All-Stars
Dave Bing, G (First Team)

Pistons in All-Star Game
Dave Bing, G

1970-71

FINAL STANDINGS

Midwest Division	W	L	Pct.	GB
Milwaukee	66	16	.805	—
Chicago	51	31	.622	15
Phoenix	48	34	.585	18
PISTONS	**45**	**37**	**.549**	**21**

Atlantic Division Winner—New York
Central Division Winner—Baltimore
Pacific Division Winner—Los Angeles

PLAYOFF RESULTS

Pistons Did Not Qualify

PISTONS PLAYOFF LEADERS

NBA CHAMPION

Milwaukee Bucks

1970-71
SEASON IN REVIEW

There was no parade through downtown Detroit, no key to the city. And for the seventh time in the last eight seasons, there was no playoff bid. But the Pistons made a historical advance in 1970-71 that brought hope to a suffering franchise. For the first time in the team's 14 years in the Motor City, the Pistons won more games than they lost, finishing 45-37 to blow away their previous best record, 40-42 in '67-68. Strangely so, they still finished last in the newly aligned Midwest Division and didn't qualify for the postseason. They slumped terribly in the final 32 games, going 11-21 and growing weary of coach Bill van Breda Kolff's high anxiety; his 41 technicals and seven ejections led the NBA. The Pistons' collapse dimmed the sheen of an incredible 34-16 start, the franchise's high-water mark to that point. With Dave Bing, who would place third in the MVP balloting, and custom-fit rookie center Bob Lanier showing the way, the Pistons won their first nine games and 12 out of 13, both still team records. But it didn't last; they immediately dropped six straight and the die was cast. They'd finish with six winning streaks of three or more, but five similar skids. Lanier's All-Rookie season (15.6 points, 8.1 boards) and Bing's greatness—his 54 points February 21 vs. Chicago set the team record—at least gave hope to the fans. Attendance climbed about 2,500 a game to 6,925, then second-best in club history.

After years of searching, the Pistons finally added a franchise center in 1970 when they drafted Bob Lanier with the first overall pick.

October 20, 1970

Bruno Kearns from *The Pontiac Press* called it "the wildest NBA game ever in Detroit." Hard to argue with at the time. The Pistons were 3-0, Milwaukee was in town for Detroit's home opener, Cobo was packed for the first time ever—11,316 in-house, 2,000 turned away—and it was the first NBA tussle between Pistons rookie Bob Lanier and Bucks star Lew Alcindor (Kareem Abdul-Jabbar). What more could a fan ask for? A Pistons win, which they got 115-114 after Bob Quick's put-back three-point play with seven seconds to go. Detroit trailed 112-105 with 1:10 left, but climbed within 113-111 behind Dave Bing, who scored 37. The Bucks intended to stall out the final 20 seconds, but Jimmy Walker (20 points) stole a pass and Detroit called time. Bing missed a driving shot with 10 seconds left, but Quick fought for the rebound, hit the layup to tie it and was fouled by Alcindor. Quick made the free throw for a 114-113 lead that held up and his teammates soon carried him off the floor. Young Lanier gave a good account of himself with 18 points, but was no match for Alcindor, who had 38 points (16-of-20 shots) and 16 boards. His MVP year would conclude with the only NBA title in Bucks history.

WHAT A NIGHT!

Kareem Abdul-Jabbar dunks for two at Cobo Arena, but the Pistons got the upper hand in his first matchup against Bob Lanier.

Premier Piston

Howie "Butch" Komives

Howie Komives never played in a postseason game in almost four seasons with the Pistons.

Before Terry Tyler made his bones as the Pistons' iron man, playing in an amazing 574 straight games from 1978-85, that title belonged to veteran point guard Howie Komives. The Toledo-born scrapper played in 264 games in a row after arriving in Detroit in '68, a streak that ended in controversy on January 21, 1972, leading to his exit to Buffalo in an off-season trade. Unfortunately, Komives holds another Pistons distinction—most games played without a playoff appearance: 298. In almost four full seasons with Detroit, Komives and Co. never got to the postseason. It's as if the basketball fathers were penalizing the Pistons for having traded hometown fave Dave DeBusschere to the Knicks for Komives and Walt Bellamy on December 19, 1968. DeBusschere became a bona fide star in the Big Apple, helping New York earn league titles in '70 and '73, while Komives fought gamely to help Detroit approach mere respectability. It was a futile chase, but Komives' Pistons career was generally solid. He alternated as a starter and sub, and averaged 9.9 points and 3.6 assists with Detroit, his best year being '69-70 when he averaged 11.2 and 3.8. He had one of his better games on December 10, 1971, dishing out 15 assists at Cleveland. But then Komives made a mistake that probably shortened his Pistons career. In January 1972, when coach Earl Lloyd held him out of a victory over Baltimore, stopping his games streak at 264, Komives accused the black coach of phasing out white players; it created a brief national stir. Komives apologized and Lloyd accepted, but the bell could not be unrung. In training camp the next September, the Pistons shipped Komives to Buffalo for a 1973 second-round draft pick.

AT A GLANCE

HOWIE KOMIVES

FULL NAME:
Howard K. Komives
BORN:
May 9, 1941; Toledo
POSITION, HEIGHT, WEIGHT:
Guard, 6-foot-1, 185 pounds
COLLEGE:
Bowling Green (Ohio), '64
ACQUIRED:
From New York, December 19, 1968, with Walt Bellamy for Dave DeBusschere
TENURE WITH PISTONS:
December 19, 1968—September 30, 1972
Also: New York 1964-68, Buffalo 1972-73, Kansas City-Omaha 1973-74
BEST SEASON WITH PISTONS:
1969-70, 82 GP, 11.2 ppg, 3.8 apg
TOTALS WITH PISTONS:
Regular season: 298 GP, 9.9 ppg, 3.6 apg
HONORS:
NBA All-Rookie Team: 1964-65

PISTON LIST

Longest-Serving Pistons Without Playoff Appearance

- Howie Komives, 298 games, 1968-72
- Otto Moore, 239 games, 1968-71, '74
- Tom Van Arsdale, 208 games, 1965-68
- Phil Hubbard, 196 games, 1979-82
- Ron Lee, 194 games, 1979-82
- Bill Hewitt, 175 games, 1969-72
- John Tresvant, 169 games, 1965-68
- Erwin Mueller, 168 games, 1969-72
- Donnis Butcher, 138 games, 1963-66
- Ben Poquette, 128 games, 1977-79
- Don Kojis, 125 games, 1964-66
- McCoy McLemore, 123 games, 1968-70

CHANGING FACES

NOT TO SOUND greedy, but besides future Hall-of-Famer Bob Lanier, the Pistons didn't add much to their lineup in 1970-71. They brought in the previous year's first-round pick, forward Terry Driscoll, who had spent a season in Italy. But unlike prior No. 4 overall Detroit draftees such as Bailey Howell ('59) and Ray Scott ('61), Driscoll was a failure with the Pistons, averaging 5.4 points in his only season with them. Detroit also added guard Harvey Marlatt out of Eastern Michigan, one of the lowest-drafted players ever to make the NBA (224th pick in '70). But the club's most significant transaction came two weeks after the season when it traded center Otto Moore to Phoenix for Mel Counts. Trouble was, Moore signed with the ABA Virginia Squires before going to the Suns. The NBA let the Suns keep both Moore and Counts while the

Otto Moore, who never met expectations in Detroit, was banished to Phoenix after the '70-71 season.

matter was in court, and the Pistons were left holding the empty bag. Detroit later got a '72 first-round pick from Phoenix, but it was small consolation.

Take a Bow

Dave Bing

Dave Bing, cutting to the basket for two more points.

It was inevitable that Dave Bing—health permitting—would one day hold every offensive record in Pistons history. After all, over his first four seasons, his lowest point average was 20.0 as a rookie and he had led the NBA in points in his second year. By '69-70, he was already the Pistons' all-time assist leader, beating Gene Shue's 1,693, and then he broke five more major records, including Bailey Howell's career points mark (8,182), during an amazing '70-71 season. Bing topped the career records for field goals and field goal attempts, points in a season with 2,213 (still the team record) and another biggie, points in a game. That happened on February 21 vs. Chicago, a Sunday afternoon at Cobo, when Bing scored 54 points in a 125-112 Detroit loss. That beat the 52 by George Yardley on February 4, 1958 vs. Syracuse. Bing had 22 baskets—still a club record—in 38 attempts and made all 10 free throws, but said, "Fifty-four points are no good if you lose." His record would stand until Kelly Tripucka scored 56 on January 29, 1983 vs.—you guessed it—Chicago.

Game Results

1970-71 REGULAR SEASON

Date	Opponent	Result	Record
10-14	at Seattle	W, 123-117	1-0
10-16	at San Francisco	W, 120-106	2-0
10-17	at Phoenix	W, 110-107	3-0
10-20	MILWAUKEE	W, 115-114	4-0
10-21	at Boston	W, 121-118	5-0
10-22	ATLANTA	W, 120-101	6-0
10-24	at Buffalo	W, 114-95	7-0
10-26	SEATTLE	W, 142-111	8-0
10-28	at Baltimore	W, 109-103	9-0
10-31	at New York	L, 89-107	9-1
11-3	CINCINNATI	W, 115-112	10-1
11-4	at Atlanta	W, 117-105	11-1
11-5	BUFFALO	W, 121-109	12-1
11-7	at Chicago	L, 99-125	12-2
11-11	L.A. LAKERS	L, 115-117	12-3
11-13	at L.A. Lakers	L, 109-122	12-4
11-14	at San Diego	L, 101-112	12-5
11-15	at Phoenix	L, 104-108	12-6
11-17	PHILADELPHIA	L, 91-113	12-7
11-19	PHOENIX	W, 112-110	13-7
11-20	at Philadelphia	W, 120-112	14-7
11-21	at Cincinnati	L, 102-114	14-8
11-24	SAN DIEGO	W, 111-104	15-8
11-25	at Milwaukee	L, 88-113	15-9
11-28	BOSTON	L, 98-121	15-10
11-29	at Cleveland	W, 120-99	16-10
12-2	NEW YORK	L, 101-82	17-10
12-4	CHICAGO	W, 107-103	18-10
12-9	SAN FRANCISCO	L, 99-110	18-11
12-11	at Boston	W, 121-118 (OT)	19-11
12-12	BUFFALO	L, 92-93	19-12
12-13	at L.A. Lakers	W, 103-100	20-12
12-15	at Portland	W, 111-103	21-12
12-17	at Phoenix	L, 114-117 (OT)	21-13
12-18	at San Diego	W, 129-116	22-13
12-20	n-Cincinnati	W, 136-125 (2OT)	23-13
12-25	at Philadelphia	L, 100-105	23-14
12-26	at Chicago	W, 117-114	24-14
12-29	ATLANTA	W, 99-97	25-14
12-30	at Cincinnati	W, 119-115	26-14
1-2	BALTIMORE	L, 99-108	26-15
1-5	at Atlanta	W, 98-90	27-15
1-6	SAN DIEGO	W, 100-99	28-15
1-8	CINCINNATI	W, 115-109	29-15
1-9	at Milwaukee	L, 110-118	29-16
1-10	L.A. LAKERS	W, 118-109	30-16
1-14	CLEVELAND	W, 108-106	31-16
1-15	at Buffalo	W, 99-97 (OT)	32-16
1-16	BOSTON	W, 121-118	33-16
1-19	SEATTLE	W, 106-102	34-16
1-22	PORTLAND	L, 112-123	34-17
1-24	NEW YORK	L, 105-117	34-18
1-27	SAN FRANCISCO	L, 112-127	34-19
1-29	SAN DIEGO	W, 131-104	35-19
1-31	n-Milwaukee	L, 104-131	35-20
2-2	BALTIMORE	W, 116-113	36-20
2-5	NEW YORK	W, 108-99	37-20
2-7	at Baltimore	L, 105-108	37-21
2-9	MILWAUKEE	L, 106-107	37-22
2-12	PHILADELPHIA	W, 118-109	38-22
2-14	BOSTON	L, 108-110	38-23
2-16	BALTIMORE	W, 110-95	39-23
2-19	at Chicago	L, 114-115 (OT)	39-24
2-20	at New York	L, 94-108	39-25
2-21	CHICAGO	L, 112-125	39-26
2-24	SAN FRANCISCO	L, 115-117	39-27
2-26	at Buffalo	W, 127-122 (OT)	40-27
2-27	PHOENIX	L, 119-124	40-28
2-28	at Atlanta	W, 106-105	41-28
3-2	PORTLAND	W, 128-122	42-28
3-5	MILWAUKEE	L, 95-108	42-29
3-6	at Philadelphia	L, 115-121	42-30
3-7	CLEVELAND	L, 100-104	42-31
3-9	PHOENIX	L, 108-114	42-32
3-11	at Seattle	L, 97-130	42-33
3-12	at Portland	W, 133-129	43-33
3-13	at San Francisco	L, 109-116	43-34
3-14	at L.A. Lakers	L, 100-110	43-35
3-17	at San Diego	L, 99-106	43-36
3-19	BUFFALO	W, 111-105	44-36
3-20	at Cleveland	L, 103-114	44-37
3-21	CHICAGO	W, 116-111	45-37

(Home games in CAPS; n-neutral site)

1971 1972

DETROIT PISTONS
BASKETBALL CLUB
NATIONAL BASKETBALL ASSN.

TIME CAPSULE

September 13, 1971:
A prison riot at Attica State Correctional Facility in New York ends, an uprising that claimed 43 lives.

February 21, 1972:
President Nixon begins his historic visit to mainland China, opening relations with the Communist nation.

June 17, 1972:
Police in Washington, D.C., arrest five men involved in a burglary at Democratic Party headquarters, beginning the famed Watergate affair.

SEASON SNAPSHOT

Most Points
Bob Lanier (2,056, 25.7 avg.)

Most Rebounds
Bob Lanier (1,132, 14.2 avg.)

Most Assists
Dave Bing (317, 7.1 avg.)

Most Minutes
Bob Lanier (3,092, 38.7 avg.)

Field-Goal Percentage
Terry Dischinger (51.4%)

Free-Throw Percentage
Jimmy Walker (82.7%)

Team Offense Average
109.1 (8,945 in 82 games)

Team Defense Average
115.9 (9,506 in 82 games)

Pistons in All-Star Game
Bob Lanier, C; Jimmy Walker, G

1971-72

FINAL STANDINGS

Midwest Division	W	L	Pct.	GB
Milwaukee	63	19	.768	—
Chicago	57	25	.695	6
Phoenix	49	33	.598	14
PISTONS	**26**	**56**	**.549**	**37**

Atlantic Division Winner—Boston
Central Division Winner—Baltimore
Pacific Division Winner—Los Angeles

PLAYOFF RESULTS

Pistons Did Not Qualify

PISTONS PLAYOFF LEADERS

NBA CHAMPION

Los Angeles Lakers

1971-72
SEASON IN REVIEW

For the first time ever, the Pistons were coming off a winning season when they gathered in 1971. Hopes were high that contender status was near. No one figured the season would crash so quickly. The Pistons lost Dave Bing to a serious eye injury in the preseason, coach Bill van Breda Kolff bailed after only 10 games and the season never straightened out; Detroit tumbled to a 26-56 record, fourth-worst in the league. Bing had October 15 surgery for a detached retina in his right eye, resulting from an accidental poke by the Lakers' Happy Hairston, his former teammate, in an exhibition. Bing gamely got 24 points in an opening-night win at New York, but blurred vision prompted the surgery and he missed the next 37 games. When he returned January 2, the Pistons were 14-24 and out of luck. While Bing healed, Detroit was 0-2 with acting coach Terry Dischinger, then longtime good soldier Earl Lloyd was named head coach November 8, but the results didn't change. The uninspired effort that bothered VBK soon sabotaged Lloyd's regime as well. Other than marvelous years by center Bob Lanier, who averaged 25.7 points and 14.2 rebounds, and fellow all-star Jimmy Walker (21.3 ppg), highlights were few. Rookie Curtis Rowe had a solid debut season, though, averaging 11.3 points and 8.5 boards.

The 1971-72 Pistons: (front row, from left) Howie Komives, Jimmy Walker, GM Ed Coil, coach Earl Lloyd, Dave Bing, Terry Dischinger; (back row) Willie Norwood, Erwin Mueller, Curtis Rowe, Bob Lanier, Jim Davis, Bill Hewitt, Bunny Wilson, trainer Bud Shockro.

WHAT A NIGHT!

January 7, 1972

Elsewhere in the NBA on this Friday night, the Lakers were pulling off a league record of amazing stature with their 33rd consecutive victory, a 134-99 win at Atlanta. But in Detroit, the Pistons were writing their names in the book, too, in a 151-132 victory over the Cincinnati Royals. Midway through their dismal 9-27 skid from November 23-February 1, the Pistons let everything hang out for one night. By outscoring Cincinnati 53-43 in the fourth quarter, the clubs tied the NBA record for combined points in a quarter with 96, set previously by Minneapolis and Boston on February 27, 1959. Though that record is now second-best, having been topped by the 99 points of San Antonio (53) and Denver (46) in 1984, the Pistons' two team records from that game are still on the books. Their 53 points in a quarter remain their most ever, as do their 87 points in the second half. At the time, their 151-point total ranked second in club history; it's now fifth. The Pistons shot 56-of-91 from the field (61.5 percent), keyed by Bill Hewitt's 6-of-6, and they fought off 41 points by Cincinnati's Tiny Archibald by having four players with 20 or more. Bob Lanier scored 29, Dave Bing 27, Terry Dischinger 21 and rookie Curtis Rowe 20.

Bill Hewitt, shown here against Milwaukee, played a vital role in one of the Pistons' biggest offensive games ever.

Earl Lloyd

After being the NBA's first black player, Earl Lloyd became a trail-blazing coach as well.

Even in 1950, as the NBA's first black player, Earl Lloyd would rather have been known simply as a player. He felt the same way when he was hired as head coach of the Pistons on November 8, 1971, becoming the fourth black in league history to attain that position. "I'm not a black coach," he said that day. "I'm a coach who is black." But despite his less-than-stellar coaching tenure, 22-55 in just under a full season, there can be no debate that Earl "Big Cat" Lloyd was a trail-blazer for blacks in the NBA. And he won a championship ring to boot, having his best season in 1954-55 to help the Syracuse Nationals win the title; the 6-6 forward averaged 10.2 points, 7.7 boards and 2.1 assists— all career highs. But even without a championship, Lloyd's name still would be prominent in NBA history. He saw to it October 31, 1950 when he was put into the game for the Washington Capitols against the Rochester Royals. By doing so, Lloyd broke the NBA's color line. Chuck Cooper had been the first black NBA draft pick and Nat Clifton was the first to sign a contract, but the first game time went to Lloyd. A small step for a 22-year-old who had grown up in segregated Virginia, but a giant leap for American culture. Lloyd had a solid career, playing six seasons with Syracuse and joining Detroit for his last two (1958-60). He served the Pistons well as head scout and assistant coach throughout the '60s. Finally, after Butch van Breda Kolff quit 10 games into '71-72, Lloyd got his chance to be head coach. Alas, Detroit wasn't a favorable setting for any coach, let alone a neophyte, and Lloyd's best intentions were crippled by dissension. He was fired seven games into '72-73, and became the team's TV analyst.

AT A GLANCE

EARL LLOYD

FULL NAME:
Earl Francis Lloyd
BORN:
April 3, 1928; Virginia
POSITION, HEIGHT, WEIGHT:
Forward, 6-foot-6, 225 pounds
COLLEGE:
West Virginia State
ACQUIRED:
Purchased June 10, 1958, from Syracuse

TENURE WITH PISTONS:
Player: 1958-59—1959-60
Coach: November 8, 1971—October 28, 1972
Also played: Washington 1950-51, Syracuse 1951-58
BEST SEASON WITH PISTONS:
Player: 1958-59, 72 GP, 8.4 ppg, 6.9 rpg
Coach: 1971-72, 70 GP, 20-50 (.286)
PLAYING TOTALS WITH PISTONS:
Regular season: 140 GP, 8,6 ppg, 5.9 rpg
Playoffs: 5 GP, 8.6 ppg, 5.4 rpg
COACHING TOTALS WITH PISTONS:
Regular season: 77 GP, 22-55 (.286)
HONORS:
Played on NBA champion, 1955

PISTON LIST

Best Home Record in 82-Game Season

- 37-4, 1988-89
- 35-6, 1989-90
- 34-7, 1987-88
- 32-9, 1986-87
- 32-9, 1990-91
- 31-10, 1985-86
- 30-11, 1976-77
- 30-11, 1983-84
- 30-11, 1995-96
- 30-11, 1996-97
- 29-12, 1973-74
- 28-13, 1992-93
- 26-15, four times

CHANGING FACES

THERE WAS NEARLY as much turnover on the coaching staff as the player roster. The coaching baton was handed from VBK to Terry Dischinger on November 1 and then to Earl Lloyd seven days later, marking the first (and only) time the Pistons had three coaches in a season. Meanwhile, there were only three new players all season: forward-center Jim Davis (via trade) and rookie draftees Curtis Rowe and Isaiah "Bunny" Wilson. Rowe was an excellent addition on the 11th overall draft pick, with the 6-foot-7 forward from UCLA quickly joining the starting five. He was the only Piston to play in all 82 games, averaging 32.4 minutes, 11.3 points and 8.5 rebounds, the latter figure ranking second on the club. Davis came to Detroit from the Houston Rockets on December 10 for a 1972 first-round pick. He would spend 3 1/2 years with the Pistons, capping an

The Pistons got Curtis Rowe with the 11th overall pick of the '71-72 draft, their best acquisition of the season.

eight-year pro career in 1975. He started sometimes, but was mostly a fill-in. Wilson, a second-round pick, suffered a preseason kidney ailment and was limited to 48 games. He went to the ABA for '72-73 and then left basketball.

Take a Bow

Bob Lanier

In his second season, Bob Lanier became a certified NBA all-star.

No center had ever led the Pistons in scoring, but Bob Lanier got rid of that bit of trivia in his second season. By averaging 25.7 points over 80 games in '71-72, he ended Dave Bing's five-year headlock on that honor. With 2,056 points, Lanier joined Bing (twice) and George Yardley as the only Pistons to top the 2,000 mark (Yardley was the NBA's first in '58). Besides making the first of his eight appearances in the All-Star Game, Lanier had four games with at least 42 points in '71-72. He racked up a season-high 44 on October 19 to spark Detroit to a 101-99 win at Portland. One game after being ejected against Houston for arguing a foul, Lanier took out his frustration on the Trail Blazers, dropping in 18 field goals, 8-of-9 free throws, and tallying his first 20-rebound NBA game. Lanier went on to score 42 on January 11 (vs. the Lakers), February 1 (at New York) and March 7 (vs. Phoenix). En route to a team rebound record (1,132), he had two games with 24: October 23 (at Golden State) and February 1 (at New York).

Game Results

1971-72 REGULAR SEASON

Date	Opponent	Result	Record
10-12	at New York	W, 91-84	1-0
10-15	L.A. LAKERS	L, 102-132	1-1
10-17	n-Houston	W, 112-99	2-1
10-19	at Portland	W, 101-99	3-1
10-22	at Phoenix	W, 116-109	4-1
10-23	at Golden State	L, 109-115 (OT)	4-2
10-26	HOUSTON	L, 103-105	4-3
10-27	at Baltimore	L, 98-128	4-4
10-29	BALTIMORE	W, 119-105	5-4
10-30	at Atlanta	W, 105-94	6-4
11-5	at Boston	L, 102-103	6-5
11-6	at Milwaukee	L, 78-106	6-6
11-10	PORTLAND	W, 139-122	7-6
11-12	at Philadelphia	L, 101-115	7-7
11-13	at New York	L, 104-127	7-8
11-16	GOLDEN STATE	L, 101-122	7-9
11-18	PHOENIX	W, 128-126	8-9
11-20	at Buffalo	W, 105-96	9-9
11-23	MILWAUKEE	L, 104-112	9-10
11-25	at Phoenix	L, 103-122	9-11
11-26	at L.A. Lakers	L, 113-132	9-12
11-27	at Seattle	L, 102-124	9-13
12-1	ATLANTA	L, 103-117	9-14
12-3	HOUSTON	W, 113-112	10-14
12-7	PORTLAND	L, 130-131 (OT)	10-15
12-9	CHICAGO	W, 110-107	11-15
12-10	at Cleveland	L, 111-112	11-16
12-11	PHILADELPHIA	L, 111-118	11-17
12-14	SEATTLE	L, 86-103	11-18
12-16	CINCINNATI	W, 107-101	12-18
12-17	at Phoenix	L, 102-123	12-19
12-18	at Golden State	L, 102-129	12-20
12-19	at Portland	L, 113-114	12-21
12-21	at Chicago	L, 92-127	12-22
12-22	CLEVELAND	W, 104-94	13-22
12-25	MILWAUKEE	W, 120-118 (OT)	14-22
12-28	NEW YORK	L, 100-119	14-23
12-30	GOLDEN STATE	L, 122-128	14-24
1-2	at Houston	W, 109-107	15-24
1-4	PHILADELPHIA	W, 127-121	15-25
1-5	at Baltimore	L, 89-111	15-26
1-7	CINCINNATI	W, 151-132	16-26
1-8	at Milwaukee	L, 119-132	16-27
1-9	BUFFALO	W, 101-96	17-27
1-11	L.A. LAKERS	L, 103-123	17-28
1-14	at Boston	L, 94-108	17-29
1-15	PHILADELPHIA	L, 121-131	17-30
1-21	BALTIMORE	W, 107-102	18-30
1-23	HOUSTON	L, 107-109	18-31
1-26	MILWAUKEE	L, 94-120	18-32
1-28	at Atlanta	L, 106-120	18-33
1-29	BOSTON	L, 112-124	18-34
1-30	at Chicago	L, 99-109	18-35
2-1	at New York	L, 106-115	18-36
2-2	CLEVELAND	W, 133-108	19-36
2-4	at Philadelphia	W, 118-113	20-36
2-5	at Cincinnati	L, 132-133 (OT)	20-37
2-9	NEW YORK	L, 102-126	20-38
2-11	at Buffalo	L, 88-95	20-39
2-12	BUFFALO	W, 113-87	21-39
2-13	at Cleveland	W, 136-121	22-39
2-15	ATLANTA	L, 105-113	22-40
2-18	CHICAGO	L, 97-122	22-41
2-20	PHILADELPHIA	L, 107-131	22-42
2-22	at L.A. Lakers	W, 135-134 (OT)	23-42
2-23	at Seattle	L, 96-97	23-43
2-24	at Golden State	L, 106-116	23-44
2-26	at Houston	L, 106-122	23-45
2-29	at Milwaukee	L, 113-131	23-46
3-1	SEATTLE	L, 102-116	23-47
3-3	BOSTON	L, 96-125	23-48
3-7	PHOENIX	L, 121-129	23-49
3-12	n-Baltimore	L, 97-102	23-50
3-14	L.A. LAKERS	L, 116-129	23-51
3-17	ATLANTA	W, 121-112	24-51
3-18	at Buffalo	L, 103-116	24-52
3-19	CHICAGO	L, 107-118	24-53
3-21	CINCINNATI	W, 120-117	25-53
3-22	at Cincinnati	L, 130-135	25-54
3-24	BUFFALO	W, 112-105	26-54
3-25	at Chicago	L, 105-121	26-55
3-26	at Boston	L, 120-133	26-56

(Home games in CAPS; n-neutral site)

1972 DETROIT PISTONS NBA 1973

TIME CAPSULE

November 7, 1972:
President Nixon is re-elected in a landslide, defeating Democratic challenger George McGovern.

January 22, 1973:
An agreement to end the Vietnam War is signed in Paris by representatives of the U.S. and North and South Vietnam.

June 9, 1973:
Secretariat, called the greatest race horse ever, wins the Belmont Stakes to become the ninth Triple Crown winner.

SEASON SNAPSHOT

Most Points
Bob Lanier (1,927, 23.8 avg.)

Most Rebounds
Bob Lanier (1,205, 14.9 avg.)

Most Assists
Dave Bing (637, 7.8 avg.)

Most Minutes
Dave Bing (3,361, 41.0 avg.)

Field-Goal Percentage
Curtis Rowe (51.9%)

Free-Throw Percentage
Dave Bing (81.4%)

Team Offense Average
110.3 (9,042 in 82 games)

Team Defense Average
110.0 (9,024 in 82 games)

Pistons in All-Star Game
Dave Bing, G; Bob Lanier, C

1972-73

FINAL STANDINGS

Midwest Division	W	L	Pct.	GB
Milwaukee	60	22	.732	—
Chicago	51	31	.622	9
PISTONS	**40**	**42**	**.488**	**20**
K.C.-Omaha	36	46	.439	24

Atlantic Division Winner—Boston
Central Division Winner—Baltimore
Pacific Division Winner—Los Angeles

PLAYOFF RESULTS

Pistons Did Not Qualify

PISTONS PLAYOFF LEADERS

NBA CHAMPION

New York Knicks

1972-73
SEASON IN REVIEW

A strong finish under yet another new coach produced renewed Pistons optimism in '72-73. They didn't wait for the season to fall apart before firing coach Earl Lloyd, doing it on October 28 with a 2-5 record. There was no guarantee that his replacement, ex-assistant Ray Scott, would do any better. But the players immediately took to Scott, easing tension in the locker room and letting the nucleus develop. Guard John Mengelt and husky forward Don Adams were acquired for draft picks, lending bench energy that had been sorely lacking. Good results weren't immediate—they dropped from playoff contention with a 7-17 midseason slump—but the Pistons were one of the NBA's hottest teams at the finish. Starting January 30, they went 20-11 the remainder of the season, their best such streak ever, to finish 40-42. Though a four-game skid marred the run and ensured their postseason absence, the Pistons also fashioned winning streaks of six, five and five, closing the season with the latter. Their 26-15 home record was the best in team history, topping their 24-17 of '70-71. Bob Lanier had another groundbreaking season in the pivot, leading the club with 23.8 points and 14.9 rebounds, the latter from his team-record 1,205 total. He tallied 48 points on November 28 vs. Portland and a Pistons-record 33 boards on December 22 vs. Seattle. Dave Bing (22.4 ppg) had a team-record 647 assists.

Bob Lanier gave more than a few opponents the hook during his record-setting '72-73 season.

February 9, 1973

WHAT A NIGHT!

As rare as it was for the Pistons to beat the Celtics, it was even rarer for Boston to lose in '72-73. The previous season's L.A. Lakers had a 69-13 record, then the best of all-time, but the proud Celtics made a strong run at breaking the mark in '72-73. Alas, they fell a game short of matching the Lakers, going 68-14 and then losing to the Knicks in the Eastern finals. Where do the Pistons enter the story? Boston lost only six home games to six different opponents, and Detroit was one of them. On February 9, 1973, the Pistons entered Boston Garden with a five-game winning streak, their longest since a 9-0 start in '70-71. When they left, it was a six-game streak courtesy of a 104-95 victory that ended Detroit's eight-game skid in the rivalry; the Pistons hadn't beaten the Celts since January 16, 1971. Bob Lanier had 19 of his 27 points in the first half, while Dave Bing scored 16 of his 22 in the second half to guide Detroit. They combined for a 10-0 run that sent the Pistons ahead by 11 points in the third quarter and they coasted from there. The Celtics got 24 points from Jo Jo White, 22 from Dave Cowens and 16 from Paul Silas. Injured captain John Havlicek was held to seven.

Dave Bing, silky smooth, continued to star in his seventh NBA season.

Premier Piston

Curtis Rowe

Curtis Rowe was a Pistons iron man, missing only three of 410 games in his five seasons.

Many NBA players can't come close to matching their college success, either individually or as a team. Curtis Rowe was one of them, but he's got a legitimate excuse. After all, how could he realistically live up to his terrific career as part of UCLA's NCAA dynasty? Rowe's eight-year NBA career—11.6 points, 7.2 boards—was workmanlike, but it wasn't anything resembling his stint with the Bruins from 1967-71. He played a starring role with the UCLA freshmen, scoring 51 points in one game as they went 19-0, and then he continued his success with the varsity. He started all 90 games for the next three years, averaging 15.2 points as the Bruins went 86-4 and breezed to the NCAA championship each year. Legendary coach John Wooden called Rowe "an unspectacular spectacular player." But it's one thing to excel next to Lew Alcindor (Kareem Abdul-Jabbar), Sidney Wicks and Lucius Allen. It's quite another to be drafted by a so-so NBA team, as Rowe was by Detroit (11th overall) in 1971. A 6-foot-7 forward with speed and an excellent midrange shot, Rowe quickly cracked the starting lineup as a rookie and averaged 11.3 points and 8.5 rebounds while playing in all 82 games. He made even greater strides in his second season, boosting his averages to 16.1 and 9.4 in '72-73 and ranking fourth in the NBA in shooting percentage (51.9). Also that season, Rowe compiled his single-game career-highs: 35 points and 23 boards. His last Pistons season, '75-76, was his best; he averaged 16.0 points and 8.7 boards and captured his only All-Star berth. Just two days before the '76-77 opener, Rowe was shipped to Boston in a three-way trade, but the Celtics were experiencing their worst period, missing the playoffs twice in Rowe's three seasons (1976-79).

AT A GLANCE

CURTIS ROWE

FULL NAME:
Curtis Rowe Jr.
BORN:
July 7, 1949; Bessemer, Alabama
POSITION, HEIGHT, WEIGHT:
Forward, 6-foot-7, 225 pounds
COLLEGE:
UCLA '71
ACQUIRED:
Drafted, first round, 1971 (11th overall)
TENURE WITH PISTONS:
1971-72 — 1975-76
Also: Boston 1976-79
BEST SEASON WITH PISTONS:
1975-76, 80 GP, 16.0 ppg, 8.7 rpg
TOTALS WITH PISTONS:
Regular season: 407 GP, 13.3 ppg, 8.0 rpg
Playoffs: 19 GP, 12.5 ppg, 7.8 rpg
HONORS:
All-Star Game: 1975-76

PISTON LIST

Most Rebounds in a Game

34
- Dennis Rodman, 3-4-92 vs. Indiana

33
- Bob Lanier, 12-22-72 vs. Seattle

32
- Walter Dukes, 12-13-59 vs. N.Y.
- Bailey Howell, 11-5-60 vs. Phila.

31
- Rodman, 3-14-92 at Sacramento
- Happy Hairston, 2-8-69 vs. San Diego

30
- Howell, 11-25-60, vs. L.A. Lakers

28
- Otto Moore, 3-17-70 vs. New York

27
- George Yardley, 2-27-58 vs. Minn.
- Rodman, 1-23-92 at Minnesota
- Rodman, 2-18-92 vs. Orlando
- Rodman, 12-23-92 at Charlotte

CHANGING FACES

THE PISTONS made big-time changes in '72-73, and most of them were productive. The bottom line was that they lost Terry Dischinger, Jimmy Walker and Howie Komives and emerged with John Mengelt, Don Adams, Stu Lantz and Fred Foster. Mengelt quickly became a fan favorite due to his non-stop effort and stayed for four seasons, averaging 10.3 points. Adams (three seasons) and Lantz (two) also became major components for a spell. The cost of the trio was the solid but disappointing Walker (to Houston for Lantz), iron man Komives (to Buffalo for a draft pick, later traded to K.C. for Mengelt) and a draft pick (to Atlanta for Adams). Foster was a pick-up from Philadelphia in the three-way trade that sent Dischinger to Portland on July 31, 1972; Foster stayed for one season. Dischinger, who threatened retirement if he was not traded, had

Don Adams' name comes first on the Pistons' all-time alphabetical roster. He averaged 8.8 points and 5.7 boards in three Detroit seasons.

given the Pistons six strong years (eight including a two-year Army stint) and averaged 12.1 points. He would play one season with Portland before quitting to become a dentist.

Take a Bow

Bob Lanier

Bob Lanier's 33 rebounds in a game were the most by any NBA player in '72-73.

By '72-73, it was obvious that the Pistons were in the presence of the greatest center in team history. Until Bob Lanier came to Detroit in '70, no Pistons pivotman had ever scored 40 points in a game. And their club rebounding record had remained static since '60-61 when Bailey Howell grabbed 1,111 to set a season-high and 32 to match the single-game record of Walter Dukes. But it didn't take long for Lanier to assume all of those records. He scored his career-high 48 points on November 28, 1972 against Portland, hitting 19-of-35 field goals. Of his 20 40-point games as a Piston, four came during '72-73 when his 23.8 average placed eighth in the NBA. A month after setting his scoring mark, Lanier compiled 33 rebounds against Seattle to break the team record, which would stand until Dennis Rodman got 34 in 1992. Lanier's was the NBA's highest total all season, edging the 32 by Dave Cowens of Boston, and his team-record 1,205 rebounds ranked sixth in the league.

Game Results

1972-73 REGULAR SEASON

Date	Opponent	Result	Record
10-11	BOSTON	L, 108-121	0-1
10-13	CHICAGO	W, 100-91	1-1
10-14	at Kansas City	L, 101-113	1-2
10-20	at Milwaukee	L, 86-109	1-3
10-21	CLEVELAND	W, 103-96	2-3
10-25	BALTIMORE	L, 105-115	2-4
10-27	at Houston	L, 118-130	2-5
10-29	at Portland	W, 118-111	3-5
10-31	at Golden State	L, 104-112	3-6
11-1	at Seattle	W, 116-106	4-6
11-3	at L.A. Lakers	L, 107-116	4-7
11-4	n-Houston	L, 108-118	4-8
11-10	GOLDEN STATE	W, 121-96	5-8
11-11	at Boston	L, 118-121	5-9
11-15	L.A. LAKERS	L, 99-110	5-10
11-17	CHICAGO	W, 109-96	6-10
11-21	ATLANTA	W, 113-110 (OT)	7-10
11-23	at Phoenix	L, 122-128	7-11
11-24	at L.A. Lakers	L, 123-140	7-12
11-26	at Seattle	L, 96-103	7-13
11-28	PORTLAND	W, 120-116	8-13
11-30	BUFFALO	W, 127-116	9-13
12-1	at Cleveland	W, 114-113	10-13
12-5	at Chicago	L, 108-130	10-14
12-6	PHOENIX	W, 114-105	11-14
12-8	K.C.-OMAHA	W, 113-100	12-14
12-9	at Milwaukee	W, 107-103	13-14
12-13	GOLDEN STATE	L, 107-110	13-15
12-15	at K.C.-Omaha	L, 132-140 (OT)	13-16
12-16	HOUSTON	L, 112-123	13-17
12-20	PHILADELPHIA	W, 141-113	14-17
12-22	SEATTLE	W, 109-87	15-17
12-23	at Baltimore	L, 97-104	15-18
12-25	at New York	L, 100-113	15-19
12-26	MILWAUKEE	W, 112-105	16-19
12-28	at Milwaukee	L, 91-115	16-20
12-29	NEW YORK	L, 94-99	16-21
1-3	PHOENIX	W, 119-105	17-21
1-5	at Kansas City	L, 100-103	17-22
1-6	ATLANTA	L, 111-116	17-23
1-7	at Portland	W, 101-96	18-23
1-9	at Golden State	L, 98-105	18-24
1-10	at Phoenix	L, 121-123	18-25
1-12	at Seattle	L, 104-113	18-26
1-15	PORTLAND	W, 112-101	19-26
1-16	at Atlanta	L, 129-130 (OT)	19-27
1-17	SEATTLE	L, 104-106	19-28
1-19	at Buffalo	L, 98-108	19-29
1-20	CHICAGO	W, 112-92	20-29
1-26	MILWAUKEE	L, 105-112	20-30
1-28	CHICAGO	L, 105-110	20-31
1-30	at Atlanta	W, 126-113	21-31
1-31	NEW YORK	W, 94-91	22-31
2-2	PHILADELPHIA	W, 114-104	23-31
2-6	at Buffalo	W, 107-105	24-31
2-7	PHOENIX	W, 113-107	25-31
2-9	at Boston	W, 104-95	26-31
2-10	at New York	L, 93-107	26-32
2-13	MILWAUKEE	L, 96-110	26-33
2-16	at Philadelphia	L, 106-119	26-34
2-17	CLEVELAND	L, 104-106	26-35
2-18	K.C.-OMAHA	W, 144-100	27-35
2-20	L.A. LAKERS	W, 106-98	28-35
2-23	BALTIMORE	W, 107-105	29-35
2-25	HOUSTON	W, 129-112	30-35
2-27	GOLDEN STATE	W, 114-100	31-35
3-2	BOSTON	L, 111-115	31-36
3-3	SEATTLE	L, 113-115	31-37
3-4	at Portland	W, 113-109	32-37
3-6	at Golden State	L, 93-108	32-38
3-10	at Phoenix	W, 117-110	33-38
3-11	at L.A. Lakers	L, 117-141	33-39
3-14	L.A. LAKERS	L, 112-121	33-40
3-16	BUFFALO	W, 121-100	34-40
3-17	at Chicago	W, 99-97	35-40
3-18	CHICAGO	L, 107-119	35-41
3-19	n-Milwaukee	L, 99-118	35-42
3-21	PORTLAND	W, 122-109	36-42
3-24	K.C.-OMAHA	W, 110-98	37-42
3-25	n-Philadelphia	W, 115-96	38-42
3-27	at Baltimore	W, 112-98	39-42
3-28	at Cleveland	W, 131-119 (OT)	40-42

(Home games in CAPS; n-neutral site)

1973 1974

DETROIT PISTONS NBA

TIME CAPSULE

December 16, 1973:
En route to a 2,000-yard season, O.J. Simpson of the Buffalo Bills sets the NFL single-season rushing record, breaking Jim Brown's mark.

April 8, 1974:
Hank Aaron of the Atlanta Braves hits his 715th home run, breaking Babe Ruth's all-time record.

August 8, 1974:
President Nixon announces that he will resign, to be succeeded by Vice President Gerald Ford, former U.S. Senator from Michigan.

SEASON SNAPSHOT

Most Points
Bob Lanier (1,822, 22.5 avg.)

Most Rebounds
Bob Lanier (1,074, 13.3 avg.)

Most Assists
Dave Bing (555, 6.9 avg.)

Most Minutes
Dave Bing (3,124, 36.6 avg.)

Field-Goal Percentage
Bob Lanier (50.4%)

Free-Throw Percentage
Stu Lantz (85.3%)

Team Offense Average
104.4 (8,560 in 82 games)

Team Defense Average
100.3 (8,227 in 82 games)

NBA All-Stars
Dave Bing, G (Second Team)

NBA Coach of the Year
Ray Scott

Pistons in All-Star Game
Dave Bing, G; Bob Lanier, C (MVP)

1973-74

FINAL STANDINGS

Midwest Division	W	L	Pct.	GB
Milwaukee	59	23	.720	—
Chicago	54	28	.659	5
PISTONS	**52**	**30**	**.634**	**7**
K.C.-Omaha	33	49	.402	26

Atlantic Division Winner—Boston
Central Division Winner—Capital
Pacific Division Winner—Los Angeles

PLAYOFF RESULTS

Western Semifinals: Chicago d. Pistons, 4-3

PISTONS PLAYOFF LEADERS

Scoring: Bob Lanier (26.3 avg.)
Rebounding: Bob Lanier (15.3)
Assists: Dave Bing (6.0)

NBA CHAMPION

Boston Celtics

1973-74
SEASON IN REVIEW

For the first time in the team's 17 undistinguished seasons in Detroit, the city finally caught Pistons fever in '73-74 and the club was worthy of fervent support. It was a season full of highlights—a franchise-best 52-30 record, new highs for home and road wins, an All-Star game MVP award for Bob Lanier, second-team All-NBA for Dave Bing. The list went on and on, including an NBA Coach of the Year award for Ray Scott. It all ended in a classic playoff series with the Chicago Bulls, lost by Detroit in seven great games. There were few early signs that the Pistons were en route to their best season; they were only 12-11 on November 30. But they went West, swept four straight and didn't look back. From December 1 to February 12, they won 28 of 36 games, including two seven-game winning skeins and a five-gamer. The run included a 16-3 home record, leading to a 29-12 overall mark at Cobo Arena, where the Pistons drew 300,000 for the first time. While placing third in the league MVP balloting, Lanier again led the team in points (22.5) and boards (13.3) and was chosen All-Star MVP with 24 points and 10 rebounds as a benchie. Though Bing's scoring average (18.8) fell below 20 for the first time, he was voted to the All-NBA second team. He hit a club-record 32 straight foul shots December 9-28.

The Pistons traded for forward George Trapp, a local product, in '73-74 and his bench production was vital. Trapp is shown here shooting a free throw.

WHAT A NIGHT!

April 13, 1974

It was a full-service playoff series—physical play, coaches parrying in the newspapers, even death threats in both cities. In short, the same kind of gamesmanship that dominated the Pistons-Bulls playoffs of the '80s and '90s. But this was 1974, Detroit vs. Chicago for the first time in the postseason in the Western semifinals. The Bulls had their way in the regular-season series, winning five of seven games, and coach Dick Motta was brimming with cockiness. That quickly disappeared when the Pistons won Game 1 at Chicago behind Bob Lanier's 27 points. The Bulls came back with two wins, but Detroit tied it 2-2 with surprise starter Stu Lantz scoring 23 points. The teams again traded victories, with the Pistons surviving 92-88 in Game 6 at home. "This series was supposed to be a piece of cake for them—and now they're choking on it," Detroit coach Ray Scott said. On April 13, 1974, the Pistons' chances in Game 7 were helped by the absence of Bulls guard Jerry Sloan (foot injury). The game hinged on two plays. Chicago forward Chet Walker hit a head-fake 10-footer with three seconds left to put his team ahead 96-94. After a timeout, Dave Bing's inbounds pass was tipped by Bulls backup big man Dennis Awtrey, leaving the Pistons two points shy and brokenhearted.

After rarely playing late in the season, Stu Lantz came up big vs. Chicago in the playoffs with games of 25 and 23 points.

Bill Davidson

Pistons owner Bill Davidson is known as "Mr. D" around The Palace.

Coach Doug Collins is prone to an occasional overstatement, but there was no bluster at all when he talked about Pistons owner Bill Davidson, lover of games, eschewer of neckties. "He is the best owner in sports," Collins said. "No owner could be better. Knowing you've got him on your side, I can't put into words what that means as a head coach. There are people all around the NBA who'd love to have my job because they know how supportive Mr. D is. Not just financially; he has great enthusiasm."

It might seem incongruous to refer to a billionaire so informally as Mr. D, but that's one reason Davidson is known as one of the most effective club owners in the NBA. When he and eight investors bought the Pistons from founder Fred Zollner in July 1974—purchase price: $8.1 million—Davidson promised a shirt-sleeve management style that's lasted more than two decades. The fact that Davidson receives the added title of Mr. is out of sheer respect, not obsequiousness.

But shirt-sleeve should not be confused with shoe-string or slapdash. The Pistons go first class in every way under Davidson; there are no half-measures. From the state-of-the-art Palace of Auburn Hills (built mostly with Davidson's funds), to the Pistons' private jet (they were the first NBA team to travel that way full-time) to their new practice facility, Davidson has utilized the same formula that made his Guardian Industries a world leader in glass manufacturing. The Pistons and The Palace are cornerstones of a larger company, Palace Sports and Enter-

tainment, that includes the Pine Knob Music Theatre, the nation's busiest ampitheatre; a championship-winning IHL hockey team, the Detroit Vipers; an indoor soccer team, the Detroit Safari; and management of the popular Meadow Brook Music Festival.

In 1988, The Palace opened for business and the Pistons presented a great christening gift—two, actually—by winning NBA titles in '89 and '90, the first in team history. But it wasn't a speedy or painless climb from also-rans to one of the league's most valuable franchises. For the first half-decade of Davidson's stewardship, there were rookie mistakes, so to speak. Trading Dave Bing, firing coach Ray Scott during practice, the comical Marvin Barnes saga, hiring overmatched head coach Dick Vitale ... not a good track record for the first few seasons. But with the hiring of general manager Jack McCloskey in 1979, Davidson placed his club in the hands of a talented "basketball man." Isiah Thomas arrived in 1981, Bill Laimbeer in '82 and Chuck Daly in '83. The club was on its way, not to look back.

Davidson, a Detroit native, was a talented track athlete in high school and college, where his love of sports was ingrained. He also served in the Navy during World War II. He's a generous contributor to a number of organizations, such as the University of Michigan and Jewish causes. The minority owners of the Pistons are: Oscar Feldman, Warren Coville, Milt Dresner, Bud Gerson, Dorothy Gerson, David Mondry, Eugene Mondry, Ann Newman, Herb Tyner and William Wetsman.

PISTON LIST

Nicknames Quiz

PLAYER	NICKNAME
1. Don Adams	a. Bird
2. Marvin Barnes	b. Buddha
3. Joe Caldwell	c. Butch
4. James Edwards	d. Chief
5. Harry Gallatin	e. Crash
6. Howie Komives	f. Geezer
7. Cliff Levingston	g. Horse
8. Kevin Loughery	h. House
9. John Mengelt	i. Murph
10. Terry Mills	j. News
11. Howard Porter	k. Pogo
12. Don Reid	l. Smart
13. John Salley	m. Spider
14. Isiah Thomas	n. Three
15. George Yardley	o. Zeke

1. 2. j, 3. k, 4. b, 5. g, 6. c, 7. h, 8. i, 9. e, 10. n, 11. f, 12. d, 13. m, 14. o, 15. a

CHANGING FACES

WHEN GEORGE TRAPP was playing his high school basketball at Highland Park in suburban Detroit, he dreamed of starring for his hometown NBA franchise. But he couldn't have conceived the circuitous route he would take to reach the Pistons. Rather than stay local, the 6-foot-8 forward traveled to California to play two years at Pasadena Junior College and two at Long Beach State. He starred so prominently at the latter, twice being named the Pacific Coast Conference MVP, that the Atlanta Hawks picked him in the first round (fifth overall) in 1971. Two solid seasons later, having rung up game-highs of 34 points and 19 rebounds with the Hawks, Trapp was swapped to Detroit for a first-round pick two weeks after the '72-73 season. He averaged 9.3 points and almost four boards as a sometimes starter in '73-74, including 22 in Game 4 of the Bulls-Pistons playoff. Trapp would be Detroit's only acquisition that season, which helps explain its success; rather than constantly fiddle with the nucleus, as they often had, the Pistons settled on a dependable rotation.

George Trapp was a Detroit-area high school star in the mid-'60s.

Take a Bow

Ray Scott

The Pistons' 52-30 record under Coach of the Year Ray Scott would remain their best ever until 1986-87 (54-28).

The Pistons weren't accustomed to having awards given to them, least of all coach Ray Scott. In his nine-year NBA playing career, he was never named to an All-Star team. He hadn't gotten any postseason honors or special recognition despite a career that included over 10,000 points and a 10.5-rebound average. So it was with genuine sincerity that Scott acknowledged a two-minute standing ovation at a packed Cobo Arena on April 11, 1974. Prior to Game 6 of the Pistons-Bulls playoff, Scott was called to center court to receive the Red Auerbach Award, better known as the NBA Coach of the Year award. In his first full season as coach, he had received a majority of votes from a nationwide panel of NBA media. "It's the greatest individual honor I've ever received," Scott said, as he thanked players, management, fans and media. The award was deserved, too. The Pistons' 52-30 record in '73-74 doubled their win total of two years earlier under Bill van Breda Kolff, Terry Dischinger and Earl Lloyd.

Game Results
1973-74
REGULAR SEASON

Date	Opponent	Result	Record
10-9	at New York	L, 100-101	0-1
10-12	ATLANTA	W, 122-105	1-1
10-13	at Chicago	L, 94-101	1-2
10-14	at Cleveland	W, 85-83	2-2
10-19	MILWAUKEE	L, 94-96	2-3
10-20	at Houston	W, 107-104	3-3
10-24	at Phoenix	W, 115-99	4-3
10-26	at L.A. Lakers	L, 92-94	4-4
10-27	at Portland	W, 111-98	5-4
10-28	at Seattle	W, 115-93	6-4
10-31	SEATTLE	W, 115-93	7-4
11-2	PHOENIX	W, 114-107	8-4
11-3	at Milwaukee	L, 115-123 (OT)	8-5
11-8	at Atlanta	W, 129-115	9-5
11-10	n-Boston	L, 97-102	9-6
11-14	PORTLAND	L, 108-111	9-7
11-16	K.C.-OMAHA	W, 125-98	10-7
11-17	at Buffalo	W, 98-94	11-7
11-18	CHICAGO	L, 102-104	11-8
11-21	PHOENIX	W, 107-104	12-8
11-24	at Chicago	L, 112-114 (OT)	12-9
11-28	CLEVELAND	L, 91-96	12-10
11-30	at Houston	L, 95-110	12-11
12-1	at Phoenix	W, 121-109	13-11
12-2	at L.A. Lakers	W, 114-108	14-11
12-4	at Golden State	W, 112-93	15-11
12-6	at Seattle	W, 113-108	16-11
12-8	PORTLAND	W, 106-91	17-11
12-9	at K.C.-Omaha	W, 86-80	18-11
12-12	L.A. LAKERS	W, 114-96	19-11
12-14	PHILADELPHIA	L, 93-96	19-12
12-15	at Philadelphia	W, 99-89	20-12
12-16	at Kansas City	L, 104-105	20-13
12-19	CHICAGO	W, 89-87	21-13
12-21	GOLDEN STATE	W, 107-104	22-13
12-22	at New York	L, 88-99	22-14
12-26	NEW YORK	L, 91-96	22-15
12-28	CAPITAL	W, 102-93	23-15
12-29	at Chicago	L, 103-105	23-16
12-30	at Milwaukee	W, 98-91	24-16
1-2	MILWAUKEE	W, 106-92	25-16
1-4	BOSTON	W, 106-101	26-16
1-5	at Capital	L, 90-93	26-17
1-9	L.A. LAKERS	W, 123-94	27-17
1-11	at Cleveland	W, 106-96	28-17
1-12	CLEVELAND	L, 112-117 (OT)	28-18
1-18	CHICAGO	W, 113-95	29-18
1-20	K.C.-OMAHA	W, 105-99	30-18
1-23	PORTLAND	W, 121-95	31-18
1-25	HOUSTON	W, 93-89	32-18
1-26	SEATTLE	W, 94-83	33-18
1-27	at Chicago	L, 91-109	33-19
1-30	BUFFALO	W, 111-96	34-19
2-1	NEW YORK	W, 96-91	35-19
2-3	at Seattle	W, 114-100	36-19
2-5	at Portland	W, 104-102	37-19
2-7	at Golden State	W, 110-86	38-19
2-8	at Phoenix	W, 99-94	39-19
2-12	K.C.-OMAHA	W, 113-106	40-19
2-14	MILWAUKEE	L, 99-102	40-20
2-15	at Buffalo	L, 116-118	40-21
2-17	at Philadelphia	W, 118-107	41-21
2-19	at Boston	L, 97-107	41-22
2-20	L.A. LAKERS	W, 120-118	42-22
2-22	CAPITAL	W, 84-83	43-22
2-23	PHOENIX	W, 119-107	44-22
2-24	at Capital	L, 84-94	44-23
2-26	BOSTON	L, 83-84	44-24
2-28	at Milwaukee	L, 90-113	44-25
3-1	SEATTLE	L, 103-105	44-26
3-3	at Portland	W, 99-95	45-26
3-5	at Golden State	W, 95-93	46-26
3-8	at L.A. Lakers	L, 113-129	46-27
3-10	at Atlanta	W, 116-111	47-27
3-11	GOLDEN STATE	L, 108-120	47-28
3-12	GOLDEN STATE	W, 113-108	48-28
3-15	MILWAUKEE	W, 93-89	49-28
3-17	BUFFALO	W, 116-109	50-28
3-20	HOUSTON	W, 103-99	51-28
3-22	at Kansas City	L, 105-107	51-29
3-23	PHILADELPHIA	L, 89-97	51-30
3-26	ATLANTA	W, 109-108	52-30

PLAYOFFS
Western Semifinals—(Best-of-Seven)

Date	Opponent	Result	Record
3-30	at Chicago	W, 97-88	1-0
4-1	CHICAGO	L, 103-108	1-1
4-5	at Chicago	L, 83-84	1-2
4-7	CHICAGO	W, 102-87	2-2
4-9	at Chicago	L, 94-98	2-3
4-11	CHICAGO	W, 92-84	3-3
4-13	at Chicago	L, 94-96	3-4

(Home games in CAPS; n-neutral site)

· T I M E O U T ·

PISTONS/BULLS RIVALRY

Isiah Thomas (11) and Michael Jordan took turns dominating the Pistons-Bulls rivalry in the '80s and '90s. Photo by Allen Einstein.

Momentum is tenuous in any great rivalry. Today's winner, puffed with pride, is tomorrow's loser, vowing payback. One team might have a brief period of domination, but the clubs essentially trade victories and it all comes out even in the end.

The Pistons-Chicago Bulls rivalry is bigger than that. These guys don't merely trade victories, they trade decades. The Pistons owned the '80s, going 52-25 vs. Chicago including the playoffs, the Bulls have had their way big-time in the '90s (31-5) and the bottom line is basically square: Chicago holds a 103-101 all-time advantage through 1997.

Along the way, the bitter series between the NBA's Midwest rivals has been a crucible of greatness, helping to forge the Pistons' back-to-back champions of '89 and '90 and teaching the Bulls the requisite lessons to dominate the league so thoroughly during the '90s. Maybe the year 2000 will herald the Pistons' return to prominence as Grant Hill succeeds the incomparable Michael Jordan as the series' (and NBA's) marquee player.

AT A GLANCE

PISTONS-BULLS

PISTONS' SERIES RECORD:
Regular Season: 86-89 (Home 55-30, Road 29-57, Neutral 2-2)
Playoffs: 15-14 (Home 10-5, Road 5-9)

TEAM RECORDS (Regular Season)
BEST SEASON:
Pistons: 6-0, 1981-82, 1988-89
Bulls: 6-0, 1994-95

HIGHEST POINT TOTAL:
Pistons: 158, March 23, 1969
Bulls: 147 (2OT), January 4, 1983

HIGHEST COMBINED SCORE
Pistons 152, Bulls 144 (296), November 3, 1982

BIGGEST WIN MARGIN:
Pistons: 44 (158-114), March 23, 1969
Bulls: 35 (127-92), December 21, 1971

MOST BLOCKED SHOTS
Pistons: 20, November 3, 1982
Bulls: 15, March 27, 1984

**INDIVIDUAL RECORDS
(Regular Season)**
MOST POINTS:
Pistons: 56, Kelly Tripucka, January 29, 1983

Bulls: 61, Michael Jordan, March 4, 1987

PLAYERS WHO PLAYED FOR BOTH TEAMS (30)
Roger Brown, Len Chappell, Ed Cureton, James Edwards, Jim Fox, Sidney Green, David Greenwood, Reggie Harding, Bill Hewitt, Charles Jones, Don Kojis, Cliff Levingston, Scott May, McCoy McLemore, John Mengelt, Erwin Mueller, Chuck Nevitt, Ben Poquette, Howard Porter, Mark Randall, Jackie Robinson, Dennis Rodman, John Salley, Brad Sellers, Steve Sheppard, Andre Wakefield, Darrell Walker, James Wilkes, Brian Williams, Orlando Woolridge.

COACHES WHO COACHED BOTH TEAMS (2)
Doug Collins, Scotty Robertson

In fact, it must be noted, the Pistons entered the '97-98 season with a winning streak—one—having beaten Chicago 108-91 on April 14, 1997 to snap their 19-game losing skid in the series. The nationally televised victory, fueled by Hill's triple-double, will be remembered for the tears shed by coach Doug Collins as the final seconds ticked away. Collins had coached the Bulls for three seasons (1986-89), getting fired just as the team was on the cusp of major success, and was previously 0-7 against them with Detroit. "My proudest moment as a coach," he called the win.

Though Detroit and Chicago locked up in a sassy seven-game playoff in 1974, finally won by the Bulls at an electric Chicago Stadium, the early stages of the rivalry were stoked more by the cities' proximity than the talent of the clubs. From 1966 through the 1979-80 season, Chicago had 43 wins in the regular-season series, Detroit 41.

Not until the arrival of Isiah Thomas and Bill Laimbeer in 1981-82 and Jordan in '84-85 did the series rocket into the stratosphere. For a spell, it featured more individual heroics than team accomplishments, such as Kelly Tripucka's Pistons-record 56 points on January 29, 1983 and Jordan's 61 on March 4, 1987, both at the Silverdome. (Or the night in 1981 when Detroit center Paul Mokeski fouled out ... in the first quarter.)

But once the Pistons put together the NBA's deepest roster in the mid-'80s and Collins' Bulls accessorized Jordan with supporting players like Scottie Pippen, Horace Grant and B.J. Armstrong, the rivalry reached its full contentious potential. For four straight springs, 1988-91, the clubs squared off in a best-of-seven playoff that contained all the subtlety of a knee to the groin. The Pistons won the first three years, getting to the NBA Finals each time and winning championships the last two. But every year, the younger Bulls made it a little closer, falling 4-1 in the second round in '88, then 4-2 and 4-3 in the Eastern Finals in '89 and '90. Every meeting was marked by physical tenacity—much of it after the whistle—like Isiah breaking his hand slugging Bill Cartwright on April 7, 1989, or Rick Mahorn tossing Collins onto the press table twice January 16, 1988.

Finally in '91, the Unstoppable Force—Jordan—budged the Immovable Object—the Pistons, starting to show their age. Chicago broke through in a convincing manner, sweeping the Pistons, 4-0, in a series marked by angry words and actions by both teams. Jordan had his say, blasting the Pistons before Game 4 at The Palace, telling *The Oakland Press* and *The Chicago Tribune* the Pistons' roughhouse style had been bad for the NBA. "Outside of Detroit, I think people will be happy they're not the reigning champions anymore," he said. "It'll mean we are getting back to a clean game and getting the Bad Boy image away from the game. ... I don't think it's been clean or sportsmanlike basketball that you'd want to advertise or endorse." The Pistons issued their reply the next day, walking off the court in the final seconds without congratulating their conquerors. They were roundly criticized as poor sports, but many Pistons fans still have not forgiven Jordan for minimizing the accomplishments of their team.

The Pistons-Bulls rivalry spawned a defensive strategy known as "The Jordan Rules," Detroit's double-teaming plot to defend him, but he's had some of his best days against them. In his 76 games vs. the Pistons, Air Jordan's 31.1-point average features 11 games of 40 or more, including 61, 59, 53, 49 (twice) and 47 (twice). His 53-point night came on March 7, 1996 at the United Center, helping to extend Detroit's continuing 21-game losing skid at Chicago, stretching back to March 16, 1990.

Pistons' seasons against Bulls

REGULAR SEASON

SEASON	HOME	AWAY	NEUTRAL	TOTAL
1966-67	1-2	3-1	1-1	5-4
1967-68	3-0	1-2	0-1	4-3
1968-69	2-1	1-2	—	3-3
1969-70	2-1	0-2	1-0	3-3
1970-71	2-1	1-2	—	3-3
1971-72	1-2	0-3	—	1-5
1972-73	3-1	1-2	—	4-3
1973-74	2-1	0-4	—	2-5
1974-75	4-1	1-3	—	5-4
1975-76	2-1	2-2	—	4-3
1976-77	1-1	1-1	—	2-2
1977-78	1-1	1-1	—	2-2
1978-79	1-1	1-1	—	2-2
1979-80	1-0	0-1	—	1-1
1980-81	1-2	0-3	—	1-5
1981-82	3-0	3-0	—	6-0
1982-83	3-0	1-2	—	4-2
1983-84	3-0	2-1	—	5-1
1984-85	2-1	1-2	—	3-3
1985-86	3-0	1-2	—	4-2
1986-87	2-1	1-2	—	3-3
1987-88	2-1	2-1	—	4-2
1988-89	3-0	3-0	—	6-0
1989-90	2-0	2-1	—	4-1
1990-91	2-1	0-2	—	2-3
1991-92	1-1	0-3	—	1-4
1992-93	1-1	0-2	—	1-3
1993-94	0-3	0-2	—	0-5
1994-95	0-2	0-3	—	0-5
1995-96	0-2	0-2	—	0-4
1996-97	1-1	0-2	—	1-3
TOTAL	**55-30**	**29-57**	**2-2**	**86-89**

PLAYOFFS

SEASON	HOME	AWAY	TOTAL
1973-74	2-1	1-3	3-4
1987-88	2-1	2-0	4-1
1988-89	2-1	2-1	4-2
1989-90	4-0	0-3	4-3
1990-91	0-2	0-2	0-4
TOTAL	**10-5**	**5-9**	**15-14**

1974 DETROIT PISTONS NBA 1975

1974-75

September 24, 1974:
Al Kaline of the Detroit Tigers becomes the 12th major-leaguer with 3,000 hits, doubling in the fourth inning at Baltimore, his hometown.

October 30, 1974:
Muhammad Ali recaptures the heavyweight boxing title with an eighth-round knockout of George Foreman in Zaire.

July 31, 1975:
Former Teamsters leader Jimmy Hoffa is missing after a meeting at a suburban Detroit restaurant; he is never seen again.

SEASON SNAPSHOT

Most Points
Bob Lanier (1,823, 24.0 avg.)

Most Rebounds
Bob Lanier (914, 12.0 avg.)

Most Assists
Dave Bing (610, 7.7 avg.)

Most Minutes
Dave Bing (3,222, 40.8 avg.)

Field-Goal Percentage
Bob Lanier (51.0%)

Free-Throw Percentage
John Mengelt (85.1%)

Team Offense Average
98.9 (8,111 in 82 games)

Team Defense Average
100.3 (8,228 in 82 games)

Pistons in All-Star Game
Dave Bing, G; Bob Lanier, C

FINAL STANDINGS

Midwest Division	W	L	Pct.	GB
Chicago	47	35	.573	—
K.C.-Omaha	44	38	.537	3
PISTONS	**40**	**42**	**.488**	**7**
Milwaukee	38	44	.463	9

Atlantic Division Winner—Boston
Central Division Winner—Washington
Pacific Division Winner—Golden State

PLAYOFF RESULTS

Western First Round: Seattle d. Pistons, 2-1

PISTONS PLAYOFF LEADERS

Scoring: Bob Lanier (20.3 avg.)
Rebounding: Bob Lanier (10.7)
Assists: Dave Bing (9.7)

NBA CHAMPION

Golden State Warriors

1974-75
SEASON IN REVIEW

All the good feelings from the previous spring quickly disappeared and the Pistons wasted '74-75 in a futile quest to find the magic again. The final results—a 40-42 record and a first-round playoff exit—weren't what fans had expected after Detroit's seven-game playoff epic vs. the Bulls in '74. The season began badly when Dave Bing and Don Adams held out from training camp, wanting their contracts reworked. Bing had two years to go and sought a raise from $190,000 to $300,000. But the Pistons' new ownership wouldn't budge, the players returned and there were hard feelings all around; both players would be gone within a year. The discord contributed to a bad start that had the Pistons stuck at 16-17 at Christmas. They perked up at midseason, improving to 31-21 after a 15-4 spurt, but that was immediately undone as Detroit lost 18 of its next 22; the skid included an 0-10 road record. The Pistons were able to squeeze into the playoffs, but lost 2-1 to Seattle. For the fourth straight season, Bob Lanier led the club in scoring (24.0) and rebounding (12.0), with games of 45, 43, 41 and 40 points as he ranked sixth in the NBA. Late in the season, though, his left knee began acting up—a grim sign. Bing's future was not in doubt at all—his troubles with management signaled a summer trade. He averaged 19 points in his last Pistons season.

John Mengelt had his best Pistons season in '74-75, averaging 11 points.

WHAT A NIGHT!

April 2, 1975

The Pistons were rather embarrassed to be in such a fix. They had been 10 games over .500 two months previous, but now they were in the final week of the season, under .500, still needing to qualify for the playoffs. They had the inside track on Milwaukee for the last Western berth, but a Tuesday loss at Milwaukee narrowed the gap. If the Pistons didn't clinch the playoff berth the next night, April 2, vs. Chicago, their season finale vs. Milwaukee could turn into a winner-take-all, loser-goes-home game. Not to worry. Before 9,336 at Cobo Arena, the Pistons beat Chicago 97-89 to reach their second straight postseason. As if the game needed any more weight, Bob Lanier got seven rebounds to top Walter Dukes' 4,986, making him the Pistons' all-time carom leader. He would raise his total to 8,063 by 1980, a figure topped only by Bill Laimbeer (9,430). Lanier's 26 points led the victory. Curtis Rowe and Howard Porter added 18 each, while John Mengelt scored 12 of his 14 in the fourth quarter to keep the Bulls at bay. Chicago, the Pistons' conqueror the year before, was led by Norm Van Lier and Tom Boerwinkle with 17 points apiece.

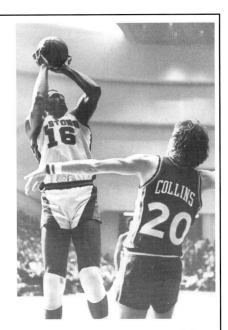

Bob Lanier, scoring over Philly's Doug Collins, became the Pistons' all-time rebound king in 1975.

Premier Piston

John "Crash" Mengelt

Blonde-locked John Mengelt became a Pistons fan favorite in the mid-'70s.

When your nickname is "Lefty" or "Red," explanations aren't required. Similarly, if you saw John Mengelt play for the Pistons from 1972-76, no one needs to explain why his nickname was "Crash." No player left more shredded skin on floors all over the NBA. Nobody scurried headlong into the stands to save more loose balls. Nobody worked harder. But Mengelt wasn't a show-off; he played all-out because he felt he had to. "I'd like to buzz around like a hummingbird, but God didn't give me that talent. I have to work harder and do the little things that might end up being big things," he said. Accordingly, Mengelt's stats were never great, but his teammates benefitted from his passion. Then again, the 6-foot-2 guard might be selling short his own athleticism. Mengelt played football and basketball at Auburn and was drafted in both, but rather than sign with the Dallas Cowboys as a linebacker, he opted for the Cincinnati Royals, who chose him in the second round in '71. Mengelt averaged 24.8 points in three seasons at Auburn and led the nation in free-throw shooting at 91.2 percent as a senior. But it soon became clear his future in the NBA was as a role player who'd have to get the most from limited minutes. A month into his second season, Detroit acquired Mengelt in trade from Kansas City and he quickly established himself as a grinder. He even showed he could score, having a 32-point game. He bumped that career high to 33 in '74-75, in which he also led the Pistons in foul shooting (85.1 percent). In '75-76, a December 9 knee injury knocked him out of the starting five, but he wound up averaging 10.7 points and 16.5 economical minutes. On November 18, 1976, the Pistons sold Mengelt to the Chicago Bulls. He would later return to Detroit as its TV color analyst.

AT A GLANCE

JOHN MENGELT

FULL NAME:
John P. Mengelt

BORN:
October 16, 1949; Lacrosse, Wisconsin

POSITION, HEIGHT, WEIGHT:
Guard, 6-foot-2, 195 pounds

COLLEGE:
Auburn '71

ACQUIRED:
1972, trade from Kansas City-Omaha

TENURE WITH PISTONS:
November 10, 1972 — 1975-76
Also: Cincinnati 1971-72, Kansas City-Omaha 1972, Chicago 1976-80, Golden State 1980

BEST SEASON WITH PISTONS:
1974-75, 80 GP, 11.0 ppg, 2.5 apg

TOTALS WITH PISTONS:
Regular season: 291 GP, 10.3 ppg, 2.3 apg
Playoffs: 16 GP, 8.1 ppg, 1.8 apg

PISTON LIST

Dave Bing's Statistical Milestones

POINTS
- January 2, 1971 — Pistons' all-time scoring leader (8,184)
- February 21, 1971 — Career-high 54 points
- February 22, 1972 — 10,000 points
- December 13, 1972 — 11,000 points
- March 14, 1973 — 12,000 points
- January 5, 1974 — 13,000 points
- November 10, 1974 — 14,000 points
- March 8, 1975 — 15,000 points

ASSISTS
- March 12, 1971 — Pistons' all-time assists leader (1,932)
- March 21, 1972 — 2,500 assists
- February 27, 1973 — 3,000 assists
- January 25, 1974 — 3,500 assists
- January 4, 1975 — 4,000 assists

CHANGING FACES

WHEN THE PISTONS dealt their 1975 No. 1 draft pick to the Knicks for 6-foot-8 forward Howard Porter, most fans remembered him for one reason. He was the guy from Villanova who was the NCAA Final Four MVP in '71, the guy who had to give back his award when it was learned he had signed a pro contract in college. Villanova, which lost the championship to UCLA, was stripped of its runner-up finish. That episode was four years old when the Pistons got Porter—nickname: Geezer—the day after Christmas 1974, and the fans soon grew to enjoy their quirky newcomer. Especially because Detroit won its first six games with him and 14 of its first 17. With an unorthodox shot and an animated playing style, Porter averaged 10.6 points and shot exactly 50 percent in 41 games for Detroit in '74-

Howard Porter, one of the Pistons' snazziest dressers, bumped his scoring average to 17.3 points in the '74-75 playoffs.

75. The season's most controversial transaction came February 18 when Don Adams was released after three seasons as a Piston. With the team in a 1-11 slump, some players, Dave Bing most prominently, felt Adams was being made a scapegoat. Within six months, Bing would also be gone.

Take a Bow

Dave Bing

In his final Pistons season, Dave Bing made great strides on NBA career lists.

Bill Russell. Dave DeBusschere. Jerry Lucas. Richie Guerin. Tricky Dick McGuire. In '74-75, Dave Bing passed every one of them in all-time NBA scoring or assists (or both) en route to his milestone 15,000th point on March 8 vs. New York. The nine-year veteran guard had begun the season with 13,734 points and quickly resumed his flight up the charts. On November 16, he topped DeBusschere and Lucas' 14,053 to reach No. 20 on the list. On January 8, he surpassed Russell's 14,522 for 19th and January 26 he nudged Guerin's 14,676 for 18th. The 17 players ahead of Bing had all scored at least 15,000 and he joined that group on March 8 with his 12th point in a 118-100 loss to the Knicks; he scored a team-leading 26 in the game. On the assists list, Bing finished the season—and his Detroit career as it turned out—ninth all-time with 4,330. He passed Russell's 4,100 on February 1 for 11th, then former Piston McGuire's 4,205 on March 1 to crack the top 10. A day later at Kansas City, the sixth of Bing's eight set-ups pushed him ahead of Guerin's 4,211.

Game Results
1974-75
REGULAR SEASON

Date	Opponent	Result	Record
10-18	at Seattle	W, 100-95	1-0
10-19	at Portland	W, 122-99	2-0
10-23	at Phoenix	L, 90-100	2-1
10-25	at L.A. Lakers	W, 110-107	3-1
10-26	at Golden State	L, 104-105	3-2
10-30	ATLANTA	L, 96-104	3-3
10-31	at Cleveland	L, 101-111	3-4
11-1	NEW ORLEANS	W, 103-93	4-4
11-2	at Philadelphia	W, 100-94	5-4
11-6	K.C.-OMAHA	W, 118-104	6-4
11-8	at Boston	W, 105-104	7-4
11-9	at Buffalo	L, 100-109	7-5
11-10	BUFFALO	L, 117-124	7-6
11-13	MILWAUKEE	W, 98-91	8-6
11-15	SEATTLE	W, 117-103	9-6
11-16	at Houston	L, 98-118	9-7
11-17	at New Orleans	W, 99-85	10-7
11-19	at Kansas City	L, 87-97	10-8
11-20	PHOENIX	L, 106-114	10-9
11-23	GOLDEN STATE	L, 98-110	10-10
11-26	at New York	W, 99-88	11-10
12-4	HOUSTON	W, 86-69	12-10
12-6	CLEVELAND	W, 117-91	13-10
12-7	at Washington	L, 89-94	13-11
12-8	K.C.-OMAHA	L, 92-96	13-12
12-10	at Milwaukee	L, 82-90	13-13
12-11	WASHINGTON	W, 103-89	14-13
12-13	at K.C.-Omaha	L, 84-88	14-14
12-14	PHILADELPHIA	W, 100-93	15-14
12-18	SEATTLE	L, 97-100	15-15
12-20	at L.A. Lakers	W, 103-102	16-15
12-21	at Portland	L, 97-108	16-16
12-22	at Seattle	L, 90-108	16-17
12-26	NEW YORK	W, 84-83	17-17
12-28	CHICAGO	W, 79-70	18-17
12-30	at Chicago	W, 86-81	19-17
1-2	NEW ORLEANS	W, 99-95	20-17
1-3	at Buffalo	W, 111-92	21-17
1-4	PHILADELPHIA	W, 89-82	22-17
1-8	MILWAUKEE	L, 92-102	22-18
1-10	at Milwaukee	W, 89-81	23-18
1-11	at Atlanta	W, 118-113	24-18
1-17	at Boston	L, 90-96	24-19
1-18	PHOENIX	W, 86-77	25-19
1-19	CLEVELAND	W, 100-98	26-19
1-22	PORTLAND	W, 96-94	27-19
1-24	ATLANTA	W, 113-103	28-19
1-25	at Chicago	L, 96-116	28-20
1-26	CHICAGO	W, 102-93 (OT)	29-20
1-29	GOLDEN STATE	W, 93-90	30-20
1-30	at Houston	L, 88-103	30-21
2-1	BUFFALO	W, 119-113	31-21
2-2	at Cleveland	L, 96-116	31-22
2-3	BOSTON	L, 100-114	31-23
2-6	at Atlanta	L, 98-111	31-24
2-7	at Chicago	L, 83-95	31-25
2-9	L.A. LAKERS	W, 97-96	32-25
2-10	at Milwaukee	L, 109-130	32-26
2-12	CHICAGO	L, 93-103	32-27
2-14	at Philadelphia	L, 101-103	32-28
2-15	K.C.-OMAHA	L, 81-93	32-29
2-16	at K.C.-Omaha	L, 99-102	32-30
2-19	NEW YORK	L, 94-109	32-31
2-21	WASHINGTON	L, 96-121	32-32
2-26	MILWAUKEE	W, 104-84	33-32
2-28	at Washington	L, 95-106	33-33
3-1	CHICAGO	W, 95-94	34-33
3-2	at K.C.-Omaha	L, 112-122	34-34
3-4	at Milwaukee	L, 83-101	34-35
3-8	at New York	L, 100-118	34-36
3-9	K.C.-OMAHA	W, 106-99	35-36
3-11	L.A. LAKERS	L, 94-95	35-37
3-14	at Chicago	L, 94-97	35-38
3-18	BOSTON	L, 90-116	35-39
3-21	HOUSTON	W, 121-110	36-39
3-23	at New Orleans	W, 125-114	37-39
3-26	PORTLAND	W, 110-107	38-39
3-27	at Phoenix	W, 91-79	39-39
3-29	at Golden State	L, 112-115	39-40
4-1	at Milwaukee	L, 91-98	39-41
4-2	CHICAGO	W, 97-89	40-41
4-5	MILWAUKEE	L, 106-119	40-42

PLAYOFFS

Western First Round—(Best-of-Three)

4-8	at Seattle	L, 77-90	0-1
4-10	SEATTLE	W, 122-106	1-1
4-12	at Seattle	L, 93-100	1-2

(Home games in CAPS)

1975 1976

DETROIT PISTONS NBA

TIME CAPSULE

September 18, 1975:
A 19-month FBI search ends when heiress Patricia Hearst is captured in San Francisco.

July 4, 1976:
The bicentennial of United States independence is celebrated.

July 20, 1976:
Viking I, launched 11 months earlier, lands on Mars.

September 5, 1976:
President Ford escapes the first of two assassination attempts within two weeks; Lynette "Squeaky" Fromme is apprehended.

SEASON SNAPSHOT

Most Points
Bob Lanier (1,366, 21.3 avg.)

Most Rebounds
Bob Lanier (746, 11.7 avg.)

Most Assists
Eric Money (338, 4.2 avg.)

Most Minutes
Curtis Rowe (2,998, 37.5 avg.)

Field-Goal Percentage
Bob Lanier (53.2%)

Free-Throw Percentage
Archie Clark (86.2%)

Team Offense Average
104.9 (8,605 in 82 games)

Team Defense Average
106.0 (8,691 in 82 games)

Pistons in All-Star Game
Curtis Rowe, F

1975-76

FINAL STANDINGS

Midwest Division	W	L	Pct.	GB
Milwaukee	38	44	.463	–
PISTONS	**36**	**46**	**.439**	**2**
Kansas City	31	51	.378	7
Chicago	24	58	.573	14

Atlantic Division Winner—Boston
Central Division Winner—Cleveland
Pacific Division Winner—Golden State

PLAYOFF RESULTS

Western First Round: Pistons d. Milwaukee, 2-1
Western Semifinals: Golden State d. Pistons, 4-2

PISTONS PLAYOFF LEADERS

Scoring: Bob Lanier (26.1 avg.)
Rebounding: Bob Lanier (12.7)
Assists: Eric Money (5.7)

NBA CHAMPION
Boston Celtics

1975-76
SEASON IN REVIEW

The Pistons made two major substitutions in '75-76 and neither made the fans especially happy. Only by gaining a playoff series victory—the club's first since 1962—did the Pistons seem to get the locals back on their side. Substitution No. 1 came before the season, August 28, when the Pistons and star guard Dave Bing parted. Having annoyed management by holding out the previous season, Bing was traded to his hometown team, the Washington Bullets, along with a first-round draft pick for reigning NBA assist leader Kevin Porter, a 5-foot-11 point guard. Though fans at Cobo Arena booed, it was impossible to judge the deal fairly, especially because Porter suffered a knee injury on December 9 and was sidelined for the rest of the season. Nevertheless, Bing was gone, exiting as the Pistons' career leader in points (15,235) and assists (4,330). Substitution No. 2 occurred January 26 when Ray Scott—not two years after being NBA Coach of the Year—was fired and replaced by assistant coach Herb Brown, the brother of Larry Brown. The new coach was razzed mercilessly, but fans eased up late in the season during a 10-1 spurt that featured eight wins in a row at home. Then in the playoffs, the Pistons slid by Milwaukee 2-1 in a best-of-three first round before losing to Golden State 4-2 in the thrilling Western Semis; the decisive loss at Cobo went into overtime.

New coach Herb Brown made a nightly fashion statement on the sidelines.

WHAT A NIGHT!

April 17, 1976

Two years earlier in the final seconds of a clinching playoff game, the Pistons had been the victims of a stolen inbounds pass. Their hearts were in tatters after the Bulls' big Dennis Awtrey deflected Dave Bing's pass, dooming Detroit in Game 7 of the Western Semifinals. The Pistons got a break in their favor in the decisive third game at Milwaukee in the first round in 1976. Having lost the opener 110-107, then rallying for a 126-123 win in Game 2, the Pistons found themselves trailing by seven points with eight minutes left in Game 3 on April 17. Sparked by George Trapp's nine points, they put together a 17-7 spurt to nudge ahead 101-98, then Archie Clark's baseline jumper restored a 103-102 lead after a Milwaukee rally. With 21 seconds left, the Bucks called timeout to draw up a potential winning play, on which rookie David Meyers was supposed to inbound to Brian Winters or Bobby Dandridge. But Chris Ford moved in front of Winters at the crucial second, stole the bounce pass and bolted for a breakaway layup and three-point lead in Detroit's 107-104 win. It was Ford's fourth steal of the game to go with 18 points. "I was lucky," he said. "I had a good angle on the ball, but where it was going was just a guess." Bob Lanier's 28 points led the Pistons, as usual.

Chris Ford's good hands fueled the Pistons' biggest victory of '75-76.

Premier Piston

Chris Ford

Chris Ford coached the Celtics for five seasons before taking over the Milwaukee Bucks in 1996.

Chris Ford is more often identified as a member of the Boston Celtics than the Pistons, which is to be expected. After all, he was the Celtics' starting two-guard for most of his three-plus seasons with them, most prominently in 1981 when Boston captured the NBA championship. Ford, multifaceted and dedicated, was the Celtics' final team MVP (1978-79) before the Larry Bird era, which began the year after Detroit dealt Ford to Boston for Earl Tatum. With the Celtics, Ford gained a distinction he will forever hold: he hit the first 3-point basket in NBA history. On October 12, 1979 at Boston Garden (Bird's NBA debut), Ford made a triple in the Celtics' 114-108 win over Houston. He finished second in the NBA in 3-point shooting (42.7 percent) that inaugural season. As a Detroit Piston for 485 games from 1972 (he was a second-round draft pick) to his October 19, 1978 trade, Ford's fortes were showing up and making steals. From 1973-78, he missed only two of 413 games and played the last 270 consecutively—a Pistons record at the time—before going to Boston. There, he expanded the streak to 417. Ford is best remembered by Detroit fans for his good hands and sharp court sense, reflected by three straight seasons in the NBA top 10 in steals (1975-78). Of course, his most famous steal came in the clinching Game 3 of the '76 first-round playoff vs. Milwaukee. On a potential winning play by the Bucks, he stepped in front of the Bucks' inbounds pass and hurried for a layup to stretch Detroit's lead to three, effectively eliminating Milwaukee. Ford now coaches the Bucks, having spent seven seasons as a Celtics assistant (1984-90) and five more as their head coach ('91-96). He was the Eastern All-Star coach in 1991.

AT A GLANCE

CHRIS FORD

FULL NAME:
Christopher Joseph Ford
BORN:
January 11, 1949; Atlantic City, New Jersey
POSITION, HEIGHT, WEIGHT:
Guard, 6-foot-5, 190 pounds
COLLEGE:
Villanova '72
ACQUIRED:
Drafted, second round, 1972 (17th overall)
TENURE WITH PISTONS:
1972-73 — October 19, 1978
Also: Boston 1978-82
BEST SEASON WITH PISTONS:
1976-77, 82 GP, 12.3 ppg, 3.3 rpg, 4.1 apg
TOTALS WITH PISTONS:
Regular season: 485 GP, 8.5 ppg, 3.5 rpg, 3.5 apg
Playoffs: 20 GP, 7.6 ppg, 4.2 rpg, 3.5 apg
HONORS:
All-Star Game coach, 1991
Coach of the Month, 1992

PISTON LIST

Best Seasonal Overtime Records

(All-time: 85-76)
1-0 (1.000)
- 1993-94
- 1974-75

4-1 (.800)
- 1996-97
- 1990-91
- 1989-90
- 1988-89

3-1 (.750)
- 1991-92
- 1987-88
- 1985-86
- 1969-70
- 1962-63

4-2 or 2-1 (.667)
- 1981-82 (4-2)
- 1970-71 (4-2)
- 1968-69 (2-1)

CHANGING FACES

THE PISTONS' new ownership had never fired a coach, so maybe they didn't know how to break the news to Ray Scott. But their removal of the popular coach on January 26 was certainly unusual. With the team in a slump of seven losses in its last nine games, management stepped in, firing Scott during a practice session as shocked players looked on; the winningest coach in club history (147-134) was escorted off the court. GM Oscar Feldman cited a "communication breakdown" for firing Scott, but the fans weren't happy about the move. Dancing Gus and the crazies in the Cobo balcony made life rough on replacement Herb Brown, booing his every coaching move. Aside from the blockbuster trade of Dave Bing to Washington for Kevin Porter—a swap of the previous year's top two assist men—the Pistons' most significant player transaction produced 10-year veteran guard Archie Clark from Seattle for a first-round pick. Clark was at the end of his career and he averaged under double-figures (7.6 points) for the only time in his career.

Archie Clark had averaged 25.2 points in 1971-72, but was only a year away from retirement when the Pistons acquired him.

The VILLAIN

Doug Collins

Philadelphia's Doug Collins definitely wasn't on the Pistons' side for most of the '70s.

Whenever his skills were not being restricted by uncooperative knees, Philadelphia 76ers guard Doug Collins was deadly to the Pistons. Others might've gotten greater acclaim, but there were few gunners who could compete with the wiry, frizzy-haired Collins if he was physically able. In '75-76, more than in any of his eight seasons, Collins was extremely able. He averaged 26 points in three games against the Pistons en route to a career-high 20.5 season average, 12th in the NBA. The only Detroit opponents to out-do Collins in their respective season series were New Orleans' "Pistol Pete" Maravich (31.0), Golden State's Phil Smith (31.0) and Kansas City's Nate Archibald (26.2). Collins had other solid seasons vs. the Pistons, averaging 20.7 in '74-75 and 27.3 in '77-78 including a 36-point effort. He had a 25-point game in '78-79, after serious knee problems set in; of 410 possible games in his last five seasons, Collins appeared in 232. Later, though, his expertise would benefit the Pistons. As their current coach, he's guided them to a 100-64 two-year record.

Game Results
1975-76
REGULAR SEASON

Date	Opponent	Result	Record
10-24	at New Orleans	L, 106-114	0-1
10-25	at Atlanta	W, 108-102	1-1
10-29	L.A. LAKERS	W, 112-99	2-1
10-31	HOUSTON	W, 131-127	3-1
11-1	at Buffalo	L, 93-97	3-2
11-4	at Milwaukee	L, 101-103	3-3
11-5	SEATTLE	W, 124-107	4-3
11-7	at Chicago	W, 124-122	5-3
11-8	BOSTON	L, 104-118	5-4
11-12	ATLANTA	L, 106-109	5-5
11-15	MILWAUKEE	W, 101-89	6-5
11-19	PORTLAND	W, 120-114	7-5
11-21	BUFFALO	W, 104-94	8-5
11-26	KANSAS CITY	W, 120-104	9-5
11-29	at New York	W, 115-110	10-5
12-3	L.A. LAKERS	L, 110-118	10-6
12-5	HOUSTON	W, 102-91	11-6
12-6	at Houston	L, 96-105	11-7
12-9	at Golden State	L, 124-129	11-8
12-12	at Seattle	L, 95-97	11-9
12-13	at Portland	L, 91-101	11-10
12-14	at L.A. Lakers	L, 100-110	11-11
12-17	GOLDEN STATE	L, 102-113	11-12
12-19	PHILADELPHIA	L, 114-115 (OT)	11-13
12-20	at Washington	L, 86-98	11-14
12-23	WASHINGTON	L, 102-120	11-15
12-26	CHICAGO	W, 101-87	12-15
12-27	at Chicago	L, 99-112	12-16
12-28	at Kansas City	W, 103-87	13-16
12-30	at Philadelphia	L, 108-114	13-17
1-2	MILWAUKEE	L, 83-98	13-18
1-3	at Cleveland	W, 104-100	14-18
1-7	CLEVELAND	W, 119-118 (OT)	15-18
1-9	at Milwaukee	L, 95-102	15-19
1-10	NEW ORLEANS	L, 99-104	15-20
1-11	at Kansas City	L, 99-105	15-21
1-16	PORTLAND	L, 104-111	15-22
1-18	PHOENIX	L, 118-123	15-23
1-20	at Washington	W, 114-107	16-23
1-21	SEATTLE	W, 111-104	17-23
1-23	at Boston	L, 91-108	17-24
1-24	NEW YORK	L, 100-117	17-25
1-27	at Cleveland	L, 83-85	17-26
1-28	CHICAGO	L, 84-87	17-27
1-30	KANSAS CITY	W, 101-94	18-27
2-1	BOSTON	L, 109-114	18-28
2-5	at Atlanta	W, 111-108	19-28
2-7	MILWAUKEE	L, 106-114	19-29
2-8	at Kansas City	W, 94-93	20-29
2-10	at L.A. Lakers	L, 88-106	20-30
2-11	at Phoenix	L, 94-123	20-31
2-14	at Golden State	L, 105-106	20-32
2-15	at Seattle	L, 107-109	20-33
2-18	PHOENIX	W, 105-94	21-33
2-20	WASHINGTON	W, 102-87	22-33
2-21	at Buffalo	W, 114-112	23-33
2-25	CLEVELAND	L, 101-108	23-34
2-27	NEW YORK	W, 97-93	24-34
2-29	PHOENIX	L, 98-109	24-35
3-2	at Kansas City	L, 113-127	24-36
3-3	SEATTLE	W, 114-110	25-36
3-5	at Philadelphia	L, 112-123	25-37
3-7	at Boston	L, 87-88	25-38
3-9	GOLDEN STATE	L, 108-112	25-39
3-12	at Milwaukee	W, 117-101	26-39
3-14	at Portland	L, 103-114	26-40
3-16	at Golden State	L, 101-110	26-41
3-18	at Phoenix	L, 100-106	26-42
3-19	at L.A. Lakers	L, 107-122	26-43
3-21	BUFFALO	W, 118-112	27-43
3-23	at New York	W, 122-116	28-43
3-24	KANSAS CITY	W, 130-117	29-43
3-26	at Chicago	W, 85-77	30-43
3-27	PORTLAND	W, 112-94	31-43
3-31	CHICAGO	W, 102-96	32-43
4-2	NEW ORLEANS	W, 116-102	33-43
4-3	at Chicago	L, 93-97 (OT)	33-44
4-4	PHILADELPHIA	W, 101-97	34-44
4-7	MILWAUKEE	W, 106-96	35-44
4-9	ATLANTA	W, 116-108	36-44
4-10	at Houston	L, 99-110	36-45
4-11	at New Orleans	L, 105-112	36-46

PLAYOFFS

Western First Round—(Best-of-Three)

Date	Opponent	Result	Record
4-13	at Milwaukee	L, 107-110	0-1
4-15	MILWAUKEE	W, 126-123	1-1
4-17	at Milwaukee	W, 107-104	2-1

Western Semifinals—(Best-of-Seven)

Date	Opponent	Result	Record
4-20	at Golden State	L, 103-127	0-1
4-22	at Golden State	W, 123-111	1-1
4-24	GOLDEN STATE	L, 96-113	1-2
4-26	GOLDEN STATE	W, 106-102	2-2
4-28	at Golden State	L, 109-128	2-3
4-30	GOLDEN STATE	L, 116-118 (OT)	2-4

(Home games in CAPS)

1976 1977

DETROIT PISTONS NBA

 TIME CAPSULE

November 2, 1976:
Former Georgia governor Jimmy Carter defeats incumbent Gerald Ford in the presidential election.

January 17, 1977:
A 10-year U.S. halt on capital punishment ends when Gary Gilmore is executed by a Utah firing squad.

July 28, 1977:
The trans-Alaska pipeline goes into full operation.

August 10, 1977:
New York City police arrest David Berkowitz as the Son of Sam killer.

SEASON SNAPSHOT

Most Points
Bob Lanier (1,616, 25.3 avg.)

Most Rebounds
Bob Lanier (745, 11.6 avg.)

Most Assists
Kevin Porter (592, 7.3 avg.)

Most Minutes
M.L. Carr (2,643, 32.2 avg.)

Field-Goal Percentage
Bob Lanier (53.4%)

Free-Throw Percentage
Howard Porter (85.8%)

Team Offense Average
109.4 (8,970 in 82 games)

Team Defense Average
110.4 (9,055 in 82 games)

Pistons in All-Star Game
Bob Lanier, C

1976-77

FINAL STANDINGS

Midwest Division	W	L	Pct.	GB
Denver	50	32	.610	—
Chicago	44	38	.537	6
PISTONS	**44**	**38**	**.537**	**6**
Kansas City	40	42	.488	10
Indiana	36	46	.439	14
Milwaukee	30	52	.366	20

Atlantic Division Winner—Philadelphia
Central Division Winner—Houston
Pacific Division Winner—Los Angeles

PLAYOFF RESULTS

Western First Round: Golden State d. Pistons, 2-1

PISTONS PLAYOFF LEADERS

Scoring: Bob Lanier (28.0 avg.)
Rebounding: Bob Lanier (16.7)
Assists: Eric Money (6.7)

NBA CHAMPION

Portland Trail Blazers

1976-77
SEASON IN REVIEW

As much as the Pistons would care to forget it, 1976-77 was the Year of Marvin Barnes. A nonstop soap opera began when the Pistons drafted him (over Moses Malone!) in the ABA dispersal when that league merged with the NBA. The 6-9 forward had been a star in the ABA, where he was known as News. Fittingly, accounts of Barnes' absences, holdouts, legal scrapes and so forth filled the papers all season long. He was eccentric, to be sure. Barnes once had 13 phones in his apartment, allowing him to answer without rising. Informed that a team flight into a Western time zone would actually arrive earlier than it left, Barnes said, "I ain't gettin' on no time machine." Queried about one of his absences, he said, "I might not be some-place, but it doesn't mean I'm lost." News made good copy, but his saga was a distraction in a season that could have been far better than its 44-38 resolution. After a 2-6 start, the Pistons went on a 35-19 tear led by Bob Lanier (25.3 ppg), streak-scoring Howard Porter and hot-shot point guard Kevin Porter, fully recovered from his 1975 knee injury. On November 20 vs. Boston, K.P. had a league-high 20 assists to set a club record he'd eventually break many times. A 4-10 finish—mostly without Lanier, who broke his right hand March 4—sent the Pistons staggering into the playoffs. They lost 2-1 to Golden State in their last postseason until '84.

When he bothered showing up, ABA refugee Marvin "News" Barnes averaged 9.6 points for the '76-77 Pistons.

WHAT A NIGHT!

November 24, 1976

It was a night of two debuts, one more honorable than the other. Cobo was packed (11,111) as Pistons fans awaited their first look at two of the defunct ABA's leading stars. Most were curious to see Philadelphia acrobat-in-Bermudas Julius "Dr. J" Erving, playing his first game ever against the Pistons. Mean-while for Detroit, forward Marvin Barnes was likely to make his NBA debut after being suspended twice already. Take a guess who had a better game. To no one's surprise, though Detroit won 118-117, Erving raised more eyebrows despite getting in early foul trouble. He scored 25 points, including 13 in the fourth quarter to help the 76ers rally from a deficit that had reached 19 at halftime. Philly finally pulled within one on George McGinnis' three-point play with nine seconds left, but the 76ers didn't get a chance to win it. Bob Lanier scored 25 to lead Detroit, Chris Ford 22 and M.L. Carr 20. For Philly, McGinnis had 29 and Lloyd (not-yet World B.) Free added 21. Barnes? The hard-to-figure forward got in for one minute in the second quarter and then the game's final minute after Detroit lost three players to fouls. He went scoreless, symbolic of his entire first season as a Piston—a big, fat zero.

Julius Erving—Dr. J—averaged 24.5 points against the Pistons in his first NBA season, including a 32-point performance in April.

Premier Piston

Kevin "K.P." Porter

Kevin Porter shoots here over the Lakers' Don Chaney—a future Pistons coach—but K.P.'s credo was pass first, shoot second.

You won't find Kevin Porter's name on a Hall of Fame plaque or a list of the best players in NBA history. He is often ignored in discussions of the top point guards of all-time. But for most of his 10 seasons, including two Pistons stints covering 190 games, the 5-foot-11 ball of energy was among the NBA's smoothest operators, winning four league assist titles. Well before John Stockton arrived on the scene, Porter held virtually every major assist record, dealing an NBA-record 1,099 for Detroit in 1978-79. Until Scott Skiles' 30 assists in 1990, Porter also owned the league single-game record of 29 (for New Jersey, '78). In fact, he still holds single-game marks for three clubs: Washington (24), New Jersey (29) and Detroit (25); he dealt 25 twice for the Pistons in '79 (March 9 vs. Boston, April 1 at Phoenix). Until Stockton repeated the feat in 1988, Porter was the only player in NBA history with back-to-back games of at least 20 assists, doing it for Washington in '75 en route to his first assist title. By now you can tell, for all of Porter's amazing quarterbacking skills, he was also much-traveled. He put in two stints each with Detroit and Washington and one for New Jersey, winning an assist title with each club. Porter's competitive nature was so intense, his quest for offensive autonomy so fierce, he wore out his welcome with more than one coach, the Pistons' Herb Brown among them. Detroit acquired Porter for Dave Bing in the summer of '75, but a knee injury limited him to 19 games that season. Though he came back strong in '76-77, averaging 7.3 assists, Brown got tired of Porter early the next season and shipped him to New Jersey. Dick Vitale got him back for '78-79 and he had a record-breaking year before being reacquired by the Bullets as a free agent.

AT A GLANCE

KEVIN PORTER

FULL NAME:
Kevin Porter
BORN:
April 17, 1950; Chicago
POSITION, HEIGHT, WEIGHT:
Point guard, 5-foot-11, 165 pounds
COLLEGE:
St. Francis (Pennsylvania), '72
ACQUIRED:
1975, trade from Washington
1978, trade from New Jersey
TENURE WITH PISTONS:
1975-76 — November 7, 1977; 1978-79
BEST SEASON WITH PISTONS:
1978-79, 82 GP, 15.4 ppg, 13.4 apg
TOTALS WITH PISTONS:
Regular season: 190 GP, 11.7 ppg, 10.1 apg
Playoffs: 3 GP, 5.3 ppg, 5.7 apg
HONORS:
NBA assist champion: 1975, 1978, 1979, 1981

PISTON LIST

Most Team Steals in a Season (Since 1973-74)

- 884, 1980-81
- 877, 1976-77
- 866, 1977-78
- 846, 1978-79
- 793, 1973-74
- 786, 1975-76
- 783, 1979-80
- 741, 1981-82
- 738, 1985-86
- 705, 1994-95
- 697, 1983-84
- 691, 1984-85
- 679, 1974-75
- 679, 1982-83

CHANGING FACES

THE PISTONS had drafted Leon Douglas for just such emergencies. When center Bob Lanier broke his right hand March 4 with Detroit trying to maintain its playoff position, rookie Douglas was thrust into the starting lineup. The 6-foot-10 muscleman from Alabama, drafted fourth overall, responded in fine form with five games in which he average 20.8 points and 13.2 rebounds, including a 30-point, 22-rebound game at Philly. The Pistons lost all five, but Douglas' emergence at least provided optimism. Douglas was second on the team in rebounds (526), but also led in fouls (294), a trend that would continue throughout his seven NBA seasons (four with Detroit). Also in '76-77, besides head case Marvin Barnes, the Pistons added two more players to their nucleus: gritty forward M.L. Carr, a free agent from the ABA pool, and former Michigan State shooting guard

Shooting guard Ralph Simpson, a Detroit native, averaged 10.9 points in two seasons with the Pistons.

Ralph Simpson. Carr was a find, becoming one of the NBA's best multipurpose forwards. Simpson was acquired from Denver on October 20 in a three-team deal that sent All-Star Curtis Rowe to Boston. Rowe had held out for a trade.

Take a Bow

Pistons "Thieves"

Blue-collar M.L. Carr led Detroit in minutes in his first season, proving a much better acquisition than fellow ABA refugee Marvin Barnes.

Mostly because of Chris Ford, the Pistons had been one of the league's better teams in steals since 1973-74 when the NBA made it an official statistic in 1973-74. Fueled by the addition of Michael Leon Carr—M.L. for short—they broke all of their team records in '76-77. They made 877 swipes, blowing away their old high of 793 in '73-74; that record would stand until they got 884 in '80-81. Detroit also eclipsed its single-game record by making 20 steals April 5 at Portland, topping the old high by one. Ford had another superb season, setting Pistons records for steals in a game (8, March 25 at Golden State) and season (179), ranking seventh in the NBA in the latter. The acquisition of Carr, who had gone undrafted in the ABA dispersal, ratcheted up the Pistons' defensive pressure twofold. That was evidenced by his own 165 steals, giving Detroit one of the NBA's top 1-2 thievery combos. Carr would top Ford's club record with a league-leading 197 steals in '78-79, but Isiah Thomas beat that mark twice (199 in '82-83, 204 a season later).

Game Results

1976-77 REGULAR SEASON

Date	Opponent	Result	Record
10-22	at Kansas City	W, 99-96	1-0
10-23	WASHINGTON	L, 97-98	1-1
10-27	SEATTLE	W, 106-92	2-1
10-29	at Seattle	L, 103-106	2-2
10-30	at Portland	L, 97-131	2-3
10-31	at L.A. Lakers	L, 101-121	2-4
11-2	at Golden State	L, 98-111	2-5
11-5	BUFFALO	L, 108-122	2-6
11-6	at Atlanta	W, 110-105	3-6
11-7	at New Orleans	W, 115-107	4-6
11-10	CLEVELAND	W, 123-112	5-6
11-12	N.Y. KNICKS	W, 111-97	6-6
11-13	at Chicago	W, 106-103	7-6
11-14	at Milwaukee	W, 104-83	8-6
11-17	NEW ORLEANS	W, 118-95	9-6
11-18	at Indiana	L, 99-104	9-7
11-20	BOSTON	W, 116-110	10-7
11-24	PHILADELPHIA	W, 118-117	11-7
11-25	at Cleveland	L, 105-111	11-8
11-26	at Buffalo	L, 119-124	11-9
11-30	at San Antonio	L, 129-130	11-10
12-1	at Houston	L, 104-110	11-11
12-3	KANSAS CITY	W, 124-115	12-11
12-8	CHICAGO	W, 107-100	13-11
12-10	at N.Y. Nets	W, 106-104	14-11
12-11	N.Y. NETS	L, 88-115	14-12
12-12	at Kansas City	W, 110-104	15-12
12-15	GOLDEN STATE	W, 136-116	16-12
12-17	INDIANA	W, 113-104	17-12
12-19	at New Orleans	W, 125-110	18-12
12-21	at N.Y. Knicks	L, 103-133	18-13
12-22	ATLANTA	W, 107-94	19-13
12-25	at Buffalo	L, 106-115	19-14
12-29	PORTLAND	W, 120-111	20-14
12-30	at Denver	L, 106-123	20-15
1-5	PHOENIX	W, 118-115	21-15
1-7	MILWAUKEE	W, 140-132	22-15
1-9	L.A. LAKERS	L, 118-124	22-16
1-11	at Golden State	W, 129-121	23-16
1-12	at Seattle	L, 99-121	23-17
1-13	at Phoenix	L, 101-131	23-18
1-15	BUFFALO	W, 121-105	24-18
1-21	HOUSTON	W, 109-86	25-18
1-23	at Washington	L, 109-119	25-19
1-25	at Boston	W, 91-89	26-19
1-26	N.Y. NETS	W, 103-101 (OT)	27-19
1-27	at Houston	L, 107-114	27-20
1-29	at Chicago	L, 101-109	27-21
1-30	INDIANA	W, 127-120	28-21
2-1	at Atlanta	W, 95-92	29-21
2-2	at Philadelphia	L, 116-138	29-22
2-4	DENVER	W, 124-111	30-22
2-6	KANSAS CITY	W, 130-111	31-22
2-9	SAN ANTONIO	L, 129-135	31-23
2-11	CLEVELAND	W, 101-94	32-23
2-15	at Boston	L, 99-101	32-24
2-16	PORTLAND	W, 125-118	33-24
2-18	WASHINGTON	W, 107-97	34-24
2-19	at Washington	L, 95-105	34-25
2-20	PHOENIX	W, 109-107	35-25
2-23	L.A. LAKERS	W, 102-101	36-25
2-25	at N.Y. Nets	W, 112-106	37-25
3-1	DENVER	L, 94-110	37-26
3-4	BOSTON	L, 92-94	37-27
3-5	at Indiana	L, 96-118	37-28
3-6	ATLANTA	W, 115-105	38-28
3-8	MILWAUKEE	W, 109-107	39-28
3-13	at San Antonio	W, 102-97	40-28
3-16	CHICAGO	L, 97-104	40-29
3-18	SEATTLE	L, 104-105	40-30
3-20	at Denver	L, 104-133	40-31
3-23	NEW ORLEANS	L, 89-95	40-32
3-25	GOLDEN STATE	W, 107-94	41-32
3-26	at Milwaukee	L, 108-128	41-33
3-27	HOUSTON	W, 115-100	42-33
3-30	at Philadelphia	L, 112-115	42-34
4-1	at Phoenix	L, 116-133	42-35
4-3	at L.A. Lakers	L, 107-115 (OT)	42-36
4-5	at Portland	L, 105-110	42-37
4-8	PHILADELPHIA	W, 116-112	43-37
4-9	at Cleveland	W, 103-96	44-37
4-10	N.Y. KNICKS	L, 126-144	44-38

PLAYOFFS

Western First Round—(Best-of-Three)

4-12	at Golden State	W, 95-90	1-0
4-14	GOLDEN STATE	L, 108-138	1-1
4-17	at Golden State	L, 101-109	1-2

(Home games in CAPS)

1977 1978

DETROIT PISTONS NBA

TIME CAPSULE

October 18, 1977:
Reggie Jackson hits a World Series-record three home runs in Game 6, leading the New York Yankees to a clinching 8-4 win over the Dodgers.

February 8, 1978:
Egyptian President Anwar el-Sadat begins a six-day U.S. visit, hoping to advance a Mideast peace settlement.

June 10, 1978:
Affirmed, ridden by jockey Steve Cauthen, wins horse racing's Triple Crown with a victory in the Belmont Stakes.

SEASON SNAPSHOT

Most Points
Bob Lanier (1,542, 24.5 avg.)

Most Rebounds
Bob Lanier (715, 11.3 avg.)

Most Assists
Kevin Porter (381, 4.6 avg.)

Most Minutes
Chris Ford (2,582, 31.5 avg.)

Field-Goal Percentage
Bob Lanier (53.7%)

Free-Throw Percentage
Jim Price (81.6%)

Team Offense Average
109.0 (8,936 in 82 games)

Team Defense Average
110.2 (9,038 in 82 games)

Pistons in All-Star Game
Bob Lanier, C

1977-78

FINAL STANDINGS

Midwest Division	W	L	Pct.	GB
Denver	48	34	.585	—
Milwaukee	44	38	.537	4
Chicago	40	42	.488	8
PISTONS	**38**	**44**	**.463**	**10**
Indiana	31	51	.378	17
Kansas City	31	51	.378	17

Atlantic Division Winner—Philadelphia
Central Division Winner—San Antonio
Pacific Division Winner—Portland

PLAYOFF RESULTS

Pistons Did Not Qualify

PISTONS PLAYOFF LEADERS

NBA CHAMPION

Washington Bullets

1977-78
SEASON IN REVIEW

The door had slammed shut on the Pistons. That became obvious in '77-78. Only a few years earlier, they believed they were one or two players from joining the NBA elite, but now they were on their way back down—a fall that is never without casualties. The first two were the Porters—Howard and Kevin—who got out of coach Herb Brown's doghouse only by being traded to New Jersey. Marvin Barnes went to Buffalo in an apparent steal for Detroit, which got power forward John Shumate, Gus Gerard and a first-round pick. And then Brown himself was fired, replaced December 15 by GM Bob Kauffman on an interim basis. The Pistons responded briefly, losing two straight in overtime, then winning eight of nine, but it didn't last; a 6-11 slump derailed them. Bob Lanier, Old Faithful, led the club in scoring in 44 of his 63 appearances, but was sidelined for the final 12 games after knee surgery, ensuring an end to Detroit's four-year playoff streak. There were other endings. It was the Pistons' final season in the Western Conference and their last as a downtown club; they'd leave Cobo for the Pontiac Silverdome in '78-79. As if to signify the finality, Denver's David Thompson victimized the Pistons for 73 points, the third-most in NBA history, in the farewell game. That's how it sounds when a door slams shut.

Guard Eric Money, passing to Bob Lanier, spent five seasons with the Pistons and averaged 11.2 points.

WHAT A NIGHT!

April 9, 1978

There were only 3,482 at Cobo Arena on April 9, 1978, and chances are you weren't one of them (c'mon, admit it). It was the Pistons' last game at Cobo after 17 seasons, as well as the end of a season gone wrong. Not even a good opponent, the Midwest-winning Denver Nuggets, was enough to bring out the fans. But it soon became obvious that history was going to be made that Sunday afternoon. Denver guard David Thompson, age 23, was attempting to pass San Antonio's George Gervin on the final day for the NBA scoring title (by average). Thompson scored 32 points in the first quarter to set a (short-lived) league record, then 19 in the second. He tired in the third (nine) and fourth (11), but finished with 73 points, the third-most in NBA history behind Wilt Chamberlain's famous 100-point game on March 2, 1962. "I'm not one who goes in for individual stats," Thompson said, fooling nobody. His 73 points lifted his average to 27.15 (rounded up to 27.2), meaning Gervin needed to score at least 58 that night at New Orleans to capture the title. Gervin, a Detroiter, did even better, scoring 63 to close at 27.22; he scored 33 in the second quarter to assume that record as well. Incidentally, the Pistons beat Denver 139-137 behind Al Skinner's meager 27 points and M.L. Carr's 25.

Denver guard David Thompson made the Pistons' Cobo Arena finale a game to remember.

Premier Piston

M.L. Carr

M.L. Carr got his stats with the Pistons, but his rings with the Celtics.

M.L. Carr wasn't an undiscovered talent when the Pistons signed him in 1976. After all, he'd been runner-up (to David Thompson) for ABA Rookie of the Year in that league's final season ('75-76), averaging 12.2 points, 6.2 rebounds and 3.0 assists. But when Carr was looking for an NBA club after the ABA's demise, the Pistons held an advantage over eight teams in bidding for the sleek 6-foot-6 forward. In Herb Brown's last previous incarnation, he had coached Carr in Israel in 1975 while both were still dreaming of the NBA. They teamed to win the European Pro League title, then returned stateside—Brown to the Pistons as an assistant and Carr to the ABA St. Louis Spirits. One year later, the two would hook up again in Detroit, starting a three-season stint in which Carr became known as one of the league's best defenders and most spirited players. His arrival in '76 immediately filled the Pistons' void at small forward and bumped their level of defensive enthusiasm. Carr twice finished second to Chris Ford in steals and then set a team record with 197 in '78-79, easily the best of his three Detroit seasons. En route to his second-team berth on the NBA All-Defensive team, Carr averaged 18.7 points, 7.4 rebounds, 3.3 assists and 2.5 steals, showing exactly the multi-purpose skills the Pistons had long been craving. His season was so solid, Boston felt compelled to sign him as a free agent in the 1979 off-season. The Pistons fouled up the subsequent compensation deal—acquiring an unhappy Bob McAdoo—but it was a great move for Carr. He played his final six seasons for the Celtics and won NBA title rings in '81 and '84, making his name as a spot defender and towel-waving substitute. He would later be Boston's coach and GM until 1997.

AT A GLANCE

M.L. CARR

FULL NAME:
Michael Leon Carr
BORN:
January 9, 1951; Wallace, North Carolina
POSITION, HEIGHT, WEIGHT:
Forward, 6-foot-6, 205 pounds
COLLEGE:
Guilford '73
TENURE WITH PISTONS:
1976-77 — 1978-79
Also: St. Louis (ABA) 1975-76, Boston 1979-85

ACQUIRED:
1976, signed as ABA free agent
BEST SEASON WITH PISTONS:
1978-79, 80 GP, 18.7 ppg, 7.4 rpg, 3.3 apg
TOTALS WITH PISTONS:
Regular season: 241 GP, 14.8 ppg, 7.4 rpg, 2.6 apg
Playoffs: 3 GP, 9.3 ppg, 5.7 rpg, 2.0 apg
HONORS:
NBA All-Defensive Team: 1978-79
ABA All-Rookie Team: 1975-76
ABA Rookie/Year runner-up: 1975-76

PISTON LIST

Pistons Records at Cobo or During Cobo Era

(Still unbroken)
INDIVIDUAL/GAME
- FGs made: 22, Dave Bing, 2-21-71
- FGs attempted: 41, Bob Lanier, 12-25-71

INDIVIDUAL/SEASON
- Points: 2,213, Bing, 1970-71
- FGs made: 836, Bing, 1967-68
- FGs attempted: 1,903, Bing, 1967-68
- Blocks: 247, Lanier, 1973-74
- Fouls: 344, Joe Strawder, 1966-67

TEAM/GAME
- Points (half): 87, Cincinnati, 1-7-72
- Points (qt.): 53, Cincinnati, 1-7-72
- Rebounds (half): 52, Seattle, 1-19-68
- Consecutive FTs: 26, K.C., 3-23-76

TEAM/SEASON
- Points: 9,725 (118.6), 1967-68

CHANGING FACES

HERB BROWN'S CRITICS—and he had plenty of them in the Cobo balcony—finally got their wish. With the Pistons staggering along at 9-15 on December 15, they dumped their renegade coach and brought new GM Bob Kauffman down from the front office to take over. Brown was canned "because the team has not been responsive," Kauffman said. Brown, whose mod sideline wardrobe recalled K.C and the Sunshine Band, expressed surprise. "I think they were wrong (to fire me)," he said. "I feel I've left a legacy here, a strong foundation. I don't intend to apologize for the job the team has done for the last several months." Brown exited with a 72-74 record, plus 5-7 in the playoffs. Kauffman, a seven-year NBA forward (1968-75), guided the Pistons to a 29-29 mark after becoming coach, while also serving as the NBA's youngest GM (31). He showed a nice touch on the trade market as well, swapping 6-foot-9 migraine Marvin Barnes to Buffalo for power forward John Shumate, Gus Gerard and a first-round pick. Shumate was Detroit's No. 3 scorer in '76-77, averaging 15.5 points in 62 games. Heart problems curtailed his career.

John Shumate—known as "Shu"—had games of 31 and 30 points after joining the Pistons in 1977.

Take a Bow

Cobo Arena

Cobo's biggest crowds were often for great opponents, like the '71-72 opener vs. the Lakers in which Bill Hewitt shoots on Wilt Chamberlain.

Gus the Dancing Vendor. The hilarity of Dick Motta kicking a ball into the balcony. Dave Bing darting, weaving, leaping for two more points. Bailey Howell outworking his opponent for a rebound. Butch van Breda Kolff, ejected yet again for too many technical fouls. Ray Scott, playing and coaching pridefully. All of those memories were fashioned during the Pistons' 17 seasons at Cobo Arena, a period that ended with 1977-78. The club announced before the season that it would leave downtown in '78-79, trucking 25 miles north to the Pontiac Silverdome to play in a 30,000-seat configuration. There was mild protest from Detroiters, but they didn't have much of a case; average attendance at Cobo had never topped 7,500, and the NBA was now starting to push its product to an upscale suburban demographic. Cobo served as the Pistons' home arena for 631 games from 1961-78, but only 14 playoff games, a sign of the club's culpability in failing to draw more fans. The Pistons had a 344-287 record at Cobo, a 54.5 winning percentage.

Game Results

1977-78 REGULAR SEASON

Date	Opponent	Result	Record
10-18	NEW JERSEY	W, 110-93	1-0
10-19	at Philadelphia	L, 96-113	1-1
10-21	at Washington	L, 109-117	1-2
10-22	DENVER	W, 126-106	2-2
10-24	BOSTON	W, 100-85	3-2
10-26	GOLDEN STATE	W, 123-107	4-2
10-29	at New York	L, 117-124	4-3
11-2	ATLANTA	L, 89-102	4-4
11-9	HOUSTON	W, 127-107	5-4
11-11	SAN ANTONIO	L, 104-107	5-5
11-13	WASHINGTON	W, 104-102	6-5
11-15	at Denver	L, 113-123	6-6
11-18	at L.A. Lakers	L, 83-116	6-7
11-19	at Golden State	L, 96-128	6-8
11-20	at Portland	L, 101-118	6-9
11-23	PHILADELPHIA	L, 105-106	6-10
11-26	CLEVELAND	L, 87-105	6-11
11-29	at Milwaukee	W, 100-99	7-11
11-30	L.A. LAKERS	W, 104-98	8-11
12-2	at Kansas City	L, 97-108	8-12
12-3	INDIANA	L, 89-103	8-13
12-7	PHOENIX	L, 107-113 (OT)	8-14
12-10	NEW ORLEANS	W, 104-96	9-14
12-14	SEATTLE	L, 92-102	9-15
12-16	at Indiana	L, 106-114 (OT)	9-16
12-17	BUFFALO	L, 122-126 (2OT)	9-17
12-18	at New Orleans	W, 117-108	10-17
12-20	at San Antonio	W, 118-117	11-17
12-22	MILWAUKEE	W, 118-102	12-17
12-23	at Chicago	W, 108-107	13-17
12-26	BOSTON	W, 122-100	14-17
12-28	PORTLAND	L, 106-111	14-18
12-30	at Buffalo	W, 103-87	15-18
1-3	at Atlanta	W, 106-103	16-18
1-4	ATLANTA	W, 111-97	17-18
1-6	at Golden State	L, 106-107	17-19
1-7	at Portland	L, 105-109	17-20
1-11	at Seattle	L, 100-106	17-21
1-13	at Phoenix	L, 100-111	17-22
1-15	CHICAGO	L, 101-107	17-23
1-18	BUFFALO	W, 113-110	18-23
1-20	at Houston	L, 108-118	18-24
1-22	at New Orleans	L, 97-100	18-25
1-24	at Washington	W, 104-101	19-25
1-25	GOLDEN STATE	W, 99-95	20-25
1-28	at Cleveland	W, 115-105	21-25
1-29	CLEVELAND	W, 120-116 (OT)	22-25
2-1	PHOENIX	W, 127-120	23-25
2-2	at Kansas City	L, 101-113	23-26
2-3	at Denver	L, 102-115	23-27
2-8	L.A. LAKERS	L, 95-105	23-28
2-10	at New Jersey	L, 112-117	23-29
2-11	NEW ORLEANS	W, 106-96	24-29
2-13	NEW JERSEY	W, 125-115	25-29
2-15	PHILADELPHIA	L, 113-116	25-30
2-17	NEW YORK	L, 108-128	25-31
2-19	KANSAS CITY	W, 110-107	26-31
2-22	HOUSTON	W, 119-108	27-31
2-25	at Seattle	L, 104-118	27-32
2-26	at L.A. Lakers	W, 127-124	28-32
3-1	at Phoenix	W, 115-102	29-32
3-3	WASHINGTON	L, 108-124	29-33
3-5	INDIANA	W, 122-110	30-33
3-7	at Atlanta	L, 109-123	30-34
3-9	at Indiana	L, 105-112	30-35
3-12	at New Jersey	W, 130-125	31-35
3-14	at Boston	L, 98-105	31-36
3-15	SAN ANTONIO	L, 106-135	31-37
3-16	at Houston	W, 106-98	32-37
3-19	CHICAGO	W, 112-92	33-37
3-21	KANSAS CITY	L, 111-116	33-38
3-24	PORTLAND	W, 107-95	34-38
3-26	at Milwaukee	L, 109-110 (OT)	34-39
3-28	at Buffalo	W, 112-118	35-39
3-29	SEATTLE	W, 121-116	36-39
3-31	at Chicago	L, 107-117	36-40
4-1	at Cleveland	L, 99-113	36-41
4-2	MILWAUKEE	L, 121-129	36-42
4-5	at Philadelphia	L, 115-126	36-43
4-6	at New York	L, 125-129 (OT)	36-44
4-7	at Boston	W, 111-109	37-44
4-9	DENVER	W, 139-137	38-44

(Home games in CAPS)

1978 🏀 1979

TIME CAPSULE

September 15, 1978:
Muhammad Ali becomes the first three-time heavyweight boxing champion, regaining the title in a 15-round decision over Leon Spinks.

November 18, 1978:
More than 900 people are found dead in Guyana in a mass suicide led by religious sect leader Jim Jones.

March 26, 1979:
Magic Johnson leads Michigan State past Larry Bird and Indiana State for the NCAA basketball championship, a preview of future battles.

March 28, 1979:
Three Mile Island nuclear plant near Harrisburg, Pennsylvania, is the site of a near-distastrous meltdown.

SEASON SNAPSHOT

Most Points
Bob Lanier (1,253, 23.6 avg.)

Most Rebounds
Leon Douglas (664, 8.5 avg.)

Most Assists
x-Kevin Porter (1,099, 13.4 avg.)

Most Minutes
M.L. Carr (3,207, 40.1 avg.)

Field-Goal Percentage
Bob Lanier (51.5%)

Free-Throw Percentage
John Long (82.6%)

Team Offense Average
110.0 (9,023 in 82 games)

Team Defense Average
112.7 (9,242 in 82 games)

Pistons in All-Star Game
Bob Lanier, C

x-led league

1978-79

FINAL STANDINGS

Central Division	W	L	Pct.	GB
San Antonio	48	34	.585	—
Houston	47	35	.573	1
Atlanta	46	36	.561	2
PISTONS	**30**	**52**	**.366**	**18**
Cleveland	30	52	.366	18
New Orleans	26	56	.317	22

Atlantic Division Winner—Washington
Midwest Division Winner—Kansas City
Pacific Division Winner—Seattle

PLAYOFF RESULTS

Pistons Did Not Qualify

PISTONS PLAYOFF LEADERS

NBA CHAMPION

Seattle SuperSonics

1978-79
SEASON IN REVIEW

A warm breeze blew through the Pistons' franchise in '78-79—or was it hot air coming from new coach Dick Vitale? Or maybe a draft blowing around the Pontiac Silverdome, the club's cavernous new home up north? Vitale, the verbose former coach at the University of Detroit, was hired to be the Pistons' head coach May 1. He immediately began spreading the word about the "ReVITALEized" Pistons, promising his club would "give 120 percent. That's 110 percent adjusted for inflation." Anybody unable to answer the bell would be broomed, he said. But Vitale turned into the first casualty, being hospitalized with stomach problems only one week into the season. With the club off to an 0-5 start, Vitale came back just in time to be forcibly ejected from the first win of the Silverdome era. There were doubts whether Vitale would last the season—so obvious was his inexperience, so uncontrollable was his passion. But he survived a 30-52 disaster whose highlights centered on Bob Lanier and Kevin Porter. Lanier's season was limited to 53 games by injuries, but he led the Pistons in scoring (23.6) and got an emotional ovation from a record house of 31,745 at the All-Star Game on February 4 at the Dome. Reacquired from the Nets, Porter set the league assist record with 1,099. Also, M.L. Carr had his best season, making the All-Defensive team, while draft picks John Long and Terry Tyler showed promise.

Toe and knee injuries caught up to Bob Lanier in '78-79, but the February 4 All-Star Game warmed his heart.

WHAT A NIGHT!

October 25, 1978

There weren't many happy moments for the Pistons in their debut season at the Silverdome. Among the few, they broke their game scoring record March 9 with a 160-117 rout over Boston. But after an 0-5 start, no win meant more to the Pistons than their first on October 25, a night made more memorable by coach Dick Vitale's wild third-quarter ejection. Detroit defeated Cleveland 110-105, using a 24-5 spurt to overcome the loss of Vitale after he protested a borderline foul against M.L. Carr. Freshly out of the hospital for treatment of stress-related stomach problems, Vitale charged on to the court to confront referee Tommy Nunez. He was quickly pulled away by team officials, then came back for more. Finally, Vitale was bearhugged by a large security guard and essentially carried up the tunnel to the nervous laughter of fans. The season was only six games old and already owner Bill Davidson was expressing concern over his coach's behavior. "I think Dick went too far," he said. Detroit bailed out Vitale behind Bob Lanier's 26 points and 13 rebounds, and rookie guard John Long scored 18. Campy Russell had 36 points for Cleveland in the Pontiac native's first game in his hometown's shining Dome.

Moments after this photo, ejected Pistons coach Dick Vitale was physically removed from the court by security.

Premier Piston

Dick Vitale

At his introductory press conference, Dick Vitale wows 'em with the arm-waving, high-decibel style that made him a TV sports star.

There's a temptation to look back on Dick Vitale's reign as coach of the Pistons and insist it was a good idea at the time. But that would be revisionism and it would be incorrect. For all of Vitale's politicking in the newspapers and high-decibel grandstanding, it was a classic bamboozle that hoodwinked an ownership group fearfully envisioning miles of empty Silverdome seats. Few coaches before or since have been less qualified to take over an NBA team, even one with a coaching pedigree as lousy as Detroit's was then.

When the Pistons hired Vitale on May 1, 1978, essentially bowing to fans' sentiment, there were few reasons to believe he could succeed, despite his fine restoration of the University of Detroit program. The Pistons' star, Bob Lanier, was aging and gimp-kneed, the team was without a first-round pick in the coming draft and there was a dearth of marketable players on the roster. Even worse, Vitale had resigned from the U-of-D job in '77 because of stomach trouble; if that kicked up again—it soon did—it could quickly derail the entire Vitale era and further delay the Pistons' needed overhaul.

Though Vitale overcame a five-day hospital stay after only three games and survived his debut season (30-52), his tenure ended predictably only 12 games into the second year. By mutual agreement, Vitale re-signed November 8, 1979, though he stuck around for one more practice so he could tell his team goodbye, an honest, genuine act by Vitale. The firing/resignation was a tacit admission that the Vitale hiring had been a mistake, but there was little malice in the switch; the front office, in fact, had grown concerned for Vitale's welfare because he took losing so hard. He admitted as much on the day he quit: "That was the one quality I lacked, the losing end of it. That's my personality. I hate failure. I totally despise it."

The hangover of the Dick Vitale era would last long after he moved on to become one of TV's most popular—and imitated—basketball commentators for ESPN and ABC. Vitale's infatuation with a declining Bob McAdoo would haunt the club for a decade. The acquisition squandered valuable Pistons assets, which the Celtics parlayed into one of the greatest front lines in NBA history. Then, though he had stolen Terry Tyler and John Long in the second round in '78, Vitale oversaw one of the lousiest drafts ever in '79. The Pistons had the fourth, 10th and 15th picks and Vitale drafted Greg Kelser, Roy Hamilton and Phil Hubbard, rejecting players like Sidney Moncrief, Vinnie Johnson and Jim Paxson.

Vitale's best work for the Pistons might've been his parting advice to Davidson, in which he told the owner he needed to hire a "basketball man" as general manager. "I told him, 'You have to bring in somebody who has a tremendous basketball background to make the day-to-day decisions,'" Vitale said. Jack McCloskey would soon be hired to clear away the rubble and finally set the team on course to championship status.

CHANGING FACES

ANYBODY WHO'S BEEN to the Silverdome knows there are revolving doors all over. Dick Vitale and the Pistons kept them spinning in '78-79, going through 20 players to set a team record that hasn't been matched. They also went through one general manager as Bob Kauffman quit July 14, 1978, a month after Vitale invested second-round picks in guard John Long and forward Terry Tyler, two of his former U-of-D stars. Both played well, though, as Tyler made the All-Rookie team and finished second on the Pistons in rebounds, and Long averaged 16.1 points. From the start, Vitale began to fiddle with his roster, getting back point guard Kevin Porter from New Jersey. Then during a ragged start, he sent co-captain Chris Ford to the Celtics for guard Earl Tatum. Other swaps brought in Rickey Green, Otis Howard and Jim Brewer, while a parade of castoffs and free agents also trouped through town: Ron Behagen, Larry McNeill, Dennis Boyd, Steve Sheppard, Andre Wakefield, Essie Hollis and Bubbles Hawkins.

The Pistons acquired guard Earl Tatum from the Boston Celtics, trading away popular co-captain Chris Ford after an 0-3 start.

Take a Bow

Kevin Porter

When Kevin Porter signed with Washington after '78-79, Detroit got two first-round picks as compensation.

In his second chance as a Piston, point guard Kevin Porter completed a trifecta. Having won NBA assist titles with Washington (1975) and New Jersey (1978), Porter was reacquired by Detroit on September 8, coming back in a trade for Eric Money. He did not disappoint, again leading the NBA in assists while setting a record with 1,099. The old league mark was 910 by Kansas City's Nate Archibald in '72-73, but Porter passed that figure March 17 with 12 games to go by passing for 20 vs. Indiana. He played in all 82 games, leading Detroit in assists in 80 of them and averaging 13.4. Going into the season, Porter held the Pistons' single-game record of 20 assists on November 20, 1976, but he destroyed that mark as well. He dealt 25 on March 9 in a 160-117 victory over Boston, then matched the total April 1 at Phoenix. Of Detroit's 19 all-time games of at least 20 assists, Porter has 10 (nine in '78-79) and Isiah Thomas nine. Porter wouldn't last long in Detroit this time, going back to Washington as a free agent July 12, 1979.

Game Results

1978-79 REGULAR SEASON

Date	Opponent	Result	Record
10-13	NEW JERSEY	L, 105-107	0-1
10-14	at Atlanta	L, 114-122	0-2
10-17	at New Orleans	L, 108-114	0-3
10-20	PHILADELPHIA	L, 117-126	0-4
10-21	at Washington	L, 99-119	0-5
10-25	CLEVELAND	W, 110-105	1-5
10-27	KANSAS CITY	W, 107-102	2-5
10-28	at San Antonio	L, 126-150	2-6
10-31	at Portland	L, 96-112	2-7
11-2	SEATTLE	L, 94-95	2-8
11-3	at Chicago	W, 99-93	3-8
11-4	GOLDEN STATE	L, 95-103	3-9
11-8	MILWAUKEE	W, 117-106	4-9
11-10	CHICAGO	W, 115-101	5-9
11-11	at Philadelphia	L, 112-135	5-10
11-12	at Boston	W, 128-123	6-10
11-15	L.A. LAKERS	L, 126-133	6-11
11-18	PHOENIX	L, 105-119	6-12
11-21	at New York	L, 79-96	6-13
11-24	ATLANTA	W, 119-117 (OT)	7-13
11-28	at L.A. Lakers	W, 105-103	8-13
11-30	at Phoenix	L, 109-119	8-14
12-1	at Denver	L, 120-125	8-15
12-2	at San Diego	W, 120-113	9-15
12-5	BOSTON	L, 112-114	9-16
12-7	CLEVELAND	W, 121-105	10-16
12-8	at Indiana	L, 107-114	10-17
12-9	at Kansas City	L, 108-132	10-18
12-12	at Cleveland	L, 110-127	10-19
12-15	WASHINGTON	L, 114-116	10-20
12-21	INDIANA	W, 121-108	11-20
12-23	SAN ANTONIO	L, 126-130	11-21
12-26	at Milwaukee	L, 84-143	11-22
12-27	HOUSTON	W, 131-119	12-22
12-29	SAN DIEGO	L, 107-111	12-23
12-30	at Houston	L, 101-112	12-24
1-2	at San Diego	L, 119-137	12-25
1-3	at Golden State	L, 81-96	12-26
1-5	at Portland	L, 96-98	12-27
1-9	at San Antonio	L, 114-116	12-28
1-11	PORTLAND	W, 104-101	13-28
1-13	GOLDEN STATE	W, 114-109	14-28
1-16	at New York	L, 110-111	14-29
1-17	at New Jersey	L, 99-106	14-30
1-18	PHOENIX	L, 87-97	14-31
1-20	KANSAS CITY	W, 122-110	15-31
1-22	at Denver	W, 121-117	16-31
1-25	L.A. LAKERS	W, 135-100	17-31
1-28	SAN DIEGO	W, 128-118	18-31
1-31	NEW YORK	L, 86-108	18-32
2-1	at Cleveland	W, 120-116	19-32
2-2	at Kansas City	L, 114-130	19-33
2-6	at Houston	L, 108-113	19-34
2-7	at Philadelphia	L, 103-114	19-35
2-8	NEW JERSEY	L, 105-106	19-36
2-10	NEW ORLEANS	L, 105-107	19-37
2-14	DENVER	W, 111-107	20-37
2-16	HOUSTON	W, 110-96	21-37
2-18	SAN ANTONIO	W, 124-104	22-37
2-21	PHILADELPHIA	W, 106-99 (OT)	23-37
2-25	PORTLAND	L, 119-126 (OT)	23-38
2-27	at Chicago	L, 117-124	23-39
3-3	NEW ORLEANS	W, 110-101	24-39
3-7	SEATTLE	L, 93-99	24-40
3-9	BOSTON	W, 160-117	25-40
3-11	at Milwaukee	W, 125-115	26-40
3-13	at Indiana	L, 120-122 (OT)	26-41
3-15	NEW YORK	W, 88-83	27-41
3-16	at Boston	L, 98-99	27-42
3-17	INDIANA	W, 105-98	28-42
3-20	at New Jersey	L, 110-117	28-43
3-21	at Atlanta	L, 104-111	28-44
3-23	WASHINGTON	W, 124-114	29-44
3-25	at Washington	L, 107-116	29-45
3-28	DENVER	L, 110-115	29-46
3-30	at L.A. Lakers	L, 113-124	29-47
3-31	at Seattle	L, 102-123	29-48
4-1	at Phoenix	L, 105-116	29-49
4-3	at Golden State	L, 100-104	29-50
4-5	at New Orleans	W, 120-104	30-50
4-6	ATLANTA	L, 96-112	30-51
4-8	CHICAGO	L, 107-117	30-52

(Home games in CAPS)

PISTONS' LOGOS AND UNIFORMS

1996-present

1978-96

1972-78

1966-72

1963-66

1958-63

1957-58

Artistically speaking, what can you do with a Piston?

That question had nagged the club for years as it attempted to revamp its primary logo, uniform and color scheme. The Pistons' red, white and blue basketball design had served them in four incarnations since 1962 but had grown tiresome.

"It was a lousy logo, but it was ours," said Tom Wilson, Palace Sports and Entertainment president.

Besides, when you have an old logo, it's hard to sell new merchandise; everyone's closet is already full.

But the question remained: What can you do with a Piston? How do you draw a logo that's attractive and incorporates the Pistons' name, while departing far enough from the previous block-letter design?

Finally, in the summer of 1996, that question was answered when the Pistons unveiled their modern new look to rave reviews. Following a horse power theme, the logo prominently shows a black and silver horse with a flaming orange mane. The horse is set against a red basketball with a ring of teal. Each "s" in "Pistons" forms a flame-spitting exhaust pipe.

With the new logo came uniforms of white (home) and teal (road) that feature stylishly baggy shorts and three-color piping.

The design was developed by Detroit-area artist Robin Brant and "Bad Boys" merchandising guru Bill Berris. It was selected from hundreds of prototypes submitted over a five-year period.

"It's like a piece of art—you aren't sure what you're looking for until you see it," Wilson said. "We like this logo a lot."

The team's earlier logos and uniforms leaned to the conservative side, the most daring being its original Piston-man logo, a smiling, animated character built totally from pistons. That ball-handling logo lasted one season, 1957-58, giving way to a dubious design that included a ball, a net

and a piston with a face carved in it. That survived five seasons.

In 1963, the logo was revamped into a basketball design which lasted—in four variations—until the horse power design replaced it in 1996. The first two circular designs promoted the Detroit Pistons Basketball Club, followed in '72 by a design that added NBA to the banner. In '78 it was changed to a solid red basketball with a blue outer ring.

The Pistons' new uniforms are a wild departure from their lackluster precursors. Their jerseys didn't deviate much from the '50s to the late '70s, usually using blue block letters and numbers on a plain background. Occasionally, "Pistons" was spelled in script. Though minor changes to the red and blue piping were made every couple of seasons, the Pistons' uniform did not become jazzy until Dick Vitale arrived as coach in '78. Players still wore "Pistons" on their chests, but the type style became a lightning bolt motif.

The uniforms were again restyled in '82, switching to a clean, block-letter concept that survived essentially untouched until '96. Except for the material, that is. The early '80s uniforms were a shiny gray, satin-like material that looked wonderful, as long as it stayed dry. But after the players got sweaty, the gray would turn a blotchy blue. Changing to cotton eventually made amends for that fashion faux pas.

In 1995, the Pistons added a new wrinkle. Instead of their usual road blues, they wore a red uniform for 15 games; it was rather popular, but not nearly so well-liked as their horse power transformation in '96.

"If you look good, you feel good. And maybe you play good, too," Grant Hill said at the introductory fashion show.

Based on the Pistons' 1996-97 success, that statement couldn't have been more prescient.

Harry Gallatin, 1957

Dave Bing, 1969

John Mengelt, 1975

Ben Poquette, 1979

Sean Elliott, 1993

Lindsey Hunter, 1997

"TRADER JACK" McCLOSKEY

The Pistons had us fooled all along. They kept saying Rick Mahorn was the Baddest of the Bad Boys. Or Bill Laimbeer. Of even Isiah Thomas. But it was all a clever ruse. The toughest of the bunch was Jack McCloskey: decorated veteran, general manager extraordinaire and the architect of a two-time NBA championship team.

After his hiring by the Pistons on December 11, 1979, replacing interim GM Oscar Feldman, McCloskey left no stone unturned to rebuild the team in his competitive image. Soon after his arrival, he offered his entire roster—not just any Piston, but all 12 at once—to the L.A. Lakers for rookie guard Magic Johnson. They turned him down, but the word was out: the Pistons had an aggressive (if inexperienced) new man in the big chair.

Until McCloskey left Detroit under somewhat unhappy circumstances in 1992, taking over as GM of the Minnesota Timberwolves, he oversaw the acquisition of 80 Pistons. Sure, that list includes the likes of Jim Zoet, Brook Steppe, Jeff Judkins and Norman Black (who?). But it's also highlighted by terrific draft picks such as Thomas, Kelly Tripucka, Joe Dumars and Dennis Rodman. It includes excellent trade additions like Laimbeer, Vinnie Johnson, Adrian Dantley, James Edwards, Mark Aguirre and Mahorn. Swaps like those—often risky, but one-sided in retrospect—earned McCloskey the nickname "Trader Jack." As GMs go, his batting average might have been lower than most, but only because he stepped to the plate more than fellow execs who couldn't match his courage.

"A lot of guys like to hide behind the salary cap. They say it prevents them from making trades, but the truth is they just don't want to take risks," McCloskey said. "I have never hesitated to make a trade if I felt it would improve our ball club. Even with all the trades we have made, we could have gambled on a lot more. But we would've been making mistakes."

Toward that end, McCloskey's strength wasn't merely spotting talent and acquiring it. He was also equipped with the self-assuredness (read: guts) to admit a failed trade and attempt to remedy it. With the maddening exception of center William Bedford, a 7-footer of marvelous potential and boundless immaturity, McCloskey was usually able to confront his mistakes. Realizing he'd erred in trading for aging power forward Dan Roundfield in 1984, McCloskey turned the deal in his favor a year later by swapping Roundfield to Washington for Mahorn. In 1989, sensing the Pistons had hit a plateau with Dantley as their offensive centerpiece, McCloskey traded his No. 1 scorer in the midst of a championship drive. He sent Dantley and a first-round pick to Dallas for Aguirre, himself a high-maintenance scoring forward. Pistons fans feared McCloskey had tinkered too much this time—and it could have blown up in his face—but with Aguirre playing an agreeable supporting role, Detroit won the next two NBA titles.

"Sometimes, winners are losers who just won't quit," McCloskey said in addressing fans at the 1989 celebration. Though never stuck with a loser's tag despite failing badly at Portland in his only NBA head coaching job, McCloskey built his career on a

AT A GLANCE

JACK McCLOSKEY

FULL NAME:
John William McCloskey
BORN:
September 19, 1925; Mahoney City, Pennsylvania
POSITION, HEIGHT, WEIGHT:
Guard, 6-foot-2, 190 pounds
COLLEGE:
Pennsylvania '48

GM TENURE WITH PISTONS:
December 11, 1979 – May 29, 1992
Also: Minnesota 1992-95
NBA COACHING CAREER:
Portland 1972-74, 48-116 (.296)
Also: L.A. Lakers assistant 1976-79, Indiana assistant 1979
NBA PLAYING CAREER:
Philadelphia, 1952-53, 1 GP, 6 pts, 3 reb, 1 ast.
Also: Sunbury (EBL)
COLLEGE COACHING CAREER:
Pennsylvania 1956-66, Wake Forest, 1966-72

never-quit attitude. It was a toughness ingrained in his youth in coal-mining Eastern Pennsylvania and his World War II experiences in the Pacific. The son of a miner in Mahoney City, Pennsylvania, McCloskey became a 19-year-old skipper of a Naval landing craft (LCT) and was part of the Okinawa and Iwo Jima invasions. Though he abhorred the war, he found the duty and comaraderie stimulating. He later discovered war parallels in the more mundane NBA. "We were sitting in Boston one time, the coaches and myself, a half-hour before a game," he said. "It was quiet in the locker room and I said, 'This sounds ridiculous, but this is just like waiting to hit the beach. After the battle ships bomb it and the planes hit it, it's your turn."

After the war, McCloskey graduated from Penn in 1948 and played for eight years in the pre-NBA American and Eastern leagues, gaining two MVP awards in the latter. In 1952-53, he played his lone NBA game for the Philadelphia Warriors, compiling six points (3-of-9 shooting) and three boards in 16 minutes. But McCloskey's future was as a coach. He put in 10 seasons as Penn's head man (1956-66), winning the Ivy League in his final season, then six seasons (1966-72) reviving a moribund Wake Forest program. In that time, he developed a reputation as a hands-on coach with an unmatched competitive drive. His success led to an NBA break as coach at Portland, where he took over an 18-win team owning the No. 1 draft pick in 1972. But McCloskey was doomed from the start, evidenced when the Blazers' owner overruled his preferred draftee, Bob McAdoo, to select Loyola center LaRue Martin, one of the great busts of all-time. Also, McCloskey's stars, Sidney Wicks and Geoff Petrie, didn't get along. After two seasons, he was fired with a 48-116 record.

After staying away from the game for two years, McCloskey was hired as an assistant with the Lakers for three years and Indiana for one before Pistons owner Bill Davidson hired him as GM in 1979. On his first day, McCloskey was already hinting at what was to come: "I won't make any impulsive trades, but I think within a two-week period, I should know each player and who has interest in our players." Within a month, peppery guard Ron Lee was acquired from Atlanta. On February 4, 1980, McCloskey granted Bob Lanier's wish, trading the veteran center to Milwaukee for Kent Benson.

Within barely two years, McCloskey acquired the makings of the two-time champi-

ons through the draft and excellent trades. Equipped with two first-round picks in 1981, he drafted Thomas second and Tripucka 12th. In the first month of the '81-82 season, he got Johnson from Seattle for Greg Kelser, then on February 16, only minutes before the annual trade deadline, he got Laimbeer and Kenny Carr from Cleveland for Phil Hubbard, Paul Mokeski and draft picks. Those swaps rank as two of his greatest, so miniscule was the cost. McCloskey's hiring of coach Chuck Daly in 1983 solidified the bench and his drafting of Dumars (18th) in '85 was a stroke of genius, as was the second-round pick-up of Rodman in '86. Drafting John Salley and acquiring Mahorn, Dantley, Edwards and Aguirre were his final

major moves to build the championship nucleus. So eager was McCloskey to see the job through, he passed up a multi-million-dollar offer in 1987 to take over the Knicks' front office.

McCloskey's loyalty and go-for-broke style played well with fans, who cheered him as loudly as any player at the championship rallies. In fact, he was largely criticism-free throughout his 13-year tenure in Detroit. But in 1992, he was badly stung by criticism from Laimbeer, who said McCloskey had wrecked the Pistons' "family atmosphere" by giving newcomer Orlando Woolridge a new contract at the expense of longer-serving players. The furor played a big role in McCloskey's decision to quit on May 29, 1992.

The Blueprint

As the Pistons' general manager from 1979-92, Jack McCloskey oversaw construction of their back-to-back NBA champions. Here is a list of his major transactions:

- January 25, 1980 — Obtained Ron Lee and 1980 second- and third-round picks from Atlanta Hawks for James McElroy.
- February 4, 1980 — Obtained Kent Benson and 1980 first-round pick from Milwaukee Bucks for Bob Lanier.
- November 21, 1981 — Obtained Vinnie Johnson from Seattle SuperSonics for Greg Kelser.
- February 16, 1982 — Obtained Bill Laimbeer and Kenny Carr from Cleveland Cavaliers for Phil Hubbard, Paul Mokeski and Pistons' 1982 first- and second-round picks.
- June 18, 1984 — Obtained Dan Roundfield from Atlanta Hawks for Cliff Levington, rights to Pistons' No. 1 pick Antoine Carr and two second-round picks.
- June 17, 1985 — Obtained Rick Mahorn and Mike Gibson from Washington Bullets for Dan Roundfield.
- August 21, 1986 — Obtained Adrian Dantley and second-round picks in 1987 and 1990 from Utah Jazz for Kelly Tripucka and Kent Benson.
- January 29, 1987 — Obtained Kurt Nimphius from Los Angeles Clippers for Pistons' 1987 first-round pick and an acquired 1987 second-round pick.
- June 22, 1987 — Obtained William Bedford from Phoenix Suns for Pistons' 1988 first-round pick.
- November 26, 1987 — Obtained Darryl Dawkins from Utah Jazz for 1988 second-round pick.
- February 24, 1988 — Obtained James Edwards from Phoenix Suns for Ron Moore and 1991 second-round pick.
- February 15, 1989 — Obtained Mark Aguirre from Dallas Mavericks for Adrian Dantley and Pistons' 1991 first-round pick.
- August 13, 1991 — Obtained Orlando Woolridge from Denver Nuggets for Scott Hastings and Pistons' 1992 second-round pick; obtained Jeff Martin and second-round pick from L.A. Clippers for James Edwards.
- September 4, 1991 — Vinnie Johnson waived; obtained Darrell Walker from Washington Bullets for second-round picks in 1993 and 1995.

1979 DETROIT PISTONS 1980

TIME CAPSULE

November 4, 1979:
Iranian revolutionaries seize the U.S. embassy in Teheran, taking 90 hostages, including 65 Americans.

February 22, 1980:
The U.S. hockey team beats the heavily favored Soviet Union 4-3 at Lake Placid, New York, setting up a gold-medal win over Finland on February 24.

May 18, 1980:
Mount St. Helens in Washington erupts for the first time since 1857, leveling about 120 square miles of forest.

SEASON SNAPSHOT

Most Points
Bob McAdoo (1,222, 21.1 avg.)

Most Rebounds
Terry Tyler (627, 7.6 avg.)

Most Assists
Eric Money (238, 4.3 avg.)

Most Minutes
M.L. Carr (2,670, 32.6 avg.)

Field-Goal Percentage
Eric Money (50.8%)

Free-Throw Percentage
John Long (82.5%)

Team Offense Average
108.9 (8,933 in 82 games)

Team Defense Average
117.2 (9,609 in 82 games)

1979-80

FINAL STANDINGS

Central Division	W	L	Pct.	GB
Atlanta	50	32	.610	—
Houston	41	41	.500	9
San Antonio	41	41	.500	9
Cleveland	37	45	.451	13
Indiana	37	45	.451	13
PISTONS	**16**	**66**	**.366**	**34**

Atlantic Division Winner—Boston
Midwest Division Winner—Milwaukee
Pacific Division Winner—Los Angeles

PLAYOFF RESULTS

Pistons Did Not Qualify

PISTONS PLAYOFF LEADERS

NBA CHAMPION

Los Angeles Lakers

1979-80
SEASON IN REVIEW

If you eventually win an NBA title, as the Pistons did, it's easier to look back on a season like 1979-80 and grin. But while you're living it, your pride is deeply wounded. The Pistons bottomed out in almost every fashion, going 16-66 (.195) for their worst record ever, while suffering a season-ending 14-game losing streak after the trading of Bob Lanier. The season was a mess before it started. Doomed coach Dick Vitale emerged from the spring draft with little to show for three top 15 picks, then acquired unhappy forward Bob McAdoo on September 6. Things only got worse. Vitale was dismissed November 8, replaced for the last 70 games by assistant Richie Adubato. As the club rode a slippery slope to embarrassment—separate losing skids of five, eight, seven, 13 and 14; a 2-29 record after January 26; a 3-38 road mark with losing streaks of 13, 12 and 13—there was nothing left but to start over. Lanier, realizing he'd never win an NBA title in Detroit, begged for liberation. He was indulged February 4 when newly hired GM Jack McCloskey dealt Detroit's all-time scoring and rebounding king to Milwaukee for Kent Benson and a first-rounder—pennies on the dollar, really. Oft-injured and occasionally interested, McAdoo led the club in scoring (21.1) before also demanding a trade. He'd have to wait; hiring a coach was No. 1 on McCloskey's Things-To-Do list.

Ill-fated Dick Vitale draws up a play during a timeout while assistant Richie Adubato looks on. Adubato would fare no better as head coach.

November 9, 1979

WHAT A NIGHT!

Coach Dick Vitale had been fired the day before, replaced by assistant Richie Adubato. The Pistons were struggling along at 4-8, with Julius Erving invading the Silverdome to compound their misery. And the club's marketing wizards—eager for a crowd over 10,000—had planned an anti-disco promotion. November 9, 1979 could've been an explosive night for the Pistons. Turns out, it was one of their 16 victories, a deserved 106-98 win over the Philadelphia 76ers before an enthusiastic house of 13,180. The surprising aspect was that Detroit won by playing energetic defense, a serious shortcoming under the frazzled Vitale. Guarded mostly by Terry Tyler, Erving was held to 13 points, well below his average, on 4-of-13 field-goal shooting. "This is the first game that we collectively played defense," Bob Lanier said after his 26-point effort. "Defense was the key. We buckled down," said Adubato, who figured his coaching tenure would last a week, but finished out the season. James McElroy scored 20 points for Detroit and Bob McAdoo supplied team-highs in rebounds (14) and assists (six). Doug Collins had 21 points to lead Philly. Incidentally, the anti-disco festivities produced no incidents—another shocker.

Philly's Doug Collins shoots over Pistons forward Terry Tyler on November 9, 1979.

John Long

John Long is the uncle of '90s Pistons forwards Terry Mills and Grant Long.

OK, the Pistons didn't have a first-round pick, but was that any reason for Dick Vitale to use up their second-rounders to give NBA jobs to his buddies from the University of Detroit? That wasn't really the case, of course, but that's how it seemed during the 1978 draft. Vitale, one year removed from coaching U-of-D, used the 23rd pick on Titans forward Terry Tyler. Fair enough. Tyler had averaged 15 points and 10.4 rebounds in his college career. But then with the 29th pick, Vitale took 6-foot-5 Titans guard John Long, and something smelled fishy. It had to seem like he hadn't done his homework and was simply reaching for two convenient players. But it soon became clear that Vitale wasn't throwing a bone to his favorites, because both of them could play. Long, who had broken Dave DeBusschere's career scoring mark at U-of-D with 2,167 points, was an immediate NBA standout. Playing all 82 games and starting 60, he placed second among rookies with a 16.1-point average. Thus began a 10-year association with the Pistons (in three stints) and a 14-year career in which he scored 12,131 points. "John Eddie" was an outstanding perimeter shooter—TV-radio voice George Blaha dubbed his jump shot the "rock-set"—and a sturdy offensive rebounder. He was also Detroit's annual leader in free-throw percentage, setting a club record of 88.4 in '83-84 when he made 51 in a row, then a team mark. Long twice led Detroit in scoring, had three 40-point games and compiled a 15.9-point average in his original eight-year stay. But his role lessened with Joe Dumars' arrival in '85 and he was traded to Seattle on September 30, 1986. He returned in '89 to be a part of the Pistons' first championship team.

AT A GLANCE

JOHN LONG

FULL NAME:
John Eddie Long
BORN:
August 28, 1956; Romulus, Michigan
POSITION, HEIGHT, WEIGHT:
Guard, 6-foot-5, 200 pounds
COLLEGE:
Detroit '78
ACQUIRED:
Drafted, second round, 1978 (29th overall)
1989, signed as free agent
1991, signed as free agent

TENURE WITH PISTONS:
1978-79 – 1985-86; 1989; 1991
Also: Indiana 1986-89, Atlanta 1989-90, Toronto 1996-97
BEST SEASON WITH PISTONS:
1979-80, 69 GP, 19.4 ppg, 4.9 rpg, 3.0 apg
TOTALS WITH PISTONS:
Regular season: 608 GP, 14.8 ppg, 3.1 apg
Playoffs: 19 GP, 9.4 ppg, 1.5 apg
HONORS:
NBA All-Rookie: 1978-79 (Second Team)

PISTON LIST

Worst Season Records (By Percentage)

- 1979-80, 16-66 (.195)
- 1993-94, 20-62 (.244)
- 1980-81, 21-61 (.256)
- 1965-66, 22-58 (.275)
- 1963-64, 23-57 (.288)
- 1971-72, 26-56 (.317)
- 1994-95, 28-54 (.341)
- 1978-79, 30-52 (.366)
- 1966-67, 30-51 (.370)
- 1969-70, 31-51 (.378)
- 1964-65, 31-49 (.388)
- 1958-59, 28-44 (.389)
- 1968-69, 32-50 (.390)
- 1959-60, 30-45 (.400)

CHANGING FACES

THE PISTONS waited too long to fire coach Dick Vitale and too long to hire GM Jack McCloskey. Had they done both immediately after '78-79, their climb out of the NBA cellar might not have been so painful. Vitale was fired November 8, but not before overseeing some of the worst decisions in club history. All McCloskey could do after his December 11 hiring was comb the rubble for heirlooms; he found none, immediately notifying the other 21 teams that all Pistons were available, even the great Bob Lanier. Vitale's misadventures as the de facto GM resulted in a miserable draft. Armed with the fourth, 10th and 15th picks, he took Greg Kelser, washout Roy Hamilton and hobbling Phil Hubbard. He even gave Milwaukee $50,000 for the No. 4 slot to make sure he got Kelser; the Bucks had wanted Sidney Moncrief anyway. In Vitale's worst move, he acquired moody scorer Bob McAdoo from Boston on September 6 for two first-rounders, also surrendering any compensation due for the Celtics' signing of free agent M.L. Carr. Boston parlayed the picks into Kevin McHale and Robert Parish.

Bob McAdoo was four years removed from his '74-75 league MVP award when the Pistons acquired him, at great cost, in 1979.

Take a Bow

Greg "Special K" Kelser

Greg Kelser, a multi-talented star at Michigan State, was the Pistons' top draftee in 1979.

There is no telling how good Greg Kelser's NBA career would have been if he'd stayed healthy. He was the Pistons' top draft choice in 1979, a versatile 6-foot-7 forward drafted fourth after a terrific NCAA championship season at Michigan State. The early returns were terrific as the Detroit native averaged 14.2 points and 5.5 rebounds to gain All-Rookie support. Two stints on the injured list with a bad ankle sprain limited him to 50 games, but he scored 34 points (his career high, as it turned out) in a February 9 loss at New York. Kelser also averaged almost 24 points and 11 boards over the final six games of the season. But he couldn't carry over his good luck. Early in '80-81, he suffered knee tendinitis that limited him to 25 games. The Pistons even traded him to Seattle on December 16, 1980, but Kelser failed the physical, killing the swap. He underwent knee surgery March 6, 1981, enabling the productive trade for Seattle's Vinnie Johnson eight months later. One of the NBA's all-time nice guys, Kelser has been a Pistons TV-radio commentator since 1992.

Game Results

1979-80 REGULAR SEASON

Date	Opponent	Result	Record
10-12	INDIANA	W, 114-105	1-0
10-13	at San Antonio	W, 112-110	2-0
10-16	at Cleveland	L, 117-137	2-1
10-18	NEW YORK	W, 129-115	3-1
10-19	at Philadelphia	L, 104-112	3-2
10-20	at Washington	L, 106-117	3-3
10-24	WASHINGTON	W, 104-103	4-3
10-26	SAN ANTONIO	L, 113-129	4-4
10-27	at Milwaukee	L, 118-132	4-5
11-1	CLEVELAND	L, 125-127	4-6
11-3	HOUSTON	L, 111-114	4-7
11-7	ATLANTA	L, 107-115	4-8
11-9	PHILADELPHIA	W, 106-98	5-8
11-10	at Houston	L, 104-112	5-9
11-14	at Boston	L, 111-115	5-10
11-17	NEW JERSEY	L, 93-98	5-11
11-20	at Atlanta	L, 105-109	5-12
11-21	UTAH	W, 98-93	6-12
11-23	MILWAUKEE	W, 119-100	7-12
11-24	at Indiana	L, 97-115	7-13
11-27	at New York	L, 114-116 (OT)	7-14
11-28	at New Jersey	L, 89-98	7-15
11-29	KANSAS CITY	L, 95-105	7-16
12-1	SAN ANTONIO	W, 134-124	8-16
12-4	BOSTON	L, 114-118 (OT)	8-17
12-5	at Kansas City	L, 93-109	8-18
12-7	at Houston	L, 109-124	8-19
12-8	at Indiana	L, 102-103	8-20
12-12	at Golden State	W, 114-96	9-20
12-14	at L.A. Lakers	L, 122-138	9-21
12-15	at Phoenix	L, 105-126	9-22
12-16	at San Diego	L, 126-133	9-23
12-18	PHILADELPHIA	L, 102-114	9-24
12-20	ATLANTA	L, 103-122	9-25
12-22	at San Antonio	L, 112-141	9-26
12-25	at Cleveland	L, 101-111	9-27
12-26	INDIANA	L, 97-98	9-28
12-28	DENVER	W, 114-98	10-28
12-29	at Atlanta	L, 104-115	10-29
1-2	at Denver	L, 116-135	10-30
1-4	at Seattle	L, 105-123	10-31
1-6	at Portland	L, 102-119	10-32
1-8	at Utah	L, 110-124	10-33
1-11	L.A. LAKERS	L, 100-123	10-34
1-12	at Indiana	L, 109-122	10-35
1-13	CHICAGO	W, 107-102	11-35
1-17	WASHINGTON	W, 110-107	12-35
1-19	HOUSTON	W, 122-110	13-35
1-22	at Chicago	L, 131-145	13-36
1-23	BOSTON	L, 104-131	13-37
1-25	at New Jersey	W, 119-116	14-37
1-27	NEW YORK	L, 93-98	14-38
1-29	GOLDEN STATE	L, 100-111	14-39
1-30	at Philadelphia	L, 108-122	14-40
2-7	SEATTLE	L, 102-119	14-41
2-9	at New York	L, 107-114	14-42
2-10	at Boston	L, 111-128	14-43
2-13	CLEVELAND	L, 102-107	14-44
2-15	PHILADELPHIA	L, 104-114	14-45
2-16	at Cleveland	L, 104-123	14-46
2-17	ATLANTA	L, 99-108	14-47
2-21	PHOENIX	L, 116-125	14-48
2-23	PORTLAND	L, 107-130	14-49
2-27	SAN DIEGO	L, 113-129	14-50
2-29	NEW JERSEY	W, 137-128 (OT)	15-50
3-2	at Boston	L, 115-118	15-51
3-4	at Washington	L, 107-135	15-52
3-5	NEW YORK	W, 120-113	16-52
3-7	WASHINGTON	L, 105-106	16-53
3-8	at New York	L, 104-110	16-54
3-9	at New Jersey	L, 100-140	16-55
3-12	NEW JERSEY	L, 119-137	16-56
3-14	SAN ANTONIO	L, 102-113	16-57
3-16	HOUSTON	L, 99-102	16-58
3-17	at Philadelphia	L, 109-123	16-59
3-18	CLEVELAND	L, 107-108 (OT)	16-60
3-20	BOSTON	L, 106-124	16-61
3-21	at Atlanta	L, 95-108	16-62
3-23	at Washington	L, 114-119	16-63
3-26	INDIANA	L, 114-124	16-64
3-28	at Houston	L, 112-128	16-65
3-30	at San Antonio	L, 124-144	16-66

(Home games in CAPS)

1980 🏀 1981

DETROIT PISTONS

TIME CAPSULE

November 21, 1980:
More than half of America's television audience tunes in "Dallas" to find out "Who Shot J.R.?"

January 20, 1981:
The Iranian hostage crisis ends on President Reagan's inauguration day, as Iran releases American captives seized 14 months earlier.

April 14, 1981:
Following its 54-hour maiden voyage, the space shuttle Columbia successfully touches down on Earth.

SEASON SNAPSHOT

Most Points
John Long (1,044, 17.7 avg.)

Most Rebounds
Phil Hubbard (586, 7.3 avg.)

Most Assists
Ron Lee (362, 4.4 avg.)

Most Minutes
Terry Tyler (2,549, 31.1 avg.)

Field-Goal Percentage
Terry Tyler (53.2%)

Free-Throw Percentage
John Long (87.0%)

Team Offense Average
99.7 (8,174 in 82 games)

Team Defense Average
106.0 (8,692 in 82 games)

1980-81

FINAL STANDINGS

Central Division	W	L	Pct.	GB
Milwaukee	60	22	.732	—
Chicago	45	37	.549	15
Indiana	44	38	.537	16
Atlanta	31	51	.378	29
Cleveland	28	54	.341	32
PISTONS	**21**	**61**	**.256**	**39**

Atlantic Division Winner—Boston
Midwest Division Winner—San Antonio
Pacific Division Winner—Phoenix

PLAYOFF RESULTS

Pistons Did Not Qualify

PISTONS PLAYOFF LEADERS

NBA CHAMPION

Boston Celtics

1980-81
SEASON IN REVIEW

The Pistons' climb out of the basement wouldn't begin in earnest for another year, when a certain cherubic guard from Indiana arrived on the scene. But the groundwork was laid in 1980-81, and not simply because Detroit's 21-61 finish accorded it the second pick in the draft. With GM Jack McCloskey firmly in control, the Pistons began putting pieces in place. Scotty Robertson, 12-29 in two NBA coaching stints, was chosen to take over when coach Richie Adubato wasn't retained. Robertson was hired after a Sixers assistant, Chuck Daly, turned down the job. "I came here to win," Robertson announced, but there wasn't much of that, as the Pistons lost their first seven games, then fell to 2-12 and 9-24. Their lineup was simply too thin to compete, and injuries to John Long, Bob McAdoo and Kent Benson made it worse. Disgruntled and politicking for a trade, McAdoo played in six games before going on the injured list for the rest of the season. That is, until he was waived March 21, delighting many in the organization. Second-year forward Phil Hubbard, the ex-Michigan star, led the Pistons in points (1,161) and Long had the highest scoring average (17.7), including Detroit's first 40-point game in three years. First-round point guard Larry Drew showed little. He would soon be superseded by a marvelous 20-year-old wunderkind.

Phil Hubbard led the Pistons in total points and rebounds in a downcast '80-81 season.

WHAT A NIGHT!

March 27, 1981

The Pistons were going to mail in the rest of the season. That's how it looked, anyway. There were two games to go and they had lost their last four, including a 39-point blowout two nights before at Philadelphia (114-75). The last thing anyone expected was the Pistons to play hard in Game 81 at Boston Garden, let alone win, especially with the Celtics fighting the 76ers for the NBA's best record and playoff home court. But the Pistons hammered the Celtics, using a 12-0 first-quarter run to breeze to a 115-90 win, their 21st against 60 losses. Detroit had a 30-17 lead after the first quarter and remained in control. "Our guys showed some pride tonight," coach Scotty Robertson said. "This was our biggest win of the year. We had a meeting yesterday after getting blown out and I knew we'd come back with a good showing." Terry Tyler had 27 points off the bench, John Long 20 and Kent Benson 19 for the Pistons. Larry Bird's 14 led the Celtics, who faced a winner-take-all finale vs. the 76ers two days later. Boston won it, tying Philly with a 62-20 mark and gaining the home court edge via the tie-breaker. It served the Celtics well en route to the NBA championship, their first since 1976.

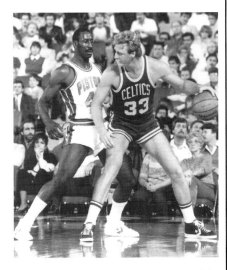

At least for one night in 1981, Terry Tyler and the Pistons got the better of Boston and the great Larry Bird.

Kent Benson

Kent Benson registered his career-highs—27 points and 22 rebounds—as a Piston.

There have been few Pistons role players as steadfast as Kent Benson. And few Pistons ever did more to help kids. No, he didn't get to stay for the championships, being shipped to Utah (with Kelly Tripucka) in 1986 for Adrian Dantley. But Benson is well-remembered by fans as someone who got the most of his abilities and was a valuable cog in the Pistons' gradual emergence from the NBA's lower echelon. All the while, the 6-foot-10 center sponsored Kent's Korner, a section of 100 season tickets he bought and set aside for kids' groups. During his six Pistons seasons, thousands of Detroit-area youths saw their first NBA game because of Benson's generosity. For the 1981-82 season, the league gave Benson its J. Walter Kennedy Citizenship Award for community service. But his good deeds off the court—he also conducted youth sports camps and was in the Fellowship of Christian Athletes —were accompaniments to his contributions on the court. Though often slowed by injuries—broken toe, foot surgery, sprained ankle—Benson was a fixture in the starting five for most of his Detroit career. He averaged a career-high 15.7 points in 59 games in '80-81, then followed with his best season, playing 75 games, averaging 12.5 points and 8.7 boards, shooting .505 from the field and .804 at the foul line, and blocking 98 shots. It should be noted that Benson played most of his career under pressure, largely because he had been the top overall draftee by Milwaukee in 1977. With Detroit, he carried additional weight since it had traded popular Bob Lanier to get him from the Bucks on February 4, 1980. He could not hope to match Lanier's stats, but his popularity stood on its own.

AT A GLANCE

KENT BENSON

FULL NAME:
Michael Kent Benson
BORN:
December 27, 1954; New Castle, Indiana
POSITION, HEIGHT, WEIGHT:
Center, 6-foot-10, 235 pounds
COLLEGE:
Indiana '77
ACQUIRED:
From Milwaukee, February 4, 1980, with 1980 first-round draft pick for Bob Lanier.
TENURE WITH PISTONS:
February 4, 1980 — 1985-86
Also: Milwaukee 1977-80, Utah 1986-87, Cleveland 1987-88
BEST SEASON WITH PISTONS:
1981-82, 75 GP, 12.5 ppg, 8.7 rpg
TOTALS WITH PISTONS:
Regular season: 398 GP, 9.6 ppg, 6.1 rpg
Playoffs: 18 GP, 6.1 ppg, 4.4 rpg
HONORS:
Kennedy Citizenship Award, 1981-82

PISTON LIST

Longest Losing Streaks (Within Same Season)

14 games
- March 7-30, 1980
- December 20, 1993-January 18, 1994

13 games
- January 27-February 27, 1980
- April 1-24, 1994

9 games
- January 14-30, 1959
- November 5-20, 1965
- February 23-March 14, 1972
- December 6-23, 1975
- January 5-19, 1981
- November 27-December 13, 1981

8 games
- 7 occasions

7 games
- 11 occasions

CHANGING FACES

THE NBA hadn't been especially fair to 50-year-old Scotty Robertson, who on June 5, 1980 was named the 16th head coach of the Pistons. He'd had two previous coaching stints, but neither lasted long enough to get a read on his skills. He was the first head coach of the expansion New Orleans Jazz in 1974, but was canned after a 1-14 start. Then with Chicago in '78-79, he coached the Bulls to an 11-15 record in the final 26 games. "I never got a good chance," Robertson said. "I feel this club can win and I'm not talking down the road. I'm talking about now." His optimism would serve him well during a difficult 21-61 season. A series of personnel moves didn't make much apparent difference. Keith Herron, a 6-foot-6 swingman, was a decent pick-up (13.7 ppg). Seven-footer Paul Mokeski was

Arkansas-born Scotty Robertson brought a folksy manner to the Pistons' head coaching job.

obtained from Houston before the season and grabbed a career-high 418 rebounds, but was not a top-of-the-line player. On January 24 vs. Cleveland, he committed six fouls in one quarter. Detroit tried to trade Greg Kelser to Seattle on December 16, but he failed the physical with a bad knee.

Take a Bow

Ron Lee

This was a common scene in Ron Lee's Pistons career—him diving to make a play. Photo by Allen Einstein.

It's fitting, and not at all surprising, that the first new Piston of the Jack McCloskey era was cut from the same cloth as the GM. Ronnie Lee, a stocky 6-foot-3 guard, was known as Kamikaze, which explains what kind of player he was: the kind who would dive to save a ball. Like John Mengelt, who came before, and Dennis Rodman, who came later, Lee spent much of the game on his belly or his posterior. In fact, in one game in 1980, the Pistons held a "Kamikaze Kontest," with fans trying to guess how often Lee would hit the floor that night. Barely more than a month after McCloskey became GM, he made his first trade January 25, 1980, acquiring Lee from Atlanta for guard James McElroy. Lee, by then a four-year veteran, had led the league with 225 steals in 1978 with Phoenix. On March 16, 1980, his nine steals tied a Pistons record, which still exists, and in '80-81 he made 166 steals to rank eighth in the NBA. Though Lee played only 2½ years for the Pistons, McCloskey later lauded him for his scrappy style, saying it was the roots of the Bad Boys.

Game Results

1980-81 REGULAR SEASON

Date	Opponent	Result	Record
10-10	WASHINGTON	L, 85-95	0-1
10-11	at Indiana	L, 87-100	0-2
10-13	at New Jersey	L, 92-108	0-3
10-14	at Cleveland	L, 91-99	0-4
10-16	SAN ANTONIO	L, 99-102	0-5
10-18	ATLANTA	L, 123-125 (2OT)	0-6
10-22	PHILADELPHIA	L, 93-94	0-7
10-25	at Houston	W, 112-109	1-7
10-29	BOSTON	L, 85-103	1-8
10-31	PHOENIX	L, 98-103 (OT)	1-9
11-1	at Chicago	L, 100-122	1-10
11-4	at Milwaukee	W, 98-96	2-10
11-5	at Philadelphia	L, 103-107	2-11
11-7	at Washington	L, 88-114	2-12
11-8	DALLAS	W, 101-73	3-12
11-11	at New York	L, 118-149	3-13
11-12	MILWAUKEE	L, 98-122	3-14
11-14	CHICAGO	W, 106-99	4-14
11-16	at New Jersey	L, 80-89	4-15
11-18	INDIANA	L, 97-102	4-16
11-20	SAN DIEGO	W, 97-90	5-16
11-22	NEW JERSEY	W, 117-103	6-16
11-26	UTAH	L, 97-104	6-17
11-28	KANSAS CITY	W, 104-94	7-17
11-29	at Atlanta	W, 98-95	8-17
12-2	BOSTON	L, 85-94	8-18
12-5	at Washington	L, 92-103	8-19
12-6	at Cleveland	L, 100-101	8-20
12-10	ATLANTA	L, 92-100	8-21
12-12	CLEVELAND	W, 101-95	9-21
12-13	at New York	L, 94-100	9-22
12-17	NEW YORK	L, 103-119	9-23
12-18	at Milwaukee	L, 104-121	9-24
12-19	INDIANA	W, 109-106	10-24
12-21	at San Diego	L, 97-117	10-25
12-23	at Phoenix	L, 104-113	10-26
12-26	HOUSTON	W, 94-114	10-27
12-27	at Chicago	L, 97-104	10-28
12-30	at Atlanta	L, 89-96	10-29
1-2	NEW YORK	W, 102-100	11-29
1-5	at Portland	L, 90-110	11-30
1-7	at Seattle	L, 94-99	11-31
1-10	at Golden State	L, 103-105	11-32
1-11	at L.A. Lakers	L, 108-117	11-33
1-13	MILWAUKEE	L, 96-119	11-34
1-14	at Indiana	L, 99-101	11-35
1-15	WASHINGTON	L, 89-106	11-36
1-17	NEW JERSEY	L, 104-116	11-37
1-19	at Boston	L, 90-92	11-38
1-20	PHILADELPHIA	W, 83-75	12-38
1-22	CHICAGO	L, 92-125	12-39
1-24	CLEVELAND	W, 117-94	13-39
1-26	at Utah	L, 99-102	13-40
1-27	at Denver	L, 123-143	13-41
1-29	at Golden State	L, 112-117	13-42
2-3	at San Antonio	L, 99-102	13-43
2-4	at Kansas City	L, 90-91	13-44
2-6	L.A. LAKERS	L, 102-111	13-45
2-7	at Chicago	L, 90-98	13-46
2-8	INDIANA	L, 101-124	13-47
2-10	at Dallas	W, 101-95	14-47
2-13	at New York	L, 92-120	14-48
2-14	WASHINGTON	W, 105-103	15-48
2-17	at Cleveland	L, 108-109	15-49
2-18	at Philadelphia	L, 97-111	15-50
2-19	PORTLAND	L, 106-115	15-51
2-21	BOSTON	L, 119-130	15-52
2-27	CLEVELAND	W, 118-109	16-52
3-1	at New Jersey	W, 117-104	17-52
3-3	at Milwaukee	L, 98-115	17-53
3-5	NEW YORK	L, 101-104	17-54
3-7	DENVER	L, 109-121	17-55
3-11	ATLANTA	W, 100-97	18-55
3-13	SEATTLE	L, 100-102	18-56
3-14	at Indiana	W, 101-94	19-56
3-18	NEW JERSEY	W, 118-115	20-56
3-20	MILWAUKEE	L, 86-104	20-57
3-22	CHICAGO	L, 103-109	20-58
3-24	at Atlanta	L, 91-96	20-59
3-25	at Philadelphia	L, 75-114	20-60
3-27	at Boston	W, 115-90	21-60
3-29	at Washington	L, 103-108	21-61

(Home games in CAPS)

113

ISIAH THOMAS

From June 9, 1981, when Isiah Thomas was drafted by the Detroit Pistons, to his no-regrets finale on April 19, 1994, his 13-year NBA career was packed with every sensory experience imaginable.

Ecstasy? He had plenty. As a pup, ecstasy was fueling a seven-point rally over Milwaukee in the final 34 seconds of a regular-season game. In later years, ecstacy was a 4-0 sweep of the L.A. Lakers in the '89 Finals and a heaven-sent triple to kick-start a 4-1 blasting of Portland for a repeat title in '90.

Agony? On and off the court, Thomas had that, too. His stolen inbounds pass—meant for Bill Laimbeer, taken by Larry Bird—in the '87 Eastern finals is his lingering Kodak Moment from Hell. His off-the-court grief was often self-inflicted, but Thomas experienced more controversy than most pro athletes would ever expect.

Satisfaction? Though greater goals loomed, who can forget the sweet delight after Thomas and Co. finally ghost-busted Boston Garden in '88 and then eliminated the Celtics at the Silverdome? No obstacle ever looked nicer in the rearview mirror.

Anger? How did Thomas' quick temper manifest itself? Let us count the ways. There was the time he swatted Washington's Rick Mahorn or the time he was ejected for drumming on Mychal Thompson's head or that strange day in '93 when Isiah broke his hand sucker-punching old pal Laimbeer during practice.

Pain? Few athletes played through more than Thomas. As a little man—6-1 on tip-toes—in a tall man's game, he staggered off the floor dizzy and bleeding so many times, toughness became part of his legacy. He broke fingers and hands so often that simply dribbling a ball became a painful undertaking. Over his eyes, solid scar tissue. Including the playoffs, he played 1,090 games despite broken ribs, detached retinas, sprained ankles by the score and a mile of stitches. He was the Evel Knievel of the NBA, a Chicago-born daredevil whose passion and inventiveness pushed his lithe body to its limits.

Contentedness? When Thomas gave his farewell address after blowing out his right Achilles tendon in his final game, he sounded genuinely at peace to get on with

AT A GLANCE

ISIAH THOMAS

FULL NAME:
Isiah Lord Thomas III
BORN:
April 30, 1961; Chicago
POSITION, HEIGHT, WEIGHT:
Guard, 6-foot-1, 185 pounds
COLLEGE:
Indiana, '81
ACQUIRED:
1981, Pistons' No. 1 draft pick (2nd overall)

TENURE WITH PISTONS:
1981-82 — 1993-94
BEST SEASON WITH PISTONS
1984-85, 81 GP, 21.2 ppg, 13.9 apg, 4.5 rpg
TOTALS WITH PISTONS:
Regular season: 979 GP, 18,822 pts. (19.2), 9,061 ast. (9.3)
Playoffs: 111 GP, 2,261 pts. (20.4), 987 ast. (8.9)
HONORS:
Top 50 Players of All-Time, 1996
All-NBA Team: First Team 1983-84, 1984-85, 1985-86; Second Team 1982-83, 1986-87
NBA Finals MVP: 1989-90
All-Star Game (12): 1981-82 — 1992-93
All-Star MVP (2): 1983-84, 1985-86
NBA All-Rookie Team: 1981-82
NBA Assist Champion: 1984-85
Kennedy Citizenship Award, 1986-87

PISTON LIST

*Isiah Thomas'
Highest-Scoring Games*

47 points
- December 13, 1983 at Denver

46 points
- February 8, 1983 at San Antonio

44 points
- March 25, 1983 at Denver
- November 15, 1991 vs. Utah

43 points
- p-June 19, 1988 at L.A. Lakers
- April 9, 1993 at Boston

42 points
- February 21, 1988 at L.A. Lakers

40 points
- Four occasions

39 points
- Four occasions

38 points
- Four occasions

p-playoff game

his post-playing career. As part-owner and GM of the up-and-coming Toronto Raptors, that career is already going fantastically.

That comes as no surprise, because Isiah was a success in the NBA from the moment he took the court for the Pistons on October 30, 1981. His 31 points, including a halfcourt basket, sparked a 118-113 Silverdome win over Milwaukee. But it wasn't just individual success; the Pistons' fortunes also improved immediately. After winning 37 games combined over the previous two seasons, Detroit went 39-43 in Thomas' first season. Fans began flocking to the Dome to see the Pistons, confident they'd see a win or an entertaining loss.

Thomas' rookie season included other triumphs, like being voted to the first of his 12 All-Star Games, but there were growing pains, too. On February 20, 1982, coach Scotty Robertson kicked him out of practice for "not being serious enough." Then he had one of the worst games ever five days later, shooting 1-for-17.

Thomas got his first taste of the playoffs in 1984, and he took a giant bite. Though the Pistons lost to the Knicks in a rugged five-game series, Thomas began building his reputation as a money player in Game 5 at Joe Louis Arena. He scored the Pistons' final 16 points in the last 1:34 of regulation to push the game into OT. Though Detroit lost, it's still one of the finest playoff performances ever.

Without team playoff success, Thomas still claimed lots of individual honors. He scored his career-high 47 points on December 13, 1983 to lead the Pistons to a 186-184 triple-OT win at Denver. In the '84 All-Star Game, he had 21 points and 15

assists to become MVP. On February 26, 1984, he hit a team-record 13 shots in a row vs. Cleveland. After the season, he got a lifetime contract: $12 million, 10 years. In 1985, he dealt a career-high 1,123 assists to break ex-Piston Kevin Porter's NBA season record.

But money and statistics didn't guarantee team success. There would be tough times before Thomas would quarterback Detroit to back-to-back NBA titles. His errant pass in Game 5 of the '87 Eastern finals, swiped by Bird, cost the Pistons a potential home clincher in Game 6 and then they lost Game 7 at steamy Boston Garden. Thomas and the Pistons came back hungry in '88 and disposed of the Celtics, the key win coming in Game 5 at Boston when they rallied from 16 down to win in overtime 102-96. Thomas scored 35 points, recovering from a six-point first half. Two days later at the Silverdome, the Pistons won the series 4-2 and went to the NBA Finals for the first time.

"When I first came to Detroit, I made a promise to the people that we would play for the NBA championship one day," Thomas said. "I've kept my promise."

It wouldn't be a happy ending for the Pistons, who lost to the Lakers 4-3 in the Finals, but not without a game for the ages by Thomas. Seeking the clinching win in Game 6 at L.A., Thomas set four NBA Finals records with an amazing performance. In the third quarter alone, he made 11-of-14 shots for 25 points to push the Pistons to the brink, but he badly sprained his right ankle in the process. Detroit lost 103-102 and Thomas' 43 points were wasted. It was a longshot that he'd be able

to play at all in Game 7, but he suited up with his ankle severely swollen. He couldn't get loose, though, and scored only 10 points in 28 minutes as Detroit lost the championship 108-105. A year later, though, with a 4-0 sweep of the banged-up Lakers, the Pistons won their first title. Thomas had 24 points in Game 1 and the Pistons were off and running.

Thomas' crowning achievement was the Pistons' repeat title over the Trail Blazers in '90 when he was Finals MVP. Detroit trailed by 10 with seven minutes left in Game 1, but Thomas scored 16 points in the fourth quarter, including 10 straight, to rally the Pistons to a 105-99 win. He went off again in Game 4 at Portland, scoring 22 in the third quarter to help the Pistons win 102-99 for a 3-1 series lead. Two days later, he scored the last two of his 29 points to tie Game 5, setting up Vinnie Johnson's winning shot. Thomas averaged 27.6 points, 7.0 assists and 5.2 rebounds in the series.

Thomas' career continued at star caliber, but injuries exacted a heavy toll in his final four seasons. He even suffered the indignity of his first DNP-CD — Did Not Play-Coach Decision. Then on April 19, 1994 at The Palace, Thomas was driving around Orlando rookie Penny Hardaway when his Achilles tendon snapped late in the third quarter. Isiah limped off the court for the last time as the Pistons' all-time leader in points, assists, steals, games, blood, sweat and tears.

"I left it all on the court," Thomas said. "From a sports standpoint, I have reached every mountaintop."

And left imposing footprints on every summit.

Isiah Thomas' Regular-Season Statistics with Detroit

SEASON	G	GS	MIN	FGM	FGA	PCT	FTM	FTA	PCT	O-RB	D-RB	TOT	AST	PF	DQ	STL	TO	BLK	PTS	PPG	HI
1981-82	72	72	2433	453	1068	.424	302	429	.704	57	152	209	565	253	2	150	299	17	1225	17.0	34
1982-83	81	81	3093	725	1537	.472	368	518	.710	105	223	328	634	318	8	199	326	29	1854	22.9	46
1983-84	82	82	3007	669	1448	.462	388	529	.733	103	224	327	914	324	8	204	307	33	1748	21.3	47
1984-85	81	81	3089	646	1410	.458	399	493	.809	114	247	361	1123	288	8	187	302	25	1720	21.2	38
1985-86	77	77	2790	609	1248	.488	365	462	.790	83	194	277	830	245	9	171	289	20	1609	20.9	39
1986-87	81	81	3013	626	1353	.463	400	521	.768	82	237	319	813	251	5	153	343	20	1671	20.6	36
1987-88	81	81	2927	621	1341	.463	305	394	.774	64	214	278	678	217	0	141	273	17	1577	19.5	42
1988-89	80	76	2924	569	1227	.464	287	351	.818	49	224	273	663	209	0	133	298	20	1458	18.2	37
1989-90	81	81	2993	579	1322	.438	292	377	.775	74	234	308	765	206	0	139	322	19	1492	18.4	37
1990-91	48	46	1657	289	665	.435	179	229	.782	35	125	160	446	118	4	75	185	10	776	16.2	32
1991-92	78	78	2918	564	1264	.446	292	378	.772	68	179	247	560	194	2	118	252	15	1445	18.5	44
1992-93	79	79	2922	526	1258	.418	278	377	.737	71	161	232	671	222	2	123	284	18	1391	17.6	43
1993-94	58	56	1750	318	763	.417	181	258	.702	46	113	159	399	126	0	68	202	6	856	14.8	31
TOTALS	979	971	35516	7194	15904	.452	4036	5316	.759	951	2527	3478	9061	2971	48	1861	3682	249	18822	19.2	47

3-point FGs: 1981-82, 17-59 (.288); 1982-83, 36-125 (.288); 1983-84, 22-65 (.338); 1984-85, 29-113 (.257); 1985-86, 26-84 (.310); 1986-87, 19-98 (.194); 1987-88, 30-97 (.309); 1988-89, 33-121 (.273); 1989-90, 42-136 (.309); 1990-91, 19-65 (.292); 1991-92, 25-86 (.291); 1992-93, 61-198 (.308); 1993-94, 39-126 (.310). TOTALS, 398-1373 (.290).

1981 1982

DETROIT PISTONS

TIME CAPSULE

September 21, 1981:
Sandra Day O'Connor becomes the first female U.S. Supreme Court justice.

January 24, 1982:
In the first Super Bowl in a northern city, the San Francisco 49ers beat the Cincinnati Bengals, 26-21, before 81,270 at the Pontiac Silverdome.

March 29, 1982:
Michael Jordan and North Carolina defeat Patrick Ewing and Georgetown for the NCAA basketball championship.

SEASON SNAPSHOT

Most Points
John Long (1,514, 21.9 avg.)

Most Rebounds
Kent Benson (653, 8.7 avg.)

Most Assists
Isiah Thomas (565, 7.8 avg.)

Most Minutes
Kelly Tripucka (3,077, 37.5 avg.)

Field-Goal Percentage
Terry Tyler (52.3%)

Free-Throw Percentage
John Long (86.5%)

Team Offense Average
111.1 (9,112 in 82 games)

Team Defense Average
112.0 (8,187 in 82 games)

Pistons in All-Star Game
Isiah Thomas, G; Kelly Tripucka, F

1981-82

FINAL STANDINGS

Central Division	W	L	Pct.	GB
Milwaukee	55	27	.671	—
Atlanta	42	40	.512	13
PISTONS	**39**	**43**	**.476**	**16**
Indiana	35	47	.427	20
Chicago	34	48	.415	21
Cleveland	15	67	.183	40

Atlantic Division Winner—Boston
Midwest Division Winner—San Antonio
Pacific Division Winner—Los Angeles

PLAYOFF RESULTS

Pistons Did Not Qualify

PISTONS PLAYOFF LEADERS

NBA CHAMPION

Los Angeles Lakers

1981-82
SEASON IN REVIEW

First Isiah Thomas. Then Kelly Tripucka. And Vinnie Johnson. And Bill Laimbeer. In a span of nine months—too quickly, really, to fathom the combined impact—the Pistons were made over from NBA doormat into a team to be feared and respected. As if to reward them for suffering in silence for two years—they'd won only 37 games combined—the NBA seemingly hauled away the tired, old Pistons and plopped down a fresh new ball club in 1981-82. GM Jack McCloskey did it, actually, using his first-round picks on Thomas (second overall) and Tripucka (12th) and then making one-sided trades for Johnson and Laimbeer during the season. A 39-43 season was the result, not good enough for the playoffs but good enough to create plenty of buzz. Keyed by the cherubic, talented Thomas and the high-strung, high-scoring Tripucka, it suddenly became fashionable to be a Pistons fan; attendance set an all-time high, nearly doubling to 406,317. Thomas was an immediate All-Star with whippet-quick drives to the basket and deft passing; he averaged 17.0 points and 7.8 assists. Fellow All-Star Tripucka topped Dave Bing's rookie scoring records with 1,772 points for the season and 49 on March 12 vs. Golden State. Laimbeer, a trade deadline acquisition from Cleveland, became an immediate starter and averaged 11.3 rebounds in the final 30 games.

Isiah Thomas and GM Jack McCloskey signed a four-year, $1.6 million contract on July 31, 1981. Photo by Allen Einstein.

WHAT A NIGHT!

October 30, 1981

It took exactly one game for rookie Isiah Thomas to show his flair for the dramatic and convince all observers he was going to be a special NBA player. On his magical debut night at the Silverdome, facing former Pistons star Bob Lanier and the Milwaukee Bucks, Thomas racked up 31 points and 11 mostly flashy assists to lead Detroit's 118-113 victory before 9,182. Still six months shy of his 21st birthday, the Pistons' 6-foot-1 ball of energy enlivened the crowd with a 50-foot halfcourt basket before halftime. He scored 27 points over the first three quarters, keeping the Pistons in contention, then asserted himself as the floor leader. His assist to Terry Tyler put Detroit ahead for good 110-109, then he stripped Quinn Buckner and fed Phil Hubbard for an easy layup. In the final 20 seconds, Thomas shot 4-of-4 free throws to wrap it up. "I didn't think I'd do that good," he said afterward. "Things just worked out." Over on the Milwaukee bench, coach Don Nelson was already having nightmares about how to defend Thomas for the next decade: "That guy is something else. He's so poised, so cool ... so damn good." Lanier said, "The Pistons have needed a leader and he looks like he's the one."

From his NBA debut, Isiah Thomas surpassed the massive expectations of being the Pistons' new leader. Photo by Allen Einstein.

Premier Piston

Kelly Tripucka

From 1981-86, Kelly Tripucka had seven games of at least 40 points, including a 56-pointer.

Scarcely two months into Kelly Tripucka's NBA career, he was already owed apologies left and right. GM Jack McCloskey had selected him with the Pistons' second 1981 first-round pick, 12th overall. It was a choice that surprised many, especially team exec Harry Hutt, who was at draft headquarters in New York to relay the Pistons' pick. Hutt would become one of Tripucka's best friends in the organization, but said, "When Jack told me we were picking Tripucka, all I knew was he was the Notre Dame guy who whined all the time. For a second, I thought, 'I'm not filling out the card. We can do better than that.' That shows you how much I know." But Hutt was not alone in his contrition, because Tripucka immediately started proving people wrong—and McCloskey right. Tripucka was more than just a solid college player. He broke virtually every Pistons rookie scoring record in 1981-82, then put together a great (but injury-shortened) second season by averaging 26.5 points and setting the club record with 56 against Chicago on January 29, 1983 at the Silverdome. "It was just one of those nights," Tripucka said. But those nights were frequent for Tripucka that season when he finished third in the league in scoring average, despite missing 23 games with a knee injury. A good outside shooter and dedicated lane-filler in transition, he was also an 85-percent foul shooter, often slapping himself if he missed. Tripucka stayed with the Pistons for five seasons, playing in two All-Star games, but was traded to Utah in 1986 after his defensive liabilities were heavily exploited by Atlanta star Dominique Wilkins in the playoffs. Tripucka retired in 1991 after a 10-year career and came back to the Pistons as a TV broadcaster in 1993, a post he still holds.

AT A GLANCE

KELLY TRIPUCKA

FULL NAME:
Peter Kelly Tripucka

BORN:
February 16, 1959; Bloomfield, New Jersey

POSITION, HEIGHT, WEIGHT:
Forward, 6-foot-6, 220 pounds

COLLEGE:
Notre Dame '81

ACQUIRED:
1981, Pistons' No. 2 draft pick (12th overall)

TENURE WITH PISTONS:
1981-82 – 1985-86

BEST SEASON WITH PISTONS:
1982-83, 58 GP, 26.5 ppg, 4.6 rpg

TOTALS WITH PISTONS:
Regular season: 352 GP, 21.6 ppg, 4.5 rpg
Playoffs: 18 GP, 19.8 ppg, 4.7 rpg

HONORS:
All-Star Game (2): 1981-82, 1983-84
NBA All-Rookie Team: 1981-82
Basketball Weekly Rookie of the Year: 1981-82
NBA Player of the Week: November 15, 1982

PISTON LIST

Most Points by a Pistons Rookie

49 points
- Kelly Tripucka, 3-12-82 vs. Golden State

47 points
- Dave Bing, 3-8-67 vs. Baltimore

40 points
- Bob Lanier, 3-19-71 vs. Buffalo

38 points
- Tripucka, 1-5-82 vs. Philadelphia

37 points
- Tripucka, 3-14-82 at Cleveland

36 points
- Tripucka, 12-10-81 vs. New York (OT)
- Tripucka, 3-6-82 at New York

34 points
- Ray Scott, 3-16-62 vs. Cincinnati
- Greg Kelser, 2-9-80 at New York
- Isiah Thomas, 2-2-82 at Atlanta
- Tripucka, 2-6-82 at New Jersey

CHANGING FACES

THE CLOCK was ticking. Midnight was fast approaching, the annual NBA trading deadline, and Jack McCloskey was waiting for his home phone to ring. He'd made an offer to Cleveland owner Ted Stepien. We'll send you Paul Mokeski, Phil Hubbard, a first-round pick and a second-rounder. All you have to send us is Kenny Carr and your backup center Bill Laimbeer. Finally the phone rang and McCloskey had his answer. It was a deal, and suddenly the Pistons had the workhorse rebounder they had waited for. It wasn't Carr, whom the newspapers portrayed as the centerpiece, but rather Laimbeer, the chunky second-year Notre Dame product. He went on to be the greatest rebounder in Pistons history (9,430). Laimbeer wasn't the only terrific trade acquisition in 1981-82. On November 21, McCloskey dealt Greg Kelser to Seattle for underutilized shooting guard Vinnie Johnson. Thus began a 798-game Detroit career for the 1979 first-round pick, a Brooklyn-bred gunner who would become one of the most beloved Pistons ever. Other new Pistons included Edgar Jones and Jeff Judkins.

In his first seven games as a Piston, Bill Laimbeer averaged 15.9 rebounds, including 20 in his home debut. Photo by Allen Einstein.

Take a Bow

Silver Anniversary Team

The Pistons couldn't have known that night, but they were drawing a demarcation line between their past and their future on April 9, 1982. At halftime vs. Milwaukee at the Silverdome, the Pistons honored their six-man Silver Anniversary Team: Dave Bing, Dave DeBusschere, Bailey Howell, Bob Lanier, Gene Shue and George Yardley. At that time, five of the men ranked in the top six in all-time scoring in Detroit, while the other—Yardley—had set an NBA record of 2,001 points in his only full season after the team moved from Fort Wayne. Of the six legends, only Lanier was still active and he scored 26 that night to fuel Milwaukee's 118-100 win. All told, the Silver stars combined for an average of 21.1 points and 8.7 rebounds in 2,669 games in a Detroit uniform. Watching from the bench were four players in their first year as Pistons—Isiah Thomas, Bill Laimbeer, Vinnie Johnson and Kelly Tripucka—a foursome that would eventually break most of the records of the All-Time stars.

Game Results

1981-82 REGULAR SEASON

Date	Opponent	Result	Record
10-30	MILWAUKEE	W, 118-113	1-0
10-31	at Chicago	W, 119-106	2-0
11-5	NEW JERSEY	W, 109-103	3-0
11-6	at Washington	L, 82-86	3-1
11-7	BOSTON	L, 88-129	3-2
11-10	PHILADELPHIA	L, 93-95	3-3
11-12	CLEVELAND	W, 130-99	4-3
11-14	at Atlanta	W, 117-104	5-3
11-18	at Cleveland	L, 103-110	5-4
11-19	WASHINGTON	W, 122-97	6-4
11-21	UTAH	W, 95-86	7-4
11-24	at Milwaukee	L, 95-103	7-5
11-25	at Kansas City	W, 129-122 (OT)	8-5
11-27	ATLANTA	L, 112-114 (OT)	8-6
11-28	at Philadelphia	L, 103-116	8-7
12-1	at New York	L, 100-112	8-8
12-2	at Boston	L, 114-115	8-9
12-4	at Indiana	L, 95-105	8-10
12-5	MILWAUKEE	L, 108-111	8-11
12-10	NEW YORK	L, 101-106 (OT)	8-12
12-12	at Seattle	L, 111-117	8-13
12-13	at Portland	L, 99-105	8-14
12-15	at Golden State	W, 108-104	9-14
12-17	INDIANA	W, 96-100	9-15
12-19	NEW YORK	W, 132-104	10-15
12-22	at Dallas	W, 106-98	11-15
12-23	at Denver	W, 124-119	12-15
12-26	CHICAGO	W, 96-94	13-15
12-29	at Washington	L, 125-129	13-16
12-30	at New Jersey	L, 119-130	13-17
1-2	at New York	L, 108-121	13-18
1-5	PHILADELPHIA	W, 124-101	14-18
1-7	PHOENIX	L, 94-110	14-19
1-9	L.A. LAKERS	L, 127-130	14-20
1-10	at Boston	L, 124-134	14-21
1-12	at Chicago	W, 122-111	15-21
1-14	WASHINGTON	L, 114-121	15-22
1-16	BOSTON	L, 120-128	15-23
1-17	at Milwaukee	W, 108-103	16-23
1-19	at Utah	L, 117-123	16-24
1-21	at San Diego	W, 120-110	17-24
1-22	at L.A. Lakers	L, 111-123	17-25
1-23	at Phoenix	L, 90-113	17-26
1-27	ATLANTA	W, 108-107	18-26
2-2	at Atlanta	W, 106-105	19-26
2-5	at Chicago	W, 110-103	20-26
2-6	NEW JERSEY	L, 120-125	20-27
2-9	CHICAGO	W, 128-123 (OT)	21-27
2-10	at New Jersey	L, 108-115	21-28
2-11	CLEVELAND	W, 123-113	22-28
2-13	PORTLAND	L, 120-128	22-29
2-16	HOUSTON	W, 111-109	23-29
2-17	at San Antonio	L, 112-126	23-30
2-20	INDIANA	W, 115-100	24-30
2-25	SAN ANTONIO	L, 116-119	24-31
2-27	KANSAS CITY	W, 127-119 (OT)	25-31
2-28	at Indiana	L, 101-112	25-32
3-2	at Milwaukee	L, 91-101	25-33
3-4	CHICAGO	W, 122-97	26-33
3-6	at New York	W, 115-111	27-33
3-8	BOSTON	L, 101-111	27-34
3-10	DENVER	L, 113-124	27-35
3-12	GOLDEN STATE	W, 121-117	28-35
3-14	at Cleveland	W, 109-103	29-35
3-16	SAN DIEGO	W, 114-110	30-35
3-18	SEATTLE	W, 119-115	31-35
3-19	at Houston	W, 111-102	32-35
3-21	at Atlanta	L, 111-119	32-36
3-25	PHILADELPHIA	W, 100-98	33-36
3-26	at Boston	L, 104-125	33-37
3-27	at New Jersey	W, 123-121	34-37
3-30	at Washington	L, 98-127	34-38
3-31	at Indiana	L, 106-108	34-39
4-1	DALLAS	L, 120-121	34-40
4-3	INDIANA	W, 105-102	35-40
4-7	ATLANTA	W, 120-115	36-40
4-9	MILWAUKEE	L, 100-118	36-41
4-11	NEW YORK	W, 97-89	37-41
4-14	at Philadelphia	L, 111-119	37-42
4-15	CLEVELAND	W, 120-110	38-42
4-17	NEW JERSEY	L, 132-147	38-43
4-18	at Cleveland	W, 116-113 (OT)	39-43

(Home games in CAPS)

BILL LAIMBEER

For all of Bill Laimbeer's clutch rebounds, put-backs, 3-pointers and irritated opponents in 12-plus seasons with the Pistons, his defining moment came not on the court, but in the locker room.

The date was June 8, 1990, two days before Game 3 of the NBA Finals. Having lost in overtime the night before, the Pistons had split the first two games against the Trail Blazers and the best-of-seven series was heading to Portland for Games 3-5. Portland, where the Pistons had not won since 1974, a span of 20 straight losses.

Getting set to fly West that afternoon, the Pistons and their coaches were meeting in the locker room when someone pointed out that they had to win at least once at Portland to bring the series back to Detroit. Laimbeer sprang to his feet and his angry voice sliced the stale air.

"Damn it!" he yelled, slamming his fist into his palm. "I'm going out there to win three games! And anybody who doesn't think we can sweep can get the hell out of the locker room!" No one stirred. The challenge had been made. "It wasn't that we didn't think we could win all three, but we

were waiting for someone to say it," Vinnie Johnson said. "Bill stepped up and said it in such a forceful way, we believed it." Assistant coach Brendan Suhr said, "That told me all I ever needed to know about Bill Laimbeer. He has an iron will."

The words would have been empty if Laimbeer and the Pistons hadn't backed them up. But they indeed swept the Trail Blazers, winning the Finals 4-1, repeating as NBA champions and solidifying the legend of Laimbeer's pain-in-the-butt reputation. He so thoroughly confounded Portland in Game 3, taking five charge—flops, the Blazers said— and hassling excitable Portland center Kevin Duckworth into a tizzy. Laimbeer's series averages—13.2 points, 13.4 rebounds— didn't symbolize his contributions as much as the sinister black top hat he donned in a champagne-soaked locker room after the Game 5 clincher.

Throughout his 14-year NBA career, Bill Laimbeer never hesitated to "wear the black hat," his terminology for playing the bad-guy role. As a player of moderate athleticism— he could scarcely run or jump—whose off-season regimen was limited to golf, fly-

AT A GLANCE

BILL LAIMBEER

FULL NAME:
William Laimbeer Jr.
BORN:
May 19, 1957; Boston
POSITION, HEIGHT, WEIGHT:
Center, 6-foot-11, 260 pounds
COLLEGE:
Notre Dame, '79

ACQUIRED:
From Cleveland, February 16, 1982, with Kenny Carr for Phil Hubbard, Paul Mokeski and 1982 first- and second-round draft picks
TENURE WITH PISTONS:
February 16, 1982 – December 1, 1993
Also: Brescia, Italy 1979-80, Cleveland 1980-82
BEST SEASON WITH PISTONS:
1985-86, 82 GP, 16.6 ppg, 13.1 rpg
TOTALS WITH PISTONS:
Regular season: 937 GP, 12,665 pts. (13.5), 9,430 reb. (10.1)
Playoffs: 113 GP, 1,354 pts. (12.0), 1,097 reb. (9.7)
HONORS:
All-Star Game (4): 1982-83, 1983-84, 1984-85, 1986-87
NBA Rebound Champion: 1983-84 (total), 1985-86 (total and average)

PISTON LIST

Bill Laimbeer's Highest-Rebounding Games

24 rebounds
- March 21, 1986 at Phoenix

23 rebounds
- December 11, 1984 vs. Chicago
- March 26, 1985 at Phoenix
- December 9, 1989 vs. Indiana
- January 26, 1990 vs. Phoenix

22 rebounds
- October 31, 1982 at Indiana
- April 10, 1984 vs. Indiana
- November 5, 1984 at Cleveland
- March 12, 1986 vs. Indiana
- April 5, 1986 at Indiana
- January 26, 1987 at Phoenix
- April 6, 1989 vs. Chicago

21 rebounds
- 11 occasions

Guard Kevin Porter, an assist man by nature, takes a jump shot against Atlanta at Cobo Arena in 1977. *Photo courtesy of The Detroit Pistons.*

Guard M.L. Carr, a Piston from 1976-79, shoots against the defense of Golden State center Robert Parish, a future Detroit nemesis, in 1978 in the sixth game ever at the Silverdome. *Photo courtesy of The Detroit Pistons.*

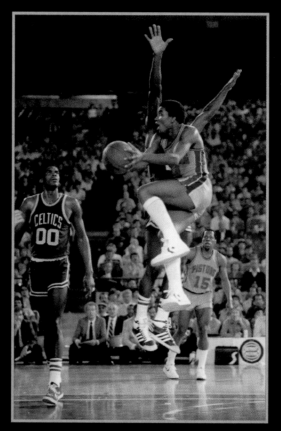

From his first day to his last,
Isiah Thomas turned on the
Pistons with his acrobatic
drives to the basket, like this
one against the Celtics in 1984.
Photo by Allen Einstein.

Coach Chuck Daly brought
style, a winning strategy
and a tremendous coiffure to
the Pistons bench. He's shown
here in 1985 with assistant
Dick Harter (left) and
ever-present trainer
Mike Abdenour.
Photo by Allen Einstein.

Kelly Tripucka exalts after scoring
a team-record 56 points against the
Chicago Bulls on January 29, 1983
at the Silverdome.
Photo by Allen Einstein.

The Collision at Boston Garden: Adrian
Dantley (foreground) and Vinnie Johnson
are a crumbled heap after colliding while
diving for a ball in Game 7 of the 1987
Eastern Conference finals.
Photo by Allen Einstein.

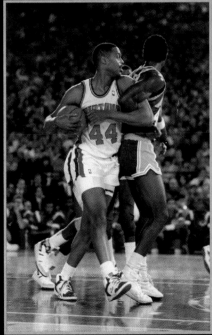

Shall we dance? Rick Mahorn locks
up with the Lakers' A.C. Green in the
1988 NBA Finals at the Silverdome.
Photo by Allen Einstein.

On a magical day at Joe Louis Arena on May 5, 1985, Vinnie Johnson lit up Robert Parish (00) and the Celtics for 22 points in the fourth quarter to rally Detroit to a playoff victory.
Photo by Allen Einstein.

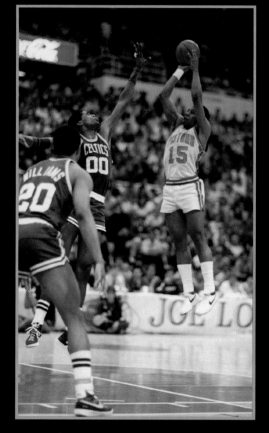

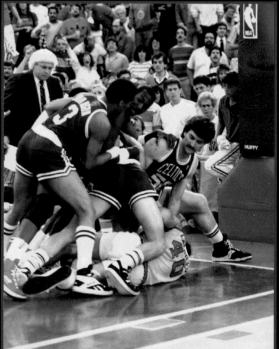

The brawl that started it all: Bill Laimbeer is stuck on the bottom of the pile after a scuffle with Larry Bird (prone over Laimbeer) in Game 3 of the 1987 Eastern Conference finals.
Photo by Allen Einstein.

Rick Mahorn, baddest of the Bad Boys, atop a float in the 1989 parade after the Pistons broomed the Lakers 4-0. Hours later, he would become an ex-Piston, stolen by Minnesota in the expansion draft.
Photo by Allen Einstein.

An emotional Dennis Rodman (left) is comforted by Isiah Thomas while addressing fans at the 1989 victory rally at The Palace.
Photo by Allen Einstein.

Isiah Thomas splits the
Portland defense for two points in
Game 1 of the 1990 NBA Finals
en route to the series MVP award
and a repeat championship for the
Pistons. *Photo by Allen Einstein.*

The 1990 NBA championship
banner is hoisted into the Palace
rafters on opening night of the
1990-91 season.
Photo by Allen Einstein.

Pistons fans show their devotion
to their team's rugged style,
waving Bad Boys cards.
Photo by Allen Einstein.

Two old pros:
Joe Dumars (left) and
Isiah Thomas talk it over
during the Pistons'
ill-fated 1991 season.
Photo by Allen Einstein.

No one dove over more press
tables or courtside seats to save
loose balls than Dennis
Rodman, shown here returning
to the court after diving
into the writers.
Photo by Allen Einstein.

Bill Laimbeer, one of the most-fined
players in NBA history, pleads his
case after a foul call.
Photo by Allen Einstein.

The Pistons' first star, jump-shooting
sensation George Yardley, was inducted to
the Basketball Hall of Fame in 1996.
Photo by Naismith Basketball Hall of Fame.

The Pistons' newest superstar,
Grant Hill, throws down a serious
dunk en route to the 1995 NBA
co-Rookie of the Year Award.
Photo by Allen Einstein.

casting and golf, Laimbeer became the NBA's consummate lunchpail player, contrary to his affluent Southern California upbringing. He possessed an indomitable will, a steely glare, a hard head and sharp elbows, rarely failing to use all of them to his advantage every time he stepped on the court. Though his modus operandi cost him roughly $85,000 in fines and salary, he called it "the cost of doing business."

But to do the kind of business Laimbeer specialized in, you've got to punch in every day and few players ever did it better. Until a one-game suspension for a fight with Cleveland's Brad Daugherty on January 27, 1989, Laimbeer played in 685 consecutive games, the fifth-longest streak in NBA history. He missed only nine games in his entire career—five to injury, three to suspension and one to coach's decision.

At his retirement press conference on December 1, 1993, Laimbeer was asked to name his proudest accomplishment. "I never went on the injured list," he said. "That was a sense of pride in me. I was paid to play. I was there every night."

When Laimbeer walked away 13 games into the '93-94 season, he went as the team's career rebounding king with 9,430, having led the NBA in total boards in 1984 (1,003) and '86 (1,075) and averaging 1,008 for his first five full seasons with the Pistons (1982-87). He also led the franchise in games played with 937, though Isiah Thomas would later top him with 979. Including Laimbeer's career-opening 1½ seasons with the Cleveland Cavaliers, he ended up with 13,790 points and 10,400 rebounds. Only 21 NBA players have ever topped 10,000 in both categories.

Those numbers are a testament to a fact only Pistons fans seemed to recognize: Bill Laimbeer could actually play the game. He wasn't merely an Ultimate Fighting champion masquerading in basketball Bermudas, as his four berths in the All-Star Game point out. He was one of the NBA's best box-out rebounders, able to hold his position like a paperweight on a Kleenex. He was one of the league's best perimeter-shooting big men, with a deadly tippy-toe jump shot that made him a 3-point threat and a major mismatch for opposing centers. He was also a master of two lost arts: outlet passes and screens.

And, of course, no one in the NBA was better at infuriating opponents and their fans. Over the years, a roster of All-Stars wanted a piece of Laimbeer at one time or another: Bob Lanier, Dominique Wilkins, Charles Barkley, Scottie Pippen, Kareem Abdul-Jabbar, Patrick Ewing, Larry Bird, Robert Parish and Kevin McHale. When Parish mugged him in Game 5 of the 1987 Eastern finals, the national media and CBS—not to mention the referees—seemed to wink at the offense.

But as opponents often said, Laimbeer was exactly the type of player they would want on their teams, and the Pistons recognized that earlier than most. GM Jack McCloskey got him from Cleveland only nine minutes before the midnight trading deadline on February 16, 1982. It was a four-player deal, with Detroit also getting forward Kenny Carr and sending Paul Mokeski, Phil Hubbard and two draft picks to the Cavs. Most observers viewed Carr as the prize, but McCloskey and coach Scotty Robertson knew better.

"We were playing at San Antonio the day after the trade and I had Laimbeer come to my hotel room at 3 in the afternoon," Robertson said. "I said, 'Bill, as of 7:30 tonight, you're my starting center. Show me what you've got.' That night, he gets 12 points and 16 rebounds—and he was really out of shape, too. He got by with position, hard work and playing smartly."

Robertson's successor, Chuck Daly, saw the same traits. "Bill's one of the best competitors I've ever seen. It doesn't matter what you're talking about — basketball, golf, darts, anything. You will never outwork Bill Laimbeer."

Or outfox him. That was never clearer than in the '90s Finals against Portland. Game 3 was Laimbeer's masterpiece. Leading the Pistons out of the locker room before the game, he ran over a photographer who got in his way. Laimbeer compiled 11 points and 12 boards, but it was his inside defense and smirking presence that spooked the Blazers. "Don't get wrapped up in Laimbeer!" Portland coach Rick Adelman yelled to his team, but it was no use. Later, with the Pistons near a 121-106 victory, Laimbeer added the crowning touch when he fouled out and bowed like a wisenheimer to the booing crowd. The Pistons followed his confident lead; four days later they were repeat NBA champs. And Laimbeer's reputation—Most-Hated NBA Player—was cemented.

"I think 'hate' is a strong word," he said. "This is an entertainment business. I wore the black hat. I accepted it. Even in high school, the other teams disliked me. It was my style."

It became his legacy.

Bill Laimbeer's Regular-Season Statistics with Detroit

SEASON	G	GS	MIN	FGM	FGA	PCT	FTM	FTA	PCT	O-RB	D-RB	TOT	AST	PF	DQ	STL	TO	BLK	PTS	PPG	HI
1981-82	30	30	935	146	283	.516	91	112	.813	110	230	340	55	126	2	17	60	34	384	12.8	24
1982-83	82	82	2871	436	877	.497	245	310	.790	282	711	993	263	320	9	51	176	118	1119	13.6	30
1983-84	82	82	2864	553	1044	.530	316	365	.866	329	674	1003	149	273	4	49	151	84	1422	17.3	33
1984-85	82	82	2892	595	1177	.506	244	306	.797	295	718	1013	154	308	4	69	129	71	1438	17.5	35
1985-86	82	82	2891	545	1107	.492	266	319	.834	305	770	1075	146	291	4	59	133	65	1360	16.6	29
1986-87	82	82	2854	506	1010	.501	245	274	.894	243	712	955	151	283	4	72	120	69	1263	15.4	30
1987-88	82	82	2897	455	923	.493	187	214	.874	165	667	832	199	284	6	66	136	78	1110	13.5	30
1988-89	81	81	2640	449	900	.499	178	212	.840	138	638	776	177	259	2	51	129	100	1106	13.7	32
1989-90	81	81	2675	380	785	.484	164	192	.854	166	614	780	171	278	4	57	98	84	981	12.1	31
1990-91	82	81	2668	372	778	.478	123	147	.837	173	564	737	157	242	3	38	98	56	904	11.0	25
1991-92	81	46	2234	342	727	.470	67	75	.893	104	347	451	160	225	0	51	102	54	783	9.7	26
1992-93	79	41	1933	292	574	.509	93	104	.894	110	309	419	127	212	4	46	59	40	687	8.7	26
1993-94	11	5	248	47	90	.522	11	13	.846	9	47	56	14	30	0	6	10	4	108	9.8	26
TOTALS	937	857	30602	5118	10275	.498	2230	2643	.844	2429	7001	9430	1923	3131	46	632	1401	857	12665	13.5	35

3-point FGs: 1981-82, 1-7 (.143); 1982-83, 2-13 (.154); 1983-84, 0-11 (.000); 1984-85, 4-18 (.222); 1985-86, 4-14 (.286); 1986-87, 6-21 (.286); 1987-88, 13-39 (.333); 1988-89, 30-86 (.349); 1989-90, 57-158 (.361); 1990-91, 37-125 (.296); 1991-92, 32-85 (.376); 1992-93, 10-27 (.370); 1993-94, 3-9 (.333). TOTALS, 199-613 (.325).

1982 1983

DETROIT PISTONS

TIME CAPSULE

September 29, 1982:
Seven people in Chicago are dead from cyanide placed in tampered-with Tylenol capsules.

December 2, 1982:
Barney Clark is the first successful recipient of an artificial heart transplant; he dies on March 23, 1983.

March 2, 1983:
More than 125 million TV viewers watch the final episode of M*A*S*H.

SEASON SNAPSHOT

Most Points
Kelly Tripucka (1,536, 26.5 avg.)

Most Rebounds
Bill Laimbeer (993, 12.1 avg.)

Most Assists
Isiah Thomas (634, 7.8 avg.)

Most Minutes
x-Isiah Thomas (3,093, 38.2 avg.)

Field-Goal Percentage
Vinnie Johnson (51.3%)

Free-Throw Percentage
Kelly Tripucka (84.3%)

Team Offense Average
112.7 (9,239 in 82 games)

Team Defense Average
113.1 (9,272 in 82 games)

NBA All-Stars
Isiah Thomas, G (Second Team)

Pistons in All-Star Game
Isiah Thomas, G; Bill Laimbeer, C

x-led league

1982-83

FINAL STANDINGS

Central Division	W	L	Pct.	GB
Milwaukee	51	31	.622	—
Atlanta	43	39	.524	8
PISTONS	**37**	**45**	**.451**	**14**
Chicago	28	54	.341	23
Cleveland	23	59	.280	28
Indiana	20	62	.244	31

Atlantic Division Winner—Philadelphia
Midwest Division Winner—San Antonio
Pacific Division Winner—Los Angeles

PLAYOFF RESULTS

Pistons Did Not Qualify

PISTONS PLAYOFF LEADERS

NBA CHAMPION

Philadelphia 76ers

1982-83
SEASON IN REVIEW

The new Pistons were a year older, but not a year better in 1982-83, and coach Scotty Robertson paid the price after the season. Despite the development of Isiah Thomas, Kelly Tripucka and Bill Laimbeer, the Pistons went 37-45—two wins fewer than 1981-82—and didn't make the playoffs. A 12-6 start was followed by a 4-10 skid, leaving Detroit 16-16, and the ship never got righted. A 1-7 March skid sealed the issue for Robertson, who was fired April 18, two days after the season. Some players had hinted in the papers that Robertson had taken the club as far as he could and a change was needed. The trouble was defense; the Pistons allowed an average of 113.1 points. "It's not just the number of points allowed, it's the percentage of shots teams are making," Detroit GM Jack McCloskey said. "Scotty did not seem to emphasize defense." It was not a totally wasted season, though. Thomas was named to the All-NBA second team (22.9 ppg, 7.8 apg), while Tripucka had one of the best scoring seasons in team history, placing third in the NBA with a 26.5 average, including a Pistons-record 56 on January 29 against Chicago. A knee injury limited him to 58 games, though. Making his first All-Star game, Laimbeer finished seven rebounds shy of 1,000, and Vinnie Johnson averaged 15.8 points. First-rounders Cliff Levingston and Ricky Pierce signed late and didn't show much.

Isiah Thomas led the league in minutes with 3,093. Photo by Allen Einstein.

WHAT A NIGHT!

January 29, 1983

It wasn't the 24-hour flu. Luckily for Kelly Tripucka, it lasted only 21 hours. He got better just in time to have the greatest individual scoring game in Pistons history on January 29, 1983. Since 1971, when Dave Bing's 54 points against Chicago set the team record, no Piston had topped 50. But on a drafty Saturday night at the Silverdome, a wrung-out Tripucka scored 56 to lead a 128-126 Detroit victory, also over the Bulls. He had 28 points in each half, tying his own team record for the most points in a first half. The night before, Tripucka had been too sick to play against Cleveland and the Pistons were defeated at home 107-106. But there he was against Chicago, making 18-of-26 field goals and a club-record 20 free throws (in 22 attempts). "I still don't feel too good," Tripucka said after a postgame rubdown. "But after what happened last night, I really wanted to play. If I knew how it happened, I would get sick more often." Coach Scotty Robertson said, "I've seen it a lot of times where a player comes back from sickness and has one of his greatest games. And it was obviously his greatest game." Bulls coach Paul Westhead, no stranger to high-scoring games, said, "From our point of view, Tripucka earned it."

Since Kelly Tripucka's 56-point night, no other Piston has scored more than 47 (Isiah Thomas). Photo by Allen Einstein.

Premier Piston

Vinnie "The Microwave" Johnson

Vinnie Johnson's amazing strength gave him an advantage on smaller shooting guards. Photo by Allen Einstein.

Anticipation followed by fruition was the essence of Vinnie Johnson's 10-year career with the Pistons. Half the fun of watching him play was trying to predict his next mind-boggling scoring streak. He would swish that first shot—usually after curling counterclockwise around a pick—and the building would suddenly perk up. Fans would move to the edge of their seats, awaiting Vinnie's next shot. If that one fell, the noise level increased noticeably. If he hit a third, strap yourself in and go along for a wild ride. That was the Vinnie Johnson who made the Pistons such fun from 1981-91, a 798-game span in which he became one of the league's best backup players and one of the most exciting Pistons ever. Along the way, he gained NBA immortality for his clinching last-second jump shot against Portland in the '90 Finals, a heaven-sent basket to complete the Pistons' 4-1 series win. Of course, it occured with only seven-tenths of a second left and the clock read :00.7, so "Double-0-7" was added to the list of Vinnie's nicknames. The rest were: "VJ," "Hoo" and, thanks to Danny Ainge in 1985, "The Microwave." But Johnson's career can't, and shouldn't, be boiled down to that one basket in Portland. He scored 11,531 points as a Piston, playoffs included, and most came from one of the greatest jump-shot forms you'll see. At 6-foot-2, 200 pounds, Johnson was built more like a longshoreman than a shooting guard, but his line-drive shot, honed on the Brooklyn schoolyards, was one of a kind. It would leave his hands on the flattest trajectory, but seemed to rip the net as if the ball had eyes. When he missed, Johnson was one of the best at rebounding his own shot. Almost half (1,165) of his 2,491 boards as a Piston were on the offensive end.

AT A GLANCE

VINNIE JOHNSON

FULL NAME:
Vincent Johnson
BORN:
September 1, 1956; Brooklyn, New York
POSITION, HEIGHT, WEIGHT:
Guard, 6-foot-2, 200 pounds
COLLEGE:
McLennan CC; Baylor '79
TENURE WITH PISTONS:
1981-82 — 1990-91
Also: Seattle 1979-81, San Antonio 1991-92

BEST SEASON WITH PISTONS:
1982-83, 82 GP, 15.8 ppg, 4.3 rpg
TOTALS WITH PISTONS:
Regular season: 798 GP, 10,146 pts. (12.7), 2,491 reb. (3.1), 2,661 ast. (3.3)
Playoffs: 111 GP, 1,385 pts. (12.5), 362 reb. (3.3), 304 ast. (2.7)

PISTON LIST

Kelly Tripucka's Highest-Scoring Games

56 points
- January 29, 1983 vs. Chicago

49 points
- March 12, 1982 vs. Golden State

45 points
- November 14, 1984 at Philadelphia

44 points
- January 14, 1984 at Cleveland

43 points
- April 1, 1983 vs. Cleveland

41 points
- February 24, 1986 vs. Chicago

40 points
- February 2, 1983 at Indiana

39 points
- November 1, 1983 vs. Milwaukee

38 points
- January 5, 1982 vs. Philadelphia
- March 23, 1983 vs. Indiana

CHANGING FACES

A YEAR EARLIER, armed with two first-round draft choices, the Pistons emerged with Isiah Thomas (2nd) and Kelly Tripucka (12th), a tidy haul indeed. But they were unable to copy their good fortune with two first-rounders in 1982-83. With the ninth pick, Detroit nabbed Wichita State forward Cliff Levingston. Nine picks later, it selected Rice guard Ricky Pierce, whose 26.8 scoring average had placed him second in the NCAA. But both players held out from training camp, wanting more money, and GM Jack McCloskey would not cave in. They finally reported, but both of them spent much of the season in coach Scotty Robertson's doghouse. A fourth-round pick, guard Walker D. Russell from Pontiac, made the club as a backup. The Pistons used 18 players this season, constantly scanning the free-agent wire. Among those making cameo appearances: Ray Tolbert, Scott May, Tom Owens, Steve Hayes and a foursome of Jims (Zoet, Johnstone, Smith and James Wilkes). Hayes and Edgar Jones were traded during the season.

Cliff Levingston's rookie year got off to a slow start with a contract holdout and a broken hand.

Take a Bow

Dave Bing

The Pistons welcomed back No. 21, Dave Bing, in 1983. Photo by Allen Einstein.

They'd been around for 25 seasons, but the Pistons had never retired a number. A wise guy might suggest they had not had any worth raising to the rafters, but that wasn't so. They were just waiting for Dave Bing to retire, that's all. On March 18, 1983, five years after Bing ended his 12-year NBA career by playing one season with the Celtics, the Pistons had a night for him at the Silverdome. With 18,057 fans in attendance and a cluster of former players on hand, the Pistons paid tribute to No. 21 with Bob Lanier and the Milwaukee Bucks in town. Bing was presented with several gifts and his jersey number was hoisted. When he was traded to Washington in the summer of 1975, Bing was the Pistons' all-time leader in points (15,235) and assists (4,330) after nine seasons. In the interim, Lanier had passed him in points, but Bing was still Detroit's assist king. Typically reserved, he said, "This is a great honor and I deeply appreciate it." He remains a frequent attendee at The Palace, sitting 10 rows behind the Detroit bench.

Game Results

1982-83 REGULAR SEASON

Date	Opponent	Result	Record
10-29	ATLANTA	W, 94-86	1-0
10-31	at Indiana	W, 118-115	2-0
11-2	at Cleveland	W, 128-119	3-0
11-3	CHICAGO	W, 152-144	4-0
11-5	PHILADELPHIA	L, 109-120	4-1
11-6	at Atlanta	L, 93-95	4-2
11-9	at Washington	W, 108-105	5-2
11-10	INDIANA	W, 115-91	6-2
11-12	MILWAUKEE	W, 111-100	7-2
11-13	at New York	L, 100-112	7-3
11-17	at Philadelphia	L, 103-120	7-4
11-19	GOLDEN STATE	W, 106-102	8-4
11-20	at Chicago	L, 128-131	8-5
11-23	at Houston	W, 128-106	9-5
11-24	at Kansas City	L, 112-122	9-6
11-26	PORTLAND	W, 132-118 (OT)	10-6
11-30	at Boston	W, 123-116	11-6
12-1	SAN ANTONIO	W, 105-97	12-6
12-4	BOSTON	L, 112-119	12-7
12-8	NEW YORK	L, 109-120	12-8
12-10	DALLAS	L, 121-122	12-9
12-11	at Philadelphia	L, 111-128	12-10
12-14	at New York	W, 104-99	13-10
12-15	BOSTON	L, 104-108	13-11
12-17	WASHINGTON	L, 110-119	13-12
12-18	at Cleveland	W, 97-90	14-12
12-19	at Boston	W, 131-114	15-12
12-21	at New Jersey	W, 102-97	16-12
12-23	DENVER	L, 127-135	16-13
12-26	at Milwaukee	L, 96-106	16-14
12-28	at Utah	L, 98-105 (OT)	16-15
12-30	at Phoenix	L, 98-115	16-16
1-1	at San Diego	W, 117-105	17-16
1-2	at L.A. Lakers	L, 112-127	17-17
1-4	at Chicago	L, 138-147 (2OT)	17-18
1-5	CLEVELAND	W, 130-116	18-18
1-7	at Milwaukee	W, 92-109	18-19
1-9	at New Jersey	L, 102-110	18-20
1-12	WASHINGTON	W, 116-100	19-20
1-14	PHILADELPHIA	L, 105-115	19-21
1-19	MILWAUKEE	W, 107-105	20-21
1-22	ATLANTA	W, 111-109	21-21
1-24	at Atlanta	W, 112-108	22-21
1-26	SEATTLE	L, 109-118	22-22
1-28	CLEVELAND	L, 106-107	22-23
1-29	CHICAGO	W, 128-126	23-23
2-2	at Indiana	L, 135-141	23-24
2-3	SAN DIEGO	L, 108-115	23-25
2-5	NEW JERSEY	W, 111-101	24-25
2-8	at San Antonio	L, 143-147 (OT)	24-26
2-9	at Dallas	L, 113-122	24-27
2-16	at Milwaukee	L, 121-126 (OT)	24-28
2-17	HOUSTON	W, 113-110	25-28
2-19	PHOENIX	W, 112-101	26-28
2-23	NEW YORK	W, 107-120	26-29
2-24	at Atlanta	L, 107-116	26-30
2-26	at Cleveland	W, 122-102	27-30
3-1	at Golden State	W, 114-103	28-30
3-3	KANSAS CITY	L, 118-125	28-31
3-5	L.A. LAKERS	L, 108-122	28-32
3-7	at Philadelphia	L, 114-123	28-33
3-8	INDIANA	W, 107-101	29-33
3-12	ATLANTA	L, 119-120	29-34
3-13	at Indiana	L, 114-118	29-35
3-15	at New Jersey	L, 90-109	29-36
3-16	UTAH	L, 115-125	29-37
3-18	MILWAUKEE	W, 103-99 (OT)	30-37
3-20	PHILADELPHIA	L, 119-121	30-38
3-22	at Chicago	W, 134-116	31-38
3-23	INDIANA	W, 109-96	32-38
3-25	at Denver	L, 120-131	32-39
3-29	at Portland	L, 107-114	32-40
3-30	at Seattle	L, 124-135	32-41
4-1	CLEVELAND	W, 120-111	33-41
4-3	CHICAGO	W, 122-107	34-41
4-5	at New York	L, 107-110 (OT)	34-42
4-6	WASHINGTON	W, 107-96	35-42
4-8	NEW JERSEY	W, 102-92	36-42
4-10	at Boston	L, 113-115	36-43
4-13	BOSTON	W, 113-101	37-43
4-15	NEW YORK	L, 83-100	37-44
4-16	at Washington	L, 95-102	37-45

(Home games in CAPS)

CHUCK DALY

A reporter once labeled Chuck Daly "The Prince of Pessimism" and he played along because it made interesting copy. But Daly knew better deep down, because the darkest cloud of his coaching career contained a brilliant silver lining. He couldn't have known it at the time, but when Daly was fired by the mismanaged and misguided Cleveland Cavaliers on March 6, 1982, it was the luckiest break he ever got.

Had Daly not been fired after 41 games—in which he endured a 9-32 record, ownership meddling and 93 straight days in a Holiday Inn—he probably wouldn't have become the Pistons' head coach one year later. While killing time as a 76ers broadcaster, Daly was hired by Detroit on May 17, 1983, beginning a fruitful nine-year relationship in which he helmed two championship teams, became the winningest coach in franchise history (467-271) and was recognized as one of the NBA's all-time greats. His selection as coach of the first U.S. Olympic Dream Team (1992) confirmed his gold-medal status.

Aside from Daly's vast basketball knowledge and ego-juggling skills, which were his strengths, he also built a marketable reputation on seemingly contradictory traits: the fashion sense of a man who takes himself seriously, countered by a self-deprecating (almost fatalistic) sense of self. Daly's sideline apparel and perfectly styled hair were a source of constant (read: excessive) media attention; he favored double-breasted suits, mostly dark blues and grays. That image led to another nickname: "Daddy Rich." But Daly's vanity was counterbalanced by a proper reading of his importance to the team. "It's a player's league," he said. "They allow you to coach them or they don't. Once they stop allowing you to coach, you're on your way out." He was also fond of saying, "Don't trust happiness." Statements like that fed his "Prince of Pessimism" rep, though Daly liked to say he was "an optimist with experience."

Daly had lots of pet phrases. When the Pistons broke a losing streak, his first whiskey-voiced words to the writers were almost certain to be: "We stopped the bleeding." When his team fell behind in a playoff series: "It's Katy-bar-the-door now." Asked

AT A GLANCE

CHUCK DALY

FULL NAME:
Charles Jerome Daly
BORN:
July 20, 1930; Kane, Pennsylvania
COLLEGE:
St. Bonaventure; Bloomsburg (Pa.) State '52

TENURE WITH PISTONS:
May 17, 1983 — May 5, 1992
Also head coach: Cleveland 1981-82, New Jersey 1992-94, Orlando 1997
Also assistant coach: Philadelphia 1978-81
BEST SEASON WITH PISTONS:
1988-89, 82 GM, 63-19 (.768), won NBA title
TOTALS WITH PISTONS:
Regular season: 738 GM, 467-271 (.633)
Playoffs: 113 GM, 71-42 (.628)
NBA PLAYING CAREER:
None
COLLEGE COACHING CAREER:
Boston College 1969-71 (26-24, .520), Pennsylvania 1971-77 (125-38, .767)
HONORS:
Top 10 Coaches of All-Time, 1996
NBA All-Star coach (1): 1989-90
U.S. Olympic coach: 1992 (8-0)

about "avenging" a previous loss: "That's High School Harry stuff." These phrases became familiar to those who followed closely from 1983-92.

Though Daly brought a strong collegiate background from Boston College and Penn, few could have envisioned his success when he arrived in the Motor City. His hiring was not popular, not only because the Cleveland disaster had been his only NBA coaching post, but because predecessor Scotty Robertson's firing had come out of the blue. Under the folksy Robertson, Detroit's win total had improved from 16 to 37 and media and fans generally felt the club had made steady progress. But the Pistons hadn't improved much defensively and that was GM Jack McCloskey's foremost reason for his second coaching switch.

The Pistons had sought Daly before. In 1980, while serving as a 76ers assistant under Billy Cunningham, Daly turned down a three-year offer from Detroit because he felt the money was insufficient. So Robertson got the gig. Then after Robertson was canned, the Pistons' first choice was Jack McKinney, the Indiana Pacers' coach, but he wanted to weigh other offers. Daly had felt he was out of contention for the job, but accepted a two-year deal, plus another year at the club's option. At age 53, he had his second shot as an NBA head coach. "This is a team of great potential," he said on his first day. "It has youth on its side. It wants to advance to a playoff situation."

Playoff situation, indeed. The Pistons never missed the playoffs under Daly, losing in the second round once and first round twice before reaching the Eastern Confer-

ence finals in 1987 for the first of five straight trips. Their three straight berths in the NBA Finals (1988-90) resulted in a seven-game loss to the Lakers and one-sided championships over the Lakers (4-0 in '89) and Portland (4-1 in '90). Until Daly showed up, the Pistons had only one 50-win season in 26 years; they won 50 or more five straight times ('87-91), including a club-record 63 in 1989.

By maintaining their basic nucleus—Isiah Thomas, Bill Laimbeer, Joe Dumars, Vinnie Johnson—the Pistons and Daly achieved rare continuity and they seemed to mature at the same pace. Sure, it was Daly's job to steer the ship, but he also received plenty of on-the-job training. During one particularly bad patch in 1985-86, Daly felt he was on the verge of being fired, only to have Thomas save him by lobbying owner Bill Davidson. A year earlier, Daly was looking to leave on his own, with an offer from Philadelphia awaiting his release by Detroit, but by demanding a first-round draft choice as compensation, the Pistons killed the swap. In time, contract negotiations became a hallmark of Daly's tenure. Especially in later seasons when NBC sought him as a color analyst, it became an annual question: Will he stay or will he go? This public tug-and-pull created the impression that Daly and McCloskey were at odds, though Daly once said, "We have a great relationship ... until contract time."

But it was a relationship that worked, probably because Daly and McCloskey had similar basketball upbringings. Daly was raised in Kane in Western Pennsylvania, while McCloskey hailed from the Eastern

part of the state, Mahoney City. Only five years separate their respective stints as head coach at Penn (McCloskey 1956-66, Daly 1971-77). In his first season there, Daly guided the Quakers to a 25-3 record, a No. 3 national ranking and the first of four Ivy League titles. He had been the head coach at Boston College (1969-71) and an assistant at Duke under Vic Bubas (1963-69). Before that he coached at Punxsutawney (Pa.) High, gaining notoriety even then as a sharp dresser, a habit he picked up from his salesman father. From Penn, Daly moved on to be a 76ers assistant for four seasons, helping them win two division titles and reach the 1980 NBA Finals. This is the vast background Daly refers to when he calls himself a coaching "lifer."

He used that term again on May 5, 1992 when he stepped down as Pistons coach after a first-round loss to the Knicks. Technically, his contract wasn't renewed, which angered some fans and players, particularly Dennis Rodman, who felt Daly was being shoved out in favor of Ron Rothstein, a former Pistons assistant groomed by Daly. But in his farewell speech, Daly agreed it was time to go: "It's my call, basically. The players need to hear a new voice. Maybe they needed it two years ago. After while, they tune you out and you start tuning them out. You can't coach that way."

But Daly wasn't done in the coaching racket. He immediately moved on to the New Jersey Nets for two seasons (1992-94), leading them to the playoffs both years. After two years as a color commentator for Turner's NBA coverage, he returned to coaching in 1997 (at age 67) with Orlando.

Chuck Daly's NBA Coaching Record

Year, Team	REGULAR SEASON				PLAYOFFS		
	W	L	Pct.	Finish/Div.	W	L	Pct.
1981-82, Cleveland	9	32	.220				
1983-84, Detroit	49	33	.598	2nd/Central	2	3	.400
1984-85, Detroit	46	36	.561	2nd/Central	5	4	.556
1985-86, Detroit	46	36	.561	3rd/Central	1	3	.250
1986-87, Detroit	52	30	.634	2nd/Central	10	5	.667
1987-88, Detroit	54	28	.659	1st/Central	14	9	.609
1988-89, Detroit	63	19	.768	1st/Central	15	2	.882
1989-90, Detroit	59	23	.720	1st/Central	15	5	.750
1990-91, Detroit	50	32	.610	2nd/Central	7	8	.467
1991-92, Detroit	48	34	.585	3rd/Central	2	3	.400
1992-93, New Jersey	43	39	.524	3rd/Atlantic	2	3	.400
1993-94, New Jersey	45	37	.549	3rd/Atlantic	1	3	.250
TOTALS, 12 years	**564**	**379**	**.598**	**TOTALS, 11 years**	**74**	**48**	**.607**

1983 1984

DETROIT PISTONS

TIME CAPSULE

October 23, 1983:
An explosive-laden truck blows up outside the U.S. Marine barracks in Beirut, Lebanon, killing 241 Marine and Navy personnel.

April 23, 1984:
Federal researchers announce the identification of a virus thought to cause acquired immune deficiency syndrome (AIDS).

July 28, 1984:
The Summer Olympic games begin in Los Angeles, highlighted by the performances of Carl Lewis and Mary Lou Retton.

SEASON SNAPSHOT

Most Points
Isiah Thomas (1,748, 21.3 avg.)
Kelly Tripucka (1,618, 21.3 avg.)

Most Rebounds
Bill Laimbeer (1,003, 12.2 avg.)

Most Assists
Isiah Thomas (914, 11.1 avg.)

Most Minutes
Isiah Thomas (3,007, 36.7 avg.)

Field-Goal Percentage
Kent Benson (55.0%)

Free-Throw Percentage
John Long (88.4%)

Team Offense Average
117.1 (9,602 in 82 games)

Team Defense Average
113.5 (9,308 in 82 games)

NBA All-Stars
Isiah Thomas, G (First Team)

Pistons in All-Star Game
Isiah Thomas, G (MVP); Bill Laimbeer, C
Kelly Tripucka, F

1983-84

FINAL STANDINGS

Central Division	W	L	Pct.	GB
Milwaukee	50	32	.610	—
PISTONS	**49**	**33**	**.598**	**1**
Atlanta	40	42	.488	10
Cleveland	28	54	.341	22
Chicago	27	55	.329	23
Indiana	26	56	.317	24

Atlantic Division Winner—Boston
Midwest Division Winner—Utah
Pacific Division Winner—Los Angeles

PLAYOFF RESULTS

Eastern First Round: N.Y. Knicks d. Pistons, 3-2

PISTONS PLAYOFF LEADERS

Scoring: Kelly Tripucka (27.4 avg.)
Rebounding: Bill Laimbeer (12.4)
Assists: Isiah Thomas (11.0)

NBA CHAMPION

Boston Celtics

1983-84
SEASON IN REVIEW

The Pistons turned one important corner this season, only to discover things were even tougher around the next corner. Guided by an unheralded new coach, Chuck Daly, the Detroit upstarts challenged for the Central Division title until the final week. Their 49-33 record (then second-best in club history) fell a game short of Milwaukee, but it earned the team's first playoff bid since 1977. Their first-round series vs. New York became a five-game classic, but the Pistons did not meet the Knicks' intensity until it was too late. Bernard King dominated them by averaging 42.6 points and not even an amazing Game 5 by Isiah Thomas (16 points in 65 seconds) could prevent Detroit's OT elimination. The lesson seared their souls, but the Pistons learned first-hand that playoff wins are gained via defensive intensity. On December 13, 1983, defense was nowhere to be found as Detroit and host Denver played the highest-scoring game in NBA history, finally won by the Pistons 186-184 in three overtimes. Besides All-Star MVP Thomas, who became Detroit's first All-NBA first-teamer since Dave Bing, Bill Laimbeer and Kelly Tripucka also made the All-Star Game. The club finished strong, winning 26 of its last 39, including a season-ending 11-3 spurt that included an OT win over the eventual champion Celtics. Detroit led the NBA in attendance for the first time, drawing an average of 15,923 to the cavernous Silverdome.

Pistons-Lakers games, like this one March 3, 1984, drew crowds in excess of 30,000. Photo by Allen Einstein.

WHAT A NIGHT!

April 27, 1984

A few miles up the road on this muggy Friday, the red-hot Tigers were playing an eventual 19-inning loss. At Cobo Arena, rock star Ted Nugent—the Motor City Madman—was in concert. Next door at Joe Louis Arena, the Pistons' season was ending, but their 127-123 overtime loss to the Knicks would go down as one of the most incredible in club history. In a magnificent 1-on-1 battle against Bernard King, Isiah Thomas played an unbelievable fourth period to nearly give Detroit its first series victory since 1976. He scored the Pistons' last 16 points in regulation in a span of 1:05 and had a chance to make the winning basket. Tied at 114 with 15 seconds left in regulation, thanks to his triple, Thomas held the ball out front as the crowd went wild in anticipation. He drove with eight seconds to go and jumped to shoot, but the ball was swiped by Darrell Walker, pushing the game into OT. Thomas would foul out with 37 seconds to go—as Bill Laimbeer had three minutes earlier—and the Pistons were doomed to a 3-2 series defeat. King scored a game-high 44, but Thomas' 35 got more acclaim. "Detroit went down swinging," Knicks coach Hubie Brown said. "Isiah's effort in the fourth quarter was a staggering punch to us."

Isiah Thomas and the Knicks' Bernard King were the stars of the 1984 playoff series. Photo by Allen Einstein.

Terry Tyler

Terry Tyler was a dependable post-up player as well as a top defender. Photo by Allen Einstein.

If the better part of greatness is simply showing up every day, there's no denying Terry Tyler's value to the Pistons. In seven years with them, beginning in 1978, the rugged 6-foot-7 forward was there every day. He never missed a game, playing all 82 each season for a team-record 574 in a row. In fact, Tyler still holds that record. Though Bill Laimbeer had a longer overall streak (685), he played only the last 561 in a row with Detroit, having carried a 124-game streak from Cleveland. Tyler is also the Pistons' career leader in blocked shots (1,070), continuing evidence of his marvelous jumping ability (his verticle leap was once 45 inches). More than a decade after Tyler left Detroit, signing with Sacramento as a free agent in 1985, he still ranks highly in several Pistons statistical categories. He is seventh in steals, eighth in games, eighth in rebounds, ninth in minutes and 14th in scoring. Though Tyler was mostly regarded as a defensive player, he could score as well. As a hometown rookie out of the University of Detroit, he set his career high (32 points) in 1978-79. In a 12-game span in 1980-81, his best season, he was the Pistons' leading scorer 11 times, averaging 22.7 points in those games. Tyler saved his best for (almost) last in 1985 in Game 3 of the Eastern semis vs. the Celtics. In a game Detroit had to win, having dropped the first two, Tyler came off the bench to score 16 of the Pistons' final 17 points and they won 125-117. "In the fourth quarter, you ask yourself, 'Do you want the pressure or don't you?' I love the pressure. It's a challenge," Tyler said. It would be his fourth-from-last game with Detroit. He signed with Sacramento, where his streak quickly ended with 11 missed games in 1986-87.

AT A GLANCE

TERRY TYLER

FULL NAME:
Terry Christopher Tyler

BORN:
October 30, 1956; Detroit

POSITION, HEIGHT, WEIGHT:
Forward, 6-foot-7, 215 pounds

COLLEGE:
Detroit '78

ACQUIRED:
Drafted, second round, 1978 (23rd overall)

TENURE WITH PISTONS:
1978-79 — 1984-85
Also: Sacramento 1985-88, Dallas 1988-89

BEST SEASON WITH PISTONS:
1980-81, 82 GP, 13.4 ppg, 6.9 rpg

TOTALS WITH PISTONS:
Regular season: 574 GP, 11.6 ppg, 6.2 rpg
Playoffs: 17 GP, 9.0 ppg, 3.2 rpg

HONORS:
NBA All-Rookie Team: 1978-79

PISTON LIST

Highest-Scoring Games (with opponent total)

x-186 points
- December 13, 1983 at Denver (184), 3OT

160 points
- March 9, 1979 vs. Boston (117)

158 points
- March 23, 1969 vs. Chicago (114)

152 points
- November 3, 1982 vs. Chicago (144)

151 points
- January 7, 1972 vs. Cincinnati (132)

148 points
- February 6, 1970 at Baltimore (153), 2OT
- December 19, 1984 at Denver (129)

147 points
- December 13, 1959 vs. New York (129)

146 points
- January 12, 1963 at Rochester (115)

x-NBA record

CHANGING FACES

WHEN CHUCK DALY took over as coach of the Pistons, he essentially did so without a first-round draft pick. Detroit chose Antoine Carr, a burly forward from Wichita State, with the eighth pick in '83, but he refused to sign with the club. The Pistons' hardline stance provoked Carr to go to Europe, where he spent the season with Milano of the Italian League. He would never play a game for Detroit. The Pistons also got rid of last year's disappointing first-round guard, Ricky Pierce, sending him to the San Diego Clippers for two second-rounders before the season. It was a bad deal, not only because Pierce went on to a 14,000-point career, but because Detroit packaged the picks for defensive guard David Thirdkill, a disappointment as well. The Pistons' finest acquisition of the season was forward Earl Cureton, a

Earl Cureton dunks over Artis Gilmore at the Silverdome. Photo by Allen Einstein.

free agent signed away from the champion 76ers. A Detroit native and another of Dick Vitale's recruits to U-of-D, Cureton contributed little in '83-84, but became a valuable role player for two seasons. Other new Pistons: Lionel Hollins and Ken Austin.

Take a Bow

Isiah Thomas

Being All-Star MVP was one of the early highlights of Isiah Thomas' career.

"I was the greatest player in the world today." For the second time in Pistons history, one of their own could make that statement. On January 29, 1984, Isiah Thomas was that player. He was chosen MVP of the All-Star game at Denver, compiling 21 points (all after halftime) and 15 assists to spark the East's 154-145 comeback win in overtime. Making his third All-Star start in as many years, Thomas joined Bob Lanier (1974) as the only Pistons to be named MVP. "You can't imagine how it feels," he said. "I imagined this happening just like me marrying Princess Di." Isiah got cooking in the third quarter, scoring 10 to help cut the West's 16-point halftime lead to eight, then he directed the East with aplomb in the fourth quarter. Winning coach K.C. Jones said, "Isiah's so good. He can make the pass and lead the fast break at 100 miles an hour. He can hit the outside jumper, too. Other than that, he's just an average player." Bill Laimbeer helped out with 13 points in 17 minutes.

Game Results
1983-84
REGULAR SEASON

Date	Opponent	Result	Record
10-28	BOSTON	W, 127-121	1-0
10-29	at Atlanta	L, 115-117	1-1
11-1	MILWAUKEE	W, 106-93	2-1
11-3	at Washington	L, 88-111	2-2
11-4	HOUSTON	L, 108-113	2-3
11-9	PHILADELPHIA	W, 120-116	3-3
11-11	at Boston	L, 118-126	3-4
11-12	KANSAS CITY	W, 131-106	4-4
11-15	at Chicago	L, 110-112	4-5
11-16	SEATTLE	W, 122-120	5-5
11-18	UTAH	W, 128-120	6-5
11-19	at New York	L, 101-104 (OT)	6-6
11-22	at Philadelphia	L, 108-112	6-7
11-23	at Indiana	W, 115-113	7-7
11-25	WASHINGTON	L, 111-120	7-8
11-27	at Boston	L, 99-114	7-9
11-29	CLEVELAND	W, 103-93	8-9
12-2	ATLANTA	W, 128-92	9-9
12-3	INDIANA	W, 117-99	10-9
12-8	at Golden State	L, 129-130	10-10
12-9	at Portland	L, 117-123	10-11
12-11	at Seattle	L, 131-135	10-12
12-13	at Denver	W, 186-184 (3OT)	11-12
12-17	BOSTON	L, 115-129	11-13
12-20	DALLAS	W, 116-104	12-13
12-21	at Cleveland	W, 119-112	13-13
12-23	PHILADELPHIA	L, 106-108	13-14
12-27	PORTLAND	W, 140-100	14-14
12-28	at New York	W, 111-108	15-14
12-30	CHICAGO	W, 103-96	16-14
1-3	at Washington	L, 102-103	16-15
1-4	PHOENIX	W, 128-114	17-15
1-6	NEW YORK	W, 118-107	18-15
1-8	at Milwaukee	W, 111-100	19-15
1-11	at Indiana	W, 112-96	20-15
1-13	CHICAGO	W, 115-104	21-15
1-14	at Cleveland	W, 132-131 (OT)	22-15
1-17	at Philadelphia	L, 117-128	22-16
1-18	NEW JERSEY	L, 115-124	22-17
1-20	ATLANTA	W, 116-94	23-17
1-21	at New Jersey	L, 103-120	23-18
1-24	INDIANA	L, 107-114	23-19
1-31	at Cleveland	L, 112-114 (OT)	23-20
2-2	at Washington	W, 139-129	24-20
2-3	SAN DIEGO	W, 126-111	25-20
2-5	at Boston	L, 134-137 (OT)	25-21
2-7	CLEVELAND	W, 130-99	26-21
2-10	GOLDEN STATE	W, 134-116	27-21
2-11	SAN ANTONIO	L, 116-123	27-22
2-14	at Houston	W, 126-119	28-22
2-18	at Dallas	W, 120-115	29-22
2-19	at San Antonio	W, 142-140 (OT)	30-22
2-21	at Kansas City	L, 112-119	30-23
2-22	NEW YORK	W, 114-111	31-23
2-24	at Indiana	L, 100-108	31-24
2-26	CLEVELAND	W, 121-109	32-24
2-28	at Atlanta	W, 101-96	33-24
2-29	WASHINGTON	W, 137-106	34-24
3-2	NEW YORK	L, 102-117	34-25
3-4	L.A. LAKERS	L, 114-118	34-26
3-6	at Chicago	W, 124-108	35-26
3-7	ATLANTA	W, 107-93	36-26
3-9	NEW JERSEY	W, 122-118	37-26
3-10	WASHINGTON	W, 115-100	38-26
3-13	at Milwaukee	L, 95-116	38-27
3-14	DENVER	L, 121-125	38-28
3-16	NEW JERSEY	L, 108-117	38-29
3-19	at Utah	L, 125-143	38-30
3-21	at San Diego	W, 132-133	39-30
3-23	at L.A. Lakers	W, 121-118	40-30
3-24	at Phoenix	W, 120-109	41-30
3-27	at Chicago	W, 111-83	42-30
3-28	CHICAGO	W, 108-101	43-30
3-29	at New Jersey	L, 116-118	43-31
3-31	MILWAUKEE	W, 107-105	44-31
4-3	PHILADELPHIA	W, 118-115	45-31
4-6	at New York	W, 115-107	46-31
4-7	at Milwaukee	L, 92-110	46-32
4-10	INDIANA	W, 100-98	47-32
4-11	at Philadelphia	W, 126-113	48-32
4-13	BOSTON	W, 128-120 (OT)	49-32
4-14	at Atlanta	L, 107-115	49-33

PLAYOFFS
Eastern First Round—(Best-of-Five)

4-17	NEW YORK	L, 93-94	0-1
4-19	NEW YORK	W, 113-105	1-1
4-22	at New York	L, 113-120	1-2
4-25	at New York	W, 119-112	2-2
4-27	NEW YORK	L, 123-127 (OT)	2-3

(Home games in CAPS)

·TIMEOUT·

HIGHEST-SCORING GAME IN NBA HISTORY

December 13, 1983:
Pistons 186, Denver Nuggets 184 (3OT)

Chuck Daly had well analyzed the situation before running into Denver coach Doug Moe prior to the Pistons-Nuggets game on December 13, 1983.

Moe's teams had a deserved reputation for defensive indifference, but Daly also knew his fledgling Pistons couldn't resist a good track meet.

Weighing those factors, Daly thought it might be a high-scoring game, maybe even a landmark, as a crowd of 9,655 filed into McNichols Arena.

"I was telling Doug Moe we should make it the first one to 140 points is the winner," Daly said. "Little did I know how prophetic I would be."

How prophetic, indeed. Three hours, 11 minutes, three overtimes, 370 points and eight league records later, the Pistons and Nuggets were the talk of the NBA. In the only overtime game ever played between the two clubs, Detroit beat Denver 186-184 in the highest-scoring game in NBA history, a feat that seems more amazing in the defensive-minded '90s.

The participants' memories haven't faded in the interim.

"I was hoping it wouldn't end—we were having too much fun," Vinnie Johnson said. "It was run-and-gun from the start. It was like a summer league game, no defense at all."

"Everybody was playing great," said Isiah Thomas, who set his career scoring high that night with 47. "It was just one of those games where everything goes in."

"Everybody was on," said Walker D. Russell (though the D. didn't apply that night; nobody played any). "From one end to the other, it was 'Bam, bam, bam.' Everything was falling. And I got mine."

Yes, the summary confirms it. Russell, the former Pontiac high school star, got in for six minutes and supplied one basket, two points and one assist. There are no insignificant numbers in a game like this.

Aside from accounting for the two highest one-team totals, the clubs' 370-point total shattered the NBA record of 316, set March 2, 1962, in the Philadelphia Warriors' 169-147 win over the New York Knicks. That was the night Wilt Chamberlain scored 100 for Philly at Hershey, Pennsylvania.

Here's how amazing the Pistons and Nuggets were: they had surpassed the Warriors-Knicks record by the end of their first overtime.

But statistics aren't foremost in Kelly Tripucka's memory, though the game was custom-made for his, uh, relaxed attitude toward defense.

"The game lasted so long, we were wondering if we could find a place to eat after the game," Tripucka said. "We were wondering, 'Is there an all-night diner in Denver?' We were just glad we didn't have a game the next day. We asked for the day off."

Though Tripucka scored all 12 Detroit points in the second OT and had 35 in the game, his total was only fifth-highest. He was topped by two teammates, Thomas (47) and John Long (41), and Denver's top two, Kiki Vandeweghe (51) and Alex English (47).

The game was close all the way, with the Pistons leading 38-34 after the first quarter and Denver battling back for a 74-74 halftime tie. The Nuggets nudged ahead 113-108 after three quarters.

"They usually say the first team to 100 points wins, but in this game, that happened

in the middle of the third quarter," Daly said. "I've never heard of anything like this, much less been involved in it."

In the fourth quarter, the game seemed to develop a momentum all its own and the players sensed it. The shots kept falling and the score kept climbing and no one was sure how—or when—it would end. English did his best to win it in regulation, scoring 17 of the Nuggets' 32 points in the final quarter, but Thomas donned the hero's wreath for Detroit.

With six seconds to play in regulation and the Pistons down 145-142, Bill Laimbeer went to the free throw line. He hit the first shot and then had to miss the second intentionally, hoping a teammate would rebound and score. That ploy rarely works, but the ball clanged hard off the rim, Thomas burst into the lane and tipped it in as time ran out to force OT.

In the first five-minute overtime, Denver claimed a 157-152 lead, but Thomas hit the Pistons' only 3-pointer of the game—imagine that—to help them tie it 159-159. The Nuggets' Dan Issel (28 points) could have

Isiah Thomas — 47 points

NBA RECORDS

- **Most points, two teams:** 370
- **Most points, one team:** Pistons 186
- **Most points, losing team:** Nuggets 184
- **Field goals, two teams:** 142 (Pistons 74, Nuggets 68)
- **Field goals, one team:** Pistons 74
- **Assists, two teams:** 93 (Pistons 47, Nuggets 46)
- **Players with 40 or more points, two teams:** 4
- **Players with 40 or more points, one team:** 2 (tied with several others)

John Long — 41 points

Kiki Vandeweghe — 51 points

Alex English — 47 points

won it, but missed a jumper in the last seconds. Thomas hurried all the way for a layup, but the officials ruled that it came after the buzzer.

Though Tripucka dominated the second OT for the Pistons, neither club could pull away. At 171-171, overtime No. 3 beckoned.

Once again, the Nuggets took the lead 179-177, but the Pistons put on an unspectacular winning surge in the final 1:41. Laimbeer hit two free throws to tie it, then Long and Thomas made breakaway layups to shove the Pistons ahead 183-179. Two Thomas free throws sealed it with 28 seconds left, though Denver's Richard Anderson closed the scoring with the Nuggets' lone 3-pointer of the night.

The final tally was eight NBA records— all still standing. But opinion seems split on how long the scoring marks will hold up.

"I think it'll be a very difficult record to break," Johnson said. "There might be a game like that if you have two expansion teams that haven't figured out the system they want to play. But they probably wouldn't be deep enough for it. You need at least eight or nine players on both teams to make it happen."

But Thomas feels the records could tumble.

"Because when we were doing it, it didn't seem too hard," he said. "It might be a while before it happens, but in the NBA, you're always going to see something phenomenal, some that just boggles your mind."

Maybe so, but until then, the Pistons-Nuggets classic of December 13, 1983 holds that record, too: Most Minds Boggled.

BOXSCORE

At Denver
DETROIT PISTONS (186)

PLAYER	MIN	FG	FGA	3P	3PA	FT	FTA	REB	A	PTS
Kelly Tripucka	39	14	25	0	0	7	9	4	2	35
Cliff Levingston	13	1	2	0	0	0	0	2	0	2
Bill Laimbeer	47	6	10	0	0	5	9	12	6	17
Isiah Thomas	52	18	34	1	2	10	19	5	17	47
John Long	46	18	25	0	0	5	6	6	8	41
Terry Tyler	28	8	15	0	0	2	3	8	1	18
Vinnie Johnson	21	4	12	0	0	4	5	5	8	12
Earl Cureton	34	3	6	0	0	3	5	7	2	9
Ray Tolbert	15	1	4	0	0	1	4	6	2	3
Walker Russell	6	1	2	0	0	0	0	0	1	2
Kent Benson	13	0	1	0	0	0	0	1	0	0
David Thirdkill	1	0	0	0	0	0	0	0	0	0
TOTALS	**315**	**74**	**136**	**1**	**2**	**37**	**60**	**56**	**47**	**186**

FG Pct.: 54.4; FT Pct.: 61.7; Team Rebounds: 16.

DENVER NUGGETS (184)

PLAYER	MIN	FG	FGA	3P	3PA	FT	FTA	REB	A	PTS
Alex English	50	18	30	0	0	11	13	12	7	47
Kiki Vandeweghe	50	21	29	0	0	9	11	9	8	51
Dan Issel	35	11	19	0	1	6	8	8	5	28
Rob Williams	21	3	8	0	0	3	4	3	5	9
T.R. Dunn	36	3	3	0	0	1	2	4	2	7
Mike Evans	40	7	13	0	0	2	2	2	7	16
Richard Anderson	14	5	6	1	1	2	3	5	1	13
Danny Schayes	24	0	1	0	0	11	12	7	2	11
Bill Hanzlik	38	0	4	0	0	2	2	7	7	2
Howard Carter	4	0	1	0	0	0	0	0	1	0
Ken Dennard	3	0	1	0	0	0	0	0	1	0
TOTALS	**315**	**68**	**115**	**1**	**2**	**47**	**57**	**57**	**46**	**184**

FG Pct.: 59.1; FT Pct.: 82.5; Team Rebounds: 13.

SCORE BY QUARTERS	1	2	3	4	OT	OT	OT	FINAL
DETROIT	38	36	34	37	14	12	15	186
DENVER	34	40	39	32	14	12	13	184

Officials: Joe Borgia, Jesse Hall.
A: 9,655. Time of game: 3:11.

1984 DETROIT PISTONS 1985

TIME CAPSULE

October 14, 1984:
Capping a near-perfect season featuring a record 35-5 start, the Detroit Tigers win the World Series over San Diego.

November 6, 1984:
Ronald Reagan is re-elected president, overwhelming Walter Mondale in the greatest Republican landslide ever.

March 4, 1985:
The Environmental Protection Agency orders a permanent ban on leaded gasoline.

SEASON SNAPSHOT

Most Points
Isiah Thomas (1,720, 21.2 avg.)

Most Rebounds
Bill Laimbeer (1,013, 12.4 avg.)

Most Assists
x-Isiah Thomas (1,123, 13.9 avg.)

Most Minutes
Isiah Thomas (3,089, 38.1 avg.)

Field-Goal Percentage
Kent Benson (50.6%)

Free-Throw Percentage
Kelly Tripucka (88.5%)

Team Offense Average
116.0 (9,508 in 82 games)

Team Defense Average
113.5 (9,304 in 82 games)

NBA All-Stars
Isiah Thomas, G (First Team)

Pistons in All-Star Game
Isiah Thomas, G; Bill Laimbeer, C

x-league record

1984-85

FINAL STANDINGS

Central Division	W	L	Pct.	GB
Milwaukee	59	23	.720	—
PISTONS	**46**	**36**	**.561**	**13**
Chicago	38	44	.463	21
Cleveland	36	46	.439	23
Atlanta	34	48	.415	25
Indiana	22	60	.268	37

Atlantic Division Winner—Boston
Midwest Division Winner—Denver
Pacific Division Winner—L.A. Lakers

PLAYOFF RESULTS

Eastern First Round: Pistons d. New Jersey, 3-0
Eastern Semifinals: Boston d. Pistons, 4-2

PISTONS PLAYOFF LEADERS

Scoring: Isiah Thomas (24.3 avg.)
Rebounding: Bill Laimbeer (10.7)
Assists: Isiah Thomas (11.2)

NBA CHAMPION

Los Angeles Lakers

1984-85
SEASON IN REVIEW

The Pistons made sure the weather wasn't the most memorable part of the 1984-85 season. Tons of snow and ice caused the Silverdome's air-supported roof to collapse March 4, only seven hours before the Pistons were to host Milwaukee. With the Dome needing millions in repairs, the Pistons simply moved back downtown for the final two months, playing at Joe Louis Arena (and one game at Cobo). Despite losing their comfort zone, the Pistons were 11-4 downtown, including a 2-0 record in their first-round playoff win over New Jersey. Detroit hadn't won a series in the postseason since 1976, but swept the Nets, 3-0. Though the Pistons suffered a 4-2 loss to the Celtics in the Eastern semis, they gave their fans a taste of things to come. After dropping Games 1 and 2 at Boston, they won Games 3 and 4 at Joe Louis as Terry Tyler and Vinnie Johnson supplied the late heroics; Johnson's 22-point fourth quarter cemented his reputation as a gamer. The Pistons' 46-36 record was enough for second place, but it was a disappointment considering that an eight-game win streak (within an 11-1 spurt) helped them to a 30-17 mark by February 4. They went on a 6-15 slump that immediately brought them back to the pack. Isiah Thomas compiled an NBA-record 1,123 assists, led the team with a 21.2 scoring average and made the All-NBA first team for a second straight year.

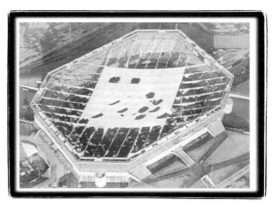

The collapse of the Silverdome's Teflon roof March 4 sent the Pistons back to downtown Detroit.

May 5, 1985

It was V.J.'s Day at JLA. It was a Sunday afternoon that created a local legend and spawned a nickname. With a national-TV audience tuned in to the game at Joe Louis Arena, Vinnie Johnson showed everyone that Isiah Thomas was not the only Pistons guard with a taste for the big moment. With Detroit trailing Boston 87-76 after three quarters, Johnson single-handedly rescued his team from a 3-1 series deficit. He pumped in 22 of the Pistons' 26 points in the fourth quarter, sparking them to a 102-99 win to tie the series 2-2. But these weren't ordinary shots Johnson was hitting en route to a then-career-high 34 points on 16-of-21 field goals in 30 minutes. He was rifling line drives from all over the court, having his way with Boston guards Dennis Johnson and Danny Ainge. All told in the quarter, Johnson hit 10-of-11 shots. "When I get it going, I feel it—even against a big man," he said. "The ball just went in. It felt good." At one point, Isiah Thomas had to tell him to keep shooting. Afterward, the amazed Ainge said, "Vinnie Johnson is The Microwave. He heated up in a hurry." The Pistons lost the next two games and the series, but Vinnie's nickname survived. He'd forever be known as The Microwave.

WHAT A NIGHT!

On a magical Sunday at Joe Louis Arena, Vinnie Johnson made almost every shot he attempted. Photo by Allen Einstein.

Dan Roundfield

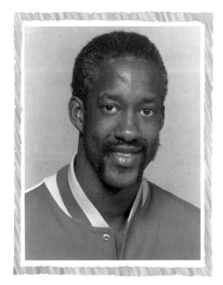

After a disappointing season in Detroit, Dan Roundfield was traded for Rick Mahorn in 1985.

Dan Roundfield, a Premier Piston? Well, he was supposed to be, though it didn't quite work out. In fact, he wound up playing only 56 games as a member of his hometown team. The Detroit Chadsey grad had acceptable averages—10.9 points, 8.1 rebounds—so he did not flop as badly as you might recall. But even GM Jack McCloskey later admitted the addition of Roundfield in the summer of 1984 was one of his worst deals. "It didn't work out," Trader Jack conceded. Then an eight-year veteran possessing career averages of 16.6 points and 10.4 rebounds, Roundfield joined the Pistons after six top-notch years with Atlanta. He'd made four NBA All-Defensive teams, including three first-team berths. The Pistons were in need of a good inside player, someone to help Bill Laimbeer on the glass and outlet to Isiah Thomas to key the fast break. Roundfield, who once had a 26-rebound game for Atlanta, seemed the perfect veteran addition. McCloskey dealt Cliff Levingston, the rights to unsigned 1983 draft pick Antoine Carr and two second-round draft picks to the Hawks on June 18, 1984. Levingston had not helped much in two years and Carr had refused to come to the Pistons, so it seemed like an OK risk. It was ineffective, though. Roundfield, 31, was soon limping on a bum knee that would need February surgery. Even when he occasionally played well—he had games of 19, 16, 15 and 14 rebounds—the Pistons weren't appreciably better. After the season, 364 days after he had arrived, Roundfield was dealt to Washington for center Mike Gibson and roundish forward Rick Mahorn. In 1987, in the Washington-Detroit first-round playoff, Roundfield left the Bullets after Game 1 and retired two days later.

AT A GLANCE

DAN ROUNDFIELD

FULL NAME:
Danny Thomas Roundfield
BORN:
May 26, 1953; Detroit
POSITION, HEIGHT, WEIGHT:
Forward, 6-foot-8, 205 pounds
COLLEGE:
Central Michigan '75
ACQUIRED:
1984, trade with Atlanta

TENURE WITH PISTONS:
1984-85
Also: Indiana 1975-78, Atlanta 1978-84, Washington 1985-87
BEST SEASON WITH PISTONS:
1984-85, 56 GP, 10.9 ppg, 8.1 rpg
TOTALS WITH PISTONS:
Regular season: 56 GP, 10.9 ppg, 8.1 rpg
Playoffs: 9 GP, 9.1 ppg, 6.7 rpg
HONORS:
All-Star Game (3): 1979-80, 1980-81, 1981-82 (Atlanta)
NBA All-Defensive: First Team 1979-80, 1981-82, 1982-83; Second Team 1983-84 (Atlanta)

PISTON LIST

Highest Career Playoff Scoring Averages

(10 games or more)
- 25.6 avg., Bob Lanier, 22 games
- 20.4, Isiah Thomas, 111 games
- 19.9, Dave Bing, 16 games
- 19.8, Adrian Dantley, 38 games
- 19.8, Kelly Tripucka, 18 games
- 19.6, Dave DeBusschere, 10 games
- 19.1, Gene Shue, 27 games
- 18.4, Don Ohl, 17 games
- 17.2, Bailey Howell, 21 games
- 16.9, Ray Scott, 14 games
- 15.9, Joe Dumars, 107 games
- 15.3, Howard Porter, 15 games
- 14.0, Eric Money, 12 games
- 13.8, Bob Ferry, 18 games
- 13.5, Mark Aguirre, 57 games
- 12.6, Walter Dukes, 30 games
- 12.5, Vinnie Johnson, 111 games
- 12.5, Curtis Rowe, 19 games
- 12.0, Bill Laimbeer, 113 games

CHANGING FACES

AFTER TWO YEARS of rookie holdouts, the Pistons were able to sign their first-round draft pick—on time—in 1984-85. Tony Campbell had been selected with the 20th pick, a 6-foot-7 small forward from Ohio State. "I think a lot of good things can happen here," he said. "The Pistons play the kind of game I like." But they were beginning to make a higher priority of defense, which wasn't Campbell's strong point, so his playing time was limited. He played only 56 of 82 games, though he appeared in 23 straight late in the season, and averaged 5.6 points. Campbell would spend three seasons with Detroit and average 6.2. The Pistons also chose Michigan guard Eric Turner in the second round, but he didn't make the squad. A summer trade for Dan Roundfield was the Pistons' most significant transaction. The deal cost them Cliff Levingston, the rights to Antoine Carr and two second-rounders. The Pistons also went through several backups: Brook Steppe, Major Jones, Lorenzo Romar, Terry Teagle, Sidney Lowe and Dale Wilkinson.

Tony Campbell's career scoring high with Detroit was 20 points. Photo by Allen Einstein.

The VILLAIN

Kevin McHale

Despite Bill Laimbeer's defense, Boston's accordian-like Kevin McHale dominated Detroit in 1984-85. Later on, too. Photo by Allen Einstein.

The Pistons had already permitted Moses Malone a 51-point game. They let a rookie named Michael Jordan score 49 on them. Bernard King got 41, Mark Aguirre got 40. But no opponent victimized Detroit in 1984-85 like Boston forward Kevin McHale. Starting only because Cedric Maxwell was hurt, the lanky 6-foot-10 Minnesotan set a (then) Celtics record by scoring 56 points on March 3, 1985, fueling a 138-129 victory over Detroit at the Boston Garden. By making 22-of-28 field goals and 12-of-13 foul shots, McHale topped Larry Bird's record of 53 points set two years before. "I'm basically a role player," McHale said. "I suppose it will sink in that there are so many legends, so many great Celtics, and I'm up there with them for one day." Bird had a triple-double with 30 points, 15 rebounds and 10 assists, but said, "Kevin could've scored 60 if he wanted." It wasn't a fluke, either. In the Pistons-Celtics playoff series two months later, McHale averaged 20.1 points, second in the series to Bird's 28.2.

Game Results
1984-85
REGULAR SEASON

Date	Opponent	Result	Record
10-26	BOSTON	L, 123-130	0-1
10-27	at New York	L, 118-137	0-2
10-30	CLEVELAND	W, 124-107	1-2
11-1	at Atlanta	W, 118-114	2-2
11-2	at Boston	L, 116-127	2-3
11-5	at Cleveland	W, 107-98	3-3
11-7	CHICAGO	L, 118-122	3-4
11-10	MILWAUKEE	W, 104-100	4-4
11-14	at Philadelphia	W, 137-133 (OT)	5-4
11-16	PHILADELPHIA	L, 90-101	5-5
11-17	at Dallas	W, 124-110	6-5
11-20	at Houston	L, 117-123	6-6
11-21	at San Antonio	W, 114-101	7-6
11-23	NEW YORK	L, 97-120	7-7
11-24	at Washington	L, 106-112	7-8
11-28	PORTLAND	W, 120-113	8-8
11-30	WASHINGTON	L, 106-114	8-9
12-1	at Indiana	W, 131-109	9-9
12-4	BOSTON	W, 104-99	10-9
12-6	at Milwaukee	L, 99-114	10-10
12-7	DENVER	W, 122-115	11-10
12-11	at Chicago	W, 108-101	12-10
12-12	CHICAGO	W, 102-95	13-10
12-14	INDIANA	W, 120-96	14-10
12-19	at Denver	W, 148-129	15-10
12-20	at Utah	L, 116-117	15-11
12-22	at Kansas City	L, 123-129	15-12
12-25	PHILADELPHIA	L, 108-109	15-13
12-26	at New Jersey	L, 97-112	15-14
12-28	at Indiana	W, 116-110	16-14
12-29	NEW JERSEY	L, 108-110	16-15
1-2	CLEVELAND	W, 108-100	17-15
1-4	ATLANTA	W, 134-111	18-15
1-5	at Washington	W, 121-113	19-15
1-9	at Philadelphia	L, 122-126	19-16
1-11	INDIANA	W, 120-109	20-16
1-13	L.A. LAKERS	W, 121-98	21-16
1-17	at New York	W, 105-89	22-16
1-19	at New Jersey	W, 109-107	23-16
1-22	at Atlanta	W, 130-113	24-16
1-24	GOLDEN STATE	W, 137-118	25-16
1-26	SEATTLE	W, 132-113	26-16
1-27	WASHINGTON	W, 115-105	27-16
1-29	at Boston	L, 130-131	27-17
1-30	KANSAS CITY	W, 120-116	28-17
2-2	ATLANTA	W, 110-102 (OT)	29-17
2-4	at Milwaukee	W, 113-111 (OT)	30-17
2-5	NEW JERSEY	L, 117-119	30-18
2-7	at Washington	L, 126-128 (2OT)	30-19
2-12	at Chicago	L, 126-139 (OT)	30-20
2-13	DALLAS	W, 124-119	31-20
2-15	at New Jersey	L, 123-124	31-21
2-16	PHILADELPHIA	L, 114-125	31-22
2-18	PHOENIX	W, 122-103	32-22
2-20	MILWAUKEE	L, 112-113	32-23
2-22	at Philadelphia	L, 99-110	32-24
2-23	NEW JERSEY	L, 103-111	32-25
2-27	CHICAGO	W, 108-99	33-25
3-1	SAN ANTONIO	L, 98-108	33-26
3-3	at Boston	L, 129-138	33-27
3-6	j-NEW YORK	W, 114-90	34-27
3-8	j-UTAH	L, 114-122	34-28
3-9	at Atlanta	W, 115-113	35-28
3-11	c-L.A. CLIPPERS	W, 121-114	36-28
3-12	at Chicago	L, 110-111	36-29
3-17	at Seattle	L, 98-106	36-30
3-18	at L.A. Clippers	L, 116-136	36-31
3-19	at Portland	L, 123-143	36-32
3-21	at Golden State	W, 122-113	37-32
3-24	at L.A. Lakers	L, 130-148	37-33
3-26	at Phoenix	W, 119-93	38-33
3-27	j-HOUSTON	W, 127-110	39-33
3-31	j-BOSTON	W, 113-105	40-33
4-1	j-ATLANTA	L, 100-114	40-34
4-2	at Indiana	W, 124-121	41-34
4-4	at Milwaukee	L, 121-130	41-35
4-5	j-CLEVELAND	L, 118-119	41-36
4-7	j-MILWAUKEE	W, 113-91	42-36
4-9	at New York	W, 107-97	43-36
4-10	j-INDIANA	W, 116-114	44-36
4-12	j-WASHINGTON	W, 102-96	45-36
4-14	at Cleveland	W, 116-113	46-36

PLAYOFFS

Eastern First Round—(Best-of-Five)

4-18	j-NEW JERSEY	W, 125-105	1-0
4-21	j-NEW JERSEY	W, 121-111	2-0
4-24	at New Jersey	W, 116-115	3-0

Eastern Semifinals—(Best-of-Seven)

4-28	at Boston	L, 99-133	0-1
4-30	at Boston	L, 114-121	0-2
5-2	j-BOSTON	W, 125-117	1-2
5-5	j-BOSTON	W, 102-99	2-2
5-8	at Boston	L, 123-130	2-3
5-10	j-BOSTON	L, 113-123	2-4

(Home games in CAPS; j-Joe Louis Arena; c-Cobo Arena)

137

JOE DUMARS

When the Pistons were preparing for the 1985 draft, their scouts had narrowed their focus to a handful of players and the time arrived for coach Chuck Daly to give his assessments. He popped in some video of McNeese State shooting guard Joe Dumars and grabbed a legal pad to make notes. But instead of scribbling, Daly just watched. Then, before the tape was over, he wrote three words on the paper: "He's a player."

It was an appraisal that proved true then, when the Pistons selected Dumars with the 18th draft pick, and remains accurate even as his All-Star career winds to a close. Along the way, Dumars' definition has been gradually broadened—from player to professional to role model—to encompass his membership in a select group of all-time Detroit stars. Al Kaline, Gordie Howe, Isiah Thomas, Steve Yzerman, Barry Sanders ... Dumars ranks with all of them, so beloved is he.

"There is no better person in the NBA than Joe Dumars," Pistons coach Doug Collins said in 1997. "I hope the people of Detroit appreciate everything he's stood for.

Guys like him are rare. He is the consummate professional."

Rare, indeed, because few players have been so respected off the court and so good on it. When Dumars scaled the 15,000-point plateau late in the 1996-97 season, it was another in a long line of signposts that have dotted his 12-year career. First-round pick. Rookie starter. Underrated star. NBA Finals MVP. Team captain. Cagey veteran. Bridge from the Bad Boys to the New Guys. Dumars has fulfilled all of those roles in a wonderfully unassuming fashion that contrasts greatly with the self-aggrandizing styles of many '90s athletes. That contrast is the root of Dumars' appeal. He does his job, does it well and doesn't make a fuss about it, and fans love him for it. We're tired of athletes telling us how great they are; we'd rather decide for ourselves, thank you. We made our decision on Joe Dumars long ago.

It took the Pistons about two seconds to draft Dumars in 1985. They'd done a lot of homework, heard he was a good kid in addition to his skills on the court, and

AT A GLANCE

JOE DUMARS

FULL NAME:
Joe Dumars III
BORN:
May 24, 1963; Natchitoches, Louisiana
POSITION, HEIGHT, WEIGHT:
Guard, 6-foot-3, 195 pounds
COLLEGE:
McNeese State, '85
ACQUIRED:
1985, Pistons' No. 1 draft pick (18th)

TENURE WITH PISTONS:
1985-86 — 1996-97
BEST SEASON WITH PISTONS:
1988-89, 69 GP, 17.2 ppg, 5.7 apg, 2.5 rpg
TOTALS WITH PISTONS:
Regular season: 908 GP, 15,030 pts. (16.6), 4,225 ast. (4.7)
Playoffs: 107 GP, 1,701 pts. (15.9), 987 ast. (4.7)
HONORS:
All-NBA Team: Second Team 1992-93; Third Team 1989-90, 1990-91
All-Star Game (6): 1989-90, 1990-91, 1991-92, 1992-93, 1994-95, 1996-97
NBA Finals MVP: 1988-89
NBA All-Rookie Team: 1985-86
NBA All-Defensive Team: First Team 1988-89, 1989-90, 1991-92, 1992-93; Second Team 1990-91
Kennedy Citizenship Award, 1993-94
NBA Sportsmanship Award, 1996-97

PISTON LIST

Joe Dumars' Highest-Scoring Games

45 points
- March 12, 1992 at Golden State
44 points
- March 9, 1994 vs. New Jersey
43 points
- February 26, 1993 vs. New York
- February 7, 1995 vs. Washington
42 points
- April 18, 1989 at Cleveland
- April 9, 1991 at Milwaukee
- April 19, 1991 at Atlanta
- February 5, 1994 vs. New Jersey
- March 5, 1994 at Milwaukee
41 points
- April 5, 1995 at Orlando
- November 8, 1995 vs. Portland
40 points
- February 19, 1994 at Dallas
- November 8, 1994 vs. Minnesota

hoped he'd be available with the 18th pick. "That might have been the easiest pick I ever made," GM Jack McCloskey said later. "We knew Dumars was the guy we wanted. But we were worried someone was going to take him before us." They didn't—and the Pistons selected the 6-foot-2 gunner. He had been a high scorer, averaging 25.8 ppg as a senior to rank seventh in the NCAA. He ranked sixth the year before at 26.4. In his McNeese State media guide, he had listed Isiah Thomas as his favorite athlete. Now they were teammates.

"I admired Isiah's game in general," Dumars said. "His mannerisms were smooth. I've always been prone to pick up on guys who handled themselves smoothly— Isiah, Gus Williams, Walt Frazier, Mo Cheeks. I naturally patterned my game after guys I liked."

But where would Dumars play? The Pistons had Isiah and steady John Long in the starting lineup and sixth man extraordinaire Vinnie Johnson. For the first half of his rookie season, Dumars showed flashes of talent in limited minutes, but the Pistons knew he would need more playing time to develop. Finally, on January 15, 1986, with the Pistons mired in a 4-15 slump, Long was yanked and Dumars was inserted in the starting lineup. He would remain there the rest of his career. The Pistons improved immediately with Dumars at shooting guard, winning 21 of their next 27, including 10 in a row. There were growing pains, too—like the 1986 game vs. Atlanta when Dumars committed six fouls in one quarter—but it was obvious the Pistons had another star-to-be.

Though Dumars was selected to the NBA All-Rookie team with a 12.4-point

average, his emergence on a national stage would not occur until the final game of his second season. With a berth in the '87 NBA Finals at stake, Dumars almost willed the Pistons to a Game 7 Eastern finals victory in the stifling heat of Boston Garden. The Celtics emerged 117-114, but only after withstanding the Pistons' best punch—and a then-career-high 35 points by Dumars. Season by season, his point average climbed in pace with his reputation as a terrific defensive player (the best defender, so spoke Michael Jordan) and big-game player. On April 18, 1989, Dumars had one of his greatest games ever to help Detroit nail down a second straight Central Division title. He scored 42 points in a 118-102 victory over the Cavs, including a team-record 24 in the third quarter to outscore Cleveland (23) all by himself.

"Joe shows up in big games as much as any player I've ever seen, in all aspects— defense and shooting," Daly said. "He's always ready to play."

Those traits were never more apparent than in Detroit's back-to-back NBA Finals victories. In 1989, Dumars led the assault as the Pistons pounded the Lakers in four straight games, averaging 27.3 points to gain MVP honors. "I'm going to Disney World!" a jubilant Dumars got to yell into the cameras, no longer an underrated accessory to Isiah. Then in 1990, Dumars trudged ahead despite his father's death prior to Game 3 at Portland. He scored 33 points that Sunday, oblivious to his father's passing, then soldiered on for two more games as the Pistons wrapped up their second title. "There aren't many guys tougher than Joe Dumars and this series proved it," assistant coach Brendan Suhr said.

Though team success was rare for the rest of Dumars' career, he was universally recognized as a star. He played in six All-Star games from 1990-97, was chosen to the All-NBA second team in 1993 when he had a career-high 23.5 scoring average and made five All-Defensive teams. With 13 games of 40 or more points, he is tied with Dave Bing for second on the Pistons' all-time list, trailing Bob Lanier's 20. In 1991, he set the team record by making 62 straight free throws.

In the latter stages of Dumars' career, he has worn well the label of elder statesman, setting a fine example for Grant Hill and other young Pistons. But he has also been a good citizen, contributing to a number of charities in and around Detroit. His annual Celebrity Tennis Classic has raised more than $1 million for Children's Hospitals of Michigan. He has also been the NBA spokesman for Second Harvest hunger relief.

For obvious reasons, Detroiters feel lucky to have witnessed Dumars' greatness for more than a decade. But they should feel even more fortunate because Dumars could have wound up in another city playing another sport. He came from a football-playing family—brother David played in the USFL—and young Joe was a terrific defensive back. It is more likely than not that he could have excelled on the pro gridiron.

"In those days, I was better at football than basketball," Dumars said. "But I felt I had topped out in football, that maybe I couldn't go much farther, and I wanted to do something different from my brothers. I had a desire to be the best I could be in basketball."

Mission accomplished. Dream fulfilled.

Joe Dumars' Regular-Season Statistics with Detroit

SEASON	G	GS	MIN	FGM	FGA	PCT	FTM	FTA	PCT	O-RB	D-RB	TOT	AST	PF	DQ	STL	TO	BLK	PTS	PPG	HI
1985-86	82	45	1957	287	597	.481	190	238	.798	60	59	119	390	200	1	66	158	11	769	9.4	22
1986-87	79	75	2439	369	749	.493	184	246	.748	50	117	167	352	194	1	83	171	5	931	11.8	24
1987-88	82	82	2732	453	960	.472	251	308	.815	63	137	200	387	155	1	87	172	15	1161	14.2	25
1988-89	69	67	2408	456	903	.505	260	306	.850	57	115	172	390	103	1	63	178	5	1186	17.2	42
1989-90	75	71	2578	508	1058	.480	297	330	.900	60	152	212	368	129	1	63	145	2	1335	17.8	34
1990-91	80	80	3046	622	1292	.481	371	417	.890	62	125	187	443	135	0	89	189	7	1629	20.4	42
1991-92	82	82	3192	587	1311	.448	412	475	.867	82	106	188	375	145	0	71	193	12	1635	19.9	45
1992-93	77	77	3094	677	1454	.466	343	397	.864	63	85	148	308	141	0	78	138	7	1809	23.5	43
1993-94	69	69	2591	505	1118	.452	276	330	.836	35	116	151	261	118	0	63	159	4	1410	20.4	44
1994-95	67	67	2544	417	970	.430	277	344	.805	47	111	158	368	153	0	72	219	7	1214	18.1	43
1995-96	67	40	2193	255	598	.426	162	197	.822	28	110	138	265	106	0	43	97	3	793	11.8	41
1996-97	79	79	2923	385	875	.440	222	256	.867	38	153	191	318	97	0	57	128	1	1158	14.7	29
TOTALS	908	834	31697	5521	11885	.465	3245	3844	.844	645	1386	2031	4225	1676	5	835	1947	79	15030	16.6	45

3-point FGs: 1985-86, 5-16 (.313); 1986-87, 9-22 (.409); 1987-88, 4-19 (.211); 1988-89, 14-29 (.483); 1989-90, 22-55 (.400); 1990-91, 14-45 (.311); 1991-92, 49-120 (.408); 1992-93, 112-299 (.375); 1993-94, 124-320 (.388); 1994-95, 103-338 (.305); 1995-96, 121-298 (.406); 1996-97, 166-384 (.432). **TOTALS, 743-1945, (.382).**

1985 1986
DETROIT PISTONS

TIME CAPSULE

September 11, 1985:
Cincinnati's Pete Rose breaks Ty Cobb's major league baseball record for hits, singling against San Diego for his 4,192nd.

January 26, 1986:
Coach Mike Ditka's personality-laden Chicago Bears defeat the New England Patriots 46-10 to win Super Bowl XX.

January 28, 1986:
Six astronauts and teacher Christa McAuliffe are killed when the space shuttle Challenger explodes 74 seconds after liftoff at Cape Canaveral, Florida.

SEASON SNAPSHOT

Most Points
Isiah Thomas (1,609, 20.9 avg.)

Most Rebounds
x-Bill Laimbeer (1,075, 13.1 avg.)

Most Assists
Isiah Thomas (830, 10.8 avg.)

Most Minutes
Bill Laimbeer (2,891, 35.3 avg.)

Field-Goal Percentage
Earl Cureton (50.5%)

Free-Throw Percentage
Kelly Tripucka (85.6%)

Team Offense Average
114.2 (9,363 in 82 games)

Team Defense Average
113.0 (9,267 in 82 games)

NBA All-Stars
Isiah Thomas, G (First Team)

Pistons in All-Star Game
Isiah Thomas, G (MVP)

x-led league

1985-86

FINAL STANDINGS

Central Division	W	L	Pct.	GB
Milwaukee	57	25	.695	—
Atlanta	50	32	.610	7
PISTONS	**46**	**36**	**.561**	**11**
Chicago	30	52	.366	27
Cleveland	29	53	.354	28
Indiana	26	56	.317	31

Atlantic Division Winner—Boston
Midwest Division Winner—Houston
Pacific Division Winner—L.A. Lakers

PLAYOFF RESULTS

Eastern First Round: Atlanta d. Pistons, 3-1

PISTONS PLAYOFF LEADERS

Scoring: Isiah Thomas (26.5 avg.)
Rebounding: Bill Laimbeer (14.0)
Assists: Isiah Thomas (12.0)

NBA CHAMPION

Boston Celtics

1985-86
SEASON IN REVIEW

It was a season of mixed signals. For all of the Pistons' individual glory, they should have done better as a team in 1985-86. They fortified their nucleus with All-Rookie shooting guard Joe Dumars, but could only match their 46-36 record of the year before. Isiah Thomas won another All-Star MVP award (30 points, 10 assists) and made the All-NBA first team, but couldn't nudge his club past the first postseason round; the Pistons were pounded 3-1 by Dominique Wilkins and the Atlanta Hawks. Bill Laimbeer captured the NBA rebounding title with 1,075 and brutish Rick Mahorn was shipped in from the Bullets, yet defensive softness continued to halt the Pistons' playoff progress. It became apparent that off-season changes were coming. Even amid all the contradictions, there were positive strides, like a club-record 10-game winning streak from February 12-28. That highlighted a 20-4 streak that roughly coincided with Dumars' permanence in the starting lineup and pushed Detroit to 40-27. A winless four-game Western trip contributed to a 6-9 finish that sent the Pistons into the postseason on a downer, though. Laimbeer was brilliant all year. He led the team in rebounds in 67 of 82 games, grabbing a career-best 24 on March 21 against Phoenix. He capped a three-year span in which he averaged 17.2 points and 12.6 rebounds over 246 games.

The Pistons' last-second 118-115 win over the Lakers on January 19 was a season highlight. Photo by Allen Einstein.

February 15, 1986

By now the Pistons were accustomed to playing in front of big crowds. Attendance had risen every year since Isiah Thomas arrived, climbing to league-high averages in 1983-84 (15,923), 1984-85 (16,867) and 1985-86 (16,957). But the really big crowds at the Silverdome were saved for once or twice a year and they usually set the NBA single-game record. It happened again February 15, 1986, 364 days after a record of 43,816 showed up to see the Pistons lose to Philadelphia. This time, also on a Saturday night, the Pistons pulled in 44,180 for a 134-133 win over the 76ers in overtime. The crowd would eventually rank only fifth in Pistons history, but it was definitely big news at the time. The fans were treated to one of the best games of the season, too, as Detroit had to rally after blowing a 16-point third-quarter lead at the hands of Philadelphia stars Moses Malone, Julius Erving and Charles Barkley, the second-year ton-of-fun. Isiah Thomas' two free throws with 52 seconds to play were the winning margin as they gave the Pistons a 134-131 lead. Andrew Toney got the Sixers within one point six seconds later, but that was all of the scoring. Thomas led Detroit with 34 points and Kelly Tripucka had 28.

WHAT A NIGHT!

Whenever Dr. J was in town, Kelly Tripucka and the Pistons drew massive crowds. Photo by Allen Einstein.

Rick Mahorn

Rick Mahorn scored his career-high 34 points as a Piston on February 26, 1988 against New Jersey.

Isiah Thomas was the Pistons' spirit and Bill Laimbeer their clenched fist, but Rick Mahorn was their kick in the pants. His unheralded arrival in 1985 turned into one of the key acquisitions in club history, providing rebounding strength and an element of danger for squeamish opponents. "If I drive to the basket, is Mahorn going to knock me into the third row?" For the first time, Pistons opponents had to ask themselves that, and it was marvelously effective. Great theatre, too. Seldom has any Pistons' public image been so opposed to the private. Ask the sick kids who received Mahorn's surprise visits in hospitals throughout metro Detroit—all of them unannounced to the media. But Pistons fans seemed to see through the tough-guy ruse anyway. Few players in Detroit have been as adored as Mahorn, a sentiment revealed in 1989 when he was lost in the expansion draft two days after the Pistons' first NBA championship. His chronic back trouble would scare off expansion teams, GM Jack McCloskey had hoped. But in the midst of the victory parade in Detroit, Mahorn was chosen by the new Minnesota Timberwolves. The fans were heartbroken, some starting a fruitless campaign to reacquire him. After four years in a Pistons jersey, Mahorn was history, but he was fun while he was here. He had arrived in trade for Dan Roundfield, but was 30 pounds too heavy. The Pistons sent him to a nutritionist and it rejuvenated his stagnating career, which started in 1980 as a backup to Bullets center Wes Unseld. Mahorn returned to Detroit in 1996-97 as a free agent, a move that was more than ceremonial. He provided his usual toughness under the basket, but a broken foot in January sidelined him until the playoffs.

AT A GLANCE
RICK MAHORN

FULL NAME:
Derrick Allen Mahorn
BORN:
September 21, 1958; Hartford, Connecticut
POSITION, HEIGHT, WEIGHT:
Forward, 6-foot-10, 260 pounds
COLLEGE:
Hampton (Virginia) Institute
ACQUIRED:
1986, trade with Washington
1996, signed as free agent
TENURE WITH PISTONS:
1985-86 — 1988-89; 1996-97
Also: Washington 1980-85, Philadelphia 1989-91, Italy 1991-92, New Jersey 1992-96
BEST SEASON WITH PISTONS:
1987-88, 67 GP, 10.7 ppg, 8.4 rpg
TOTALS WITH PISTONS:
Regular season: 304 GP, 6.8 ppg, 6.3 rpg
Playoffs: 61 GP, 5.4 ppg, 5.4 rpg

PISTON LIST

Most Decisive Victories Ever

46 points
- 119-73 vs. Indiana, 4-2-87

44 points
- 158-114 vs. Chicago, 3-23-69
- 144-100 vs. K.C.-Omaha, 2-18-73
- 118-74 vs. Toronto, 1-4-97

43 points
- 160-117 vs. Boston, 3-9-79

42 points
- 143-101 vs. New York, 11-28-62

40 points
- 131-91 vs. Cincinnati, 12-26-58
- 137-97 vs. St. Louis, 1-7-66
- 140-100 vs. Portland, 12-27-83
- 121-81 at Orlando, 1-26-91

CHANGING FACES

IT DIDN'T SOUND like much at the time, but it turned into a marvelous deal for Detroit. When veteran forward Terry Tyler signed with the Sacramento Kings as a free agent on November 18, 1985—with the season already a month old—the Pistons were entitled to compensation, per NBA rules. The clubs announced their agreement two days later: the Pistons were given the choice of flip-flopping first-round draft slots with the Kings in 1986 or '87. It wouldn't take long for GM Jack McCloskey to go for the switch. In the '86 draft, facing a No. 17 pick, he elected to give it to the Kings and take their No. 11 slot. He selected 7-foot center John Salley, who would become a key ingredient in the Pistons' future champions; at No. 17, Sacramento wound up with unspectacular Harold Pressley. In addition to drafted McNeese State guard Joe

The exit of Terry Tyler in 1985 led to the drafting of John Salley in '86.

Dumars, who led all NBA rookies with 390 assists, Detroit had four other new players in '85-86: Rick Mahorn and Mike Gibson (by trade with Washington) and free-agent centers Chuck Nevitt (7-foot-5) and Ron Crevier (7-foot).

The VILLAIN

Dominique Wilkins

Atlanta's Dominique Wilkins dominated everyone in 1985-86, but the Pistons were high on the list.

Every year in the mid-80s, there were one or two players who seemed to specialize in embarrassing the Pistons. In 1985-86, Atlanta forward Dominique Wilkins took his turn. Took it to extremes, in fact. The Hawks met Detroit 10 times, including four in the opening round of the Eastern playoffs, and Wilkins averaged 32.6 points. "The Human Highlight Film" didn't save all of his big games for the Pistons—he led the league with a 30.3 average—but he simply 30'd Detroit to death. In the regular season Wilkins had consecutive games of 30, 32, 26, 30, 36 and 35 as the Hawks went 4-2 in the rivalry. In the playoffs, he scored 28, 50, 21 and 38 as Atlanta claimed the series 3-1. Of Atlanta's 354 shots in the series, 'Nique took almost one-third (114, making 53). He was incomparable in Game 2, reaching the half-century mark by hitting 19-of-28 field goals and 12-of-15 free throws in the Hawks' 137-125 victory. Of course, by holding Wilkins to 21 in Game 3, the Pistons got their only victory.

Game Results

1985-86 REGULAR SEASON

Date	Opponent	Result	Record
10-25	MILWAUKEE	W, 118-116	1-0
10-26	at Chicago	L, 118-121	1-1
10-29	NEW JERSEY	W, 124-107	2-1
10-30	at Philadelphia	L, 125-132 (OT)	2-2
11-1	INDIANA	W, 124-116	3-2
11-2	at Indiana	W, 128-117	4-2
11-6	CHICAGO	W, 122-105	5-2
11-8	at Washington	W, 117-110	6-2
11-9	BOSTON	L, 105-124	6-3
11-12	WASHINGTON	W, 124-122 (OT)	7-3
11-13	at Milwaukee	L, 118-137	7-4
11-15	at Atlanta	L, 118-122	7-5
11-20	NEW YORK	W, 109-98	8-5
11-22	GOLDEN STATE	W, 115-96	9-5
11-23	at Philadelphia	W, 119-114	10-5
11-26	CLEVELAND	W, 113-98	11-5
11-27	at Boston	L, 124-132	11-6
11-29	MILWAUKEE	W, 111-102	12-6
11-30	at Washington	W, 119-133	12-7
12-3	PHILADELPHIA	L, 107-127	12-8
12-5	NEW JERSEY	W, 113-111	13-8
12-7	SACRAMENTO	L, 112-122	13-9
12-10	at Cleveland	W, 130-120	14-9
12-11	WASHINGTON	L, 100-108	14-10
12-13	SAN ANTONIO	L, 113-119	14-11
12-15	at L.A. Lakers	L, 119-132	14-12
12-17	at Sacramento	L, 121-132	14-13
12-19	at Seattle	W, 99-97	15-13
12-21	at New York	L, 110-112	15-14
12-26	at New Jersey	L, 116-124	15-15
12-27	CLEVELAND	L, 105-119	15-16
12-30	at Milwaukee	L, 110-121	15-17
1-2	at Chicago	L, 122-131	15-18
1-3	at Atlanta	L, 101-111	15-19
1-7	BOSTON	W, 113-109	16-19
1-9	ATLANTA	L, 99-110	16-20
1-11	PHILADELPHIA	L, 101-102	16-21
1-15	CHICAGO	W, 123-115	17-21
1-17	DENVER	W, 129-113	18-21
1-19	L.A. LAKERS	W, 118-115	19-21
1-20	at Indiana	L, 99-105	19-22
1-22	at Cleveland	W, 107-104	20-22
1-24	at Dallas	W, 129-120	21-22
1-25	at Houston	L, 112-117	21-23
1-27	at San Antonio	W, 118-117	22-23
1-29	ATLANTA	W, 107-94	23-23
1-31	at Atlanta	L, 103-116	23-24
2-1	WASHINGTON	W, 116-101	24-24
2-4	at Chicago	W, 117-115	25-24
2-6	at Washington	W, 111-109 (OT)	26-24
2-11	at New Jersey	L, 122-130	26-25
2-12	NEW YORK	W, 113-99	27-25
2-14	DALLAS	W, 119-110	28-25
2-15	PHILADELPHIA	W, 134-133 (OT)	29-25
2-17	UTAH	W, 117-96	30-25
2-19	SEATTLE	W, 118-113	31-25
2-20	at Cleveland	W, 109-107	32-25
2-22	PORTLAND	W, 113-106	33-25
2-24	CHICAGO	W, 110-100	34-25
2-26	L.A. CLIPPERS	W, 111-104	35-25
2-28	ATLANTA	W, 115-103	36-25
3-2	at Boston	L, 109-129	36-26
3-4	NEW JERSEY	W, 120-103	37-26
3-7	at New Jersey	W, 104-102	38-26
3-10	PHOENIX	L, 109-120	38-27
3-12	INDIANA	W, 111-101	39-27
3-14	NEW YORK	W, 112-89	40-27
3-16	at Portland	L, 109-119	40-28
3-17	at Utah	L, 106-107	40-29
3-19	at Denver	L, 98-114	40-30
3-21	at Phoenix	L, 103-105	40-31
3-22	at L.A. Clippers	W, 119-99	41-31
3-25	at Golden State	L, 121-125	41-32
3-28	HOUSTON	W, 116-107	42-32
3-29	at Milwaukee	L, 121-130	42-33
4-1	INDIANA	W, 116-108	43-33
4-2	at Boston	L, 106-122	43-34
4-4	MILWAUKEE	L, 108-115	43-35
4-5	at Indiana	W, 115-106	44-35
4-7	CLEVELAND	W, 128-104	45-35
4-8	at Philadelphia	L, 112-116	45-36
4-11	at New York	W, 108-95	46-36

PLAYOFFS

Eastern First Round—(Best-of-Five)

4-17	at Atlanta	L, 122-140	0-1
4-19	at Atlanta	L, 125-137	0-2
4-22	ATLANTA	W, 106-97	1-2
4-25	ATLANTA	L, 113-114 (2OT)	1-3

(Home games in CAPS)

143

DENNIS "WORM" RODMAN

Not to assert that Dennis Rodman has ever been boring. Freaks are rarely dull.

But long before he became Dennis Rodman and his Amazing Technicolor Dreamhair, he was simply "Worm." Before he became MTV Dennis, Madonna-dating Dennis, tattooed-like-motel-curtains Dennis and pierced-eyelids Dennis, he was just Dennis Rodman, revolutionary rebounder and energetic curiosity.

That's surely the way Detroiters prefer to remember the lanky 6-foot-8 forward who played there for seven mindboggling seasons (1986-93). Pistons fans view Rodman not so much as the '90s cultural phenomenon whose sunglassed persona rarely leaves our consciousness, but as the earnest waif rescued from a nowhere existence by a sudden growth spurt and dogged determination. Not as an addled cross-dresser who talks in circles as dizzying as a 360-degree dunk, but as a one-of-a-kind discovery who overcame a laundry list of allergies to turn the NBA on its then-unpierced ear.

He's an unlikely star, to be sure, but there is no debating that in his 11-year career, Rodman has been one of the NBA's greats. It's not just his rebounds, either, though that is the biggest part. After 1996-97, Rodman had led the NBA in rebound average six straight years with three clubs, compiling numbers not seen since the early 1970s when a headbanded Wilt Chamberlain played for the Lakers. Injuries and suspensions have greatly curtailed Rodman's playing time, but his career average is a remarkable 12.97 rebounds in 796 regular-season games. In the last six years, it's 17.1 in 391 games, though only twice in that span did he play more than 64 games in a season.

But again, it's not just the rebounds. It was the downright adhesive defense that helped Rodman win two NBA Defensive Player of the Year awards (1990, '91) in Detroit. It was the boundless intensity that sometimes reduced him to tears after wins as well as losses. It was the clapping, high-fiving and fist-pumping that brought Pistons

AT A GLANCE

DENNIS RODMAN

FULL NAME:
Dennis Keith Rodman
BORN:
May 13, 1961; Trenton, N.J.
POSITION, HEIGHT, WEIGHT:
Forward, 6-foot-8, 220 pounds
COLLEGE:
SE Oklahoma State, '86
ACQUIRED:
1986, Pistons' No. 2 draft pick (27th)
TENURE WITH PISTONS:
1986-87 – 1992-93
Also: San Antonio 1993-95, Chicago 1995-97

BEST SEASON WITH PISTONS:
1991-92, 82 GP, 9.8 ppg, 18.7 rpg, 2.3 apg
TOTALS WITH PISTONS:
Regular season: 549 GP, 4,844 pts. (8.8), 6,299 reb. (11.5)
Playoffs: 94 GP, 716 pts. (7.6), 766 reb. (8.1)
HONORS:
Defensive Player of the Year (2): 1989-90, 1990-91
IBM Award: 1991-92
All-NBA Team: Second Team 1991-92 (Detroit); Third Team 1994-95 (San Antonio)
All-Star Game (2): 1989-90, 1991-92
NBA All-Defensive Team: First Team 1988-89, 1989-90, 1990-91, 1991-92, 1992-93 (Detroit), 1994-95 (San Antonio), 1995-96 (Chicago); Second Team 1993-94 (San Antonio)
NBA Rebound Champion: Detroit 1991-92, 1992-93, San Antonio 1993-94, 1994-95, Chicago 1995-96, 1996-97

PISTON LIST

Dennis Rodman's Best Rebounding Games

34 rebounds
- March 4, 1992 vs. Indiana (OT)

32 rebounds
- January 28, 1992 at Charlotte (OT)

31 rebounds
- March 14, 1992 at Sacramento

27 rebounds
- January 23, 1992 at Minnesota
- February 18, 1992 vs. Orlando
- December 23, 1992 at Charlotte

26 rebounds
- January 11, 1993 vs. San Antonio
- February 16, 1992 at Philadelphia
- February 6, 1992 at Cleveland

25 rebounds
- 8 occasions

fans out of their padded seats and made back-to-back NBA championships a lot more fun.

And it's the winning, too. During his 11 seasons, no NBA player has won more than Rodman. Including a playoff mark of 103-48 (68.2 percent) in which he's missed only three games, Rodman's teams have amassed a record of 727-326 (69.0). That includes 429-240 (64.1) with Detroit, 127-56 (69.4) in two years with San Antonio (1993-95) and an amazing 171-30 (85.1) in two years with the champion Bulls (1995-97). It can be argued that everywhere Rodman has been, he's played alongside a lynchpin superstar — Isiah Thomas in Detroit, David Robinson in San Antonio, Michael Jordan and Scottie Pippen with the Bulls. Also, missing 109 of his teams' 1,053 games due to injuries, holdouts and disciplinary measures diminishes Rodman's overall contribution.

But though Rodman was fortunate to catch the Pistons when he did, the Pistons were even luckier to get him, stealing him in the second round of the 1986 draft out of tiny NAIA Southeastern Oklahoma State. It's no coincidence that their emergence as an NBA power was due to improved defense and intangibles and that Rodman was one of their main suppliers of both. "He's a throwback," coach Chuck Daly said. "He has made his name for everything but scoring. He's changed the game."

It's a small miracle that Rodman wound up in the NBA at all, let alone with the Pistons. Growing up in Dallas, he didn't play high school ball. He tried out, but at only 5-foot-9, was cut. He got a custodial job at Dallas-Fort Worth Airport, but that only led to trouble. One night, he used his mop handle to reach through a gate guarding gift-shop watches. Stole about 50 of them, he did, and gave them to friends. Charges were dropped after he went through the indignity of recovering the booty.

In the meantime, Rodman was experiencing a two-year growth spurt that would boost him to 6-foot-8 and draw the attention of Cooke County College in Gainesville, Texas, in 1982. He soon quit the team, but resurfaced the next year at Southeastern Oklahoma, where he proved to be a basketball natural. Overcoming gawkiness—better yet, exploiting it—and nurtured by the rare kinship of a white family with whom he lived, Rodman became a scoring and rebounding machine. He was named All-NAIA three straight years, averaging 25.7 points and 15.7 rebounds in 96 games. Though already 25, three years older than his college contemporaries, NBA scouts were wildly intrigued by Rodman.

The Pistons were most interested. They scouted Rodman extensively and planned to draft him in the first round, 11th overall. But in the predraft camps at Portsmouth (Virginia), Honolulu and Chicago, Rodman played dreadfully. By the Chicago camp, "He was awful, just terrible," Pistons GM Jack McCloskey said. But in Chicago, Rodman's agent Bill Pollack contacted his friend, Pistons trainer Mike Abdenour, and asked him to come to the hotel and examine Rodman, who was feeling lousy. What Abdenour discovered was this: "Dennis had allergies to almost everything. Cat hair, you name it. In Chicago, it was so hot and humid, the kid could hardly breathe, let alone play basketball."

Armed with this exclusive information, the Pistons sat back as Rodman's draft stock plummeted. It dropped so far that McCloskey now decided to draft a big man at No. 11 and hope Rodman would be around for the third pick of the second round (No. 27). After picking center John Salley 11th, the waiting began. Finally ... bingo! Rodman was still on the board and McCloskey grabbed him for one of the great steals in draft history (assist: Abdenour). The Pistons were immediately struck by Rodman's quickness as a leaper, which made him a relentless rebounder. "It's like a spring. Once it hits, boom, he's gone again," McCloskey said. "Some guys have to bend and gather themselves to make two jumps, but Dennis already has two leaps in by then."

It was this magnificent athleticism that served Rodman so well in his Pistons career. He also became a student of rebounding, trying to figure out which way the ball would carom off the board. He would position himself, then almost invariably outleap his competition. Those skills came in handy as Rodman set the Pistons' season rebound record with 1,530 in 1991-92 and one-game mark with 34 on March 4, 1992. His 6,299 boards rank third on the Pistons' career list behind Bill Laimbeer (9,430) and Bob Lanier (8,063).

With those accomplishments in hand, as well as championship rings from 1989 and '90, Rodman began growing trouble-some and distracted by personal matters in 1992. He alarmed many when he was discovered at The Palace early one morning, sleeping in his truck with a loaded rifle. He held out to begin the '92-93 season and became a constant source of upheaval until being traded to San Antonio for Sean Elliott on October 1, 1993. The Pistons had gotten a first-hand preview of the Dennis to come. Earrings and tattoos and TV shows would soon follow. But that is not the Rodman who will remain in the memories of Pistons fans.

Dennis Rodman's Regular-Season Statistics with Detroit

SEASON	G	GS	MIN	FGM	FGA	PCT	FTM	FTA	PCT	O-RB	D-RB	TOT	AST	PF	DQ	STL	TO	BLK	PTS	PPG	HI
1986-87	77	1	1155	213	391	.545	74	126	.587	163	169	332	56	166	1	38	93	48	500	6.5	21
1987-88	82	32	2147	398	709	.561	152	284	.535	318	397	715	110	273	5	75	156	45	953	11.6	30
1988-89	82	8	2208	316	531	.595	97	155	.626	327	445	772	99	292	4	55	126	76	735	9.0	32
1989-90	82	43	2377	288	496	.581	142	217	.654	336	456	792	72	276	2	52	90	60	719	8.8	18
1990-91	82	77	2747	276	560	.493	111	176	.631	361	665	1026	85	281	7	65	94	55	669	8.2	34
1991-92	82	80	3301	342	635	.539	84	140	.600	523	1007	1530	191	248	0	68	140	70	800	9.8	20
1992-93	62	55	2410	183	429	.427	87	163	.534	367	765	1132	102	201	0	48	103	45	468	7.5	18
TOTALS	549	296	16345	2016	3751	.537	747	1261	.592	2395	3904	6299	715	1737	19	401	802	399	4844	8.8	34

3-point FGs: 1986-87, 0-1 (.000); 1987-88, 5-17 (.294); 1988-89, 6-26 (.231); 1989-90, 1-9 (.111); 1990-91, 6-30 (.200); 1991-92, 32-101 (.317); 1992-93, 15-73 (.205). TOTALS, 65-257 (.253).

1986 DETROIT PISTONS 1987

TIME CAPSULE

November 22, 1986:
Twenty-year-old Mike Tyson knocks out Trevor Berbick, becoming the youngest heavyweight boxing champion ever.

April 12, 1987:
Larry Mize sinks a 50-yard wedge shot on the second playoff hole to beat Greg Norman and Seve Ballesteros at The Masters.

August 16, 1987:
A Northwest Airlines jet crashes on takeoff from Detroit Metropolitan Airport, killing 156 of 157 passengers.

SEASON SNAPSHOT

Most Points
Adrian Dantley (1,742, 21.5 avg.)

Most Rebounds
Bill Laimbeer (955, 11.6 avg.)

Most Assists
Isiah Thomas (813, 10.0 avg.)

Most Minutes
Isiah Thomas (3,013, 37.2 avg.)

Field-Goal Percentage
John Salley (56.2%)

Free-Throw Percentage
Bill Laimbeer (89.4%)

Team Offense Average
111.2 (9,118 in 82 games)

Team Defense Average
107.8 (8,836 in 82 games)

NBA All-Stars
Isiah Thomas, G (Second Team)

Pistons in All-Star Game
Isiah Thomas, G; Bill Laimbeer, C

FINAL STANDINGS

Central Division	W	L	Pct.	GB
Atlanta	57	25	.695	—
PISTONS	**52**	**30**	**.634**	**5**
Milwaukee	50	32	.610	7
Indiana	41	41	.500	16
Chicago	40	42	.488	17
Cleveland	31	51	.378	26

Atlantic Division Winner—Boston
Midwest Division Winner—Dallas
Pacific Division Winner—L.A. Lakers

PLAYOFF RESULTS

Eastern First Round: Pistons d. Washington, 3-0
Eastern Semifinals: Pistons d. Atlanta, 4-1
Eastern Finals: Boston d. Pistons, 4-3

PISTONS PLAYOFF LEADERS

Scoring: Isiah Thomas (24.1 avg.)
Rebounding: Bill Laimbeer (10.4)
Assists: Isiah Thomas (8.7)

NBA CHAMPION

Los Angeles Lakers

1986-87
SEASON IN REVIEW

An off-season of upheaval developed into a season full of hope, then a postseason full of heartbreak. Searing, tearful heartbreak. After grappling with Atlanta for the Central title much of the season, the Pistons settled for second place while matching their all-time best record (52-30). They slipped by Washington and Atlanta in the playoffs, but were bitterly defeated by Boston in the seven-game Eastern finals, reaching that round for the first time under the modern playoff format.

If not for one of the greatest plays in NBA history—a Larry Bird steal that cost the Pistons Game 5—they might have earned their first berth in the NBA Finals. Instead they went home to ponder why the basketball gods turned against them just when they felt their time had arrived.

The season began with a revamped nucleus, a consequence of Detroit's 3-1 first-round playoff defeat by Atlanta the previous spring. The ease with which the Pistons lost convinced them their mix was insufficient for postseason success, especially defensively.

The tweaking process started with the June 17 draft that produced 6-11 Georgia Tech center John Salley on the 11th pick—they had hoped to get Ohio State's Brad Sellers—and a gangly, 25-year-old jumping bean with ears out to here, 6-8 Dennis Rodman from small-college Southeast Oklahoma State. Detroit got him with the third pick of the second round (27th overall); his stock had fallen because of poor showings at college camps, but the Pistons discovered he'd been sapped by severe allergies.

But the overhaul had only begun. On August 21, GM Jack McCloskey traded for two-time NBA scoring champ Adrian Dantley from Utah, costing the Pistons fan favorites Kelly Tripucka and Kent Benson. A day later, they added 6-9 rebounding ace Sidney Green from the Bulls, shipping out Earl Cureton. John Long was sent to Seattle for draft picks in training camp.

The acquisition of Adrian Dantley in the summer of 1986 gave Detroit a bona fide post-up threat. Photo by Allen Einstein.

It took time for the Pistons to meld the talent and develop a rotation, evidenced by their 3-6 start, but once they began to click, they became one of the NBA's best teams. A run of 22 wins in 27 games pushed their record to 25-11 on January 19. The spurt featured a 119-114 home victory over the Lakers on December 13 and a 111-100 victory at Atlanta three days later, keyed by Bill Laimbeer's 28 points and 20 rebounds. After a brief skid—four losses in five games—the Pistons put together another hot streak, winning 18 of 23 to climb to 44-20 by March 16.

The off-season acquisitions were proving excellent. Dantley was their leading scorer with 21.5 points a game, becoming at age 30 the reliable isolation man they had needed—someone who could draw double-teams. Green was strong defensively, his 653 boards second to Laimbeer's 955. And the youngsters, Rodman and Salley, showed vast improvement. They provided energetic defense and fresh-legged enthusiasm.

The Pistons didn't close strong, however. They went 8-10 in their last 18 games to finish five games behind Atlanta. In the midst of their cold stretch, the Pistons had a great chance to end a 13-game Boston Garden losing skid, but squandered a 10-point fourth-quarter lead and suffered a 119-115 overtime loss. The teams would meet again soon thereafter.

But before the Pistons and Celtics could lock up in one of the greatest playoff series ever, Detroit had to take the first two steps. Washington was a first-round speed-bump, falling 3-0, and then the Pistons routed nemesis Atlanta 4-1 to win two playoff series in a season for the first time. They turned the Hawks series in their favor by stealing Game 1 at Atlanta, 112-111, then by holding serve in Games 3 and 4 at home. Isiah Thomas scored 35 in Game 3, including a then-NBA playoff record 25 in the third period, and won Game 4 with a brilliant shot. His high-arching 8-foot runner in the final seconds gave the Pistons an 89-88 victory.

(continued...)

1986-87
SEASON IN REVIEW
(continued)

In his second season, Joe Dumars emerged as a star, scoring 35 points in the final playoff loss to Boston. Photo by Allen Einstein.

The Eastern finals against the Celtics turned into a memorable series of "Can You Top This?" At home, Boston took Games 1 and 2 to stretch its Garden mastery of the Pistons to 16 straight games, but Detroit rose to the challenge at home, winning a physical Game 3 by 18 and breezing in Game 4 145-119, the most points allowed by Boston in a playoff game.

Then came the pivotal Game 5. The Pistons, overcoming a non-ejection to Celtics center Robert Parish after he sucker-punched Laimbeer in the first half, found themselves ahead 107-106 on Thomas' 17-foot jumper with 17 seconds left. Could it be? Was the streak finally going to end?

No. Emphatically no. The Pistons were bringing the ball inbounds in the Celtics' end with five seconds to play, needing only to run out the clock. But with Thomas triggering the pass to Laimbeer, suddenly Bird flew in from nowhere and stole it. In one motion, he spun along the baseline and found Dennis Johnson cutting to the basket. D.J. made the layup, dooming Detroit, 108-107, and carving Larry Legend's name deeper in NBA annals.

Even though the Pistons recovered at home to beat the Celtics in Game 6—without Parish, who was suspended for the game—they had missed their best chance. Game 7 in musty Boston Garden had always been a bad proposition for opposing teams, and the Pistons couldn't buck history. On a Saturday in which the temperature in the Garden soared as high as 93, the Pistons hung tough and were tied at 99 with 4:37 left. But they just couldn't hold on, having lost both Dantley and Vinnie Johnson when they knocked heads diving for a ball at the end of the third quarter. Despite a career-high 35 points by Joe Dumars, the drained and weakened Pistons lost, 117-114. Afterward, their tears flowed easily, as did their venom.

It had been the finest season in team history, but the sour taste was a good sign in a way. It showed that the Pistons, longtime NBA pushovers, were not going to settle for less ever again.

Game Results

1986-87 REGULAR SEASON

Date	Opponent	Result	Record
10-31	MILWAUKEE	L, 104-120	0-1
11-1	at Indiana	L, 89-92	0-2
11-5	WASHINGTON	W, 109-85	1-2
11-7	CHICAGO	W, 115-109	2-2
11-8	at Milwaukee	L, 89-103	2-3
11-12	PHOENIX	W, 108-100	3-3
11-14	ATLANTA	L, 100-105	3-4
11-15	BOSTON	L, 111-118	3-5
11-19	at Washington	L, 105-119	3-6
11-21	at Philadelphia	W, 120-110	4-6
11-22	CLEVELAND	W, 93-84	5-6
11-28	MILWAUKEE	W, 120-99	6-6
12-3	at New Jersey	W, 107-106 (OT)	7-6
12-4	at Cleveland	L, 105-113	7-7
12-6	DENVER	W, 128-113	8-7
12-10	SACRAMENTO	W, 108-101	9-7
12-12	WASHINGTON	W, 115-116	9-8
12-13	L.A. LAKERS	W, 119-114	10-8
12-16	at Atlanta	W, 111-100	11-8
12-17	UTAH	W, 122-107	12-8
12-19	SAN ANTONIO	W, 114-84	13-8
12-20	at Philadelphia	W, 98-88	14-8
12-23	at Indiana	L, 98-111	14-9
12-26	GOLDEN STATE	W, 121-106	15-9
12-27	at Washington	W, 107-105	16-9
12-30	at Milwaukee	W, 103-99	16-9
1-2	NEW JERSEY	W, 129-128	18-9
1-3	at Chicago	L, 119-124	18-10
1-7	NEW YORK	W, 122-111	19-10
1-9	L.A. CLIPPERS	W, 131-123	20-10
1-10	BOSTON	W, 118-101	21-10
1-13	at Cleveland	W, 103-101	22-10
1-14	CLEVELAND	W, 104-87	23-10
1-16	HOUSTON	L, 106-112	23-11
1-17	at New Jersey	W, 123-113	24-11
1-19	ATLANTA	W, 108-98	25-11
1-21	at Utah	L, 108-112	25-12
1-23	at L.A. Clippers	W, 100-97	26-12
1-24	at Sacramento	L, 113-138	26-13
1-26	at Phoenix	L, 118-120 (OT)	26-14
1-27	at San Antonio	L, 107-118	26-15
1-29	WASHINGTON	W, 112-101	27-15
1-31	at New York	W, 114-113	28-15
2-1	CHICAGO	W, 94-92	29-15
2-5	INDIANA	L, 93-98	29-16
2-11	at Philadelphia	W, 123-113 (OT)	30-16
2-12	at Cleveland	W, 113-109	31-16
2-14	PHILADELPHIA	W, 125-107	32-16
2-17	at Atlanta	L, 103-107	32-17
2-19	SEATTLE	W, 117-105	33-17
2-21	ATLANTA	W, 102-97	34-17
2-22	NEW YORK	W, 122-110	35-17
2-24	at New Jersey	W, 120-112	36-17
2-25	CLEVELAND	W, 106-105	37-17
2-27	PORTLAND	L, 111-123	37-18
3-1	at Boston	L, 102-112	37-19
3-4	CHICAGO	L, 120-125 (OT)	37-20
3-6	DALLAS	W, 125-115	38-20
3-8	BOSTON	W, 122-119 (OT)	39-20
3-10	at New York	W, 116-93	40-20
3-11	at Indiana	W, 107-98	41-20
3-13	at Chicago	W, 100-99	42-20
3-14	PHILADELPHIA	W, 98-85	43-20
3-16	INDIANA	W, 115-95	44-20
3-18	NEW JERSEY	L, 112-113	44-21
3-21	at Dallas	L, 118-122	44-22
3-23	at Houston	W, 114-110	45-22
3-25	at Golden State	L, 115-127	45-23
3-26	at L.A. Lakers	L, 111-128	45-24
3-28	at Denver	W, 121-109	46-24
3-29	at Seattle	W, 109-108	47-24
3-31	at Portland	L, 111-113	47-25
4-2	INDIANA	W, 119-73	48-25
4-3	at Boston	L, 115-119 (OT)	48-26
4-5	MILWAUKEE	W, 125-107	49-26
4-7	at Chicago	L, 86-116	49-27
4-10	at Atlanta	L, 99-101	49-28
4-12	at Washington	W, 98-103	49-29
4-13	at New York	W, 120-100	50-29
4-15	NEW YORK	W, 118-114	51-29
4-17	NEW JERSEY	W, 130-117	52-29
4-18	at Milwaukee	L, 110-124	52-30

PLAYOFFS

Eastern First Round (Best-of-Five)

Date	Opponent	Result	Record
4-24	WASHINGTON	W, 106-92	1-0
4-26	WASHINGTON	W, 128-85	2-0
4-29	at Washington	W, 97-96	3-0

Eastern Semifinals (Best-of-Seven)

Date	Opponent	Result	Record
5-3	at Atlanta	W, 112-111	1-0
5-5	at Atlanta	L, 102-115	1-1
5-8	ATLANTA	W, 108-99	2-1
5-10	ATLANTA	W, 89-88	3-1
5-13	at Atlanta	W, 104-96	4-1

Eastern Finals (Best-of-Seven)

Date	Opponent	Result	Record
5-19	at Boston	L, 91-104	0-1
5-21	at Boston	L, 101-110	0-2
5-23	BOSTON	W, 122-104	1-2
5-24	BOSTON	W, 145-119	2-2
5-26	at Boston	L, 107-108	2-3
5-28	BOSTON	W, 113-105	3-3
5-30	at Boston	L, 114-117	3-4

(Home games in CAPS)

SPOTLIGHT
Game

MAY 26, 1987

Here he is, Larry Bird, the Celtic who cut out the hearts of the Pistons and their fans in Game 5.

First Robert Parish punched out Bill Laimbeer—literally—then Larry Bird figuratively threw a 1-2 knockout combination to the solar plexus of the entire Pistons franchise.

With the Eastern Conference finals deadlocked 2-2 on Boston Garden's storied parquet floor, Game 5 started innocently enough. As the Celtics built an early 12-point lead, there was no more than the usual elbowing and posturing for most of the first half.

Then it got ugly fast. Robert Parish, reacting not to anything Laimbeer did at the moment so much as the cumulative frustration of the Detroit center's hands-on defense, took enforcement into his own hands late in the half. He slap-punched Laimbeer three times from behind on the head and shoulders, pulling him down. The referees called nothing on Parish.

Against that contentious background, Detroit rallied and moved ahead on Vinnie Johnson's layup in the third quarter. The clubs traded the lead in the fourth before Boston nursed it to three, but jumpers by Laimbeer and Isiah Thomas put Detroit ahead 107-106 with only 17 seconds left.

On what the Celtics feared was their last possession, Bird's shot from the left side was smartly blocked by Dennis Rodman and careened out of bounds off the Celtics with five seconds left. A clean

inbounds pass and probably two free throws were all that stood between the Pistons and a 3-2 series lead, plus the end of their 16-game Garden losing streak.

But no Pistons looked to the bench, where the coaches were screaming for a timeout. Deep in Detroit's own end, Thomas hurriedly attempted to inbound to Laimbeer. But Thomas' pass hung in the air slightly, Laimbeer was slow to meet the ball and Bird, using the sixth sense that had made him one of the NBA's money players, leapt in front of the pass. He quickly wheeled and dished the ball to Dennis Johnson for a winning layup.

"I figured if we got the ball in fast, they'd foul us quick and we'd have it won," Thomas said. "I never saw (Bird). It was probably a bad pass."

Laimbeer said: "We should've called timeout, but we made a mistake in the heat of the battle. It was nobody's fault and everybody's fault."

Boston broadcaster Johnny Most, the gravel-voiced Piston-hater, made one of his immortal calls: "Now there's the steal by Bird! Underneath to D.J., he lays it in! And Boston has ... a one-point lead! Oh, my, this place is going cra-zeeee!"

To this day, it's a film clip guaranteed to rumble the stomach of every Piston and every fan who couldn't believe—or did not want to believe —what they had just seen.

SUMMARY—Game 5
Celtics 108, Pistons 107

PISTONS (107)

Player	Min	FG M-A	3P M-A	FT M-A	Reb O-T	A	PF	Pts
Mahorn	23	2-3	0-0	0-0	0-4	0	5	4
Dantley	37	10-15	0-0	5-5	1-3	2	4	25
Laimbeer	43	7-20	0-0	2-4	1-14	6	5	16
Dumars	26	2-5	0-0	0-0	0-1	6	1	4
Thomas	43	6-16	0-2	5-8	1-3	11	5	17
V.Johnson	27	8-13	0-0	4-4	1-2	3	1	20
Salley	17	3-8	0-0	1-2	4-8	2	6	7
Rodman	21	7-7	0-0	0-0	0-3	1	5	14
Green	1	0-0	0-0	0-0	0-0	0	0	0
Totals	**240**	**45-87**	**0-2**	**17-23**	**8-38**	**31**	**32**	**107**

Percentages: FG .517, 3P .000, FT .739. Team Rebounds: 10. Blocked shots: 2 (Laimbeer, Rodman). Turnovers: 15 (Thomas 4, Laimbeer 3, Dantley 2, Dumars 2, Rodman 2, Mahorn, Salley). Steals: 8 (Thomas 3, Dantley 2, Laimbeer 2, V.Johnson). Technical fouls: Illegal defense, 3:21 second. Illegal defense: 2.

CELTICS (108)

Player	Min	FG M-A	3P M-A	FT M-A	Reb O-T	A	PF	Pts
McHale	27	8-9	0-0	4-4	1-7	1	5	20
Bird	47	12-25	0-2	12-12	1-12	9	1	36
Parish	38	3-10	0-0	5-6	3-8	0	1	11
D.Johnson	45	5-13	0-0	8-10	2-7	5	3	18
Ainge	36	5-12	2-6	0-0	0-1	4	3	12
Daye	22	2-3	0-0	3-5	0-2	1	6	7
Vincent	10	1-4	0-0	2-2	1-1	1	1	4
Sichting	6	0-1	0-0	0-0	0-0	0	1	0
Roberts	7	0-0	0-0	0-0	0-0	0	0	0
Kite	2	0-1	0-0	0-0	1-2	0	2	0
Totals	**240**	**36-78**	**2-8**	**34-39**	**9-40**	**21**	**23**	**108**

Percentages: FG .462, 3P .250, FT .872. Team Rebounds: 7. Blocked shots: 3 (Bird, McHale, Parish). Turnovers: 18 (Bird 5, McHale 3, Parish 3, Ainge 3, D.Johnson 2, Daye, Vincent). Steals: 7 (Daye 3, McHale 2, Bird, Parish). Technical fouls: Illegal defense, 4:41 fourth. Illegal defense: 2.

DETROIT	29	27	29	22	— 107
BOSTON	38	20	28	22	— 108

A—14,890 (sellout). T—2:24. Officials—Jack Madden, Jess Kersey

Premier Piston

Adrian "A.D." Dantley

Adrian Dantley led the Pistons in scoring for his entire 2½ seasons with them. Photo by Allen Einstein.

There is no denying that Adrian Dantley's greatest individual moments in the NBA came in another team's uniform. After all, the high-scoring forward played for six teams in 15 seasons and he spent less than three seasons in Detroit. Out of his 23,177 points, more than 19,000 were for other clubs, namely Utah, with whom he won two NBA scoring crowns in a seven-year stay. But it's also certain that A.D.'s finest team moments came with Detroit after he was acquired from Utah on August 21, 1986 for Kelly Tripucka and Kent Benson. Though he wasn't on their NBA champion clubs, having been dealt to Dallas for Mark Aguirre in 1989, Dantley was never closer than in 1988 when the Pistons lost to the L.A. Lakers in the NBA Finals. He played a major role in Detroit's emergence, providing the post-up threat it had lacked. Dantley was unstoppable on isolations and clear-outs, seeming to beat his defender and score the basket or get fouled on every play. In his first season with Detroit, 1986-87, he led the club in scoring with 21.5 points per game (41 vs. Boston on November 15) and then 20.5 during the playoffs that ended so bitterly against Boston. Among the enduring images of Dantley's career occurred in Game 7 of the '87 Eastern finals. Diving for a ball near the end of the third quarter, he and Vinnie Johnson collided head-on and were knocked out of the game. Dantley was sent to the hospital with a concussion and Detroit lost. When the Pistons' quest resumed in 1987-88, Dantley was again their scoring leader at 20.0 per game. He had 45 points in a November 21 OT win against Chicago, the Pistons' season high. Alas, the Pistons lost the Finals despite A.D.'s 21.3 average and then he was traded controversially four months before the '89 title. Dantley left without a ring, but with a secure spot in Pistons history.

AT A GLANCE

ADRIAN DANTLEY

FULL NAME:
Adrian Delano Dantley
BORN:
February 28, 1956; Washington, D.C.
POSITION, HEIGHT, WEIGHT:
Forward, 6-foot-5, 208 pounds
COLLEGE:
Notre Dame, '76
ACQUIRED:
1986, traded from Utah Jazz
TENURE WITH PISTONS:
1986-87 — 1988-89
Also: Buffalo 1976-77, Indiana 1977, L.A. Lakers 1977-79, Utah 1979-1986, Dallas 1989-90, Milwaukee 1991
BEST SEASON WITH PISTONS:
1986-87, 81 GP, 21.5 ppg, 4.1 rpg

TOTALS WITH PISTONS:
Regular season: 192 GP, 3,894 pts. (20.3), 723 reb. (3.8)
Playoffs: 38 GP, 754 pts. (19.8), 175 reb. (4.6)
HONORS:
NBA Rookie of the Year, 1976-77 (Buffalo)
NBA All-Rookie Team, 1976-77 (Buffalo)
All-NBA Team: Second Team 1980-81, 1983-84 (Utah)
All-Star Game (6): 1979-80, 1980-81, 1981-82, 1983-84, 1984-85, 1985-86 (Utah)
NBA Comeback Player of the Year, 1983-84 (Utah)
NBA Scoring Champion: 1980-81, 1983-84 (Utah)

Isiah Thomas

Robert Parish

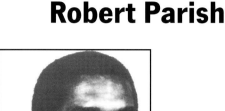

Isiah Thomas beat Atlanta almost singlehandedly in the Eastern semis. Photo by Allen Einstein.

Robert Parish's attack on Bill Laimbeer went unpunished by the refs and perhaps underpunished by the NBA.

Wait a minute. How can Isiah be the Pistons' playoff hero when he was the guy who threw the ball to Larry Bird and cost the Pistons Game 5 of the Eastern finals? Easy, because without Thomas' late-game wizardry, the Pistons probably wouldn't have advanced as far as they did. At least they would not have done it so stylishly. In 15 playoff games over three series, Thomas led the team in scoring (24.1 ppg) and assists (8.7 apg). He was especially flashy in Detroit's 4-1 series win over Atlanta in the Eastern semis. He scored 30 in a 112-111 Game 1 victory, including the decisive free throw with only 16 seconds left. In Game 3, he set an NBA playoff record—since broken—and dominated Atlanta chum Doc Rivers by scoring 25 points in the third quarter of a 108-99 win. For the game, he compiled 35 points, eight rebounds, eight assists and five steals. But his greatest glory would come in the final seconds of Game 4 on Sunday— Mother's Day. With his mother at Indiana to accept his degree, Thomas hit an 8-foot running jumper to hand the Pistons a landmark 89-88 win. Thomas' spinning war dance after the shot is one of the most vivid film clips in team history. Detroit clinched the series at Atlanta three days later to dance into the conference finals for the first time in 25 years.

The stage had been set three days earlier at the Silverdome in Game 3 of the conference finals vs. Boston. Down 2-0 in the series, the Pistons knew they'd have to get more physical and Bill Laimbeer volunteered. In the fourth quarter, he pulled down Larry Bird on a layup, causing Bird to punch him while they were tangled on the floor, and Bird later fired the ball off Laimbeer's shoulder. The combatants were ejected, the Pistons won twice to tie the series and Boston vowed retribution. That's where Parish comes in. The veteran center got the Celtics' revenge in the first half of Game 5 at Boston, punching Laimbeer three times from behind in an unprovoked attack. Ref Jess Kersey, standing a few feet away, called a foul away from the play, but nothing on Parish. He later said, "I didn't see any punches." The Pistons were irate, holding a press conference to rap the Celtics, the refs and the NBA. That Parish was suspended by the league for Game 6 and fined $7,500 did not boost their mood, especially after Bird's legendary steal cost them Game 5—and probably the series—in a most deflating way. Not even the Pistons' NBA titles of 1989 and '90 fully eased the sting of Parish's punches, at least for the fans. They booed him for the rest of his career.

February 14, 1987

This Valentine's Night clash appealed to the eye, ear and viscera. On a chilled Saturday at the Silverdome, with Julius Erving and the Sixers in town, a new NBA record 52,745 fans packed the joint to see the Pistons pound Philadelphia 125-107. With the crowd roaring from the start, the teams engaged in a physical game that culminated in a scuffle between Adrian Dantley and Erving midway through the fourth quarter. The small forwards turned the game into a 1-on-1 battle, trying to embarrass the other on successive trips. Finally, after Dantley flew around Dr. J for a layup, Erving wanted the same chance on the other end. He got free from Dantley and was headed to the hoop when Dantley fouled him around the neck. They got into a brief wrestling match before being pulled away by teammates and both getting a technical foul. The Pistons' win, keyed by Dantley's 35 points, gave them a 4-0 edge in the season series with the 76ers. Philly got 23 points from center Tim McCormick, who'd grown up just 10 minutes from the Dome. No one knew it that day, but it would be Erving's last game against Detroit. The Sixers came back to the Dome on March 14, but the injured Dr. J didn't suit up for Detroit's 98-95 win. He retired after the season.

Julius Erving (right) gets a hug from Isiah Thomas to commemorate his final game against the Pistons. Photo by Allen Einstein.

Nothing the Pistons did could stop Michael Jordan on his magical 61-point night.

March 4, 1987

Doug Collins, in his first season as coach of the Chicago Bulls, tabbed it "the finest performance I've ever been associated with." The Pistons were in no position to quibble with the assessment. Michael Jordan had just torched them for 61 points —his highest regular-season total ever—in the Bulls' 125-120 overtime win. He made 22 of 39 field goals and 17 of 18 free throws, topping Kelly Tripucka's Silverdome record of 56 points on January 29, 1983 vs. Chicago. In the fourth quarter, Jordan scored 26 points, including 24 of the Bulls' first 25 in the first eight minutes. "Jordan was unbelievable," Pistons coach Chuck Daly said. "He's almost unstoppable. He's just incredible. Amazing." Jordan was so good that he surprised himself: "You never feel unstoppable, but this was close to it. This has to be the best streak I've ever had. I kept coming up with shots that I myself haven't seen." Collins said, "He had that look. Michael put on an unbelievable show." But Jordan did more than just score. With the game tied at 111 in the last five seconds of regulation, he made a steal to prevent the Pistons from getting off a final shot. For Detroit, Adrian Dantley compiled 32 points, Isiah Thomas 31 with 18 assists.

CHANGING FACES

IN ORDER to get, you have to give. The Pistons did plenty of both before and during the 1986-87 season, essentially rounding out a nucleus that would reach the Eastern Conference finals five straight seasons. To get two-time scoring champ Adrian Dantley, strong rebounder Sidney Green and four second-round draft picks before the season, the Pistons had to send away a group of crowd favorites: Kelly Tripucka, Kent Benson, Earl Cureton and John Long. The foursome had 21,806 points in 1,292 games with the Pistons, including Long's brief later stints. Tripucka's 56 points vs. the Bulls on January 29, 1983 remain the most ever by a Piston. Detroit wasn't done retooling after adding Dantley and Green via trade and John Salley and Dennis Rodman in the draft. Just before the trade deadline, they got power forward Kurt Nimphius from the L.A. Clippers on January 29 for their 1987 first-round draft pick. Nimphius would last only one season in the Motor City and the same for Green, whose 23 rebounds vs. Milwaukee on December 20 were the Pistons' game high for the season.

John "Spider" Salley's long-armed rebounds boosted the Pistons' defense in his rookie season. Photo by Allen Einstein.

Take a Bow
Vinnie Johnson

Baseball has its Rolaids Relief Man, the NBA has its Sixth Man Award. In 1986-87, Vinnie Johnson was one of the NBA's finest relief gunners, finishing second in the Sixth Man balloting to ex-Piston Ricky Pierce of the Milwaukee Bucks. Averaging 27.7 minutes in 78 games, Johnson had a 15.7-point average—the second-highest output of his career—while scoring in double-figures 66 times. He had 23 games with more than 20 points. But The Microwave did some of his best work as a starter. When Joe Dumars injured his right ankle in late March, Johnson was sent into the starting five and responded immediately. He scored 30 points in his first start, setting his season high to help the Pistons coast at Denver. Three games later, he pumped in a game-leading 25 in a 119-73 rout of Indiana, the biggest victory margin in Pistons history. All told, Johnson averaged 18.4 points in seven straight starts. "He could start full-time on most teams," coach Chuck Daly said. "Vinnie's one of the best streak shooters I've ever seen."

Vinnie Johnson proved his worth to the Pistons both as a substitute and starter. Photo by Allen Einstein.

PISTON LIST

Highest-Scoring Playoff Games

145 points—
- Game 4 vs. Boston, May 24, 1987 (W)

132 points—
- Game 5 vs. L.A. Lakers, March 31, 1962 (W)

128 points—
- Game 2 vs. Washington, April 26, 1987 (W)

126 points—
- Game 2 vs. Boston, March 25, 1968 (W)
- Game 2 vs. Milwaukee, April 15, 1976 (W)

125 points—
- Game 1 vs. New Jersey, April 18, 1985 (W)
- Game 3 vs. Boston, May 2, 1985 (W)
- Game 2 vs. Atlanta, April 19, 1986 (L)

124 points—
- Game 2 vs. Cincinnati, March 16, 1958 (W)
- Game 3 vs. L.A. Lakers, March 17, 1961 (W)

123 points—
- 5 times

1987 DETROIT PISTONS 1988

TIME CAPSULE

October 19, 1987:
The worst crash in the modern history of the New York Stock Exchange occurs when the Dow Jones Industrial Average tumbles by 508 points.

February 5, 1988:
A federal grand jury in Miami indicts Panamanian General Manuel Noriega in connection with illegal drug dealing.

April 23, 1988:
A ban on smoking on domestic passenger flights goes into effect.

SEASON SNAPSHOT

Most Points
Adrian Dantley (1,380, 20.0 avg.)

Most Rebounds
Bill Laimbeer (832, 10.1 avg.)

Most Assists
Isiah Thomas (678, 8.4 avg.)

Most Minutes
Isiah Thomas (2,927, 36.1 avg.)

Field-Goal Percentage
Rick Mahorn (57.4%)

Free-Throw Percentage
Bill Laimbeer (87.4%)

Team Offense Average
119.2 (8,957 in 82 games)

Team Defense Average
104.1 (8,533 in 82 games)

Pistons in All-Star Game
Isiah Thomas, G

1987-88

FINAL STANDINGS

Central Division	W	L	Pct.	GB
PISTONS	**54**	**28**	**.659**	**—**
Chicago	50	32	.610	4
Atlanta	50	32	.610	4
Milwaukee	42	40	.512	12
Cleveland	42	40	.512	12
Indiana	38	44	.463	16

Atlantic Division Winner—Boston
Midwest Division Winner—Denver
Pacific Division Winner—L.A. Lakers

PLAYOFF RESULTS

Eastern First Round: Pistons d. Washington, 3-2
Eastern Semifinals: Pistons d. Chicago, 4-1
Eastern Finals: Pistons d. Boston, 4-2
NBA Finals: L.A. Lakers d. Pistons, 4-3

PISTONS PLAYOFF LEADERS

Scoring: Isiah Thomas (21.9 avg.)
Rebounding: Bill Laimbeer (9.6)
Assists: Isiah Thomas (8.7)

NBA CHAMPION

Los Angeles Lakers

1987-88
SEASON IN REVIEW

In the Pistons' locker room at the L.A. Forum, the celebration podium was being constructed. Underlings were hauling in champagne on ice—good stuff for drinking, cheaper stuff for spraying. Pistons owner Bill Davidson had been asked to come to the locker room to accept the NBA championship trophy, a scene he had rehearsed in his head for 14 years.

One minute later—one lousy minute!—the podium was broken down, the champagne was carted away and the party was off. There would be no celebration today. Just when it appeared the Pistons would win their first title, they were beaten by the Lakers in the final minute of Game 6, tying the NBA Finals 3-3. Two days later, the Lakers would capture their second straight title with a 108-105 victory, leaving the Pistons to contemplate how things went so wrong in their grandest moment.

After a season full of rousing triumphs and memorable moments, the Pistons' first and possibly only trip to the Finals—no guarantee you'll ever get back—ended with tears. Isiah Thomas, who almost willed his team to a title on a swollen ankle, and Bill Laimbeer sat on the shower floor at the Forum, their tears mingling with the water. Having stolen a couple of bottles of the Lakers' bubbly, the veterans sat there for what seemed like hours, vowing to win it all next season, the depth of their disappointment surpassed only by their unsatisfied hunger.

One lousy minute! After finishing 54-28 to win the division for the first time in club history, then excusing surprisingly tough Washington, the Chicago Jordans and the previously unbeatable Celtics in the first three playoff rounds, the Pistons pulled ahead of the Lakers 3-2 in the Finals. They won Games 1, 4 and 5, the latter a 104-94 victory before a playoff record crowd of 41,732 in their final game at the Silverdome. A win in Game 6 or 7 at Los Angeles would produce the first championship in the topsy-turvy 31-year history of NBA basketball in Detroit.

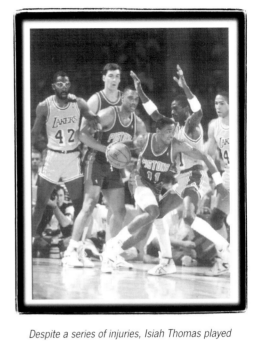

Despite a series of injuries, Isiah Thomas played a gallant Finals series against the Lakers. Photo by Andrew Bernstein/NBA.

If not for a couple of off-balance jump shots and a shaky but expected foul call in the final minute of Game 6, the Pistons would have done it. But despite the magnificence of Thomas, whose heroic 43-point performance ranks as the finest in team history, the Pistons fell short that Sunday. They led 102-101 and set up for a possible back-breaking shot, but Isiah missed an off-balance 18-footer and the Lakers hurried downcourt, eyeing the lead. The ball was fed to Kareem Abdul-Jabbar on the right baseline and he tried his skyhook. Tweet! Foul, Laimbeer. The Pistons were incensed. Replays showed minimal (if any) contact, but it didn't matter. Abdul-Jabbar hit both free throws for a 103-102 Lakers lead. Detroit had one more chance, but Joe Dumars' double-clutch six-footer clanged off the rim to Byron Scott with eight seconds left. Even after Scott missed both free throws, the Pistons had no timeouts and couldn't get off a final shot. Their best chance to win had disappeared.

The ending marred a miraculous game by Isiah. He had been incredible, setting a Finals record with a 25-point third quarter on 11-of-13 field goals, turning an eight-point Pistons deficit into a two-point lead. In the midst of his burst, he had landed badly on his right ankle, suffering a severe sprain, but it didn't stop him. He scored 14 straight Pistons points in one stretch. He also set a Finals record with six steals. "I felt we needed a lift," Thomas said, sitting sideways on the locker room bench to support his grapefruit-sized ankle. "My shot was falling and the guys were working hard to get me open." Of the loss, he said, "Sometimes in this crazy game, things just don't go your way. This just proves it's very difficult to win a championship. No one said it would be easy."

Thomas' injury figured to prevent him from playing Game 7. He suited up, but was unable to play at full speed and the Pistons paid for it. With Thomas sidelined for the final 10:22, they couldn't muster the big plays they needed down the stretch. Behind 102-100, they could've gone ahead on Laimbeer's missed triple with 1:11 left or tied on Dennis Rodman's ill-advised pull-up 14-footer with :39 left. They finally pulled within 106-105 after a Dumars layup

(continued...)

1987-88
SEASON IN REVIEW
(continued)

In Game 5, the Pistons' last game at the Silverdome, Bill Laimbeer controls a rebound against Lakers' Kurt Rambis. Photo by Allen Einstein.

and Laimbeer triple with six seconds to play, but A.C. Green's breakaway layup capped the Lakers' repeat title.

"We got beat, but we gave it our best shot," Laimbeer said. "I think our teams are even. The ball bounces different ways, and tonight it bounced a lot of different ways." Thomas sounded the same theme: "To be a champion, you have to be good and lucky. We are a good team, but we are just not lucky." GM Jack McCloskey added, "We need to be a little smarter. If we're smarter, we'll be better. I think we've got a real shot at it next season."

The regular season had been highlighted by a 20-4 spurt that gave the Pistons a 45-20 record by March 22. Just before their hot streak, they gained a landmark victory, pounding the Celtics 125-108 on Jan. 29 to thrill an NBA-record crowd of 61,983 at the Silverdome. Unless an NBA team returns to a football stadium, that record will never be broken.

The Pistons' greatest postseason moments also occurred against the Celtics, only they were at Boston, where Detroit hadn't won since December 19, 1982, a 21-game span. In the Eastern finals, the Pistons opened the series with a 104-96 victory at Boston Garden to break the streak and won there again in Game 5, prevailing 102-96 in overtime. Thomas was amazing throughout, compiling 35 in both wins at Boston. The Pistons finally killed off the Celtics in Game 6 at the Silverdome, erasing the bitter memories of the previous spring and reaching the NBA Finals for the first time. But instead of a championship trophy, the Pistons were given another painful playoff lesson, administered by the Lakers, filed away for future reference.

Game Results

1987-88
REGULAR SEASON

Date	Opponent	Result	Record
11-6	NEW YORK	W, 110-99	1-0
11-7	at Milwaukee	L, 105-119	1-1
11-10	at Indiana	L, 118-121	1-2
11-13	at Philadelphia	W, 113-94	2-2
11-14	at Cleveland	W, 128-113	3-2
11-18	PHILADELPHIA	L, 109-113	3-3
11-20	GOLDEN STATE	W, 131-108	4-3
11-21	at Chicago	W, 144-132 (OT)	5-3
11-24	at Houston	W, 97-83	6-3
11-25	at Dallas	L, 107-113	6-4
11-27	SAN ANTONIO	W, 143-111	7-4
11-28	at Washington	L, 102-124	7-5
12-1	at New Jersey	W, 124-115 (OT)	8-5
12-2	MILWAUKEE	W, 115-105	9-5
12-4	BOSTON	W, 128-105	10-5
12-8	PORTLAND	W, 127-117	11-5
12-11	WASHINGTON	W, 114-108	12-5
12-12	NEW YORK	W, 124-96	13-5
12-15	CHICAGO	W, 127-123 (OT)	14-5
12-18	DALLAS	W, 117-112	15-5
12-25	at New York	W, 91-87	16-5
12-26	NEW JERSEY	W, 110-75	17-5
12-29	HOUSTON	L, 91-101	17-6
12-30	at Indiana	W, 105-95	18-6
1-2	DENVER	L, 142-151	18-7
1-5	at Atlanta	L, 71-81	18-8
1-6	ATLANTA	W, 90-87	19-8
1-8	L.A. LAKERS	L, 104-106	19-9
1-13	at Boston	L, 105-143	19-10
1-15	CLEVELAND	W, 97-93	20-10
1-16	at Chicago	L, 99-115	20-11
1-18	at Denver	W, 123-116	21-11
1-20	at Utah	W, 120-117	22-11
1-22	at Seattle	L, 106-109	22-12
1-24	at Portland	L, 111-119	22-13
1-27	INDIANA	W, 103-86	23-13
1-29	BOSTON	W, 125-108	24-13
1-30	at New Jersey	L, 104-116	24-14
2-1	at Cleveland	L, 83-94	24-15
2-2	at Milwaukee	W, 99-97	25-15
2-4	at New York	L, 93-100	25-16
2-9	at Chicago	W, 89-74	26-16
2-10	NEW YORK	W, 98-87	27-16
2-12	ATLANTA	W, 108-92	28-16
2-13	CHICAGO	W, 82-73	29-16
2-15	PHILADELPHIA	W, 102-95	30-16
2-18	SEATTLE	W, 108-95	31-16
2-19	at Milwaukee	L, 108-119	31-17
2-21	at L.A. Lakers	L, 110-117	31-18
2-23	at Sacramento	W, 121-105	32-18
2-24	at Golden State	W, 107-93	33-18
2-26	NEW JERSEY	W, 137-109	34-18
2-28	BOSTON	W, 106-101	35-18
3-1	at Atlanta	W, 117-104	36-18
3-2	L.A. CLIPPERS	W, 103-90	37-18
3-5	at Washington	L, 97-101	37-19
3-6	MILWAUKEE	W, 109-99	38-19
3-8	at Indiana	L, 104-117	38-20
3-9	UTAH	W, 103-98	39-20
3-11	PHOENIX	W, 116-88	40-20
3-12	CLEVELAND	W, 104-100	41-20
3-14	SACRAMENTO	W, 109-97	42-20
3-17	at Cleveland	W, 102-99	43-20
3-20	WASHINGTON	W, 118-110	44-20
3-22	INDIANA	W, 123-104	45-20
3-25	at San Antonio	L, 106-107	45-21
3-26	at Phoenix	W, 108-103	46-21
3-28	at L.A. Clippers	L, 100-102	46-22
3-30	ATLANTA	L, 102-103	46-23
4-1	at Boston	L, 110-121	46-24
4-3	CHICAGO	L, 110-112	46-25
4-5	at New Jersey	W, 107-95	47-25
4-8	at Philadelphia	W, 96-86	48-25
4-9	at Atlanta	W, 115-102	49-25
4-11	at New York	L, 111-114	49-26
4-13	CLEVELAND	W, 115-98	50-26
4-15	MILWAUKEE	W, 92-91	51-26
4-16	NEW JERSEY	W, 114-96	52-26
4-19	at Boston	L, 110-121	52-27
4-21	at Washington	W, 99-87	53-27
4-22	INDIANA	L, 98-103	53-28
4-24	PHILADELPHIA	W, 128-118	54-28

PLAYOFFS
Eastern First Round—(Best-of-Five)

Date	Opponent	Result	Record
4-28	WASHINGTON	W, 96-87	1-0
4-30	WASHINGTON	W, 102-101	2-0
5-2	at Washington	L, 106-114 (OT)	2-1
5-4	at Washington	L, 103-106	2-2
5-8	WASHINGTON	W, 99-78	3-2

Eastern Semifinals—(Best-of-Seven)

Date	Opponent	Result	Record
5-10	CHICAGO	W, 93-82	1-0
5-12	CHICAGO	L, 95-105	1-1
5-14	at Chicago	W, 101-79	2-1
5-15	at Chicago	W, 96-77	3-1
5-18	CHICAGO	W, 102-95	4-1

Eastern Finals—(Best-of-Seven)

Date	Opponent	Result	Record
5-25	at Boston	W, 104-96	1-0
5-26	at Boston	L, 115-119 (OT)	1-1
5-28	BOSTON	W, 98-94	2-1
5-30	BOSTON	L, 78-79	2-2
6-1	at Boston	W, 102-96 (OT)	3-2
6-3	BOSTON	W, 95-90	4-2

NBA Finals—(Best-of-Seven)

Date	Opponent	Result	Record
6-7	at L.A. Lakers	W, 105-93	1-0
6-9	at L.A. Lakers	L, 96-108	1-1
6-12	L.A. LAKERS	L, 86-99	1-2
6-14	L.A. LAKERS	W, 111-86	2-2
6-16	L.A. LAKERS	W, 104-94	3-2
6-19	at L.A. Lakers	L, 102-103	3-3
6-21	at L.A. Lakers	L, 105-108	3-4

(Home games in CAPS)

SPOTLIGHT Game

MAY 25, 1988

Isiah Thomas saved his best for the Lakers, but also sparked the Pistons' conquest of the Celtics. Photo by Allen Einstein.

After nearly six years of constant trying, the Little Engine That Could finally did. No more "I think I can, I think I can" from the Pistons when it came to winning in the Celtics' home arena. With a hard-earned 104-96 victory in Game 1 of the 1988 Eastern finals, the Pistons halted their 21-game losing streak at Boston Garden.

With Isiah Thomas compiling 35 points and 12 assists, the Pistons won in the House That Red Auerbach Built for the first time since December 19, 1982, grabbing away the Celtics' precious homecourt advantage, which would come in handy to Detroit later in the series. The sellout crowd —the 368th in a row at the Garden—sat dumbfounded.

"We had great determination. I thought our defense was as good as it's ever been," coach Chuck Daly said, though he'd been around far too long to get overly excited. "It's a seven-game series. You've got to win four. We know Boston will come back. We know what kind of pride they have. We know what we're in for the rest of the way."

The Pistons showed grit of their own, overcoming Bill Laimbeer's exit with a right shoulder strain in the third quarter. James Edwards filled in with six points and six rebounds in 22 minutes, leading a 33-4 edge for Detroit's bench. The Celtics, so

accustomed to hitting vital shots, didn't do it this time; they made only 16-of-45 after halftime.

"It's frustrating," said Boston star Larry Bird, who scored 20. "At the start of the series, you want to get that first game under your belt. Our shots wouldn't go in."

The Pistons took the lead for good early in the fourth quarter on two straight Adrian Dantley jumpers that snapped an 80-80 tie. The Celtics got back within two on a hook shot by Kevin McHale, who led them with 31 points, but Thomas answered with a three-point play and 3-pointer to make it 90-82 with 5:30 left.

"Vinnie (Johnson) came off a screen, passed it to me and said, 'Shoot it,' " Thomas said of his 3-pointer. "I didn't take the shot and he kind of looked at me weird, so I dribbled back and let the shot go. Thank God it went in."

A week later at Boston, the Pistons would be similarly thankful. In the pivotal game of the series, Game 5, Thomas again scored 35 and rallied Detroit from a 16-point second-half deficit for a 102-96 win in overtime. It gave the Pistons a 3-2 series advantage, setting the stage for their Friday clincher at the Silverdome and first NBA Finals berth.

But it all began May 25, 1988, the night The Streak finally ended.

SUMMARY—Game 1
Pistons 104, Celtics 96

PISTONS (104)

Player	Min	FG M-A	3P M-A	FT M-A	Reb O-T	A	PF	Pts
Mahorn	32	2-4	0-0	0-1	0-10	1	4	4
Dantley	29	7-14	0-0	0-1	1-6	2	5	14
Laimbeer	21	4-7	0-1	0-2	2-7	1	3	8
Dumars	31	3-8	0-0	4-4	0-0	5	1	10
Thomas	44	12-19	2-3	9-10	0-2	12	1	35
Rodman	19	2-4	0-0	1-4	2-9	1	3	5
Salley	21	5-6	0-0	0-2	1-3	1	5	10
V.Johnson	21	5-9	0-0	2-4	0-2	3	0	12
Edwards	22	3-6	0-0	0-0	1-6	1	4	6
Russell DNP-Coach's Decision								
Ra.Lewis DNP-Coach's Decision								
Nevitt DNP-Coach's Decision								
Totals	**240**	**43-77**	**2-4**	**16-28**	**7-45**	**27**	**26**	**104**

CELTICS (96)

Player	Min	FG M-A	3P M-A	FT M-A	Reb O-T	A	PF	Pts
McHale	43	13-17	0-0	5-7	3-6	2	4	31
Bird	44	8-20	1-2	3-5	1-9	6	3	20
Parish	36	5-14	0-0	4-5	5-13	2	3	14
D.Johnson	43	3-14	0-2	2-4	0-5	10	3	8
Ainge	42	7-18	2-5	3-4	1-2	6	5	19
Acres	6	0-0	0-0	0-0	0-0	0	1	0
Jm.Paxson	11	1-3	0-0	0-0	0-1	1	1	2
Roberts	3	0-2	0-0	0-0	0-1	0	0	0
Gilmore	8	0-0	0-0	0-0	0-0	0	2	0
Re.Lewis	4	1-3	0-0	0-0	0-1	0	1	2
Minniefield DNP-Coach's Decision								
Lohaus DNP-Coach's Decision								
Totals	**240**	**38-91**	**3-9**	**17-25**	**10-38**	**27**	**23**	**96**

Percentages: FG .558, 3P .500, FT .571. Team Rebounds: 15. Blocked shots: 3 (Mahorn, Salley, Edwards). Turnovers: 13 (Mahorn 2, Dantley 2, Laimbeer 2, Thomas 2, Salley 2, Dumars, Rodman, Edwards). Steals: 2 (Dantley, Thomas). Technical fouls: Mahorn, 1:42 third.

Percentages: FG .418, 3P .333, FT .680. Team Rebounds: 9. Blocked shots: 5 (McHale 2, Bird 2, Parish). Turnovers: 8 (McHale 3, Bird 2, Ainge 2, Jm.Paxson). Steals: 5 (Bird 2, Ainge, Jm.Paxson, Re.Lewis). Technical fouls: illegal defense, 1:20 second; McHale, 1:42 third.

DETROIT	30	22	23	29	— 104
BOSTON	28	25	20	23	— 96

A—14,890 (sellout). T—2:14. Officials—Earl Strom, Paul Mihalak.

Premier Piston

John "Spider" Salley

John Salley's playoff averages—8.1 points, 5.4 rebounds—were even better than his regular-season stats—7.5 and 4.6.

No matter how he tried, Chuck Daly couldn't stay mad at John Salley. It was impossible. Salley was so likable, such an engaging personality, Daly would always give in to his amiable nature. It was a constant struggle, though, because for all of Salley's terrific athletic gifts, he was among the most maddening players of the Pistons' championship era. While the ratio was certainly better than 1:1 for his six-year career in Detroit, it sometimes seemed like Salley would make one poor play for every good one. For every blocked shot into the fourth row, a blown layup. For every productive hustle play, a fumbled pass or a bite on a Kevin McHale head-fake. But the bottom line of Salley's career was consistency. There was the occasional upward spike on the chart, like his surprising 1987 game with 28 points, 10 boards and five blocks, and his "Mr. May" postseason exploits. But Salley's season averages usually wound up the same: seven points, five rebounds, two blocks. Those would be journeyman statistics anywhere else, as when Salley was traded to Miami in 1992, but for the championship Pistons, they were needed and appreciated. The fans loved Salley, no doubt for his personality as much as his production, and their devotion was rewarded. Few Pistons made more public appearances than Salley and a better ambassador would be hard to find; his winning smile and sense of humor were a guaranteed hit. It was a personality honed as a youth in Brooklyn, New York, going door-to-door for Jehovah's Witness. Two championship banners and 709 blocked shots (fourth in club history) are the most prominent reminders of Salley's stint in Detroit, but his happy countenance and snappy comebacks will surely remain as memorable.

AT A GLANCE

JOHN SALLEY

FULL NAME:
John Thomas Salley
BORN:
May 16, 1964; Brooklyn, New York
POSITION, HEIGHT, WEIGHT:
Center, 6-foot-11, 230 pounds
COLLEGE:
Georgia Tech '86
TENURE WITH PISTONS:
1986-87 — 1991-92
Also: Miami 1992-95, Toronto 1995-96, Chicago 1996
BEST SEASON WITH PISTONS:
1987-88, 82 GP, 8.5 ppg, 4.9 rpg, 137 blocks
TOTALS WITH PISTONS:
Regular season: 459 GP, 7.5 ppg, 4.6 rpg, 709 blocks
Playoffs: 95 GP, 8.1 ppg, 5.4 rpg, 146 blocks

PISTON LIST

Isiah Thomas' 25-Point Third Quarter vs. Lakers

(Game 6, June 19, 1988)
- 11:01 — 2-of-2 free throws
- 10:31 — 5-foot put-back
- 10:06 — 18-footer, top key
- 9:37 — 12-footer, right wing
- 8:14 — 14-footer, left wing
- 7:38 — 12-footer, left wing
- 6:22 — Breakaway layup
- 4:21 — Injures ankle, exits
- 3:46 — Re-enters game
- 3:29 — 12-footer, left baseline
- 2:59 — 14-foot bank shot
- 1:13 — 26-foot 3-pointer
- :46 — Fast-break layup
- :02 — 20-footer, left corner

TOTAL: 11-of-13 shots, 25 points

Isiah Thomas

Jeff Malone

Throughout the '88 playoffs, Isiah Thomas was the Pistons' prime-time performer. Photo by Allen Einstein.

In the first four playoff games vs. Detroit, Washington's Jeff Malone averaged 31 points and shot 49-of-85 (57.6 percent).

Health permitting, and oftentimes not, Isiah Thomas did his best work under the hottest spotlights. It was always that way. But as wonderful as he was in the 1988 NBA Finals, highlighted by his record 25-point third quarter in Game 6, Thomas was just as amazing in the early rounds. In the Pistons' 23 playoff games, he averaged a team-high 21.9 points and 8.7 assists, leading them in scoring in each of the first three series. He averaged 25.2 points vs. Washington in the five-game first round, 20.4 against Chicago in the five-game second round and 23.0 in the six-game win over Boston in the Eastern finals. Included in those conquests were games of 30, 34, 35 and 35 points, the latter two at Boston. But he was only warming up for the seven-game Finals that re-emphasized his greatness on a national stage. Though Adrian Dantley led Detroit with a 21.3 average, Thomas was close behind at 19.7, a figure that doesn't do justice to the signature game of his career. It was Game 6, the Pistons' possible clincher. Sensing the moment slipping away, Thomas took over in the third quarter with 25 points, the last 11 on a badly sprained ankle. Despite the loss, his 43-point performance is widely regarded among the greatest Finals games ever.

As marvelous as the Pistons' playoff run was in 1988, they almost didn't make it out of the first round thanks to Washington shooting guard Jeff Malone. The five-year veteran played well vs. Detroit in the regular season, averaging 22.4 points in five meetings, but he was amazing in the playoffs, averaging 25.6 and causing the Central champs substantial unease. The Pistons felt they had the series well under control, winning Games 1 and 2 at the Silverdome despite 33 and 31 points by Malone. But the series moved to Washington and Malone carried his team on his back. In Game 3, a 114-106 Bullets win in overtime, Malone scored 35 on 15-of-22 shooting. He scored nine of their last 13 in regulation, then shot 4-of-4 in OT. "I don't know what we're going to do with Malone," Chuck Daly said. Joe Dumars, faced with a defensive challenge akin to Michael Jordan, said, "They're setting three or four picks for Malone on every play, sometimes five." Their exasperation grew in Game 4 when Malone scored 25 and Washington tied the series with a 106-103 win, but Daly switched 6-foot-8 Dennis Rodman on to Malone and it began to wear down the 6-foot-4 guard. In Game 5, Malone shot 1-of-12 and had only four points in the Pistons' clinching 99-78 home rout.

January 29, 1988

It was a feat of Barnumesque proportions—stuffing 61,983 fans into the Silverdome for an NBA game—and the Pistons responded by giving them the greatest show on Earth. Sure, many of the tickets were 2-for-1's, discounts and outright freebies, but compared to the old days when fans wouldn't even show up for free, the overflow house was a terrific testament to the home team's popularity. Keyed by a 21-7 third-period spurt, the Pistons beat the Celtics, 125-108, to send their fans into the traffic jam with smiles. "We didn't let anyone down. We gave everyone a good show," Dennis Rodman said. The crowd topped the previous NBA (and Pistons) record of 52,745 on February 14, 1987. "It was amazing," Isiah Thomas said. "When that many people come out to see a game, it shows they like the way we play basketball."

The biggest crowd in NBA history gathered at the Silverdome on January 29, 1988. Photo by Allen Einstein.

Added coach Chuck Daly, "It was mind-boggling to look up and see people all the way around the arena. It is hard to believe that many people would be here. It's a great show for our marketing department and our fans." It was a great win, too, the Pistons' second of the season over Boston. The Celtics had entered with a 30-11 record, including 13-2 in January. The win lifted the Pistons to 24-13.

December 15, 1987

Adrian Dantley's constant drives to the basket caused headaches for Scottie Pippen and the Bulls on December 15. Photo by Allen Einstein.

Neither rain nor Michael Jordan nor overtime could stay the Pistons from their appointed rounds as the NBA's hottest team. They had to fight off all three on December 15 to gain a 127-123 victory over the Chicago Bulls, stretching their winning streak to seven. Playing seemingly through a steady drizzle dripping from the Silverdome ceiling, the Pistons raised their record to an NBA-best 14-5 and earned their second OT win over the Bulls in less than a month, having won at Chicago 144-132 on November 21. Forced into overtime after Jordan swished an amazing turnaround three-pointer at the buzzer, Detroit pulled out the second win when Joe Dumars made a smart play with 16 seconds left. The Pistons led 124-123 when Chicago came down for the potential winning shot. Jordan wanted to drive the left baseline, but Dumars jumped in his path and Jordan was whistled for his sixth foul. He exited with 38 points. Bill Laimbeer's 29 led Detroit, while Adrian Dantley scored 27 (with 19-of-22 free throws) and Rick Mahorn 18 with 14 boards.

"The Bulls are going to be very difficult to beat in the playoffs. To get to the Eastern finals, whoever it is will have to get through them," Pistons coach Chuck Daly said, correctly predicting the future.

CHANGING FACES

THE PISTONS spent most of the season looking for a helpful big man and Jack McCloskey's search was finally successful. Having already traded for 7-foot-1 William Bedford from Phoenix, 7-foot rookie Ron Moore and mercurial 6-foot-11 veteran Darryl Dawkins, McCloskey struck gold on February 24. He dealt Moore and a 1991 second-rounder to Phoenix for 11-year veteran James Edwards, a 7-foot-1 center who had parlayed a smooth fallaway jumper into a 15-point career average. His contributions were not immediately felt because it took time for Chuck Daly to blend Edwards' skills, but he would prove a valuable acquisition over the next three seasons. McCloskey had high hopes for the eminently talented but immature Bedford, for whom he'd traded a 1988 No. 1 pick, but Bedford quickly wound up in the NBA's drug rehab program. Dawkins was acquired Thanksgiving Day, but quit the NBA only two weeks later. Near the trade deadline, Houston offered broken-down 7-foot-4 Ralph Sampson to Detroit, but McCloskey refused to part with Joe Dumars.

How's this for a pious matchup: "Buddha" (James Edwards) shooting over Moses (Malone). Photo by Allen Einstein.

Take a Bow

Adrian Dantley

Adrian Dantley's place in basketball history was secure long before he stepped on to the Silverdome floor on December 8, 1987. But he confirmed his spot by reaching the 20,000-point mark in the closing seconds of a 127-117 win over Portland. On a banked-in fast-break layup with 14 seconds left, Dantley became the 13th player in NBA history to attain 20,000. He completed the feat in his 12th season. "I'm glad we won because when I scored my 10,000th (for Utah, 1982), we didn't," said Dantley, who also recalled shooting 3-of-17 in his NBA debut. "I was a little uptight. You want to go out and shoot the ball, but you also want to stay in the flow. You don't want to mess up the team." Coach Chuck Daly was lavish in his praise of Dantley. "He's phenomenal. The guy is 6-foot-6, playing against guys up to 7-foot-2—he's a dinosaur, really. Only a guy with great discipline could approach anything like this." Dantley's next goal was to pass idol Elgin Baylor's 23,149 points. He did, retiring in 1991 with 23,177.

Since Adrian Dantley, 11 NBA players have topped 20,000 points, bringing the total to 24.

PISTON LIST

Highest-Scoring Playoff Games

(with opponent total)

145 points
- 5-24-87 vs. Boston (119)

132 points
- 3-31-62 at L.A. Lakers (125)

128 points
- 4-26-87 vs. Washington (85)

126 points
- 3-25-68 vs. Boston (116)
- 4-15-76 vs. Milwaukee (123)

125 points
- 4-18-85 vs. New Jersey (108)
- 5-2-85 vs. Boston (117)
- 4-19-86 at Atlanta (137)

124 points
- 3-16-58 at Cincinnati (104)
- 3-17-61 vs. L.A. Lakers (113)

123 points
- 5 times

HOMES OF THE PISTONS

After three decades of renting, squatting and essentially crashing on someone else's couch, the Pistons finally found a home in 1988. It was no handyman's special, either. It was a palace.

With the construction of the state-of-the-art Palace of Auburn Hills, nestled 30 miles into Detroit's sparkling northern suburbs, the Pistons had a place to call their own for the first time since the franchise left Fort Wayne in 1957.

No more sharing an arena with hockey's Red Wings.

No more carpetbagging in a college field house.

No more neutral-site games ... in their own city.

No more games squeezed into the corner of a domed football stadium, with the pillowy Teflon roof leaking on your head and a constant draft.

And no more games in high school gymnasiums.

Yes, that's right. The Pistons got so hard up for a place to play in '60, with their two home arenas otherwise in use, they had to annex Grosse Pointe High School for their first-round playoff opener vs. Minneapolis. It was the ultimate indignity, the game being shown on national TV. As if to live down to the absurdity of the situation, Detroit lost 113-112.

Including their one-time voyage into schoolboy territory, the Pistons have played home games in seven arenas over 40 years. Considering the NBA championships of 1989 and '90, it's no surprise that The Palace is the most favorable home court of the bunch. Through '97, having played exactly 400 games there since '88, they had a .683 winning percentage (273-127), including a 24-7 record (.774) in the postseason.

The Pistons' first home was Olympia Stadium, a red brick building on Grand River Avenue that provokes fond memories among Detroiters. But most of their recollections aren't about the Pistons, but rather the Red Wings, who spent 52 seasons there from 1927-79. They captured seven Stanley Cups during that span and were runners-up 11 times. The Motor City upstarts, the Pistons, struggled along with losing records, meager crowds and second-class status. In case of schedule conflicts, Olympia (capacity 15,000) was kept for the Red Wings, while the Pistons had to play at the University of Detroit Memorial Building (9,000). The crowds were so routinely small, attendance figures emerged from midair more often than not; many fans attended on discounted (read: free) tickets.

After four seasons at Olympia, U-D and, all right, Grosse Pointe High, the Pistons reached a deal March 21, 1961 to move to the 10,939-seat Convention Arena on Detroit's riverfront. Not only would the team save on arena rental — $600 a game, compared to $2,500 at Olympia — but it would be the main tenant. The Pistons played in that building, renamed Cobo Arena, for 17 seasons (1961-78) in its longest stint in any arena. They racked up a 344-287 record (.545) in 631 games at Cobo, but only 14 were playoff games, so there are relatively few important memories from the Pistons' tenure there. In fact, their last game at Cobo on April 9, 1978 is one of the most memorable, but only because Denver's David Thompson scored 73 points, still the third-most in an NBA game.

The Pistons' move from Cobo to the Pontiac Silverdome for the 1978-79 season signified more than a move to a larger stadium. The Pistons hadn't drawn well downtown; their best attendance average was 7,492 in '74-75 (though critics would argue that their quality of play did not deserve greater support). In addition, the Red Wings were preparing to become the main tenant in Detroit's new riverfront arena in 1979 (Joe Louis Arena) and Pistons owner Bill Davidson was not interested in his club becoming entrenched as a second-rate attraction in Detroit. So on September 26, 1977, he announced he was moving his team to Pontiac where it would play in a 30,000-seat configuration at the Silverdome. If city fans wouldn't support the Pistons, perhaps suburban fans would.

Cobo Arena (lower right) highlights the Detroit riverfront as it appeared in 1962.

It was a logistical accomplishment to put on basketball at the Dome, the Detroit Lions' home since the 80,000-seat stadium opened in 1975. The court was set up in the Southeast corner, an amazing feat in itself because the concrete floor had a 10-inch crown. A four-ton scoreboard was held in place by a hydraulic hoisting system attached to the upper rim of the stadium. To create relative intimacy, a 3,000-pound curtain—402 feet long, 75 feet tall—was suspended along the 50-yard line.

If not for the arrival of Isiah Thomas in 1981, the Pistons might have failed commercially at the Silverdome as they had in Detroit. But after they became an entertaining attraction and an annual playoff club, fans turned out in record numbers. With a winning product, lots of seats and imaginative marketing, the Pistons made attendance gains for the last seven of their 10 seasons at the Silverdome. They led the NBA the final five seasons, averaging a record 26,012 and nabbing every single-game league mark. Their crowning glory came on January 29, 1988 when an NBA-record 61,983 fans crammed the Silverdome for a victory over Boston, breaking their own record of 52,745 set February 14, 1987 vs. Philadelphia. From 1985-88, the Pistons attracted 10 crowds of more than 40,000, the last occurring June 16, 1988 when 41,732 attended the final game at the Silverdome—Game 5 of the NBA Finals vs. the Lakers. Fittingly, the Pistons' final points in the stadium were two free throws by guard Walker D. Russell, who grew up on the hardscrabble courts of Pontiac.

But the Pistons' stay at the Silverdome was not uninterrupted. With a moto-cross inexplicably scheduled at the Dome on April 27, 1984, they returned to Detroit, to Joe Louis Arena, to play the deciding fifth game of their first-round playoff series against Bernard King and the Knicks. New York won 127-123 in overtime, but only after withstanding one of Thomas' highlight-reel accomplishments: 16 points in the final 1:34 to force a 114-114 tie. Then March 4, 1985, merely seven hours before the Pistons were to host Milwaukee, the inflated Silverdome roof collapsed under tons of snow and ice, causing $10 million in damage. The stadium was closed six months for repairs, so the Pistons went back downtown for their last 10 home games and the playoffs. Every game was at Joe Louis Arena except one, a 121-114 win over the L.A. Clippers at Cobo Arena on March 11—a final nod to the franchise's formative years.

The culmination of those years arrived November 5, 1988 when the Pistons met the expansion Charlotte Hornets in the first game at The Palace, a 94-85 Detroit victory. The privately financed, $80 million arena was a showpiece. Housing three levels of suites, 21,454 padded seats, a huge video scoreboard and a vast array of concessions, The Palace set a new standard for a sports and entertainment venue. The potent combination of a championship team and a beautiful arena made the Pistons the hot ticket in town; they sold out the first 245 games at The Palace, a span of more than five seasons. It took them three decades, but the Pistons' embarrassment had finally been erased. They graduated high school, so to speak.

PISTONS RECORDS IN HOME ARENAS

OLYMPIA STADIUM (1957-61)
Regular	54-50 (.519)
Playoffs	3-2 (.600)

UNIVERSITY OF DETROIT (1958-61)
Regular	10-6 (.625)
Playoffs	2-0 (1.000)

GROSSE POINTE H.S. (March 12, 1960)
Playoffs	0-1 (.000)

COBO ARENA (1961-78, '85)
Regular	337-280 (.546)
Playoffs	7-7 (.500)

PONTIAC SILVERDOME (1978-88)
Regular	241-159 (.603)
Playoffs	18-5 (.783)

JOE LOUIS ARENA (1984-85)
Regular	6-3 (.667)
Playoffs	4-2 (.667)

PALACE OF AUBURN HILLS (1989-97)
Regular	249-120 (.675)
Playoffs	24-7 (.774)

TOTALS (1957-97)
Regular	897-618 (.592)
Playoffs	58-24 (.707)
OVERALL	**955-642 (.598)**

The Pistons came of age during 10 seasons at the Pontiac Silverdome, setting practically every NBA attendance record.

Under construction in 1987, The Palace takes shape in the woods of Auburn Hills.

1988 DETROIT PISTONS 1989

November 8, 1988:
Vice President George Bush defeats Governor Michael Dukakis of Massachusetts in the presidential election.

January 22, 1989:
The San Francisco 49ers win their third Super Bowl, beating Cincinnati 20-16 behing Joe Montana's record 357 yards passing.

March 24, 1989:
The oil tanker Exxon Valdez strikes a reef in Prince William Sound, Alaska, leaking more than a million barrels of crude oil into the water.

SEASON SNAPSHOT

Most Points
Isiah Thomas (1,458, 18.2 avg.)

Most Rebounds
Bill Laimbeer (776, 9.6 avg.)

Most Assists
Isiah Thomas (663, 8.3 avg.)

Most Minutes
Isiah Thomas (2,924, 36.6 avg.)

Field-Goal Percentage
x-Dennis Rodman (59.5%)

Free-Throw Percentage
Joe Dumars (85.0%)

Team Offense Average
106.6 (8,740 in 82 games)

Team Defense Average
100.8 (8,264 in 82 games)

Pistons in All-Star Game
Isiah Thomas, G

NBA Finals MVP
Joe Dumars, G

x-led league

1988-89

FINAL STANDINGS

Central Division	W	L	Pct.	GB
PISTONS	**63**	**19**	**.768**	**—**
Cleveland	57	25	.695	6
Atlanta	52	30	.634	11
Milwaukee	49	33	.598	14
Chicago	47	35	.573	16
Indiana	28	54	.341	35

Atlantic Division Winner—New York
Midwest Division Winner—Utah
Pacific Division Winner—L.A. Lakers

PLAYOFF RESULTS

Eastern First Round: Pistons d. Boston, 3-0
Eastern Semifinals: Pistons d. Milwaukee, 4-0
Eastern Finals: Pistons d. Chicago, 4-2
NBA Finals: Pistons d. L.A. Lakers, 4-0

PISTONS PLAYOFF LEADERS

Scoring: Isiah Thomas (18.2 avg.)
Rebounding: Dennis Rodman (10.0)
Assists: Isiah Thomas (8.3)

NBA CHAMPION

DETROIT PISTONS

1988-89
SEASON IN REVIEW

When Neil Armstrong became the first man to walk on the moon July 20, 1969, they were the easiest steps of all. Everything that led up to that moment, the perilous journey, that was the hard part.

Such was the case 20 years later when the Pistons ascended to the first NBA title in club history. Their final steps were the easiest of all. A 4-0 sweep of the injury-riddled Los Angeles Lakers, the two-time defending champions, could not be considered easy, to be sure. But set against their decade-long climb from the 16 wins of 1979-80, their quest for respectability and their long struggle to overcome the invincible Celtics, the '89 Finals were a Sunday stroll.

The anticlimactic ease with which the Pistons vanquished the Lakers didn't take away any of the satisfaction, though. They had gambled and won, trading away top scorer Adrian Dantley for Mark Aguirre on February 15, leading to a 30-4 finishing kick for a 63-19 final record, their best ever. Then they swept the Celtics and Bucks in the first two rounds, eliminated Chicago in six games in the Eastern finals and did exactly what they were supposed to in the NBA Finals—pound a wounded team into submission. The Lakers were without their starting guards, Magic Johnson and Byron Scott, due to hamstring pulls, and that duo's absence played to the Pistons' strength—"The Palace Guard" trio of Isiah Thomas, Joe Dumars and Vinnie Johnson.

The 1988-89 NBA champions. First row, from left, Bill Laimbeer, John Long, head coach Chuck Daly, chief executive officer Thomas S. Wilson, owner William M. Davidson, general manager Jack McCloskey, legal counsel Oscar H. Feldman, John Salley, James Edwards, Rick Mahorn. Second row, from left, trainer Mike Abdenour, chief scout Stan Novak, assistant to the general manager Will Robinson, assistant coach Brendan Suhr, Micheal Williams, Vinnie Johnson, Fennis Dembo, Dennis Rodman, Mark Aguirre, Joe Dumars, Isiah Thomas, assistant coach Brendan Malone, broadcaster George Blaha. Photo by Allen Einstein.

It's likely the Pistons would have beaten a healthy L.A. lineup—we'll never know for sure—based on their NBA-best record, their near-miss against the Lakers in the 1988 Finals and the deepest lineup in the league. The Lakers had the second-deepest, but the loss of Scott before the series and Johnson in Game 2 tested them. Michael Cooper and ex-Piston Tony Campbell were thrust into the starting five and were no match for the likes of Thomas, Dumars and Johnson. Likewise, by borrowing from their bench, the Lakers could no longer fully cope with Detroit super subs Dennis Rodman, John Salley and James Edwards.

The Pistons opened the Finals with a 109-97 victory at The Palace, leading by at least 11 for the final 20 minutes. Then the Lakers wasted their best chance to assert themselves, losing Game 2 108-105 after James Worthy missed a free throw that should've sent the game into overtime. Johnson pulled his hamstring with 4:39 left in the third quarter and was done for the series; the Lakers were now rudderless. But the Pistons were having their way even before he exited, getting terrific play from Dumars, who would take home series MVP honors with a 27.3 scoring average. It was Dumars who saved Detroit's 114-110 victory in Game 3, preserving a last-minute three-point lead by blocking David Rivers' 3-point attempt from the left corner.

Game 4 at L.A. on June 13 was a coronation, a formality. The Pistons were hitting on all cylinders and the Lakers had nothing left. Chanting "Baaaaad Boys, Baaaaad Boys!" on the bench in the closing seconds, the Pistons turned aside the Lakers 105-97 to set off a wild celebration in their Forum locker room and back home in Detroit, where fans filled The Palace to view the game. In a champagne shower that soaked everyone from owner Bill Davidson to the ball boys, more than three decades of Pistons frustration were suddenly over. As Isiah Thomas kissed and hugged the championship trophy and Bill Laimbeer soaked everyone he could see through his champagne fog, all those years of anemic teams, apathetic attendance and a nomadic existence had been forgotten. They hadn't been erased, just superceded in the collective memory bank of Detroit basketball fans.

"It means so much, so much," Isiah Thomas said with a faraway, contented look. "Winning four (in the Finals) is so much sweeter after you've lost four, believe me." "We wanted it more than anyone else," Laimbeer said. Coach Chuck Daly, his well-styled coif now matted with champagne, said matter-of-factly, "I think our depth finally won out."

(continued...)

1988-89
SEASON IN REVIEW
——— (continued) ———

After winning their first NBA championship, the Pistons were fittingly saluted by "The Breakfast of Champions."

The Pistons' celebration had a nickname—"Bad Boys"—and a theme—"Hammer Time"—from the song by rapper M.C. Hammer. Yes, they had put the hammer down on the Lakers, but this time they had been lucky too. Unlike the previous spring when Isiah's ankle sprain likely robbed Detroit of the title, this time it was the Pistons' opponents who were shorthanded. They swept Boston without Larry Bird (heel surgery) in the first round, then Milwaukee without Terry Cummings; the Bucks had a 4-2 record against the Pistons in the regular season and expected to give them trouble, but injuries left them with only seven players for Game 4. Only the Bulls were at full strength, but Doug Collins' club wasn't quite ready to challenge the savvier Pistons.

Despite their league-best record, the regular season hadn't been a walkover for the Pistons. After a 9-1 start, they fell into second place for most of December and January, trailing Cleveland by five full games on January 27 despite a 26-13 record. Dumars suffered a broken hand on January 12, sidelining him for 12 games. Though the Pistons were still beating most teams, they struggled against New York, Milwaukee and Cleveland. There was tension between Daly and Dantley; the coach felt he was holding the ball too long, leaving the offense scrambling for last-second shots. The Pistons also felt A.D. wasn't getting to the foul line enough.

On February 15, GM Jack McCloskey made the boldest stroke of his career, trading Dantley (and a first-round pick) to Dallas for Aguirre, who had worn out his welcome there. It was a massive gamble that worked. "Our mix wasn't right," McCloskey explained. "This deal makes us younger." The fans and Dantley blamed Isiah, who had long been friends with Aguirre, but he denied involvement. "People didn't give me credit for trading Paul Mokeski for Laimbeer and I'm not the one who traded A.D., either," the captain said.

Four months later, as the Pistons celebrated an NBA championship for the first time in 32 years in Detroit, the complaints had been replaced by cheers.

Game Results

1988-89 REGULAR SEASON

Date	Opponent	Result	Record
11-4	at Chicago	W, 107-94	1-0
11-5	CHARLOTTE	W, 94-85	2-0
11-8	at Philadelphia	W, 116-109	3-0
11-9	ATLANTA	W, 101-95 (OT)	4-0
11-11	at Boston	W, 116-107	5-0
11-15	at Dallas	W, 108-99	6-0
11-16	at San Antonio	W, 94-88	7-0
11-18	at Phoenix	W, 121-105	8-0
11-19	at Houston	L, 98-109	8-1
11-22	at Charlotte	W, 99-93	9-1
11-23	NEW YORK	L, 111-133	9-2
11-26	L.A. LAKERS	W, 102-99	10-2
11-29	at Indiana	L, 98-107	10-3
11-30	INDIANA	W, 114-111	11-3
12-2	at Washington	W, 120-114	12-3
12-4	at New Jersey	W, 102-99	13-3
12-6	at Milwaukee	L, 84-109	13-4
12-7	CHICAGO	W, 102-89	14-4
12-9	at Atlanta	W, 92-82	15-4
12-10	PHILADELPHIA	W, 106-100	16-4
12-14	MILWAUKEE	L, 110-119	16-5
12-15	at Cleveland	L, 98-119	16-6
12-17	CHARLOTTE	W, 100-91	17-6
12-20	MIAMI	W, 116-100	18-6
12-22	at New York	L, 85-88	18-7
12-28	PHOENIX	W, 106-100	19-7
12-30	HOUSTON	W, 95-83	20-7
1-3	at Atlanta	L, 104-123	20-8
1-6	ATLANTA	W, 111-88	21-8
1-7	at Indiana	L, 99-113	21-9
1-11	NEW YORK	L, 93-100	21-10
1-13	WASHINGTON	W, 119-103	22-10
1-15	at Milwaukee	L, 112-120	22-11
1-16	BOSTON	W, 96-87	23-11
1-18	NEW JERSEY	W, 103-90	24-11
1-20	INDIANA	W, 132-99	25-11
1-22	at Boston	L, 99-112	25-12
1-25	GOLDEN STATE	W, 105-104	26-12
1-27	CLEVELAND	L, 79-80	26-13
1-29	SACRAMENTO	W, 122-97	27-13
1-31	at Chicago	W, 104-98 (OT)	28-13
2-3	at Philadelphia	W, 124-106	29-13
2-5	CHICAGO	W, 113-102	30-13
2-8	MILWAUKEE	W, 107-96	31-13
2-14	at L.A. Lakers	W, 111-103	32-13
2-16	at Sacramento	W, 95-84	33-13
2-18	at Golden State	L, 119-121 (OT)	33-14
2-20	at Denver	L, 101-103	33-15
2-22	PORTLAND	W, 105-94	34-15
2-25	at New Jersey	W, 113-95	35-15
2-26	L.A. CLIPPERS	W, 110-98	36-15
2-28	at Cleveland	L, 99-115	36-16
3-1	UTAH	W, 96-85	37-16
3-3	CLEVELAND	W, 96-90	38-16
3-5	at Miami	W, 109-100	39-16
3-6	DENVER	W, 129-112	40-16
3-8	SEATTLE	W, 112-96	41-16
3-11	at Philadelphia	W, 111-106	42-16
3-12	WASHINGTON	W, 110-104	43-16
3-14	at Indiana	W, 129-117	44-16
3-17	BOSTON	W, 106-98	45-16
3-18	at Milwaukee	L, 100-117	45-17
3-21	at Atlanta	W, 110-95	46-17
3-22	SAN ANTONIO	W, 115-94	47-17
3-24	NEW JERSEY	W, 112-96	48-17
3-25	at Charlotte	W, 113-101	49-17
3-27	DALLAS	W, 90-77	50-17
3-29	at Utah	W, 108-104 (2OT)	51-17
3-31	at Seattle	W, 111-108	52-17
4-2	at L.A. Clippers	W, 117-101	53-17
4-4	at Portland	L, 100-118	53-18
4-6	CHICAGO	W, 115-108	54-18
4-7	at Chicago	W, 114-112 (OT)	55-18
4-9	MILWAUKEE	W, 100-91	56-18
4-10	at Washington	W, 124-100	57-18
4-12	CLEVELAND	W, 107-95	58-18
4-14	at New York	L, 100-104	58-19
4-16	WASHINGTON	W, 104-98	59-19
4-18	at Cleveland	W, 118-102	60-19
4-19	INDIANA	W, 115-105	61-19
4-21	PHILADELPHIA	W, 100-91	62-19
4-23	ATLANTA	W, 99-81	63-19

PLAYOFFS

Eastern First Round—(Best-of-Five)

Date	Opponent	Result	Record
4-28	BOSTON	W, 101-91	1-0
4-30	BOSTON	W, 102-95	2-0
5-2	at Boston	W, 100-85	3-0

Eastern Semifinals—(Best-of-Seven)

Date	Opponent	Result	Record
5-10	MILWAUKEE	W, 85-80	1-0
5-12	MILWAUKEE	W, 112-95	2-0
5-14	at Milwaukee	W, 110-90	3-0
5-15	at Milwaukee	W, 96-94	4-0

Eastern Finals—(Best-of-Seven)

Date	Opponent	Result	Record
5-21	CHICAGO	L, 88-94	0-1
5-23	CHICAGO	W, 100-91	1-1
5-27	at Chicago	L, 97-99	1-2
5-29	at Chicago	W, 86-80	2-2
5-31	CHICAGO	W, 94-85	3-2
6-2	at Chicago	W, 103-94	4-2

NBA Finals—(Best-of-Seven)

Date	Opponent	Result	Record
6-6	L.A. LAKERS	W, 109-97	1-0
6-8	L.A. LAKERS	W, 108-105	2-0
6-11	at L.A. Lakers	W, 114-110	3-0
6-13	at L.A. Lakers	W, 105-97	4-0

(Home games in CAPS)

SPOTLIGHT
Game

JUNE 13, 1989

After the heartbreak of 1988, the conquering Pistons got to spray champagne at The Forum in '89. Photo by Andrew Bernstein/NBA.

By Game 4 of the Finals, it was a foregone conclusion that the Pistons were going to supplant the L.A. Lakers as NBA champions. Detroit held a 3-0 lead and the Lakers' starting backcourt of Magic Johnson and Byron Scott was sidelined with matching hamstring pulls. It was obvious that the Pistons' time had arrived.

Coupled with the anticipation of the Pistons' first league title, there was also sadness in Detroit because the series probably wouldn't make it back home. With Games 4 and 5 at The Forum, the Pistons seemed sure to clinch the series on television, rather than at The Palace.

So the Pistons did the next best thing—they combined the two. They opened the arena so their fans could watch Game 4 on the PalaceVision scoreboard and share the experience en masse. On June 13, 1989, more than 20,000 fans packed The Palace, cheering their heroes all the way as the Pistons finished the sweep with a 105-97 conquest of the Lakers.

"My obsession has been realized," Isiah Thomas said in a champagne-soaked locker room. "It feels just like I thought it would—awesome," said Joe Dumars, the modest Finals MVP who emerged from Thomas' considerable shadow in the series with a 27.3 scoring average. "I can't tell you how proud I am of this group," coach Chuck

Daly said, his natty suit coat replaced by a championship T-shirt.

The Lakers didn't go quietly, but there was a certain fatalism at The Forum that Tuesday night. The Pistons trailed by as much as 16 in the first half as L.A.'s James Worthy began shaping a 40-point game, but there was a detectable feeling that the deeper Detroiters would have the final say.

They did. The Pistons pulled within 78-76 after the third quarter, then took control as James Edwards—a 1977 Lakers draftee—scored all of his 13 points in the final 12 minutes. His three-point play and a pair of Thomas layups sent Detroit ahead 93-87 with 7:10 left. In the last minute, Dumars hit a 15-footer and Bill Laimbeer a 17-footer to ensure the fantastic final outcome.

The Pistons' first championship wasn't the only history to come out of Game 4. It was also the last NBA game for all-time scoring king Kareem Abdul-Jabbar, the Lakers' 42-year-old center. In November, in his final regular-season game at The Palace, the Pistons had given him a rocking chair. In Game 4, they sent the 20-year veteran into retirement after an unpoetic seven-point game. With 19 seconds to go, Kareem exited to the cheers of a full Forum and a standing ovation by the conquering Pistons.

Back home at The Palace, the victory party had already begun.

SUMMARY—Game 4
Pistons 105, L.A. Lakers 97

PISTONS (105)

Player	Min	FG M-A	3P M-A	FT M-A	Reb O-T	A	PF	Pts
Aguirre	23	1-5	0-0	0-0	0-2	0	2	2
Mahorn	35	5-7	0-0	3-4	3-7	1	6	13
Laimbeer	30	5-8	2-2	4-4	1-6	2	4	16
Dumars	37	5-13	0-0	13-17	0-1	6	0	23
Thomas	32	5-9	0-1	4-6	0-3	5	4	14
Rodman	13	1-5	0-0	0-0	3-4	1	2	2
Salley	20	3-4	0-0	2-4	1-3	1	2	8
V.Johnson	29	5-11	0-0	4-7	0-6	5	2	14
Edwards	21	4-8	0-0	5-9	1-4	0	4	13
Dembo DNP-Coach's Decision								
Long DNP-Coach's Decision								
Williams DNP-Coach's Decision								
Totals	**240**	**34-70**	**2-3**	**35-51**	**9-36**	**21**	**26**	**105**

Percentages: FG .486, 3P .667, FT .686. Team Rebounds: 15. Blocked shots: 4 (Salley 3, Edwards). Turnovers: 9 (Thomas 3, Aguirre 2, Dumars 2, Mahorn, Rodman). Steals: 3 (Thomas 2, Mahorn). Technical fouls: Mahorn, 10:31 first; coach Daly, 2:18 first.

L.A. LAKERS (97)

Player	Min	FG M-A	3P M-A	FT M-A	Reb O-T	A	PF	Pts
Green	38	2-5	0-1	2-4	3-12	0	3	6
Worthy	46	17-26	2-3	4-6	0-3	3	3	40
Abdul-Jabbar	29	2-8	0-0	3-4	1-3	3	3	7
Campbell	14	2-3	0-0	2-2	2-3	2	6	6
Cooper	46	4-14	1-7	2-3	0-3	9	4	11
Rivers	12	1-5	0-0	0-0	0-1	2	3	2
Thompson	24	3-10	0-0	5-6	3-7	1	3	11
Woolridge	25	4-7	0-0	5-6	1-7	3	3	13
Lamp	5	0-1	0-0	1-2	0-1	0	2	1
McNamara	1	0-0	0-0	0-0	0-0	0	0	0
M.Johnson DNP-Pulled hamstring								
Scott DNP-Pulled hamstring								
Totals	**240**	**35-79**	**3-11**	**24-33**	**10-40**	**23**	**30**	**97**

Percentages: FG .443, 3P .273, FT .727. Team Rebounds: 14. Blocked shots: 6 (Worthy 3, Abdul-Jabbar 2, Woolridge). Turnovers: 7 (Abdul-Jabbar 2, Rivers 2, Worthy, Campbell, Woolridge). Steals: 3 (Cooper 2, Green). Technical fouls: Cooper, 10:31 first; illegal defense, 1:33 second.

DETROIT	23	26	27	29	—	105
L.A. LAKERS	35	20	23	19	—	97

A—17,505 (sellout). T—2:36. Officials—Earl Strom, Jack Madden, Jess Kersey.

Mark Aguirre

The Pistons' acquisition of Mark Aguirre (for Adrian Dantley) on February 15, 1989 was the biggest NBA trade of the season.

Through little fault of his own, Mark Aguirre began his Pistons career with a massive I-told-you-so hanging over his head. Sure, he had asked to be traded from Dallas, where the Mavs' all-time scoring leader had grown restless in his eighth season. But when he was acquired by the Pistons on February 15, 1989, exchanged for Adrian Dantley, public opinion didn't fall in Aguirre's favor. Not only had Dantley been beloved by the locals, but Aguirre had a malcontent's reputation; his Dallas teammates expressed glee to see him go. So when the 6-foot-6 scoring forward arrived in Detroit, the prevailing attitude among fans and teammates was essentially, "We've got a good thing going. Screw it up and you're history." Instead, he helped the Pistons make history, playing a crucial (and generally agreeable) role in their back-to-back NBA titles. Let the record state that Detroit went 45-8 in '89 after Aguirre showed up, 44-6 when he was a starter. In 1989-90, he was willing to be benched for Dennis Rodman at midseason, allowing the Pistons to field their best defensive lineup en route to another championship. All told in Aguirre's four-plus seasons, the Pistons were 266-155 (63.2 percent). Did he catch them at the right time? No question, but Aguirre's contributions were also substantial and fairly seamless. He averaged 15.5 points in 1989, lending inside offense by using his Mahorn-like backside to keep low-post defenders at bay. Aguirre followed with full seasons of 14.1 points ('89-90) and 14.2 ('90-91). Though meager compared to his 24.6 career average for Dallas, which drafted him No. 1 over Isiah Thomas in 1981, stats like those earned Aguirre two NBA championship rings. I-told-you-so, indeed.

AT A GLANCE

MARK AGUIRRE

FULL NAME:
Mark Anthony Aguirre
BORN:
December 10, 1959; Chicago
POSITION, HEIGHT, WEIGHT:
Forward, 6-foot-6, 232 pounds
COLLEGE:
DePaul '81
ACQUIRED:
1989, trade from Dallas
TENURE WITH PISTONS:
February 15, 1989 – 1992-93
Also: Dallas 1981-89, L.A. Clippers 1993-94
BEST SEASON WITH PISTONS:
1988-89, 36 GP, 15.5 ppg, 4.2 rpg
TOTALS WITH PISTONS:
Regular season: 318 GP, 12.9 ppg, 3.8 rpg
Playoffs: 57 GP, 13.5 ppg, 4.1 rpg
HONORS:
All-Star Game (3): Dallas 1983-84, 1986-87, 1987-88
No. 1 overall draft pick, 1981

PISTON LIST

Highest Seasonal Field Goal Percentage

- .494, 1988-89
- .493, 1987-88
- .490, 1986-87
- .484, 1985-86
- .483, 1976-77
- .482, 1981-82
- .480, 1983-84
- .480, 1984-85
- .480, 1979-80
- .478, 1977-78
- .478, 1989-90
- .477, 1982-83
- .475, 1978-79

PLAYOFF HERO

PLAYOFF VILLAIN

Joe Dumars

Michael Jordan

Joe Dumars' last-second blocked shot on David Rivers clinched Game 3 for the Pistons.

In 22 playoff games against the Pistons from 1988-91, Michael Jordan averaged 30.0 points, 6.7 rebounds and 6.6 assists.

For years, it seemed like Joe Dumars' first name wasn't Joe at all, it was Underrated. That's what he was called: Underrated Joe Dumars. But after Detroit's tidy 15-2 NBA championship run, Dumars was no longer Underrated, he was Joe, the MVP of the Finals. After being somewhat of a disappointment in the '88 Finals, missing some shots that could've swung the series Detroit's way, Dumars was terrific in the '89 sweep of the Lakers. He shot nearly 58 percent and averaged 27.3 points to capture series scoring honors. It capped a marvelous postseason in which Dumars averaged 17.6 points. "Winning the championship is the most special part. You dream about it when you're a kid," he said. "But I'm also honored to win the award. There have been a lot of great players who've won it and I'm proud to be among them." So humble. So typical of Dumars. He could've been haughtier; he'd earned it. He was steady in the early rounds, having a 25-point game in the playoff opener vs. Boston, then a team-high 22 in the clincher at Milwaukee. His offense suffered against the Bulls, having to guard Michael Jordan, but he starred in the Finals with 22, 33, 31 and 23 points, leading Detroit in the final three games. "Dumars was just amazing," Lakers coach Pat Riley said.

The Pistons called them "The Jordan Rules" and released details on a need-to-know basis. That is to say, the media and fans were out of the loop. But for all of the cloak-and-dagger insinuations, it was not as if the Pistons were guarding U.S. nuclear secrets. It was just their own way of getting into the head of Chicago's Michael Jordan, needing every edge they could muster. The "Rules" were nothing revolutionary—make him go left, force him to the "help" side, make him get rid of the ball — but the Pistons' deep backcourt (and the versatile Dennis Rodman) gave them sufficient defensive flexibility to implement the tactics better than most teams. Detroit entered the 1989 Eastern finals undefeated in seven playoff games, having pounded Indiana and Milwaukee. Though the Pistons were 6-0 against Chicago during the season, Jordan and the Bulls didn't go as quietly in the playoffs, forcing Detroit to six games. Jordan made it interesting, giving Chicago a 2-1 series lead by scoring 32 in Game 1 and 46 in Game 3. But the Pistons held Jordan to 23 in Game 4 and 18 in Game 5, winning both, then overcame Jordan's 32 to clinch in Game 6. Jordan averaged 29.7 for the series, leading his team in five games. He would be heard from again.

169

April 18, 1989

Everything came together for the Pistons on April 18, 1989. They won their second straight Central Division title, they reached the 60-win plateau for the only time in club history, Joe Dumars scored a then-career-high 42 points and Isiah Thomas returned to top form after breaking his left hand six games previous. With a 118-102 win at Cleveland (and a champagne-less postgame), the Pistons officially stamped themselves as playoff-ready; they couldn't have dreamed up a more satisfying victory. Dumars was so good, he outscored the Cavaliers by himself in the third quarter 24-23, tying the Pistons' record for most points in a quarter and helping them break open a close game. Though Thomas' 17 points were his most since his hand injury, Dumars' 42 were especially needed. "Joe's was a sensational performance—absolutely incredible for such a duressful situation, if there is such a word," coach Chuck Daly said. In his big third quarter, Dumars scored 17 straight Detroit points. He shot 18-of-26 for the game, including 4-of-5 3-pointers. "Our plan was to have fun and if you feel like you've got a shot, take it," Dumars understated. "That third quarter took a lot out of (Cleveland), but it also took a lot out of me. I was tired after that."

Since his 42-point night against the Cavs, Joe Dumars has beaten or matched that total eight times. Photo by Allen Einstein.

"How did I get down here if I wasn't pushed?" Bill Laimbeer pleads his case to the referees. Photo by Allen Einstein.

"Fight Nights"

From preseason to postseason, 1988-89 was full of fights, flagrant fouls and fines. The Pistons were docked $30,000 in fines and $56,000 in salary throughout the season, with the heavyweight bouts resulting in suspensions for Bill Laimbeer and Isiah Thomas. On January 27 at The Palace, Laimbeer and Cleveland center Brad Daugherty got into a tussle under the basket and started throwing punches. The next day, the league office handed down a $5,000 fine and one-game suspension that halted Laimbeer's NBA-leading iron man streak at 685 games. He'd also made 561 straight starts, another league high. He was unapologetic. "That's the first time I have swung back—ever," Laimbeer said. "I've told the league that when people come swinging at me, I will protect myself." On April 7 at Chicago, with Detroit steaming toward another division title, Thomas got into a first-quarter scuffle with Bulls center Bill Cartwright. After Isiah absorbed an elbow from Cartwright, they fell to the court and started swinging. Thomas landed three punches, but the result was a broken left hand, a $5,000 fine and a two-game sit-down. "I stole the ball from him and he hit me," Thomas said. "We've played the Bulls six times this year and Cartwright has hit me five times."

CHANGING FACES

IN 1983-84, the NBA's top scorers had been a trio of small forwards: Utah's Adrian Dantley (30.6 ppg), Dallas' Mark Aguirre (29.5) and Denver's Kiki Vandeweghe (29.4). In 1989, they were still being lumped together, but as the subject of intense trade talks. A month before Detroit and Dallas rocked the NBA by swapping Dantley for Aguirre on February 15, the Pistons were negotiating to acquire Vandeweghe from Portland. As The Oakland Press reported, the Pistons would trade the much-traveled Dantley and rookie point guard Micheal Williams to the Blazers for nine-year veteran Vandeweghe and center Steve Johnson. Though Vandeweghe offered to defer some salary to make the deal happen, Portland balked and Detroit turned its attention to Dallas; the Aguirre deal was soon consummated. Fennis Dembo and Williams were second-round draftees who lasted all season with Detroit. John Long returned for a second Pistons stint and also earned a championship ring. Cameo appearances were made by Darryl Dawkins, Steve Harris, Pace Mannion and Jim "Incredible Hulk" Rowinski.

Adrian Dantley's famous fallaway jumper couldn't prevent him from being traded to Dallas. Photo by Allen Einstein.

Take a Bow

Rick Mahorn

Take a bow, he did. Rick Mahorn gazed out into the darkened Palace, a microphone in hand, and told 15,000 friends, "I'm glad to be the baddest Bad Boy you've ever seen!" He didn't know it was his farewell speech. On the afternoon of the Pistons' NBA title celebration, two days after the clincher in L.A., 100,000 fans gathered for a downtown parade before the party moved to The Palace. All the while, GM Jack McCloskey was on the phone with the new Minnesota TimberWolves, trying to convince them not to pick Mahorn in that day's NBA expansion draft. He offered two first-round picks and Micheal Williams, but the T-Wolves were immovable, selecting Mahorn in the midst of the celebration. Unaware of his fate, Mahorn told McCloskey during the ceremony, "Thank you for sticking with me through my weight problem." It nearly broke the GM's heart, for he would soon have to break the news to his starting power forward. "It's a business deal," a shaken Mahorn said, trying to smile through his tears. It didn't work, but at least he got to take one last bow.

The loss of Rick Mahorn in the 1989 expansion draft was deflating for the Pistons and their fans. Photo by Allen Einstein.

PISTON LIST

Longest Home Winning Streaks

(Within Same Season)

21 games
- January 29-April 23, 1989

18 games
- January 15-March 22, 1988

15 games
- January 26-April 3, 1990
- January 15-March 4, 1986

12 games
- December 19, 1990-January 30, 1991

10 games
- November 20-December 26, 1987

9 games
- December 13, 1986-January 14, 1987
- January 2-February 2, 1985

8 games
- 5 occasions

7 games
- 2 occasions

1989 1990
DETROIT PISTONS

TIME CAPSULE

October 17, 1989:
An earthquake measuring 6.9 on the Richter Scale hits San Francisco, killing more than 60 and causing widespread damage.

February 28, 1990:
Black nationalist Nelson Mandela meets with President Bush, two weeks after having spent 27 years in prison in South Africa.

August 7, 1990:
Responding to the Middle East crisis, American troops leave for Saudi Arabia as "Operation Desert Shield" begins.

SEASON SNAPSHOT

Most Points
Isiah Thomas (1,492, 18.4 avg.)

Most Rebounds
Dennis Rodman (792, 9.7 avg.)

Most Assists
Isiah Thomas (765, 9.4 avg.)

Most Minutes
Isiah Thomas (2,993, 37.0 avg.)

Field-Goal Percentage
Dennis Rodman (58.1%)

Free-Throw Percentage
Joe Dumars (90.0%)

Team Offense Average
104.3 (8,556 in 82 games)

Team Defense Average
98.3 (8,057 in 82 games)

NBA All-Stars
Joe Dumars, G (Third Team)

NBA Defensive Player of Year
Dennis Rodman

Pistons in All-Star Game
Isiah Thomas, G; Joe Dumars, G; Dennis Rodman, F

NBA Finals MVP
Isiah Thomas, G

1989-90

FINAL STANDINGS

Central Division	W	L	Pct.	GB
PISTONS	**59**	**23**	**.720**	**—**
Chicago	55	27	.671	4
Milwaukee	44	38	.537	15
Cleveland	42	40	.512	17
Indiana	42	40	.512	17
Atlanta	41	41	.500	18
Orlando	18	64	.220	41

Atlantic Division Winner—Philadelphia
Midwest Division Winner—San Antonio
Pacific Division Winner—L.A. Lakers

PLAYOFF RESULTS

Eastern First Round: Pistons d. Indiana, 3-0
Eastern Semifinals: Pistons d. New York, 4-1
Eastern Finals: Pistons d. Chicago, 4-3
NBA Finals: Pistons d. Portland, 4-1

PISTONS PLAYOFF LEADERS

Scoring: Isiah Thomas (20.5 avg.)
Rebounding: Bill Laimbeer (10.6)
Assists: Isiah Thomas (8.2)

NBA CHAMPION

DETROIT PISTONS

1989-90
SEASON IN REVIEW

To those who attempted to classify the Pistons' 1989 NBA title as a fluke over a wounded Lakers team, an emphatic rejoinder was issued in 1990: "U Can't Touch This." It wasn't merely another rap song co-opted to market a sequel championship, it truly fit the Pistons' situation. It was their way of declaring, "If you thought we got lucky last year, now we're two-time champs—and just try to take this one from us."

The Pistons' method for winning their second title—three straight victories at Portland, where they hadn't won since 1974—sent a clear message to all detractors that they indeed belonged among the Lakers, Celtics and 76ers as the great teams of the decade. With a 4-1 Finals conquest of the Trail Blazers, capped by Vinnie Johnson's last-second jump shot in Game 5, the Pistons became only the second repeat NBA champion since 1969. In addition, they became the lone visiting team in Finals history to sweep the middle three games. When you do all that after losing your starting power forward to expansion, you're no fluke.

"People doubted we could do it this time. This is definitely sweeter," Finals MVP Isiah Thomas said in the victorious locker room at Portland on June 14. Villain supreme Bill Laimbeer said, "This came about as a bit of a grudge because of a lack of respect from last year. But we accomplished something we were supposed to. We repeated."

In the end, it was Johnson's trademark 17-foot jump shot over Jerome Kersey that decided Detroit's 92-90 clinching victory. It completed a 9-0 burst by the Pistons after Portland had taken a 90-83 lead with 2:02 to play. Johnson scored seven of his 16 points in the spurt and Thomas, who led Detroit with 29, hit the tying 15-footer with 36 seconds left.

Having swept the Trail Blazers three straight in Portland, the Pistons celebrate their second straight NBA title. Photo by Allen Einstein.

The game was surely Johnson's crowning moment in a Pistons uniform. He started the winning rally by making a 15-footer and a free throw as Portland star Clyde Drexler fouled out. A miss by Blazers center Kevin Duckworth was rebounded by Laimbeer, his last of 17 boards, and then Johnson muscled in a jumper from the right baseline to nudge the Pistons within 90-88. Thomas, who had sat out five minutes down the stretch after catching a Cliff Robinson forearm in the nose, made the tying 15-footer from the right side after Johnson won a jump ball from Danny Young. The Pistons got their chance to win it after Blazers guard Terry Porter threw away a pass with 20 seconds left. "I honestly thought when we came out of the timeout that somebody would make the shot. I just knew it." said Joe Dumars, who played a strong series (20.6 ppg) despite the sorrow of his father's death prior to Game 3.

On the Pistons' final play, Thomas drained the clock to three seconds and threw a short pass to Johnson on the deep right wing. With Kersey defending, Johnson took two left-handed dribbles to create space for himself, then jumped and fired his shot over Kersey's outstretched right hand. The ball swished cleanly with seven-tenths of a second left, stunning the Portland crowd. Hadn't their team just led by seven points?

"I'm not going to say I knew the shot was going in, but it felt good. It was just beautiful to see it go in," Johnson said. "That's just Vinnie. He hits those shots every day in practice," his pal Laimbeer said. "Vinnie came through big-time. It was vintage Vinnie," Thomas said. And coach Chuck Daly said, "Those were great plays by a great 1-on-1 player."

The final sequence was vindication for Johnson, who had decried suggestions of a slump despite shooting 1-for-10 in Games 1 and 2. "Some guys get 10 shots in a half. If you're not getting shots, it's hard to score," The Microwave said.

(continued...)

SEASON IN REVIEW

(continued)

In a series loaded with heroes, Bill Laimbeer's low-post play against Portland's Kevin Duckworth was pivotal. Photo by Allen Einstein.

But there were heroes at other lockers, too. There was Thomas, who averaged 27.6 points in the Finals and hit 11-of-16 three-pointers for a five-game record. "You can say what you want about me, but you can't say I'm not a winner," he said. There was Dumars, who learned of his father's death after scoring 33 points in Game 3, then bravely remained with the team. "I know my Pop would have wanted me to stay, fight it out, be tough about it," the '89 Finals MVP said. There was Laimbeer, who averaged 13.4 rebounds, got inside the Blazers' heads and served as the Pistons' defensive lightning rod and emotional touchstone throughout the series. And there was Dennis Rodman, the NBA Defensive Player of the Year, playing 30 stoic minutes in the clincher after missing Games 3 and 4 with a sore ankle.

Just as in the playoffs, when the Pistons got past Indiana (in three games), New York (five) and Chicago (seven) in the early rounds, the regular season was a well-rounded team effort. Despite losing burly enforcer Rick Mahorn in the expansion draft two days after the '89 championship, the Pistons' defense grew even more suffocating, holding opponents to 98.3 points a game. Rodman led the charge, ending Laimbeer's seven-year reign as team rebound king, edging him 792-780. Rodman also played in his first All-Star game, joining Thomas, Dumars and Eastern coach Daly.

In fact, it was no coincidence that the Pistons reached their full potential after Rodman entered the starting lineup for good on January 23, replacing Mark Aguirre. What followed was the most amazing period in team history: winning streaks of 13 (a team record) and 12 sandwiched around a loss to Atlanta. Holding opponents under 100 points 17 times, the Pistons' 25-1 streak lifted them to 51-15 on March 20 and they chugged to a 59-23 record for their third straight division title. "There were nights when we walked on the court and the other team was already beat," Dumars admitted. "We just knew we were going to win. We had so much confidence."

It was the kind of swagger that would enable the Pistons to silence their critics and join the short list of the NBA's all-time great teams.

Game Results

1988-89
REGULAR SEASON

Date	Opponent	Result	Record
11-4	NEW YORK	W, 106-103	1-0
11-5	at Washington	W, 95-93	2-0
11-7	at Chicago	L, 114-117	2-1
11-8	at Indiana	L, 74-95	2-2
11-10	at Orlando	W, 125-121	3-2
11-11	at Miami	L, 84-88	3-3
11-15	MIAMI	W, 130-94	4-3
11-17	MILWAUKEE	W, 106-79	5-3
11-18	BOSTON	W, 103-86	6-3
11-21	ATLANTA	L, 96-103	6-4
11-24	CLEVELAND	W, 101-83	7-4
11-26	at Portland	L, 82-102	7-5
11-28	at Sacramento	W, 93-81	8-5
11-29	at Phoenix	W, 111-103	9-5
12-1	at L.A. Lakers	W, 108-97 (OT)	10-5
12-2	at Seattle	L, 95-120	10-6
12-6	WASHINGTON	W, 116-107	11-6
12-8	at Philadelphia	L, 101-107	11-7
12-9	INDIANA	W, 121-93	12-7
12-12	at Denver	W, 121-108	13-7
12-13	at L.A. Clippers	L, 79-83	13-8
12-15	at Utah	L, 91-94	13-9
12-16	at Golden State	L, 92-104	13-10
12-19	SEATTLE	W, 94-77	14-10
12-22	at New Jersey	W, 96-90	15-10
12-23	ORLANDO	W, 106-100	16-10
12-27	at Cleveland	W, 99-82	17-10
12-29	MILWAUKEE	L, 85-99	17-11
12-30	NEW JERSEY	W, 117-106	18-11
1-2	at Orlando	W, 115-113	19-11
1-3	L.A. CLIPPERS	W, 84-80	20-11
1-5	INDIANA	W, 122-99	21-11
1-6	NEW YORK	W, 117-106	22-11
1-9	CHICAGO	W, 100-90	23-11
1-10	at Boston	L, 84-97	23-12
1-12	MINNESOTA	W, 97-86	24-12
1-13	PORTLAND	W, 111-106	25-12
1-17	at Philadelphia	L, 108-112	25-13
1-19	GOLDEN STATE	W, 125-118	26-13
1-21	L.A. LAKERS	L, 97-107	26-14
1-23	at Chicago	W, 107-95	27-14
1-26	PHOENIX	W, 107-103	28-14
1-27	at Minnesota	W, 85-83	29-14
1-30	at Atlanta	W, 112-95	30-14
1-31	WASHINGTON	W, 133-109	31-14
2-3	at Cleveland	W, 105-100	32-14
2-4	UTAH	W, 115-83	33-14
2-6	CLEVELAND	W, 105-96	34-14
2-8	at Milwaukee	W, 104-101	35-14
2-13	DENVER	W, 106-96	36-14
2-17	at Miami	W, 99-79	37-14
2-19	MIAMI	W, 94-85	38-14
2-21	ORLANDO	W, 140-109	39-14
2-23	at Atlanta	L, 103-112	39-15
2-25	at New York	W, 98-87	40-15
2-27	HOUSTON	W, 106-102 (OT)	41-15
3-1	at Washington	W, 99-85	42-15
3-2	PHILADELPHIA	W, 115-112 (OT)	43-15
3-4	INDIANA	W, 111-105	44-15
3-6	SACRAMENTO	W, 101-91	45-15
3-9	at New Jersey	W, 99-95	46-15
3-11	at Charlotte	W, 98-88	47-15
3-15	SAN ANTONIO	W, 110-98	48-15
3-16	at Chicago	W, 106-81	49-15
3-18	DALLAS	W, 114-84	50-15
3-20	at Milwaukee	W, 117-96	51-15
3-22	at Houston	L, 110-115	51-16
3-24	at San Antonio	L, 98-105	51-17
3-25	at Dallas	L, 96-98	51-18
3-28	CHARLOTTE	W, 106-97	52-18
3-30	at Boston	L, 111-123	52-19
4-3	BOSTON	W, 93-82	53-19
4-5	at Atlanta	W, 104-99	54-19
4-6	MILWAUKEE	L, 84-92	54-20
4-8	at Cleveland	L, 97-100	54-21
4-10	at New York	W, 108-98	55-21
4-11	NEW YORK	W, 98-93	56-21
4-13	ATLANTA	L, 111-115	56-22
4-14	ORLANDO	W, 111-107	57-22
4-19	PHILADELPHIA	L, 97-107	57-23
4-20	at Indiana	W, 121-115 (OT)	58-23
4-22	CHICAGO	W, 111-106	59-23

PLAYOFFS
Eastern First Round—(Best-of-Five)

4-26	INDIANA	W, 104-94	1-0
4-28	INDIANA	W, 100-87	2-0
5-1	at Indiana	W, 108-96	3-0

Eastern Semifinals—(Best-of-Seven)

5-8	NEW YORK	W, 112-77	1-0
5-10	NEW YORK	W, 104-97	2-0
5-12	at New York	L, 103-111	2-1
5-13	at New York	W, 102-90	3-1
5-15	NEW YORK	W, 95-84	4-1

Eastern Finals—(Best-of-Seven)

5-20	CHICAGO	W, 86-77	1-0
5-22	CHICAGO	W, 102-93	2-0
5-26	at Chicago	L, 102-107	2-1
5-28	at Chicago	L, 101-108	2-2
5-30	CHICAGO	W, 97-83	3-2
6-1	at Chicago	L, 91-109	3-3
6-3	CHICAGO	W, 93-74	4-3

NBA Finals—(Best-of-Seven)

6-5	PORTLAND	W, 105-99	1-0
6-7	PORTLAND	L, 105-106 (OT)	1-1
6-10	at Portland	W, 121-106	2-1
6-12	at Portland	W, 112-109	3-1
6-14	at Portland	W, 92-90	4-1

(Home games in CAPS)

SPOTLIGHT Game

JUNE 10, 1990

With a heavy heart, Joe Dumars continued to play in the NBA Finals despite his father's death. Photo by Allen Einstein.

The Pistons were in trouble.

The NBA Finals were tied 1-1 after Detroit blew Game 2 at home and now the series was continuing with three games in Portland, where the Pistons had lost 20 straight since 1974. Robo-rebounder Dennis Rodman was sidelined with an ankle sprain and Vinnie Johnson, despite his statements to the contrary, was in a scoring slump. This was the Trail Blazers' chance to take command of the series.

And then, another punch to the gut occurred before Game 3 when word reached the Pistons that Joe Dumars' father, Joe II, had died from heart failure in an Alexandria, Louisiana, hospital. By prior agreement with his wife Debbie, Dumars wasn't notified of his dad's death before the game. Only Isiah Thomas, the coaches and PR director Matt Dobek knew about it.

How fitting, indeed, that on one of the worst days of his life, Dumars played one of his greatest games, leading the Pistons to a 121-106 win that set them back on course for a second straight NBA championship. Dumars scored 33 points, his 1990 playoff high, helping the Pistons gradually pull away for their highest postseason output since 1987.

Even before Dumars' family tragedy was revealed, it was a game full of subplots. Not only had Johnson finally broken out with a 21-point game on 9-of-13 shooting, but Bill Laimbeer had thoroughly rattled Portland's big men with his low-post defense. In one stretch, he drew offensive fouls on Jerome Kersey, Buck Williams and Kevin Duckworth, causing the less-experienced Blazers to come unglued and essentially sealing the outcome.

But it was Dumars' day. He shot 11-of-22 from the field, hitting a vast arsenal of jumpers, and making 9-of-9 at the foul line. Two baskets were especially tough on the Blazers. He nailed a long 3-pointer to make it 71-68 in the third quarter, quelling a Portland rally, and later hit a high-arc 14-footer over Drazen Petrovic with the shot clock running out.

"Joe threw it real high in the air and it went in. We kind of looked at each other and smiled," Thomas said afterward. "I said to myself, 'Your dad threw that one in. You didn't have anything to do with that.' "

The immediate word was that Dumars would fly home to Natchitoches, Louisiana, to attend the funeral, but in accordance with his family's wishes, the services were delayed and he remained with the team. Four days later, the Pistons would be world champions all over again and Joe Dumars would go home to honor the greatest man he ever knew. He wasn't alone; most of his teammates attended as well.

SUMMARY—Game 3
Pistons 121, Trail Blazers 106

PISTONS (121)

Player	Min	FG M-A	3P M-A	FT M-A	Reb O-T	A	PF	Pts
Aguirre	28	4-7	1-2	2-4	1-3	1	2	11
Edwards	25	5-10	0-0	1-5	1-2	2	2	11
Laimbeer	40	4-12	0-3	3-3	1-12	2	6	11
Dumars	43	11-22	2-3	9-9	1-1	5	3	33
Thomas	41	6-8	0-1	9-11	2-3	5	3	21
Salley	21	3-7	0-0	4-4	3-7	1	3	10
Greenwood	13	1-1	0-0	1-2	1-5	0	4	3
Hastings	3	0-1	0-1	0-0	0-0	0	1	0
V.Johnson	25	9-13	0-0	3-3	1-1	0	1	21
Henderson	1	0-0	0-0	0-0	0-0	0	0	0
Rodman DNP-Sprained ankle								
Bedford DNP-Coach's Decision								
Totals	**240**	**43-81**	**3-10**	**32-41**	**10-36**	**19**	**26**	**121**

PORTLAND (106)

Player	Min	FG M-A	3P M-A	FT M-A	Reb O-T	A	PF	Pts
Kersey	38	10-21	0-0	7-7	3-7	0	5	27
Williams	27	1-3	0-0	3-4	3-6	1	6	5
Duckworth	27	8-13	0-0	2-2	2-4	0	5	18
Drexler	43	9-23	1-6	5-6	6-13	8	4	24
Porter	42	6-13	1-4	7-7	2-3	9	4	20
Robinson	14	1-7	0-1	0-0	0-1	1	5	2
Bryant	7	0-0	0-0	1-2	0-1	0	3	1
Cooper	16	2-3	0-0	0-0	2-5	0	1	4
Young	18	2-5	0-1	1-3	0-2	1	2	5
Petrovic	8	0-5	0-1	0-0	0-0	2	3	0
Irvin DNP-Coach's Decision								
Johnston DNP-Coach's Decision								
Totals	**240**	**39-93**	**2-13**	**26-31**	**18-42**	**22**	**38**	**106**

Percentages: FG .531, 3P .300, FT .780. Team Rebounds: 13. Blocked shots: 4 (Salley 2, V.Johnson, Laimbeer). Turnovers: 14 (Thomas 6, Dumars 4, V.Johnson 3, Greenwood). Steals: 3 (Aguirre, Laimbeer, Thomas). Technical fouls: coach Daly, Edwards, Laimbeer.

Percentages: FG .419, 3P .154, FT .839. Team Rebounds: 15. Blocked shots: 1 (Drexler). Turnovers: 20 (Duckworth 5, Drexler 5, Porter 4, Williams 2, Kersey, Bryant, Cooper, Petrovic). Steals: 7 (Drexler 3, Porter 2, Robinson, Young). Technical fouls: coach Adelman, Kersey.

DETROIT	31	27	32	31	— 121
PORTLAND	27	24	31	24	— 106

A—12,884 (sellout). T—2:32. Officials—Jake O'Donnell, Joe Crawford, Jess Kersey.

Premier Piston

James "Buddha" Edwards

James Edwards scored 32 points three times in his Pistons career, including once in the '90 playoffs.

The most enduring memory of James Edwards in a Pistons uniform? That's easy. Picture him swishing a 10-foot fallaway jumper, grinning through his Fu Manchu mustache, then quietly running downcourt with that long, loping stride. Why, if you listen really carefully, you can still hear P.A. announcer Ken Calvert's booming voice in the distance. "Boo-duh!" There was no need to explain who he was talking about. In Detroit, there was only one Buddha: Edwards, the lanky 7-foot-1 center who joined the Pistons in 1988 and became a central figure in their back-to-back NBA championships. He was an 11-year veteran of four teams by the time the Pistons got him from Phoenix on February 24, 1988. The trade was the last great heist of GM Jack McCloskey's tenure, costing only Ron Moore and a second-round pick. Edwards quickly assumed a new nickname—he seemingly was known overnight as Buddha—and a vital reserve role in Detroit's failed quest for the '88 NBA title. He continued as a backup en route to the '89 championship (7.3 ppg), but became a starter for good in '89-90. With the Pistons mired in a 7-5 start, coach Chuck Daly inserted Edwards into the starting lineup and he averaged 16.0 points over the final 70 games; the Pistons had a 52-18 record in that span. Then in the playoffs, Edwards led the team in scoring four times and averaged 14.3 points, including a career playoff high 32 in Game 2 of the second round against Patrick Ewing and the Knicks. Daly's strategy with Edwards was quite elementary. He would feature him for the first 6-8 minutes of each half, feeding him mid-post for his familiar fallaway. No, Edwards wasn't a contact player like most 7-footers, but with a reliable jumper like that, he didn't need to be.

AT A GLANCE

JAMES EDWARDS

FULL NAME:
James Franklin Edwards
BORN:
November 22, 1955; Seattle, Washington
POSITION, HEIGHT, WEIGHT:
Center, 7-foot-1, 260 pounds
COLLEGE:
Washington '77
ACQUIRED:
1988, trade from Phoenix
TENURE WITH PISTONS:
February 24, 1988 — 1990-91
Also: L.A. Lakers 1977, Indiana 1977-81, Cleveland 1981-83, Phoenix 1983-88,
L.A. Clippers 1991-92, L.A. Lakers 1992-94, Portland 1994-95, Chicago 1995-96
BEST SEASON WITH PISTONS:
1989-90, 82 GP, 14.5 ppg, 4.2 rpg
TOTALS WITH PISTONS:
Regular season: 256 GP, 11.2 ppg, 3.6 rpg
Playoffs: 75 GP, 9.4 ppg, 2.8 rpg

PLAYOFF HERO

PLAYOFF VILLAIN

Isiah Thomas

Bill Laimbeer

In the '90 Finals, Isiah Thomas had consecutive games with 33, 23, 21, 32 and 29 points to become MVP. Photo by Allen Einstein.

The Trail Blazers never found a solution for Bill Laimbeer's 3-point shooting and sledgehammer defense in the Finals.

Isiah Thomas built his reputation as a jitterbug, a little guy more likely to beat you with a dribble-drive layup than a jump shot. Give him an alley, no matter how slim, and he'll drive right through, get to the basket, hit the shot and probably make you foul him. Thomas still had those talents in 1989-90, but when he took his game beyond the 3-point arc in the playoffs, opponents didn't have a clue. Do we guard him close and risk him going around us? Or do we play off him and hope he'll miss the 23-footer? Frankly, it didn't seem to matter which strategy they used, because Thomas was terrific in every aspect, especially in winning the Finals MVP award. En route to his team-leading 20.5 scoring average in Detroit's 20 playoff games, Thomas averaged 27.6 vs. Portland and set a Finals record with 11 3-pointers in a five-game series. He was amazing throughout, starting with his 33-point bailout job in Game 1 and ending with a tidy 29 points in the Game 5 clincher. In Game 1, he scored 10 in a row, including two triples over wide-eyed Terry Porter, to kick-start a 23-4 rally. In Game 5, having missed five minutes after absorbing a forearm to his nose, Thomas hit the Pistons' tying basket with 36.5 seconds left, setting up Vinnie Johnson's winner.

Yes, Bill Laimbeer was the villain, but to the Pistons' benefit and the chagrin of four playoff opponents who couldn't ignore his antagonistic style. He wore the black hat, literally and figuratively, donning a black top-hat during the Finals vs. Portland and becoming the focus of the Blazers' nonstop bellyaching in Games 3-5. But it wasn't only Laimbeer's hands-on defense that made him so effective. Like few big men before him, he was a 3-point threat throughout the postseason. He wrote his name in the record book in Game 2 with six triples (in nine attempts). Three of the 3-pointers came in overtime, a remarkable feat that's been largely forgotten because Detroit lost 106-105. But that merely set the stage for some of Laimbeer's finest moments as a Piston. Leading the team out of the tunnel for Game 3 at Portland, he set the tone by running over a photographer who happened to get in his way. His statistics—12 points, 11 rebounds, six fouls—don't do justice to Laimbeer's villainous performance that day. He drew five charges on the Blazers, who accused him of flopping, and knocked them off their game. "Maybe only Bill can be like that," coach Chuck Daly said. "He was unbelievable." Ever modest, Laimbeer said, "It was just hard work."

April 19, 1990

It was a game the Pistons didn't need to win, having already clinched the Central Division, but they wanted to send a succinct message to the Philadelphia 76ers on the regular season's final weekend: to get to the Finals, you'll have to beat us first. But on this night, it was the 76ers who did the sending, defeating the Pistons 107-97 at The Palace and meeting Detroit's physical nature head-on. A wild brawl with 14.8 seconds left served as a fitting (and frightening) conclusion to a game that included all manner of ice glares, errant elbows and angry words. When it was over, Bill Laimbeer and Charles Barkley were ejected for the heavyweight bout that started it all and Detroit's Scott Hastings was booted for punching Barkley in what he called a peacemaking role. The hostilities even spread to the stands after a fan hit Barkley and the Sixers' star spat at him before security regained control. The fight had been brewing all season and was almost triggered earlier in the quarter when Isiah Thomas hit ex-teammate Rick Mahorn and was ejected. The night resulted in $162,500 in fines, the most ever for one game. Each team was docked $50,000 for losing control of its players, Laimbeer $20,000, Barkley $20,000, Hastings $10,000 and Thomas $7,500.

76ers star Charles Barkley is led away from the brawl by referee Jake O'Donnell. Photo by Allen Einstein.

Isiah Thomas' 3-pointer and steal triggered the Pistons' most exciting finish of the regular season.

March 2, 1990

A good portion of the sellout crowd was already in the Palace parking lot. The Pistons were trailing Philadelphia 103-99 with 10.8 seconds to go and it didn't look good. "We could have thrown the ball in the air and given up. But we've learned that you don't give up," Joe Dumars said. The Pistons' savvy served them greatly in the final seconds as they made an incredible rally for the lead, then beat the Sixers 115-112 in overtime. Isiah Thomas ignited the comeback when he hit a 3-pointer under heavy pressure, boosting Detroit within one. Then with Philly's Mike Gminski trying desperately to inbound the ball, James Edwards jumped into his sight line and Thomas slid in front of Hersey Hawkins for a steal. Isiah drove the lane to draw the 76ers, then passed to a slashing Dumars for a layup and 104-103 lead with 2.5 seconds left. Detroit could not hold the lead, as Charles Barkley's free throw forced overtime, but Dumars' three-point play with 39 seconds left in OT was decisive. It snapped a 110-110 tie and gave him a game-high 34 points (with 18-of-19 free throws). Prior to tipoff, Philly forward Rick Mahorn was cheered as he received his 1989 championship ring, though they turned to boos after he shoved Dumars in the third quarter.

CHANGING FACES

FOR THREE SEASONS, John Salley had been the Pistons' king of the quips. But the team signed a challenger to the throne for '89-90, bringing in free-agent center Scott Hastings, who had spent most of his career in Atlanta. "I'll just follow Salley around and when he runs out of stuff to say, I'll jump in," Hastings said. "And when Bill Laimbeer gets tired of signing autographs, I'll jump in. But I won't sign his name because that's an invitation for a death threat in a lot of cities." Yuk, yuk, yuk. Hastings became the Pistons' designated sitter, playing in only 40 games, but he added extra personality to a team that didn't lack for it. The Pistons' other acquisitions were two tested veterans, forward David Greenwood (October 4) and guard Gerald Henderson (December 6). Greenwood's shining moment was Game 3 of the Finals when he got five rebounds in 13 needed minutes. Also appearing during the season were guards Stan Kimbrough and Ralph Lewis. In the draft, Detroit emerged with 6-foot-9 forward Anthony Cook from Arizona, but he decided to play in Greece.

Before two Pistons stints, Gerald Henderson was a playoff hero for the Celtics. Photo by Allen Einstein.

Take a Bow
Dennis Rodman

We had seen Dennis Rodman cry once before—at the Pistons' NBA title celebration the previous June. His tears flowed afresh May 7, 1990, when he was named NBA Defensive Player of the Year, getting 49 of 92 votes to beat Houston's Hakeem Olajuwon (35). Rodman thought he had deserved the award in '89 when Utah man-mountain Mark Eaton won it, even joking that he'd retire if he was snubbed again. However, when he mounted the podium to accept the award, Rodman's humility returned. "I wanted this award so bad," he said, breaking down in sobs. Pistons GM Jack McCloskey stepped up, patted Rodman on the back and led him away to compose himself. "I tried not to cry, but it didn't work," Rodman said later. "It's great that someone could feel so strongly about this. Dennis is the best defensive player I've ever seen," McCloskey said. "He is a credit to basketball," Chuck Daly said. "The game today is based on scoring, the selfish aspect of the game. Here is a guy who does all of the little things opposite of that."

"I went numb when I heard," Dennis Rodman said after being named NBA Defensive Player of the Year. Photo by Allen Einstein.

PISTON LIST

Best Home Record in 82-Game Season

(After Neutral-Site Era)

- 1988-89, 37-4
- 1989-90, 35-6
- 1987-88, 34-7
- 1986-87, 32-9
- 1990-91, 32-9
- 1985-86, 31-10
- 1976-77, 30-11
- 1983-84, 30-11
- 1995-96, 30-11
- 1996-97, 30-11
- 1992-93, 28-13

"A FINE MESS"
BAD BOYS BECOME SCOURGE OF NBA

Rick Mahorn boxes out Charlotte's Kurt Rambis, so to speak, in 1989 game at Palace. Photo by Allen Einstein.

Seemingly every Detroit-Chicago game led to fisticuffs, such as in this 1991 meeting. Photo by Allen Einstein.

After waiting 30 years to become the poster children for NBA success, the Pistons finally got their wish in the late 1980s and early '90s. But they didn't know it would be a "Wanted" poster. For the greater part of a decade, no professional sports team had a reputation for rugged play as notorious as the Detroit Pistons.

Borrowing on the outlaw image of the NFL's Los Angeles Raiders—by then a caricature of their former selves—the Pistons adopted a take-no-prisoners physicality, a mind-set of intimidation and an appropriate nickname. They became known as the Bad Boys—feared administers of hard fouls, sharp elbows and, in their jaundiced view, frontier justice. It was a winning formula, resulting in NBA titles in 1989 and '90.

The NBA's response was predictably severe. Though the league office couldn't decide how it really felt about the Pistons—at once punishing them while profiting from Bad Boys videos—its public stance was to paddle them. Starting in 1985, oddly coinciding with their acquisition of 6-foot-10 Mack truck Rick Mahorn, the Pistons were fined more than $220,000 by the NBA over the next eight years, not including about $85,000 in lost salaries from suspensions.

To many, trading for Mahorn was akin to throwing logs on a flash fire because the Pistons already had an incendiary nucleus in the mid-'80s. They had Bill Laimbeer, regarded as a provocative pest by Detroit fans, but a clumsy, low-skilled, cheapshot artist in most other venues, especially his Boston birthplace. They had Isiah Thomas, whose backers viewed him as a little man with a take-no-guff attitude; detractors suspected him as the smiling mastermind of a back-alley basketball team. And they had coach Chuck Daly, whose defensive strategy—"No easy baskets!"—tacitly endorsed hard fouls.

Upon his 1993 retirement, Laimbeer was no doubt the most penalized player in NBA history, compiling roughly $69,000 in fines over a dozen incidents, plus $17,000 in lost pay; Dennis Rodman and Charles Barkley, among others, have since blown his totals out of the water. The oddest part of the equation is that Laimbeer seldom reared back with a punch. He slugged Cleveland's Brad Daugherty in a January 27, 1989 fight, leading to a $5,000 fine and one-game suspension that halted Laimbeer's 685-game streak, but most of his trespasses were flagrant fouls that escalated into brawls. Isiah Thomas racked up just over $31,000 in penalties, plus $50,000 more in lost salary, and Mahorn was levied $16,000 from four incidents. Even the non-fighters like Joe Dumars got into the act; in December 1990, he was fined $1,000 three weeks apart for fighting brothers Harvey (Washington) and Horace Grant (Chicago).

After a while, it seemed like every Pistons game produced some sort of altercation, though most occurred against Eastern Conference clubs like Boston, Chicago, Atlanta and Philadelphia. The most heinous incidents drew speedy responses from the league, but others seemed to go unpunished as the Pistons gradually stretched the boundaries of "Bad" manners; a shoving match came to be excused as a harmless faux pas.

Though the biggest altercation occurred against Philadelphia—more on that later—the Bulls and Celtics seemed to bring out the Baddest in the Pistons. In April 1987, Michael Jordan spoke out, saying, "Laimbeer is the dirtiest player in the NBA," when the teams brawled at Chicago. After a first-period steal by Jordan, he was shoved down by Laimbeer to prevent an easy layup. "He was out to get me, something he likes to do," Jordan said. Laimbeer's reaction: "I don't know what all the fuss was about. I was just trying to block the shot and all of the sudden Jordan's coming after me." Bulls coach Doug Collins said, "Just look in our media guide. There's a picture of Jordan going up for a slam dunk with Laimbeer's knee buried in his groin."

The pattern was set; the clubs would scuffle regularly in later years. On January 16, 1988, Mahorn and Charles Oakley fought, causing Collins to run off the bench to protect his player. Mahorn shoved Collins on to the press table twice. On April 7, 1989, Thomas busted his hand by hitting Bill Cartwright on the head, having tired of the Bull's active elbows. On May 27, 1991, Rodman was fined $5,000 for shoving Scottie Pippen with two hands from behind, the teams' last significant incident of the Bad Boys era.

Countless tussles with the Celtics centered around Laimbeer. He pulled down Larry Bird on a layup in Game 3 of the 1987 Eastern finals at the Silverdome, leading to his national-televised mugging by Robert Parish two games later. They would fight again in '88.

Weary of NBA scrutiny, Thomas tried to quell the Pistons' reputation after the first championship in '89, declaring during their White House visit that the Bad Boys were no more. It made nice copy, but there was little change, as the following preseason showed when the Pistons got into brawls with Phoenix and Philadelphia.

The Pistons and 76ers would renew their hostilities late that season at The Palace. On April 19, 1990, with the 76ers trying to claim the Atlantic Division, Laimbeer and Barkley got into a fight with 14 seconds left on the baseline near the Pistons bench. As the twosome wrestled, Pistons forward Scott Hastings ran off the bench, dove on to the pile and began pummeling Barkley, causing both benches to clear. It didn't help that a fan tried to get after Barkley as he was being led off the court, nearly reigniting the brawl. "Everyone on both benches will be fined," referee Jake O'Donnell predicted. He was darn near correct as the clubs were assessed a combined $162,500 in fines, the most ever for one game. Each team was fined $50,000 for losing control of its players, Laimbeer $20,000, Hastings $10,000 and Thomas $7,500 for a third-quarter incident with one of Philadelphia's newly acquired ruffians, one Rick Mahorn. Barkley was fined $20,000 to lead the 76ers' $72,500 total, suffering a one-game suspension along with Laimbeer and Hastings.

Incidentally, the man in charge of handing out all of these penalties? NBA vice president Rod Thorn, Detroit Piston, 1964-66.

Pistons' major fines and suspensions, 1986-97

1986-87
- **May 23, 1987** — Bill Laimbeer fined $5,000 for flagrant foul on Boston's Larry Bird in Game 3 of Eastern Conference finals.

1987-88
- **December 12, 1987** — Isiah Thomas fined $3,000 for fight with New York's Sidney Green. Six Pistons fined $500 for leaving the bench.
- **December 18, 1987** — Adrian Dantley fined $1,000 and suspended one game ($11,600 in salary) for bumping referee Ed T. Rush during game against Dallas.
- **January 16, 1988** — Rick Mahorn fined $5,000 and suspended one game ($5,500 in salary) for fight with Chicago's Michael Jordan and Charles Oakley.

1988-89
- **October 28, 1988** — Rick Mahorn fined $5,000 for fight with Washington's Dave Feitl in preseason game.
- **November 9, 1988** — Rick Mahorn fined $1,000 for flagrant fouls against Atlanta's Moses Malone and Doc Rivers.
- **November 11, 1988** — Bill Laimbeer fined $1,000 for fight with Boston's Robert Parish.
- **January 27, 1989** — Bill Laimbeer fined $5,000 and suspended one game ($7,300 in salary) for fight with Cleveland's Brad Daugherty.
- **February 28, 1989** — Rick Mahorn fined $5,000 for "an intentional flagrant elbow" against Cleveland's Mark Price.
- **March 3, 1989** — Coach Chuck Daly fined $1,500 for communicating with his team's bench after being ejected against Cleveland.
- **March 14, 1989** — James Edwards fined $3,500 for fight with Indiana's Stuart Gray. John Long and Dennis Rodman fined $500 for leaving the bench.
- **April 7, 1989** — Isiah Thomas fined $5,000 and suspended two games ($48,780 in salary) for fight with Chicago's Bill Cartwright. Mark Aguirre fined $2,000 for "acting other than a peacemaker."

1989-90
- **October 27, 1989** — Isiah Thomas fined $1,250 for fight with Phoenix's Armon Gilliam in preseason game. Bill Laimbeer and William Bedford fined $500 for leaving the bench.
- **October 30, 1989** — James Edwards fined $2,750 and Isiah Thomas $1,750 for fight with Philadelphia's Mike Gminski in preseason game.
- **November 7, 1989** — Scott Hastings fined $1,500 for fight with Chicago's Stacey King.
- **January 21, 1990** — Isiah Thomas fined $2,500 for slapping L.A. Lakers' Mychal Thompson.
- **April 14, 1990** — Bill Laimbeer fined $750 for scuffle with Orlando. William Bedford, Scott Hastings and James Edwards fined $500 for leaving the bench.
- **April 19, 1990** — Fight Night with Philadelphia: Pistons fined $50,000 for players' actions. Bill Laimbeer fined $20,000 and suspended one game ($9,500 in salary) for fight with Charles Barkley. Scott Hastings fined $10,000 and suspended one game ($8,000) for punching Barkley. Isiah Thomas fined $7,500 for punching 76ers' Rick Mahorn. John Salley, William Bedford, Gerald Henderson, Mark Aguirre and David Greenwood fined $500 for leaving the bench. (76ers fined combined $72,500: Team fined $50,000 for players' actions. Barkley fined $20,000 and suspended one game. Ron Anderson, Kurt Nimphius, Kenny Payne, Scott Brooks and Lanard Copeland fined $500 for leaving the bench.)

1990-91
- **October 27, 1990** — Bill Laimbeer fined $500 for fight with Phoenix in preseason game.
- **November 27, 1990** — Bill Laimbeer fined $2,000 for fight with Atlanta's Dominique Wilkins. Vinnie Johnson fined $750 for "escalation." James Edwards, William Bedford and John Salley fined $500 for leaving the bench.
- **December 1, 1990** — Joe Dumars fined $1,000 for fight with Washington's Harvey Grant.
- **December 21, 1990** — Isiah Thomas fined $1,500 for punching Atlanta's Trevor Wilson.
- **December 25, 1990** — Joe Dumars fined $1,000 for fight with Chicago's Horace Grant.
- **March 11, 1991** — Dennis Rodman fined $5,000 for elbowing Milwaukee's Danny Schayes.
- **May 27, 1991** — Dennis Rodman fined $5,000 for shoving Chicago's Scottie Pippen from behind.

1991-92
- **November 27, 1991** — Isiah Thomas fined $3,000 for fight with Atlanta's Kevin Willis.

1992-93
- **October 22, 1992** — Bill Laimbeer fined $7,500 for flagrant foul on San Antonio's David Wood in preseason game.
- **October 23, 1992** — Olden Polynice fined $8,000 for fight with Phoenix's Tom Chambers in preseason game.
- **December 23, 1992** — Bill Laimbeer fined $6,500 for fight with Charlotte's Alonzo Mourning. Mark Randall fined $500 for leaving the bench.
- **January 30, 1993** — Isiah Thomas fined $2,000 for delay in leaving court after ejection.
- **March 30, 1993** — Alvin Robertson fined $7,500 for fight with Orlando's Shaquille O'Neal. Terry Mills and Isaiah Morris fined $500 for leaving the bench.
- **April 12, 1993** — Bill Laimbeer fined $12,000 for fight with Chicago. Six Pistons fined $500 for leaving the bench.
- **April 17, 1993** — Isiah Thomas fined $4,000 for kicking New York's Doc Rivers.

1993-94
- **November 12, 1993** — Bill Laimbeer fined $5,000 and suspended one game ($15,853 in salary) for flagrant foul on Utah's Karl Malone.

1995-96
- **March 19, 1996** — Coach Doug Collins fined $5,000 for telling players not to defend on final play against Orlando.

1990 DETROIT PISTONS 1991

TIME CAPSULE

October 3, 1990:
Cecil Fielder of the Detroit Tigers slams his 50th and 51st homers of the season, joining Hank Greenberg (58) as the only Tigers to top 50.

January 16, 1991:
Allied planes attack Iraq in "Operation Desert Storm;" six weeks later, the Iraqi army is driven from Kuwait.

March 3, 1991:
Los Angeles policemen beat African-American motorist Rodney King, and the inflammatory incident is videotaped by an observer.

SEASON SNAPSHOT

Most Points
Joe Dumars (1,629, 20.4 avg.)

Most Rebounds
Dennis Rodman (1,026, 12.5 avg.)

Most Assists
Isiah Thomas (446, 9.3 avg.)

Most Minutes
Joe Dumars (3,046, 38.1 avg.)

Field-Goal Percentage
Dennis Rodman (49.3%)

Free-Throw Percentage
Joe Dumars (89.0%)

Team Offense Average
100.1 (8,205 in 82 games)

Team Defense Average
96.8 (7,937 in 82 games)

NBA All-Stars
Joe Dumars, G (Third Team)

NBA Defensive Player of Year
Dennis Rodman

Pistons in All-Star Game
Joe Dumars, G; Isiah Thomas, G

1990-91

FINAL STANDINGS

Central Division	W	L	Pct.	GB
Chicago	61	21	.671	—
PISTONS	**50**	**32**	**.610**	**11**
Milwaukee	48	34	.585	13
Atlanta	43	39	.524	18
Indiana	41	41	.500	20
Cleveland	33	49	.402	28
Charlotte	26	56	.317	35

Atlantic Division Winner—Boston
Midwest Division Winner—San Antonio
Pacific Division Winner—Portland

PLAYOFF RESULTS

Eastern First Round: Pistons d. Atlanta, 3-2
Eastern Semifinals: Pistons d. Boston, 4-2
Eastern Finals: Chicago d. Pistons, 4-0

PISTONS PLAYOFF LEADERS

Scoring: Joe Dumars (20.6 avg.)
Rebounding: Dennis Rodman (11.8)
Assists: Isiah Thomas (7.4)

NBA CHAMPION

182

1990-91
SEASON IN REVIEW

Characteristic of a team nicknamed the Bad Boys, the Pistons' two-year run as NBA champions ended amid bitterness and bad feelings in 1990-91.

After a regular season that had as many lows as highs, the defending champs seemed to enter the playoffs with their fingers crossed, hoping to have enough gas in the tank to do it again. The Pistons showed some spunk in eliminating Atlanta and Boston in the playoffs, reaching their fifth straight conference finals, but then the bottom fell out against the Chicago Bulls, who had learned well as the Pistons' feet.

In a best-of-seven series that was more competitive off the court than on it, Detroit suffered the indignity of a 4-0 sweep by the Bulls, losing the last two at home and walking off the court—a singular (and signature) act of defiance that would stain the franchise for years.

It wasn't unexpected that the Bulls would beat the Pistons. After all, Chicago had finally won the division, its 61-21 mark easily beating out second-place Detroit (50-32). And though the Pistons had eliminated the Bulls from the previous three playoffs, the Bulls had extended Detroit one game farther each time, from five games in 1988 to six in '89 and then seven in '90 when the home team won every game.

But it was the manner of the Bulls' conquest that Pistons fans found most galling. The end of Detroit's glory era occurred not so much with Chicago's 115-94 Game 4 clincher on Memorial Day, but the day before when Michael Jordan attempted to discredit the Pistons' two titles.

"Outside of Detroit, I think people will be happy they're not the reigning champions anymore," Jordan said. "It'll mean we are getting back to a clean game and getting the Bad Boy image away from the game. I think people want to see that type of basketball out."

He wasn't through yet.

After eliminating the Bulls from three straight playoffs, Isiah Thomas and the Pistons got a taste of some bad medicine in 1991. Photo by Allen Einstein.

"I don't think it's been clean basketball or sportsmanlike basketball that you'd want to advertise or endorse," Jordan said. "I think because they've been successful, other teams have tried to do it and I don't think it's been good for the game."

Those were fightin' words, but the Pistons didn't have much fight left in them. Aside from Bill Laimbeer's flagrant foul on Scottie Pippen and Dennis Rodman's subsequent two-handed shove of Pippen, resulting in a $5,000 fine, the Pistons went quietly in Game 4. So quietly, in fact, that most of them left without congratulating the Bulls. Led by Isiah Thomas and Laimbeer—over the protests of coach Chuck Daly—most of them walked off the court, past the Bulls bench, with 15 seconds left.

"Why should we give them any credit? They didn't give us any," Rodman said. "The NBA got what they wanted, Jordan in the Finals. You read their script and you play by it. Michael Jordan is God."

"I don't think Michael is God," John Salley said, "but I got my second foul today for looking at him wrong."

While the inimitable Laimbeer answered most every postgame querie with the same two-word answer—"They won"—Thomas was a bit more philosophical in summing up the moment.

"Had we not accomplished all we did, this might be a tough pill to swallow," the captain said. "Had we been as good as we are and not cashed in our chips (for two championships), we might be bitter. But we're maxed out. And when you're maxed out, you're maxed out."

Though most of the Pistons' cast would stick around for 1991-92 and lose to the Knicks in the first round, this really was the end of the Bad Boys. Two NBA championships, three Central Division titles, five trips to the Eastern Conference finals, a five-year record of 339-161 in exactly 500 games and 10 times that many memories.

Though the '90-91 season didn't resolve itself as well as the previous two, it contained several highlights. Joe Dumars had his best season to date, leading the Pistons in scoring (20.4 ppg) for the first time and being named to the All-NBA third team. He started in the All-Star game, had two 42-point games and also broke John Long's team record by

(continued...)

Dennis Rodman was second in the NBA in rebounding in 1990-91, but would finish first for the next six seasons. Photo by Allen Einstein.

making 62 straight free throws, then the fourth-longest streak in NBA history (Long had 51). On February 15, Daly was announced as coach of the Olympic basketball Dream Team, the first U.S. entry to use NBA players. During the playoffs, Rodman won his second straight Defensive Player of the Year award in a landslide, receiving 51 of 96 votes.

But many of the Pistons' brighter moments came early in the season. There was a 10-game winning streak during a 13-2 start, then an 11-gamer and five-gamer that gave them a 33-13 record February 1. However, coinciding with Thomas' right wrist surgery that kept him out for 32 games (January 23-April 5), Detroit went into a late-season slide. A 17-19 finish produced a 50-32 record and left the Pistons wondering if they had the energy to gear up for another grueling playoff run.

"This is a good team, a proud team, and I worry," Daly said. "They've got to decide how they want the story to end. We can't keep saying, 'We'll get to the playoffs and make everything right again.' "

And Thomas sounded an ominous tone April 10 when he said, "Nobody even gives a (bleep) anymore, the coaches included. There are too many different agendas. Everybody's part-time this and part-time that. We can't keep fooling ourselves and say, 'Yeah, we're going to be all right.' Someday you have to get started."

Accordingly, the early playoff rounds were a struggle, more so than in the preceding years. The Pistons needed the maximum five games to subdue an ordinary Atlanta club in the first round, then finally excused the aging Celtics in six games in the Eastern semis. The Palace clincher was a blast, though, as Detroit beat Boston 117-113 in overtime with a trademark rescue job by Thomas. But it would be the Pistons' last win of the season. The hungry Bulls were next. The party was over.

Game Results

1990-91
REGULAR SEASON

Date	Opponent	Result	Record
11-2	MILWAUKEE	W, 115-104	1-0
11-3	CLEVELAND	W, 106-97	2-0
11-6	at Seattle	L, 92-100	2-1
11-7	at L.A. Clippers	W, 110-83	3-1
11-9	at Portland	L, 101-113	3-2
11-13	MIAMI	W, 118-93	4-2
11-16	at New Jersey	W, 105-96	5-2
11-17	ATLANTA	W, 91-83	6-2
11-20	at Miami	W, 106-90	7-2
11-21	at Indiana	W, 108-100 (OT)	8-2
11-23	WASHINGTON	W, 97-88	9-2
11-25	SACRAMENTO	W, 105-92	10-2
11-27	at Atlanta	W, 120-97	11-2
11-28	NEW YORK	W, 90-83	12-2
11-30	at Philadelphia	W, 96-94	13-2
12-1	at Washington	L, 83-94	13-3
12-4	at L.A. Lakers	L, 90-114	13-4
12-5	at Utah	L, 85-106	13-5
12-7	at Golden State	L, 110-113	13-6
12-8	at Sacramento	W, 104-93	14-6
12-11	SAN ANTONIO	L, 86-95	14-7
12-14	at Boston	L, 100-108	14-8
12-18	at Milwaukee	L, 101-106	14-9
12-19	CHICAGO	W, 105-84	15-9
12-21	ATLANTA	W, 113-87	16-9
12-22	at Philadelphia	L, 99-106	16-10
12-25	at Chicago	L, 86-98	16-11
12-26	CHARLOTTE	W, 102-94	17-11
12-28	at Minnesota	W, 97-85	18-11
12-29	HOUSTON	W, 99-84	19-11
1-2	DENVER	W, 118-107	20-11
1-4	at Cleveland	W, 98-94	21-11
1-5	NEW JERSEY	W, 99-83	22-11
1-8	at Charlotte	W, 101-98	23-11
1-11	PORTLAND	W, 100-98 (OT)	24-11
1-12	MIAMI	W, 109-103 (OT)	25-11
1-14	at Dallas	W, 89-81	26-11
1-17	at Houston	W, 97-91 (OT)	27-11
1-18	at Phoenix	L, 102-103	27-12
1-21	BOSTON	W, 101-90	28-12
1-23	at Boston	L, 94-111	28-13
1-25	DALLAS	W, 84-82	29-13
1-26	at Orlando	W, 121-81	30-13
1-28	WASHINGTON	W, 87-81	31-13
1-30	CLEVELAND	W, 93-84	32-13
2-1	at Washington	W, 80-75	33-13
2-3	PHOENIX	L, 97-112	33-14
2-5	PHILADELPHIA	W, 107-98	34-14
2-7	CHICAGO	L, 93-95	34-15
2-13	INDIANA	L, 101-105	34-16
2-14	at Milwaukee	W, 102-94	35-16
2-17	at New York	L, 88-116	35-17
2-18	SEATTLE	W, 85-83	36-17
2-20	ATLANTA	W, 97-89	37-17
2-22	at Charlotte	L, 114-122	37-18
2-24	L.A. LAKERS	L, 96-102 (OT)	37-19
2-26	at Cleveland	L, 103-106	37-20
2-28	at Miami	L, 98-100	37-21
3-1	UTAH	L, 92-94	37-22
3-3	L.A. CLIPPERS	W, 107-98	38-22
3-6	NEW YORK	L, 99-102	38-23
3-9	at Indiana	W, 114-112	39-23
3-11	MILWAUKEE	L, 85-96	39-24
3-13	CHARLOTTE	W, 94-83	40-24
3-14	at New Jersey	L, 110-118	40-25
3-16	ORLANDO	W, 106-99	41-25
3-20	at Philadelphia	L, 103-107	41-26
3-22	NEW JERSEY	W, 109-93	42-26
3-24	at San Antonio	L, 78-85	42-27
3-25	at Denver	W, 118-94	43-27
3-27	INDIANA	W, 102-93	44-27
3-29	GOLDEN STATE	W, 111-105	45-27
4-2	at Charlotte	W, 83-78	46-27
4-5	MINNESOTA	W, 101-82	47-27
4-6	at New York	L, 88-101	47-28
4-9	at Milwaukee	L, 95-105	47-29
4-10	CLEVELAND	W, 90-94	47-30
4-12	CHICAGO	W, 95-91	48-30
4-14	at Indiana	L, 107-125	48-31
4-16	BOSTON	W, 118-90	49-31
4-19	at Atlanta	W, 126-120	50-31
4-21	at Chicago	L, 100-108	50-32

PLAYOFFS
Eastern First Round—(Best-of-Five)

Date	Opponent	Result	Record
4-26	ATLANTA	L, 98-103	0-1
4-28	ATLANTA	W, 101-88	1-1
4-30	at Atlanta	W, 103-91	2-1
5-2	at Atlanta	L, 111-123	2-2
5-5	ATLANTA	W, 113-81	3-2

Eastern Semifinals—(Best-of-Seven)

5-7	at Boston	W, 86-75	1-0
5-9	at Boston	L, 103-109	1-1
5-11	BOSTON	L, 83-115	1-2
5-13	BOSTON	W, 104-97	2-2
5-15	at Boston	W, 116-111	3-2
5-17	BOSTON	W, 117-113 (OT)	4-2

Eastern Finals—(Best-of-Seven)

5-19	at Chicago	L, 83-94	0-1
5-21	at Chicago	L, 97-105	0-2
5-25	CHICAGO	L, 107-113	0-3
5-27	CHICAGO	L, 94-115	0-4

(Home games in CAPS)

SPOTLIGHT Game

MAY 17, 1991

Gimpy Isiah Thomas came off the bench to spark the Pistons' clinching win over the Celtics. Photo by Allen Einstein.

Isiah Thomas was often rapped for ball-hogging, and his critics were unmistakably correct on this night. How fortunate for the Pistons.

Like a bolt of lightning from on high, Thomas pumped electricity into a listless team in overtime, singlehandedly leading the Pistons to a clinching 117-113 playoff victory over the proud, aging Boston Celtics.

The victory gave the two-time defending champions a 4-2 win in the best-of-seven series and pushed them into the Eastern Conference finals for the fifth straight season. Their opponent, for the third straight time, would be the Chicago Bulls.

At a sold-out Palace, Thomas rallied the Pistons from a 109-105 overtime deficit after they had blown an 80-63 lead in the final 15:34 of regulation. Isiah burned the Celtics with a 3-pointer, two long jump shots and a free throw in the last 2:23 of OT, jumping on the press table to celebrate at the final buzzer.

Though Thomas built his reputation on such moments, he was an unlikely hero in this case. After spraining his right foot in Game 1, he had missed Games 2 and 4 completely, then shot 0-for-2 in 15 minutes of Detroit's Game 5 win. He came off the bench in Game 6 as well, but was inserted for the OT stretch run after Joe Dumars (32 points) got tired.

"I didn't feel I had to take over, but everybody was waiting for me to do something," said Thomas, who scored 14 points in 31 minutes. "I just didn't want to lose. We had worked so hard to get here. This has been a hard year for us. Everything's been stacked against us.

"Had (the Celtics) won, they would've won the series, because they'd have broken our spirit. I didn't want to go back to Boston (for Game 7). Damn it, I didn't want to see Boston Garden again this year."

Thomas made sure the Pistons did not. Despite his injury, his closing burst was highly reminiscent of his MVP performance in the NBA Finals the previous spring. Boston coach Chris Ford, himself a former Pistons playoff hero, tipped his hat. "Isiah made some great clutch shots," he said. "I can't fault Dee Brown's defense. Isiah was possessed. It took a great player making great plays to beat us."

Tops on the list was Thomas' 3-pointer from the deep right wing with 2:23 left. It came with one second on the 24-second clock and gave the Pistons a 110-109 lead. Though Boston and Thomas would trade baskets again, Detroit built a decisive five-point lead when Bill Laimbeer hit a 15-footer and Thomas converted his own steal into a long jumper.

The Pistons' subsequent loss to the Bulls removed much of the luster from their season, no question, but Thomas' terrific 2:23 ranks with the greatest scoring sprees in team history.

SUMMARY—Game 6
Pistons 117, Celtics 113

CELTICS (113)

Player	Min	FG M-A	3P M-A	FT M-A	Reb O-T	A	PF	Pts
Bird	45	4-14	0-0	4-4	1-4	4	3	12
Gamble	18	0-0	0-0	0-0	0-0	0	1	0
Kleine	7	1-3	0-0	0-0	2-4	0	4	2
Lewis	51	9-27	0-1	5-5	3-7	5	2	23
Shaw	18	3-10	0-0	2-2	1-1	1	1	8
McHale	46	11-19	1-1	11-14	1-8	3	5	34
D.Brown	39	9-13	0-0	3-4	0-5	4	1	21
Pinckney	40	6-6	0-0	1-3	5-9	1	3	13
M.Smith	1	0-0	0-0	0-0	0-0	0	1	0
Totals	**265**	**43-92**	**1-2**	**26-32**	**13-38**	**18**	**20**	**113**

PISTONS (117)

Player	Min	FG M-A	3P M-A	FT M-A	Reb O-T	A	PF	Pts
Rodman	39	2-5	0-0	0-0	6-13	2	4	4
Edwards	24	4-11	0-0	9-10	1-5	2	4	17
Laimbeer	39	7-11	0-0	1-3	5-14	2	5	15
Dumars	45	14-25	3-5	1-3	1-3	10	2	32
V.Johnson	31	5-15	0-0	0-0	2-5	4	1	10
Salley	29	5-7	0-0	2-4	3-8	0	5	12
Aguirre	26	5-10	0-3	0-0	0-1	3	2	10
Thomas	31	7-14	2-5	1-2	1-3	6	3	17
Hastings	1	0-0	0-0	0-0	0-1	2	2	0
Totals	**265**	**49-98**	**5-13**	**14-22**	**19-53**	**31**	**28**	**117**

Percentages: FG .467, 3P .500, FT .813. Team Rebounds: 10. Blocked shots: 3 (Lewis, D.Brown, Pinckney). Turnovers: 7 (Lewis 2, McHale 2, D.Brown 2, Kleine). Steals: 4 (Bird 2, Lewis 2). Technical fouls: McHale, 10:36 second; Kleine, 1:07 third. Flagrant foul: Bird, 1:36 second.

Percentages: FG .500, 3P .385, FT .636. Team Rebounds: 11. Blocked shots: 2 (Rodman, Salley). Turnovers: 10 (Rodman 2, Edwards 2, Laimbeer, Dumars, Johnson, Salley, Aguirre, Thomas). Steals: 2 (Rodman, Thomas). Technical fouls: Salley, 10:36 second.

BOSTON	23	27	25	30	8	—	113
DETROIT	29	27	26	23	12	—	117

A—21,454 (sellout). T—2:36. Officials—Jack Madden, Mike Mathis, Dick Bavetta.

Scott Hastings and "Cult Heroes"

Fun-loving Scott Hastings was the Pistons' designated sitter for two seasons. Photo by Allen Einstein.

At the beginning of a game, an NBA coach has 240 minutes to dole out— five positions, 48 minutes apiece—and it would seem like enough to go around. But it rarely happens that way. A couple of players don't get in, and usually it's the same guys from night to night. Like most teams, the Pistons have had several designated sitters and few filled the role with the good humor of Scott Hastings, a 6-foot-11 journeyman center who played two seasons with Detroit (1989-91). Like others who came before—Darrall Imhoff, Roger Brown, Chuck Nevitt, Walker D. Russell— Hastings developed cult-hero status among the fans while playing only 279 minutes in 67 games. If you wanted tips on how to defend Kareem Abdul-Jabbar, you went to somebody else. But if you wanted to find out which bench had the most comfortable seats, you went to Hastings. "In Boston, the chairs were made of really thin tubing and cheap plastic. If you sat down with any firmness, the legs did the splits on you. I don't know how many of them we busted," Hastings said. On the best vantage points, he said, "I hate back-to-back games where you watch the game from the same side. You get a little crick in your neck. You think, 'Dang, can't we look the other way for a while?' " Even opposing fans grew to love Hastings. "When you're sitting there the whole game, like I am, the fans get on you at first. You laugh and say, 'Hey, that's a funny one.' But after while, they say, 'Man, how come you never play?' It's like they're on your side all of the sudden." After being traded to Denver in '91 and playing two seasons, giving him an 11-year career, Hastings retired in 1993. He now brings his witty style to Turner's NBA coverage.

AT A GLANCE

"CULT HEROES"

ON THE BENCH

DARRALL IMHOFF — Went on to a solid career with Lakers, but with the Pistons from 1962-64, "Big D" (6-foot-10) averaged 3.9 points, 4.3 rebounds and 12.9 minutes.

ROGER BROWN — Backup center from 1975-77, Brown (6-foot-11) played 776 minutes over 72 games, but 51 minutes were in OT game vs. Bulls on April 3, 1976. Often razzed at Cobo.

CHUCK NEVITT — The Human Victory Cigar, Nevitt (7-foot-5) spent three seasons with Detroit (1985-88), averaging 5.2 minutes in 83 games. Had 12 points, 10 boards, five blocks January 7, 1987 vs. Knicks.

WALKER D. RUSSELL — Pontiac's own. Campy Russell's kid brother, Walker D. played 87 games in three Pistons stints (879 minutes). Had a 16-point game as rookie in 1982-83.

BEHIND THE SCENES

MORRIE MOORAWNICK — Official scorer since 1957 and still going strong. His box scores remain meticulous.

ED RIVERO — Nearing two decades as the Pistons' locker room attendant and a statistician for radio broadcasts.

JERRY DZIEDZIC — Spent 27 seasons as equipment manager.

LEON THE BARBER — Like Cobo predecessor Dancing Gus, Leon "The Barber" Bradley was a Pistons fixture, razzing the opposing bench.

CHEERLEADERS — From "Don Massey's Classy Chassis" in the '80s to "Automotion" in the '90s.

MASCOTS — Regrettable predecessors, like the Magic Cylinder at Cobo (Dziedzic in a goofy get-up) and Sir Slam-A-Lot, have been replaced by Hooper the Horse.

CHANGING FACES

THE PISTONS reached in their closet and John Long's familiar No. 25 jersey was waiting for him. They kept it handy, just in case. On January 25, 1991, Long emerged from semi-retirement for his third stint with the Pistons. He took the roster spot of Isiah Thomas, who had hand surgery and was put on the injured list. "I've kept in good shape, but I haven't played under the whistle in a while," said Long, the 1978 Pistons draftee who was traded in 1986 but came back in 1989 for a championship ring. "Getting a ring was the highlight of my career. Now I've got a chance for another one," he said. Coach Chuck Daly joked, "John will sign a 10-day contract when he's 50," and he was fairly prescient. In 1996, having been out of the NBA for five seasons, the 40-year-old Long was brought back by Toronto for the final five months of the season. Aside from Long, the Pistons were mostly static in '90-91. They used the No. 26 draft pick on Texas guard Lance Blanks, who would make little impact in two seasons.

The last of John Long's three stints with the Pistons was in '90-91. Photo by Allen Einstein.

Take a Bow
Bill Laimbeer

Bill Laimbeer broke an important Pistons record and coined a term—"duration player"—on January 11, 1991 when Detroit edged Portland 100-98 in overtime in a rematch of 1990 NBA finalists. With Laimbeer's fifth rebound of the night, gathering a miss by Buck Williams with 8:50 left in the third quarter, it gave him 8,064 in his Pistons career to top Bob Lanier's team record. He would finish with 9,430 after retiring in '94, ranking first in total rebounds and third in average (10.1) behind Lanier (11.8) and Dennis Rodman (11.5). Laimbeer, typically curt, downplayed the career record. "It means I've been around a long time," he said. "It may mean more to me later when I look through the record book. I'm just proud that I've been a duration player in this league." He sells himself short with that term. Laimbeer was not merely Detroit's annual rebound leader from 1983-89, he led the NBA by total in '84 (1,003) and total and average in '86 (1,075, 13.1). That's not merely duration, that's domination.

Bill Laimbeer's box-out skills were vital to his rebounding proficiency. Photo by Allen Einstein.

PISTON LIST

Last Previous Player to Wear Popular Numbers

Lindsey Hunter's No. 1
- Kevin Porter, 1975-79

Joe Dumars' No. 4
- Never worn

Dennis Rodman's No. 10
- Glenn Hagan, 1981-82

x-Isiah Thomas' No. 11
- Bob McAdoo, 1979-81

x-Vinnie Johnson's No. 15
- Larry Wright, 1980-82

x-Bob Lanier's No. 16
- Dave Gambee, 1968-69

x-Dave Bing's No. 21
- Earl Evans, 1979-80

Grant Hill's No. 33
- Cadillac Anderson, 1993-94

x-Bill Laimbeer's No. 40
- Wayne Robinson, 1980-81

x-retired number

1991 1992

DETROIT PISTONS

TIME CAPSULE

November 7, 1991:
Magic Johnson retires from basketball, announcing that he has tested positive for HIV, the virus that causes AIDS.

December 25, 1991:
Mikhail Gorbachev resigns as leader of the Soviet Union.

May 1, 1992:
Federal troops are ordered into Los Angeles due to riots triggered by the acquittal of four policemen charged with beating Rodney King.

May 22, 1992:
Johnny Carson's final "Tonight Show" is aired to 50 million viewers.

SEASON SNAPSHOT

Most Points
Joe Dumars (1,635, 19.9 avg.)

Most Rebounds
Dennis Rodman (1,530, 18.7 avg.)

Most Assists
Isiah Thomas (560, 7.2 avg.)

Most Minutes
Dennis Rodman (3,301, 40.3 avg.)

Field-Goal Percentage
Dennis Rodman (53.9%)

Free-Throw Percentage
Bill Laimbeer (89.3%)

Team Offense Average
98.9 (8,113 in 82 games)

Team Defense Average
96.9 (7,946 in 82 games)

NBA All-Stars
Dennis Rodman, F (Third Team)

Pistons in All-Star Game
Isiah Thomas, G; Joe Dumars, G; Dennis Rodman, F

1991-92

FINAL STANDINGS

Central Division	W	L	Pct.	GB
Chicago	67	15	.817	—
Cleveland	57	25	.695	10
PISTONS	**48**	**34**	**.585**	**19**
Indiana	40	42	.488	27
Atlanta	38	44	.463	29
Charlotte	31	51	.378	36
Milwaukee	31	51	.378	36

Atlantic Division Winner—(tie) Boston, New York
Midwest Division Winner—Utah
Pacific Division Winner—Portland

PLAYOFF RESULTS

Eastern First Round: N.Y. Knicks d. Pistons, 3-2

PISTONS PLAYOFF LEADERS

Scoring: Joe Dumars (16.8 avg.)
Rebounding: Dennis Rodman (10.2)
Assists: Isiah Thomas (7.4)

NBA CHAMPION

Chicago Bulls

1991-92
SEASON IN REVIEW

This time, there could be no doubts. The Pistons' era of greatness was over. In '91-92, they spent nine months trying to duplicate the formulas that won two NBA championships, but the futility of that exercise was laid bare. A tense 48-34 season ended with a first-round playoff loss to the Knicks—Detroit's earliest elimination since 1986—as well as the resignations of coach Chuck Daly (after nine seasons) and embattled GM Jack McCloskey (after 13). The season had deteriorated into a chase for personal statistics. Dennis Rodman's 1,530 rebounds led the league, his 18.7 average being the NBA's highest since Wilt Chamberlain's 19.2 in '71-72. Isiah Thomas scored 44 points on November 15 against Utah's John Stockton, and then topped Bob Lanier's 15,488 points to become the Pistons' all-time scoring king December 1 vs. Houston. Thomas needed 100 games more than Lanier (781-681) to reach the total. But from a team standpoint, everything slid downward. James Edwards had been traded and Vinnie Johnson waived, but their de facto replacements, Orlando Woolridge and Darrell Walker, didn't fit in as well. Bill Laimbeer even missed a game because of an injury for the first time in his career February 29 vs. New Jersey. Winning streaks of seven in March and six in April were deceiving, as the playoff loss to the Knicks would prove. It was time to start anew.

Dennis Rodman had a second straight 1,000-rebound season, joining Bob Lanier and Bill Laimbeer with that distinction. Photo by Allen Einstein.

November 15, 1991

It wasn't John Stockton's fault that he was named to the 1992 Dream Team over Isiah Thomas. That was Michael Jordan's doing; he didn't want to play with Thomas because of long-standing feuds. But the next time Thomas and Stockton played each other November 15, 1991 at Detroit, the Pistons' star made his point—lots of them—that he should have been a Dream Teamer. Thomas torched Stockton for 44 points, his highest total in nearly 10 years, as Detroit beat Utah 123-115. Though Thomas pleaded ignorance—"It just sort of happened," he said—there was little doubt he had an agenda. He made all seven shots in the third quarter and his first three in the fourth quarter. "I'll bet the last time he scored like that was, like, 1985," new teammate Orlando Woolridge said. Close enough. Thomas' three previous games of 44 or more (47, 46, 44) were all in 1983. The Jazz were mindful to pay back Thomas only a month later, December 14 at Utah. Just 4:28 into the game, as Thomas drove up the right baseline, Karl Malone hammered him with a flagrant elbow to the head. The deep cut required 40 stitches and resulted in a $10,000 fine and one-game suspension for Malone. "If Bill Laimbeer does that, they suspend him for the whole season," Thomas complained.

Isiah Thomas didn't make the first Dream Team, but he proved he belonged on it. Photo by Allen Einstein.

WHAT A NIGHT!

Premier Piston

"Healing Hands"

Trainer Mike Abdenour tends to Bob Lanier's sore left shoulder in 1976.

The rosin dot tells you exactly how Mike Abdenour approaches his job as the Pistons' trainer. He is so meticulous, so darn organized, so tuned in to details, Abdenour put a magic marker dot on the Pistons' padded press table next to the bench. The bottle of rosin goes there. If a player carries it to center court with him, Abdenour scurries after it, placing it back on the dot for the next user. In 18 seasons with the Pistons (plus three more with the 76ers), Abdenour has become known as a leader in his field and one of the NBA's most enthusiastic trainers. He has even received four technical fouls, though none since the Silverdome era. Fans know him as the guy who keeps track of timeouts on the bench and bellows "Go to it, go to it!" to notify the Pistons that the 24-second clock is expiring; his alertness has saved countless possessions over the years. A lot of years, at that. A Detroit native and Wayne State grad, Abdenour joined the Pistons as a 23-year-old head trainer in 1975 and he stayed for 16 of the next 17 seasons, missing only 1977-78. After leaving in 1992 for three years with the 76ers, he came back in 1995. Before Abdenour, the Pistons' trainers were Stan Kenworthy (1957-63), Don Friederichs (1963-66) and Harold "Bud" Shockro (1966-75). Mike Kostich (1977-78) and Tony Harris (1992-95) filled the gaps in

Abdenour's tenure. Detroit also has one of the NBA's top team physicians in Dr. Benjamin Paolucci, D.O., who has served the club since 1972. Among Metro Detroit's leading general surgeons, Paolucci oversees the diagnosis and treatment of all Pistons injuries. Known around the team as "Palooch," he headed up the medical team for the 1994 World Cup soccer matches at the Silverdome. Since 1992, the Pistons' staff has included Arnie Kander, widely known as the NBA's most innovative strength and conditioning coach. He blends nontraditional and standard methods to tailor programs unique to each player. Kander's techniques stress balance and flexibility as well as strength.

Dr. Benjamin Paolucci

PISTON LIST

Best Road Records in 82-Game Season

- 26-15, 1988-89
- 24-17, 1989-90
- 24-17, 1996-97
- 23-17, 1973-74
- 23-18, 1991-92
- 20-19, 1970-71
- 20-21, 1984-85
- 20-21, 1986-87
- 20-21, 1987-88
- 19-22, 1983-84
- 18-23, 1990-91
- 16-25, 1981-82

CHANGING FACES

THE SEASON began with upheaval and ended with more of the same, but the early part involved players and the latter involved management. The changes began August 13, 1991 when the Pistons made two deals, getting high-scoring forward Orlando Woolridge from Denver for lovable bench rider Scott Hastings and shipping James Edwards to the L.A. Clippers. Edwards said he would hold out if he didn't get a new contract, so the Pistons dumped him for guard Jeff Martin and a second-round pick. Then September 4, Vinnie Johnson was waived after his 10th Pistons season and veteran guard Darrell Walker was acquired from Washington. Johnson, 1990's playoff hero, said, "I'm hurt and disappointed, but I know it's part of the business." GM Jack McCloskey said, "It was a very, very tough day. Vinnie is one of my all-time favorites." There were tougher days ahead for McCloskey. As the season progressed, he was publicly criticized by Bill Laimbeer for poor management. McCloskey would resign May 29, a week after naming Ron Rothstein as coach to replace the resigned Chuck Daly.

Orlando Woolridge averaged 14 points in '91-92, joining Mark Aguirre as a clear-out offensive threat. Photo by Allen Einstein.

Take a Bow

Chuck Daly

steps down as coach of the Pistons. Photo by Allen Einstein.

Chuck Daly never used the words "resign" or "quit." He didn't have to. It was simply "time to go." After nine seasons as the winningest coach in club history, Daly stepped down on May 5, 1992, eager for his Dream Team assignment and unregretful about bidding the Pistons goodbye. He had notified his players on April 4. "You just know when it's time," Daly said, a month short of his 62nd birthday. "It's my call, basically. The players need to hear a new voice. Maybe they needed it two years ago. I've got John Salley on the floor and I keep hollering at him. How long can they keep listening?" Dennis Rodman was unhappy to say so-long to the only NBA coach he'd ever had. "I can't believe he's leaving," he said. Including a 71-42 playoff record (.628), Daly was 538-313 (.632) since joining the Pistons in 1983. He would coach the Dream Team to an 8-0 record and Olympic gold medal, then become coach of the Nets for two seasons. After a stint with TNT, he returned to the NBA in 1997 as Orlando's coach.

Game Results

1991-92 REGULAR SEASON

Date	Opponent	Result	Record
11-1	MILWAUKEE	L, 99-109	0-1
11-2	at Atlanta	W, 89-87	1-1
11-5	CHARLOTTE	W, 117-93	2-1
11-9	at New Jersey	W, 110-100	3-1
11-10	WASHINGTON	W, 85-79	4-1
11-12	at Chicago	L, 93-110	4-2
11-13	at Miami	L, 102-107	4-3
11-15	UTAH	W, 123-115	5-3
11-16	PHILADELPHIA	L, 86-89	5-4
11-18	at Indiana	L, 101-118	5-5
11-20	SEATTLE	L, 86-91	5-6
11-22	NEW YORK	L, 90-99	5-7
11-23	at Cleveland	L, 89-96	5-8
11-26	at Atlanta	W, 103-93	6-8
11-27	ATLANTA	W, 100-91	7-8
11-30	at New York	L, 96-103	7-9
12-1	HOUSTON	W, 94-87	8-9
12-3	INDIANA	L, 99-108	8-10
12-5	CLEVELAND	L, 101-110	8-11
12-6	at Washington	W, 105-94	9-11
12-10	at Phoenix	L, 93-102	9-12
12-11	at L.A. Clippers	L, 96-101	9-13
12-13	at Portland	W, 113-103	10-13
12-14	at Utah	L, 100-102	10-14
12-16	DENVER	W, 103-89	11-14
12-18	CHARLOTTE	W, 117-97	12-14
12-20	L.A. LAKERS	W, 112-93	13-14
12-26	at Orlando	W, 112-100	14-14
12-27	ORLANDO	W, 106-94	15-14
12-30	PHOENIX	L, 103-110	15-15
1-2	at Houston	W, 106-83	16-15
1-3	at Dallas	W, 106-96	17-15
1-6	at San Antonio	L, 90-100	17-16
1-8	SACRAMENTO	W, 114-95	18-16
1-10	PORTLAND	W, 86-81	19-16
1-11	NEW JERSEY	W, 90-88	20-16
1-13	DALLAS	W, 84-81	21-16
1-15	at Indiana	W, 118-104	22-16
1-19	CHICAGO	L, 85-87	22-17
1-23	at Minnesota	W, 111-100	23-17
1-24	at Chicago	L, 93-117	23-18
1-26	at Boston	L, 91-106	23-19
1-28	at Charlotte	W, 100-95 (OT)	24-19
1-29	CLEVELAND	L, 90-95	24-20
1-31	MIAMI	W, 109-98	25-20
2-1	at Atlanta	W, 89-80	26-20
2-5	MILWAUKEE	W, 102-94	27-20
2-6	at Cleveland	W, 112-95	28-20
2-11	at Milwaukee	L, 87-104	28-21
2-13	MINNESOTA	L, 93-96	28-22
2-16	at Philadelphia	W, 90-83	29-22
2-18	ORLANDO	W, 117-95	30-22
2-19	at New Jersey	L, 102-106	30-23
2-21	at Orlando	W, 114-100	31-23
2-22	at Miami	L, 98-107	31-24
2-25	CHICAGO	W, 108-106	32-24
2-27	MILWAUKEE	W, 104-98	33-24
2-29	NEW JERSEY	L, 90-99	33-25
3-2	WASHINGTON	W, 99-89	34-25
3-4	INDIANA	W, 110-107 (OT)	35-25
3-6	at Denver	W, 106-91	36-25
3-8	at L.A. Lakers	W, 98-93	37-25
3-10	at Seattle	W, 98-92	38-25
3-12	at Golden State	W, 119-112	39-25
3-14	at Sacramento	W, 89-83	40-25
3-16	ATLANTA	L, 77-89	40-26
3-18	PHILADELPHIA	W, 91-85	41-26
3-20	BOSTON	L, 99-104 (OT)	41-27
3-22	at Charlotte	L, 101-113	41-28
3-25	GOLDEN STATE	L, 99-103	41-29
3-27	at Boston	L, 87-106	41-30
3-29	SAN ANTONIO	W, 107-103	42-30
3-31	L.A. CLIPPERS	L, 81-97	42-31
4-3	at Washington	L, 85-119	42-32
4-5	MIAMI	W, 104-80	43-32
4-7	at New York	W, 103-94	44-32
4-8	at Philadelphia	W, 89-71	45-32
4-10	CHARLOTTE	W, 125-106	46-32
4-12	NEW YORK	W, 72-61	47-32
4-14	at Milwaukee	W, 98-94 (OT)	48-32
4-15	BOSTON	L, 89-92	48-33
4-19	at Chicago	L, 85-103	48-34

PLAYOFFS

Eastern First Round—(Best-of-Five)

Date	Opponent	Result	Record
4-24	at New York	L, 75-109	0-1
4-26	at New York	W, 89-88	1-1
4-28	NEW YORK	L, 87-90 (OT)	1-2
5-1	NEW YORK	W, 86-82	2-2
5-3	at New York	L, 87-94	2-3

(Home games in CAPS)

191

1992 1993

DETROIT PISTONS

TIME CAPSULE

November 3, 1992:
Bill Clinton wins the presidential election, defeating incumbent George Bush and independent candidate Ross Perot.

December 8, 1992:
United Nations troops arrive in Somalia to assist a starving populace.

February 26, 1993:
The World Trade Center in New York City is bombed by terrorists.

April 19, 1993:
Nearly 100 people perish in a fire to end the 51-day standoff between David Koresh's Branch Davidians and federal agents in Waco, Texas.

SEASON SNAPSHOT

Most Points
Joe Dumars (1,809, 23.5 avg.)

Most Rebounds
Dennis Rodman (1,132, 18.3 avg.)

Most Assists
Isiah Thomas (671, 8.5 avg.)

Most Minutes
Joe Dumars (3,094, 40.2 avg.)

Field-Goal Percentage
Bill Laimbeer (50.9%)

Free-Throw Percentage
Bill Laimbeer (89.4%)

Team Offense Average
100.6 (8,252 in 82 games)

Team Defense Average
102.0 (8,366 in 82 games)

NBA All-Stars
Joe Dumars, G (Second Team)

Pistons in All-Star Game
Isiah Thomas, G; Joe Dumars, G

1992-93

FINAL STANDINGS

Central Division	W	L	Pct.	GB
Chicago	57	25	.695	—
Cleveland	54	28	.659	3
Charlotte	44	38	.537	13
Atlanta	43	39	.524	14
Indiana	41	41	.500	16
PISTONS	**40**	**42**	**.488**	**17**
Milwaukee	28	54	.341	29

Atlantic Division Winner—New York
Midwest Division Winner—Houston
Pacific Division Winner—Phoenix

PLAYOFF RESULTS

Pistons Did Not Qualify

PISTONS PLAYOFF LEADERS

NBA CHAMPION

Chicago Bulls

1992-93
SEASON IN REVIEW

The Pistons' nine-year playoff run finally ended in '92-93. Though they finished only one game out of qualifying, it was such a trying season that no one seemed too upset to just go home and try again next year. Coach Ron Rothstein wouldn't be back, though. The crowned successor to Chuck Daly lost his veteran support and was fired after the season, going 40-42, but he never had a chance. The tearing-down of a championship team is never pretty, and the season was full of ill-fated personnel moves and odd incidents, even a brief hunger strike by new center Olden Polynice. It was the season when Dennis Rodman's behavior moved from eccentric to weird and dangerous. He held out of camp, angry that Daly was "forced out," then was sidelined with tendinitis and a three-game suspension for insubordination. The Pistons tried to trade him, but were unsuccessful. He hadn't helped by tearing a calf muscle in January and being discovered at The Palace one morning, sleeping in his truck with a loaded rifle. Nevertheless, Rodman led the NBA in rebounding (18.3) despite playing only 62 games. Joe Dumars had a great season, as his 23.5 scoring average ranked seventh in the NBA, the highest finish by a Piston in 10 years. Free-agent forward Terry Mills showed promise, averaging 14.8 points and 5.8 rebounds.

The Pistons acquired center Olden Polynice in the summer of '92 to shore up their front line. Photo by Allen Einstein.

WHAT A NIGHT!

February 16, 1993

It was a painful realization, but in 1993 the Pistons and Orlando Magic were heading in opposite directions. Detroit was in rapid retreat and Orlando was loading up for a happy future with massive rookie center Shaquille O'Neal (7-foot-1, 300). But the Pistons were still undefeated in the all-time series, having won all 13 meetings since the Magic's entry in 1989. The perfect record survived the 14th game, but barely so, as Detroit overcame a Palace-record 46 points by O'Neal to claim a 124-120 overtime victory. Obviously, the Pistons' old guard wasn't going to go quietly. Joe Dumars made 16-of-26 shots en route to 39 points, Isiah Thomas dealt a season-high 19 assists and Dennis Rodman returned from a 14-game injury layoff to grab 12 rebounds. O'Neal was unstoppable, making 19-of-25 shots, including 16-of-18 after the first quarter, and grabbing 21 boards. But he wore the goat's horns after Detroit rallied from a 107-100 deficit in the final 2:07 of regulation for a 113-111 lead. O'Neal made the tying layup with 5.1 seconds left, but blew the free throw, forcing overtime. In OT, with Detroit fouling intentionally, O'Neal bricked two more foul shots, ending an 8-of-16 night at the line. "We weren't stopping him any other way," coach Ron Rothstein said.

Joe Dumars scored 39 points in 50 minutes against Orlando on February 16, 1993. Photo by Allen Einstein.

Terry "Three" Mills

Detroit-area product Terry Mills has averaged 13.5 points and 6.2 rebounds in five seasons with the Pistons.

Coach Doug Collins calls them "heat-check shots." "That's when you're so hot, you've got to shoot one more to make sure it's real," Collins said. Just call Terry Mills the master of the heat-check shot. Especially in '96-97 when he made a team-leading 175 3-pointers and ranked eighth in the league at 42.2 percent, Mills was one of the best streak shooters in club history. Often left unattended as opponents double-teamed Grant Hill, Mills would spot up behind the arc and fire away. Just when you thought he was a step too deep, he'd swish another 23-footer and the Palace announcer got to exclaim, "Threeeeee Millllls!" For one wild week in December 1996, Mills scrawled his name into the NBA record book by nailing 13 straight 3-point attempts, tying Brent Price's mark. He made his final six in a home win over Atlanta, then was 6-of-6 against Cleveland. A night later at New Jersey, he hit his first triple for No. 13, but missed his next attempt. In that four-game week, Mills had 64 points in 75 minutes on 22-of-31 shooting, including 17-of-22 triples. "It's like every shot I take, I know it's going in. It's fun that way," he said. "When I come in the game, other teams are saying, 'This guy is going to make a difference.' I love that role." When Mills signed with the Pistons in '92-93, stolen from New Jersey as a free agent, Detroit fans were quite familiar with him from his prep days at Romulus High and Michigan. Playing starter's minutes, he developed into a talented scorer. His second Pistons season was his best as he registered career highs of 17.3 points and 8.4 boards in 80 games. Collins' arrival in 1995 signaled a change in Mills' role and he embraced it after initial hesitation. In the summer of 1997, he left the Pistons for the Miami Heat, accepting half the money Detroit offered.

AT A GLANCE

TERRY MILLS

FULL NAME:
Terry Richard Mills
BORN:
December 21, 1967; Romulus, Michigan
POSITION, HEIGHT, WEIGHT:
Forward, 6-foot-10, 250 pounds
COLLEGE:
Michigan '90
ACQUIRED:
1992, signed as free agent
TENURE WITH PISTONS:
1992-93 — 1996-97
Also: Denver 1990-91, New Jersey 1991-92
BEST SEASON WITH PISTONS:
1993-94, 80 GP, 17.3 ppg, 8.4 rpg
TOTALS WITH PISTONS:
Regular season: 394 GP, 13.5 ppg, 6.2 rpg
Playoffs: 8 GP, 9.4 ppg, 5.0 rpg
HONORS:
NBA Player of the Week, December 9, 1996

PISTON LIST

40-Point Games in One Season

10 games
- George Yardley, 1957-58 (52, 51, 49, 48, 48, 44, 44, 43, 41, 41)

5 games
- Dave Bing, 1967-68 (45, 43, 42, 41, 40)

4 games
- Bob Lanier, 1971-72 (44, 42, 42, 42)
- Bob Lanier, 1972-73 (48, 42, 42, 40)
- Bob Lanier, 1974-75 (45, 43, 41, 40)
- Joe Dumars, 1993-94 (44, 42, 42, 40)

3 games
- Dave Bing, 1969-70 (44, 42, 40)
- Dave Bing, 1970-71 (54, 49, 40)
- Bob Lanier, 1976-77 (40, 40, 40)
- Kelly Tripucka, 1982-83 (56, 43, 40)
- Joe Dumars, 1994-95 (43, 41, 40)

CHANGING FACES

RON ROTHSTEIN tried to replace a local legend. So did Billy McKinney. Neither would fare well. Rothstein, Chuck Daly's former assistant, followed him as Detroit's coach with predictable results. With a fading team and many in the organization still loyal to Daly, Rothstein didn't last. After a 40-42 season, he was replaced by assistant Don Chaney on May 3, 1993, not yet a year after being hired by outgoing GM Jack McCloskey. McKinney, meanwhile, was selected to fill McCloskey's job, though he was given the title of player personnel director. A seven-year NBA guard who once shot 14-of-14 in a game for Kansas City, McKinney received more slack than Rothstein, but not much. Though responsible for drafting Grant Hill, Allan Houston and Lindsey Hunter, McKinney would be fired after three seasons (1995). The major acquisitions of '92-93 were forward Terry Mills,

Ron Rothstein was a valuable assistant in the Bad Boys era, but didn't succeed as the Pistons' head coach in '92-93.

defensive center Olden Polynice and oft-injured guard Alvin Robertson, the latter coming from Milwaukee for Orlando Woolridge. Before the season, the Pistons traded John Salley (Miami) and William Bedford (L.A. Clippers).

Take a Bow

Bob Lanier

Bob Lanier's No. 16 has been retired by both Detroit and Milwaukee. Photo by Allen Einstein.

The honor was several years overdue, but that didn't detract from the festivities on January 9, 1993 when the Pistons raised Bob Lanier's No. 16 to the Palace rafters, joining Dave Bing's 21 as the team's only retired numbers. No Piston had worn 16 since Lanier was dealt to Milwaukee in 1980, but this ceremony made it official. More than 20 former players, coaches and NBA executives were in attendance to speak about Lanier's career of basketball greatness and community service. Framed jerseys, artwork and other gifts were presented to the eight-time Detroit point leader and one-time career scoring king. "This is a moment I'll forever be proud of. This is truly a day that I've looked forward to," Lanier said. He became the sixth player in league history to be similarly honored by two teams, the others being Julius Erving, Kareem Abdul-Jabbar, Oscar Robertson, Wilt Chamberlain and Nate Thurmond. Addressing the packed house, Lanier dedicated the night to his late father: "He's looking down with a big smile on his face. I know he'd be proud of me."

Game Results

1992-93 REGULAR SEASON

Date	Opponent	Result	Record
11-6	MILWAUKEE	L, 81-86	0-1
11-7	INDIANA	W, 89-87	1-1
11-11	at Chicago	L, 96-98 (OT)	1-2
11-12	MIAMI	W, 95-88	2-2
11-14	INDIANA	L, 100-104	2-3
11-17	at L.A. Clippers	L, 106-115 (OT)	2-4
11-19	at Denver	L, 87-99	2-5
11-21	at Seattle	L, 101-138	2-6
11-22	at Portland	L, 90-115	2-7
11-25	CHARLOTTE	L, 97-101	2-8
11-28	at Minnesota	L, 80-82	2-9
11-29	at New York	W, 92-76	3-9
12-4	at Philadelphia	W, 101-99	4-9
12-5	PHILADELPHIA	W, 112-88	5-9
12-9	ORLANDO	W, 108-103	6-9
12-11	CLEVELAND	W, 107-103	7-9
12-12	at New York	L, 88-95	7-10
12-15	at Atlanta	W, 107-94	8-10
12-16	ATLANTA	W, 89-88	9-10
12-18	INDIANA	W, 122-106	10-10
12-19	at Milwaukee	W, 103-90	11-10
12-22	HOUSTON	W, 98-84	12-10
12-23	at Charlotte	L, 95-107	12-11
12-26	at Washington	W, 99-97	13-11
12-28	at Cleveland	L, 89-98	13-12
12-30	WASHINGTON	W, 118-110	14-12
1-2	at Orlando	W, 98-97	15-12
1-5	at Miami	L, 83-89	15-13
1-6	L.A. CLIPPERS	W, 110-103	16-13
1-8	ATLANTA	L, 92-101	16-14
1-9	GOLDEN STATE	L, 104-108	16-15
1-11	SAN ANTONIO	L, 91-109	16-16
1-13	DALLAS	W, 112-96	17-16
1-14	at Atlanta	L, 91-108	17-17
1-16	at Philadelphia	L, 108-123	17-18
1-19	at Dallas	L, 103-113	17-19
1-21	at Houston	L, 120-126	17-20
1-22	at San Antonio	L, 109-123	17-21
1-25	PHOENIX	L, 119-121	17-22
1-27	BOSTON	W, 103-94	18-22
1-29	MINNESOTA	W, 112-103	19-22
1-30	at Indiana	L, 106-110	19-23
2-5	at Cleveland	L, 89-109	19-24
2-7	SEATTLE	L, 101-103	19-25
2-9	MIAMI	L, 105-106	19-26
2-10	at New Jersey	L, 86-109	19-27
2-12	NEW JERSEY	W, 106-97	20-27
2-14	at Charlotte	L, 106-117	20-28
2-16	ORLANDO	W, 124-120 (OT)	21-28
2-17	at Miami	L, 107-111	21-29
2-23	PHILADELPHIA	W, 101-89	22-29
2-26	NEW YORK	W, 108-80	23-29
2-27	MILWAUKEE	L, 93-95	23-30
3-1	BOSTON	W, 99-95	24-30
3-3	UTAH	L, 98-106	24-31
3-5	at Boston	L, 101-105	24-32
3-7	at Milwaukee	W, 98-91	25-32
3-9	L.A. LAKERS	L, 121-123	25-33
3-11	DENVER	W, 112-104	26-33
3-14	CHICAGO	W, 101-99	27-33
3-16	at Sacramento	W, 113-110	28-33
3-17	at Utah	L, 80-104	28-34
3-19	at Phoenix	L, 97-127	28-35
3-21	at L.A. Lakers	W, 106-101	29-35
3-22	at Golden State	L, 91-96	29-36
3-26	CHARLOTTE	W, 115-107	30-36
3-28	CLEVELAND	W, 91-78	31-36
3-30	at Orlando	L, 91-105	31-37
3-31	PORTLAND	W, 120-111	32-37
4-2	SACRAMENTO	W, 109-100	33-37
4-6	WASHINGTON	W, 91-79	34-37
4-8	at New Jersey	W, 100-98	35-37
4-9	at Boston	W, 105-90	36-37
4-11	at Washington	W, 106-94	37-37
4-12	CHICAGO	L, 95-98	37-38
4-14	ATLANTA	W, 87-84	38-38
4-16	at Charlotte	L, 93-127	38-39
4-17	at New York	L, 85-95	38-40
4-20	at Cleveland	L, 81-105	38-41
4-22	at Chicago	L, 103-109 (OT)	38-42
4-23	INDIANA	W, 109-104	39-42
4-25	NEW JERSEY	W, 116-110	40-42

(Home games in CAPS)

VOICES OF THE PISTONS

George Blaha

Fred McLeod

When fans dial in a Pistons radio or TV broadcast, they get more than just the score, how much time remains or a garden-variety description of who has the ball. They get a crash course in shorthand.

"Joe D. two-timed, gets rid of it to Zeke for the flying finger-roll off the window! He fills it up!" Translation: Joe Dumars eluded a double-team by passing to Isiah Thomas, who drove and banked a short basket off the backboard.

"Worm blows the bunny!" Dennis Rodman missed a layup, in other words.

"Eight and 20 to go in the second." That means eight minutes and 20 seconds are left in the second quarter.

"Reggie with the triple try, he air-mailed it from 22! Pulled down by Spider!" Indiana's Reggie Miller shot a 3-point airball, caught by John Salley.

The shorthand teacher is the longtime Voice of the Pistons, George Blaha, whose unique play-by-play style is as sure a sign of winter in Michigan as a snowstorm, only much more welcome. Contrary to the spelling, there is no blah in Blaha, his bucolic upbringing in Iowa, northern Michigan and Wisconsin notwithstanding.

For more than half of their history, since 1976, Blaha has been the Pistons' primary radio broadcaster, TV announcer or both — often on the same night. For years, his play-by-play aired simultaneously on radio and TV. Since the addition of cable coverage on PASS (Pro-Am Sports Systems) in 1984, with popular Fred McLeod at the mike, Blaha handles only the WWJ radio broadcast when PASS is televising. When Pistons flagship Channel 50 is airing the game, Blaha calls the telecasts and turns over the radio mike to WWJ's Larry Henry. On March 29, 1991, on his 47th birthday, Blaha called his 1,000th Pistons game.

Having once said, "If wanting the Pistons to win makes me a homer, then I stand convicted," Blaha sprinkles his call with unique witticisms and shortcuts that are immediately recognizable to regular listeners. They are spoken less out of over-familiarity with the players than as a time-saver, allowing himself and listeners to keep up with a fast game, especially on radio where he must paint a word-picture.

Pistons fans have never required an explanation when Blaha referred to "Billy" (Laimbeer), "the Dobber" (Bob Lanier) or "John Eddie" (John Long) and his "rock-set J," Long's jump-shot on which he would rock on the balls of his feet. When Blaha mentioned "V.J." in his play-by-play, he didn't need to tell anybody he was talking about Vinnie Johnson, his radio partner since 1994. When he said "Kelly" or "K.T.," listeners knew that meant Kelly Tripucka, his TV color analyst since 1993.

Johnson and Tripucka are the most recent on a long list of Blaha's broadcast partners. Beginning with Tom Hemmingway in 1976, he has shared the mike with all sorts of former players, coaches killing time between jobs and guys who actually make their living on the airwaves. Among them: Dave Bing, John "Crash" Mengelt, Greg Kelser, Mike Fratello, Hubie Brown, Ron Rothstein, Dick Motta, John MacLeod, Ray Scott, Frank Beckmann, Stu Klitenic and Skip Macholz.

On the cable side, McLeod has been the Pistons' play-by-play man for all 13 seasons, bringing an enthusiastic and informative style to the coverage. He, too, has had several broadcast partners over the years, ranging from Pistons president Tom Wilson, whose company position didn't inhibit him from voicing critical opinions, to Detroit-area NBA products Tim McCormick and Kelser, the latter McLeod's current partner.

Before the '70s — essentially before Lanier showed up — Pistons on-the-air coverage was sporadic at best, especially in the early days. WJBK's Bill Flemming, later of ABC fame, was the Pistons' first radio play-by-play man, calling occasional games in the late-'50s and early-'60s. More often than not, the team's only broadcast presence consisted of a phoned-in report to Al Ackerman's late-night sports show.

Flemming was succeeded in 1962 by Don Wattrick, who later served as the Pistons' general manager from November 1964 until his death of a heart attack the following October. Milt Hopwood spent six seasons on the radio mike — five as the play-by-play man and then as Paul Carey's analyst when WJR took over the broadcasts in 1969. For the first time in team history, all home games were aired by WJR, sponsored by Stroh Brewery. When Carey joined Ernie Harwell on the Tigers' broadcasts in '73, the Pistons hired Don Howe and he handled the duties until Blaha's '76 arrival. Paul Keels and Mark Champion preceded Henry as the stand-in radio voice on WWJ when Blaha was working games on Channel 50.

The team's TV presence was also hit-and-miss in the '60s, some years not getting on the tube at all. Hemmingway called 13 games in 1967-68, sponsored by Carling, and then Ray Lane and ex-coach Earl Lloyd were the telecast team in '71-72, with Lane soon succeeded by Dave Diles. Bob Wolff bridged the TV gap until Blaha took over.

The list of predecessors is long, but for many, the Voice of the Pistons is, was and always will be George Blaha.

That's "G.B." in shorthand.

Primary Pistons Broadcasters

TELEVISION

Tenure	Broadcaster
1967-68	Tom Hemmingway
1971-72	Ray Lane
1973-75	Dave Diles
1975-78	Bob Wolff
1978-97	George Blaha (Ch. 50)
1984-97	Fred McLeod (PASS)

RADIO

Tenure	Broadcaster
1957-62	Bill Flemming
1962-64	Don Wattrick
1964-69	Milt Hopwood
1969-73	Paul Carey
1973-76	Don Howe
1976-80	George Blaha
1980-82	Paul Keels
1982-97	George Blaha
1991-96	Mark Champion
1996-97	Larry Henry

Dave Diles

Paul Carey (center) and Milt Hopwood (right) took over the radio duties for WJR-760 in 1969.

1993 1994

DETROIT PISTONS

TIME CAPSULE

October 6, 1993:
Having led the Chicago Bulls to three straight NBA titles, Michael Jordan shocks the sports world by announcing his retirement.

January 17, 1994:
An earthquake in Southern California kills 57.

June 17, 1994:
Former NFL star O.J. Simpson, charged with murdering his ex-wife and her friend, leads police on a 60-mile highway chase before returning home.

August 12, 1994:
Major League baseball players go on strike, leading to the September 14 cancellation of the season, including the World Series.

SEASON SNAPSHOT

Most Points
Joe Dumars (1,410, 20.4 avg.)

Most Rebounds
Terry Mills (672, 8.4 avg.)

Most Assists
Isiah Thomas (399, 6.9 avg.)

Most Minutes
Terry Mills (2,773, 34.7 avg.)

Field-Goal Percentage
Cadillac Anderson (54.3%)

Free-Throw Percentage
Joe Dumars (83.6%)

Team Offense Average
96.9 (7,949 in 82 games)

Team Defense Average
104.7 (8,587 in 82 games)

1993-94

FINAL STANDINGS

Central Division	W	L	Pct.	GB
Atlanta	57	25	.695	—
Chicago	55	27	.671	2
Cleveland	47	35	.573	10
Indiana	47	35	.573	10
Charlotte	41	41	.500	16
Milwaukee	20	62	.244	37
PISTONS	**20**	**62**	**.244**	**37**

Atlantic Division Winner—New York
Midwest Division Winner—Houston
Pacific Division Winner—Seattle

PLAYOFF RESULTS

Pistons Did Not Qualify

PISTONS PLAYOFF LEADERS

NBA CHAMPION

Houston Rockets

1993-94
SEASON IN REVIEW

More than any season in Pistons history, 1993-94 was one of true transition. Out with the old, in with the new. Too proud to hang on past their primes, Isiah Thomas and Bill Laimbeer said goodbye, the latter a month into the season. Dennis Rodman was traded to San Antonio before the season for All-Star forward Sean Elliott; it seemed like a good deal at the time. And Lindsey Hunter (10th pick) and Allan Houston (11th) became the first lottery draftees in team history. But the transition year wouldn't be complete until after the Pistons compiled a dreadful 20-62 record, their second-worst ever behind the 16-66 in '79-80. The poor finish left the Pistons with the No. 3 draft slot, which they would spend in June on franchise-star-to-be Grant Hill. But to qualify for Hill, Detroit had to endure a season featuring losing streaks of 14 (tying the team record) and 13, as well as a 1-20 skid. Laimbeer's retirement December 1 after 13 games foretold the collapse, then Thomas followed him out the door April 19 after tearing his Achilles tendon in Game 79 against Orlando. It was hard to believe any team with Isiah could go 20-62, but it did. Laimbeer's retirement left the low post manned by Terry Mills (17.3) and the overmatched Olden Polynice and Cadillac Anderson, while Elliott (12.1 ppg) was a huge disappointment. Joe Dumars (20.4) kept the club afloat.

Terry Mills' excellent season on both ends was a bright spot in '93-94. Photo by Allen Einstein.

April 19, 1994

WHAT A NIGHT!

"I left it all on the court—my heart, guts and soul. You're not supposed to save anything." With those words, Isiah Thomas bid a contented farewell to his NBA playing career on April 19, 1994 after an embarrassing 132-104 Palace loss to Orlando. It was somehow poetic that Thomas, one of the toughest guys ever to lace up high-tops, limped into retirement with a torn right Achille tendon. He blew it out with 1:37 left in the third quarter, trying to drive around Magic rookie Penny Hardaway. "It felt like I got shot with a cannon," he said. "Or I thought someone kicked me or somebody threw something out of the stands." Throughout his 13-year career, Isiah overcame countless busted fingers, swollen eyes and ankle sprains, but the last injury underscored the toll a big man's game exacted on the most courageous of 6-footers. Many had anticipated it would be Isiah's final home game and he confirmed as much during pregame introductions, bowing as the fans gave him a two-minute ovation. But he couldn't follow the script, scoring only 12 points in 26 minutes and shooting 4-of-18 with four airballs. "I was very nervous, the most nervous I've ever been for a game, even the NBA Finals," Isiah admitted. "My concentration wasn't 100 percent on the game."

On Isiah Thomas' final night in a Pistons uniform, the fans let him know what he meant to them. Photo by Allen Einstein.

Lindsey Hunter

After two years on the trading block, Lindsey Hunter became a functional part of the Pistons' nucleus.

The Lindsey Hunter drafted by the Pistons in 1993 wasn't the same one who emerged as a dependable starter in '96-97. When Detroit drafted him 10th overall, making the Jackson State guard its first-ever lottery pick, many hoped Hunter would become Isiah Thomas' successor. Isiah fed the perception, saying, "He's the first one I've seen come into the league since myself and Tim Hardaway in terms of doing things with the ball and dribbling on the move." But it wasn't so cut and dried. Just because a player is 6-foot-2 doesn't make him a point guard. Hunter struggled with the finer points, especially fast-break decision-making. For all of his athletic greatness—his first NBA basket was a breakaway dunk off a steal—Hunter seemed like a player without a position. A broken right foot in his second season set him back further, costing him 40 games and sending him to the trading block. Enter coach Doug Collins. "My first goal is to restore Lindsey's confidence," he said in 1995 on the day he became coach. "I want to make him the best defensive point guard in the NBA." Collins' plan was to take the ball from Hunter on offense, letting him float as a perimeter shooter, while having him concentrate on defending the opponent's lead guard. It was a stroke of brilliance. Hunter began to emerge in '95-96, starting half the season and averaging 8.5 points, and then fully bloomed in '96-97. Starting 76 games and playing all 82, he averaged a career-best 14.2 points while making 166 3-pointers to rank second on the team; his 129 steals also ranked second. Hunter made an amazing overhead tip-in to force OT in an eventual victory February 28 at Boston and then scored a career-high 30 points in the '96-97 finale at Indiana.

AT A GLANCE

LINDSEY HUNTER

FULL NAME:
Lindsey Benson Hunter Jr.

BORN:
December 3, 1970; Jackson, Mississippi

POSITION, HEIGHT, WEIGHT:
Guard, 6-foot-2, 195 pounds

COLLEGE:
Jackson (Mississippi) State, '93

TENURE WITH PISTONS:
1993-94 — 1996-97

BEST SEASON WITH PISTONS:
1996-97, 82 GP, 14.2 ppg, 2.8 rpg

TOTALS WITH PISTONS:
Regular season: 286 GP, 10.5 ppg, 3.1 apg
Playoffs: 7 GP, 11.6 ppg, 2.9 rpg

HONORS:
All-Rookie Team: Second Team 1993-94

PISTON LIST

Highest Overall Draft Picks

1. Jimmy Walker, Providence, 1967
1. Bob Lanier, St. Bonnie, 1970
2. Charlie Tyra, Louisville, 1957
2. Dave Bing, Syracuse, 1966
2. Isiah Thomas, Indiana, 1981
3. Grant Hill, Duke, 1994
4. Bailey Howell, Mississippi State, 1959
4. Jackie Moreland, Lousiana Tech., 1960
4. Ray Scott, Portland, 1961
4. Joe Caldwell, Arizona State, 1964
4. Sonny Dove, St. John's, 1967
4. Terry Driscoll, Boston College, 1969
4. Leon Douglas, Alabama, 1976
4. Greg Kelser, Michigan State, 1979
5. Eddie Miles, Seattle, 1963

CHANGING FACES

THE PISTONS couldn't get rid of Dennis Rodman fast enough. Then they couldn't replace his replacement fast enough. New GM Billy McKinney was hailed as a Jack McCloskey clone on October 1, 1993 when he traded the increasingly unmanageable Rodman, getting All-Star forward Sean Elliott from San Antonio. The trouble was, Elliott never fit into the tougher Eastern style, mainly because he was no longer alongside a dominant center like David Robinson. On February 4, Detroit thought it had traded Elliott to Houston for Robert Horry and Matt Bullard, but the Rockets nixed the deal because they feared Elliott's kidney condition. The retirements of Bill Laimbeer and Isiah Thomas were the season's big personnel moves. "I don't have the desire to compete anymore. It's just gone," Laimbeer said. Aside from the elevation of assistant Don Chaney to head coach, the Pistons altered their look by signing center Cadillac Anderson and waiving Mark Aguirre. Other additions were Mark Macon (for Alvin Robertson), Pete Chilcutt (for Olden Polynice) and Charles Jones.

The Sean Elliott trade was a titanic failure for the Pistons.

Take a Bow

Vinnie Johnson

Vinnie Johnson and Isiah Thomas enjoy Vinnie's big night. Isiah would join him in retirement three months later. Photo by Allen Einstein.

The Pistons gave Hoo his due February 5, 1994. In doing so, they gave The Microwave (what else?) an engraved microwave oven. Vinnie Johnson, known as Hoo to teammates and The Microwave to fans, had his familiar No. 15 retired to the delight of a sold-out Palace. He joined Dave Bing (21) and Bob Lanier (16) whose jerseys already hung in the rafters. Johnson had made himself a Pistons immortal with a last-second jumper to clinch the 1990 NBA Finals against Portland. When he was waived in 1991, Johnson had played more games (798) than anyone in Pistons history. "The greatest thrills of my career were us winning the back-to-back championships, hitting the winning shot and having my number retired," Johnson said in a halftime ceremony featuring lots of gifts, fireworks and speeches. "When Vinnie had it going, nobody on the planet could stop him," said emcee George Blaha, Johnson's TV-radio partner. Isiah Thomas said, "All of us know Vinnie could have gone to any other team and been a superstar."

Game Results

1993-94 REGULAR SEASON

Date	Opponent	Result	Record
11-5	MINNESOTA	W, 104-99	1-0
11-6	at Indiana	W, 113-107	2-0
11-9	WASHINGTON	L, 112-118	2-1
11-11	at L.A. Clippers	L, 99-111	2-2
11-12	at Utah	L, 89-109	2-3
11-14	at Portland	L, 111-114	2-4
11-17	ORLANDO	W, 98-92	3-4
11-19	SAN ANTONIO	W, 95-86	4-4
11-21	PHILADELPHIA	W, 103-89	5-4
11-24	BOSTON	L, 103-118	5-5
11-27	at New York	L, 85-112	5-6
11-28	GOLDEN STATE	L, 88-91	5-7
11-30	at Cleveland	L, 74-92	5-8
12-2	PHOENIX	L, 101-102	5-9
12-7	at Orlando	L, 89-91	5-10
12-8	ATLANTA	L, 97-105	5-11
12-10	MILWAUKEE	L, 88-90	5-12
12-11	at Minnesota	W, 92-80	6-12
12-14	L.A. LAKERS	L, 93-99	6-13
12-16	at Washington	W, 97-95	7-13
12-18	CLEVELAND	W, 98-92 (OT)	8-13
12-20	at Philadelphia	L, 92-121	8-14
12-21	CHARLOTTE	L, 97-108	8-15
12-23	CHICAGO	L, 72-81	8-16
12-27	at Charlotte	L, 94-109	8-17
12-28	at Atlanta	L, 101-119	8-18
12-30	SACRAMENTO	L, 91-97	8-19
1-2	MIAMI	L, 85-93	8-20
1-4	at Chicago	L, 91-97	8-21
1-8	INDIANA	L, 92-101	8-22
1-11	DENVER	L, 86-94	8-23
1-13	NEW YORK	L, 80-94	8-24
1-15	at New York	L, 88-97	8-25
1-17	UTAH	L, 94-109	8-26
1-18	at Milwaukee	L, 91-123	8-27
1-21	at Miami	W, 118-98	9-27
1-22	at Washington	L, 93-98	9-28
1-24	CHICAGO	L, 86-92	9-29
1-26	at Golden State	L, 92-108	9-30
1-28	at L.A. Lakers	L, 97-105	9-31
1-29	at Denver	L, 110-125	9-32
1-31	CLEVELAND	L, 103-107	9-33
2-2	MILWAUKEE	W, 104-90	10-33
2-4	SEATTLE	L, 84-108	10-34
2-5	NEW JERSEY	L, 100-107	10-35
2-7	at Atlanta	L, 97-141	10-36
2-9	at Boston	W, 102-95	11-36
2-10	HOUSTON	L, 81-104	11-37
2-15	WASHINGTON	W, 100-93	12-37
2-17	at San Antonio	L, 96-115	12-38
2-19	at Dallas	W, 105-96	13-38
2-21	DALLAS	L, 88-98	13-39
2-25	at Indiana	L, 90-110	13-40
2-26	MIAMI	L, 100-105	13-41
3-1	at New Jersey	L, 98-108	13-42
3-2	PORTLAND	L, 107-131	13-43
3-5	at Milwaukee	L, 108-117	13-44
3-7	NEW YORK	L, 85-99	13-45
3-9	NEW JERSEY	W, 114-97	14-45
3-11	CLEVELAND	W, 98-96	15-45
3-12	ATLANTA	L, 92-104	15-46
3-14	at Sacramento	W, 108-102	16-46
3-15	at Seattle	W, 89-87	17-46
3-18	at Phoenix	L, 114-113	18-46
3-19	at Houston	L, 88-106	18-47
3-23	L.A. CLIPPERS	W, 111-107	19-47
3-25	CHARLOTTE	L, 92-106	19-48
3-27	at Cleveland	L, 99-111	19-49
3-29	at Miami	W, 123-115	20-49
4-1	at Chicago	L, 95-102	20-50
4-3	CHICAGO	L, 93-96	20-51
4-5	at Indiana	L, 89-105	20-52
4-8	at Orlando	L, 103-117	20-53
4-10	BOSTON	L, 111-116	20-54
4-12	PHILADELPHIA	L, 107-134	20-55
4-13	at Boston	L, 96-109	20-56
4-15	at New Jersey	L, 114-119	20-57
4-17	INDIANA	L, 99-104	20-58
4-19	ORLANDO	L, 104-132	20-59
4-20	at Milwaukee	L, 78-103	20-60
4-23	at Charlotte	L, 103-108	20-61
4-24	at Philadelphia	L, 102-110	20-62

(Home games in CAPS)

GRANT HILL

After three straight seasons of missing the playoffs, the Pistons had gotten used to bad news and bad luck. It seemed to be their payback for the success of the Bad Boys, a karmic balancing of the ledgers.

Then, suddenly, look who falls into their lap: Grant Hill, too good to be true.

The Pistons would not have dared predict a greater turnaround for the franchise than the 1994 draft addition of Hill, a multi-talented 6-foot-8 small forward from Duke. To succeed in the NBA, a team must have at least one superstar. How lucky for the Pistons that merely two months after losing their touchstone player, Isiah Thomas, to retirement, they acquired Hill, a player capable of breaking Thomas' records.

In fact, there are parallels in how the Pistons drafted Thomas and Hill. In 1981, with Dallas picking first and Detroit second, the Pistons were hot for Thomas, but feared that Dallas would draft him. No problem. In a predraft visit to Dallas, Thomas intentionally gave a bad impression. He made it clear to the Mavericks they'd be making a mistake to draft him. So the Mavs took DePaul's

Mark Aguirre, leaving Thomas for the Pistons.

In Hill's case, with Milwaukee set on taking Glenn Robinson No. 1, that left Dallas (No. 2) and Detroit (No. 3) to battle over Hill and Jason Kidd. Hill visited Detroit first and was so taken after meeting with GM Billy McKinney, coach Don Chaney and Joe Dumars that he decided to call off his visit to Dallas. The Mavs, fearing drafting an unhappy camper, went with Kidd instead, leaving Hill for the Pistons. In Detroit's draft room at The Palace, McKinney excitedly leapt into the arms of club president Tom Wilson. In announcing the pick to the media, McKinney fought back tears and said, "I promised God an awful lot of things last night." And Dumars said, "In 15 years, I'll be telling my children, 'See that guy? I played with him.' Grant's going to be a very special player."

At Indianapolis, where the draft was being held at the RCA Dome, Hill was similarly thrilled. "I don't mind being picked third because Detroit is where I wanted to go all along," he said, not wearing the painted-

---

AT A GLANCE

GRANT HILL

FULL NAME:
Grant Henry Hill
BORN:
October 5, 1972; Dallas
POSITION, HEIGHT, WEIGHT:
Forward-guard, 6-foot-8, 225 pounds
COLLEGE:
Duke, '94
ACQUIRED:
1994, Pistons' No. 1 draft pick (3rd overall)

TENURE WITH PISTONS:
1994-95 — present
BEST SEASON WITH PISTONS:
1996-97, 80 GP, 21.4 ppg, 9.0 rpg, 7.3 apg, 1.8 spg
TOTALS WITH PISTONS:
Regular season: 230 GP, 4,722 pts. (20.5), 1,949 reb. (8.5), 1,484 ast. (6.5)
Playoffs: 8 GP, 175 pts. (21.9), 56 reb. (7.0), 38 ast. (4.8)
HONORS:
NBA Rookie of the Year: 1994-95
NBA All-Rookie Team: First Team 1994-95
NBA IBM Award: 1996-97
All-NBA Team: First Team 1996-97; Second Team 1995-96
All-Star Game (3): 1994-95, 1995-96, 1996-97
All-Star vote leader: 1994-95, 1995-96
NBA Triple-Double Leader: 1995-96 (10), 1996-97 (13)

PISTON LIST

Grant Hill's Highest-Scoring Games

38 points
- April 20, 1997 at Indiana (OT)

35 points
- April 1, 1997 at Dallas
- March 2, 1996 at L.A. Clippers
- November 22, 1995 vs. Washington

34 points
- January 18, 1997 at L.A. Lakers (OT)
- January 29, 1996 at Utah

33 points
- January 22, 1997 at Sacramento
- November 30, 1995 vs. Miami
- April 21, 1995 at Atlanta
- April 2, 1995 vs. Washington
- March 25, 1995 vs. Boston

32 points
- March 23, 1995 vs. Dallas

31 points
- 6 occasions

on smile of a draftee for a losing team. "I'm happy for the guys who went in front of me and behind me, but I'm really happy for myself. To me, Detroit represents all that's good about pro sports. They've won before, they have good players and good fans. It's a good fit. The Pistons are struggling a little now, but they'll be back. I think I can help them."

Help? Starting with Hill's shared Rookie to the Year award (with Kidd) and culminating with his All-NBA first-team selection in 1996-97, he's led the Pistons to an amazing transformation in three years. From 20 wins the season before he arrived, the Pistons have won 28, 46 and 54 with Hill in command. So far, playoff success has been elusive for Hill, with first-round losses to Orlando (1996) and Atlanta ('97), and that is how his career will eventually be judged. But coach Doug Collins, hired after Hill's first season to aid his development, said there is no reason to worry that Hill will never be a postseason star. "People forget that Michael Jordan lost nine of his first 10 playoff games," said Collins, who coached Jordan from 1986-89. "Grant's still learning. It's a process you have to go through. As much as you'd like to rush it, you can't."

Though Hill's abundant skills — quick first step, great leaper, terrific floor sense — are more akin to Scottie Pippen, it's Jordan to whom Hill is usually compared. Collins winces at the comparisons, but concedes that there are certain similarities.

"Grant's like Michael in that they're handsome, they come from great families and they're also tremendous athletes," Collins said. "There's almost a magnetic thing that draws you to certain people. Michael has that greatness and Grant has it.

He's got an aura about him and people are attracted to him. Grant's the kind of guy people feel they can go up and talk to or ask for an autograph. Certain guys give you a sense of 'Don't come near me,' but Grant has an attractive aura like Michael."

It's that nice-guy reputation that quickly made Hill the darling of fans and media, as well as Madison Avenue. He has become one of the leading product endorsers in all of sports. But Hill chuckles at his Mr. Clean rep. "Anybody who knows me knows I'm not perfect," he said. "My parents (ex-NFL star Calvin and Janet Hill) know that more than anyone. I think they're kind of amused by a lot of stuff they see written about me. But I sense that they're proud of their child, that he's doing well and people like him and think he's a good person."

Despite Hill's claims of imperfection, it's difficult to find anyone to say anything bad about him. Like, maybe doesn't tip well. Or he leaves a sloppy hotel room. Or he doesn't help little old ladies across the street. Or perhaps once, with nobody watching, he liberated too much change from the take-a-penny, leave-a-penny dish at 7-Eleven. Sorry, nothing to report. Three years after he burst into the NBA, all arms and legs and gangly enthusiasm, the Grant Hill love-fest continues in full pucker. If Jordan is the NBA's king, Hill is surely its handsome, dutiful prince, beloved by the masses, but never failing to bow before wise elders.

With today's young NBA players being criticized left and right — too unpolished, too worried about their contract, too many oily hangers-on — Hill is almost always excluded from such rants. Old-timers cite him as a museum-quality replica of a bygone era

when players at least feigned respect for coaches, front-office types and the game. On and off the court, Hill is the perfect camera-friendly personality to lead the NBA into the new millenium.

"Grant is a very special player, both in the way he plays the game and how he carries himself off the court," Utah Jazz veteran John Stockton said at the 1997 All-Star Game in Cleveland. "Grant's just beginning his career. We're just seeing the tip of the iceberg, and it's exciting to wonder what's underneath that."

"Grant's game is all about making everyone else better. That's why he's a superstar," Magic Johnson said. "I'm glad he's stopped listening to the media comparing him to Michael Jordan and just be Grant Hill. Michael Jordan is Michael Jordan. Grant should just be himself. Grant will make his mark by making people better, by being a triple-double guy. His game isn't flash, it's delivering every single night."

Which is essentially what Hill has done. While leading the Pistons in scoring all three seasons (19.9, 20.2 and 21.4), he has also joined a rare group of NBA players who have led their team in scoring, rebounding and assists in the same season. He became the 15th player to do so in 1995-96, then repeated the feat in '96-97. He has played in three All-Star games, leading the fan balloting his first two years with record totals. In '97, while becoming the Pistons' first All-NBA first-teamer since Thomas in '86, Hill also won the NBA's IBM Award, a sort of MVP award that uses a statistical formula to determine the player who contributed most to his team's success.

Pistons fans could've answered that without a calculator.

Grant Hill's Regular-Season Statistics with Detroit

SEASON	G	GS	MIN	FGM	FGA	PCT	FTM	FTA	PCT	O-RB	D-RB	TOT	AST	PF	DQ	STL	TO	BLK	PTS	PPG	HI
1994-95	70	69	2678	508	1064	.477	374	511	.732	125	320	445	353	203	1	124	202	62	1394	19.9	33
1995-96	80	80	3260	564	1221	.462	485	646	.751	127	656	783	548	242	1	100	263	48	1618	20.2	35
1996-97	80	80	3147	625	1259	.496	450	633	.711	123	598	721	583	186	0	144	259	48	1710	21.4	38
TOTALS	230	229	9085	1697	3544	.479	1309	1790	.731	375	1574	1949	1484	631	2	368	724	158	4722	20.5	38

3-point FGs: 1994-95, 4-27 (.148); 1995-96, 5-26 (.192); 1996-97, 10-33 (.303). TOTALS, 19-86 (.221).

1994 1995

DETROIT PISTONS

TIME CAPSULE

November 5, 1994:
George Foreman, age 45, becomes the oldest heavyweight champion in boxing history by knocking out Michael Moorer.

April 19, 1995:
The deadliest terrorist attack ever on U.S. soil occurs in Oklahoma City, where 168 people are killed in the bombing of the Murrah Federal Building.

June 24, 1995:
Bidding for their first Stanley Cup since 1955, the Detroit Red Wings are swept in the Finals by the defensive-minded New Jersey Devils.

SEASON SNAPSHOT

Most Points
Grant Hill (1,394, 19.9 avg.)

Most Rebounds
Terry Mills (558, 7.8 avg.)

Most Assists
Joe Dumars (368, 5.5 avg.)

Most Minutes
Grant Hill (2,678, 38.3 avg.)

Field-Goal Percentage
Mark West (55.6%)

Free-Throw Percentage
Allan Houston (86.0%)

Team Offense Average
98.2 (8,053 in 82 games)

Team Defense Average
105.5 (8,651 in 82 games)

NBA Rookie of the Year
Grant Hill

Pistons in All-Star Game
Grant Hill, F (led balloting); Joe Dumars, G

1994-95

FINAL STANDINGS

Central Division	W	L	Pct.	GB
Indiana	52	30	.634	—
Charlotte	50	32	.610	2
Chicago	47	35	.573	5
Cleveland	43	39	.524	9
Atlanta	42	40	.512	10
Milwaukee	34	48	.415	18
PISTONS	**28**	**54**	**.341**	**24**

Atlantic Division Winner—Orlando
Midwest Division Winner—San Antonio
Pacific Division Winner—Phoenix

PLAYOFF RESULTS

Pistons Did Not Qualify

PISTONS PLAYOFF LEADERS

NBA CHAMPION

Houston Rockets

1994-95
SEASON IN REVIEW

hree seasons of post-Bad Boys depression, ill-fated personnel moves and rotten luck were washed away in one marvelous moment: the June 29 drafting of Grant Hill, the 6-foot-8 All-American guard-forward from Duke. Shorn of their franchise star, the retired Isiah Thomas, the lucky Pistons immediately replaced him with Hill on the No. 3 pick. It was quickly obvious Hill could be the one to break Thomas' countless team records. With the awesome first step of Michael Jordan, the versatility of Scottie Pippen and, refreshingly, the earnestness lacking in other entry-level players, Hill became the poster child for the Pistons' future and the NBA's as well. Despite missing 12 games with a sore foot, Hill confirmed all the great expectations by averaging a club-high 19.9 points, plus 6.4 rebounds. Only two other rookies, Dave Bing and Kelly Tripucka, had ever led the Pistons in scoring. At midseason, Hill became the first rookie to lead the All-Star voting (1,289,585), scoring 10 points for the East. After the season, in sharing Rookie of the Year honors with Dallas' Jason Kidd, Hill joined Bing as the only Pistons to win the award. But not even Hill's greatness could save Detroit from an injury-plagued 28-54 season. Allan Houston emerged as a potential star, but Lindsey Hunter was a disappointment before suffering a broken foot.

Grant Hill makes a speech to accept the NBA Rookie of the Year Award he shared with Dallas' Jason Kidd. Photo by Allen Einstein.

WHAT A NIGHT!

April 7, 1995

As amazing as Grant Hill had been in his rookie season, he hadn't been able to finish a triple-double—double-figures in points, rebounds and assists—and the Pistons hadn't had one since Isiah Thomas' in 1987. But Hill finally achieved the feat on April 7, 1995, helping Detroit end two long losing streaks. With Hill compiling 21 points, 11 rebounds and 10 assists, the Pistons upset Eastern Conference-leading Orlando 104-94 at The Palace. It was their first Friday win in more than a year and their first victory over a plus-.500 team in 19 games. Hill finished his triple-double with 2:18 to play, getting his 10th assist on an Oliver Miller dunk. A week earlier, Hill had fallen one assist short (26-12-9) vs. the Knicks, so he knew it was a matter of time. "It wasn't something I was pressing for," he said. "It was against the best team in the league and it's on national TV. But it's better that we won." Over the next two seasons, Hill's 23 triple-doubles would lead the NBA in both 1996 (10) and '97 (13). The Pistons had lost 17 straight Friday games, last winning March 18, 1994 at Phoenix. Also in the game, Allan Houston's four 3-pointers gave him a team-record 128 for the season.

This quickly became a familiar sight to Pistons fans: Grant Hill flying in for a layup. Photo by Allen Einstein.

Allan Houston

Once Allan Houston began getting regular minutes, his offensive skills overshadowed his defensive liabilities.

There are millionaires, and then there are Millionaires. In a span of 21 months, Allan Houston made an amazing transition from lower case to upper case. In doing so, he went from a potential-laden bench rider with a gorgeous jump shot to one of the NBA's top-paid shooting guards with a seven-year $56 million contract. Only one problem for the Pistons: he went somewhere else to get his checks, leaving Detroit after his third season for the monied New York Knicks, who acquired him during their free-agent blitz of July 1996. The defection shook the Pistons not only because Houston had told them he intended to re-sign, but because it left them with a 20-point hole in their lineup. Though they prospered despite his absence, with Lindsey Hunter admirably filling his buddy's old role, Houston's decision was especially baffling to the Pistons. Yes, he had languished on their bench, untested, for more than a year—his defense was too weak, Don Chaney contended—but the fact remains that new coach Doug Collins and Grant Hill's defense-drawing presence on the court helped Houston become the scorer who charmed the Knicks. Coaxed by Collins to supplement his stand-still jump shot with drives to the basket, Houston averaged 19.7 points in '95-96. He had averaged 24.8 over the last 24 games of '94-95, having emerged from the bench, "But they weren't winning points," Collins pointed out in 1996. "Now, these are meaningful points against teams that respect the Pistons." Then in the '96 playoffs, Houston led the club in scoring with a 25.0 average in a three-game loss to Orlando. Barely two months later he was gone to New York, leaving Detroit holding a bag full of unwanted cash.

AT A GLANCE

ALLAN HOUSTON

FULL NAME:
Allan Wade Houston
BORN:
April 4, 1971; Louisville, Kentucky
POSITION, HEIGHT, WEIGHT:
Guard, 6-foot-6, 210 pounds
COLLEGE:
Tennessee '93
TENURE WITH PISTONS:
1993-94 — 1995-96
Also: New York 1996-97
BEST SEASON WITH PISTONS:
1995-96, 82 GP, 19.7 ppg, 3.7 rpg
TOTALS WITH PISTONS:
Regular season: 237 GP, 14.3 ppg, 2.5 rpg
Playoffs: 3 GP, 25.0 ppg, 2.7 rpg

PISTON LIST

Allan Houston's Top-Scoring Games

38 points
- March 23, 1996 at Atlanta

36 points
- March 10, 1995 vs. Denver
- April 11, 1995 at Milwaukee (OT)

35 points
- March 14, 1995 at Phoenix
- March 19, 1995 at Golden State
- Nov. 26, 1995 vs. Houston

33 points
- Feb. 17, 1995 at Chicago

32 points
- Jan. 24, 1995 vs. Philadelphia
- March 29, 1995 vs. New York

31 points
- 4 occasions

30 points
- 2 occasions

CHANGING FACES

THERE WASN'T ANYONE in the Pistons' organization who didn't want Don Chaney to succeed as head coach. It's safe to say few people in Pistons history have been better liked than Chaney, who became coach on May 3, 1993 after the firing of one-year head man Ron Rothstein. Chaney fared little better, overseeing two seasons with a 48-116 total record and getting fired on April 25, 1995. He gave no parting speech, but said two weeks earlier, "The front office never told me the agenda has changed, that we had to make the playoffs. I hope we are still on the same page, because rebuilding can take four or five years." But it was no use. Management cleaned house, securing the resignation of GM Billy McKinney as well. "I feel I've done a great job and I wish I could stay to reap the benefits," McKinney said. Besides drafting Hill, Detroit's major acquisitions of '94-95 were the free-agent signings of portly Oliver Miller, Johnny Dawkins and Negele Knight and trades for centers Bill Curley (for Sean Elliott), Mark West and Eric Leckner.

Don Chaney had few answers for the Pistons' losing ways in '94-95. Photo by Allen Einstein.

Take a Bow

Bill Laimbeer

Bill Laimbeer's No. 40 hangs in the Palace rafters next to the Hammer Time banner he helped earn. Photo by Allen Einstein.

You'd have thought the Pistons were retiring Mother Teresa's jersey on February 4, 1995. The good Mother led mankind in assists, sure enough, but she couldn't rebound, swish the 3-pointer or throw the long outlet pass like Bill Laimbeer. Never were so many nice things said about Laimbeer in one place than during a 35-minute pregame ceremony that concluded with his old No. 40 hoisted to the rafters. Surrounded by family, former teammates and luminaries, Detroit's all-time rebounding king (9,430) accepted the kind words and gifts with humble grace. "Please sit down, please sit," he said, urging the fans to cut short their ovation. "I had a great run. I had a lot of fun. We had quite a ride all those years." Joe Dumars told Big Bill, "You were the consummate pro, the consummate player. If I had to pick one guy to get in a foxhole with, this is the guy I'd choose." And Isiah Thomas, next in line for jersey retirement, said despite differences in upbringing, politics and religion, "I fell in love with Bill Laimbeer as a man and a teammate."

Game Results

1994-95
REGULAR SEASON

Date	Opponent	Result	Record
11-4	L.A. LAKERS	L, 98-115	0-1
11-5	at Atlanta	W, 114-109 (OT)	1-1
11-8	MINNESOTA	W, 126-112	2-1
11-10	INDIANA	W, 112-110	3-1
11-12	at Charlotte	L, 100-113	3-2
11-15	PHILADELPHIA	W, 99-98	4-2
11-17	at Denver	W, 94-92	5-2
11-18	at Utah	L, 96-121	5-3
11-20	at Portland	L, 96-98	5-4
11-23	MILWAUKEE	W, 113-108	6-4
11-25	MIAMI	L, 97-111	6-5
11-27	GOLDEN STATE	W, 106-91	7-5
11-30	at Boston	L, 115-118	7-6
12-2	at Washington	L, 104-115	7-7
12-3	PHOENIX	W, 107-97	8-7
12-6	at Indiana	L, 83-90	8-8
12-9	CHICAGO	L, 96-117	8-9
12-10	at Cleveland	L, 79-87	8-10
12-13	at Chicago	L, 78-98	8-11
12-14	CHARLOTTE	L, 93-106	8-12
12-17	at Philadelphia	W, 97-92	9-12
12-21	at New Jersey	L, 99-117	9-13
12-23	ATLANTA	L, 77-97	9-14
12-27	MILWAUKEE	L, 88-98	9-15
12-28	at New York	L, 93-101	9-16
12-30	BOSTON	L, 107-124	9-17
1-3	at L.A. Lakers	L, 96-105	9-18
1-5	at Sacramento	L, 88-94	9-19
1-8	ORLANDO	L, 88-108	9-20
1-10	NEW JERSEY	W, 98-84	10-20
1-11	at Orlando	L, 107-124	10-21
1-13	at Minnesota	L, 92-104	10-22
1-16	at Philadelphia	W, 116-110	11-22
1-18	UTAH	L, 86-99	11-23
1-20	HOUSTON	L, 96-106	11-24
1-21	at Milwaukee	L, 100-120	11-25
1-24	PHILADELPHIA	W, 116-105	12-25
1-26	PORTLAND	L, 89-106	12-26
1-28	MIAMI	W, 89-85	13-26
1-30	L.A. CLIPPERS	W, 102-95	14-26
2-1	at Miami	L, 75-98	14-27
2-2	CLEVELAND	W, 85-83	15-27
2-4	ATLANTA	W, 84-78	16-27
2-6	at New Jersey	L, 97-101	16-28
2-7	WASHINGTON	W, 119-115	17-28
2-8	CHARLOTTE	L, 78-106	17-29
2-14	NEW YORK	W, 106-94	18-29
2-15	at Indiana	L, 88-114	18-30
2-17	at Chicago	L, 102-117	18-31
2-18	at Charlotte	L, 88-110	18-32
2-20	SACRAMENTO	W, 99-93	19-32
2-23	at Houston	L, 99-100	19-33
2-24	at San Antonio	L, 97-114	19-34
2-27	MILWAUKEE	W, 97-89	20-34
3-1	INDIANA	W, 92-79	21-34
3-3	at Atlanta	L, 78-94	21-35
3-4	at Dallas	W, 98-91	22-35
3-7	at Cleveland	L, 81-89	22-36
3-8	at Washington	W, 114-105	23-36
3-10	DENVER	L, 88-99	23-37
3-12	SEATTLE	L, 94-134	23-38
3-14	at Phoenix	L, 109-116	23-39
3-15	at L.A. Clippers	L, 87-117	23-40
3-18	at Seattle	L, 110-133	23-41
3-19	at Golden State	L, 115-117	23-42
3-21	NEW JERSEY	W, 102-95	24-42
3-23	DALLAS	L, 94-102	24-43
3-25	BOSTON	W, 104-103	25-43
3-27	SAN ANTONIO	L, 93-114	25-44
3-29	NEW YORK	L, 97-107	25-45
4-2	WASHINGTON	W, 110-105	26-45
4-5	at Orlando	L, 125-128	26-46
4-7	ORLANDO	W, 104-94	27-46
4-8	at New York	L, 96-113	27-47
4-11	at Milwaukee	L, 109-114 (OT)	27-48
4-12	CHICAGO	L, 113-124	27-49
4-14	CHARLOTTE	L, 86-94	27-50
4-15	at Boston	L, 104-129	27-51
4-18	CLEVELAND	W, 85-76	28-51
4-20	at Chicago	L, 105-120	28-52
4-21	at Atlanta	L, 111-128	28-53
4-23	at Miami	L, 105-129	28-54

(Home games in CAPS)

DOUG COLLINS

When the Pistons hired Doug Collins as coach on April 29, 1995, luring him back to the NBA after six years behind a TNT microphone, they gave him a five-year contract, a mandate and a mission. His assignment: grab the franchise by the lapels and promptly turn it in the right direction.

Though Collins inherited a club with two enviable talents—superstar-to-be Grant Hill and Joe Dumars—plus a No. 7 lottery pick in its pocket, it was still a team that had won only 28 games in 1994-95. Despite his admirable 137-109 record as coach of the Chicago Bulls from 1986-89, there were no guarantees Collins could revive the moribund Pistons.

Well, except in his own mind. Supremely confident and driven by the same core fire that made him a four-time All-Star guard in the 1970s, Collins had no intention of failing with his new club. In two seasons, he has mostly fulfilled his Detroit assignment, setting the franchise firmly on course to be a contender into the next century.

The turnaround has been nothing short of dizzying. In 1995-96, the Pistons made an 18-win gain—the most of any team—for a 46-

36 record, predictably losing the first round of the playoffs to Orlando. Then they bumped their win total to 54 in 1996-97, including a 24-17 road record, before losing to Atlanta in the first round. Not only did the latter season make Collins the fastest Pistons coach to 100 victories, it reversed the 28-54 record that led to his hiring.

"A hundred wins means a lot," Collins said. "It means we've averaged 50 wins a season for a franchise that was averaging 24 for the two years before. It means that we're doing things right." Joe Dumars said, "I'm happy for Doug. He came in and delivered."

The most amazing facet of the Pistons' transformation was that they did it essentially with leftovers from their 28-win club. They parlayed the 1996 lottery pick into power forward Otis Thorpe, but he was the only major acquisition in the two years. In addition, they had to overcome the loss of free agent Allan Houston to the Knicks in the summer of '96. They survived, and thrived, not only because of Grant Hill's development into an All-NBA player, but because Collins greatly improved Detroit's depth.

AT A GLANCE

DOUG COLLINS

FULL NAME:
Paul Douglas Collins
BORN:
July 28, 1951; Benton, Illinois
POSITION, HEIGHT, WEIGHT:
Guard, 6-foot-6, 180 pounds
COLLEGE:
Illinois State, '73

COACHING TENURE WITH PISTONS:
1995-97
Also: Chicago 1986-89
BEST SEASON WITH PISTONS:
1996-97, 82 GP, 54-28 (.659)
COACHING TOTALS WITH PISTONS:
Regular season: 164 GP, 100-64 (.610)
Playoffs: 8 GP, 2-6 (.250)
NBA PLAYING TENURE:
Philadelphia 1973-81
NBA PLAYING TOTALS:
Regular season: 421 GP, 16.0 ppg, 10.7 rpg
Playoffs: 14 GP, 16.9 ppg, 13.8 rpg
HONORS:
All-Star Game coach: 1996-97
All-Star Game player (4): 1976-80
No. 1 overall draft pick, 1973

PISTON LIST

Pistons' Improvement Since Collins' Hiring

	1994-95	1996-97
Wins	28	54
Finish	7th	T-3rd
Home Rec.	22-19	30-11
Road Rec.	6-35	24-17
Def. Avg.	105.5	88.9
Opp. FG Pct.	47.6	44.4
Opp. Reb	3,579	3,228
Reb. Deficit	-417	-78
Turnovers	1,318	1,041
Turn. Deficit	-32	154
Foul Deficit	-405	132
FG Pct.	46.1	46.4
FT Pct.	74.1	74.5

His most vital construction project was Lindsey Hunter. By turning the 1993 lottery pick into a defensive point guard, Collins allowed him to relax enough on the offensive end to become a steady scorer as well. Collins also found a new role for 6-foot-10 Terry Mills, letting him roam the perimeter for 3-pointers over shorter defenders. The addition of hardnosed backups like Don Reid and Michael Curry added a tougher edge.

"I'm very proud of the strides this group has made," Collins said. "The first year, we had to clean up the mess and see what we had. We had to establish ourselves as a team that would compete every night. This year, everybody predicted gloom and doom for us (after Houston left). Our players were out to prove we could be an excellent team and they did that. Anyone who would look at our team now—as opposed to 24 months ago—would have to say we've been successful."

The success confirms that Collins was correct in leaving his job with Turner Sports. Having been fired by the Bulls in 1989, Collins turned into one of the best basketball commentators in the business. In that six-year span, he turned down numerous coaching offers. When the Pistons started fishing for a new coach in 1995, Collins was strongly recommended by ex-Detroit coach Chuck Daly. "Chuck told me, 'Doug's the guy you should get, but you will never get him,' " Pistons president Tom Wilson said.

Indeed, Collins was in no hurry to leave TV. But he was greatly intrigued by the Pistons' offer, especially the opportunity to coach a player like Hill through his NBA infancy. "When I began looking at this job, no red flags came up like they had with other teams," he said. "I already had a great job, working 40 nights a year, but I felt if I passed this up, something this good might not come again."

On his first day on the job, Collins set the tone with an enthusiastic, blunt style. He declared an immediate end to post-Bad Boys softness; passive Pistons were put on notice. "I'll be very honest. This (previous) Pistons team was soft," he said. "When's the last time you heard of that? I mean, Rick Mahorn threw me over a press table twice." Collins was referring to a 1988 Pistons-Bulls brawl in which he tried to control the Detroit forward, only to be tossed aside. "When we played the Pistons in their glory days, if you drove the lane, you were looking at Mahorn, (Bill) Laimbeer, (Dennis) Rodman and (John) Salley. Their guards would rip your head off, too."

But Collins wasn't advocating brutishness for his new Pistons. "I'm just talking about playing tough. I'm talking about that five-minute period—not necessarily the last five minutes of the game—when a team says, 'Are we going to dig in here?' That's what we need to find out."

Aside from getting opponents to quit laughing at the Pistons, Collins' grand prescription surprised no one—make Hill the Pistons' go-to guy, rejuvenate the dispirited Dumars and deepen the talent base. Of Hill, he said, "There will be days when he's not very happy with me, because I'm not going to let him float. I'm not going to let him hide in the last three minutes of the game. He will not be a decoy."

Clearly, Collins' intensity for the game hadn't disappeared during his six seasons away from the game, it merely simmered. That became clear early in the 1995-96 season. When the Pistons got their first win after losing their first three games, tears could be seen in Collins' eyes afterward. In 1996-97, after a key 3-pointer by Mills, Collins jumped out and kissed him as he ran upcourt. Late in the season, in the closing seconds of a home win over his old Bulls, Collins quietly sobbed on the bench as NBC recorded the moment.

Oftentimes, his emotions have gone the other way, like after a Thanksgiving Eve loss to an inferior Washington team in 1995. "I hope everyone has a happy Thanksgiving, because I won't," Collins said, dead serious, in a live postgame press conference. That weekend, the call-in shows lit up with fans wondering which would come first: midseason or a counseling session between Collins and a licensed professional.

Collins' ultracompetitive nature hasn't been a hit with every player. Thorpe couldn't deal with it and was traded to Vancouver. Others have voiced occasional displeasure, but the results have been too fantastic for that to cause much of a ripple. Besides, Hill and Dumars have been vocal in their support of Collins. The coach, for his part, doesn't bother fighting his reputation, deserved or not.

"There might be a negative perception of me out there, but as a coach, your team will let you know whether they want to play for you," Collins said. "You'll see it in how they perform every day, how they approach their jobs, how they compete. If they didn't want me, I'd know by now. I think this team believes in me and appreciates me."

Doug Collins' NBA Coaching Record

		REGULAR SEASON				PLAYOFFS		
Year	Team	W	L	Pct.	Finish/Div.	W	L	Pct.
1986-87	Chicago	40	42	.488	5th/Central	0	3	.000
1987-88	Chicago	50	32	.610	2nd/Central	4	6	.400
1988-89	Chicago	47	35	.573	5th/Central	9	8	.529
1995-96	Detroit	46	36	.561	4th/Central	0	3	.000
1996-97	Detroit	54	28	.659	3rd/Central	2	3	.400
TOTALS	5 years	237	173	.578	TOTALS, 5 years	15	23	.395

1995 1996

TIME CAPSULE

September 6, 1995:
Cal Ripken of the Baltimore Orioles plays his 2,131st consecutive game, breaking the 56-year-old major league record of Lou Gehrig.

October 3, 1995:
After a yearlong trial, a jury finds O.J. Simpson not guilty of all charges in the slaying of his ex-wife and an acquaintance.

May 12, 1996:
A group of climbers is caught in a blizzard on Mount Everest; eight die, while others survive after days without food, water or sleep.

SEASON SNAPSHOT

Most Points
Grant Hill (1,618, 20.2 avg.)

Most Rebounds
Grant Hill (783, 9.8 avg.)

Most Assists
Grant Hill (548, 6.9 avg.)

Most Minutes
Grant Hill (3,260, 40.8 avg.)

Field-Goal Percentage
Otis Thorpe (53.0%)

Free-Throw Percentage
Allan Houston (82.3%)

Team Offense Average
95.4 (7,822 in 82 games)

Team Defense Average
92.9 (7,617 in 82 games)

NBA All-Stars
Grant Hill, F (Second Team)

Pistons in All-Star Game
Grant Hill, F (led balloting)

1995-96

FINAL STANDINGS

Central Division	W	L	Pct.	GB
Chicago	72	10	.878	—
Indiana	52	30	.634	20
Cleveland	47	35	.573	25
Atlanta	46	36	.561	26
PISTONS	**46**	**36**	**.561**	**26**
Charlotte	41	41	.500	31
Milwaukee	25	57	.305	47
Toronto	21	61	.256	51

Atlantic Division Winner—Orlando
Midwest Division Winner—San Antonio
Pacific Division Winner—Seattle

PLAYOFF RESULTS

Eastern First Round: Orlando d. Pistons, 3-0

PISTONS PLAYOFF LEADERS

Scoring: Allan Houston (25.0 avg.)
Rebounding: Otis Thorpe (11.7)
Assists: Grant Hill (3.7)

NBA CHAMPION

Chicago Bulls

1995-96
SEASON IN REVIEW

The Pistons finally learned how to win again in 1995-96. They learned how to compete for every loose ball, every minute, every night, and they were rewarded with the franchise's first playoff berth since 1992. It ended predictably with a 3-0 sweep by far-superior Orlando, but that took none of the luster off a 46-36 season that proved the value of good coaching. Doug Collins, the former Chicago coach, had been hired in May. His task? Take Grant Hill, exploit his star talent and surround him with a competitive supporting cast, as he had done in the late '80s with Michael Jordan and the Bulls. Not for a second did anyone think the Pistons were suddenly contenders, but they were no longer pushovers. Early victories over Seattle and Houston proved that, then road streaks of 4-1 and 6-2 reinforced it. The difference was defense, as the Pistons reduced their average allowance to 92.9 points, 12.6 less than the season before. The incomparable Hill, a savvy veteran in his second year, led the charge by lifting his averages to 20.1 points, 9.8 rebounds and 6.9 assists; he topped the NBA with 10 triple-doubles. Joe Dumars' injury-plagued year was offset by the emergence of shooting guard Allan Houston (19.7 ppg), the trade addition of forward Otis Thorpe (14.2 ppg, 8.4 rpg) and the nightly doggedness that made people quit laughing at the Pistons.

Grant Hill was the only NBA player to lead his team in points, rebounds and assists in 1995-96. Photo by Allen Einstein.

November 26, 1995

The Pistons had already beaten an excellent Seattle team two weeks earlier, so they had some idea that a new day had dawned in 1995-96. But that point was driven home November 26 when Terry Mills swished a rainbow 3-pointer in the final seconds to give them a 102-100 Palace victory over Houston, the two-time defending NBA champions. Mills broke out a personal slump in the fourth quarter, scoring 13 of his 19 points. He got the ball with the Rockets leading 100-99, courtesy of a 15-foot basket by Hakeem Olajuwon with 3.5 minutes left. Mills toed up behind the 3-point arc and fired. When the ball went through the hoop, he was mobbed by his teammates and they fell on the scorer's table at center court. "I knew I had time to shoot it; 3.5 seconds is a long time," Mills said. "It was a real confidence-builder." The victory lifted the Pistons to 5-6, prompting coach Doug Collins to say, "This team needs rewards. We're committed to doing things right and we need to win these games to get that reinforced." Mills wasn't Detroit's only hero. Allan Houston scored 35 points, one short of his then-career-high, while the normally dominant Olajuwon was limited to 19. The Rockets' 3-for-25 3-point shooting helped the Pistons' cause.

Terry Mills became the Pistons' designated 3-point bomber in 1995-96. Photo by Allen Einstein.

WHAT A NIGHT!

Otis Thorpe

It seemed like a great marriage, but the honeymoon was short and then divorce became inevitable. Otis Thorpe gave the Pistons one good season and one so-so season and he was suddenly gone, traded to Vancouver for a draft pick August 7, 1997. Like his previous three teams, the Pistons were never able to figure out Thorpe. He didn't have a malcontent's reputation when the Pistons acquired him in 1995, the first major addition of Doug Collins' regime. The 6-foot-10 power forward had helped Houston claim the 1994 NBA title, benefitting greatly from all the defensive attention paid to center Hakeem Olajuwon. Thorpe was traded to Portland in 1995 for Clyde Drexler, then came to the Pistons on September 20, 1995 for center Bill Curley, Randolph Childress and a flip-flopped first-round draft slot. The Pistons had needed a power player of Thorpe's ability for years—even in the Bad Boys era—and the early returns were positive. In '95-96, still remarkably durable in his 12th season, Thorpe was the only Piston to start every game and he averaged 14.2 points and 8.4 rebounds. After the season, he got a new three-year contract for $18 million. But the marriage quickly disintegrated in Thorpe's second season in Detroit. By nature taciturn and quiet, he didn't mesh well with Collins' keyed-up coaching style. The two began to clash, including a conspicuous sideline disagreement on February 2, 1997, Thorpe's 1,000th game. The situation eroded quickly after that, as Thorpe refused to speak to Collins, forcing the coach to relay instructions through assistants. Thorpe demanded a trade and got his wish, though he was dealt to the NBA's worst team, the 14-win Grizzlies. Detroit got a first-round pick between 1998 and 2003.

In 1996-97, Otis Thorpe surpassed 15,000 points, 9,000 rebounds and 1,000 games in his 13-year NBA career.

AT A GLANCE

OTIS THORPE

FULL NAME:
Otis Henry Thorpe
BORN:
August 5, 1962; Boynton Beach, Florida
POSITION, HEIGHT, WEIGHT:
Forward, 6-foot-10, 246 pounds
COLLEGE:
Providence
ACQUIRED:
1992, trade with Portland
TENURE WITH PISTONS:
1995-96 — 1996-97
BEST SEASON WITH PISTONS:
1995-96, 82 GP, 14.2 ppg, 8.4 rpg
TOTALS WITH PISTONS:
Regular season: 161 GP, 13.6 ppg, 8.1 rpg
Playoffs: 8 GP, 10.5 ppg, 8.4 rpg
HONORS:
All-Star Game (1): 1991-92 (Houston)

PISTON LIST

Most-Decisive Wins on Opening Night

(Record: 18-22)
23 points
- 10-17-67 vs. Cincinnati, 131-108
17 points
- 10-18-77 vs. New Jersey, 110-93
13 points
- 11-4-88 at Chicago, 107-94
11 points
- 11-6-87 vs. New York, 110-99
- 11-2-90 vs. Milwaukee, 115-104
Nine points
- 10-12-79 vs. Indiana, 114-105
Eight points
- 10-29-82 vs. Atlanta, 94-86
Seven points
- 10-12-71 at New York, 91-84
Six points
- 10-14-70 at Seattle, 123-117
- 10-28-83 vs. Boston, 127-121
- 11-1-96 vs. Indiana, 95-89

CHANGING FACES

MICHAEL CURRY had spanned the globe, looking for his basketball home. Italy. Spain. Germany. Belgium. France. Omaha. He'd been everywhere, a journeyman guard-forward, trying to fit in somewhere for more than a season. Starting January 31, 1996, Curry found a home with the Pistons as a backup defensive specialist. He signed a pair of 10-day contracts and coach Doug Collins liked him so well, the Pistons kept him for the rest of the season. Adding the energetic, team-oriented Curry was symbolic of the Pistons' refound competitiveness, as was the drafting of 6-foot-8 forward-center Don Reid on the final pick of the draft (58th). Though undersized, his nonstop effort made him a fixture in the rotation. Reid, from Georgetown, started 46 games at center and the Pistons went 30-16. The Pistons' other draft picks were lean shot-blocking center Theo Ratliff from Wyoming, guard Randolph Childress and small forward Lou Roe. Childress was traded to Portland (with Bill Curley) on September 20 for Otis Thorpe.

Michael Curry dunks over the Knicks' Patrick Ewing. Photo by Allen Einstein.

Take a Bow

Isiah Thomas

Isiah Thomas acknowledged the cheers on his special night. Photo by Allen Einstein.

Pistons owner Bill Davidson isn't known for speech-making, but he summed it up best February 17, 1996. "In 1981, we drafted Isiah Thomas. I had a dream and Isiah fulfilled it," Davidson told the packed Palace on the night of Isiah's jersey retirement. A festive Saturday culminated with a No. 11 banner raised to the rafters and the renaming of the arena's main entrance to Isiah Thomas Drive. It was a night to reflect on all that he'd meant to the franchise. Most conceded that without Thomas, The Palace would never have been built; the franchise was a loser before he showed up. Almost every prominent name in franchise history was in attendance and their words were glowing. "They're retiring your number, but they'll never retire your spirit," Chuck Daly said. "You were like the brother I never had," Bill Laimbeer said. Representing the old-timers, Bob Lanier said, "I bow to you. This is from someone who toiled here before you and never had their dream realized. We lived vicariously through you during the championship years."

Game Results

1995-96 REGULAR SEASON

Date	Opponent	Result	Record
11-3	NEW YORK	L, 100-106	0-1
11-4	at Washington	L, 89-100	0-2
11-7	at Charlotte	L, 96-108	0-3
11-8	PORTLAND	W, 107-100 (OT)	1-3
11-10	CLEVELAND	W, 100-80	2-3
11-15	SEATTLE	W, 94-87	3-3
11-17	UTAH	L, 81-86	3-4
11-18	at Cleveland	L, 90-93	3-5
11-22	WASHINGTON	L, 97-98	3-6
11-24	PHILADELPHIA	W, 101-78	4-6
11-26	HOUSTON	W, 102-100	5-6
11-27	at Orlando	L, 95-96	5-7
11-29	at Boston	L, 96-100	5-8
11-30	MIAMI	L, 107-118	5-9
12-2	ATLANTA	W, 104-96	6-9
12-4	at Denver	L, 82-85	6-10
12-7	at Vancouver	W, 93-84	7-10
12-8	at Golden State	W, 121-114 (OT)	8-10
12-10	at L.A. Lakers	L, 82-87	8-11
12-13	L.A. LAKERS	L, 98-101	8-12
12-15	NEW JERSEY	W, 105-98	9-12
12-16	at New York	L, 82-86	9-13
12-19	at Toronto	W, 94-82	10-13
12-20	MILWAUKEE	W, 102-77	11-13
12-22	at Miami	W, 84-75	12-13
12-23	ORLANDO	L, 79-94	12-14
12-26	GOLDEN STATE	W, 100-90	13-14
12-28	TORONTO	W, 113-91	14-14
12-30	CHARLOTTE	W, 102-100 (OT)	15-14
1-3	at Milwaukee	L, 82-96	15-15
1-6	WASHINGTON	W, 90-82	16-15
1-11	at Charlotte	W, 95-93	17-15
1-13	at New Jersey	W, 91-80	18-15
1-15	at Atlanta	L, 88-96	18-16
1-18	SAN ANTONIO	W, 100-98	19-16
1-19	at Indiana	L, 81-89	19-17
1-21	CHICAGO	L, 96-111	19-18
1-24	at San Antonio	W, 85-84	20-18
1-25	at Dallas	W, 93-92	21-18
1-27	at Houston	L, 85-105	21-19
1-29	at Utah	L, 97-106	21-20
2-1	INDIANA	W, 87-70	22-20
2-3	SACRAMENTO	L, 85-94	22-21
2-5	at New York	L, 91-97	22-22
2-7	ORLANDO	W, 97-83	23-22
2-14	at Philadelphia	W, 102-83	24-22
2-15	CHICAGO	L, 109-112 (OT)	24-23
2-17	TORONTO	W, 108-95	25-23
2-19	MINNESOTA	W, 113-83	26-23
2-21	NEW YORK	L, 110-113 (OT)	26-24
2-23	at Minnesota	L, 93-94	26-25
2-25	at Portland	W, 93-81	27-25
2-26	at Sacramento	W, 93-78	28-25
2-28	at Seattle	L, 80-96	28-26
3-1	at Phoenix	W, 102-97	29-26
3-2	at L.A. Clippers	W, 107-103	30-26
3-4	ATLANTA	W, 99-93	31-26
3-5	at Toronto	W, 105-84	32-26
3-7	at Chicago	L, 81-102	32-27
3-9	DALLAS	W, 92-91	33-27
3-11	L.A. CLIPPERS	W, 100-90	34-27
3-13	PHOENIX	W, 118-115	35-27
3-15	CLEVELAND	W, 80-69	36-27
3-17	DENVER	W, 91-81	37-27
3-19	at Orlando	L, 91-113	37-28
3-20	at Miami	L, 93-102	37-29
3-22	NEW JERSEY	W, 105-98	38-29
3-23	at Atlanta	L, 84-92	38-30
3-26	VANCOUVER	W, 86-75	39-30
3-30	MIAMI	L, 85-95	39-31
4-2	at Milwaukee	L, 98-105	39-32
4-3	CHARLOTTE	W, 98-83	40-32
4-5	at Philadelphia	W, 108-87	41-32
4-7	at Boston	L, 97-98	41-33
4-9	at New Jersey	W, 111-94	42-33
4-10	PHILADELPHIA	W, 92-76	43-33
4-13	at Indiana	L, 86-91	43-34
4-14	BOSTON	W, 105-96	44-34
4-17	INDIANA	W, 102-93	45-34
4-18	at Chicago	L, 79-110	45-35
4-20	at Cleveland	L, 73-75	45-36
4-21	MILWAUKEE	W, 108-92	46-36

PLAYOFFS

Eastern First Round—(Best-of-Five)

Date	Opponent	Result	Record
4-26	at Orlando	L, 92-112	0-1
4-28	at Orlando	L, 77-92	0-2
4-30	ORLANDO	L, 98-101	0-3

(Home games in CAPS)

1996 1997

TIME CAPSULE

December 26, 1996:
Coach Wayne Fontes is fired by the NFL's Detroit Lions after eight topsy-turvy seasons in which the club won one playoff game.

June 7, 1997:
Ending a 42-year drought, the Detroit Red Wings sweep the Philadelphia Flyers to win the Stanley Cup at Joe Louis Arena in Detroit.

July 4, 1997:
Pathfinder lands on Mars after a six-month flight, beaming back amazing panoramic photos and conducting scientific tests.

SEASON SNAPSHOT

Most Points
Grant Hill (1,710, 21.4 avg.)

Most Rebounds
Grant Hill (721, 9.0 avg.)

Most Assists
Grant Hill (583, 7.3 avg.)

Most Minutes
Grant Hill (3,147, 39.3 avg.)

Field-Goal Percentage
Otis Thorpe (53.2%)

Free-Throw Percentage
Michael Curry (89.8%)

Team Offense Average
94.2 (7,723 in 82 games)

Team Defense Average
88.9 (7,293 in 82 games)

NBA All-Stars
Grant Hill, F (First Team)

Pistons in All-Star Game
Grant Hill, F; Joe Dumars, G

FINAL STANDINGS

Central Division	W	L	Pct.	GB
Chicago	69	13	.841	—
Atlanta	56	26	.683	13
PISTONS	**54**	**28**	**.659**	**15**
Charlotte	54	28	.659	15
Cleveland	42	40	.512	27
Indiana	39	43	.476	30
Milwaukee	33	49	.402	36
Toronto	30	52	.366	39

Atlantic Division Winner—Miami
Midwest Division Winner—Utah
Pacific Division Winner—Seattle

PLAYOFF RESULTS

Eastern First Round: Atlanta d. Pistons 3-2

PISTONS PLAYOFF LEADERS

Scoring: Grant Hill (23.6 avg.)
Rebounding: Terry Mills (7.0)
Assists: Grant Hill (5.4)

NBA CHAMPION

Chicago Bulls

1996-97
SEASON IN REVIEW

The Pistons faced higher pressure and raised expectations in 1996-97. Surprisingly, they overcame the prior and surpassed the latter, steadfastly refusing to fall back on a convenient excuse.

Having suffered an off-season bruise when 20-point free agent Allan Houston accepted a big-money contract from the Knicks, the Pistons didn't waste energy whining about it. They simply moved on without him and continued to make rebuilding strides, going 54-28 to match the third-best record in franchise history.

If not for a disheartening five-game loss to Atlanta in the first round of the Eastern playoffs, the Pistons' season would've been an unqualified success. They blew two chances, one on their own court, to clinch their first winning series since 1991. That leftover goal presumably shoots to the top of their list for 1997-98.

1996-97 was the year in which Grant Hill's accolades caught up to the hype. He was a legitimate NBA star upon debuting in 1994, but he climbed to mega-stardom in his third season. He was chosen to the All-NBA first team, a notch higher than the year before, and placed third in the MVP voting behind Karl Malone and Michael Jordan. No Piston had achieved first team since Isiah Thomas' three straight berths from 1984-86 and none had finished as high for MVP since Bob Lanier was third in '73-74.

Hill also won the IBM Award, a pseudo-MVP award that uses a computer formula to decide which player contributed most to his team. "I think Grant is the most valuable player in the NBA because of what he means to us," coach Doug Collins said. "I've always believed the NBA should have two awards—the Best Player Award and the MVP for the guy who's most valuable to his team. Every year, you could give the Best Player Award to Michael Jordan, then give out the MVP."

For the second straight year, Hill led the team in the major categories: points (1,710), rebounds (721), assists (583) and steals (144). Accordingly, his 13 triple-doubles led the NBA for a second straight season, and he fell short by one rebound or assist six other times. He was twice NBA player of the week and also player of the month for January, in which he averaged 22.0 points, 7.3 rebounds and 9.7 assists in 14 games. For a third straight year, Hill started the All-Star game and contributed 11 points to the East's 132-120 comeback victory.

Terry Mills hit his last six 3-pointers December 4 vs. Atlanta, starting his NBA-record streak of 13 straight. Photo by Allen Einstein.

The winning All-Star coach? Collins, who received the honor by virtue of the Pistons' surprising 30-11 record at the break. The All-Star berth highlighted Collins' turbulent season in which he pondered his coaching future more than once. He considered heading back to TV after enduring a late-season slump, at which time he was the object of a pout by forward Otis Thorpe and the subject of unfounded firing rumors. But buoyed by the biggest win of the season—a 108-91 rout of Chicago on April 13—and a summer getaway, Collins decided to return, convinced that a tweaked roster would bring continued success in '97-98.

Hill and Collins weren't the only stars of the season. Joe Dumars, a full-time starter again in his 12th year, was Detroit's No. 2 scorer at 14.7 and ranked fourth in the NBA in 3-point shooting (43.2 percent). Lindsey Hunter, whom Collins sought to revitalize, was one of the league's most improved players while settling into a starting role as a hybrid guard. His 14.2-point average was a career best and he honed his reputation as a defensive stopper. Terry Mills continued as a 3-point threat, benefitting from size mismatches on the perimeter and Hill's double-teams. He tied an NBA record December 4-7 by hitting 13 straight triples. Thorpe was solid for the first half of the season, but faded so badly down the stretch that teammates began criticizing his effort.

At the outset, there were few clues that the season would resolve itself so well, mainly because of the surprise exit of Houston, who had emerged as a 19.7-point scorer at shooting guard. He privately assured the Pistons he would re-sign, then jumped at the Knicks' seven-year, $56 million offer July 13 without giving Detroit a chance to counter. Just like that, the Pistons were one building block short and that in turn hindered their ability to attract top-line free agents like Juwan Howard.

(continued...)

1996-97
SEASON IN REVIEW
(continued)

It was a turbulent season for coach Doug Collins, but the Pistons' 54 wins gave him 100 in his two seasons. Photo by Allen Einstein.

Strangely, though the Pistons never really replaced Houston's scoring, they didn't seem to miss him once the season began. They went 11-2 to challenge their best start ever (12-1 in 1970-71) and gradually bumped the record even higher over .500—19-4, then 28-9, 33-11, 39-13 and finally the high-water mark of 47-17 on March 16. A 7-11 finish left them 54-28, giving them exactly 100 wins in Collins' two seasons. Their 24-17 road record was their second-best ever, trailing the 26-15 mark of 1988-89.

To approach records like that, there were numerous exciting victories, keyed mostly by a suffocating defense that allowed only 88.9 points a game, a team record. The Pistons' 1,041 turnovers were the fewest in NBA history (counted since 1970-71) and they set a team single-game record with only four giveaways February 26 vs. Golden State.

Among the landmark wins, nothing could beat the emotional trouncing of Chicago, the Pistons' first since 1993, a span of 19 straight losses in the rivalry. There were two overtime games that also ranked highly. On January 18, Detroit beat the host Lakers 100-97 in two overtimes, fueled by Hill's triple-double and his banked-in 3-pointer to force the first OT. On February 28 at Boston, Hunter's last-second over-the-head tip-in sent the game into overtime and the Pistons went on to a 106-100 win.

In the playoffs, Detroit mustered victories in Games 2 and 3, the first one coming at Atlanta. In the possible Game 4 clincher at home, the Pistons gave a lackluster effort and were beaten 94-82. In Game 5 at Atlanta, the Hawks took command in the final three minutes to win the series and end the Pistons' season of surprises.

Game Results

1996-97
REGULAR SEASON

Date	Opponent	Result	Record
11-1	INDIANA	W, 95-89	1-0
11-2	at Atlanta	W, 90-78	2-0
11-5	at Philadelphia	W, 83-81	3-0
11-6	DALLAS	W, 103-84	4-0
11-8	CHICAGO	L, 80-98	4-1
11-12	at Washington	W, 92-79	5-1
11-13	DENVER	W, 95-94 (OT)	6-1
11-15	WASHINGTON	W, 95-84	7-1
11-16	at Cleveland	W, 102-98	8-1
11-20	at Boston	W, 108-85	9-1
11-21	NEW JERSEY	W, 96-88	10-1
11-23	at Charlotte	L, 85-93	10-2
11-27	VANCOUVER	W, 87-78	11-2
11-29	L.A. LAKERS	L, 76-84	11-3
12-1	SACRAMENTO	W, 95-66	12-3
12-4	ATLANTA	W, 100-90	13-3
12-6	CLEVELAND	W, 93-81	14-3
12-7	at New Jersey	W, 95-69	15-3
12-10	at Milwaukee	W, 93-85	16-3
12-12	at Houston	L, 96-115	16-4
12-15	BOSTON	W, 99-89	17-4
12-16	at Toronto	W, 98-92	18-4
12-18	NEW YORK	W, 112-78	19-4
12-20	at Indiana	W, 84-75	20-4
12-21	at New York	L, 92-95	20-5
12-25	at Chicago	L, 83-95	20-6
12-26	INDIANA	L, 89-95 (OT)	20-7
12-28	CHARLOTTE	W, 97-75	21-7
12-30	ORLANDO	W, 97-85	22-7
1-2	BOSTON	W, 99-87	23-7
1-4	TORONTO	W, 118-74	24-7
1-7	MILWAUKEE	L, 76-86	24-8
1-10	SAN ANTONIO	W, 84-78	25-8
1-11	UTAH	W, 87-77	26-8
1-14	at Portland	L, 86-95	26-9
1-15	at Vancouver	W, 103-79	27-9
1-18	at L.A. Lakers	W, 100-97 (2OT)	28-9
1-20	at Phoenix	L, 86-89	28-10
1-22	at Sacramento	L, 92-97	28-11
1-23	at Golden State	W, 94-79	29-11
1-25	PHILADELPHIA	W, 104-95	30-11
1-28	at Milwaukee	W, 93-84	31-11
1-29	PORTLAND	W, 98-89	32-11
2-1	at New Jersey	W, 90-75	33-11
2-2	PHOENIX	L, 91-106	33-12
2-6	HOUSTON	W, 96-87	34-12
2-11	at Miami	L, 91-104	34-13
2-12	ORLANDO	W, 96-87	35-13
2-14	at Charlotte	W, 109-103	36-13
2-16	at Toronto	W, 92-89	37-13
2-19	WASHINGTON	W, 100-85	38-13
2-21	NEW JERSEY	W, 98-84	39-13
2-23	at Washington	W, 85-79	40-13
2-24	at Orlando	L, 84-93	40-14
2-26	GOLDEN STATE	W, 117-84	41-14
2-28	at Boston	W, 106-100 (OT)	42-14
3-2	ATLANTA	W, 82-75	43-14
3-4	MIAMI	L, 99-108	43-15
3-5	at Minnesota	W, 92-88	44-15
3-7	at Utah	L, 88-95	44-16
3-8	at L.A. Clippers	W, 91-85	45-16
3-11	at Seattle	L, 80-93	45-17
3-13	at Denver	W, 102-82	46-17
3-16	SEATTLE	W, 86-83	47-17
3-17	at Cleveland	L, 82-85	47-18
3-19	TORONTO	L, 97-99	47-19
3-21	MINNESOTA	W, 112-98	48-19
3-22	at Chicago	L, 88-103	48-20
3-26	at New York	L, 94-105	48-21
3-28	L.A. CLIPPERS	W, 113-85	49-21
3-30	PHILADELPHIA	L, 92-96	49-22
4-1	at Dallas	W, 100-82	50-22
4-2	at San Antonio	W, 99-92	51-22
4-4	at Atlanta	L, 89-103	51-23
4-7	MIAMI	L, 88-94	51-24
4-10	at Miami	L, 83-93	51-25
4-11	CHARLOTTE	L, 85-93	51-26
4-13	CHICAGO	W, 108-91	52-26
4-14	at Orlando	L, 91-100	52-27
4-16	MILWAUKEE	W, 92-85	53-27
4-18	CLEVELAND	L, 75-82	53-28
4-20	at Indiana	W, 124-120 (OT)	54-28

PLAYOFFS
Eastern First Round—(Best-of-Five)

Date	Opponent	Result	Record
4-25	at Atlanta	L, 75-89	0-1
4-27	at Atlanta	W, 93-80	1-1
4-29	ATLANTA	W, 99-91	2-1
5-2	ATLANTA	L, 82-94	2-2
5-4	at Atlanta	L, 79-84	2-3

(Home games in CAPS)

SPOTLIGHT *Game*

APRIL 13, 1997

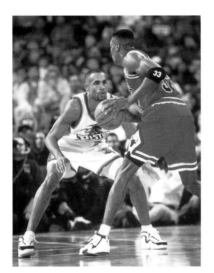

Grant Hill was winless against Scottie Pippen and the Bulls until April 13, 1997. Photo by Allen Einstein.

Doug Collins swallowed hard. He stared at the floor. He fidgeted with his tie. Anything to keep the tears from coming. But it was no use.

With about two minutes left in a 108-91 Sunday win over the Chicago Bulls—on national TV, after four straight losses, amid rumors of team discord—Collins had no defenses left. His chin quivered and tears trickled down the cheeks of the Pistons' coach, with an NBC camera panning in for a close-up.

After two weeks of turmoil on and off the court, the Pistons and their emotional coach soothed their wounds in the most satisfying way they could imagine. They easily beat the defending NBA champs at The Palace to end a 19-game losing streak in the rivalry; they hadn't beaten the Bulls since March 19, 1993. It was also Chicago's worst loss of the season.

"This is probably my proudest moment as a coach," Collins said, his renewed spirit contrasting sharply with his sweaty shirt and red eyes. "Not because we beat the Bulls and that's my former team (as coach), but because of what we've gone through for a couple of weeks."

Aside from four losses to 50-win teams in a 10-day span, it had been reported that Collins might be fired because of player unrest. Though the reports proved erroneous, the strain on the coach was obvious.

"I told the players the greatest compliment they could ever give their coach was to do what they did today—play with courage from start to finish, withstand anything Chicago tried to throw at us, play with poise and confidence, and play together as we have all season," Collins said.

"It was a great win. I'm happy for Doug," said Terry Mills, who scored a season-high 29 points as a surprise starter at center. "Coach has always shaded this game as not being that important, but I think he showed today that it really meant something to him."

"We played today like Doug coaches—with passion," Grant Hill said after his 12th triple-double of the season (27 points, 12 rebounds, 10 assists).

Sure, Chicago was without the injured Dennis Rodman and Toni Kukoc, and Michael Jordan turned his ankle three minutes into the game. Then Scottie Pippen sat out briefly with a right hand injury. But there would be no apologies from the Pistons, who desperately needed a victory. It was the first win over the Bulls for both Collins and Hill.

"The only other time I've beaten Michael and Scottie was on my (Sony) Playstation at home," Hill said. "I scored 50 points on them, too."

SUMMARY
Pistons 108, Bulls 91

BULLS (91)

Player	Min	FG M-A	3P M-A	FT M-A	Reb O-T	A	PF	Pts
Pippen	39	9-19	2-5	1-2	2-5	3	2	21
Caffey	33	6-12	0-0	3-6	5-10	2	3	15
Longley	26	5-13	0-0	0-0	4-8	2	3	10
Jordan	38	7-16	0-3	4-4	1-9	7	1	18
Harper	18	1-3	0-2	0-0	0-1	2	0	2
Kerr	33	3-4	2-2	0-0	0-0	4	0	8
B.Williams	16	5-9	0-0	0-0	0-3	2	2	10
Buechler	21	0-2	0-0	0-0	2-2	1	1	0
Simpkins	12	2-3	0-0	2-2	0-2	3	1	6
Steigenga	4	0-2	0-1	1-2	0-1	0	0	1
Totals	**240**	**38-83**	**4-13**	**11-16**	**14-41**	**26**	**13**	**91**

Percentages: FG .458, 3P .308, FT .688. Team Rebounds: 8. Blocked shots: 1 (Longley). Turnovers: 10 (Jordan 4, Longley 2, B.Williams 2, Pippen, Steigenga). Steals: 2 (Kerr, Simpkins). Technical fouls: Coach Jackson, 10:10 fourth. Flagrant fouls: Pippen, 6:05 fourth.

PISTONS (108)

Player	Min	FG M-A	3P M-A	FT M-A	Reb O-T	A	PF	Pts
Hill	43	11-23	0-1	5-6	4-12	10	3	27
Thorpe	30	6-13	0-0	2-2	2-7	0	5	14
Mills	39	11-16	5-9	2-2	0-9	1	4	29
Dumars	42	3-10	3-7	1-1	0-2	9	1	10
Hunter	39	4-10	0-3	2-2	0-2	2	2	10
Curry	14	2-3	0-0	0-1	0-1	1	0	4
Ratliff	21	4-6	0-0	0-0	2-2	0	4	8
McKie	9	3-5	0-0	0-0	3-4	0	2	6
J.Williams	1	0-0	0-0	0-0	1-2	0	0	0
Green	1	0-0	0-0	0-0	0-0	0	0	0
Reid	1	0-1	0-0	0-0	0-0	0	0	0
Totals	240	44-87	8-20	12-14	12-41	23	21	108

Percentages: FG .506, 3P .400, FT .857. Team Rebounds: 5. Blocked shots: 3 (Ratliff 3). Turnovers: 7 (Hill 2, Thorpe 2, Mills, McKie, J.Williams). Steals: 7 (Thorpe 2, Hunter 2, Hill, Dumars, McKie). Illegal defenses: 1.

CHICAGO	28	21	27	15	— 91
DETROIT	35	28	20	25	— 108

A—21,454 (sellout). T—2:12. Officials—Derrick Stafford, Billy Oakes, Sean Corbin.

Premier Piston

Aaron McKie

Aaron McKie is regarded as a promising Piston for the late 90s.

When the phone rang in his Phoenix hotel room on January 24, 1997, Aaron McKie thought to himself, "Must be my wake-up call." He was correct in an abstract manner. It was Portland coach P.J. Carlesimo, calling to tell him he was being traded to the Pistons. So far, the swap appears to be a wake-up call for McKie's NBA career, which was stagnating in its third year with the Trail Blazers. The Pistons acquired the 6-foot-5 shooting guard in the Stacey Augmon deal to ease the strain on Joe Dumars. What they might have found was Dumars' eventual successor. "I see Aaron as a Chevy version of Joe," coach Doug Collins said. "He has a great upside. He's a tough strong guard. He can post up, defend and rebound." Portland wasn't getting much use from McKie, whom it drafted in the first round (17th) out of Temple in 1994. He supplied 6.5 points a game as a rookie, then 10.7 in 75 starts in a promising second year. But when the Pistons got him, he was languishing on Portland's bench, averaging only 18.9 minutes and shooting 34 percent. "My minutes were limited because we had J.R. Rider," McKie said. "I was trying to deal with it, but it can wear on you after a while. My friends said they could see it in my body language." In Detroit, McKie played 42 games (starting three) and showed versatility at both guard spots and post-up small forward. Averaging 20.2 minutes, he scored in double-figures 10 times, with a season high of 18 on April 16 vs. Milwaukee. McKie started for flu-ridden Grant Hill that night and also had a career-high 12 rebounds and eight assists, falling two short of his first NBA triple-double. Over the final four games of the season, he averaged 12.3 points, 6.3 rebounds and 4.8 assists.

AT A GLANCE

AARON McKIE

FULL NAME:
Aaron Fitzgerald McKie
BORN:
October 2, 1972; Philadelphia
POSITION, HEIGHT, WEIGHT:
Guard, 6-foot-5, 209 pounds
COLLEGE:
Temple '94
ACQUIRED:
1997, traded from Portland
TENURE WITH PISTONS:
1996-97
Also: Portland 1994-96
BEST SEASON WITH PISTONS:
1996-97, 42 GP, 6.3 ppg, 3.0 rpg
TOTALS WITH PISTONS:
Regular season: 42 GP, 6.3 ppg, 3.0 rpg
Playoffs: 5 GP, 3.0 ppg, 2.0 rpg, 2.0 apg

PISTON LIST

Grant Hill's 1996-97 Triple-Doubles

Date	Opp.	Pts-Reb-Ast
December 18	Knicks	17-10-11
January 18	Lakers	34-15-14
January 25	76ers	21-16-10
February 1	Nets	22-11-11
February 12	Magic	31-10-10
February 28	Celtics	29-12-12
March 21	Minn.	22-11-10
March 30	76ers	22-16-10
April 2	Spurs	31-11-10
April 4	Hawks	22-12-12
April 11	Hornets	20-14-10
April 13	Bulls	27-12-10
April 14	Magic	12-15-13

PLAYOFF HERO

PLAYOFF VILLAIN

Grant Hill

Grant Hill led the Pistons in scoring in four of their five playoff games.

Dikembe Mutombo

Atlanta's Dikembe Mutombo dominated the Pistons in the playoffs.

Such is the fate of the star player. You're entrusted with the big shot. Sometimes you make it and wear the hero's wreath. Other times you miss it and wear the goat's horns. Grant Hill, not unexpectedly, played both roles in the Pistons' first-round playoff loss to the Hawks in 1996-97. He was clearly their hero, leading the club with averages of 23.6 points and 5.4 assists. He scored at least 20 in every game (20, 25, 24, 28 and 21) and his 14 rebounds in Game 1 were the Pistons' high for the series, as were his eight assists in Game 3. Hill was able to dictate the action on the perimeter, going around helpless defender Tyrone Corbin. But the Hawks had an advantage the Pistons did not—a 7-footer camped in the middle to clean up their defensive mistakes. If Hill drove past Corbin or Steve Smith, he became fair game for center Dikembe Mutombo and that made matters tough on Hill in the late stages of games. For instance, Hill was shut out in the fourth quarter of Game 1 and the Pistons were beaten by 14. In Game 5, Mutombo blocked three of his shots in the last five minutes and Detroit lost by five, going home for the summer. "This was Grant's second shot at (the playoffs). Now he realizes what they're about," coach Doug Collins said.

The Pistons simply couldn't avoid Dikembe Mutombo in 1996-97, not before the season, especially not in the playoffs. The 7-foot-2 center from Zaire had been part of their summer plan, as they had considered making him a rich free-agent offer. But once Allan Houston left them, the Pistons felt leery about giving a seven-year contract to a mostly defensive center who wouldn't make them an immediate contender. So they passed on Mutombo, letting him join the Atlanta Hawks, but they helped the Hawks create salary-cap room by accepting Grant Long and Stacey Augmon in trade. Those machinations would come back to haunt Detroit in the postseason. Mutombo would become Defensive Player of the Year and his long-armed presence was too much for the Pistons to overcome in their 3-2 playoff loss. He was especially dominant in the fifth game, blocking six shots, giving him 13 in the series. He blocked Grant Hill's dunk with 1:36 left, preserving a 77-77 tie. Then Mutombo blocked a Hill layup with 45 seconds to go, resulting in Steve Smith's killer triple. "You think you're past Mutombo and then those long arms come out of nowhere," Hill conceded. In the series, Mutombo averaged 18.2 points, including 26 in Game 1, as well as 13.6 rebounds.

December 18, 1996

Allan Houston had bolted the Pistons in the dead of the off-season and the fans hadn't had a chance to weigh in with their feelings. They got their say, rather loudly, when the Knicks made their first Palace visit of the season December 18. Well-liked in Detroit before he joined New York as a free agent, Houston was booed passionately from start to finish and had a dreadful game as the Pistons rolled 112-78, improving to 19-4. Clearly shaken by the boos, Houston tried only four shots in 20 minutes, making one, and committed five turnovers and four fouls. A worse perfor-mance, he couldn't have imagined, but it set a trend for his rough season against the Pistons. In three meetings, Houston had a combined 11 points on 5-of-18 shooting, hitting only 1-of-7 3-pointers. He had more fouls (13) than points, in fact. The Pistons, meanwhile, played one of their best games of the season in the first matchup vs. the Knicks. Wearing their throw-back Fort Wayne uniforms, the Pistons were "close to a perfect game," Grant Hill said. Sparked by Lindsey Hunter's 28 points and Hill's first triple-double of the season (17-10-11), Detroit led by 15 in the first quarter and coasted. "I hope fans are starting to recognize what we're building here," coach Doug Collins said.

Grant Hill thunder-dunks over the Knicks' John Starks and John Wallace. Photo by Allen Einstein.

Grant Hill played a career-high 53 minutes in a double-OT win over the Lakers. Photo by Allen Einstein.

January 18, 1997

Rather than shrink from the pressure against a marquee team in a marquee town, Grant Hill and the Pistons embraced it figuratively and literally on this Saturday night in Los Angeles. Hill got the Pistons into overtime with the Lakers by banking in a 25-foot 3-pointer at the buzzer, then he had six points and three assists in the second overtime to lead Detroit to a memorable 100-97 victory. The Pistons hadn't beaten the Lakers since 1993, spanning seven games, and coach Doug Collins punctuated the win in L.A. style. Nearly into the tunnel, he bolted back across the court to high-five actor Jack Nicholson, the very embodiment of Lakers hep-cat cool. But Jack was only a supporting player in this story. Hill wrested away top billing with an MVP-style performance: 34 points, 15 rebounds and 14 assists for his second triple-double of the season. His tying 3-pointer was lucky, he admitted. Detroit got the ball with 2.2 seconds left in regulation. Hill took one dribble to evade Robert Horry and banked in his off-balance shot. "This was my first time beating the Lakers and it was fun because my idol, Magic Johnson, was in the stands," Hill said. "I was starting to think I would never beat the Lakers." "Grant was sensa-tional," Collins said.

CHANGING FACES

WHEN GRANT LONG and Stacey Augmon were traded to Detroit in Summer 1996, their reputations preceded them: hard workers, defensive demons, Doug Collins' kind of players. Maybe something was lost in transit from Atlanta, because both turned into disappointing acquisitions before the season was out. With the Pistons scrambling after Allan Houston bolted to New York in free agency, the July 15 get-well trade was this: Detroit got Long and Augmon and Atlanta got Detroit's first-round pick in 1998, a conditional first-rounder (between Nos. 16-29) from Sacramento and two second-round picks. But Augmon was quickly exposed as a careless defender and offensive liability, and Long's intermittent play soon left him out of the rotation. Coincidentally, one day before his No. 2 would be retired in honor of Chuck Daly, Augmon was traded January 24 to Portland for three guards: Aaron McKie, Randolph Childress and Reggie Jordan. The Pistons also signed free-agent veterans Rick Mahorn (age 38) and Kenny Smith, though the latter lasted barely a month.

Rick Mahorn began his second go-around with the Pistons in 1996—a real crowd-pleasing move. Photo by Allen Einstein.

Take a Bow

Chuck Daly

Whenever things were going really, really well for his Pistons, Chuck Daly feared impending doom. "You can't trust happiness," he'd say with a throaty exhale, like a 10-game losing streak was lurking just around the corner. But Isiah Thomas, Bill Laimbeer and dozens of his olds pals might have convinced Daly otherwise on January 25, 1997. The gang was in attendance to applaud the coach they once nicknamed Daddy Rich. In his honor, the No. 2 was retired, signifying the two NBA championships the Pistons won under his tutelage. Daly

Chuck Daly, flanked by his retired No. 2 and two retirees, Vinnie Johnson (left) and Bill Laimbeer. Photo by Allen Einstein.

had left in 1992 as the winningest coach in team history with a 538-313 record including the playoffs. He pointed out to the packed Palace that he didn't reach prominence until he was over 50. "Most of the good things that happened to me happened after I was 52. So those of you in your 30s and 40s ... don't worry. Good things happen," he said. Thomas told Daly, "You took a bunch of boys and turned us into men. We wanted to win, but we had no idea how to do it." Rick Mahorn said simply, "Without you, there wouldn't be us."

PISTON LIST

Best Seasonal Defensive Average

- 88.9, 1996-97 (7,293 points)
- 92.9, 1995-96 (7,617)
- 96.8, 1990-91 (7,937)
- 96.9, 1991-92 (7,946)
- 98.3, 1989-90 (8,057)
- 100.3, 1973-74 (8,227)
- 100.3, 1974-75 (8,228)
- 100.8, 1988-89 (8,264)
- 102.0, 1992-93 (8,366)
- 104.1, 1987-88 (8,533)
- 104.7, 1993-94 (8,587)
- 105.5, 1994-95 (8,651)
- 106.0, 1975-76 (8,691)
- 106.0, 1980-81 (8,692)

THE FUTURE

Brian Williams

Scot Pollard

The Pistons' foremost goal entering the summer of 1997 was to add an All-Star caliber player to start alongside Grant Hill. With the signing of free-agent center Brian Williams, they believe they did that.

Fresh from helping Chicago win another NBA championship, Williams was regarded as the best catch of the free-agent market. The Pistons had planned to sit out the bidding in preparation for the expected free-agent bonanza of 1998, but on August 16 signed Williams to the biggest contract (by average) in team history: seven years, $45 million.

Bringing in Williams (6-foot-11, 260 lb.) was clearly the highlight of an off-season in which Detroit re-signed four players, added four new ones and lost four via trades, free-agent signings or renouncements.

The summer's first order of business was the reaffirmation of Doug Collins as coach. He briefly considered returning to television, so exhausted was he after nearly two seasons without significant time off. But buoyed by a 10-day vacation—and the public support of Grant Hill and Joe Dumars—Collins continued under a revised contract.

"I had to make sure I wanted to continue to take the grind necessary to be successful in this business," Collins said. "When I came back from vacation, I talked to Grant and Joe and Lindsey (Hunter). In essence, I wanted to see if I was the guy they wanted as their coach. I never really wanted not to come back. I want to win a championship. I want to win it in Detroit, and I want to win it for Bill Davidson. He has been so great to me."

On June 25, the Pistons began tweaking their roster, drafting Kansas forward-center Scot Pollard (6-10) with the 19th overall pick and UCLA swingman Charles O'Bannon (6-5) with the 32nd. The pair, born 11 days apart in February 1975, are regarded as projects.

"I don't want to throw rose petals and flowers and say these guys are going to come in and knock our socks off," Collins

conceded. "We're not kidding ourselves. We took a chance on the biggest guy (Pollard) who we think has a chance to be a good player."

Pollard averaged 9.4 points and 6.6 rebounds in his college career as Kansas made four straight trips to the NCAA Sweet Sixteen. He was a starter the last two seasons, gaining honorable mention all-America. "I come from a program where nothing less than your best effort is accepted," he said. "I think I should be able to fit in well in Detroit."

Collins said he feels O'Bannon was a first-round prospect who slipped into the second round "because of his brother." (Ed O'Bannon was the ninth overall pick by New Jersey in 1995, but hasn't panned out.) Charles, who started 122 of 124 college games, averaged 14.4 points and 6.5 rebounds in his UCLA career. He averaged 17.7 points as a senior.

Detroit's first summer signing was a familiar face: Dumars, who re-upped for one year on July 30, the day after backup swingman Michael Curry signed with the Milwaukee Bucks as a free agent. By accepting a conservative contract, reportedly around $3 million, Dumars allowed the Pistons salary cap flexibility that came in handy to sign Williams.

"When Mr. Davidson asked me to help out the team with the salary cap, I decided I would," Dumars said. "You can make a truckload of money and be the most unhappy guy in the world if you're playing on a losing team and not surrounded by the best players."

A week later, August 7, the Pistons cleared $6 million from their salary cap by honoring Otis Thorpe's trade request. The disgruntled power forward was sent to his fifth NBA team, the 14-win Vancouver Grizzlies, for a conditional first-round pick from 1998 to 2003.

"We recaptured the asset we gave up to get Otis (in 1995)," player personnel director Rick Sund said.

"I think it's very important to note that we didn't just get rid of Otis," Collins said. "He asked to be traded after the season was over and we said we'd do our best, but only if we could get equity for him."

A day later, the Pistons locked up another starter on a long-term basis, re-signing Hunter to a seven-year deal for a reported $20 million.

"I'm very happy we were able to sign Lindsey," Collins said. "His outside shooting and great defensive pressure on the ball are a perfect fit for us. I believe he'll become an NBA all-defensive first-team player in the next couple of seasons."

Sund said, "Lindsey's defense is especially important to us. There are so many point guards in the East who take the ball to the basket—(Tim) Hardaway, Mookie (Blaylock), (Terrell) Brandon, (Allen) Iverson, (Damon) Stoudamire. Lindsey can match up with them on a game-by-game basis. It was important for us to get him on board."

The August 16 addition of Williams, a six-year veteran, was regarded around the NBA as one of the most prudent summer acquisitions by any team. He sat out most of 1996-97, unable to reach a contract with the L.A. Clippers and having minor knee surgery, then signed with the Bulls in April. He played the final nine regular-season games and all 17 in the playoffs to help Chicago win the championship again. With the Clippers the year before, Williams averaged 15.7 points and 7.6 rebounds, both career highs, becoming a dependable back-to-the-basket player.

"The Pistons' future is very bright and I wanted to be a part of that," Williams said. "Playing next to Grant Hill and for Doug Collins made it a very easy decision for me to sign with the Pistons."

Collins said, "Brian is one of the top 10 centers in the league. He will give us tremendous flexibility on the front line. He was a big part of the Bulls' championship and he knows what it takes to be a winner. He fits in with our goal of adding an All-Star caliber player to our lineup."

On August 21, the Pistons suffered a free-agent defection, losing Terry Mills to Miami despite offering three times more money than the Heat for 1997-98. Unwilling to hamstring their salary cap, the Pistons resisted Mills' unbending demand for a six-year contract. But their $3 million offer clobbered the $1 million he accepted from Miami.

On August 25, Detroit signed 6-foot-8 swingman Malik Sealy, a former Clippers teammate of Williams. Sealy was coming off the best of his five NBA seasons, starting 79 games and averaging 13.5 points as Los Angeles' second-leading scorer. Three times, he went scoreless in the first half and scored at least 25 in the second half, but the Clippers gave up his free-agent rights because of an overload of guards.

"I think there's a great opportunity for me," the St. John's product said. "With the (offers) available to me, I think this was the best place for me, as far as playing, being on a team that wins and possibly having a long-term future."

Coach Doug Collins, "We had to have somebody who could score off our bench. We feel Malik can give us that."

Charles O'Bannon

Malik Sealy

REFERENCES AND SOURCES

Green, Jerry. (1991). *The Detroit Pistons: Capturing a Remarkable Era.* Chicago: Bonus Books Inc.

Kreiser, John & Friedman, Lou. (1996). *The New York Rangers: Broadway's Longest-Running Hit.* Champaign, Ill.: Sagamore Publishing.

Lazenby, Roland. (1988). *The Official Detroit Pistons Yearbook, 1988-89.* Dallas: Taylor Publishing Co.

Lazenby, Roland. (1989). *The Official Detroit Pistons Yearbook, 1989-90.* Dallas: Taylor Publishing Co.

Lazenby, Roland. (1990). *The Official Detroit Pistons Yearbook, 1990-91.* Dallas: Taylor Publishing Co.

Nelson, Rodger. (1995). *The Zollner Piston Story.* Fort Wayne, Ind.: Allen County Public Library Foundation.

Pearson, Mike. (1995). *Illini Legends, Lists & Lore.* Champaign, Ill.: Sagamore Publishing.

Sachare, Alex, Ed. (1994). *The Official NBA Basketball Encyclopedia.* New York: Villard Books (a division of Random House Inc.)

Smith, Sam. (1992). *The Jordan Rules.* New York: Simon and Schuster.

Stauth, Cameron. (1990). *The Franchise.* New York: William Morrow and Company, Inc.

TEAM AND LEAGUE BOOKS:
Detroit Pistons. (1957-97). Detroit Pistons Media Guides. Auburn Hills, Mich: Detroit Pistons.
The Sporting News. (1957-97). The Sporting News Official NBA Guide. St. Louis: The Sporting News Publishing Co.
The Sporting News. (1957-97). The Sporting News Official NBA Register. St. Louis: The Sporting News Publishing Co.

NEWSPAPERS:
The Oakland Press
The Detroit News
The Detroit Free Press
The Detroit Times
The Flint Journal
The Associated Press
United Press International

PERIODICALS
The Pistons Insider
HOOP Magazine

STATISTICAL
APPENDICES

PISTONS ALL-TIME ROSTER

(A complete listing of all 265 Detroit Pistons from 1957-58 through 1996-97)

#	Name (College)	TERM	Yrs.	GP	REGULAR SEASON REB	AST	PTS	AVG.	GP	PLAYOFFS REB	AST	PTS	AVG.
A													
10	Don Adams (Northwestern)	1972-73 – 1974-75	3	195	1111	328	1710	8.8	7	51	20	64	9.1
7	Rafael Addison (Syracuse)	1994-95	1	79	242	109	545	8.5	-	-	-	-	-
23	Mark Aguirre (DePaul)	1988-89 – 1992-93	5	318	1218	604	4115	12.9	57	236	96	772	13.5
16	Gary Alcorn (Fresno)	1959-60	1	58	279	22	230	4.0	-	-	-	-	-
33	Greg Anderson (Houston)	1993-94	1	77	571	51	491	6.4	-	-	-	-	-
7	Dick Atha (Indiana State)	1957-58	1	18	24	19	44	2.4	-	-	-	-	-
2	Stacey Augmon (UNLV)	1996-97	1	20	49	15	90	4.5	-	-	-	-	-
34	Ken Austin (Rice)	1983-84	1	7	3	1	12	1.7	-	-	-	-	-
B													
25	Stephen Bardo (Illinois)	1995-96	1	9	22	15	22	2.4	-	-	-	-	-
21	John Barnhill (Tennessee State)	1965-66	1	45	112	112	337	7.5	-	-	-	-	-
24	Marvin Barnes (Providence)	1976-77 – 1977-78	2	65	344	64	630	9.7	-	-	-	-	-
00	William Bedford (Memphis State)	1987-88 – 1991-92	5	172	317	52	605	3.5	14	26	4	29	2.1
27	Ron Behagen (Minnesota)	1978-79	1	1	1	0	0	0.0	-	-	-	-	-
8	Walt Bellamy (Indiana)	1968-69 – 1969-70	2	109	1113	154	1554	14.3	-	-	-	-	-
54	Kent Benson (Indiana)	1979-80 – 1985-86	6	398	2437	784	3810	9.6	18	79	11	109	6.1
21	Dave Bing (Syracuse)	1966-67 – 1974-75	9	675	2828	4330	15235	22.6	16	61	100	319	19.9
24	Norman Black (St. Joseph's, Pa.)	1980-81	1	3	2	2	8	2.7	-	-	-	-	-
32	Lance Blanks (Texas)	1990-91 – 1991-92	2	81	42	45	128	1.6	1	1	3	2	2.0
8	Doug Bolstorff (Minnesota)	1957-58	1	3	0	0	4	1.3	-	-	-	-	-
9	Walter Bond (Minnesota)	1994-95	1	5	5	7	10	2.0	-	-	-	-	-
32	Jim Bostic (New Mexico State)	1977-78	1	4	16	3	26	6.5	-	-	-	-	-
11	Dennis Boyd (Detroit)	1978-79	1	5	2	7	6	1.2	-	-	-	-	-
42	Jim Brewer (Minnesota)	1978-79	1	25	95	13	57	2.3	-	-	-	-	-
11	Wayman Britt (Michigan)	1977-78	1	7	4	2	9	1.3	-	-	-	-	-
20	Roger Brown (Kansas)	1975-76 – 1976-77	2	72	220	24	132	1.8	11	14	2	10	0.9
17	Bill Buntin (Michigan)	1965-66	1	42	252	36	324	7.7	-	-	-	-	-
24	Donnis Butcher (Pikeville, Ky.)	1963-64 – 1965-66	3	138	495	330	967	7.0	-	-	-	-	-
C													
10	Barney Cable (Bradley)	1958-59	1	32	88	12	109	3.4	-	-	-	-	-
21	Joe Caldwell (Arizona State)	1964-65 – 1965-66	2	99	631	183	1055	10.7	-	-	-	-	-
00	Tony Campbell (Ohio State)	1984-85 – 1986-87	3	178	383	88	1102	6.2	8	9	1	20	2.5
32	Kenny Carr (N.C. State)	1981-82	1	28	137	23	207	7.4	-	-	-	-	-
30	M.L. Carr (Guilford)	1976-77 – 1978-79	3	241	1777	628	3568	14.8	3	17	6	28	9.3
12	George Carter (St. Bonaventure)	1967-68	1	1	0	1	3	3.0	-	-	-	-	-
45	Cornelius Cash (Bowling Green)	1976-77	1	6	16	1	21	3.5	-	-	-	-	-
19	Len Chappell (Wake Forest)	1967-68	1	57	346	48	570	10.0	5	12	0	7	1.5
34	Pete Chilcutt (North Carolina)	1993-94	1	30	100	15	115	3.8	-	-	-	-	-
3	Randolph Childress (Wake Forest)	1996-97	1	4	1	2	10	2.5	-	-	-	-	-
11	Archie Clark (Minnesota)	1975-76	1	79	137	218	600	7.6	3	6	15	25	8.3
24	Nat Clifton (Xavier, La.)	1957-58	1	68	403	76	525	7.7	7	23	4	28	4.0
51	Ben Coleman (Maryland)	1993-94	1	9	26	0	28	3.1	-	-	-	-	-
12	Eddie Conlin (Fordham)	1958-59 – 1959-60	2	85	437	143	958	11.3	5	11	4	18	3.6
42	Ron Crevier (Boston College)	1985-86	1	2	1	0	0	0.0	-	-	-	-	-
23	Earl Cureton (Detroit)	1983-84 – 1985-86	3	234	1210	256	1376	5.9	18	104	15	105	5.8
17	Bill Curley (Boston College)	1994-95	1	53	124	25	143	2.7	-	-	-	-	-
12	Michael Curry (Georgia Southern)	1995-96 – 1996-97	2	122	199	69	519	4.3	5	4	1	8	1.6
D													
45	Adrian Dantley (Notre Dame)	1986-87 – 1988-89	3	192	723	426	3894	20.3	38	175	81	754	19.8
20	Jim Davis (Colorado)	1971-72 – 1974-75	4	309	1035	270	1285	4.2	9	20	5	33	3.7
50	Darryl Dawkins (No College)	1987-88 – 1988-89	2	16	7	2	31	1.9	-	-	-	-	-
12	Johnny Dawkins (Duke)	1994-95	1	50	113	205	325	6.5	-	-	-	-	-
22	Dave DeBusschere (Detroit)	1962-63 – 1969-70	7	440	4947	1152	7096	16.1	10	160	19	196	19.6
16	Archie Dees (Indiana)	1959-60 – 1960-61	2	101	491	70	852	8.4	2	4	2	11	5.5

#	Name (College)	TERM	Yrs.	GP	REGULAR SEASON REB	AST	PTS	AVG.	PLAYOFFS GP	REB	AST	PTS	AVG.
34	Fennis Dembo (Wyoming)	1988-89	1	31	23	5	36	1.2	2	0	0	2	1.0
22	Henry Dickerson (Morris Harvey)	1975-76	1	17	3	8	28	1.6	-	-	-	-	-
18	Terry Dischinger (Purdue)	1964-65; 1967-72	6	456	2341	716	5522	12.1	6	29	9	56	9.3
13	Leon Douglas (Alabama)	1976-77 — 1979-80	4	309	2273	375	2939	9.5	3	10	3	10	3.3
44	Sonny Dove (St. John's)	1967-68 — 1968-69	2	57	114	23	174	3.1	2	2	0	4	2.0
6	Dan Doyle (Belmont Abbey)	1962-63	1	4	8	3	16	4.0	-	-	-	-	-
22	Larry Drew (Missouri)	1980-81	1	76	120	249	504	6.6	-	-	-	-	-
17	Terry Driscoll (Boston College)	1970-71	1	69	402	54	372	5.4	-	-	-	-	-
42	Terry Duerod (Detroit)	1979-80	1	67	98	117	624	9.3	-	-	-	-	-
25	Bob Duffy (Colgate)	1963-64 — 1964-65	2	46	58	79	228	5.0	-	-	-	-	-
23	Walter Dukes (Seton Hall)	1957-58 — 1962-63	6	422	4986	515	4580	10.9	30	358	46	379	12.6
4	Joe Dumars (McNeese State)	1985-86 —	12	908	2031	4225	15030	16.6	107	250	499	1701	15.9

E

#	Name (College)	TERM	Yrs.	GP	REB	AST	PTS	AVG.	GP	REB	AST	PTS	AVG.
6	Bill Ebben (Detroit)	1957-58	1	8	8	4	15	1.9	-	-	-	-	-
44	Al Eberhard (Missouri)	1974-75 — 1977-78	4	220	760	175	1490	6.8	11	35	9	55	5.0
53	James Edwards (Washington)	1987-88 — 1990-91	4	256	930	182	2867	11.2	75	212	45	705	9.4
25	John Egan (Providence)	1961-62 — 1963-64	3	128	207	332	860	6.7	5	9	16	68	13.6
32	Sean Elliott (Arizona)	1993-94	1	73	263	197	885	12.1	-	-	-	-	-
21	Earl Evans (UNLV)	1979-80	1	36	75	37	157	4.4	-	-	-	-	-

F

#	Name (College)	TERM	Yrs.	GP	REB	AST	PTS	AVG.	GP	REB	AST	PTS	AVG.
22	Dick Farley (Indiana)	1958-59	1	70	195	124	491	7.0	3	6	3	11	3.7
17	Bob Ferry (St. Louis)	1960-61 — 1963-64	4	312	1968	538	3851	12.3	18	139	35	249	13.8
42	Chris Ford (Villanova)	1972-73 — 1978-79	7	485	1686	1698	4120	8.5	20	83	69	151	7.6
25	Fred Foster (Miami, Ohio)	1972-73	1	63	183	94	547	8.7	-	-	-	-	-
23	Jim Fox (South Carolina)	1967-68 — 1968-69	2	49	274	40	222	4.5	6	37	3	27	4.5
43	Tony Fuller (Pepperdine)	1980-81	1	15	42	28	60	4.0	-	-	-	-	-

G

#	Name (College)	TERM	Yrs.	GP	REB	AST	PTS	AVG.	GP	REB	AST	PTS	AVG.
10	Harry Gallatin (NE Missouri)	1957-58	1	72	749	86	1072	14.9	7	70	11	90	12.9
16	Dave Gambee (Oregon State)	1968-69	1	25	78	15	169	6.8	-	-	-	-	-
22	Gus Gerard (Virginia)	1977-78 — 1978-79	2	49	147	44	375	7.7	-	-	-	-	-
35	Mike Gibson (S.C.-Spartanburg)	1985-86	1	32	40	5	48	1.5	-	-	-	-	-
25	Gerald Glass (Mississippi)	1992-93	1	56	139	68	296	5.3	-	-	-	-	-
9	Litterial Green (Georgia)	1996-97	1	45	22	41	90	2.0	-	-	-	-	-
24	Rickey Green (Michigan)	1978-79	1	27	40	63	179	6.6	-	-	-	-	-
12	Sidney Green (UNLV)	1986-87	1	80	653	62	631	7.9	9	9	1	17	1.9
33	David Greenwood (UCLA)	1989-90	1	37	78	12	60	1.6	5	9	0	5	1.0

H

#	Name (College)	TERM	Yrs.	GP	REB	AST	PTS	AVG.	GP	REB	AST	PTS	AVG.
5	Happy Hairston (New York U.)	1967-68 — 1969-70	3	122	1309	157	2113	17.3	6	37	7	70	11.7
45	Lindsay Hairston (Michigan State)	1975-76	1	47	179	21	273	5.8	-	-	-	-	-
24	Roy Hamilton (UCLA)	1979-80	1	72	107	192	333	4.6	-	-	-	-	-
19	Reggie Harding (No College)	1963-64 — 1964-65	2	117	1316	231	1357	11.7	-	-	-	-	-
24	Alan Hardy (Michigan)	1981-82	1	38	34	20	142	3.7	-	-	-	-	-
35	Steve Harris (Tulsa)	1988-89	1	3	2	0	4	1.3	-	-	-	-	-
35	Scott Hastings (Arkansas)	1989-90 — 1990-91	2	67	60	15	90	1.3	15	6	3	10	0.7
11	Bubbles Hawkins (Illinois State)	1978-79	1	4	6	4	18	4.5	-	-	-	-	-
52	Steve Hayes (Idaho State)	1981-82	1	26	100	24	117	4.5	-	-	-	-	-
12	Gerald Henderson (Va. Commonwealth)	1989-90 — 1991-92	3	77	74	128	255	3.3	18	4	10	10	0.6
34	Keith Herron (Villanova)	1980-81	1	80	211	148	1094	13.7	-	-	-	-	-
31	Bill Hewitt (Southern Cal)	1969-70 — 1971-72	3	175	1037	231	986	5.6	-	-	-	-	-
12	Wayne Hightower (Kansas)	1966-67	1	29	164	28	248	8.6	-	-	-	-	-
33	Grant Hill (Duke)	1994-95 —	3	230	1949	1484	4722	20.5	8	56	38	175	21.9
9	Lionel Hollins (Arizona State)	1983-84	1	32	22	62	59	1.8	2	0	0	0	0.0
22	Essie Hollis (St. Bonaventure)	1978-79	1	25	45	6	69	2.8	-	-	-	-	-
20	Bob Hogsett (Tennessee)	1966-67	1	7	3	1	16	2.3	-	-	-	-	-
16	Joe Holup (George Washington)	1957-58 — 1958-59	2	105	529	96	779	7.4	10	44	6	54	5.4
17	Bob Houbregs (Washington)	1957-58	1	17	65	19	128	7.5	-	-	-	-	-
20	Allan Houston (Tennessee)	1993-94 — 1995-96	3	237	587	514	3386	14.3	3	8	6	75	25.0
32	Otis Howard (Austin Peay)	1978-79	1	11	34	4	49	4.5	-	-	-	-	-
18	Bailey Howell (Mississippi State)	1959-60 — 1963-64	5	387	4583	882	8182	21.1	21	201	59	361	17.2
35	Phil Hubbard (Michigan)	1979-80 — 1981-82	3	196	1178	287	2266	11.6	-	-	-	-	-
1	Lindsey Hunter (Jackson State)	1993-94 —	4	286	691	891	3002	10.5	7	20	7	81	11.6

I

#	Name (College)	TERM	Yrs.	GP	REB	AST	PTS	AVG.	GP	REB	AST	PTS	AVG.
17	Darrall Imhoff (California)	1962-63 — 1963-64	2	103	438	84	397	3.9	1	1	0	0	0.0

#	Name (College)	TERM	Yrs.	GP	REB	AST	PTS	AVG.	GP	REB	AST	PTS	AVG.
				REGULAR SEASON					**PLAYOFFS**				

#	Name (College)	TERM	Yrs.	GP	REB	AST	PTS	AVG.	GP	REB	AST	PTS	AVG.
J													
9	Lee Johnson (E. Tennessee State)	1980-81	1	2	2	0	0	0.0	-	-	-	-	-
9	Ron Johnson (Minnesota)	1960-61	1	6	14	1	18	4.5	-	-	-	-	-
15	Vinnie Johnson (Baylor)	1981-82 — 1990-91	10	798	2491	2661	10146	12.7	111	362	304	1385	12.5
34	Jim Johnstone (Wake Forest)	1982-83	1	16	30	10	24	1.5	-	-	-	-	-
42	Edgar Jones (Nevada-Reno)	1981-82 — 1982-83	2	97	488	109	784	8.1	-	-	-	-	-
23	Charles Jones (Albany State)	1993-94	1	42	235	29	91	2.2	-	-	-	-	-
35	Major Jones (Albany State)	1984-85	1	47	128	15	129	2.7	1	0	0	2	2.0
9	Wali Jones (Villanova)	1975-76	1	1	0	2	8	8.0	-	-	-	-	-
5	Willie Jones (Northwestern)	1960-61 — 1964-65	5	272	767	545	2016	7.4	16	37	43	157	9.8
16	Phil Jordon (Whitworth)	1957-58 — 1958-59	2	118	871	115	1442	12.1	9	36	7	84	9.3
22	Jeff Judkins (Utah)	1981-82	1	30	34	14	79	2.6	-	-	-	-	-
K													
32	Gregory Kelser (Michigan State)	1979-80 — 1981-82	3	86	435	165	1114	13.0	-	-	-	-	-
5	Ben Kelso (Central Michigan)	1973-74	1	46	31	18	85	1.8	1	1	1	0	0.0
6	Billy Kenville (St. Bonaventure)	1957-58, 1959-60	2	60	173	112	385	6.4	7	19	5	46	6.6
3	Stan Kimbrough (Xavier)	1989-90	1	10	7	5	16	1.6	-	-	-	-	-
32	Negele Knight (Dayton)	1994-95	1	44	58	116	181	4.1	-	-	-	-	-
16	Don Kojis (Marquette)	1964-65 — 1965-66	2	125	503	105	862	6.9	-	-	-	-	-
30	Howard Komives (Bowling Green)	1968-69 — 1971-72	4	298	721	1081	2957	9.9	-	-	-	-	-
L													
40	Bill Laimbeer (Notre Dame)	1981-82 — 1993-94	13	937	9430	1923	12665	13.5	113	1097	195	1354	12.0
16	Bob Lanier (St. Bonaventure)	1970-71 — 1979-80	10	681	8063	2256	15488	22.7	22	303	76	564	25.6
22	Stu Lantz (Nebraska)	1972-73 — 1973-74	2	101	285	235	937	9.3	7	29	14	84	12.0
50	Ed Lawrence (McNeese State)	1980-81	1	3	4	1	12	4.0	-	-	-	-	-
45	Eric Leckner (Wyoming)	1994-95 — 1995-96	2	75	208	15	269	3.6	1	0	0	0	0.0
12	George Lee (Michigan)	1960-61 — 1961-62	2	149	839	153	1467	9.9	11	42	15	104	9.5
30	Ron Lee (Oregon)	1979-80 — 1981-82	3	194	465	848	844	4.4	-	-	-	-	-
53	Cliff Levingston (Wichita State)	1982-83 — 1983-84	2	142	777	161	929	6.5	5	24	1	40	8.0
35	Ralph Lewis (LaSalle)	1987-88, 1989-90	2	54	51	14	83	1.5	10	8	1	4	0.4
30	Marcus Liberty (Illinois)	1993-94	1	35	56	15	100	2.9	-	-	-	-	-
26	Bill Ligon (Vanderbilt)	1974-75	1	38	26	25	126	3.3	2	0	0	2	1.0
17	Earl Lloyd (West Virginia State)	1958-59 — 1959-60	2	140	822	179	1207	8.6	5	27	10	43	8.6
43	Grant Long (Eastern Michigan)	1996-97	1	65	222	39	326	5.0	5	11	3	25	5.0
25	John Long (Detroit)	1978-79 — 1985-86 1988-89; 1990-91	10	608	1857	1136	9023	14.8	19	29	15	179	9.4
25	Paul Long (Wake Forest)	1967-68; 1969-70	2	41	26	29	140	3.4	1	0	1	6	6.0
21	Kevin Loughery (St. John's)	1962-63 — 1963-64	2	58	109	106	363	6.3	2	0	4	3	1.5
34	Sidney Lowe (N.C. State)	1984-85	1	6	1	8	4	0.7	-	-	-	-	-
M													
2	Mark Macon (Temple)	1993-94 — 1995-96	3	113	132	119	477	4.2	-	-	-	-	-
44	Rick Mahorn (Hampton Inst.)	1985-86 — 1988-89 1996-97 —	5	304	1901	227	2074	6.8	61	331	25	330	5.4
44	Steve Malovic (San Diego State)	1979-80	1	10	28	15	26	2.6	-	-	-	-	-
12	Pace Mannion (Utah)	1988-89	1	5	3	0	4	0.8	-	-	-	-	-
26	Harvey Marlatt (Eastern Michigan)	1970-71 — 1971-72	2	54	85	90	221	4.1	-	-	-	-	-
8	Tom Marshall (Western Kentucky)	1957-58	1	9	7	3	21	2.3	-	-	-	-	-
24	Scott May (Indiana)	1982-83	1	9	26	12	59	6.6	-	-	-	-	-
11	Bob McAdoo (North Carolina)	1979-80 — 1980-81	2	64	508	220	1294	20.2	-	-	-	-	-
30	Bob McCann (Morehead State)	1991-92	1	26	30	6	30	1.2	1	2	0	6	6.0
33	James McElroy (Central Michigan)	1979-80	1	36	50	159	422	11.7	-	-	-	-	-
15	Dick McGuire (St. John's)	1957-58 — 1959-60	3	208	840	1255	1695	8.1	12	54	68	125	10.4
23	Aaron McKie (Temple)	1996-97 —	1	42	128	77	263	6.3	5	10	10	15	3.0
18	McCoy McLemore (Drake)	1968-69 — 1969-70	2	123	572	127	851	6.9	-	-	-	-	-
6	Shellie McMillon (Bradley)	1958-59 — 1961-62	4	215	1267	179	1831	8.5	9	39	9	78	8.7
32	Larry McNeill (Marquette)	1978-79	1	11	10	3	29	2.6	-	-	-	-	-
41	Cozell McQueen (N.C. State)	1986-87	1	3	8	0	6	2.0	-	-	-	-	-
15	John Mengelt (Auburn)	1972-73 — 1975-76	4	291	671	585	2987	10.3	16	29	25	129	8.1
14	Eddie Miles (Seattle)	1963-64 — 1969-70	7	497	1673	1094	7419	14.9	6	22	15	87	14.5
25	Oliver Miller (Arkansas)	1994-95	1	64	475	93	545	8.5	-	-	-	-	-
6	Terry Mills (Michigan)	1992-93 — 1996-97	5	394	2431	645	5324	13.5	8	40	11	75	9.4
23	Steve Mix (Toledo)	1969-70 — 1971-72	3	61	251	53	446	7.3	-	-	-	-	-
44	Paul Mokeski (Kansas)	1980-81 — 1981-82	2	119	540	159	691	5.8	-	-	-	-	-
15	Eric Money (Arizona)	1974-75 — 1977-78 1979-80	5	350	725	1276	4123	11.8	12	31	71	168	14.0

#	Name (College)	TERM	Yrs.	GP	REGULAR SEASON REB	AST	PTS	AVG.	PLAYOFFS GP	REB	AST	PTS	AVG.
35	Otto Moore (Pan American)	1968-69 — 1970-71 1974-75	4	239	2126	261	2274	9.5	-	-	-	-	-
54	Ron Moore (West Virginia State)	1987-88	1	9	2	1	10	1.1	-	-	-	-	-
23	Tracy Moore (Tulsa)	1993-94	1	3	1	0	6	2.0	-	-	-	-	-
15	Jackie Moreland (Louisiana Tech)	1960-61 — 1964-65	5	348	1779	432	2684	7.7	14	62	16	103	7.4
35	Isaiah Morris (Arkansas)	1992-93	1	25	12	4	55	2.2	-	-	-	-	-
51	Erwin Mueller (San Francisco)	1969-70 — 1971-72	3	168	839	369	1250	7.4	-	-	-	-	-
41	Tod Murphy (Cal-Irvine)	1993-94	1	7	9	3	15	2.1	-	-	-	-	-
19	Dorie Murrey (Detroit)	1966-67	1	36	102	12	98	2.8	-	-	-	-	-

N

#	Name (College)	TERM	Yrs.	GP	REB	AST	PTS	AVG.	GP	REB	AST	PTS	AVG.
33	Bob Nash (Hawaii)	1972-73 — 1973-74	2	71	108	30	149	2.1	-	-	-	-	-
42	Chuck Nevitt (N.C. State)	1985-86 — 1987-88	3	83	126	9	132	1.6	7	9	0	6	0.9
23	Melvin Newbern (Minnesota)	1992-93	1	33	37	57	119	3.6	-	-	-	-	-
52	Ivano Newbill (Georgia Tech)	1994-95	1	34	81	17	40	1.2	-	-	-	-	-
19	Rich Niemann (St. Louis)	1968-69	1	16	41	9	48	3.0	-	-	-	-	-
41	Kurt Nimphius (Arizona State)	1986-87	1	28	54	7	96	3.4	4	10	0	8	2.0
5	Chuck Noble (Louisville)	1957-58 — 1961-62	5	285	679	882	2114	7.4	17	30	41	91	5.4
8	Willie Norwood (Alcorn A&M)	1971-72 — 1974-75 1977-78	5	381	1011	187	2172	5.7	5	3	1	18	3.6

O

#	Name (College)	TERM	Yrs.	GP	REB	AST	PTS	AVG.	GP	REB	AST	PTS	AVG.
45	Dan O'Sullivan (Fordham)	1993-94	1	13	10	3	17	1.3	-	-	-	-	-
10	Don Ohl (Illinois)	1960-61 — 1963-64	4	307	942	1059	5137	16.7	17	58	58	312	18.4
10	Bud Olsen (Louisville)	1968-69	1	10	11	7	20	2.0	-	-	-	-	-
44	Tom Owens (South Carolina)	1982-83	1	49	186	44	207	4.2	-	-	-	-	-

P

#	Name (College)	TERM	Yrs.	GP	REB	AST	PTS	AVG.	GP	REB	AST	PTS	AVG.
20	George Patterson (Toledo)	1967-68	1	59	159	51	120	2.0	1	1	1	0	0.0
54	Mike Peplowski (Michigan State)	1994-95	1	6	3	1	11	1.8	-	-	-	-	-
22	Ricky Pierce (Rice)	1982-83	1	39	35	14	85	2.2	-	-	-	-	-
0	Olden Polynice (Virginia)	1992-93 — 1993-94	2	104	847	51	972	9.3	-	-	-	-	-
50	Ben Poquette (Central Michigan)	1977-78 — 1978-79	2	128	481	77	737	5.8	-	-	-	-	-
54	Howard Porter (Villanova)	1974-75 — 1977-78	4	202	986	97	2173	10.8	15	79	8	229	15.3
1	Kevin Porter (St. Francis, Pa.)	1975-76 — 1978-79	4	190	366	1920	2217	11.7	3	6	17	16	5.3
15	Jim Price (Louisville)	1977-78	1	34	101	102	390	11.5	-	-	-	-	-

Q

#	Name (College)	TERM	Yrs.	GP	REB	AST	PTS	AVG.	GP	REB	AST	PTS	AVG.
14	Bob Quick (Xavier)	1969-70 — 1971-72	3	93	344	78	695	7.5	-	-	-	-	-

R

#	Name (College)	TERM	Yrs.	GP	REB	AST	PTS	AVG.	GP	REB	AST	PTS	AVG.
42	Mark Randall (Kansas)	1992-93	1	35	55	10	97	2.8	-	-	-	-	-
42	Theo Ratliff (Wyoming)	1995-96 —	2	151	553	26	780	5.2	4	4	1	8	2.0
17	Hub Reed (Oklahoma City)	1964-65	1	62	206	38	208	3.4	-	-	-	-	-
20	Ron Reed (Notre Dame)	1965-66 — 1966-67	2	118	762	173	951	8.1	-	-	-	-	-
52	Don Reid (Georgetown)	1995-96 —	2	116	304	25	395	3.4	4	2	1	7	1.8
26	George Reynolds (Houston)	1969-70	1	10	14	12	21	2.1	-	-	-	-	-
3	Alvin Robertson (Arkansas)	1992-93	1	30	132	107	279	9.3	-	-	-	-	-
9	Jackie Robinson (UNLV)	1979-80	1	7	5	9	27	3.9	-	-	-	-	-
40	Wayne Robinson (Virginia Tech)	1980-81	1	81	294	112	643	7.9	-	-	-	-	-
10	Dennis Rodman (SE Oklahoma St.)	1986-87 — 1992-93	7	549	6299	715	4844	8.8	94	766	80	716	7.6
3	Lou Roe (Massachusetts)	1995-96	1	49	78	15	90	1.8	2	2	0	0	0.0
30	Tree Rollins (Clemson)	1990-91	1	37	42	4	36	1.0	6	3	0	4	0.7
14	Lorenzo Romar (Washington)	1984-85	1	5	0	10	9	1.8	-	-	-	-	-
32	Dan Roundfield (Central Michigan)	1984-85	1	56	453	102	611	10.9	9	60	15	82	9.1
18	Curtis Rowe (UCLA)	1971-72 — 1975-76	5	407	3256	711	5407	13.3	19	148	52	237	12.5
41	Jim Rowinski (Purdue)	1988-89	1	6	2	0	4	0.7	-	-	-	-	-
43	Jeff Ruland (Iona)	1992-93	1	11	18	2	12	1.1	-	-	-	-	-
33	Walker D. Russell (W. Michigan)	1982-83 — 1983-84 1985-86; 1987-88	4	87	92	155	226	2.6	7	0	1	6	0.9

S

#	Name (College)	TERM	Yrs.	GP	REB	AST	PTS	AVG.	GP	REB	AST	PTS	AVG.
22	John Salley (Georgia Tech)	1986-87 — 1991-92	6	459	2095	495	3420	7.5	95	515	86	771	8.1
35	John Schweitz (Richmond)	1986-87	1	3	1	0	0	0.0	-	-	-	-	-
12	Ray Scott (Portland)	1961-62 — 1966-67	6	421	4508	1228	6724	16.0	14	193	40	236	16.9
2	Brad Sellers (Ohio State)	1991-92 — 1992-93	1	43	42	14	102	2.4	2	0	2	6	3.0
12	Phil Sellers (Rutgers)	1976-77	1	44	41	25	198	4.5	1	2	0	3	3.0
27	Steve Sheppard (Maryland)	1978-79	1	20	19	4	32	1.6	-	-	-	-	-
21	Gene Shue (Maryland)	1957-58 — 1961-62	5	368	1783	1693	7247	19.7	27	114	120	515	19.1

#	Name (College)	TERM	Yrs.	GP	REB	AST	PTS	AVG.	GP	REB	AST	PTS	AVG.
					REGULAR SEASON					**PLAYOFFS**			
34	John Shumate (Notre Dame)	1977-78; 1979-80	2	71	624	131	1045	14.7	-	-	-	-	-
32	Ralph Simpson (Michigan State)	1976-77 — 1977-78	2	109	263	267	1190	10.9	3	3	1	0	0.0
35	Al Skinner (Massachusetts)	1977-78	1	69	172	113	485	7.0	-	-	-	-	-
32	Jim Smith (Ohio State)	1982-83	1	4	5	0	8	2.0	-	-	-	-	-
30	Kenny Smith (North Carolina)	1996-97	1	9	5	10	23	2.6	-	-	-	-	-
24	Larry Staverman (Villa Madonna)	1963-64	1	20	69	12	114	5.7	-	-	-	-	-
31	Brook Steppe (Georgia Tech)	1984-85	1	54	57	36	253	4.7	4	3	2	8	2.0
16	Joe Strawder (Bradley)	1965-66 — 1967-68	3	231	2296	245	1977	8.6	6	65	9	42	7.0
T													
43	Earl Tatum (Marquette)	1978-79	1	76	121	72	594	7.8	-	-	-	-	-
35	Jeff Taylor (Texas Tech)	1986-87	1	12	4	3	21	1.8	-	-	-	-	-
22	Terry Teagle (Baylor)	1984-85	1	2	0	0	2	1.0	-	-	-	-	-
9	Bill Thieben (Hofstra)	1957-58	1	27	65	7	100	3.7	-	-	-	-	-
31	Justus Thigpen (Weber State)	1972-73	1	18	9	8	46	2.6	-	-	-	-	-
22	David Thirdkill (Bradley)	1983-84 — 1984-85	2	56	39	28	106	1.9	-	-	-	-	-
14	Charles Thomas (Eastern Michigan)	1991-92	1	37	22	22	48	1.3	-	-	-	-	-
11	Isiah Thomas (Indiana)	1981-82 — 1993-94	13	979	3478	9061	18822	19.2	111	524	987	2261	20.4
50	Terry Thomas (Detroit)	1975-76	1	28	36	3	77	2.8	4	1	0	0	0.0
10	Rod Thorn (West Virginia)	1964-65 — 1965-66	2	101	367	225	1192	11.8	-	-	-	-	-
50	Otis Thorpe (Providence)	1995-96 — 1996-97	2	161	1310	291	2197	13.6	8	67	11	84	10.5
24	Ray Tolbert (Indiana)	1982-83 — 1983-84	2	77	189	44	293	3.8	1	0	0	0	0.0
31	George Trapp (Long Beach)	1973-74 — 1976-77	4	242	828	197	2092	8.6	19	79	15	192	10.1
23	John Tresvant (Seattle)	1965-66 — 1967-68	3	169	1302	264	1792	10.6	-	-	-	-	-
7	Kelly Tripucka (Notre Dame)	1981-82 — 1985-86	5	352	1579	1135	7597	21.6	18	85	53	357	19.8
41	Terry Tyler (Detroit)	1978-79 — 1984-85	7	574	3583	776	6638	11.6	17	55	8	153	9.0
V													
5	Tom Van Arsdale (Indiana)	1965-66 — 1967-68	3	208	782	477	2128	10.2	-	-	-	-	-
10	Charles Vaughn (Southern Illinois)	1965-66	1	37	63	104	280	7.6	-	-	-	-	-
W													
26	Andre Wakefield (Loyola, Ill.)	1978-79	1	71	76	69	170	2.4	-	-	-	-	-
5	Darrell Walker (Arkansas)	1991-92 — 1992-93	2	83	257	214	395	4.8	5	12	4	10	2.0
24	Jimmy Walker (Providence)	1967-68 — 1971-72	5	388	972	1278	6262	16.1	6	9	9	76	12.7
18	Bob Warlick (Pepperdine)	1965-66	1	10	16	10	24	2.4	-	-	-	-	-
41	Mark West (Old Dominion)	1994-95 — 1995-96	2	114	541	24	650	5.7	3	16	1	28	9.3
34	James Wilkes (UCLA)	1982-83	1	9	19	10	34	3.8	-	-	-	-	-
31	Dale Wilkinson (Idaho State)	1984-85	1	2	1	0	0	0.0	-	-	-	-	-
12	Cliff Williams (Bowling Green)	1968-69	1	3	3	2	4	1.3	-	-	-	-	-
55	Earl Williams (Winston-Salem)	1975-76	1	46	251	18	168	3.7	-	-	-	-	-
13	Jerome Williams (Georgetown)	1996-97 —	1	33	50	7	49	1.5	1	3	0	4	4.0
24	Michael Williams (Baylor)	1988-89	1	49	27	70	127	2.6	4	2	2	2	0.5
10	Isaiah Wilson (Baltimore)	1971-72	1	48	47	41	167	3.5	-	-	-	-	-
10	Tony Windis (Wyoming)	1959-60	1	9	47	32	36	4.0	-	-	-	-	-
12	David Wood (Nevada-Reno)	1993-94	1	78	239	51	322	4.1	-	-	-	-	-
0	Orlando Woolridge (Notre Dame)	1991-92 — 1992-93	2	132	436	200	1801	13.6	5	10	3	55	11.0
32	Tom Workman (Seattle)	1969-70	1	2	0	0	0	0.0	-	-	-	-	-
15	Larry Wright (Grambling)	1980-81 — 1981-82	2	46	80	153	335	7.3	-	-	-	-	-
Y													
12	George Yardley (Stanford)	1957-58 — 1958-59	2	118	1095	137	2959	25.1	7	72	17	164	23.4
20	Danny Young (Wake Forest)	1992-93	1	65	47	119	188	2.9	-	-	-	-	-
Z													
34	Jim Zoet (Kent State)	1982-83	1	7	8	1	2	0.3	-	-	-	-	-

PISTONS YEAR-BY-YEAR RESULTS

Season	W	L	Pct.	GB	Div. Finish	Playoff Results (w/opponent)
1957-58	33	39	.458	8	T-2nd Western	Lost Western Finals (St. Louis)
1958-59	28	44	.389	21	3rd Western	Lost Western Semifinals (Minneapolis)
1959-60	30	45	.400	16	2nd Western	Lost Western Semifinals (Minneapolis)
1960-61	34	45	.430	17	3rd Western	Lost Western Semifinals (L.A. Lakers)
1961-62	37	43	.463	18	3rd Western	Lost Western Finals (L.A. Lakers)
1962-63	34	46	.425	19	3rd Western	Lost Western Semifinals (St. Louis)
1963-64	23	57	.288	25	5th Western	Did Not Qualify
1964-65	31	49	.388	18	4th Western	Did Not Qualify
1965-66	22	58	.275	23	5th Western	Did Not Qualify
1966-67	30	51	.370	14	5th Western	Did Not Qualify
1967-68	40	42	.488	22	4th Eastern	Lost Eastern Semifinals (Boston)
1968-69	32	50	.390	25	6th Eastern	Did Not Qualify
1969-70	31	51	.378	29	7th Eastern	Did Not Qualify
1970-71	45	37	.549	21	4th Midwest	Did Not Qualify
1971-72	26	56	.549	37	4th Midwest	Did Not Qualify
1972-73	40	42	.488	20	3rd Midwest	Did Not Qualify
1973-74	52	30	.634	7	3rd Midwest	Lost Western Semifinals (Chicago)
1974-75	40	42	.488	7	3rd Midwest	Lost Western First Round (Seattle)
1975-76	36	46	.439	2	2nd Midwest	Lost Western Semifinals (Golden State)
1976-77	44	38	.537	6	T-2nd Midwest	Lost Western First Round (Golden State)
1977-78	38	44	.463	10	4th Midwest	Did Not Qualify
1978-79	30	52	.366	18	T-4th Central	Did Not Qualify
1979-80	16	66	.366	34	6th Central	Did Not Qualify
1980-81	21	61	.256	39	6th Central	Did Not Qualify
1981-82	39	43	.476	16	3rd Central	Did Not Qualify
1982-83	37	45	.451	14	3rd Central	Did Not Qualify
1983-84	49	33	.598	1	2nd Central	Lost Eastern First Round (N.Y. Knicks)
1984-85	46	36	.561	13	2nd Central	Lost Eastern Semifinals (Boston)
1985-86	46	36	.561	11	3rd Central	Lost Eastern First Round (Atlanta)
1986-87	52	30	.634	5	2nd Central	Lost Eastern Finals (Boston)
1987-88	54	28	.659	—	1st Central	Lost NBA Finals (L.A. Lakers)
1988-89	63	19	.786	—	1st Central	Won NBA Finals (L.A. Lakers)
1989-90	59	23	.720	—	1st Central	Won NBA Finals (Portland)
1990-91	50	32	.610	11	2nd Central	Lost Eastern Finals (Chicago)
1991-92	48	34	.585	19	3rd Central	Lost Eastern First Round (N.Y. Knicks)
1992-93	40	42	.488	17	6th Central	Did Not Qualify
1993-94	20	62	.244	37	T-6th Central	Did Not Qualify
1994-95	28	54	.341	24	7th Central	Did Not Qualify
1995-96	46	36	.561	26	T-4th Central	Lost Eastern First Round (Orlando)
1996-97	54	28	.659	15	T-3rd Central	Lost Eastern First Round (Atlanta)

ALL-TIME RECORD: 1524-1715 (.471)

PISTONS CAREER LEADERS 1957-97

(Regular season only; Detroit only)

TOTAL POINTS

Isiah Thomas	18,822
Bob Lanier	15,488
Dave Bing	15,235
Joe Dumars	15,030
Bill Laimbeer	12,664
Vinnie Johnson	10,146
John Long	9,023
Bailey Howell	8,182
Kelly Tripucka	7,597
Eddie Miles	7,419
Gene Shue	7,247
Dave DeBusschere	7,096
Ray Scott	6,724
Terry Tyler	6,638
Jimmy Walker	6,262
Terry Dischinger	5,522
Curtis Rowe	5,407
Terry Mills	5,324
Don Ohl	5,137
Grant Hill	4,722
Walter Dukes	4,580

SCORING AVERAGE
(Minimum 120 games)

Bob Lanier (681 gm.)	22.7
Dave Bing (675)	22.6
Grant Hill (230)	20.5
Kelly Tripucka (352)	21.6
Bailey Howell (387)	21.1
Adrian Dantley (192)	20.3
Gene Shue (368)	19.7
Isiah Thomas (979)	19.2
Happy Hairston (122)	17.3
Don Ohl (307)	16.7
Joe Dumars (908)	16.6
Dave DeBusschere (440)	16.1
Eddie Miles (497)	14.9
John Long (608)	14.8
M.L. Carr (241)	14.8
Allan Houston (237)	14.3
Walt Bellamy (109)	14.3
Otis Thorpe (161)	13.6
Bill Laimbeer (937)	13.5
Terry Mills (394)	13.5

REBOUNDS

Bill Laimbeer	9,430
Bob Lanier	8,063
Dennis Rodman	6,299
Walter Dukes	4,986
Dave DeBusschere	4,947
Bailey Howell	4,583
Ray Scott	4,508
Terry Tyler	3,583
Isiah Thomas	3,478
Curtis Rowe	3,256
Dave Bing	2,828
Vinnie Johnson	2,491
Kent Benson	2,437
Terry Dischinger	2,341
Joe Strawder	2,296
Leon Douglas	2,273

ASSISTS

Isiah Thomas	9,061
Dave Bing	4,330
Joe Dumars	4,225
Vinnie Johnson	2,661
Bob Lanier	2,256
Bill Laimbeer	1,923
Kevin Porter	1,920
Chris Ford	1,698
Gene Shue	1,693
Grant Hill	1,484
Jimmy Walker	1,278
Eric Money	1,276
Dick McGuire	1,255
Ray Scott	1,228
Dave DeBusschere	1,152
John Long	1,136
Kelly Tripucka	1,135
Howie Komives	1,081
Don Ohl	1,059

GAMES

Isiah Thomas	979
Bill Laimbeer	937
Joe Dumars	908
Vinnie Johnson	798
Bob Lanier	681
Dave Bing	675
John Long	583
Terry Tyler	574
Dennis Rodman	549
Eddie Miles	497
Chris Ford	485
John Salley	459
Terry Dischinger	456
Dave DeBusschere	440
Walter Dukes	422
Ray Scott	421
Curtis Rowe	407

MINUTES

Isiah Thomas	35,516
Joe Dumars	31,697
Bill Laimbeer	30,602
Dave Bing	26,052
Bob Lanier	24,640
Vinnie Johnson	20,218
Dennis Rodman	16,345
John Long	16,226
Terry Tyler	15,919
Dave DeBussch1ere	15,235
Gene Shue	14,920
Curtis Rowe	13,954
Eddie Miles	13,890
Ray Scott	13,885
Bailey Howell	13,826
Chris Ford	12,985
Kelly Tripucka	12,123
Jimmy Walker	11,941
Terry Dischinger	11,761
Walter Dukes	11,515
Terry Mills	11,123

John Salley	10,261
Don Ohl	10,025

STEALS
(Since 1973-74)

Isiah Thomas	1,861
Joe Dumars	835
Chris Ford	785
Vinnie Johnson	708
John Long	649
Bill Laimbeer	632
Terry Tyler	615
M.L. Carr	509
Bob Lanier	504
Eric Money	437

BLOCKED SHOTS
(Since 1973-74)

Terry Tyler	1,070
Bob Lanier	859
Bill Laimbeer	830
John Salley	709
Dennis Rodman	399
Kent Benson	331
Isiah Thomas	249
Leon Douglas	246
Theo Ratliff	227
Rick Mahorn	222
Vinnie Johnson	213
Joe Dumars	210

FIELD GOALS MADE

Isiah Thomas	7,194
Bob Lanier	6,276
Dave Bing	5,772
Joe Dumars	5,421
Bill Laimbeer	5,071
Vinnie Johnson	4,202
John Long	3,851
Eddie Miles	3,019
Bailey Howell	2,905
Kelly Tripucka	2,807
Dave DeBusschere	2,783
Gene Shue	2,667

FIELD GOALS ATTEMPTED

Isiah Thomas	15,904
Dave Bing	13,119
Bob Lanier	12,347
Joe Dumars	11,885
Bill Laimbeer	10,275
Vinnie Johnson	9,094
John Long	8,060
Eddie Miles	6,804
Gene Shue	6,584
Dave DeBusschere	6,553

THREE-POINTERS MADE

Joe Dumars	743
Lindsey Hunter	463
Terry Mills	400

Isiah Thomas	398
Allan Houston	346
Bill Laimbeer	199
Mark Aguirre	112
Dennis Rodman	65
Vinnie Johnson	63
Michael Curry	43
Ron Lee	42

THREE-POINTERS ATTEMPTED

Joe Dumars	1,945
Isiah Thomas	1,373
Lindsey Hunter	1,309
Terry Mills	1,016
Allan Houston	817
Bill Laimbeer	613
Mark Aguirre	400
Vinnie Johnson	260
Dennis Rodman	257
Ron Lee	128
Michael Curry	127

THREE-POINT PERCENTAGE
(120 attempts)

Allan Houston	.424
Terry Mills	.394
Joe Dumars	.382
Lindsey Hunter	.354
Michael Curry	.339
Ron Lee	.328
Bill Laimbeer	.325
Isiah Thomas	.290
Mark Aguirre	.280
Dennis Rodman	.253

FREE THROWS MADE

Isiah Thomas	4,036
Dave Bing	3,691
Joe Dumars	3,245
Bob Lanier	2,936
Bailey Howell	2,372
Bill Laimbeer	2,230
Kelly Tripucka	1,948
Gene Shue	1,913
Vinnie Johnson	1,669
Ray Scott	1,590
Dave DeBusschere	1,530

FREE THROWS ATTEMPTED

Isiah Thomas	5,316
Dave Bing	4,789
Joe Dumars	3,844
Bob Lanier	3,797
Bailey Howell	3,063
Bill Laimbeer	2,621
Kelly Tripucka	2,340
Gene Shue	2,279
Ray Scott	2,256
Dave DeBusschere	2,222
Vinnie Johnson	2,137

PISTONS YEAR-BY-YEAR STATISTICAL LEADERS

(x - league leader)

SCORING AVERAGE

YEAR	PLAYER	GP	AVG
1957-58	x-George Yardley	72	27.8
1958-59	Gene Shue	72	17.6
1959-60	Gene Shue	75	22.8
1960-61	Bailey Howell	77	23.6
1961-62	Bailey Howell	79	19.9
1962-63	Bailey Howell	79	22.7
1963-64	Bailey Howell	77	21.6
1964-65	Terry Dischinger	80	18.2
1965-66	Eddie Miles	80	19.6
1966-67	Dave Bing	80	20.0
1967-68	x-Dave Bing	79	27.1
1968-69	Dave Bing	77	23.4
1969-70	Dave Bing	70	22.9
1970-71	Dave Bing	82	27.0
1971-72	Bob Lanier	80	25.7
1972-73	Bob Lanier	81	23.8
1973-74	Bob Lanier	81	22.5
1974-75	Bob Lanier	76	24.0
1975-76	Bob Lanier	64	21.3
1976-77	Bob Lanier	64	25.3
1977-78	Bob Lanier	63	24.5
1978-79	Bob Lanier	53	23.6
1979-80	Bob McAdoo	58	21.1
1980-81	John Long	59	17.7
1981-82	John Long	69	21.9
1982-83	Kelly Tripucka	58	26.5
1983-84	Isiah Thomas	82	21.3
	Kelly Tripucka	76	21.3
1984-85	Isiah Thomas	81	21.2
1985-86	Isiah Thomas	77	20.9
1986-87	Adrian Dantley	81	21.5
1987-88	Adrian Dantley	69	20.0
1988-89	Isiah Thomas	80	18.2
1989-90	Isiah Thomas	81	18.4
1990-91	Joe Dumars	80	20.4
1991-92	Joe Dumars	82	19.9
1992-93	Joe Dumars	77	23.5
1993-94	Joe Dumars	69	20.4
1994-95	Grant Hill	70	19.9
1995-96	Grant Hill	80	20.2
1996-97	Grant Hill	80	21.4

TOTAL POINTS

YEAR	PLAYER	PTS
1957-58	x-George Yardley	2,001
1958-59	Gene Shue	1,266
1959-60	Gene Shue	1,712
1960-61	Bailey Howell	1,815
1961-62	Bailey Howell	1,576
1962-63	Bailey Howell	1,793
1963-64	Bailey Howell	1,666
1964-65	Terry Dischinger	1,456
1965-66	Eddie Miles	1,566
1966-67	Dave Bing	1,601
1967-68	x-Dave Bing	2,142
1968-69	Dave Bing	1,800
1969-70	Jimmy Walker	1,687
1970-71	Dave Bing	2,213
1972-73	Bob Lanier	1,927
1973-74	Bob Lanier	1,822
1974-75	Bob Lanier	1,823
1975-76	Bob Lanier	1,366
1976-77	Bob Lanier	1,616
1977-78	Bob Lanier	1,542
1978-79	M.L. Carr	1,497
1979-80	John Long	1,337
1980-81	Phil Hubbard	1,161
1981-82	Kelly Tripucka	1,772
1982-83	Isiah Thomas	1,854
1983-84	Isiah Thomas	1,748
1984-85	Isiah Thomas	1,720
1985-86	Kelly Tripucka	1,622
1986-87	Adrian Dantley	1,742
1987-88	Isiah Thomas	1,577
1988-89	Isiah Thomas	1,458
1989-90	Isiah Thomas	1,492
1990-91	Joe Dumars	1,629
1991-92	Joe Dumars	1,635
1992-93	Joe Dumars	1,809
1993-94	Joe Dumars	1,410
1994-95	Grant Hill	1,394
1995-96	Grant Hill	1,618
1996-97	Grant Hill	1,710

REBOUNDING

YEAR	PLAYER	GP	REB	AVG
1957-58	Walter Dukes	72	954	13.3
1958-59	Walter Dukes	72	958	13.3
1959-60	Walter Dukes	66	883	13.4
1960-61	Bailey Howell	77	1,111	14.4
1961-62	Bailey Howell	79	996	12.6
1962-63	Bailey Howell	79	910	11.5
1963-64	Ray Scott	80	1,078	13.5
1964-65	Reggie Harding	78	906	11.6
1965-66	Dave DeBusschere	79	916	11.6
1966-67	Dave DeBusschere	78	924	11.8
1967-68	Dave DeBusschere	80	1,081	13.5
1968-69	Happy Hairston	81	959	11.8
1969-70	Otto Moore	81	900	11.2
1970-71	Otto Moore	82	700	8.5
1971-72	Bob Lanier	80	1,132	14.2
1972-73	Bob Lanier	81	1,205	14.9
1973-74	Bob Lanier	81	1,074	13.3
1974-75	Bob Lanier	76	914	12.0
1975-76	Bob Lanier	64	746	11.7
1977-78	Bob Lanier	63	715	11.3
1978-79	Leon Douglas	78	664	8.5
1979-80	Terry Tyler	82	627	7.6
1980-81	Phil Hubbard	80	586	7.3
1981-82	Kent Benson	75	653	8.7
1982-83	Bill Laimbeer	82	993	12.1
1983-84	Bill Laimbeer	82	1,003	12.2
1984-85	Bill Laimbeer	82	1,013	12.4
1985-86	x-Bill Laimbeer	82	1,075	13.1
1986-87	Bill Laimbeer	82	955	11.6
1987-88	Bill Laimbeer	82	832	10.1
1988-89	Bill Laimbeer	81	776	9.6
1989-90	Dennis Rodman	82	792	9.7
1990-91	Dennis Rodman	82	1,026	12.5
1991-92	x-Dennis Rodman	82	1,530	18.7
1992-93	x-Dennis Rodman	62	1,132	18.3
1993-94	Terry Mills	80	672	8.4
1994-95	Terry Mills	72	558	7.8
1995-96	Grant Hill	80	783	9.8
1996-97	Grant Hill	80	721	9.0

ASSISTS

YEAR	PLAYER	GP	AST	AVG
1957-58	Dick McGuire	69	454	6.6
1958-59	Dick McGuire	71	443	6.2
1960-61	Gene Shue	78	530	6.8
1961-62	Gene Shue	80	465	5.8
1962-63	Don Ohl	80	325	4.1
1963-64	Ray Scott	80	244	3.1
1964-65	Dave DeBusschere	79	253	3.2
1965-66	Ray Scott	79	238	3.0
1966-67	Dave Bing	80	330	4.1
1967-68	Dave Bing	79	509	6.4
1968-69	Dave Bing	77	546	7.1
1969-70	Dave Bing	70	418	6.0
1970-71	Dave Bing	82	408	5.0
1971-72	Dave Bing	45	317	7.1
1972-73	Dave Bing	82	637	7.8
1973-74	Dave Bing	81	555	6.9
1974-75	Dave Bing	79	610	7.7
1975-76	Eric Money	80	338	4.2
1976-77	Kevin Porter	81	592	7.3
1977-78	Chris Ford	82	381	4.6
1978-79	x-Kevin Porter	82	1,099	13.4
1979-80	Eric Money	55	238	4.3
1980-81	Ron Lee	82	362	4.4
1981-82	Isiah Thomas	72	565	7.8
1982-83	Isiah Thomas	81	634	7.8
1983-84	Isiah Thomas	82	914	11.1
1984-85	x-Isiah Thomas	81	1,123	13.9
1985-86	Isiah Thomas	77	830	10.8
1987-88	Isiah Thomas	81	678	8.4
1988-89	Isiah Thomas	80	653	8.2
1989-90	Isiah Thomas	81	765	9.4
1990-91	Isiah Thomas	48	446	9.3
1991-92	Isiah Thomas	78	560	7.2
1992-93	Isiah Thomas	79	671	8.5
1993-94	Isiah Thomas	58	399	6.9
1994-95	Joe Dumars	67	368	5.5
1995-96	Grant Hill	80	548	6.9
1996-97	Grant Hill	80	583	7.3

MINUTES

YEAR	PLAYER	GP	MIN	AVG
1957-58	George Yardley	72	2,843	39.5
1958-59	Gene Shue	72	2,745	38.1
1959-60	x-Gene Shue	75	3,338	44.5
1960-61	Gene Shue	78	3,361	43.1
1961-62	Gene Shue	80	3,143	39.3
1962-63	Bailey Howell	79	2,971	37.6
1963-64	Ray Scott	80	2,964	37.1
1964-65	Dave DeBusschere	79	2,769	35.1
1965-66	Eddie Miles	80	2,788	34.9
1966-67	Dave DeBusschere	78	2,897	37.1
1967-68	Dave Bing	79	3,209	40.6
1968-69	Dave Bing	77	3,039	39.5

1969-70	Jimmy Walker	81	2,869	35.4
1970-71	Dave Bing	82	3,065	37.4
1971-72	Bob Lanier	80	3,092	38.7
1972-73	Dave Bing	82	3,361	41.0
1973-74	Dave Bing	81	3,124	38.6
1974-75	Dave Bing	79	3,222	40.8
1975-76	Curtis Rowe	80	2,998	37.5
1976-77	M.L. Carr	82	2,643	32.2
1977-78	Chris Ford	82	2,582	31.5
1978-79	M.L. Carr	80	3,207	40.1
1979-80	Terry Tyler	82	2,670	32.6
1980-81	Terry Tyler	82	2,549	31.1
1981-82	Kelly Tripucka	82	3,077	37.5
1982-83	x-Isiah Thomas	81	3,092	38.1
1983-84	Isiah Thomas	82	3,007	36.7
1984-85	Isiah Thomas	81	3,089	38.1
1985-86	Bill Laimbeer	82	2,891	35.3
1986-87	Isiah Thomas	81	3,013	37.2
1987-88	Isiah Thomas	81	2,927	36.1
1988-89	Isiah Thomas	80	2,924	36.6
1989-90	Isiah Thomas	81	2,993	37.0
1990-91	Joe Dumars	80	3,046	38.1
1991-92	Dennis Rodman	82	3,301	40.3
1992-93	Joe Dumars	77	3,094	40.2
1993-94	Terry Mills	80	2,773	34.7
1995-96	Grant Hill	80	3,260	40.8
1996-97	Grant Hill	80	3,147	39.3

STEALS

(Since 1973-74)

YEAR	PLAYER	GP	STL	AVG
1973-74	Chris Ford	82	148	1.8
1974-75	Dave Bing	79	116	1.5
1975-76	Chris Ford	82	178	2.2
1976-77	Chris Ford	82	179	2.2
1977-78	Chris Ford	82	166	2.0
1978-79	x-M.L. Carr	80	197	2.5
1979-80	John Long	69	129	1.9
1980-81	Ron Lee	82	166	2.0
1981-82	Isiah Thomas	82	150	1.8
1982-83	Isiah Thomas	81	199	2.5
1983-84	Isiah Thomas	82	204	2.5
1984-85	Isiah Thomas	81	187	2.3
1985-86	Isiah Thomas	77	171	2.2
1986-87	Isiah Thomas	81	153	1.9
1987-88	Isiah Thomas	81	141	1.7
1988-89	Isiah Thomas	80	133	1.7
1989-90	Isiah Thomas	81	139	1.7
1990-91	Joe Dumars	80	89	1.1
1991-92	Isiah Thomas	78	118	1.5
1992-93	Isiah Thomas	79	123	1.6
1993-94	Lindsey Hunter	82	121	1.5
1995-96	Grant Hill	80	100	1.3
1996-97	Grant Hill	80	144	1.8

BLOCKED SHOTS

(Since 1973-74)

YEAR	PLAYER	GP	BLK	AVG
1973-74	Bob Lanier	81	247	3.1
1974-75	Bob Lanier	76	172	2.3
1975-76	Bob Lanier	64	86	1.3
1976-77	Bob Lanier	64	126	1.9
1977-78	Bob Lanier	63	93	1.5
1978-79	Terry Tyler	82	201	2.5
1979-80	Terry Tyler	82	220	2.7
1980-81	Terry Tyler	82	180	2.2
1981-82	Terry Tyler	82	160	2.0
1982-83	Terry Tyler	82	160	2.0
1983-84	Bill Laimbeer	82	84	1.0
1984-85	Terry Tyler	82	90	1.1
1985-86	Bill Laimbeer	82	65	0.8
1986-87	John Salley	82	125	1.5
1987-88	John Salley	82	137	1.7
1988-89	Bill Laimbeer	81	100	1.2
1989-90	John Salley	82	153	1.9
1990-91	John Salley	74	112	1.5
1991-92	John Salley	72	110	1.5
1992-93	Terry Mills	81	50	0.6
1993-94	Cadillac Anderson	77	68	0.9
1994-95	Oliver Miller	64	116	1.8
1995-96	Theo Ratliff	75	116	1.5
1996-97	Theo Ratliff	76	111	1.5

FIELD GOAL SHOOTING

YEAR	PLAYER	FG	FGA	PCT
1957-58	George Yardley	673	1,624	.413
1958-59	Shellie McMillon	127	289	.439
1959-60	Bailey Howell	510	1,119	.456
1960-61	Bailey Howell	607	1,293	.469
1961-62	Bailey Howell	553	1,193	.464
1962-63	Bailey Howell	637	1,235	.516
1963-64	Bailey Howell	598	1,267	.493
1964-65	Terry Dischinger	568	1,153	.493
1965-66	Eddie Miles	634	1,418	.447
1966-67	Reggie Harding	172	382	.450
1967-68	Len Chappell	255	458	.513
1968-69	Terry Dischinger	264	513	.515
1969-70	Terry Dischinger	342	650	.526
1970-71	Terry Dischinger	304	568	.535
1971-72	Terry Dischinger	295	574	.514
1972-73	Curtis Rowe	547	1,053	.519
1973-74	Bob Lanier	748	1,483	.504
1974-75	Bob Lanier	731	1,438	.510
1975-76	Bob Lanier	541	1,017	.532
1976-77	Bob Lanier	678	1,269	.534
1977-78	Bob Lanier	622	1,159	.537
1978-79	Bob Lanier	489	948	.516
1979-80	Eric Money	259	510	.508
1980-81	Terry Tyler	476	895	.532
1981-82	Terry Tyler	336	643	.523
1982-83	Vinnie Johnson	520	1,013	.513
1983-84	Kent Benson	248	451	.550
1984-85	Kent Benson	201	397	.506
1985-86	Earl Cureton	285	564	.505
1986-87	John Salley	163	290	.562
1987-88	Rick Mahorn	276	481	.574
1988-89	x-Dennis Rodman	316	531	.595
1989-90	Dennis Rodman	288	496	.581
1990-91	Dennis Rodman	276	560	.493
1991-92	Dennis Rodman	342	635	.539
1992-93	Bill Laimbeer	292	574	.509
1993-94	Cadillac Anderson	201	370	.543
1994-95	Mark West	217	390	.556
1995-96	Otis Thorpe	452	853	.530
1996-97	Otis Thorpe	419	787	.532

THREE-POINT SHOOTING

(At least 50 attempts)

YEAR	PLAYER	3P	3PA	PCT
1979-80	Ron Lee	22	56	.393
1980-81	(Phil Hubbard	1	3	.333)
1981-82	Ron Lee	18	59	.305
1982-83	(Kelly Tripucka	14	37	.378)
1983-84	Isiah Thomas	22	65	.338
1984-85	Isiah Thomas	29	113	.257
1985-86	Isiah Thomas	26	84	.310

(At least 80 attempts)

YEAR	PLAYER	3P	3PA	PCT
1986-87	Isiah Thomas	19	98	.194
1987-88	Isiah Thomas	30	97	.309
1988-89	Isiah Thomas	33	121	.273
1989-90	Bill Laimbeer	57	158	.361
1990-91	Bill Laimbeer	37	125	.296
1991-92	Joe Dumars	49	120	.408
1992-93	Joe Dumars	112	299	.375
1993-94	Joe Dumars	124	320	.388
1994-95	Allan Houston	158	373	.424
1995-96	Allan Houston	191	447	.427
1996-97	Joe Dumars	166	384	.432

FREE THROW SHOOTING

YEAR	PLAYER	FT	FTA	PCT
1957-58	Gene Shue	276	327	.844
1958-59	Gene Shue	338	421	.803
1959-60	Gene Shue	472	541	.872
1960-61	Gene Shue	465	543	.856
1961-62	Gene Shue	362	447	.810
1962-63	Bailey Howell	519	650	.798
1963-64	Bailey Howell	470	581	.809
1964-65	Terry Dischinger	320	424	.755
1965-66	Ray Scott	323	435	.743
1966-67	Tom Van Arsdale	272	347	.784
1967-68	Jimmy Walker	134	175	.766
1968-69	Jimmy Walker	182	229	.795
1969-70	McCoy McLemore	119	145	.821
1970-71	Jimmy Walker	344	414	.831
1971-72	Jimmy Walker	397	480	.827
1972-73	Dave Bing	456	560	.814
1973-74	Stu Lantz	139	163	.853
1974-75	John Mengelt	211	248	.851
1975-76	Archie Clark	100	116	.862
1976-77	Howard Porter	103	120	.858
1977-78	Jim Price	84	103	.815
1978-79	John Long	157	190	.826
1979-80	John Long	160	194	.825
1980-81	John Long	160	184	.870
1981-82	John Long	238	275	.865
1982-83	Kelly Tripucka	392	465	.843
1983-84	John Long	243	275	.884
1984-85	Kelly Tripucka	255	288	.885
1985-86	Kelly Tripucka	380	444	.856
1986-87	Bill Laimbeer	245	274	.894
1987-88	Bill Laimbeer	187	214	.874
1988-89	Joe Dumars	260	306	.850
1989-90	Joe Dumars	297	330	.900
1990-91	Joe Dumars	371	417	.890
1991-92	Bill Laimbeer	67	75	.893
1992-93	Bill Laimbeer	93	104	.894
1993-94	Joe Dumars	276	330	.836
1994-95	Allan Houston	147	171	.860
1995-96	Allan Houston	298	362	.823
1996-97	Michael Curry	97	108	.898

TURNOVERS

(Since 1977-78)

YEAR	PLAYER	GP	TO	AVG
1977-78	Eric Money	76	322	4.2
1978-79	Kevin Porter	82	340	4.1
1979-80	Bob McAdoo	58	238	4.1
1980-81	Kent Benson	59	190	3.2
1981-82	x-Isiah Thomas	72	299	4.2
1982-83	Isiah Thomas	81	326	4.0
1983-84	Isiah Thomas	82	307	3.7
1984-85	Isiah Thomas	81	302	3.7
1985-86	Isiah Thomas	77	289	3.8
1986-87	Isiah Thomas	81	343	4.2
1987-88	Isiah Thomas	81	273	3.4
1988-89	Isiah Thomas	80	298	3.7
1989-90	x-Isiah Thomas	81	322	4.0
1990-91	Joe Dumars	80	189	2.4
1991-92	Isiah Thomas	78	252	3.2
1992-93	Isiah Thomas	79	284	3.6
1993-94	Isiah Thomas	58	202	3.5
1994-95	Joe Dumars	67	219	3.3
1995-96	Grant Hill	80	263	3.3
1996-97	Grant Hill	80	259	3.2

PERSONAL FOULS

YEAR	PLAYER	GP	PF	AVG
1957-58	x-Walter Dukes	72	311	4.3
1958-59	x-Walter Dukes	72	332	4.6
1959-60	Walter Dukes	66	310	4.7
1960-61	Walter Dukes	73	313	4.3
1961-62	Walter Dukes	77	327	4.2
1962-63	Bailey Howell	79	301	3.8
1963-64	Ray Scott	80	296	3.7
1964-65	Reggie Harding	78	258	3.3
1965-66	Joe Strawder	79	305	3.9
1966-67	x-Joe Strawder	79	344	4.4
1967-68	Joe Strawder	73	312	4.3
1968-69	Dave Bing	77	256	3.3
1969-70	Howie Komives	82	247	3.0
1970-71	Bob Lanier	82	272	3.3
1971-72	Bob Lanier	80	297	3.7
1972-73	Bob Lanier	81	278	3.4
1973-74	Bob Lanier	81	273	3.4
1974-75	Bob Lanier	76	237	3.1
1975-76	Al Eberhard	81	250	3.1
1976-77	Leon Douglas	82	294	3.6
1977-78	Leon Douglas	79	295	3.7
1978-79	Kevin Porter	82	302	3.7
1979-80	Leon Douglas	70	219	3.6
1980-81	Phil Hubbard	80	317	4.0
1981-82	Isiah Thomas	72	253	3.5
1982-83	Bill Laimbeer	82	320	3.9
1983-84	Isiah Thomas	82	324	3.9
1984-85	Bill Laimbeer	82	308	3.8
1985-86	Bill Laimbeer	82	291	3.6
1986-87	Bill Laimbeer	82	283	3.5
1987-88	John Salley	82	294	3.6
1988-89	Dennis Rodman	82	292	3.6
1989-90	James Edwards	82	295	3.6
1990-91	Dennis Rodman	82	281	3.4
1991-92	Dennis Rodman	82	248	3.0
1992-93	Terry Mills	81	282	3.5
1993-94	Terry Mills	80	309	3.9
1994-95	Terry Mills	72	253	3.5
1995-96	x-Otis Thorpe	82	300	3.7
1996-97	Otis Thorpe	79	298	3.8

• APPENDIX E •

PISTONS SINGLE-SEASON LEADERS

(x-league leader)

POINTS

PLAYER	YEAR	PTS
Dave Bing	1970-71	2,213
x-Dave Bing	1967-68	2,142
Bob Lanier	1971-72	2,056
x-George Yardley	1957-58	2,001
Bob Lanier	1972-73	1,927
Isiah Thomas	1982-83	1,854
Dave Bing	1972-73	1,840
Bob Lanier	1974-75	1,823
Bob Lanier	1973-74	1,822
Bailey Howell	1960-61	1,815
Joe Dumars	1992-93	1,809
Dave Bing	1968-69	1,800
Bailey Howell	1962-63	1,793
Kelly Tripucka	1981-82	1,772
Gene Shue	1960-61	1,765
Isiah Thomas	1983-84	1,748
Adrian Dantley	1986-87	1,742
Isiah Thomas	1984-85	1,720
Gene Shue	1959-60	1,712
Grant Hill	1996-97	1,710
Jimmy Walker	1969-70	1,687
Isiah Thomas	1986-87	1,671
Bailey Howell	1963-64	1,666
Jimmy Walker	1971-72	1,665
Joe Dumars	1991-92	1,635
Joe Dumars	1990-91	1,629
Kelly Tripucka	1985-86	1,622
Kelly Tripucka	1983-84	1,618
Grant Hill	1995-96	1,618
Bob Lanier	1976-77	1,616
Isiah Thomas	1985-86	1,609
Dave Bing	1969-70	1,604
Dave Bing	1966-67	1,601
Bailey Howell	1961-62	1,576
Eddie Miles	1965-66	1,566
Don Ohl	1962-63	1,547
Bob Lanier	1977-78	1,542
Kelly Tripucka	1982-83	1,536
Gene Shue	1961-62	1,522
Dave Bing	1973-74	1,522
John Long	1981-82	1,514

REBOUNDS

PLAYER	YEAR	REB
x-Dennis Rodman	1991-92	1,530
Bob Lanier	1972-73	1,205
x-Dennis Rodman	1992-93	1,132
Bob Lanier	1971-72	1,132
Bailey Howell	1960-61	1,111
Dave DeBusschere	1967-68	1,081
Ray Scott	1963-64	1,078
x-Bill Laimbeer	1985-86	1,075
Bob Lanier	1973-74	1,074
Walter Dukes	1960-61	1,028
Dennis Rodman	1990-91	1,026
Bill Laimbeer	1984-85	1,013
Bill Laimbeer	1983-84	1,003
Bailey Howell	1961-62	996
Bill Laimbeer	1982-83	993
Happy Hairston	1968-69	959
Walter Dukes	1958-59	958
Bill Laimbeer	1986-87	955
Walter Dukes	1957-58	954
Dave DeBusschere	1966-67	924
Dave DeBusschere	1965-66	916
Bob Lanier	1974-75	914
Bailey Howell	1962-63	910
Reggie Harding	1964-65	906
Otto Moore	1969-70	900

ASSISTS

PLAYER	YEAR	AST
x-Isiah Thomas	1984-85	1,123
x-Kevin Porter	1978-79	1,099
Isiah Thomas	1983-84	914
Isiah Thomas	1985-86	830
Isiah Thomas	1986-87	813
Isiah Thomas	1989-90	765
Isiah Thomas	1987-88	678
Isiah Thomas	1992-93	671
Isiah Thomas	1988-89	653
Dave Bing	1972-73	637
Isiah Thomas	1982-83	634
Dave Bing	1974-75	610
Kevin Porter	1976-77	592
Grant Hill	1996-97	583
Isiah Thomas	1981-82	565

Isiah Thomas	1991-92	560
Dave Bing	1973-74	555
Grant Hill	1995-96	548
Dave Bing	1968-69	546
Gene Shue	1960-61	530
Dave Bing	1967-68	509

MINUTES

PLAYER	YEAR	MIN
Gene Shue	1960-61	3,361
Dave Bing	1972-73	3,361
x-Gene Shue	1959-60	3,338
Dennis Rodman	1991-92	3,301
Grant Hill	1995-96	3,260
Dave Bing	1974-75	3,222
Dave Bing	1967-68	3,209
M.L. Carr	1978-79	3,207
Joe Dumars	1991-92	3,192
Grant Hill	1996-97	3,147
Gene Shue	1961-62	3,143
Dave DeBusschere	1967-68	3,125
Dave Bing	1973-74	3,124

STEALS
(Since 1973-74)

PLAYER	YEAR	STL
Isiah Thomas	1983-84	204
Isiah Thomas	1982-83	199
x-M.L. Carr	1978-79	197
Isiah Thomas	1984-85	187
Chris Ford	1976-77	179
Chris Ford	1975-76	178
Isiah Thomas	1985-86	171
Ron Lee	1980-81	166
Chris Ford	1977-78	166
M.L. Carr	1976-77	165
Kevin Porter	1978-79	158
Isiah Thomas	1986-87	153
Isiah Thomas	1981-82	150

BLOCKED SHOTS
(Since 1973-74)

PLAYER	YEAR	STL
Bob Lanier	1973-74	247
Terry Tyler	1979-80	220

235

Terry Tyler	1978-79	201
Terry Tyler	1980-81	180
Bob Lanier	1974-75	172
Terry Tyler	1981-82	160
Terry Tyler	1982-83	160
John Salley	1989-90	153
John Salley	1987-88	137
Bob Lanier	1976-77	126
John Salley	1986-87	125

FIELD GOAL SHOOTING

PLAYER	YEAR	PCT
x-Dennis Rodman	1988-89	.595
Dennis Rodman	1989-90	.581
Rick Mahorn	1987-88	.574
John Salley	1987-88	.566
John Salley	1986-87	.562
Dennis Rodman	1987-88	.561
Mark West	1994-95	.556
Oliver Miller	1994-95	.555
Kent Benson	1983-84	.550
Olden Polynice	1993-94	.547
Dennis Rodman	1986-87	.545
Cadillac Anderson	1993-94	.543
Dennis Rodman	1991-92	.539
Bob Lanier	1977-78	.537
Terry Dischinger	1970-71	.535
Adrian Dantley	1986-87	.534
Bob Lanier	1976-77	.534

THREE-POINT SHOOTING

(80 attempts)

PLAYER	YEAR	PCT
Joe Dumars	1996-97	.432
Allan Houston	1995-96	.427

Allan Houston	1994-95	.424
Terry Mills	1996-97	.422
Joe Dumars	1991-92	.408
Joe Dumars	1995-96	.406
Lindsey Hunter	1995-96	.405
Terry Mills	1995-96	.396
Joe Dumars	1993-94	.388
Terry Mills	1994-95	.382
Joe Dumars	1992-93	.375
Bill Laimbeer	1989-90	.361
Mark Aguirre	1992-93	.361

FREE THROW SHOOTING

PLAYER	YEAR	PCT
Joe Dumars	1989-90	.900
Michael Curry	1996-97	.898
Bill Laimbeer	1986-87	.894
Bill Laimbeer	1992-93	.894
Bill Laimbeer	1991-92	.893
Joe Dumars	1990-91	.890
Kelly Tripucka	1984-85	.885
John Long	1983-84	.884
Bill Laimbeer	1987-88	.874
Gene Shue	1959-60	.872
John Long	1980-81	.870

TURNOVERS

(Since 1977-78)

PLAYER	YEAR	TO
Isiah Thomas	1986-87	343
Kevin Porter	1978-79	340
Isiah Thomas	1982-83	326
Eric Money	1977-78	322
x-Isiah Thomas	1989-90	322
Isiah Thomas	1983-84	307

Isiah Thomas	1984-85	302
x-Isiah Thomas	1981-82	299
Isiah Thomas	1988-89	298
Isiah Thomas	1985-86	289
Isiah Thomas	1992-93	284
Kelly Tripucka	1981-82	280
Isiah Thomas	1987-88	273
Grant Hill	1995-96	263
Grant Hill	1996-97	259
Isiah Thomas	1991-92	252

PERSONAL FOULS

PLAYER	YEAR	PF
x-Joe Strawder	1966-67	344
x-Walter Dukes	1958-59	332
Walter Dukes	1961-62	327
Isiah Thomas	1983-84	324
Bill Laimbeer	1982-83	320
Isiah Thomas	1982-83	318
Phil Hubbard	1980-81	317
Walter Dukes	1960-61	313
Joe Strawder	1967-68	312
x-Walter Dukes	1957-58	311
Walter Dukes	1959-60	310
Terry Mills	1993-94	309
Bill Laimbeer	1984-85	308
Joe Strawder	1965-66	305
Dave DeBusschere	1967-68	304
Kevin Porter	1978-79	302
Bailey Howell	1962-63	301
x-Otis Thorpe	1995-96	300

· A P P E N D I X F ·
PISTONS YEAR-BY-YEAR
SCORING STATISTICS

1957-58

REGULAR SEASON (33-39)

PLAYER	G	MIN	FGM	FGA	PCT	FTM	FTA	PCT	REB	AST	PF	DQ	PTS	PPG
George Yardley	72	2843	673	1624	.414	655	808	.811	768	97	226	3	2001	27.8
Gene Shue	63	2333	353	919	.384	276	327	.844	333	172	150	1	982	15.6
Harry Gallatin	72	1990	340	898	.379	392	498	.787	749	86	217	5	1072	14.9
Walter Dukes	72	2184	278	796	.349	247	366	.675	954	52	311	17	803	11.2
Phil Jordon	46	822	177	433	.409	59	87	.678	277	32	91	1	413	9.0
Dick McGuire	69	2311	203	544	.373	150	225	.667	291	454	178	0	556	8.1
Nat Clifton	68	1435	217	597	.363	91	146	.623	403	76	202	3	525	7.7
Bob Houbregs	17	302	49	137	.358	30	43	.698	65	19	36	0	128	7.5
Chuck Noble	61	1363	199	601	.331	56	77	.727	140	153	166	0	454	7.4
Billy Kenville	35	649	106	280	.379	46	75	.613	102	66	68	0	258	7.4
Joe Holup	37	607	77	211	.365	55	71	.775	177	23	82	2	209	5.6
Bill Thieben	27	243	42	143	.294	16	27	.593	65	7	44	0	100	3.7
Dick Atha	18	160	17	47	.362	10	12	.833	24	19	24	0	44	2.4
Tom Marshall	9	62	7	21	.333	7	8	.875	7	3	6	0	21	2.3
Bill Ebben	8	50	6	28	.214	3	4	.750	8	4	5	0	15	1.9
Doug Bolstorff	3	21	2	5	.400	0	0	.000	0	0	1	0	4	1.3
PISTONS	72	—	2746	7295	.376	2093	2774	.755	5168	1264	1807	32	7585	105.3

PLAYOFFS (3-4)

PLAYER	G	MIN	FGM	FGA	PCT	FTM	FTA	PCT	REB	AST	PF	DQ	PTS	PPG
George Yardley	7	254	52	127	.409	60	67	.896	72	17	26	0	164	23.4
Gene Shue	7	281	45	123	.366	40	43	.930	46	33	15	0	130	18.6
Walter Dukes	7	286	37	101	.366	37	56	.661	97	4	38	3	111	15.9
Harry Gallatin	7	182	32	87	.368	26	37	.703	70	11	27	1	90	12.9
Dick McGuire	7	236	25	60	.417	17	24	.708	33	40	13	0	67	9.6
Billy Kenville	7	99	18	44	.409	10	18	.556	19	5	12	0	46	6.6
Phil Jordon	6	62	12	30	.400	15	20	.750	12	2	15	0	39	6.5
Joe Holup	7	134	15	43	.349	12	16	.750	36	3	20	0	42	6.0
Nat Clifton	7	74	11	30	.367	6	8	.750	23	4	11	0	28	4.0
Chuck Noble	7	72	8	38	.211	4	8	.500	13	6	9	0	20	2.9
PISTONS	7	—	255	683	.373	227	297	.764	505	125	186	4	737	105.3

1958-59
REGULAR SEASON (28-44)

PLAYER	G	MIN	FGM	FGA	PCT	FTM	FTA	PCT	REB	AST	PF	DQ	PTS	PPG
George Yardley	46	1419	350	842	.416	258	313	.824	327	40	122	1	958	20.8
Gene Shue	72	2745	464	1197	.388	338	421	.803	335	231	129	1	1266	17.6
Phil Jordon	72	2058	399	967	.413	231	303	.762	594	83	193	1	1029	14.3
Walter Dukes	72	2338	318	904	.352	297	452	.657	958	64	332	22	933	13.0
Ed Conlin	15	344	68	179	.380	41	63	.651	91	17	32	1	177	11.8
Dick McGuire	71	2063	232	543	.427	191	258	.740	285	443	147	1	655	9.2
Earl Lloyd	72	1796	234	670	.349	137	182	.753	500	90	291	15	605	8.4
Joe Holup	68	1502	209	580	.360	152	200	.760	352	73	239	12	570	8.4
Chuck Noble	65	939	189	560	.338	83	113	.735	115	114	126	0	461	7.1
Dick Farley	70	1280	177	448	.395	137	186	.737	195	124	130	2	491	7.0
Shellie McMillon	48	700	127	289	.439	55	104	.529	285	26	110	2	309	6.4
Barney Cable	31	271	43	126	.341	23	29	.793	88	12	30	0	109	3.5
PISTONS	72	—	2811	7305	.385	1943	2627	.740	4860	1317	1881	58	7565	105.1

PLAYOFFS (1-2)

PLAYER	G	MIN	FGM	FGA	PCT	FTM	FTA	PCT	REB	AST	PF	DQ	PTS	PPG
Gene Shue	3	118	28	60	.467	27	33	.818	14	10	7	0	83	27.7
Dick McGuire	3	109	20	32	.625	7	11	.636	17	19	10	0	47	15.7
Phil Jordon	3	99	15	45	.333	15	18	.833	24	5	9	0	45	15.0
Walter Dukes	3	113	15	30	.500	13	17	.765	40	3	15	1	43	14.3
Earl Lloyd	3	87	9	28	.321	8	8	1.000	18	7	12	0	26	8.7
Shellie McMillon	3	54	7	23	.304	5	6	.833	14	0	16	1	19	6.3
Joe Holup	3	36	3	14	.214	6	7	.857	8	3	7	0	12	4.0
Chuck Noble	3	28	5	17	.294	2	2	1.000	0	1	3	0	12	4.0
Dick Farley	3	33	5	12	.417	1	1	1.000	6	3	6	0	11	3.7
Ed Conlin	3	43	4	16	.250	2	4	.500	7	4	5	0	10	3.3
PISTONS	3	—	111	277	.401	86	107	.804	183	55	90	2	308	102.7

1959-60
REGULAR SEASON (30-45)

PLAYER	G	MIN	FGM	FGA	PCT	FTM	FTA	PCT	REB	AST	PF	DQ	PTS	PPG
Gene Shue	75	3338	620	1501	.413	472	541	.872	409	295	146	2	1712	22.8
Bailey Howell	75	2346	510	1119	.456	312	422	.739	790	63	282	13	1332	17.8
Walter Dukes	66	2140	314	871	.361	376	508	.740	883	80	310	20	1004	15.2
Chuck Noble	58	1621	276	774	.357	101	138	.732	201	265	172	2	653	11.3
Eddie Conlin	70	1636	300	831	.361	181	238	.761	346	126	158	2	781	11.2
Archie Dees	73	1244	271	617	.439	165	204	.809	397	43	188	3	707	9.7
Shellie McMillon	75	1416	267	627	.426	132	199	.663	431	49	198	3	666	8.9
Earl Lloyd	68	1610	237	665	.356	128	160	.800	322	89	226	1	602	8.9
Dick McGuire	68	1466	179	402	.445	124	201	.617	264	358	112	0	482	7.1
Billy Kenville	25	365	47	131	.359	33	41	.805	71	46	31	0	127	5.1
Gary Alcorn	58	670	91	312	.292	48	84	.571	279	22	123	4	230	4.0
Tony Windis	9	193	16	60	.267	4	6	.667	47	32	20	0	36	4.0
PISTONS	75	—	3146	7920	.397	2075	2847	.729	5491	1472	1983	50	8367	111.6

PLAYOFFS (0-2)

PLAYER	G	MIN	FGM	FGA	PCT	FTM	FTA	PCT	REB	AST	PF	DQ	PTS	PPG
Walter Dukes	2	78	16	31	.516	16	22	.727	33	2	9	1	48	24.0
Gene Shue	2	89	15	38	.395	18	20	.900	12	6	5	0	48	24.0
Bailey Howell	2	72	14	41	.341	6	8	.750	17	3	8	0	34	17.0
Shellie McMillon	2	47	8	21	.381	4	5	.800	16	2	5	0	20	10.0
Earl Lloyd	2	53	6	24	.250	5	8	.625	9	3	11	1	17	8.5
Chuck Noble	2	51	6	27	.269	0	0	.000	9	13	6	0	14	7.0
Archie Dees	2	18	4	12	.333	3	3	1.000	4	2	2	0	11	5.5
Dick McGuire	2	42	5	12	.417	1	3	.333	4	9	3	0	11	5.5
Eddie Conlin	2	20	3	10	.300	2	2	1.000	4	0	2	0	8	4.0
PISTONS	2	—	78	215	.363	55	71	.775	108	40	51	2	211	105.5

1960-61
REGULAR SEASON (34-45)

PLAYER	G	MIN	FGM	FGA	PCT	FTM	FTA	PCT	REB	AST	PF	DQ	PTS	PPG
Bailey Howell	77	2952	607	1293	.469	601	798	.753	1111	196	297	10	1815	23.6
Gene Shue	78	3361	650	1545	.421	465	543	.856	334	530	207	1	1765	22.6
Don Ohl	79	2172	427	1085	.394	200	278	.719	256	265	224	3	1054	13.3
George Lee	74	1735	310	776	.399	276	394	.701	490	89	158	1	896	12.1
Walter Dukes	73	2044	286	706	.405	281	400	.703	1028	139	313	16	853	11.7
Bob Ferry	79	1657	350	776	.451	189	255	.741	500	129	205	1	889	11.3
Shellie McMillon	78	1636	322	752	.428	140	201	.697	487	98	238	6	784	10.1
Jackie Moreland	64	1003	191	477	.400	86	132	.652	315	52	174	3	468	7.3
Chuck Noble	75	1655	196	566	.346	82	115	.713	180	287	195	4	474	6.3
Willie Jones	35	452	78	216	.361	40	63	.635	94	63	90	2	196	5.6
Archie Dees	28	308	53	135	.393	39	47	.830	94	17	50	0	145	5.2
Ron Johnson	6	60	11	30	.367	9	14	.643	14	1	6	0	31	5.2
PISTONS	79	—	3481	8357	.417	2408	3240	.743	5813	1866	2157	47	9370	118.6

PLAYOFFS (2-3)

PLAYER	G	MIN	FGM	FGA	PCT	FTM	FTA	PCT	REB	AST	PF	DQ	PTS	PPG
Bob Ferry	5	167	30	74	.405	41	49	.836	63	11	12	0	101	20.2
Gene Shue	5	186	35	72	.486	23	29	.793	12	22	11	0	93	18.6
George Lee	5	135	29	70	.414	20	27	.741	34	14	11	0	78	15.6
Don Ohl	5	130	25	78	.320	13	19	.684	19	14	13	0	63	12.6
Bailey Howell	5	144	20	57	.351	16	23	.696	46	22	22	1	56	11.2
Jack Moreland	3	45	14	31	.415	4	5	.800	18	3	10	0	32	10.7
Walter Dukes	5	152	20	53	.377	10	18	.555	49	11	25	2	50	10.0
Willie Jones	3	40	12	29	.414	6	7	.857	7	6	6	0	30	10.0
Shellie McMillon	4	67	13	27	.481	13	18	.722	9	7	16	2	39	9.8
Chuck Noble	5	124	20	45	.444	5	7	.714	8	21	18	1	45	9.0
PISTONS	5	—	218	536	.407	151	202	.747	327	131	144	6	587	117.4

1961-62
REGULAR SEASON (37-43)

PLAYER	G	MIN	FGM	FGA	PCT	FTM	FTA	PCT	REB	AST	PF	DQ	PTS	PPG
Bailey Howell	79	2857	553	1193	.464	470	612	.768	996	186	317	10	1576	19.9
Gene Shue	80	3143	580	1422	.408	362	447	.810	372	465	192	1	1522	19.0
Don Ohl	77	2526	555	1250	.444	201	280	.718	267	244	173	2	1311	17.0
Bob Ferry	80	1918	411	939	.438	286	422	.678	503	145	199	2	1108	13.9
Ray Scott	75	2087	370	956	.387	255	388	.657	865	132	232	6	995	13.3
Walter Dukes	77	1896	256	647	.396	208	291	.715	803	125	327	20	720	9.4
George Lee	75	1351	179	500	.358	213	280	.761	349	64	128	1	571	7.6
Jackie Moreland	74	1219	205	487	.421	139	186	.747	427	76	179	2	549	7.4
Willie Jones	69	1006	177	475	.373	64	101	.634	177	115	137	1	418	6.1
Johnny Egan	58	696	128	301	.425	64	84	.762	86	102	64	0	320	5.5
Shellie McMillon	14	140	26	83	.313	20	36	.556	64	6	37	0	72	5.1
Chuck Noble	26	361	32	113	.283	8	15	.533	43	63	55	1	72	2.8
PISTONS	80	—	3472	8366	.415	2290	3142	.729	5823	1723	2040	46	9234	115.4

PLAYOFFS (5-5)

PLAYER	G	MIN	FGM	FGA	PCT	FTM	FTA	PCT	REB	AST	PF	DQ	PTS	PPG
Don Ohl	8	317	71	171	.415	22	27	.815	27	25	22	0	164	20.5
Bailey Howell	10	378	69	163	.423	62	75	.827	96	23	48	3	200	20.0
Ray Scott	10	400	69	170	.406	35	67	.522	145	43	39	2	173	17.3
Gene Shue	10	369	62	151	.410	37	48	.771	30	49	29	0	161	16.1
Johnny Egan	5	106	29	62	.467	10	10	1.000	9	16	8	0	68	13.6
Walter Dukes	10	342	39	91	.428	46	61	.754	138	24	52	5	124	12.4
Bob Ferry	9	156	37	81	.457	26	43	.605	41	13	20	0	100	11.1
Willie Jones	9	180	43	101	.426	13	14	.928	23	31	27	2	99	11.0
Jack Moreland	7	96	17	33	.515	4	7	.571	24	7	22	0	38	5.4
George Lee	6	50	10	20	.500	6	7	.857	8	1	6	0	26	4.3
PISTONS	10	—	446	1043	.428	261	359	.727	635	232	273	12	1153	115.3

1962-63
REGULAR SEASON (34-46)

PLAYER	G	MIN	FGM	FGA	PCT	FTM	FTA	PCT	REB	AST	PF	DQ	PTS	PPG
Bailey Howell	79	2971	637	1235	.516	519	650	.798	910	232	300	9	1793	22.7
Don Ohl	80	2961	636	1450	.439	275	380	.724	239	325	234	3	1547	19.3
Ray Scott	76	2538	460	1110	.414	308	457	.674	772	191	263	9	1228	16.2
Bob Ferry	79	2479	426	984	.433	220	339	.649	537	170	246	1	1072	13.6
Dave DeBusschere	80	2352	406	944	.430	206	287	.718	694	207	247	2	1018	12.7
Willie Jones	79	1470	305	730	.418	118	164	.720	233	188	207	4	728	9.2
Jackie Moreland	78	1516	271	622	.436	145	214	.678	449	114	226	5	687	8.8
Kevin Loughery	57	845	146	397	.368	71	100	.710	109	104	135	1	363	6.4
Johnny Egan	46	752	110	296	.372	53	69	.768	59	114	70	0	273	5.9
Walter Dukes	62	913	83	255	.325	101	137	.737	360	55	183	5	267	4.3
Danny Doyle	4	25	6	12	.500	4	5	.800	8	3	4	0	16	4.0
Darrall Imhoff	45	458	48	153	.314	24	50	.480	155	28	66	1	120	2.7
PISTONS	80	—	3534	8188	.432	2044	2852	.717	5315	1731	2181	40	9112	113.9

PLAYOFFS (1-3)

PLAYER	G	MIN	FGM	FGA	PCT	FTM	FTA	PCT	REB	AST	PF	DQ	PTS	PPG
Don Ohl	4	155	33	83	.398	19	22	.863	12	19	18	0	85	21.3
Dave DeBusschere	4	159	25	59	.424	30	44	.682	63	6	14	1	80	20.0
Bailey Howell	4	163	24	64	.375	23	27	.852	42	11	19	1	71	17.8
Ray Scott	4	155	27	77	.351	9	13	.692	48	9	19	0	63	15.8
Bob Ferry	4	143	20	45	.444	8	24	.333	35	11	10	0	48	12.0
Jack Moreland	4	82	13	26	.500	7	10	.700	20	6	18	1	33	8.3
Willie Jones	4	67	11	28	.393	6	8	.750	7	6	10	0	28	7.0
Kevin Loughery	2	26	1	10	.100	1	1	1.000	0	4	3	0	3	1.5
Walter Dukes	3	8	0	0	.000	3	3	1.000	1	2	3	0	3	1.0
Darrall Imhoff	1	2	0	0	.000	0	0	.000	1	0	0	0	0	0.0
PISTONS	4	—	154	392	.393	106	152	.697	269	74	114	3	414	103.5

1963-64
REGULAR SEASON (23-57)

PLAYER	G	MIN	FGM	FGA	PCT	FTM	FTA	PCT	REB	AST	PF	DQ	PTS	PPG
Bailey Howell	77	2700	598	1267	.472	470	581	.809	776	205	290	9	1666	21.6
Ray Scott	80	2964	539	1307	.412	328	456	.719	1078	244	296	7	1406	17.6
Don Ohl	71	2366	500	1224	.408	225	331	.680	180	225	219	3	1225	17.3
Johnny Egan	24	838	105	256	.410	57	68	.838	62	116	(181)	(3)	267	11.1
Reggie Harding	39	1158	184	460	.400	61	98	.622	410	52	119	1	429	11.0
Bob Ferry	74	1522	298	670	.445	186	279	.667	428	94	174	2	782	10.6
Jackie Moreland	78	1780	272	639	.426	164	210	.781	405	121	268	9	708	9.1
Donnis Butcher	52	1553	165	392	.421	117	190	.616	262	178	(249)	(4)	447	8.6
Dave DeBusschere	15	304	52	133	.391	25	43	.581	105	23	32	1	129	8.6
Willie Jones	77	1539	265	680	.390	100	141	.709	253	172	211	5	630	8.2
Larry Staverman	20	380	44	82	.537	26	41	.634	69	12	50	2	114	5.7
Eddie Miles	60	811	131	371	.353	62	87	.713	95	58	92	0	324	5.4
Bob Duffy	42	552	88	207	.425	38	56	.679	54	74	(48)	0	214	5.1
Darrall Imhoff	58	871	104	251	.414	69	114	.605	283	56	167	5	277	4.8
Kevin Loughery	1	2	1	4	.250	0	0	.000	0	0	2	0	2	2.0
PISTONS	80	–	3346	7943	.421	1928	2685	.718	5145	1633	2235	50	8620	107.8

()-includes totals with two or more teams

1964-65
REGULAR SEASON (31-49)

PLAYER	G	MIN	FGM	FGA	PCT	FTM	FTA	PCT	REB	AST	PF	DQ	PTS	PPG
Terry Dischinger	80	2698	568	1153	.493	320	424	.755	479	198	253	5	1456	18.2
Dave DeBusschere	79	2769	508	1196	.425	306	437	.700	874	253	242	5	1322	16.7
Ray Scott	66	2167	402	1092	.368	220	314	.701	634	239	209	5	1024	15.5
Eddie Miles	76	2074	439	994	.442	166	223	.744	258	157	201	1	1044	13.7
Reggie Harding	78	2699	405	987	.410	128	209	.612	906	179	258	5	938	12.0
Rod Thorn	74	1770	320	750	.427	176	243	.724	266	161	122	0	816	11.0
Joe Caldwell	66	1543	290	776	.374	129	210	.614	441	118	171	3	709	10.7
Don Kojis	65	836	180	416	.433	62	98	.633	243	63	115	1	422	6.5
Donnis Butcher	71	1157	143	353	.405	126	204	.618	200	122	183	4	412	5.8
Jackie Moreland	54	732	103	296	.348	66	104	.635	183	69	151	4	272	5.0
Willie Jones	12	101	21	52	.404	2	6	.333	10	7	13	0	44	3.7
Bob Duffy	4	26	4	11	.364	6	7	.857	4	5	4	0	14	3.5
Hub Reed	62	753	84	221	.380	40	58	.690	206	38	136	2	208	3.4
PISTONS	80	–	3467	8297	.418	1747	2537	.689	5394	1609	2058	35	8681	108.5

1965-66
REGULAR SEASON (22-58)

PLAYER	G	MIN	FGM	FGA	PCT	FTM	FTA	PCT	REB	AST	PF	DQ	PTS	PPG
Eddie Miles	80	2788	634	1418	.447	298	402	.741	302	221	203	2	1566	19.6
Ray Scott	79	2652	544	1309	.416	323	435	.743	755	238	209	1	1411	17.9
Dave DeBusschere	79	2696	524	1284	.408	249	378	.659	916	209	252	5	1297	16.4
Rod Thorn	27	815	143	343	.417	90	123	.732	101	64	67	0	376	13.9
Tom Van Arsdale	79	2041	312	834	.374	209	290	.721	309	205	251	1	833	10.5
Joe Caldwell	33	716	143	338	.423	60	88	.682	190	65	63	0	346	10.5
Joe Strawder	79	2180	250	613	.408	176	256	.688	820	78	305	10	676	8.6
John Tresvant	46	756	134	322	.416	115	158	.728	279	62	136	2	383	8.3
Bill Buntin	42	713	118	299	.395	88	143	.615	252	36	119	4	324	7.7
Charles Vaughn	37	774	110	282	.390	60	82	.732	63	104	60	0	280	7.6
Ron Reed	57	997	186	524	.355	54	100	.540	339	92	133	1	426	7.5
John Barnhill	45	926	139	363	.383	59	98	.602	112	113	76	0	337	7.5
Don Kojis	60	783	182	439	.415	76	141	.539	260	42	94	0	440	7.3
Donnis Butcher	15	285	45	96	.469	18	34	.529	33	30	40	1	108	7.2
Bob Warlick	10	78	11	38	.289	2	6	.333	16	10	8	0	24	2.4
PISTONS	80	–	3475	8502	.409	1877	2734	.687	5427	1569	2016	27	8827	110.3

1966-67
REGULAR SEASON (30-51)

PLAYER	G	MIN	FGM	FGA	PCT	FTM	FTA	PCT	REB	AST	PF	DQ	PTS	PPG
Dave Bing	80	2762	664	1522	.436	273	370	.738	359	330	217	2	1601	20.0
Dave DeBusschere	78	2897	531	1278	.415	361	512	.705	924	216	297	7	1423	18.2
Eddie Miles	81	2419	582	1363	.427	261	338	.772	298	181	216	2	1425	17.6
Ray Scott	45	1477	252	681	.370	156	206	.757	404	84	132	1	660	14.7
Tom Van Arsdale	79	2134	347	887	.391	272	347	.784	341	193	241	3	966	12.2
John Tresvant	68	1553	256	585	.438	164	234	.701	483	88	246	8	676	9.9
Joe Strawder	79	2156	281	660	.426	188	262	.718	791	82	344	19	750	9.5
Ron Reed	61	1248	223	600	.372	79	133	.594	423	81	145	2	525	8.6
Wayne Hightower	29	564	92	259	.355	64	86	.744	164	28	80	1	248	8.6
Reggie Harding	74	1367	172	383	.449	63	103	.612	455	94	164	2	407	5.5
Charles Vaughn	50	680	85	226	.376	50	74	.676	67	75	54	0	220	4.4
Dorie Murrey	35	311	33	82	.402	32	54	.593	102	12	57	2	98	2.8
Bob Hogsett	7	22	5	16	.313	6	6	1.000	3	1	5	0	16	2.3
PISTONS	81	–	3523	8542	.412	1969	2725	.723	5511	1465	2198	49	9015	111.3

1967-68
REGULAR SEASON (40-42)

PLAYER	G	MIN	FGM	FGA	PCT	FTM	FTA	PCT	REB	AST	PF	DQ	PTS	PPG
Dave Bing	79	3209	835	1893	.441	472	668	.707	373	509	254	2	2142	27.1
Happy Hairston	26	892	164	357	.459	162	226	.717	262	37	72	0	490	18.8
Eddie Miles	76	2303	561	1180	.475	282	369	.764	264	215	200	3	1404	18.5
Dave DeBusschere	80	3125	573	1295	.442	289	435	.664	1081	181	304	3	1435	17.9
John Tresvant	55	1671	275	597	.461	183	278	.658	540	114	239	15	733	13.3
Terry Dischinger	78	1936	394	797	.494	237	311	.762	483	114	247	6	1025	13.1
Len Chappell	57	999	220	428	.514	130	184	.707	346	48	113	1	570	10.0
Jimmy Walker	81	1585	289	733	.394	134	175	.766	135	226	204	1	712	8.8
Joe Strawder	73	2029	206	456	.452	139	215	.647	685	85	312	18	551	7.5
Tom Van Arsdale	50	832	114	307	.371	101	136	.743	132	79	119	3	329	6.6
Jim Fox	24	380	34	82	.415	30	52	.577	135	17	51	0	98	4.1
Paul Long	16	93	23	51	.451	11	15	.733	15	12	13	0	57	3.6
George Carter	1	5	1	2	.500	1	1	1.000	0	1	0	0	3	3.0
George Patterson	59	559	44	133	.331	32	38	.842	159	51	85	0	120	2.0
Sonny Dove	28	162	22	75	.293	12	26	.462	52	11	27	0	56	2.0
PISTONS	82	–	3755	8386	.448	2215	3129	.708	5452	1700	2240	52	9725	118.6

PLAYOFFS (2-4)

PLAYER	G	MIN	FGM	FGA	PCT	FTM	FTA	PCT	REB	AST	PF	DQ	PTS	PPG
Dave Bing	6	254	68	166	.410	33	45	.733	24	29	21	0	169	28.2
Dave DeBusschere	6	263	45	106	.425	26	45	.578	97	13	23	0	116	19.3
Eddie Miles	6	197	39	95	.411	9	12	.750	22	15	16	0	87	14.5
Jimmy Walker	6	121	31	67	.463	14	17	.824	9	9	17	1	76	12.7
Happy Hairston	6	149	29	71	.408	12	20	.600	37	7	22	1	70	11.7
Terry Dischinger	6	154	21	56	.375	14	19	.737	29	9	19	0	56	9.3
Joe Strawder	6	177	14	42	.333	14	22	.636	65	9	27	1	42	7.0
Jim Fox	6	90	6	19	.316	15	19	.789	37	3	11	1	27	4.5
Len Chappell	5	21	2	7	.286	3	6	.500	12	0	3	0	7	1.4
Paul Long	1	4	3	3	1.000	0	0	.000	0	1	1	0	6	6.0
Sonny Dove	2	6	2	4	.500	0	0	.000	2	0	0	0	4	2.0
George Patterson	1	4	0	0	.000	0	0	.000	1	1	0	0	0	0.0
PISTONS	6	–	260	636	.409	140	205	.683	335	96	160	4	660	110.0

1968-69
REGULAR SEASON (32-50)

PLAYER	G	MIN	FGM	FGA	PCT	FTM	FTA	PCT	REB	AST	PF	DQ	PTS	PPG
Dave Bing	77	3039	678	1594	.425	444	623	.713	382	546	256	3	1800	23.4
Walt Bellamy	53	2023	359	701	.512	276	416	.663	716	99	197	4	994	18.8
Happy Hairston	81	2889	530	1131	.469	404	553	.731	959	109	255	3	1464	18.1
Dave DeBusschere	29	1092	189	423	.447	94	130	.723	353	63	111	1	472	16.3
Eddie Miles	80	2252	441	983	.449	182	273	.667	283	180	201	0	1064	13.3
Howie Komives	53	1726	272	665	.409	138	178	.775	204	266	178	1	682	12.9
Jimmy Walker	69	1639	312	670	.466	182	229	.795	157	221	172	1	806	11.7
Terry Dischinger	75	1456	264	513	.515	130	178	.730	323	93	230	5	658	8.8
Otto Moore	74	1605	241	544	.443	88	168	.524	524	68	182	2	570	7.7
McCoy McLemore	50	910	141	356	.396	84	104	.808	236	44	113	3	366	7.3
Dave Gambee	25	302	60	142	.423	49	62	.790	78	15	60	0	169	6.8
Jim Fox	25	375	45	96	.469	34	53	.642	139	23	56	1	124	5.0
Sonny Dove	29	236	47	100	.470	24	36	.667	62	12	49	0	118	4.1
Rich Niemann	16	123	20	47	.426	8	10	.800	41	9	30	0	48	3.0
Bud Olsen	10	70	8	23	.348	4	12	.333	11	7	8	0	20	2.0
Cliff Williams	3	18	2	9	.222	0	0	.000	3	2	7	0	4	1.3
PISTONS	82	–	3609	7997	.451	2141	3025	.708	4471	1757	2105	24	9359	114.1

1969-70
REGULAR SEASON (31-51)

PLAYER	G	MIN	FGM	FGA	PCT	FTM	FTA	PCT	REB	AST	PF	DQ	PTS	PPG
Dave Bing	70	2334	575	1295	.444	454	580	.783	299	418	196	0	1604	22.9
Jimmy Walker	81	2869	666	1394	.478	355	440	.807	242	248	203	4	1687	20.8
Eddie Miles	44	1243	231	531	.435	130	170	.765	173	82	99	0	592	13.5
Otto Moore	81	2523	383	805	.476	194	305	.636	900	104	232	3	960	11.9
Terry Dischinger	75	1754	342	650	.526	174	241	.722	369	106	213	5	858	11.4
Howie Komives	82	2418	363	878	.413	190	234	.812	193	312	247	2	916	11.2
Happy Hairston	15	282	57	103	.553	45	63	.714	88	11	36	0	159	10.6
Erwin Mueller	74	2284	287	614	.467	185	254	.728	469	199	186	1	759	10.3
Walt Bellamy	56	1173	210	384	.547	140	249	.562	397	55	163	3	560	10.0
McCoy McLemore	73	1421	233	500	.466	119	145	.821	336	83	159	3	585	8.0
Bob Quick	19	297	49	111	.441	37	53	.698	63	11	41	0	135	7.1
Steve Mix	18	276	48	100	.480	23	39	.590	64	15	31	0	119	6.6
Bill Hewitt	45	801	85	210	.405	38	63	.603	213	36	91	1	208	4.6
Paul Long	25	130	28	62	.452	27	38	.711	11	17	22	0	83	3.3
George Reynolds	10	44	8	19	.421	5	7	.714	14	12	10	0	21	2.1
Tom Workman	2	6	0	1	.000	0	0	.000	0	0	1	0	0	0.0
PISTONS	82	–	3565	7657	.466	2116	2881	.734	3831	1709	1930	22	9246	112.8

1970-71
REGULAR SEASON (45-37)

PLAYER	G	MIN	FGM	FGA	PCT	FTM	FTA	PCT	REB	AST	PF	DQ	PTS	PPG
Dave Bing	82	3065	799	1710	.467	615	772	.797	364	408	228	4	2213	27.0
Jimmy Walker	79	2765	524	1201	.436	344	414	.831	207	268	173	0	1392	17.6
Bob Lanier	82	2017	504	1108	.455	273	376	.726	665	146	272	4	1281	15.6
Terry Dischinger	65	1855	304	568	.535	161	211	.763	339	113	189	2	769	11.8
Otto Moore	82	1926	310	696	.445	121	219	.553	700	88	182	0	741	9.0
Steve Mix	35	731	111	294	.378	68	89	.764	164	34	72	0	290	8.3
Howie Komives	82	1932	275	715	.385	121	151	.801	152	262	184	0	671	8.2
Bob Quick	56	1146	155	341	.455	138	176	.784	230	56	142	1	448	8.0
Bill Hewitt	62	1725	203	435	.467	69	120	.575	454	124	189	5	475	7.7
Erwin Mueller	52	1224	126	309	.408	60	108	.556	223	113	99	0	312	6.0
Terry Driscoll	69	1255	132	318	.415	108	154	.701	402	54	212	2	372	5.4
Harvey Marlatt	23	214	25	80	.313	15	18	.833	23	30	27	0	65	2.8
PISTONS	82	−	3468	7730	.449	2093	2808	.745	3923	1696	1969	18	9029	110.1
OPPONENTS	82	−	3525	7713	.457	2040	2703	.755	4292	1912	2087	30	9090	110.9

1971-72
REGULAR SEASON (26-56)

PLAYER	G	MIN	FGM	FGA	PCT	FTM	FTA	PCT	REB	AST	PF	DQ	PTS	PPG
Bob Lanier	80	3092	834	1690	.493	388	505	.768	1132	248	297	6	2056	25.7
Dave Bing	45	1936	369	891	.414	278	354	.785	186	317	138	3	1016	22.6
Jimmy Walker	78	3083	634	1386	.457	397	480	.827	231	315	198	2	1665	21.3
Curtis Rowe	82	2661	369	802	.460	192	287	.669	699	99	171	1	930	11.3
Terry Dischinger	79	2062	295	574	.514	156	200	.780	338	92	289	7	746	9.4
Howie Komives	79	2071	262	702	.373	164	203	.808	172	291	196	9	688	8.7
Willie Norwood	78	1272	222	440	.505	140	215	.651	316	43	229	4	584	7.5
Bob Quick	18	204	39	82	.476	34	45	.756	51	11	29	0	112	6.2
Jim Davis	52	684	121	251	.482	64	98	.653	196	38	106	1	306	5.9
Harvey Marlatt	31	506	60	149	.403	36	42	.857	62	60	64	1	156	5.0
Steve Mix	8	104	15	47	.319	7	12	.583	23	4	7	0	37	4.6
Bill Hewitt	68	1203	131	277	.473	41	82	.500	370	71	134	1	303	4.5
Erwin Mueller	42	605	68	197	.345	43	74	.581	147	57	64	0	179	4.3
Isaiah Wilson	48	322	63	177	.356	41	56	.732	47	41	32	0	167	3.5
PISTONS	82	−	3482	7665	.454	1981	2653	.747	3970	1687	1954	26	8945	109.1
OPPONENTS	82	−	3822	8106	.472	1862	2464	.753	4377	2214	1931	25	9506	115.9

1972-73
REGULAR SEASON (40-42)

PLAYER	G	MIN	FGM	FGA	PCT	FTM	FTA	PCT	REB	AST	PF	DQ	PTS	PPG
Bob Lanier	81	3150	810	1654	.490	307	397	.773	1205	260	278	4	1927	23.8
Dave Bing	82	3361	692	1545	.448	456	560	.814	298	637	229	1	1840	22.4
Curtis Rowe	81	3009	547	1053	.519	210	327	.642	760	172	191	0	1304	16.1
John Mengelt	67	1435	294	583	.504	116	141	.823	159	128	124	0	704	10.5
Stu Lantz	51	1603	185	455	.407	120	150	.800	172	138	117	0	490	9.6
Don Adams	70	1798	257	640	.402	138	176	.784	419	112	220	2	652	9.3
Fred Foster	63	1460	243	627	.388	61	87	.701	183	94	150	0	547	8.7
Willie Norwood	79	1282	249	504	.494	154	225	.684	324	56	182	0	652	8.3
Chris Ford	74	1537	208	434	.479	60	93	.645	266	194	133	1	476	6.4
Jim Davis	73	771	131	257	.510	72	114	.632	261	56	126	2	334	4.6
Justus Thigpen	18	99	23	57	.404	0	0	.000	9	8	18	0	46	2.6
Bob Nash	36	169	16	72	.222	11	17	.647	34	16	30	0	43	1.2
Erwin Mueller	21	80	9	31	.290	5	7	.714	14	7	13	0	23	1.1
Harvey Marlatt	7	26	2	4	.500	0	0	.000	1	4	1	0	4	0.6
PISTONS	82	−	3666	7916	.463	1710	2294	.745	4105	1882	1812	10	9042	110.3
OPPONENTS	82	−	3803	8064	.472	1418	1862	.762	4019	2263	1891	22	9024	110.0

1973-74
REGULAR SEASON (52-30)

PLAYER	G	MIN	FGM	FGA	PCT	FTM	FTA	PCT	O-RB	D-RB	TOT	AST	PF	DQ	STL	BLK	PTS	PPG	HG
Bob Lanier	81	3047	748	1483	.504	326	409	.797	269	805	1074	343	273	7	10	247	1822	22.5	45
Dave Bing	81	3124	582	1336	.436	356	438	.813	108	173	281	555	216	1	109	17	1520	18.8	33
Curtis Rowe	82	2499	380	769	.494	118	169	.698	167	348	515	136	177	1	49	36	878	10.7	28
Don Adams	74	2298	303	742	.408	153	201	.761	133	315	448	141	242	2	110	12	759	10.3	25
George Trapp	82	1489	333	693	.481	99	134	.739	97	216	313	81	226	2	47	33	765	9.3	22
Stu Lantz	50	980	154	361	.427	139	163	.853	34	79	113	97	79	0	38	3	447	8.9	24
John Mengelt	77	1555	249	558	.446	182	229	.795	40	166	206	148	164	2	68	7	680	8.8	30
Willie Norwood	74	1178	247	484	.510	95	143	.664	95	134	229	58	156	2	60	9	589	8.0	29
Chris Ford	82	2059	264	595	.444	57	77	.740	109	195	304	279	159	1	148	14	585	7.1	24
Jim Davis	78	947	117	283	.413	90	139	.647	102	191	293	86	158	1	39	30	324	4.2	15
Bob Nash	35	281	41	115	.357	24	39	.615	31	43	74	14	35	0	3	10	106	3.0	16
Ben Kelso	46	298	35	96	.365	15	22	.682	16	31	47	18	45	0	12	1	85	1.8	8
PISTONS	82	—	3453	7515	.459	1654	2164	.764	1200	2681	3881	1956	1930	19	793	419	8560	104.4	129
OPPONENTS	82	—	3376	7499	.450	1475	1932	.763	1173	2632	3805	1980	1996	30	772	410	8227	100.3	129

PLAYOFFS (3-4)

PLAYER	G	MIN	FGM	FGA	PCT	FTM	FTA	PCT	O-RB	D-RB	TOT	AST	PF	DQ	STL	BLK	PTS	PPG	HG
Bob Lanier	7	303	77	152	.507	30	38	.789	26	81	107	21	28	0	4	14	184	26.3	38
Dave Bing	7	312	55	131	.420	22	30	.733	6	20	26	42	20	0	3	1	132	18.9	23
Stu Lantz	7	227	28	59	.475	28	32	.875	10	19	29	14	19	0	2	0	84	12.0	25
Don Adams	7	256	28	73	.342	8	14	.571	17	34	51	20	26	0	6	1	64	9.1	23
George Trapp	7	119	30	51	.588	2	2	1.000	4	18	22	2	23	0	0	4	62	8.9	22
Curtis Rowe	7	229	25	52	.481	8	13	.615	16	36	52	11	23	0	3	5	58	8.3	18
John Mengelt	4	39	5	14	.357	7	8	.875	2	5	7	6	6	0	2	0	17	4.3	7
Chris Ford	5	94	8	17	.412	4	6	.667	4	11	15	7	10	0	2	1	20	4.0	7
Jim Davis	7	69	11	19	.579	4	6	.667	4	12	16	5	7	0	2	0	26	3.7	10
Willie Norwood	5	31	7	11	.636	4	4	1.000	1	2	3	1	7	0	3	1	18	3.6	6
Ben Kelso	1	1	0	2	.000	0	0	.000	0	1	1	1	0	0	0	0	0	0.0	0
PISTONS	7	—	274	581	.472	117	153	.765	90	239	329	130	173	0	26	27	665	95.0	103
BULLS	7	—	266	625	.426	117	151	.775	107	210	317	140	151	0	54	34	649	92.7	108

1974-75
REGULAR SEASON (40-42)

PLAYER	G	MIN	FGM	FGA	PCT	FTM	FTA	PCT	O-RB	D-RB	TOT	AST	PF	DQ	STL	BLK	PTS	PPG	HG
Bob Lanier	76	2987	731	1433	.510	361	450	.802	225	689	914	350	237	1	75	172	1823	24.0	45
Dave Bing	79	3222	578	1333	.434	343	424	.809	86	200	286	610	222	3	116	26	1499	19.0	32
Curtis Rowe	82	2787	422	874	.483	171	227	.753	174	411	585	121	190	0	50	44	1015	12.4	26
John Mengelt	80	1995	336	701	.479	211	248	.851	38	153	191	201	198	2	72	4	883	11.0	33
Howard Porter	41	1030	188	376	.500	59	70	.843	66	150	216	17	76	0	20	25	435	10.6	22
George Trapp	78	1472	288	652	.442	99	131	.756	71	205	276	63	210	1	37	14	675	8.7	24
Willie Norwood	24	347	64	123	.520	31	42	.738	31	57	88	16	51	0	23	0	159	6.6	18
Chris Ford	80	1962	206	435	.474	63	95	.663	93	176	269	230	187	0	113	26	475	5.9	18
Don Adams	51	1376	127	315	.403	45	78	.577	63	181	244	75	179	1	69	20	299	5.9	19
Eric Money	66	889	144	319	.451	31	45	.689	27	61	88	101	121	3	33	2	319	4.8	21
Jim Davis	79	1078	118	260	.454	85	117	.726	96	189	285	90	129	2	50	36	321	4.1	21
Jim Ligon	38	272	55	143	.385	16	25	.640	14	12	26	25	31	0	8	9	126	3.3	15
Al Eberhard	34	277	31	85	.365	17	21	.810	18	29	47	16	33	0	13	1	79	2.3	11
Otto Moore	2	11	1	4	.250	1	2	.500	0	2	2	1	2	0	0	1	3	1.5	3
PISTONS	82	—	3289	7053	.466	1533	1975	.776	1002	2515	3517	1916	1866	13	679	380	8111	98.9	125
OPPONENTS	82	—	3409	7257	.470	1410	1793	.786	1104	2550	3654	2012	1875	24	663	306	8228	100.3	130

PLAYOFFS (1-2)

PLAYER	G	MIN	FGM	FGA	PCT	FTM	FTA	PCT	O-RB	D-RB	TOT	AST	PF	DQ	STL	BLK	PTS	PPG	HG
Bob Lanier	3	128	26	51	.510	9	12	.750	5	27	32	19	10	0	4	12	61	20.3	29
Howard Porter	3	92	23	42	.548	6	7	.857	8	12	20	0	5	0	5	1	52	17.3	21
Dave Bing	3	134	20	47	.426	8	13	.615	3	8	11	29	12	0	5	0	48	16.0	20
Curtis Rowe	3	115	17	33	.515	10	19	.526	8	18	26	15	6	0	1	5	44	14.7	22
George Trapp	3	81	18	33	.545	5	7	.714	5	17	22	4	6	0	0	0	41	13.7	24
John Mengelt	3	65	9	23	.391	7	9	.778	2	6	8	9	9	0	1	1	25	8.3	9
Chris Ford	3	82	6	11	.545	0	0	.000	2	11	13	10	8	0	1	0	12	4.0	8
Jim Davis	2	16	2	4	.500	3	5	.600	2	2	4	0	1	0	1	0	7	3.5	7
Bill Ligon	2	7	1	1	1.000	0	0	.000	0	0	0	0	1	0	0	0	2	1.0	2
PISTONS	3	—	122	245	.498	48	72	.667	35	101	136	86	58	0	18	19	292	97.3	122

1975-76
REGULAR SEASON (36-46)

PLAYER	G	MIN	FGM	FGA	PCT	FTM	FTA	PCT	O-RB	D-RB	TOT	AST	PF	DQ	STL	BLK	PTS	PPG	HG
Bob Lanier	64	2363	541	1017	.532	284	370	.768	217	529	746	217	203	2	79	86	1366	21.3	41
Curtis Rowe	80	2998	514	1098	.468	252	342	.737	231	466	697	183	209	3	47	45	1280	16.0	29
Eric Money	80	2267	449	947	.474	145	180	.806	77	130	207	338	243	4	137	11	1043	13.0	26
Kevin Porter	19	687	99	235	.421	42	56	.750	14	30	44	193	83	3	35	3	240	12.6	23
John Mengelt	67	1105	264	540	.489	192	237	.810	27	88	115	108	138	1	40	5	720	10.7	32
Al Eberhard	81	2066	283	683	.414	191	229	.834	139	251	390	83	250	5	87	15	757	9.3	30
Howard Porter	75	1482	298	635	.469	73	97	.753	81	214	295	25	133	0	31	36	669	8.9	28
Chris Ford	82	2198	301	707	.426	83	115	.722	80	211	291	272	222	0	178	24	685	8.4	24
George Trapp	76	1091	278	602	.462	63	88	.716	79	150	229	50	167	3	33	23	619	8.1	27
Wali Jones	1	19	4	11	.364	0	0	.000	0	0	0	2	2	0	2	0	8	8.0	8
Archie Clark	79	1589	250	577	.433	100	116	.862	27	110	137	218	157	0	62	4	600	7.6	18
Lindsey Hairston	47	651	104	228	.456	65	112	.580	65	114	179	21	84	2	21	32	273	5.8	25
Earl Williams	46	562	73	152	.480	22	44	.500	103	148	251	18	81	0	22	20	168	3.7	13
Terry Thomas	28	136	28	65	.431	21	29	.724	15	21	36	3	21	1	4	2	77	2.8	18
Roger Brown	29	454	29	72	.403	14	18	.778	47	83	130	12	76	1	6	25	72	2.5	11
Henry Dickerson	17	112	9	29	.310	10	16	.625	3	0	3	8	17	1	2	1	28	1.6	11
PISTONS	82	—	3524	7598	.464	1557	2049	.760	1205	2545	3750	1751	2086	26	786	332	8605	104.9	131
OPPONENTS	82	—	3492	7479	.467	1707	2211	.772	1218	2690	3908	2014	1914	21	724	437	8691	106.0	129

PLAYOFFS (4-5)

PLAYER	G	MIN	FGM	FGA	PCT	FTM	FTA	PCT	O-RB	D-RB	TOT	AST	PF	DQ	STL	BLK	PTS	PPG	HG
Bob Lanier	9	359	95	172	.552	45	50	.900	39	75	114	30	34	1	8	21	235	26.1	35
Curtis Rowe	9	346	53	111	.477	29	34	.853	25	45	70	26	27	1	6	8	135	15.0	33
Howard Porter	9	213	51	97	.526	15	17	.882	22	20	42	6	24	0	7	5	117	13.0	27
Eric Money	9	273	48	105	.457	17	21	.810	10	12	22	51	36	1	14	1	113	12.6	18
George Trapp	9	153	37	89	.416	15	18	.833	12	23	35	9	26	0	4	4	89	9.9	17
John Mengelt	9	119	34	56	.607	19	27	.704	2	12	14	10	22	0	4	1	87	9.7	16
Chris Ford	9	276	33	81	.407	12	15	.800	6	30	36	40	33	1	11	5	78	8.7	22
Archie Clark	9	192	30	62	.484	12	18	.667	2	19	21	29	25	0	6	0	72	8.0	15
Al Eberhard	8	182	17	39	.436	14	19	.737	11	15	26	7	14	0	8	4	48	6.0	16
Henry Dickerson	5	15	4	9	.444	1	2	.500	4	0	4	3	1	0	1	0	9	1.8	5
Roger Brown	4	51	4	9	.444	2	4	.500	7	7	14	2	10	0	0	1	10	1.1	2
Terry Thomas	4	6	0	5	.000	0	0	.000	1	0	1	0	1	0	0	0	0	0.0	0
PISTONS	9	—	406	835	.486	181	225	.804	141	258	399	213	253	4	69	50	993	110.3	126
OPPONENTS	9	—	410	836	.490	216	272	.794	144	259	403	214	236	4	92	55	1036	115.1	128

1976-77
REGULAR SEASON (44-38)

PLAYER	G	MIN	FGM	FGA	PCT	FTM	FTA	PCT	O-RB	D-RB	TOT	AST	PF	DQ	STL	BLK	PTS	PPG	HG
Bob Lanier	64	2446	678	1269	.534	260	318	.818	200	545	745	214	174	0	70	126	1616	25.3	40
M.L. Carr	82	2643	443	931	.476	205	279	.735	211	420	631	181	287	8	165	58	1091	13.3	29
Howard Porter	78	2200	465	962	.483	103	120	.858	155	303	458	53	202	0	50	73	1033	13.2	27
Chris Ford	82	2539	437	918	.476	131	170	.771	96	174	270	337	192	1	179	26	1005	12.3	33
Ralph Simpson	77	1597	356	834	.427	138	195	.708	48	133	181	180	100	0	68	5	850	11.0	25
Eric Money	73	1586	329	631	.521	90	114	.789	43	81	124	243	199	3	91	14	748	10.2	32
Marvin Barnes	53	989	202	452	.447	106	156	.679	69	184	253	45	139	1	38	33	510	9.6	33
Kevin Porter	81	2117	310	605	.512	97	133	.729	28	70	98	592	271	8	88	8	717	8.9	28
Leon Douglas	82	1626	245	512	.479	127	229	.555	181	345	526	68	294	10	44	81	617	7.5	30
Al Eberhard	68	1219	181	380	.476	109	138	.790	76	145	221	50	197	4	45	15	471	6.9	24
George Trapp	6	68	15	29	.517	3	4	.750	4	6	10	3	13	0	0	1	33	5.5	15
Phil Sellers	44	329	73	190	.384	52	72	.722	19	22	41	25	56	0	22	0	198	4.5	17
Cornelius Cash	6	49	9	23	.391	3	6	.500	8	8	16	1	8	0	2	1	21	3.5	11
Roger Brown	43	322	21	56	.375	18	26	.692	31	59	90	12	68	4	15	18	60	1.4	10
PISTONS	82	—	3764	7792	.483	1442	1960	.736	1169	2495	3664	2004	2200	39	877	459	8970	109.4	140
OPPONENTS	82	—	3561	7639	.466	1933	2543	.760	1317	2637	3954	1952	1827	15	793	381	9055	110.4	144

PLAYOFFS (1-2)

PLAYER	G	MIN	FGM	FGA	PCT	FTM	FTA	PCT	O-RB	D-RB	TOT	AST	PF	DQ	STL	BLK	PTS	PPG	HG
Bob Lanier	3	118	34	54	.630	16	19	.842	13	37	50	6	10	0	3	7	84	28.0	33
Howard Porter	3	98	29	47	.617	2	4	.500	6	11	17	2	7	0	2	4	60	20.0	30
Eric Money	3	103	22	44	.500	11	13	.846	2	7	9	20	9	0	6	0	55	18.3	31
Chris Ford	3	101	18	44	.409	5	9	.556	8	11	19	12	11	0	7	0	41	13.7	22
M.L. Carr	3	112	12	31	.387	4	7	.571	9	8	17	6	9	0	1	3	28	9.3	16
Kevin Porter	3	61	5	14	.357	6	9	.667	1	5	6	17	7	0	1	0	16	5.3	9
Leon Douglas	3	57	4	13	.308	2	7	.286	4	6	10	3	11	0	1	5	10	3.3	6
Phil Sellers	1	6	1	4	.250	1	4	.250	1	1	2	0	2	0	0	0	3	3.0	3
Al Eberhard	3	42	1	9	.111	5	8	.625	2	7	9	2	6	0	1	0	7	2.3	4
Roger Brown	2	5	0	1	.000	0	0	.000	0	0	0	0	0	0	0	1	0	0.0	0
Ralph Simpson	2	17	0	9	.000	0	0	.000	1	2	3	1	1	0	0	0	0	0.0	0
PISTONS	3	—	126	270	.467	52	80	.650	47	95	142	69	73	0	22	20	304	101.3	108
OPPONENTS	3	—	140	307	.456	57	72	.792	72	97	169	73	69	0	21	16	337	112.3	138

1977-78
REGULAR SEASON (38-44)

PLAYER	G	GS	MIN	FGM	FGA	PCT	FTM	FTA	PCT	O-RB	D-RB	TOT	AST	PF	DQ	STL	TO	BLK	PTS	PPG	HG
Bob Lanier	63	63	2311	622	1159	.537	298	386	.772	197	518	715	216	185	2	82	225	93	1542	24.5	41
Eric Money	76	72	2557	600	1200	.500	214	298	.718	90	119	209	356	237	5	123	322	12	1414	18.6	39
John Shumate	62	56	2170	316	622	.508	326	409	.797	125	429	554	122	142	1	76	186	43	958	15.5	31
M.L. Carr	79	60	2556	390	857	.455	200	271	.738	202	355	557	185	243	4	147	210	27	980	12.4	28
Jim Price	34	23	839	153	363	.421	84	103	.816	27	74	101	102	82	0	45	74	5	390	11.5	26
Leon Douglas	79	23	1993	321	667	.481	221	345	.641	181	401	582	112	295	6	57	197	48	863	10.9	28
Ralph Simpson	32	17	739	143	346	.413	54	64	.844	27	55	82	87	48	1	32	78	3	340	10.6	23
Chris Ford	82	49	2582	374	777	.481	113	154	.734	117	151	268	381	182	2	166	232	17	861	10.5	25
Marvin Barnes	12	8	269	53	118	.449	14	29	.483	28	63	91	19	43	2	7	29	11	120	10.0	15
Gus Gerard	47	16	805	154	355	.434	64	93	.688	49	97	146	44	96	1	34	54	22	372	7.9	20
Al Skinner	69	2	1274	181	387	.468	123	159	.774	53	119	172	113	208	4	52	132	15	485	7.0	27
Jim Bostic	4	0	48	12	22	.545	2	5	.400	8	8	16	3	5	0	0	3	0	26	6.5	12
Willie Norwood	16	4	260	34	82	.415	20	29	.690	27	27	54	14	45	0	13	17	3	88	5.5	13
Al Eberhard	37	6	576	71	160	.444	41	61	.672	37	65	102	26	64	0	13	23	4	183	4.9	20
Kevin Porter	8	0	127	14	31	.452	9	13	.692	5	10	15	36	18	0	5	12	0	37	4.6	14
Ben Poquette	52	7	626	95	225	.422	42	60	.700	50	95	145	20	69	1	10	40	22	232	4.5	18
Howard Porter	8	2	107	16	43	.372	4	7	.571	5	12	17	2	15	0	3	5	5	36	4.5	10
Wayman Britt	7	0	16	3	10	.300	3	4	.750	1	3	4	2	3	0	1	1	0	9	1.3	4
PISTONS	82	—	—	3552	7424	.478	1832	2490	.735	1229	2601	3830	1840	1980	29	866	1842	330	8936	109.0	130
OPPONENTS	82	—	—	3688	7606	.485	1662	2177	.763	1244	2494	3738	2105	2088	27	902	1698	395	9038	110.2	135

1978-79
REGULAR SEASON (30-52)

PLAYER	G	GS	MIN	FGM	FGA	PCT	FTM	FTA	PCT	O-RB	D-RB	TOT	AST	PF	DQ	STL	TO	BLK	PTS	PPG	HG
Bob Lanier	53	53	1835	489	950	.515	275	367	.749	164	330	494	140	181	5	20	175	75	1253	23.6	38
M.L. Carr	80	79	3207	587	1143	.514	323	435	.743	219	370	589	262	279	2	197	255	46	1497	18.7	36
John Long	82	60	2498	581	1240	.469	157	190	.826	127	139	266	121	224	1	102	137	19	1319	16.1	28
Kevin Porter	82	82	3064	534	1110	.481	192	266	.722	62	147	209	1099	302	5	158	337	5	1260	15.4	32
Terry Tyler	82	36	2560	456	946	.482	144	219	.658	211	437	648	89	254	3	104	141	201	1056	12.9	32
Leon Douglas	78	64	2215	342	698	.490	208	328	.634	248	416	664	74	319	13	39	190	55	892	11.4	24
Chris Ford	3	3	108	13	35	.371	7	8	.875	9	9	18	5	9	1	1	10	1	33	11.0	22
Earl Tatum	76	16	1195	272	607	.448	48	66	.727	40	81	121	72	158	3	78	85	33	592	7.8	20
Ben Poquette	76	16	1337	198	464	.427	111	142	.782	99	237	336	57	198	4	38	65	98	507	6.7	28
Rickey Green	27	1	431	67	177	.379	45	67	.672	15	25	40	63	37	0	25	44	1	179	6.6	17
Otis Howard	11	0	91	19	45	.422	11	23	.478	13	21	34	4	16	0	2	5	2	49	4.5	16

PLAYER	G	GS	MIN	FGM	FGA	PCT	FTM	FTA	PCT	O-RB	D-RB	TOT	AST	PF	DQ	STL	TO	BLK	PTS	PPG	HG
Bubbles Hawkins	4	0	28	6	16	.375	6	6	1.000	3	3	6	4	7	0	5	2	0	18	4.5	10
Essie Hollis	25	0	154	30	75	.400	9	12	.750	21	24	45	6	28	0	11	14	1	69	2.8	10
Larry McNeill	11	0	46	9	20	.450	11	12	.917	3	7	10	3	7	0	0	4	0	29	2.6	19
Andre Wakefield	71	0	578	62	176	.352	48	69	.696	25	51	76	69	68	0	19	71	2	172	2.4	17
Jim Brewer	25	1	310	27	60	.450	3	15	.200	34	71	105	13	38	0	13	19	10	57	2.3	7
Steve Sheppard	20	0	76	12	25	.480	8	15	.533	9	10	19	4	10	0	3	4	1	32	1.6	15
Gus Gerard	2	0	6	1	3	.333	1	2	.500	1	0	1	0	0	0	2	0	1	3	1.5	3
Dennis Boyd	5	0	40	3	12	.250	0	0	.000	0	2	2	7	5	0	0	6	0	6	1.2	2
Ron Behagen	1	0	1	0	0	.000	0	0	.000	0	0	0	0	1	0	0	1	0	0	0.0	0
PISTONS	82	—	—	3708	7802	.475	1607	2242	.717	1303	2380	3683	2092	2142	38	846	1599	550	9023	110.0	160
OPPONENTS	82	—	—	3765	7623	.494	1734	2295	.756	1301	2628	3929	2407	1912	21	666	1739	506	9243	112.7	150

1979-80
REGULAR SEASON (16-66)

PLAYER	G	GS	MIN	FGM	FGA	PCT	FTM	FTA	PCT	O-RB	D-RB	TOT	AST	PF	DQ	STL	TO	BLK	PTS	PPG	HG
Bob Lanier	37	37	1392	319	584	.546	164	210	.781	108	265	373	122	130	2	38	113	60	802	21.7	34
Bob McAdoo	58	51	2097	492	1025	.480	235	322	.730	100	367	467	200	178	3	73	238	65	1222	21.1	37
John Long	69	66	2364	588	1164	.505	160	194	.825	152	185	337	206	221	4	129	206	26	1337	19.4	38
Greg Kelser	50	26	1233	280	593	.472	146	203	.719	124	152	276	108	176	5	60	140	34	709	14.2	34
Terry Tyler	82	59	2670	430	925	.465	143	187	.765	228	399	627	129	237	3	107	175	220	1005	12.3	29
Kent Benson	17	10	502	86	187	.460	33	44	.750	30	90	120	51	68	3	19	51	18	206	12.1	26
Jim McElroy	36	26	1012	162	356	.455	95	119	.798	12	38	50	162	78	1	25	88	14	422	11.7	33
Eric Money	55	35	1467	259	510	.508	81	104	.779	28	69	97	238	135	3	53	143	10	599	10.9	26
John Shumate	9	8	228	35	65	.538	17	25	.680	18	52	70	9	16	0	9	14	5	87	9.7	20
Terry Duerod	67	10	1331	282	598	.472	45	66	.682	29	69	98	117	102	0	41	79	11	624	9.3	28
Phil Hubbard	64	13	1189	210	451	.466	165	220	.750	114	206	320	70	202	9	48	120	10	585	9.1	30
Leon Douglas	70	37	1782	221	455	.486	125	185	.676	171	330	501	121	249	10	30	127	62	567	8.1	26
Ron Lee	31	19	803	84	214	.393	35	53	.660	29	61	90	174	107	4	84	68	13	225	7.3	23
Roy Hamilton	72	10	1116	115	287	.401	103	150	.687	45	62	107	192	82	0	48	118	5	333	4.6	17
Earl Evans	36	2	381	63	140	.450	24	42	.571	26	49	75	37	64	0	14	36	1	157	4.4	16
Jackie Robinson	7	0	51	9	17	.529	9	11	.818	3	2	5	0	8	0	3	2	3	27	3.9	10
Steve Malovic	10	1	162	8	25	.320	10	14	.714	9	19	28	14	16	0	2	9	5	26	2.6	9
PISTONS	82	—	—	3643	7596	.480	1590	2149	.740	1226	2415	3641	1950	2069	46	783	1742	562	8933	108.9	137
OPPONENTS	82	—	—	3847	7761	.496	1858	2405	.773	1319	2572	3891	2306	1871	13	874	1583	470	9609	117.2	145

3-point FG: Detroit 57-219 (.260), Lanier 0-5 (.000), McAdoo 3-24 (.125), Long 1-12 (.083), Kelser 3-15 (.200), Tyler 2-12 (.167), Benson 1-4 (.250), McElroy 3-14 (.214), Duerod 15-53 (.283), Hubbard 0-2 (.000), Douglas 0-1 (.000), Lee 22-56 (.393), Hamilton 0-2 (.000), Evans 7-18 (.389), Robinson 0-1 (.000). Opponents 57-206 (.277).

1980-81
REGULAR SEASON (21-61)

PLAYER	G	GS	MIN	FGM	FGA	PCT	FTM	FTA	PCT	O-RB	D-RB	TOT	AST	PF	DQ	STL	TO	BLK	PTS	PPG	HG
John Long	59	54	1750	441	957	.461	160	184	.870	95	102	197	106	164	3	95	151	22	1044	17.7	40
Kent Benson	59	57	1956	364	770	.473	196	254	.772	124	276	400	172	184	1	72	190	67	924	15.7	27
Phil Hubbard	80	62	2289	433	880	.492	294	426	.690	236	350	586	150	317	14	80	229	20	1161	14.5	29
Keith Herron	80	33	2270	432	954	.453	228	267	.854	98	113	211	148	154	1	91	153	26	1094	13.7	29
Terry Tyler	82	67	2549	476	895	.532	148	250	.592	198	369	567	136	215	2	112	163	180	1100	13.4	31
Greg Kelser	25	16	654	120	285	.421	68	106	.642	53	67	120	45	89	0	34	78	29	308	12.3	33
Bob McAdoo	6	4	168	30	82	.366	12	20	.600	9	32	41	20	16	0	8	18	7	72	12.0	16
Wayne Robinson	81	0	1592	234	509	.460	175	240	.729	117	177	294	112	186	2	46	149	24	643	7.9	19
Larry Wright	45	38	997	140	303	.462	53	66	.803	26	62	88	153	114	1	42	74	7	335	7.4	19
Paul Mokeski	80	34	1815	224	458	.489	120	200	.600	141	277	418	135	267	7	38	160	73	568	7.1	18
Larry Drew	76	16	1581	197	484	.407	106	133	.797	24	96	120	249	125	0	88	166	7	504	6.6	23
Ron Lee	82	28	1829	113	323	.350	113	156	.724	65	155	220	362	260	4	166	173	29	341	4.2	15
Tony Fuller	15	2	248	24	66	.364	12	16	.750	13	29	42	28	25	0	10	23	1	60	4.0	9
Ed Lawrence	3	0	19	5	8	.625	2	4	.500	2	2	4	1	6	0	1	1	0	12	4.0	6
Norman Black	3	0	28	3	10	.300	2	8	.250	0	2	2	2	2	0	1	1	0	8	2.7	4
Lee Johnson	12	0	90	7	25	.280	0	0	.000	6	16	22	1	18	0	0	7	5	14	1.2	6
PISTONS	82	—	—	3236	6986	.463	1689	2330	.725	1201	2111	3312	1819	2125	35	884	1759	492	8174	99.7	123
OPPONENTS	82	—	—	3499	6869	.509	1663	2217	.750	1090	2396	3486	2033	2095	20	793	1797	585	8692	106.0	149

3-point FG: Detroit 13-84 (.155), Long 2-11 (.182), Benson 0-4 (.000), Hubbard 1-3 (.333), Herron 2-11 (.182), Tyler 0-8 (.000), Kelser 0-2 (.000), Robinson 0-6 (.000), Wright 2-7 (.286), Mokeski 0-1 (.000), Drew 4-17 (.235), Lee 2-13 (.154), Fuller 0-1 (.000). Opponents 31-127 (.244).

1981-82
REGULAR SEASON (39-43)

PLAYER	G	GS	MIN	FGM	FGA	PCT	FTM	FTA	PCT	O-RB	D-RB	TOT	AST	PF	DQ	STL	TO	BLK	PTS	PPG	HG
John Long	69	66	2211	637	1294	.492	238	275	.865	95	162	257	148	173	0	65	167	25	1514	21.9	41
Kelly Tripucka	82	82	3077	636	1281	.496	495	621	.797	219	224	443	270	241	0	89	280	16	1772	21.6	49
Isiah Thomas	72	72	2433	453	1068	.424	302	429	.704	57	152	209	565	253	2	150	299	17	1225	17.0	34
Bill Laimbeer	30	30	935	146	283	.516	91	112	.813	110	230	340	55	126	2	17	60	34	384	12.8	24
Kent Benson	75	72	2467	405	802	.505	127	158	.804	219	434	653	159	214	2	66	160	98	940	12.5	27
Phil Hubbard	52	38	1104	207	410	.505	106	163	.650	101	171	272	67	176	1	38	99	16	520	10.0	20
Terry Tyler	82	0	1989	336	643	.523	142	192	.740	154	339	493	126	182	1	77	121	160	815	9.9	22
Greg Kelser	11	0	183	35	86	.407	27	41	.659	13	26	39	12	32	0	5	22	7	97	8.8	14
Edgar Jones	48	19	802	142	259	.548	90	129	.698	70	137	207	40	149	3	28	66	92	375	7.8	25
Vinnie Johnson	67	15	1191	208	422	.493	98	130	.754	75	69	144	160	93	0	50	91	23	517	7.7	20
Kenny Carr	28	6	444	77	168	.458	53	82	.646	53	84	137	23	69	0	6	40	6	207	7.4	16
Steve Hayes	26	0	416	46	93	.495	25	41	.610	32	68	100	24	54	0	3	17	18	117	4.5	9

PLAYER	G	GS	MIN	FGM	FGA	PCT	FTM	FTA	PCT	O-RB	D-RB	TOT	AST	PF	DQ	STL	TO	BLK	PTS	PPG	HG
Alan Hardy	38	0	487	54	111	.486	18	29	.621	14	20	34	20	32	0	9	20	4	142	3.7	13
Ron Lee	81	8	1467	88	246	.358	84	119	.706	35	120	155	312	221	3	116	123	20	278	3.4	11
Paul Mokeski	39	3	523	49	111	.441	25	33	.758	35	87	122	24	103	2	13	39	23	123	3.2	9
Jeff Judkins	30	0	251	31	81	.383	16	26	.615	14	20	34	14	33	0	6	9	5	79	2.6	8
Glenn Hagan	4	0	25	3	7	.429	1	1	1.000	2	2	4	8	7	0	3	1	0	7	1.8	5
Larry Wright	1	0	6	0	1	.000	0	0	.000	0	0	0	0	2	0	0	1	0	0	0.0	0
PISTONS	82	—	—	3561	7391	.482	1938	2581	.751	1298	2345	3643	2027	2160	16	741	1629	564	9112	111.1	132
OPPONENTS	82	—	—	3743	7362	.508	1648	2211	.745	1159	2434	3593	2191	2383	40	782	1637	581	9187	112.0	147

3-point FG: Detroit 52-213 (.244), Long 2-15 (.133), Tripucka 5-22 (.227), Thomas 17-59 (.288), Laimbeer 1-7 (.143), Benson 3-11 (.273), Hubbard 0-3 (.000), Tyler 1-4 (.250), Kelser 0-3 (.000), Jones 1-2 (.500), Johnson 3-11 (.273), Carr 0-1 (.000), Hardy 0-5 (.000), Lee 18-59 (.305), Mokeski 0-1 (.000), Judkins 1-10 (.100). Opponents 41-175 (.234).

1982-83
REGULAR SEASON (37-45)

PLAYER	G	GS	MIN	FGM	FGA	PCT	FTM	FTA	PCT	O-RB	D-RB	TOT	AST	PF	DQ	STL	TO	BLK	PTS	PPG	HG
Kelly Tripucka	58	58	2252	565	1156	.489	392	464	.845	126	138	264	237	157	0	67	187	20	1536	26.5	56
Isiah Thomas	81	81	3093	725	1537	.472	368	518	.710	105	223	328	634	318	8	199	326	29	1854	22.9	46
Vinnie Johnson	82	51	2511	520	1013	.513	245	315	.778	167	186	353	301	263	2	93	152	49	1296	15.8	33
Bill Laimbeer	82	82	2871	436	877	.497	245	310	.790	282	711	993	263	320	9	51	176	118	1119	13.6	30
Terry Tyler	82	56	2543	421	880	.478	146	196	.745	180	360	540	157	221	3	103	120	160	990	12.1	32
John Long	70	30	1485	312	692	.451	111	146	.760	56	124	180	105	130	1	44	144	12	737	10.5	29
Kent Benson	21	15	599	85	182	.467	38	50	.760	53	102	155	49	61	0	14	35	17	208	9.9	18
Edgar Jones	49	25	1036	145	294	.493	117	172	.680	80	191	271	69	160	5	28	103	77	409	8.3	19
Scott May	9	1	155	21	50	.420	17	21	.810	10	16	26	12	24	1	5	13	2	59	6.6	11
Cliff Levingston	62	5	879	131	270	.485	84	147	.571	104	128	232	52	125	2	23	73	36	346	5.6	24
Ray Tolbert	28	0	395	57	124	.460	28	59	.475	26	65	91	19	56	0	10	32	23	142	5.1	20
Tom Owens	49	4	725	81	192	.422	45	66	.682	66	120	186	44	115	0	12	48	14	207	4.2	12
James Wilkes	9	0	129	11	34	.324	12	15	.800	9	10	19	10	22	0	3	5	1	34	3.8	8
Walker D. Russell	68	1	757	67	184	.364	47	58	.810	19	54	73	131	71	0	16	92	1	183	2.7	16
Ricky Pierce	39	1	265	33	88	.375	18	32	.563	15	20	35	14	42	0	8	18	4	85	2.2	13
Jim Smith	4	0	18	3	4	.750	2	4	.500	0	5	5	0	4	0	0	0	0	8	2.0	5
Jim Johnstone	16	0	137	9	20	.450	6	15	.400	11	19	30	10	24	0	2	11	6	24	1.5	4
Jim Zoet	7	0	30	1	5	.200	0	0	.000	3	5	8	1	9	0	1	4	3	2	0.3	2
PISTONS	82	—	—	3623	7602	.477	1921	2588	.742	1312	2477	3789	2108	2122	31	679	1557	572	9239	112.7	152
OPPONENTS	82	—	—	3802	7679	.495	1647	2287	.720	1266	2594	3860	2252	2326	43	761	1580	561	9272	113.1	147

3-point FG: Detroit 72-272 (.265), Tripucka 14-37 (.378), Thomas 36-125 (.288), Johnson 11-40 (.275), Laimbeer 2-13 (.154), Tyler 2-15 (.133), Long 2-7 (.286), Benson 0-1 (.000), Jones 2-6 (.333), Levingston 0-1 (.000), Tolbert 0-1 (.000), Wilkes 0-1 (.000), Russell 2-18 (.111), Pierce 1-7 (.143). Opponents 21-182 (.115).

1983-84
REGULAR SEASON (49-33)

PLAYER	G	GS	MIN	FGM	FGA	PCT	FTM	FTA	PCT	O-RB	D-RB	TOT	AST	PF	DQ	STL	TO	BLK	PTS	PPG	HG
Isiah Thomas	82	82	3007	669	1448	.462	388	529	.733	103	224	327	914	324	8	204	307	33	1748	21.3	47
Kelly Tripucka	76	75	2493	595	1296	.459	426	523	.815	119	187	306	228	190	0	65	151	17	1618	21.3	44
Bill Laimbeer	82	82	2864	553	1044	.530	316	365	.866	329	674	1003	149	273	4	49	151	84	1422	17.3	33
John Long	82	82	2514	545	1155	.472	243	275	.884	139	150	289	205	199	1	93	143	18	1334	16.3	41
Vinnie Johnson	82	0	1909	426	901	.473	207	275	.753	130	107	237	271	196	1	44	135	19	1063	13.0	28
Terry Tyler	82	7	1602	313	691	.453	94	132	.712	104	181	285	76	151	1	63	78	59	722	8.8	20
Cliff Levingston	80	24	1746	229	436	.525	125	186	.672	234	311	545	109	281	7	44	77	78	583	7.3	22
Kent Benson	82	58	1734	248	451	.550	83	101	.822	117	292	409	130	230	4	71	79	53	579	7.1	23
Ray Tolbert	49	0	475	64	121	.529	23	45	.511	45	53	98	26	88	1	12	26	20	151	3.1	10
Earl Cureton	73	0	907	81	177	.458	31	59	.525	86	201	287	36	143	3	24	55	31	193	2.6	13
Walker D. Russell	16	0	119	14	42	.333	12	13	.923	6	13	19	22	25	0	4	9	0	41	2.6	13
Lionel Hollins	32	0	216	24	63	.381	11	13	.846	4	18	22	62	26	0	13	24	1	59	1.8	8
David Thirdkill	46	0	291	31	72	.431	15	31	.484	9	22	31	27	44	0	10	19	3	77	1.7	9
Ken Austin	7	0	28	6	13	.462	0	0	.000	2	1	3	1	7	0	3	1	1	12	1.7	6
PISTONS	82	—	—	3798	7910	.480	1974	2547	.775	1430	2434	3861	2256	2177	30	697	1310	417	9612	117.2	186
OPPONENTS	82	—	—	3657	7369	.496	1941	2577	.753	1163	2457	3620	2193	2187	46	621	1478	522	9318	113.6	184

3-point FG: Detroit 32-141 (.227), Thomas 22-65 (.338), Tripucka 2-17 (.118), Laimbeer 0-11 (.000), Long 1-5 (.200), Johnson 4-19 (.211), Tyler 2-13 (.154), Levingston 0-3 (.000), Benson 0-1 (.000), Tolbert 0-1 (.000), Cureton 0-1 (.000), Russell 1-2 (.500), Hollins 0-2 (.000), Thirdkill 0-1 (.000). Opponents 53-202 (.262).

PLAYOFFS (2-3)

PLAYER	G	GS	MIN	FGM	FGA	PCT	FTM	FTA	PCT	O-RB	D-RB	TOT	AST	PF	DQ	STL	TO	BLK	PTS	PPG	HG
Kelly Tripucka	5	5	208	48	102	.471	41	51	.804	10	13	23	15	22	1	11	18	0	137	27.4	40
Isiah Thomas	5	5	198	39	83	.470	27	35	.771	7	12	19	55	22	1	13	23	6	107	21.4	35
Bill Laimbeer	5	5	165	29	51	.569	18	20	.900	14	48	62	12	23	2	4	12	3	76	15.2	31
John Long	5	5	149	20	55	.364	15	15	1.000	7	4	11	2	15	0	7	10	0	55	11.0	14
Vinnie Johnson	5	0	132	17	46	.370	17	19	.895	5	9	14	12	9	0	1	4	1	51	10.2	16
Cliff Levingston	5	0	101	15	19	.789	10	16	.625	11	13	24	1	15	0	1	3	2	40	8.0	17
Kent Benson	5	5	129	16	37	.432	6	10	.600	9	21	30	7	14	0	5	3	7	38	7.6	18
Earl Cureton	5	0	93	15	31	.484	2	6	.333	14	19	33	2	9	0	2	5	1	32	6.4	12
Terry Tyler	5	0	42	10	24	.417	5	9	.556	5	2	7	1	4	0	0	1	3	25	5.0	8
Lionel Hollins	2	0	6	0	1	.000	0	0	.000	0	0	0	0	0	0	0	2	0	0	0.0	0
Ray Tolbert	1	0	2	0	0	.000	0	0	.000	0	0	0	0	0	0	0	0	0	0	0.0	0
PISTONS	5	—	—	209	449	.465	141	181	.779	82	141	223	107	133	4	44	81	24	561	112.2	123
KNICKS	5	—	—	218	444	.491	117	158	.741	73	150	223	133	151	4	46	89	30	558	111.6	127

3-point FG: Detroit 2-9 (.222), Tripucka 0-1 (.000), Thomas 2-6 (.333), Long 0-1 (.000), Johnson 0-1 (.000). Knicks 5-14 (.357).

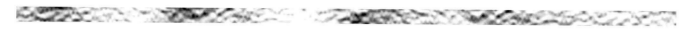

1984-85
REGULAR SEASON (46-36)

PLAYER	G	GS	MIN	FGM	FGA	PCT	FTM	FTA	PCT	O-RB	D-RB	TOT	AST	PF	DQ	STL	TO	BLK	PTS	PPG	HG
Isiah Thomas	81	81	3089	646	1410	.458	399	493	.809	114	247	361	1123	288	8	187	302	25	1720	21.2	38
Kelly Tripucka	55	43	1675	396	831	.477	255	288	.885	66	152	218	135	118	1	49	118	14	1049	19.1	45
Bill Laimbeer	82	82	2892	595	1177	.506	244	306	.797	295	718	1013	154	308	4	69	129	71	1438	17.5	35
John Long	66	55	1820	431	885	.487	106	123	.862	81	109	190	130	139	0	71	98	14	973	14.7	28
Vinnie Johnson	82	16	2093	428	942	.454	190	247	.769	134	118	252	325	205	2	71	135	20	1051	12.8	28
Terry Tyler	82	53	2004	422	855	.494	106	148	.716	148	275	423	63	192	0	49	76	90	950	11.6	28
Dan Roundfield	56	43	1492	236	505	.467	139	178	.781	175	278	453	102	147	0	26	123	54	611	10.9	27
Kent Benson	72	35	1401	201	397	.506	76	94	.809	103	221	324	93	207	4	53	68	44	478	6.6	15
Earl Cureton	81	1	1642	207	428	.484	82	144	.569	169	250	419	83	216	1	56	114	42	496	6.1	18
Tony Campbell	56	0	625	130	262	.496	56	70	.800	41	48	89	24	107	1	28	69	3	316	5.6	17
Brook Steppe	54	0	486	83	178	.466	87	104	.837	25	32	57	35	61	0	16	43	4	253	4.7	13
David Thirdkill	10	1	115	12	23	.522	5	11	.455	4	4	8	1	16	0	3	12	2	29	2.9	8
Major Jones	47	0	418	48	87	.552	33	51	.647	48	80	128	15	58	0	9	35	14	129	2.7	15
Lorenzo Romar	5	0	35	2	8	.250	5	5	1.000	0	0	0	10	5	0	4	5	0	9	1.8	5
Terry Teagle	2	0	5	1	2	.500	0	0	.000	0	0	0	0	2	0	0	1	0	2	1.0	2
Sidney Lowe	6	0	31	2	7	.286	0	0	.000	0	1	1	8	5	0	0	2	0	4	0.7	4
Dale Wilkinson	2	0	7	0	2	.000	0	0	.000	0	1	1	0	2	0	0	0	0	0	0.0	0
PISTONS	82	—	—	3840	7999	.480	1783	2262	.788	1403	2534	3937	2302	2076	21	691	1341	397	9508	116.0	148
OPPONENTS	82	—	—	3700	7457	.496	1826	2404	.760	1109	2563	3672	2107	2017	30	642	1486	508	9304	113.5	148

3-point FG: Detroit 45-199 (.226), Thomas 29-113 (.257), Tripucka 2-5 (.400), Laimbeer 4-18 (.222), Long 5-15 (.333), Johnson 5-27 (.185), Tyler 0-8 (.000), Roundfield 0-2 (.000), Benson 0-3 (.000), Cureton 0-3 (.000), Campbell 0-1 (.000), Steppe 0-1 (.000), Thirdkill 0-1 (.000), Romar 0-2 (.000). Opponents 78-249 (.313).

PLAYOFFS (5-4)

PLAYER	G	GS	MIN	FGM	FGA	PCT	FTM	FTA	PCT	O-RB	D-RB	TOT	AST	PF	DQ	STL	TO	BLK	PTS	PPG	HG
Isiah Thomas	9	9	355	83	166	.500	47	62	.758	11	36	47	101	39	2	19	30	4	219	24.3	37
Kelly Tripucka	9	9	288	49	118	.415	35	40	.875	19	20	39	29	22	0	4	19	3	133	14.8	24
Bill Laimbeer	9	9	325	48	107	.449	36	51	.706	36	60	96	15	32	1	7	16	7	132	14.7	27
Vinnie Johnson	9	0	235	53	103	.515	22	28	.786	15	12	27	29	24	0	6	15	1	128	14.2	34
Terry Tyler	9	0	179	49	100	.490	22	27	.815	15	25	40	3	17	0	6	9	4	120	13.3	23
John Long	9	9	255	48	105	.457	15	15	1.000	10	7	17	13	22	0	14	11	2	112	12.4	20
Dan Roundfield	9	9	215	33	68	.485	16	17	.941	19	41	60	15	21	0	4	15	6	82	9.1	22
Kent Benson	9	1	142	25	46	.543	13	15	.867	9	27	36	4	27	0	8	6	2	63	7.0	13
Earl Cureton	9	0	133	16	34	.471	5	9	.556	10	31	41	4	20	0	9	4	2	37	4.1	9
Major Jones	1	0	4	1	1	1.000	0	0	.000	0	0	0	0	0	0	0	0	0	2	2.0	2
Brook Steppe	4	0	20	2	7	.286	4	6	.667	1	2	3	2	3	0	0	2	0	8	2.0	6
Tony Campbell	2	0	9	1	3	.333	0	0	.000	0	2	2	1	1	0	0	0	0	2	1.0	2
PISTONS	9	—	—	408	858	.476	215	270	.796	145	263	408	216	228	3	77	127	31	1038	115.3	125
OPPONENTS	9	—	—	411	812	.506	223	274	.814	129	280	409	235	2	72	147	43	1054	117.1	133

3-point FG: Detroit 7-28 (.250), Thomas 6-15 (.400), Tripucka 0-1 (.000), Laimbeer 0-2 (.000), Johnson 0-3 (.000), Tyler 0-1 (.000), Long 1-4 (.250), Cureton 0-1 (.000), Steppe 0-1 (.000). Opponents 9-29 (.310).

1985-86
REGULAR SEASON (46-36)

PLAYER	G	GS	MIN	FGM	FGA	PCT	FTM	FTA	PCT	O-RB	D-RB	TOT	AST	PF	DQ	STL	TO	BLK	PTS	PPG	HG
Isiah Thomas	77	77	2790	609	1248	.488	365	462	.790	83	194	277	830	245	9	171	289	20	1609	20.9	39
Kelly Tripucka	81	81	2626	615	1236	.498	380	444	.856	116	232	348	265	167	0	93	183	10	1622	20.0	41
Bill Laimbeer	82	82	2891	545	1107	.492	266	319	.834	305	770	1075	146	291	4	59	133	65	1360	16.6	29
Vinnie Johnson	79	12	1978	465	996	.467	165	214	.771	119	107	226	269	180	2	80	88	23	1097	13.9	35
John Long	62	30	1176	264	548	.482	89	104	.856	47	51	98	82	92	0	41	59	13	620	10.0	28
Joe Dumars	82	45	1957	287	597	.481	190	238	.798	60	59	119	390	200	1	66	158	11	769	9.4	22
Earl Cureton	80	19	2017	285	564	.505	117	211	.555	198	306	504	137	239	3	58	150	58	687	8.6	25
Tony Campbell	82	1	1292	294	608	.484	58	73	.795	83	153	236	45	164	0	62	86	7	648	7.9	20
Kent Benson	72	51	1344	201	415	.484	66	83	.795	118	258	376	80	196	3	58	58	51	469	6.5	21
Rick Mahorn	80	12	1442	157	345	.455	81	119	.681	121	291	412	64	261	4	40	109	61	395	4.9	22
Chuck Nevitt	25	0	101	12	32	.375	15	20	.750	10	15	25	5	29	0	2	7	17	39	1.6	8
Mike Gibson	32	0	161	20	51	.392	8	11	.727	15	25	40	5	35	0	8	6	4	48	1.5	9
Walker D. Russell	1	0	2	0	1	.000	0	0	.000	0	0	0	1	0	0	0	0	0	0	0.0	0
Ron Crevier	2	0	3	0	2	.000	0	2	.000	1	0	1	0	2	0	0	0	0	0	0.0	0
PISTONS	82	—	—	3754	7750	.484	1800	2300	.783	1276	2461	3737	2319	2101	26	738	1343	340	9363	114.2	134
OPPONENTS	82	—	—	3620	7365	.492	1956	2589	.756	1180	2538	3718	2083	1977	25	662	1490	500	9267	113.0	137

3-point FG: Detroit 55-182 (.302), Thomas 26-84 (.310), Tripucka 12-25 (.480), Laimbeer 4-14 (.286), Johnson 2-13 (.154), Long 3-16 (.188), Dumars 5-16 (.313), Cureton 0-2 (.000), Campbell 2-9 (.222), Benson 1-2 (.500), Mahorn 0-1 (.000). Opponents 71-258 (.275).

PLAYOFFS (1-3)

PLAYER	G	GS	MIN	FGM	FGA	PCT	FTM	FTA	PCT	O-RB	D-RB	TOT	AST	PF	DQ	STL	TO	BLK	PTS	PPG	HG
Isiah Thomas	4	4	163	41	91	.451	24	36	.667	8	14	22	48	17	0	9	17	3	106	26.5	36
Bill Laimbeer	4	4	168	34	68	.500	21	23	.913	20	36	56	1	19	1	2	8	3	90	22.5	27
Kelly Tripucka	4	4	175	33	71	.465	21	23	.913	10	13	23	9	14	1	3	16	2	87	21.8	33
Joe Dumars	4	4	147	25	41	.610	10	15	.667	6	7	13	25	16	0	4	7	0	60	15.0	18
Vinnie Johnson	4	0	85	22	49	.449	7	13	.538	8	9	17	11	9	0	3	5	0	51	12.8	23
Earl Cureton	4	4	126	17	31	.548	2	8	.250	12	18	30	9	14	0	3	5	0	36	9.0	14
John Long	1	0	13	2	5	.400	3	3	1.000	0	1	1	0	1	0	1	2	0	7	7.0	7
Tony Campbell	2	0	16	4	10	.400	1	2	.500	0	2	2	0	5	0	0	1	0	9	4.5	8
Rick Mahorn	4	0	61	5	13	.385	2	2	1.000	3	9	12	0	14	0	1	3	0	12	3.0	6
Kent Benson	4	0	55	4	10	.400	0	0	.000	3	10	13	0	11	0	0	1	2	8	2.0	4
Chuck Nevitt	1	0	1	0	0	.000	0	0	.000	0	0	0	0	0	0	0	0	0	0	0.0	0
PISTONS	4	—	—	187	389	.481	91	125	.728	70	119	189	103	120	2	26	65	10	466	116.5	125
HAWKS	4	—	—	182	354	.514	121	164	.738	53	128	181	115	110	5	26	60	25	488	121.1	140

3-point FG: Detroit 1-10 (.100), Thomas 0-5 (.000), Laimbeer 1-1 (1.000), Johnson 0-3 (.000), Cureton 0-1 (.000). Hawks 3-7 (.429).

1986-87
REGULAR SEASON (52-30)

PLAYER	G	GS	MIN	FGM	FGA	PCT	FTM	FTA	PCT	O-RB	D-RB	TOT	AST	PF	DQ	STL	TO	BLK	PTS	PPG	HG
Adrian Dantley	81	81	2736	601	1126	.534	539	664	.812	104	228	332	162	193	1	63	181	7	1742	21.5	41
Isiah Thomas	81	81	3013	626	1353	.463	400	521	.768	82	237	319	813	251	5	153	343	20	1671	20.6	36
Vinnie Johnson	78	8	2166	533	1154	.462	158	201	.786	123	134	257	300	159	0	92	133	16	1228	15.7	30
Bill Laimbeer	82	82	2854	506	1010	.501	245	274	.894	243	712	955	151	283	4	72	120	69	1263	15.4	30
Joe Dumars	79	75	2439	369	749	.493	184	246	.748	50	117	167	352	194	1	83	171	5	931	11.8	24
Sidney Green	80	69	1792	256	542	.472	119	177	.672	196	457	653	62	197	0	41	127	50	631	7.9	22
Dennis Rodman	77	1	1155	213	391	.545	74	126	.587	163	169	332	56	166	1	38	93	48	500	6.5	21
Rick Mahorn	63	6	1278	144	322	.447	96	117	.821	93	282	375	38	221	4	32	73	50	384	6.1	17
John Salley	82	2	1463	163	290	.562	105	171	.614	108	188	296	54	256	5	44	74	125	431	5.3	28
Tony Campbell	40	0	332	57	145	.393	24	39	.615	21	37	58	19	40	0	12	34	1	138	3.5	17
Kurt Nimphius	28	5	277	36	78	.462	24	32	.750	22	32	54	7	38	0	4	16	13	96	3.4	12
Cozell McQueen	3	0	7	3	3	1.000	0	0	.000	3	5	8	0	1	0	0	0	1	6	2.0	4
Chuck Nevitt	41	0	267	31	63	.492	14	24	.583	36	47	83	4	73	0	7	21	30	76	1.9	12
Jeff Taylor	12	0	44	6	10	.600	9	10	.900	1	3	4	3	4	0	2	8	1	21	1.8	6
John Schweitz	3	0	7	0	1	.000	0	0	.000	0	1	1	0	2	0	0	2	0	0	0.0	0
PISTONS	82	—	—	3544	7237	.490	1991	2602	.765	1245	2649	3894	2021	2078	21	643	1417	436	9118	111.2	131
OPPONENTS	82	—	—	3376	7307	.462	1951	2608	.748	1143	2339	3482	2029	2067	28	670	1294	472	8836	107.8	138

3-point FG: Detroit 39-169 (.231), Dantley 1-6 (.167), Thomas 19-98 (.194), Johnson 4-14 (.286), Laimbeer 6-21 (.286), Dumars 9-22 (.409), Green 0-2 (.000), Rodman 0-1 (.000), Salley 0-1 (.000), Campbell 0-3 (.000), Nimphius 0-1 (.000). Opponents 133-419 (.317).

PLAYOFFS (10-5)

PLAYER	G	GS	MIN	FGM	FGA	PCT	FTM	FTA	PCT	O-RB	D-RB	TOT	AST	PF	DQ	STL	TO	BLK	PTS	PPG	HG
Isiah Thomas	15	1	562	134	297	.451	83	110	.755	21	46	67	130	51	1	39	42	4	361	24.1	36
Adrian Dantley	15	15	500	111	206	.539	86	111	.775	29	39	68	35	36	0	13	33	0	308	20.5	32
Vinnie Johnson	15	0	388	95	207	.459	31	36	.861	20	24	44	62	33	0	9	23	4	221	14.7	25
Joe Dumars	15	15	473	78	145	.538	32	41	.780	8	11	19	72	26	0	12	27	1	190	12.7	35
Bill Laimbeer	15	15	543	84	163	.515	15	24	.625	30	126	156	37	53	2	15	20	12	184	12.3	20
Rick Mahorn	15	15	483	59	109	.541	28	35	.800	42	100	142	5	60	1	6	16	11	146	9.7	17
Dennis Rodman	15	0	245	40	74	.541	18	32	.563	32	39	71	3	48	0	6	17	17	98	6.5	14
John Salley	15	0	311	33	66	.500	27	42	.643	30	42	72	11	60	1	3	14	17	93	6.2	15
Tony Campbell	4	0	13	3	6	.500	2	2	1.000	0	5	5	0	1	0	0	0	0	9	2.3	7
Kurt Nimphius	4	0	30	3	9	.333	2	4	.500	5	5	10	0	10	0	0	3	2	8	2.0	4
Sidney Green	9	0	42	6	10	.600	5	6	.833	3	6	9	1	2	0	1	3	2	17	1.9	6
Chuck Nevitt	3	0	10	1	5	.200	2	2	1.000	1	5	6	0	1	0	0	3	3	4	1.3	2
PISTONS	15	—	—	647	1297	.499	331	445	.744	221	448	669	356	381	5	104	201	73	1639	109.3	145
OPPONENTS	15	—	—	581	1237	.470	368	464	.793	199	418	617	350	369	4	91	204	76	1549	103.3	119

3-point FG: Detroit 14-45 (.311), Thomas 10-33 (.303), Johnson 0-2 (.000), Dumars 2-3 (.667), Laimbeer 1-5 (.200), Mahorn 0-1 (.000), Campbell 1-1 (1.000). Opponents 19-78 (.244).

1987-88
REGULAR SEASON (54-28)

PLAYER	G	GS	MIN	FGM	FGA	PCT	FTM	FTA	PCT	O-RB	D-RB	TOT	AST	PF	DQ	STL	TO	BLK	PTS	PPG	HG
Adrian Dantley	69	50	2144	444	863	.514	492	572	.860	84	143	227	171	144	0	39	135	10	1380	20.0	45
Isiah Thomas	81	81	2927	621	1341	.463	305	394	.774	64	214	278	678	217	0	141	273	17	1577	19.5	42
Joe Dumars	82	82	2732	453	960	.472	251	308	.815	63	137	200	387	155	1	87	172	15	1161	14.2	25
Bill Laimbeer	82	82	2897	455	923	.493	187	214	.874	165	667	832	199	284	6	66	136	78	1110	13.5	30
Vinnie Johnson	82	1	1935	425	959	.443	147	217	.677	90	141	231	267	164	0	58	152	18	1002	12.2	27
Dennis Rodman	82	32	2147	398	709	.561	152	284	.535	318	397	715	110	273	5	75	156	45	953	11.6	30
Rick Mahorn	67	64	1963	276	481	.574	164	217	.756	159	406	565	60	262	4	43	119	42	717	10.7	34
John Salley	82	16	2003	258	456	.566	185	261	.709	166	236	402	113	294	4	53	120	137	701	8.5	21
James Edwards	26	2	328	48	101	.475	45	61	.738	22	55	77	5	57	0	2	22	5	141	5.4	16
William Bedford	38	0	298	44	101	.436	13	23	.565	27	38	65	4	47	0	8	19	17	101	2.7	14
Darryl Dawkins	2	0	7	1	2	.500	2	3	.667	0	0	0	1	4	0	0	3	1	4	2.0	4
Ralph Lewis	50	0	310	27	87	.310	29	48	.604	17	34	51	14	36	0	13	19	4	83	1.7	10
Ron Moore	9	0	25	4	13	.308	2	4	.500	2	0	2	1	8	0	2	3	0	10	1.1	4
Chuck Nevitt	17	0	63	7	21	.333	3	6	.500	4	14	18	0	12	0	1	2	5	17	1.0	4
Walker D. Russell	1	0	1	0	1	.000	0	0	.000	0	0	0	0	0	0	0	0	0	0	0.0	0
PISTONS	82	—	—	3461	7018	.493	1977	2612	.757	1181	2482	3663	2011	1957	20	588	1348	394	8957	109.2	144
OPPONENTS	82	—	—	3334	7134	.467	1751	2298	.762	1144	2276	3420	1964	2164	32	649	1328	406	8533	104.1	132

3-point FG: Detroit 58-202 (.287), Dantley 0-2 (.000), Thomas 30-97 (.309), Dumars 4-19 (.211), Laimbeer 13-39 (.333), Johnson 5-24 (.208), Rodman 5-17 (.294), Mahorn 1-2 (.500), Lewis 0-1 (.000), Russell 0-1 (.000). Opponents 114-394 (.289).

PLAYOFFS (14-9)

PLAYER	G	GS	MIN	FGM	FGA	PCT	FTM	FTA	PCT	O-RB	D-RB	TOT	AST	PF	DQ	STL	TO	BLK	PTS	PPG	HG
Isiah Thomas	23	23	911	183	419	.437	125	151	.828	26	81	107	201	71	2	66	85	8	504	21.9	43
Adrian Dantley	23	23	804	153	292	.524	140	178	.787	37	70	107	46	50	0	19	51	1	446	19.4	34
Joe Dumars	23	23	804	113	247	.457	56	63	.889	18	32	50	112	50	1	13	40	2	284	12.3	29
Bill Laimbeer	23	23	779	114	250	.456	40	45	.889	43	178	221	44	77	2	18	30	19	273	11.9	29
Vinnie Johnson	23	0	477	101	239	.423	33	50	.660	35	40	75	43	48	0	17	21	4	236	10.3	24
Dennis Rodman	23	0	474	71	136	.522	22	54	.407	51	85	136	21	87	1	14	31	14	164	7.1	23
John Salley	23	0	623	56	104	.538	49	69	.710	64	91	155	21	88	2	15	23	37	161	7.0	17
James Edwards	22	0	308	56	110	.509	27	41	.659	23	45	68	11	55	0	2	10	10	139	6.3	18
Rick Mahorn	23	21	409	31	90	.344	13	19	.684	19	70	89	13	64	2	5	16	10	75	3.3	11
Walker D. Russell	7	0	10	2	5	.400	2	2	1.000	0	0	0	1	1	0	1	1	0	6	0.9	2
Chuck Nevitt	3	0	4	1	2	.500	0	0	.000	2	1	3	0	1	0	0	1	0	2	0.7	2
Ralph Lewis	10	0	17	2	6	.333	0	0	.000	3	5	8	1	2	0	0	0	0	4	0.4	2
PISTONS	23	—	—	883	1900	.465	507	672	.754	321	698	1019	514	594	10	170	318	105	2294	99.7	115
OPPONENTS	23	—	—	812	1830	.444	530	695	.763	271	640	911	502	542	6	143	338	97	2189	95.2	119

3-point FG: Detroit 21-81 (.259), Thomas 13-44 (.295), Dantley 0-2 (.000), Dumars 2-6 (.333), Laimbeer 5-17 (.294), Johnson 1-7 (.143), Rodman 0-2 (.000), Salley 0-1 (.000), Edwards 0-1 (.000), Lewis 0-1 (.000). Opponents 35-117 (.299).

NBA FINALS (3-4)

PLAYER	G	GS	MIN	FGM	FGA	PCT	FTM	FTA	PCT	O-RB	D-RB	TOT	AST	PF	DQ	STL	TO	BLK	PTS	PPG	HG
Adrian Dantley	7	7	255	47	82	.573	55	64	.859	14	21	35	16	18	0	4	18	1	149	21.3	34
Isiah Thomas	7	7	262	49	115	.426	35	42	.833	5	26	31	63	23	1	20	26	2	138	19.7	43
Joe Dumars	7	7	233	40	78	.513	13	14	.929	6	10	16	32	15	0	4	8	0	94	13.4	25
Vinnie Johnson	7	0	164	34	84	.405	8	18	.444	12	14	26	21	16	0	5	6	1	77	11.0	16
Bill Laimbeer	7	7	235	27	69	.391	10	10	1.000	12	50	62	13	25	1	3	8	7	66	9.4	13
Dennis Rodman	7	0	174	22	35	.629	11	21	.524	15	33	48	4	32	1	6	4	7	55	7.9	15
John Salley	7	0	177	18	31	.581	14	20	.700	12	32	44	6	25	0	5	7	9	50	7.1	17
James Edwards	7	0	96	21	44	.477	7	11	.636	10	11	21	7	18	0	1	4	3	49	7.0	14
Rick Mahorn	7	7	74	9	22	.409	5	6	.833	5	12	17	1	14	0	0	1	4	23	3.3	11
Chuck Nevitt	1	0	1	1	2	.500	0	0	.000	2	0	2	0	1	0	0	0	0	2	2.0	2
Walker D. Russell	3	0	5	1	3	.333	2	2	1.000	0	0	0	0	1	0	0	0	0	4	1.3	2
Ralph Lewis	3	0	4	1	2	.500	0	0	.000	2	1	3	0	0	0	0	0	0	2	0.7	2
PISTONS	7	—	—	270	567	.476	160	208	.769	95	210	305	163	188	3	48	82	34	709	101.3	111
LAKERS	7	—	—	248	531	.535	185	247	.749	72	191	263	166	154	0	41	92	21	691	98.7	108

3-point FG: Detroit 9-31 (.290), Thomas 5-17 (.294), Dumars 1-2 (.500), Johnson 1-6 (.167), Laimbeer 2-6 (.333). Lakers 10-40 (.250).

1988-89
REGULAR SEASON (63-19)

PLAYER	G	GS	MIN	FGM	FGA	PCT	FTM	FTA	PCT	O-RB	D-RB	TOT	AST	PF	DQ	STL	TO	BLK	PTS	PPG	HG
Adrian Dantley	42	42	1341	258	495	.521	256	305	.839	53	111	164	93	99	1	23	81	6	772	18.4	35
Isiah Thomas	80	76	2924	569	1227	.464	287	351	.818	49	224	273	663	209	0	133	298	20	1458	18.2	37
Joe Dumars	69	67	2408	456	903	.505	260	306	.850	57	115	172	390	103	1	63	178	5	1186	17.2	42
Mark Aguirre	36	32	1068	213	441	.483	110	149	.738	56	95	151	89	101	2	16	68	7	558	15.5	31
Vinnie Johnson	82	21	2073	462	996	.464	193	263	.734	109	146	255	242	155	0	74	105	17	1130	13.8	34
Bill Laimbeer	81	81	2640	449	900	.499	178	212	.840	138	638	776	177	259	2	51	129	100	1106	13.7	32
Dennis Rodman	82	8	2208	316	531	.595	97	155	.626	327	445	772	99	292	4	55	126	76	735	9.0	32
James Edwards	76	1	1254	211	422	.500	133	194	.686	68	163	231	49	226	1	11	72	31	555	7.3	18
Rick Mahorn	72	61	1795	203	393	.517	116	155	.748	141	355	496	59	206	1	40	97	66	522	7.3	19
John Salley	67	21	1458	166	333	.498	135	195	.692	134	201	335	75	197	3	40	100	72	467	7.0	19
Micheal Williams	49	0	358	47	129	.364	31	47	.660	9	18	27	70	44	0	13	42	3	127	2.6	11
John Long	24	0	152	19	40	.475	11	13	.846	2	9	11	15	16	0	0	9	2	49	2.0	17
Darryl Dawkins	14	0	48	9	19	.474	9	18	.500	3	4	7	1	13	0	0	4	1	27	1.9	8
Steve Harris	3	0	7	1	4	.250	2	2	1.000	0	2	2	0	1	0	1	0	0	4	1.3	4
Fennis Dembo	31	0	74	14	42	.333	8	10	.800	8	15	23	5	15	0	1	7	0	36	1.2	8
Pace Mannion	5	0	14	2	2	1.000	0	0	.000	0	3	3	0	3	0	1	0	0	4	0.8	4
Jim Rowinski	6	0	8	0	2	.000	4	4	1.000	0	2	2	0	0	0	0	0	0	4	0.7	4
PISTONS	82	—	—	3395	6879	.494	1830	2379	.769	1154	2546	3700	2027	1939	15	522	1336	406	8740	106.6	132
OPPONENTS	82	—	—	3140	7022	.447	1826	2325	.785	1131	2188	3319	1855	2088	28	646	1225	341	8264	100.8	133

3-point FG: Detroit 120-400 (.300), Thomas 33-121 (.273), Dumars 14-29 (.483), Aguirre 22-75 (.293), Johnson 13-44 (.295), Laimbeer 30-86 (.349), Rodman 6-26 (.231), Edwards 0-2 (.000), Mahorn 0-2 (.000), Salley 0-2 (.000), Williams 2-9 (.222), Dembo 0-4 (.000). Opponents 158-554 (.285).

PLAYOFFS (15-2)

PLAYER	G	GS	MIN	FGM	FGA	PCT	FTM	FTA	PCT	O-RB	D-RB	TOT	AST	PF	DQ	STL	TO	BLK	PTS	PPG	HG
Isiah Thomas	17	17	633	115	279	.412	71	96	.740	24	49	73	141	39	0	27	43	4	309	18.2	33
Joe Dumars	17	17	620	106	233	.455	87	101	.861	11	33	44	96	31	0	12	31	1	300	17.6	33
Vinnie Johnson	17	0	372	91	200	.455	47	62	.758	16	29	45	43	32	0	4	21	3	239	14.1	25
Mark Aguirre	17	17	462	89	182	.489	28	38	.737	26	49	75	28	38	0	8	20	3	214	12.6	25
Bill Laimbeer	17	17	497	66	142	.465	25	31	.806	26	114	140	31	55	1	6	19	8	172	10.1	19
John Salley	17	0	392	58	99	.586	36	54	.667	34	45	79	9	58	0	9	12	25	12	8.9	23
James Edwards	17	0	317	40	85	.471	40	51	.784	11	25	36	12	53	0	1	15	8	120	7.1	15
Dennis Rodman	17	0	409	37	70	.529	24	35	.686	56	114	170	16	58	0	6	24	12	98	5.8	12
Rick Mahorn	17	17	360	40	69	.580	17	26	.654	30	57	87	7	59	1	9	11	13	97	5.7	17
John Long	4	0	8	1	1	1.000	3	3	1.000	0	0	0	0	0	0	0	0	0	5	1.3	3
Fennis Dembo	2	0	4	1	1	1.000	0	0	.000	0	0	0	0	1	0	0	1	0	2	1.0	2
Micheal Williams	4	0	6	0	0	.000	2	2	1.000	1	1	2	2	1	0	1	0	0	2	0.5	2
PISTONS	17	—	—	644	1361	.473	380	499	.762	235	516	751	385	425	2	83	205	77	1710	100.6	114
OPPONENTS	17	—	—	583	1300	.448	368	491	.749	178	462	640	357	431	7	97	215	60	1579	92.9	110

3-point FG: Detroit 42-142 (.296), Thomas 8-30 (.267), Dumars 1-12 (.083), Johnson 10-24 (.417), Aguirre 8-29 (.276), Laimbeer 15-42 (.357), Edwards 0-1 (.000), Rodman 0-4 (.000). Opponents 45-160 (.281).

NBA FINALS (4-0)

PLAYER	G	GS	MIN	FGM	FGA	PCT	FTM	FTA	PCT	O-RB	D-RB	TOT	AST	PF	DQ	STL	TO	BLK	PTS	PPG	HG
Joe Dumars	4	4	147	38	66	.576	33	38	.868	1	6	7	24	4	0	2	7	1	109	27.3	33
Isiah Thomas	4	4	141	32	66	.485	19	25	.760	2	8	10	29	13	0	6	10	1	85	21.3	26
Vinnie Johnson	4	0	95	30	50	.600	7	11	.636	3	10	13	11	9	0	0	2	1	68	17.0	19
James Edwards	4	0	97	12	27	.444	12	16	.750	6	8	14	3	16	0	0	3	3	36	9.0	15
Bill Laimbeer	4	4	94	12	22	.545	6	7	.857	3	18	21	9	15	0	2	3	0	32	8.0	16
Mark Aguirre	4	4	107	12	33	.364	6	8	.750	9	15	24	6	13	0	2	8	0	30	7.5	14
John Salley	4	0	81	13	19	.684	4	7	.571	2	8	10	5	14	0	1	2	11	30	7.5	9
Rick Mahorn	4	4	98	10	18	.556	4	6	.667	6	15	21	4	17	1	1	1	3	24	6.0	13
Dennis Rodman	4	0	94	7	15	.467	6	7	.857	13	27	40	5	12	0	2	9	1	20	5.0	12
John Long	1	0	2	1	1	1.000	0	0	.000	0	0	0	0	0	0	0	0	0	2	2.0	2
Fennis Dembo	1	0	2	0	0	.000	0	0	.000	0	0	0	0	1	0	0	0	0	0	0.0	0
Micheal Williams	1	0	2	0	0	.000	0	0	.000	0	0	0	1	1	0	0	0	0	0	0.0	0
PISTONS	4	—	—	167	317	.527	97	125	.776	45	115	160	97	115	1	16	45	21	436	109.0	114
LAKERS	4	—	—	144	310	.465	108	144	.750	47	98	145	92	104	2	22	47	16	409	102.3	110

3-point FG: Detroit 5-20 (.250), Dumars 0-2 (.000), Thomas 2-6 (.333), Johnson 1-5 (.200), Laimbeer 2-3 (.667), Aguirre 0-3 (.000), Rodman 0-1 (.000). Lakers 13-43 (.302).

1989-90
REGULAR SEASON (59-23)

PLAYER	G	GS	MIN	FGM	FGA	PCT	FTM	FTA	PCT	O-RB	D-RB	TOT	AST	PF	DQ	STL	TO	BLK	PTS	PPG	HG
Isiah Thomas	81	81	2993	579	1322	.438	292	377	.775	74	234	308	765	206	0	139	322	19	1492	18.4	37
Joe Dumars	75	71	2578	508	1058	.480	297	330	.900	60	152	212	368	129	1	63	145	2	1335	17.8	34
James Edwards	82	70	2283	462	928	.498	265	354	.749	112	233	345	63	295	4	23	133	37	1189	14.5	32
Mark Aguirre	78	40	2005	438	898	.488	192	254	.756	117	188	305	145	201	2	34	121	19	1099	14.1	31
Bill Laimbeer	81	81	2675	380	785	.484	164	192	.854	166	614	780	171	278	4	57	98	84	981	12.1	31
Vinnie Johnson	82	12	1972	334	775	.431	131	196	.668	108	148	256	255	143	0	71	123	13	804	9.8	25
Dennis Rodman	82	43	2377	288	496	.581	142	217	.654	336	456	792	72	276	2	52	90	60	719	8.8	18
John Salley	82	12	1914	209	408	.512	174	244	.713	154	285	439	67	282	7	51	97	153	593	7.2	21
William Bedford	42	0	246	54	125	.432	9	22	.409	15	43	58	4	39	0	3	21	17	118	2.8	13
Gerald Henderson	46	0	335	42	83	.506	10	13	.769	8	23	31	61	36	0	8	16	2	108	2.3	13
David Greenwood	37	0	205	22	52	.423	16	29	.552	24	54	78	12	40	0	4	16	9	60	1.6	6
Stan Kimbrough	10	0	50	7	16	.438	2	2	1.000	4	3	7	5	4	0	4	4	0	16	1.6	4
Scott Hastings	40	0	166	10	33	.303	19	22	.864	7	25	32	8	31	0	3	7	3	42	1.1	9
Ralph Lewis	4	0	6	0	1	.000	0	0	.000	0	0	0	0	1	0	0	1	0	0	0.0	0
PISTONS	82	—	—	3333	6980	.478	1713	2252	.761	1185	2458	3643	1996	1961	20	512	1233	418	8556	104.3	140
OPPONENTS	82	—	—	3043	6809	.447	1785	2342	.762	1040	2281	3321	1764	2072	29	606	1248	304	8057	98.3	123

3-point FG: Detroit 177-541 (.327), Thomas 42-136 (.309), Dumars 22-55 (.400), Edwards 0-3 (.000), Aguirre 31-93 (.333), Laimbeer 57-158 (.361), Johnson 5-34 (.147), Rodman 1-9 (.111), Salley 1-4 (.250), Bedford 1-6 (.167), Henderson 14-31 (.452), Hastings 3-12 (.250). Opponents 186-558 (.333).

PLAYOFFS (15-5)

PLAYER	G	GS	MIN	FGM	FGA	PCT	FTM	FTA	PCT	O-RB	D-RB	TOT	AST	PF	DQ	STL	TO	BLK	PTS	PPG	HG
Isiah Thomas	20	20	758	148	320	.463	81	102	.794	21	88	109	163	65	1	43	72	7	409	20.5	36
Joe Dumars	20	20	754	130	284	.458	99	113	.876	18	26	44	95	37	0	22	54	0	364	18.2	33
James Edwards	20	20	536	114	231	.494	58	96	.604	24	47	71	13	74	0	5	31	11	286	14.3	32
Bill Laimbeer	20	20	667	91	199	.457	25	29	.862	41	170	211	28	77	3	23	16	18	222	11.1	26
Mark Aguirre	20	3	439	86	184	.467	39	52	.750	31	60	91	27	51	0	10	30	3	219	11.0	25
Vinnie Johnson	20	0	463	85	184	.462	34	43	.791	28	28	56	54	38	0	8	31	4	206	10.3	21
John Salley	20	0	547	58	122	.475	74	98	.755	57	60	117	20	76	2	9	22	33	190	9.5	20
Dennis Rodman	19	17	560	54	95	.568	18	35	.514	55	106	161	17	62	1	9	31	13	126	6.6	20
David Greenwood	5	0	47	2	4	.500	1	4	.250	2	7	9	0	11	0	2	2	0	5	1.0	3
William Bedford	5	0	19	1	6	.167	2	2	1.000	0	2	2	0	4	0	0	0	1	4	0.8	2
Scott Hastings	5	0	16	1	4	.250	0	0	.000	0	0	0	0	4	0	1	0	0	2	0.4	2
Gerald Henderson	8	0	19	1	5	.200	0	0	.000	2	1	3	4	3	0	2	1	0	2	0.3	2
PISTONS	20	—	—	771	1638	.471	431	574	.751	279	595	874	421	502	7	134	302	90	2035	101.8	121
OPPONENTS	20	—	—	698	1604	.435	449	570	.788	245	543	788	410	521	8	132	305	75	1895	94.8	111

3-point FG: Detroit 62-138 (.369), Thomas 32-68 (.471), Dumars 5-19 (.263), Edwards 0-1 (.000), Laimbeer 15-43 (.349), Aguirre 8-24 (.333), Johnson 2-7 (.286), Hastings 0-3 (.000), Henderson 0-3 (.000). Opponents 50-183 (.273).

NBA FINALS (4-1)

PLAYER	G	GS	MIN	FGM	FGA	PCT	FTM	FTA	PCT	O-RB	D-RB	TOT	AST	PF	DQ	STL	TO	BLK	PTS	PPG	HG
Isiah Thomas	5	5	192	52	96	.542	23	31	.742	8	18	26	35	19	1	8	25	2	138	27.6	33
Joe Dumars	5	5	210	34	82	.415	33	37	.892	5	9	14	28	11	0	4	18	0	103	20.6	33
James Edwards	5	5	138	29	65	.446	14	25	.560	8	11	19	4	20	0	2	5	3	72	14.4	26
Bill Laimbeer	5	5	191	24	54	.444	10	10	1.000	12	55	67	12	25	2	7	1	3	66	13.2	26
Vinnie Johnson	5	5	113	25	46	.543	11	14	.786	7	3	10	6	11	0	1	8	3	61	12.2	21
Mark Aguirre	5	3	120	15	45	.333	14	21	.667	6	12	18	4	12	0	2	6	0	48	9.6	18
John Salley	5	0	143	12	32	.375	9	13	.692	18	14	32	2	18	1	1	4	12	33	6.6	10
Dennis Rodman	4	2	79	4	9	.444	1	4	.250	6	16	22	3	13	1	2	6	2	9	2.3	6
David Greenwood	3	0	33	1	3	.333	1	2	.500	2	7	9	0	8	0	1	2	0	3	1.0	3
Gerald Henderson	2	0	2	1	1	1.000	0	0	.000	0	0	0	0	0	0	0	0	0	2	1.0	2
Scott Hastings	2	0	4	0	1	.000	0	0	.000	0	0	0	0	1	0	0	0	0	0	0.0	0
PISTONS	5	—	—	197	434	.454	116	157	.739	72	145	217	94	138	5	28	75	25	535	107.0	121
PORTLAND	5	—	—	187	410	.456	125	169	.740	57	145	202	103	149	5	36	82	17	510	102.0	109

3-point FG: Detroit 25-56 (.446), Thomas 11-16 (.688), Dumars 2-7 (.286), Edwards 0-1 (.000), Laimbeer 8-22 (.364), Johnson 0-1 (.000), Aguirre 4-8 (.500), Hastings 0-1 (.000). Trail Blazers 11-47 (.234).

1990-91
REGULAR SEASON (50-32)

PLAYER	G	GS	MIN	FGM	FGA	PCT	FTM	FTA	PCT	O-RB	D-RB	TOT	AST	PF	DQ	STL	TO	BLK	PTS	PPG	HG
Joe Dumars	80	80	3046	622	1292	.481	371	417	.890	62	125	187	443	135	0	89	189	7	1629	20.4	42
Isiah Thomas	48	46	1657	289	665	.435	179	229	.782	35	125	160	446	118	4	75	185	10	776	16.2	32
Mark Aguirre	78	13	2006	420	909	.462	240	317	.757	134	240	374	139	209	2	47	128	20	1104	14.2	30
James Edwards	72	70	1903	383	792	.484	215	295	.729	91	186	277	65	249	4	12	126	30	982	13.6	32
Vinnie Johnson	82	28	2390	406	936	.434	135	209	.646	110	170	280	271	166	0	75	118	15	958	11.7	32
Bill Laimbeer	82	81	2668	372	778	.478	123	147	.837	173	564	737	157	242	3	38	98	56	904	11.0	25
Dennis Rodman	82	77	2747	276	560	.493	111	176	.631	361	665	1026	85	281	7	65	94	55	669	8.2	34
John Salley	74	1	1649	179	377	.475	186	256	.727	137	190	327	70	240	7	52	91	112	544	7.4	24
Gerald Henderson	23	10	392	50	117	.427	16	21	.762	8	29	37	62	43	0	12	28	2	123	5.3	24
William Bedford	60	4	562	106	242	.438	55	78	.705	55	76	131	32	76	0	2	32	36	272	4.5	20
John Long	25	0	256	35	85	.412	24	25	.960	9	23	32	18	17	0	9	14	2	96	3.8	14
Scott Hastings	27	0	113	16	28	.571	13	13	1.000	14	14	28	7	23	0	0	7	0	48	1.8	7
Lance Blanks	38	0	214	26	61	.426	10	14	.714	4	16	20	26	35	0	9	18	2	64	1.7	7
Tree Rollins	37	0	202	14	33	.424	8	14	.571	13	29	42	4	35	0	2	15	20	36	1.0	6
PISTONS	82	—	—	3194	6875	.465	1686	2211	.763	1206	2452	3658	1825	1869	27	487	1181	367	8205	100.1	126
OPPONENTS	82	—	—	3053	6743	.453	1674	2173	.770	1002	2274	3276	1736	1987	24	581	1127	289	7937	96.8	125

3-point FG: Detroit 131-440 (.298), Dumars 14-45 (.311), Thomas 19-65 (.292), Aguirre 24-78 (.308), Edwards 1-2 (.500), Johnson 11-34 (.324), Laimbeer 37-125 (.296), Rodman 6-30 (.200), Salley 0-1 (.000), Henderson 7-21 (.333), Bedford 5-13 (.385), Long 2-6 (.333), Hastings 3-4 (.750), Blanks 2-16 (.125). Opponents 157-504 (.312).

PLAYOFFS (7-8)

PLAYER	G	GS	MIN	FGM	FGA	PCT	FTM	FTA	PCT	O-RB	D-RB	TOT	AST	PF	DQ	STL	TO	BLK	PTS	PPG	HG
Joe Dumars	15	15	588	105	245	.429	82	97	.845	21	29	50	62	33	1	16	17	1	309	20.6	32
Mark Aguirre	15	2	397	90	178	.506	42	51	.824	17	44	61	29	41	0	12	20	1	234	15.6	34
Vinnie Johnson	15	3	438	102	220	.464	22	31	.710	37	39	76	43	33	0	11	17	4	228	15.2	29
Isiah Thomas	13	11	436	60	149	.403	50	69	.725	13	41	54	111	41	1	13	41	2	176	13.5	29
Bill Laimbeer	15	15	446	66	148	.446	27	31	.871	42	80	122	19	54	0	5	17	12	164	10.9	24
James Edwards	15	11	345	61	150	.407	38	55	.691	15	22	37	9	43	0	2	24	3	160	10.7	19
John Salley	15	0	308	38	70	.543	36	60	.600	20	42	62	11	58	1	6	13	20	112	7.5	13
Dennis Rodman	15	14	495	41	91	.451	10	24	.417	67	110	177	14	55	1	11	13	10	94	6.3	15
William Bedford	8	3	65	5	24	.208	9	14	.643	9	13	22	4	14	0	2	4	4	19	2.4	7
Scott Hastings	10	0	35	3	6	.500	0	0	.000	2	4	6	3	6	0	0	1	1	8	0.8	5
Gerald Henderson	10	1	40	4	16	.250	0	0	.000	1	0	1	6	4	0	1	0	0	8	0.8	2
Tree Rollins	6	0	32	2	2	1.000	0	0	.000	1	2	3	0	6	0	1	2	1	4	0.7	4
PISTONS	15	—	—	577	1299	.444	316	432	.731	245	426	671	311	388	4	80	173	59	1516	101.1	117
OPPONENTS	15	—	—	554	1202	.461	399	510	.782	200	441	641	302	356	3	96	173	63	1533	102.2	123

3-point FG: Detroit 46-145 (.317), Dumars 17-42 (.405), Aguirre 12-33 (.364), Johnson 2-13 (.154), Thomas 6-22 (.273), Laimbeer 5-17 (.294), Rodman 2-9 (.222), Bedford 0-2 (.000), Hastings 2-4 (.500), Henderson 0-3 (.000). Opponents 26-97 (.268).

1991-92
REGULAR SEASON (48-34)

PLAYER	G	GS	MIN	FGM	FGA	PCT	FTM	FTA	PCT	O-RB	D-RB	TOT	AST	PF	DQ	STL	TO	BLK	PTS	PPG	HG
Joe Dumars	82	82	3192	587	1311	.448	412	475	.867	82	106	188	375	145	0	71	193	12	1635	19.9	45
Isiah Thomas	78	78	2918	564	1264	.446	292	378	.772	68	179	247	560	194	2	118	252	15	1445	18.5	44
Orlando Woolridge	82	61	2113	452	907	.498	241	353	.683	109	151	260	88	154	0	41	133	33	1146	14.0	34
Mark Aguirre	75	12	1582	339	787	.431	158	230	.687	67	169	236	126	171	0	51	105	11	851	11.3	27
Dennis Rodman	82	80	3301	342	635	.539	84	140	.600	523	1007	1530	191	248	0	68	140	70	800	9.8	20
Bill Laimbeer	81	46	2234	342	727	.470	67	75	.893	104	347	451	160	225	0	51	102	54	783	9.7	26
John Salley	72	38	1774	249	486	.512	186	260	.715	106	190	296	116	222	1	49	102	110	684	9.5	23
Darrell Walker	74	4	1541	161	381	.423	65	105	.619	85	153	238	205	134	0	63	79	18	387	5.2	19
William Bedford	32	8	363	50	121	.413	14	22	.636	24	39	63	12	56	0	6	15	18	114	3.6	11
Brad Sellers	43	1	226	41	88	.466	20	26	.769	15	27	42	14	20	0	1	15	10	102	2.4	13
Gerald Henderson	8	0	62	8	21	.381	5	5	1.000	0	6	6	5	8	0	3	4	0	24	3.0	8
Lance Blanks	43	0	189	25	55	.455	8	11	.727	9	13	22	19	26	0	14	14	1	64	1.5	12
Charles Thomas	37	0	156	18	51	.353	10	15	.667	6	16	22	22	20	0	4	17	1	48	1.3	11
Bob McCann	26	0	129	13	33	.394	4	13	.308	12	18	30	6	23	0	6	7	4	30	1.2	10
PISTONS	82	—	—	3191	6867	.465	1566	2108	.743	1210	2421	3631	1899	1646	3	546	1212	357	8113	98.9	125
OPPONENTS	82	—	—	3157	6973	.453	1421	1866	.762	1115	2255	3370	1894	1916	21	642	1117	373	7946	96.9	119

3-point FG: Detroit 165-526 (.314), Dumars 49-120 (.408), I.Thomas 25-86 (.291), Woolridge 1-9 (.111), Aguirre 15-71 (.211), Rodman 32-101 (.317), Laimbeer 32-85 (.376), Salley 0-3 (.000), Walker 0-10 (.000), Bedford 0-1 (.000), Henderson 3-5 (.600), Sellers 0-1 (.000), Blanks 6-16 (.375), C.Thomas 2-17 (.118), McCann 0-1 (.000). Opponents 211-625 (.338).

PLAYOFFS (2-3)

PLAYER	G	GS	MIN	FGM	FGA	PCT	FTM	FTA	PCT	O-RB	D-RB	TOT	AST	PF	DQ	STL	TO	BLK	PTS	PPG	HG
Joe Dumars	5	5	221	32	68	.471	15	19	.789	5	3	8	16	11	0	5	7	1	84	16.8	23
Isiah Thomas	5	5	200	22	65	.338	22	28	.786	3	23	26	37	18	0	5	16	0	70	14.0	31
John Salley	5	1	149	20	44	.455	23	38	.821	10	20	30	14	18	0	3	9	14	63	12.6	20
Orlando Woolridge	5	5	128	23	52	.442	9	16	.563	5	5	10	3	14	0	1	6	1	55	11.0	16
Mark Aguirre	5	0	113	16	48	.333	12	16	.750	4	5	9	12	9	0	2	13	1	45	9.0	13
Bill Laimbeer	5	4	145	17	46	.370	5	5	1.000	5	28	33	8	18	1	4	5	1	41	8.2	15
Dennis Rodman	5	5	156	16	27	.593	4	8	.500	16	35	51	9	17	0	4	7	2	36	7.2	12
Bob McCann	1	0	13	3	6	.500	0	0	.000	1	1	2	0	2	0	0	2	1	6	6.0	6
William Bedford	1	0	9	3	6	.500	0	0	.000	0	2	2	0	1	0	0	0	0	6	6.0	6
Brad Sellers	2	0	13	2	4	.500	2	2	1.000	0	0	0	2	0	0	0	0	2	6	3.0	6
Darrell Walker	5	0	68	3	9	.333	4	4	1.000	5	7	12	4	7	0	1	5	0	10	2.0	6
Lance Blanks	1	0	10	1	2	.500	0	0	.000	0	1	1	3	2	0	3	1	0	2	2.0	2
PISTONS	5	—	—	158	377	.419	96	126	.762	54	130	184	108	117	1	29	76	23	424	84.8	89
KNICKS	5	—	—	173	418	.414	103	138	.746	92	150	242	107	122	1	36	69	25	463	92.6	109

3-point FG: Detroit 12-39 (.308), Dumars 5-10 (.500), Thomas 4-11 (.364), Salley 0-1 (.000), Aguirre 1-5 (.200), Laimbeer 2-10 (.500), Rodman 0-2 (.000). Opponents 14-46 (.304).

1992-93
REGULAR SEASON (40-42)

PLAYER	G	GS	MIN	FGM	FGA	PCT	FTM	FTA	PCT	O-RB	D-RB	TOT	AST	PF	DQ	STL	TO	BLK	PTS	PPG	HG
Joe Dumars	77	77	3094	677	1454	.466	343	397	.864	63	85	148	308	141	0	78	138	7	1809	23.5	43
Isiah Thomas	79	79	2922	526	1258	.418	278	377	.737	71	161	232	671	222	2	123	284	18	1391	17.6	43
Terry Mills	81	46	2183	494	1072	.461	201	254	.791	176	296	472	111	282	6	44	142	50	1199	14.8	41
Orlando Woolridge	50	47	1477	271	566	.479	113	168	.673	84	92	176	112	114	1	26	73	25	655	13.1	36
Mark Aguirre	51	15	1056	187	422	.443	99	129	.767	43	109	152	105	101	1	16	68	7	503	9.9	29
Alvin Robertson	30	22	941	108	249	.434	40	58	.690	60	72	132	107	98	1	65	56	9	279	9.3	26
Bill Laimbeer	79	41	1933	292	574	.509	93	104	.894	110	309	419	127	212	4	46	59	40	687	8.7	24
Dennis Rodman	62	55	2410	183	429	.427	87	163	.534	367	765	1132	102	201	0	48	103	45	468	7.5	18
Olden Polynice	67	18	1299	210	429	.490	66	142	.465	181	237	418	29	126	0	31	54	21	486	7.3	27
Gerald Glass	56	5	777	134	312	.429	21	33	.636	60	79	139	68	98	1	30	30	18	296	5.3	22
Melvin Newbern	33	1	311	42	113	.372	34	60	.567	19	18	37	57	42	0	23	32	1	119	3.6	20
Danny Young	65	2	836	69	167	.413	28	32	.875	13	34	47	119	36	0	31	30	5	188	2.9	15
Mark Randall	35	0	240	40	79	.506	16	26	.615	27	28	55	10	32	0	4	16	2	97	2.8	12
Isaiah Morris	25	0	102	26	57	.456	3	4	.750	6	6	12	4	14	0	3	8	1	55	2.2	11
Jeff Ruland	11	0	55	5	11	.455	2	4	.500	9	9	18	2	16	0	2	6	0	12	1.1	4
Darrell Walker	9	2	144	3	19	.158	2	6	.333	4	15	19	9	12	0	10	13	0	8	0.9	3
PISTONS	82	—	—	3267	7211	.453	1426	1957	.729	1293	2315	3608	1941	1747	16	580	1152	249	8252	100.6	124
OPPONENTS	82	—	—	3321	6906	.481	1463	2036	.719	1099	2442	3541	2048	1804	16	623	1219	363	8366	102.0	138

3-point FG: Detroit 292-908 (.322), Dumars 112-299 (.375), Thomas 61-198 (.308), Mills 10-36 (.278), Woolridge 0-9 (.000), Aguirre 30-83 (.361), Robertson 23-67 (.343), Laimbeer 10-27 (.370), Rodman 15-73 (.205), Polynice 0-1 (.000), Glass 7-31 (.226), Newbern 1-8 (.125), Randall 1-7 (.143), Young 22-68 (.324), Walker 0-1 (.000). Opponents 261-769 (.339).

1993-94
REGULAR SEASON (20-62)

PLAYER	G	GS	MIN	FGM	FGA	PCT	FTM	FTA	PCT	O-RB	D-RB	TOT	AST	PF	DQ	STL	TO	BLK	PTS	PPG	HG
Joe Dumars	69	69	2591	505	1118	.452	276	330	.836	35	116	151	261	118	0	63	159	4	1410	20.4	44
Terry Mills	80	74	2773	588	1151	.511	181	227	.797	193	479	672	177	309	6	64	153	62	1381	17.3	35
Isiah Thomas	58	56	1750	318	763	.417	181	258	.702	46	113	159	399	126	0	68	202	6	856	14.8	31
Olden Polynice	37	36	1350	222	406	.547	42	92	.457	148	308	456	22	108	1	24	49	36	486	13.1	27
Sean Elliott	73	73	2409	360	791	.455	139	173	.803	68	195	263	197	174	3	54	129	27	885	12.1	27
Lindsey Hunter	82	26	2172	335	893	.375	104	142	.732	47	142	189	390	174	1	121	184	10	843	10.3	29
Bill Laimbeer	11	5	248	47	90	.522	11	13	.846	9	47	56	14	30	0	6	10	4	108	9.8	26
Allan Houston	79	20	1519	272	671	.405	89	108	.824	19	101	120	100	165	2	34	99	13	668	8.5	31
Cadillac Anderson	77	47	1624	201	370	.543	88	154	.571	183	388	571	51	234	4	55	94	68	491	6.4	23
Pete Chilcutt	30	0	391	51	120	.425	10	13	.769	29	71	100	15	48	0	10	18	11	115	3.8	12
David Wood	78	3	1182	119	259	.459	62	82	.756	104	135	239	51	201	3	39	35	19	322	4.1	14
Mark Macon	35	1	370	55	139	.396	15	24	.625	15	19	34	40	56	0	33	26	0	127	3.6	11
Ben Coleman	9	0	77	12	25	.480	4	8	.500	10	16	26	0	9	0	2	7	2	28	3.1	8
Marcus Liberty	35	0	274	36	116	.310	18	37	.486	26	30	56	15	29	0	11	22	4	100	2.9	23
Charles Jones	42	0	877	36	78	.462	19	34	.559	89	146	235	29	136	3	14	12	43	91	2.2	9
Tod Murphy	7	0	57	6	12	.500	3	6	.500	4	5	9	3	8	0	2	1	0	15	2.1	5
Tracy Moore	3	0	10	2	3	.667	2	2	1.000	0	1	1	0	0	0	0	0	0	6	2.0	6
Dan O'Sullivan	13	0	56	4	12	.333	9	12	.750	2	8	10	3	10	0	0	3	0	17	1.3	6
PISTONS	82	—	—	3169	7017	.452	1253	1715	.731	1027	2320	3347	1767	1935	23	602	1236	309	7949	96.9	123
OPPONENTS	82	—	—	3255	6878	.473	1805	2451	.736	1191	2590	3581	2097	1602	9	721	1169	368	8587	104.7	141

3-point FG: Detroit 358-1041 (.344), Dumars 124-320 (.388), Mills 24-73 (.329), Thomas 39-126 (.310), Polynice 0-1 (.000), Elliott 26-87 (.299), Hunter 69-207 (.333), Laimbeer 3-9 (.333), Houston 35-117 (.299), Anderson 1-3 (.333), Wood 22-49 (.449), Chilcutt 3-14 (.214), Macon 2-7 (.286), Liberty 10-27 (.370), Jones 0-1 (.000). Opponents 272-814 (.334).

1994-95
REGULAR SEASON (28-54)

PLAYER	G	GS	MIN	FGM	FGA	PCT	FTM	FTA	PCT	O-RB	D-RB	TOT	AST	PF	DQ	STL	TO	BLK	PTS	PPG	HG
Grant Hill	70	69	2678	508	1064	.477	374	511	.732	125	320	445	353	203	1	124	202	62	1394	19.9	33
Joe Dumars	67	67	2544	417	970	.430	277	344	.805	47	111	158	368	153	0	72	219	7	1214	18.1	43
Terry Mills	72	69	2514	417	933	.447	175	219	.799	124	434	558	160	253	5	68	144	33	1118	15.5	37
Allan Houston	76	39	1996	398	859	.463	147	171	.860	29	138	167	164	182	0	61	113	14	1101	14.5	36
Oliver Miller	64	22	1558	232	418	.555	78	124	.629	162	313	475	93	217	1	60	115	116	545	8.5	21
Rafael Addison	79	16	1776	279	586	.476	74	99	.747	67	175	242	109	236	2	53	76	25	656	8.3	25
Mark West	67	58	1543	217	390	.556	66	138	.478	160	248	408	18	247	8	27	85	102	500	7.5	19
Lindsey Hunter	42	26	944	119	318	.374	40	55	.727	24	51	75	159	94	1	51	79	7	314	7.5	24
Johnny Dawkins	50	9	1170	125	270	.463	50	55	.909	28	85	113	205	74	1	52	86	1	325	6.5	17
Mark Macon	55	6	721	101	265	.381	54	68	.794	29	47	76	63	97	1	67	41	1	276	5.0	17
Negele Knight	44	17	665	78	199	.392	14	21	.667	20	38	58	116	65	0	20	45	5	181	4.1	15
Eric Leckner	57	11	623	87	165	.527	51	72	.708	47	127	174	14	122	1	15	39	15	225	3.9	16
Bill Curley	53	1	595	58	134	.433	27	36	.750	54	70	124	25	128	3	21	25	21	143	2.7	15
Walter Bond	5	0	51	3	12	.250	3	4	.750	1	4	5	7	10	0	1	3	0	10	2.0	5
Mike Peplowski	6	0	21	5	5	1.000	1	2	.500	1	2	3	1	10	0	1	2	0	11	1.8	5
Ivano Newbill	34	0	331	16	45	.356	8	22	.364	40	41	81	17	60	0	12	12	11	40	1.2	6
PISTONS	82	—	—	3060	6633	.461	1439	1941	.741	958	2204	3162	1872	2151	24	705	1318	420	8053	98.2	126
OPPONENTS	82	—	—	3120	6558	.476	1963	2720	.722	1147	2432	3579	2013	1746	9	693	1286	439	8651	105.5	134

3-point FG: Detroit 494-1396 (.354), Hill 4-27 (.148), Dumars 103-338 (.305), Mills 109-285 (.382), Houston 158-373 (.424), Miller 3-13 (.231), Addison 24-83 (.289), Hunter 36-108 (.333), Dawkins 25-73 (.342), Macon 20-62 (.323), Knight 11-28 (.393), Leckner 0-2 (.000), Bond 1-4 (.250). Opponents 448-1235 (.363).

1995-96
REGULAR SEASON (46-36)

PLAYER	G	GS	MIN	FGM	FGA	PCT	FTM	FTA	PCT	O-RB	D-RB	TOT	AST	PF	DQ	STL	TO	BLK	PTS	PPG	HG
Grant Hill	80	80	3260	564	1221	.462	485	646	.751	127	656	783	548	242	1	100	263	48	1618	20.2	35
Allan Houston	82	75	3072	564	1244	.453	298	362	.823	54	246	300	250	233	1	61	233	16	1617	19.7	38
Otis Thorpe	82	82	2841	452	852	.530	257	362	.710	211	477	688	158	300	7	53	195	39	1161	14.2	27
Joe Dumars	67	40	2193	255	598	.426	162	197	.822	28	110	138	265	106	0	43	97	3	793	11.8	41
Terry Mills	82	5	1656	283	675	.419	121	157	.771	108	244	352	98	197	0	42	98	20	769	9.4	24
Lindsey Hunter	80	48	2138	239	628	.381	84	120	.700	44	150	194	188	185	0	84	80	18	679	8.5	21
Michael Curry	41	1	749	70	151	.464	41	58	.707	25	55	80	26	89	1	23	23	2	201	4.9	17
Theo Ratliff	75	2	1305	128	230	.557	85	120	.708	110	187	297	13	144	1	16	56	116	341	4.5	21
Don Reid	69	46	997	106	187	.567	51	77	.662	78	125	203	11	199	2	47	41	40	263	3.8	12
Mark Macon	23	0	287	29	67	.433	9	11	.818	10	12	22	16	34	0	15	9	0	74	3.2	12
Mark West	47	21	682	61	126	.484	28	45	.622	49	84	133	6	135	2	6	35	37	150	3.2	15
Steve Bardo	9	0	123	9	23	.391	4	6	.667	2	20	22	15	17	1	4	5	1	22	2.4	8
Eric Leckner	18	8	155	18	29	.621	8	13	.615	8	26	34	1	30	0	2	11	4	44	2.4	13
Lou Roe	49	2	372	32	90	.356	24	32	.750	30	48	78	15	42	0	10	17	8	90	1.8	14
PISTONS	82	—	—	2810	6122	.459	1657	2206	.751	884	2440	3324	1610	1953	16	506	1215	352	7822	95.4	121
OPPONENTS	82	—	—	2827	6375	.443	1458	2039	.715	964	2268	3232	1729	1887	19	556	1153	385	7617	92.9	118

3-point FG: Detroit 545-1350 (.404), Hill 5-26 (.192), Houston 191-447 (.427), Thorpe 0-4 (.000), Dumars 121-298 (.406), Mills 82-207 (.396), Hunter 117-289 (.405), Curry 20-50 (.400), Ratliff 0-1 (.000), Macon 7-15 (.467), Bardo 0-4 (.000), Roe 2-9 (.222). Opponents 505-1380 (.366).

PLAYOFFS (0-3)

PLAYER	G	GS	MIN	FGM	FGA	PCT	FTM	FTA	PCT	O-RB	D-RB	TOT	AST	PF	DQ	STL	TO	BLK	PTS	PPG	HG
Allan Houston	3	3	136	25	58	.431	18	20	.900	1	7	8	6	11	0	0	11	1	75	25.0	33
Grant Hill	3	3	115	22	39	.564	12	14	.857	4	18	22	11	13	0	3	8	0	57	19.0	21
Joe Dumars	3	3	123	16	35	.457	4	4	1.000	5	8	13	11	5	0	0	7	0	41	13.7	15
Otis Thorpe	3	3	101	13	24	.542	9	12	.750	14	21	35	7	9	0	0	7	0	35	11.7	15
Mark West	3	3	78	11	21	.524	6	13	.462	6	10	16	1	12	0	1	2	1	28	9.3	11
Terry Mills	3	0	48	5	20	.250	5	6	.833	3	2	5	4	6	0	1	1	0	16	5.3	10
Lindsey Hunter	2	0	36	2	8	.250	1	2	.500	1	1	2	1	2	0	1	0	0	6	3.0	3
Michael Curry	3	0	43	3	7	.429	0	0	.000	1	2	3	1	5	0	1	0	1	6	2.0	2
Don Reid	3	0	26	1	3	.333	1	3	.333	0	1	1	1	8	0	0	1	2	3	1.0	3
Eric Leckner	1	0	3	0	0	.000	0	0	.000	0	0	0	0	2	0	0	0	0	0	0.0	0
Lou Roe	2	0	7	0	1	.000	0	0	.000	1	1	2	1	1	0	1	0	0	0	0.0	0
PISTONS	3	—	—	98	216	.454	56	74	.757	36	71	107	43	74	0	8	40	5	267	89.0	98
ORLANDO	3	—	—	114	220	.518	53	83	.639	34	78	112	77	70	1	17	34	14	305	101.7	112

3-point FG: Detroit 15-50 (.300), Houston 7-21 (.333), Hill 1-2 (.500), Dumars 5-14 (.357), Mills 1-8 (.125), Hunter 1-4 (.250), Curry 0-1 (.000). Opponents 24-53 (.453).

1996-97
REGULAR SEASON (54-28)

PLAYER	G	GS	MIN	FGM	FGA	PCT	FTM	FTA	PCT	O-RB	D-RB	TOT	AST	PF	DQ	STL	TO	BLK	PTS	PPG	HG
Grant Hill	80	80	3147	625	1259	.496	450	633	.711	123	598	721	583	186	0	144	259	48	1710	21.4	38
Joe Dumars	79	79	2923	385	875	.440	222	256	.867	38	153	191	318	97	1	57	128	1	1158	14.7	29
Lindsey Hunter	82	76	3023	421	1042	.404	158	203	.778	59	174	233	154	206	1	129	96	24	1166	14.2	30
Otis Thorpe	79	79	2661	419	787	.532	198	303	.653	226	396	622	133	298	7	59	145	17	1036	13.1	27
Terry Mills	79	5	1997	312	702	.444	58	70	.829	68	309	377	99	161	1	35	85	27	857	10.8	29
Aaron McKie	42	3	850	97	209	.464	51	61	.836	27	101	128	77	69	0	43	42	7	263	6.3	18
Theo Ratliff	76	38	1292	179	337	.531	81	116	.698	109	147	256	13	181	2	29	56	111	439	5.8	25
Grant Long	65	24	1166	123	275	.447	63	84	.750	88	134	222	39	106	0	43	48	6	326	5.0	15
Stacey Augmon	20	3	292	31	77	.403	28	41	.683	14	35	49	15	29	0	10	27	10	90	4.5	12
Michael Curry	81	2	1217	99	221	.448	97	108	.898	23	96	119	43	128	0	31	28	12	318	3.9	17
Don Reid	47	14	462	54	112	.482	24	32	.750	36	65	101	14	105	1	16	23	15	132	2.8	14
Kenny Smith	9	0	64	8	20	.400	2	2	1.000	0	5	5	10	2	0	1	3	0	23	2.6	7
Rick Mahorn	22	7	218	20	54	.370	16	22	.727	19	34	53	6	34	0	4	10	3	56	2.5	13
Randolph Childress	4	0	30	4	10	.400	0	0	.000	0	1	1	2	5	0	2	5	0	10	2.5	8
Litterial Green	45	0	311	30	64	.469	30	47	.638	6	16	22	41	27	0	16	15	1	90	2.0	8
Jerome Williams	33	0	177	20	51	.392	9	17	.529	22	28	50	7	18	0	13	13	1	49	1.5	9
PISTONS	82	—	—	2827	6095	.464	1487	1995	.745	858	2292	3150	1554	1652	12	632	1041	283	7723	94.2	124
OPPONENTS	82	—	—	2768	6231	.444	1229	1668	.737	964	2264	3228	1795	1784	18	488	1195	282	7293	88.9	120

3-point FG: Detroit 582-1499 (.388), Hill 10-33 (.303), Dumars 166-384 (.432), Hunter 166-468 (.355), Thorpe 0-2 (.000), Mills 175-415 (.422), McKie 18-48 (.375), Long 17-47 (.362), Curry 23-77 (.299), Reid 0-1 (.000), Smith 5-10 (.500), Mahorn 0-1 (.000), Childress 2-3 (.667), Green 0-10 (.000). Opponents 528-1430 (.369).

PLAYOFFS (2-3)

PLAYER	G	GS	MIN	FGM	FGA	PCT	FTM	FTA	PCT	O-RB	D-RB	TOT	AST	PF	DQ	STL	TO	BLK	PTS	PPG	HG
Grant Hill	5	5	203	45	103	.437	28	39	.718	13	21	34	27	14	0	4	19	5	118	23.6	28
Lindsey Hunter	5	5	201	29	66	.439	5	7	.714	4	14	18	6	9	0	6	1	1	75	15.0	26
Joe Dumars	5	5	214	22	61	.361	19	20	.950	2	7	9	10	9	0	5	6	0	69	13.8	17
Terry Mills	5	4	196	24	55	.436	2	4	.500	4	31	35	7	14	0	6	4	0	59	11.8	17
Otis Thorpe	5	5	152	21	41	.512	7	9	.778	12	20	32	4	21	0	2	9	0	49	9.8	16
Grant Long	5	0	86	8	18	.444	9	11	.818	4	7	11	3	11	0	4	0	0	25	5.0	17
Don Reid	1	0	3	0	0	.000	4	4	1.000	0	1	1	0	0	0	0	0	0	4	4.0	4
Jerome Williams	1	0	5	2	2	1.000	0	0	.000	0	3	3	0	0	0	1	1	0	4	4.0	4
Aaron McKie	5	0	97	7	20	.350	0	0	.000	1	9	10	10	12	0	6	3	2	15	3.0	7
Theo Ratliff	3	0	18	3	4	.750	2	4	.500	2	2	4	1	5	0	1	3	4	8	2.7	5
Michael Curry	2	0	7	1	2	.500	0	1	.000	0	1	1	0	1	0	0	0	0	2	1.0	2
Rick Mahorn	2	1	18	0	2	.000	0	0	.000	1	0	1	0	5	0	0	0	0	0	0.0	0
PISTONS	5	—	—	162	374	.433	76	99	.768	43	116	159	68	101	0	35	47	12	428	85.6	99
HAWKS	5	—	—	157	346	.454	95	117	.812	51	158	209	83	94	0	22	79	23	438	87.6	94

3-point FG: Detroit 28-85 (.329), Hunter 12-29 (.414), Dumars 6-23 (.261), Mills 9-26 (.346), Long 0-2 (.000), McKie 1-5 (.200). Hawks 29-110 (.264).

ALL-TIME PISTONS TEAM RECORDS

(x-NBA record)

REGULAR SEASON RECORDS

SEASON

STAT	RECORD	SEASON
Points	8,725	1967-68
Scoring Average	118.6	1967-68
Defensive Average	88.9	1996-97
Field Goals	3,840	1984-85
Field Goal Attempts	8,502	1965-66
Field Goal Percentage	.494	1988-89
3-Point Goals	582	1996-97
3-Point Goal Attempts	1,499	1996-97
3-Point Goal Percentage	.404	1995-96
Free Throws	2,408	1960-61
Free Throw Attempts	3,220	1960-61
Free Throw Percentage	.788	1984-85
Rebounds	5,823	1961-62
Offensive Rebounds	1,430	1983-84
Defensive Rebounds	2,649	1986-87
Assists	2,319	1985-86
Personal Fouls	2,240	1967-68
Disqualifications	58	1958-59
Steals	884	1980-81
Blocked shots	572	1982-83
Most Turnovers	1,858	1977-78
Victories	63	1988-89
Best Winning Pct.	.768 (63-19)	1988-89
Poorest Winning Pct.	.195 (16-66)	1979-80
Most Home Victories	37	1988-89
Fewest Home Victories	9	1963-64
Most Road Victories	26 (of 41)	1988-89
Fewest Road Victories	3 (of 19)	1960-61
	3 (of 41)	1979-80
Wins Over .500	44 (63-19)	April 23, 1989
100-Point Games	78	1983-84
	78	1985-86
Defensive Sub-100 Games	71	1996-97

GAME (OR PORTION)

STAT	RECORD	OPPONENT	DATE
Most Points			
x-Game	186	at Denver (3-OT)	Dec. 13, 1983
Half (1st)	83	vs. Chicago	March 23, 1969
Half (2nd)	87	vs. Cincinnati	Jan. 7, 1972
Quarter (1st)	46	vs. Chicago	March 23, 1969
Quarter (2nd)	43	vs. San Antonio	Feb. 9, 1977
	43	vs. Milwaukee	April 2, 1978
Quarter (3rd)	44	vs. Golden State	Jan. 24, 1985
Quarter (4th)	53	vs. Cincinnati	Jan. 7, 1972
Fewest Points			
Home Game	72	vs. New York	April 12, 1992
Road Game	71	at Atlanta	Jan. 5, 1988
Half	25	at Atlanta (1st)	Nov. 6, 1989
x-Quarter	6	at Orlando (4th)	Dec. 7, 1993
Most Points Allowed			
Home Game	162	vs. Syracuse	Feb. 8, 1963
Road Game	184	at Denver (3-OT)	Dec. 13, 1983
Half	91	at Boston (2nd)	Feb. 10, 1960
	91	at Syracuse (2nd)	Jan. 13, 1963
Quarter	52	at Baltimore (3rd)	Dec. 18, 1965

Fewest Points Allowed

Home Game	61	vs. New York	April 12, 1992
Road Game	69	at Cincinnati	Jan. 10, 1959
Half	25	at Washington (1st)	Feb. 1, 1991
Quarter	7	vs. Charlotte (4th)	Dec. 28, 1996
	7	vs. Orlando (4th)	Feb. 7, 1996

Most Field Goals

x-Game	74	vs. Denver (3-OT)	Dec. 13, 1983
Half	37	at L.A. Lakers	Nov. 24, 1972
	37	vs. Boston	March 9, 1979
Quarter	22	vs. Chicago (1st)	March 23, 1969

Most Field Goal Attempts

Game	142	vs. Boston (2-OT)	Nov. 17, 1959
Half	65	vs. Boston (2nd)	Nov. 17, 1959
Quarter	45	vs. L.A. Lakers (4th)	Nov. 28, 1965

Most Three-Point Goals

Game	14	vs. Minnesota	Nov. 8, 1994
	14	at Orlando	April 5, 1995
Half	9	vs. New York (2nd)	Feb. 26, 1993
	9	vs. Minnesota (1st)	Nov. 8, 1994
	9	vs. Orlando (2nd)	April 5, 1995
Quarter	7	vs. Denver (4th)	March 10, 1995

Most Three-Points Goal Attempts

Game	29	vs. Indiana (OT)	Dec. 26, 1996
Half	21	vs. Denver (2nd)	March 10, 1995
Quarter	12	vs. Denver (4th)	March 10, 1995

Most Free Throws

Game	48	vs. Syracuse (at Phila.)	Jan. 5, 1962
Half	34	vs. New Jersey (w/OT)	Feb. 29, 1980
Quarter	21	vs. Cincinnati (4th)	Jan. 7, 1972

Most Free Throws Attemped

Game	65	at Seattle	Feb. 16, 1962
Half	45	vs. Baltimore (2nd)	Jan. 15, 1966
Quarter	25	vs. Cincinnati (4th)	Jan. 7, 1972

Most Rebounds

Game	107	vs. Boston (at N.Y.)	Nov. 15, 1960
Half	52	vs. Seattle (2nd)	Jan. 19, 1968
Quarter	38	vs. St. Louis (2nd)	Dec. 7, 1960

Offensive Rebounds (since 1973-74)

Game	36	at L.A. Lakers	Dec. 14, 1975
Half	19	vs. L.A. Lakers (1st)	Dec. 12, 1973
Quarter	14	at L.A. Lakers (2nd)	Dec. 14, 1975

Defensive Rebounds (since 1973-74)

Game	46	at Cleveland	Jan. 17, 1974
Half	27	vs. Kansas City (1st)	Nov. 6, 1974
Quarter	17	vs. Golden State (1st)	Jan. 25, 1989

Most Assists

Game	48	at Cleveland (OT)	March 28, 1973
Half	26	vs. Chicago (1st)	Nov. 3, 1982
Quarter	16	vs. Boston (1st)	April 13, 1983

Most Personal Fouls

Game	44	at Denver (3-OT)	Dec. 13, 1983
Half	23	vs. New Jersey (2nd)	Oct. 13, 1978
Quarter	15	vs. Milwaukee (4th)	April 9, 1982

Most Disqualifications

Game	4	vs. Buffalo	Nov. 11, 1974
	4	vs. New Jersey	Feb. 29, 1980

Most Technical Fouls

Game	8	at New Jersey	March 12, 1978

Most Steals

Game	22	at New Jersey	Nov. 16, 1980
Half	14	vs. Phoenix (2nd)	Feb. 1, 1978
Quarter	9	at Phoenix (3rd)	Jan. 13, 1978

Most Turnovers

Game	38	vs. Atlanta (OT)	Oct. 18, 1980
Half	21	vs. Atlanta (1st)	Dec. 29, 1979
	21	vs. Atlanta (1st)	Oct. 18, 1980
Quarter	13	at Kansas City (3rd)	Dec. 5, 1979

Most Blocked Shots

Game	21	vs. Atlanta	Oct. 18, 1980
Half	15	vs. Washington (2nd)	Nov. 19, 1981
Quarter	10	vs. Washington (4th)	Nov. 19, 1981

PLAYOFF RECORDS

GAME (OR PORTION)

STAT	RECORD	OPPONENT	DATE
Most Points			
Game	145	vs. Boston	May 24, 1987
Half (1st)	78	at L.A. Lakers	March 31, 1962
Half (2nd)	83	vs. Boston	May 24, 1987
Quarter (1st)	39	at Golden State	April 22, 1976
	39	vs. New Jersey	April 18, 1985
Quarter (2nd)	42	vs. L.A. Lakers	March 18, 1961
Quarter (3rd)	42	vs. Boston	May 24, 1987
Quarter (4th)	41	at Boston	April 22, 1984
	41	vs. Boston	May 24, 1987
Fewest Points			
Game	75	vs. New York	April 22, 1992
	75	vs. Atlanta	April 25, 1997
Half	32	vs. Atlanta (2nd)	April 25, 1997
Quarter	10	vs. Boston (1st, 4th)	May 30, 1988
Most Points Allowed			
Game	145	vs. St. Louis	March 25, 1958
Half	76	at L.A. Lakers (1st)	March 19, 1961
Quarter	51	at L.A. Lakers (4th)	March 31, 1962
Most Field Goals			
Game	61	vs. Boston	May 24, 1987
Half	34	vs. Boston (2nd)	May 24, 1987
Quarter	17	vs. Boston (3rd, 4th)	May 24, 1987
Most Field Goal Attempts			
Game	113	vs. Boston	March 25, 1968
Half	57	vs. Boston (2nd)	March 25, 1968
Quarter	32	at Milwaukee (1st)	April 13, 1976

Most Free Throws

Game	41	at New York	April 22, 1984
Half	33	at New York (2nd)	April 22, 1984
Quarter	22	at New York (3rd)	April 22, 1984

Most Free Throws Attemped

Game	51	at L.A. Lakers	June 13, 1989
Half	39	at New York (2nd)	April 22, 1984
Quarter	27	at New York (3rd)	April 22, 1984

Most Rebounds

Game	74	at Boston	March 27, 1968
Half	39	at Boston (2nd)	March 25, 1968
Quarter	23	at Boston (3rd)	March 25, 1968

Offensive Rebounds (since 1973-74)

Game	27	vs. Boston	May 10, 1985
Half	16	Six occasions	
Quarter	13	vs. Chicago (4th)	May 21, 1989

Defensive Rebounds (since 1973-74)

Game	45	vs. Washington	April 26, 1987
Half	26	at Golden State (2nd)	April 12, 1977
Quarter	16	vs. Washington (4th)	April 26, 1987

Most Assists

Game	34	vs. Boston	May 24, 1987
Half	21	at L.A. Lakers (1st)	March 19, 1961
Quarter	12	at L.A. Lakers (2nd)	March 19, 1961

Most Personal Fouls

Game	40	vs. Los Angeles	April 3, 1962
Half	23	at Chicago (2nd)	May 21, 1961
Quarter	15	at Chicago (2nd)	May 21, 1961

Most Steals

Game	13	at Boston	April 30, 1985
	13	at L.A. Lakers	June 21, 1988
Half	10	vs. Washington (1st)	April 30, 1988
Quarter	7	vs. Boston (2nd)	April 28, 1989

Most Blocked Shots

Game	12	vs. Washington	April 26, 1987
Half	8	vs. Golden State (1st)	April 24, 1976
	8	vs. Boston (1st)	April 28, 1989
Quarter	7	vs. Boston (2nd)	April 28, 1989

STREAKS AND STARTS

GAME (OR PORTION)

STAT	RECORD	OPPONENT	DATE
Consecutive Points			
	20	at Atlanta (3rd)	Nov. 6, 1982
Consecutive FTs Made			
	26	vs. Kansas City	March 23, 1976

Season

STAT	RECORD	DATES
Winning Streak	13	Jan. 23-Feb. 21, 1990
Home Winning Streak	21	Jan. 29-April 23, 1989
Home Winning Streak (2 sea.)		
	25	Jan. 29-Nov. 18, 1989
Road Winning Streak	6	Oct. 14-28, 1970
		Nov. 4-18, 1988
		Jan. 23-Feb. 17, 1990
		Feb. 25-March 20, 1990
Best Start	9-0	Oct. 14-28, 1970
Best Finish	5-0	March 21-28, 1973
		April 7-14, 1985
		April 16-23, 1989
Winning Streak w/1 loss		
	25-1	Jan. 23-March 20, 1990
Losing Streak	14	March 7-30, 1980
Losing Streak (2 seasons)		
	21	March 7-Oct. 22, 1980
Home Losing Streak	10	Jan. 23-Feb. 27, 1980
Home Losing Streak (2 sea.)		
	13	March 7-Oct. 31, 1980
Road Losing Streak	19	Dec. 5, 1980-Feb. 7, 1981
Poorest Start	0-7	1963-64; Oct. 10-22, 1980
Poorest Finish	0-14	March 7-30, 1980

• APPENDIX H •

PISTONS IN THE ALL-STAR GAME

ALL-STAR STATISTICS
(x-denotes starter; y-MVP)

Year	Player	Min	Pts	Reb	Ast
1958	x-George Yardley	32	19	9	1
	Gene Shue	25	18	2	0
	Dick McGuire	31	4	7	10
1959	x-Gene Shue	31	13	4	3
	George Yardley	17	6	4	0
	Dick McGuire	24	5	3	3
1960	x-Gene Shue	34	13	6	6
	x-Walter Dukes	26	4	15	1
	Chuck Noble	11	0	1	3
1961	x-Gene Shue	23	15	3	6
	Walter Dukes	17	8	4	1
	Bailey Howell	16	13	3	3
1962	Bailey Howell	8	2	0	1
	Gene Shue	17	7	5	4
1963	Don Ohl	12	3	0	2
	Bailey Howell	11	4	1	1
1964	Don Ohl	18	8	2	0
	Bailey Howell	6	2	2	0
1965	Terry Dischinger	24	5	5	1
1966	Dave DeBusschere	22	4	6	1
	Eddie Miles	28	17	1	0
1967	Dave DeBusschere	25	22	6	0
1968	x-Dave Bing	20	9	2	4
	Dave DeBusschere	12	0	4	0
1969	Dave Bing	13	3	0	3
1970	Jimmy Walker	14	1	1	0
1971	x-Dave Bing	19	4	2	2
1972	Jimmy Walker	16	10	2	1
	Bob Lanier	5	2	3	0
1973	Dave Bing	19	2	3	0
	Bob Lanier	12	10	6	0
1974	y-Bob Lanier	26	24	10	2
	Dave Bing	16	5	6	2
1975	Bob Lanier	12	2	7	2
	Dave Bing	12	2	0	1
1976	Curtis Rowe	8	1	2	0
1977	Bob Lanier	20	17	10	4
1978	Bob Lanier	4	1	2	0
1979	Bob Lanier	31	10	4	4
1982	x-Isiah Thomas	17	12	1	4
	Kelly Tripucka	15	6	1	2
1983	x-Isiah Thomas	29	19	4	7
	Bill Laimbeer	6	2	1	0
1984	xy-Isiah Thomas	39	21	5	15
	Bill Laimbeer	17	13	5	0
	Kelly Tripucka	6	1	0	2
1985	x-Isiah Thomas	25	22	2	5
	Bill Laimbeer	11	5	3	1
1986	xy-Isiah Thomas	36	30	1	10
1987	Isiah Thomas	24	16	3	9
	Bill Laimbeer	11	8	2	1
1988	x-Isiah Thomas	28	8	2	15
1989	x-Isiah Thomas	33	19	2	14

1990	x-Isiah Thomas	27	15	4	9
	Joe Dumars	18	9	1	5
	Dennis Rodman	11	4	4	1
1991	x-Joe Dumars	15	2	2	1
	x-Isiah Thomas		DNP-injured		
1992	x-Isiah Thomas	28	15	1	5
	Joe Dumars	17	4	1	3
	Dennis Rodman	25	4	13	0
1993	x-Isiah Thomas	32	8	2	4
	Joe Dumars	17	5	2	4
1995	x-Grant Hill	20	10	0	3
	Joe Dumars	22	11	0	6
1996	x-Grant Hill	26	14	3	2
1997	x-Grant Hill	22	11	3	2
	Joe Dumars	10	3	1	1

PISTONS COACHES IN ALL-STAR GAMES

1990 — Chuck Daly, East (W 130-113)
1997 — Doug Collins, East (W 132-120)

ALL-STAR APPEARANCES

Player	Games
Isiah Thomas	11
Bob Lanier	7
Dave Bing	6
Joe Dumars	6
Gene Shue	5
Bailey Howell	4
Bill Laimbeer	4
Dave DeBusschere	3
Grant Hill	3
Walter Dukes	2
Dick McGuire	2
Don Ohl	2
Dennis Rodman	2
Kelly Tripucka	2
Jimmy Walker	2
George Yardley	2
Terry Dischinger	1
Eddie Miles	1
Chuck Noble	1
Curtis Rowe	1

· APPENDIX I ·

PISTONS EARNING NBA HONORS

50TH ANNIVERSARY TEAM
(Chosen 1996-97)
Top 50 Players of All-Time
Dave Bing, 1966-75
Dave DeBusschere, 1962-70
Isiah Thomas, 1981-94
Top 10 Coaches of All-Time
Chuck Daly, 1983-92

COACH OF THE YEAR
(Red Auerbach Award)
1973-74   Ray Scott

ROOKIE OF THE YEAR
(Eddie Gottlieb Trophy)
1966-67   Dave Bing
1994-95   Grant Hill

DEFENSIVE PLAYER OF THE YEAR
1989-90   Dennis Rodman
1990-91   Dennis Rodman

IBM AWARD
(By computer formula)
1991-92   Dennis Rodman
1996-97   Grant Hill

NBA FINALS MVP
1989   Joe Dumars
1990   Isiah Thomas

SPORTSMANSHIP AWARD
1996   Joe Dumars

ALL-NBA TEAM
First Team
1957-58   George Yardley
1959-60   Gene Shue
1967-68   Dave Bing
1970-71   Dave Bing
1983-84   Isiah Thomas
1984-85   Isiah Thomas
1985-86   Isiah Thomas
1996-97   Grant Hill
Second Team
1960-61   Gene Shue
1962-63   Bailey Howell
1968-69   Dave DeBusschere
1973-74   Dave Bing
1982-83   Isiah Thomas
1986-87   Isiah Thomas
1992-93   Joe Dumars
1995-96   Grant Hill
Third Team
1989-90   Joe Dumars
1990-91   Joe Dumars
1991-92   Dennis Rodman

ALL-ROOKIE TEAM
First Team
1962-63   Dave DeBusschere
1964-65   Joe Caldwell
1965-66   Tom Van Arsdale
1966-67   Dave Bing
1970-71   Bob Lanier
1978-79   Terry Tyler
1981-82   Isiah Thomas
        Kelly Tripucka
1985-86   Joe Dumars
1994-95   Grant Hill
Second Team
1993-94   Lindsey Hunter

ALL-DEFENSIVE TEAM
First Team
1988-89   Dennis Rodman
        Joe Dumars
1989-90   Dennis Rodman
        Joe Dumars
1990-91   Dennis Rodman
1991-92   Dennis Rodman
        Joe Dumars
1992-93   Dennis Rodman
        Joe Dumars
Second Team
1978-79   M.L. Carr
1990-91   Joe Dumars

PISTONS IN BASKETBALL HALL OF FAME

PLAYERS (9)
(With year elected)
Walt Bellamy, 1968-70 (1993)
Dave Bing, 1966-75 (1991)
Dave DeBusschere, 1962-70 (1982)
Harry Gallatin, 1957-58 (1991)
Bob Houbregs, 1957-58 (1987)
Bailey Howell, 1959-64 (1997)
Bob Lanier, 1970-80 (1992)
Dick McGuire, 1957-60 (1993)
George Yardley, 1957-59 (1996)

COACHES (1)
(With year elected)
Chuck Daly, 1983-92 (1994)

PISTONS MANAGEMENT & COACHES

PISTONS MANAGEMENT

Owner	Tenure
Fred Zollner	1941-July 29, 1974
William Davidson	July 29, 1974-present

President	Tenure
Fred Zollner	1941-July 29, 1974
Thomas S. Wilson	May 18, 1992-present

General Managers	Tenure
Fred DeLano	April 1957 to May 1958
W. Nick Kerbawy	June 1958 to March 1961
Fran Smith	March 1961 to November 1964
Don Wattrick	November 1964 to October 1965
Fred Zollner	October 1965 to May 1966
Ed Coil	May 1966 to June 1975
Oscar Feldman	June 1975 thru 1976-77
Bob Kauffman	1977-78 thru July 14, 1978
Oscar Feldman	July 15, 1978 to December 11, 1979
Jack McCloskey	Dec. 11, 1979 to May 29, 1992
Billy McKinney	June 23, 1992 to April 26, 1995
Rick Sund	June 3, 1995-present

PISTONS COACHES & RECORDS

Coach	Tenure	Regular Season				Playoffs			
		Gm	W	L	Pct.	Gm	W	L	Pct.
Charles Eckman	10/10/57 - 12/19/57	25	9	16	.360	-	-	-	-
Ephraim "Red" Rocha	12/19/57 - 12/28/59	153	65	88	.425	10	4	6	.400
Dick McGuire	12/28/59 - 5/1/63	280	122	158	.436	21	8	13	.381
Charley Wolf	5/1/63 - 11/9/64	91	25	66	.274	-	-	-	-
Dave DeBusschere	11/9/64 - 3/7/67	222	79	143	.356	-	-	-	-
Donnis Butcher	3/7/67 - 12/2/68	112	52	60	.464	6	2	4	.333
Paul Seymour	12/2/68 - 5/16/69	60	22	38	.367	-	-	-	-
Bill van Breda Kolff	5/21/69 - 11/1/71	174	82	92	.471	-	-	-	-
Terry Dischinger	11/1/71 -11/8/71	2	0	2	.000	-	-	-	-
Earl Lloyd	11/8/71 - 10/28/72	77	22	55	.286	-	-	-	-
Ray Scott	10/28/72 - 1/26/76	281	147	134	.523	10	4	6	.400
Herb Brown	1/26/76 - 12/15/77	147	72	74	.493	12	5	7	.417
Bob Kauffman	12/15/77 - 4/9/78	58	29	29	.500	-	-	-	-
Dick Vitale	5/1/78 - 11/8/79	94	34	60	.362	-	-	-	-
Richie Adubato	11/8/79 - 4/1/80	70	12	58	.171	-	-	-	-
Scotty Robertson	6/5/80 - 4/18/83	246	97	149	.395	-	-	-	-
Chuck Daly	5/17/83 - 5/5/92	738	467	271	.633	113	71	42	.628
Ron Rothstein	5/21/92 - 5/3/93	82	40	42	.488	-	-	-	-
Don Chaney	5/3/93 - 4/25/95	164	48	116	.297	-	-	-	-
Doug Collins	4/29/95 - present	164	100	64	.610	8	2	6	.250

PISTONS' ALL-TIME DRAFT

Round/ Overall	Player	College
1957, April 17		
1/2	Charlie Tyra	Louisville
2/10	Bob McCoy	Grambling
3/18	Bill Ebben	Detroit
4/26	Kurt Englebert	St. Joseph's (Pa.)
5/34	Ron Kramer	Michigan
6/42	Walt Adamushko	St. Francis (N.Y.)
7/50	Carl Boldt	San Francisco
8/57	Doug Bolstorff	Minnesota
9/64	Bob Lazor	Pittsburgh
1958		
1/3	Traded pick to New York	
2/22	Barney Cable	Bradley
3/18	Roy DeWitz	Kansas State
4/26	Ralph Croswaite	Western Kentucky
5/34	Hank Morano	St. Peter's
6/42	Shellie McMillon	Bradley
7/50	Ed Blair	Western Michigan
8/58	Jack Quiggle	Michigan State
9/65	Harry Marske	N. Dakota State
10/71	Pete Gaudin	Loyola (La.)
11/76	Herb Merritt	Tennessee Tech
12/80	Jim Drew	Alabama State
1959		
1/4	Bailey Howell	Mississippi State
2/9	Tom Robitaille	Rice
2/10	Don Goldstein	Louisville
3/18	Gary Alcorn	Fresno State
4/26	George Lee	Michigan
5/34	Tony Windis	Wyoming
6/42	Lou Jordan	Cornell
7/50	Doug Smart	Washington
8/57	Chuck Curtis	Pacific Lutheran
9/63	Doyle Edmiston	Hardin-Simmons
10/69	Bruno Bain	Washington
11/75	M.C. Burton	Michigan
1960		
1/4	Jack Moreland	Louisiana Tech
2/12	Ron Johnson	Minnesota
3/20	Frank Case	Dayton
4/28	Ken Remley	W.Va. Wesleyan
5/36	Willie Jones	Northwestern
6/44	Bill Lowery	Christian Brothers
7/52	Doug Moe	North Carolina
8/59	Mike Yugovich	Youngstown
9/66	Martin Holland	Kentucky Wesleyan
10/73	Joe Kennelly	Dayton
11/78	Mel Peterson	Wheaton
12/83	Don Dobbert	Wheaton
13/87	Lee Hopfenspirger	Hamline
1961		
1/4	Ray Scott	Portland
2/12	Johnny Egan	Providence
3/26	Doug Kistler	Duke
4/35	George Finley	Tennessee A&I
5/44	Dan Doyle	Belmont Abbey
6/53	Lee Patrone	West Virginia
7/62	Burt Price	Wittenberg
8/71	Walter Ward	Hampton Institute

9/79	Peter Baltic	Penn State
10/86	Wayne Monson	Northern Michigan
11/94	Richard Kraft	Brockport
1962		
T/1	Dave DeBusschere	Detroit
2/13	Kevin Loughery	St. John's
3/22	Harry Hudgens	Texas Tech
4/31	Reggie Harding	Detroit Eastern H.S.
5/40	Lindbergh Moody	South Carolina
6/49	Ed Noe	Morehead State
7/58	John Bradley	Lawrence Tech
8/66	Mike Rice	Duquesne
9/75	Bill Nelson	Hamline
10/84	Glenn Moore	Oregon
T-denotes territorial pick		
1963		
1/5	Eddie Miles	Seattle
2/13	Jerry Smith	Furman
3/22	Mike McCoy	Miami
4/31	Dave Erickson	Marquette
5/40	Bill Small	Illinois
6/49	Reggie Harding	Detroit Eastern H.S.
7/58	Ira Harge	New Mexico
8/67	Gary Silc	Northern Michigan
9/72	Ernie Dunston	Seattle
1964		
1/4	Joe Caldwell	Arizona State
2/11	Les Hunter	Loyola (Ill.)
3/20	Wali Jones	Villanova
4/29	Jim Davis	Colorado
5/38	Ray Wolford	Toledo
6/47	Larry Phillips	Rice
7/56	Jerry Jackson	Ohio
8/65	Ralph Telken	Rockhurst
1965		
T/1	Bill Buntin	Michigan
2	No selection	
3/19	Tom Van Arsdale	Indiana
4/28	Ron Reed	Notre Dame
5/37	Jim King	Oklahoma State
6/46	Ted Manning	N.C. College
7/55	Barry Smith	High Point
T-denotes territorial pick		
1966		
1/2	Dave Bing	Syracuse
2/12	Dorie Murrey	Detroit
3/22	Oliver Darden	Michigan
4/32	Jeff Congdon	Brigham Young
5/42	William Pickens	Georgia Southern
6/52	Carroll Hooser	Southern Methodist
7/61	Ted Manning	N.C. College
8/70	George McNeil	Southern Illinois
1967, May 3		
1/1	Jimmy Walker	Providence
1/4	Sonny Dove	St. John's
2/14	Steve Sullivan	Georgetown
3/21	Darrell Hardy	Baylor
4/33	Ron Franz	Kansas

5/45	Paul Long	Wake Forest
6/57	Vaughn Harper	Syracuse
7/69	Bob Lloyd	Rutgers
8/81	George Carter	St. Bonaventure
9	No selection	
10	No selection	
11	No selection	
12/125	George Dalzell	Colgate
13/135	Matthew Aitch	Michigan State
1968		
1/6	Otto Moore	Pan American
2/20	Manny Leaks	Niagara
3/25	Don Dee	St. Mary of the Plains
3/28	Traded pick to Cincinnati	
4/42	Rich Niemann	St. Louis
5/56	Carl Fuller	Bethune-Cookman
6/70	Wally Anderzunas	Creighton
7/84	Larry Newbold	Long Island U.
8/98	Harry Laurie	St. Peter's
9/112	Vaughn Harper	Syracuse
10/126	Tom Baack	Nebraska
1969		
1/4	Terry Driscoll	Boston College
2/19	Willie Norwood	Alcorn A&M
3/33	Traded pick to Phoenix	
4/47	Ted Wierman	Washington State
5/61	Steve Mix	Toledo
6/75	Larry Jeffries	Trinity (Tex.)
7/89	Steve Vandenberg	Duke
8/103	Bob Arnzen	Notre Dame
9/117	George Reynolds	Houston
10/131	Bill English	Winston-Salem
11/145	Rusty Clark	North Carolina
1970, March 20		
1/1	Bob Lanier	St. Bonaventure
2/20	Traded pick to Seattle	
2/32	Ken Warzynski	DePaul
3/37	Bob St. Pierre	Hanover
3/47	Jim Hayes	Boston University
4/54	Traded pick to Baltimore	
5/71	Bill Jankans	Long Beach State
6/88	Sevira Brown	DePaul
7/105	Marv Copeland	Michigan Lutheran
8/122	Dan Issel	Kentucky
9/139	Alex Wynn	Dartmouth
10/156	Bruce Chapman	Nevada
11/172	Rick Anheuser	N.C. State
12/185	Don Ogletree	Cincinnati
13/195	Ernest Hardy	Harvard
14/205	Randy Smith	Buffalo State
15/215	Dennis Clark	Springfield
16/224	Harvey Marlatt	Eastern Michigan
1971, March 29		
1/11	Curtis Rowe	UCLA
2/29	Bunny Wilson	Baltimore
3/45	Marv Roberts	Utah State
4/62	Jarrett Durham	Duquesne
5/79	Vincent White	Savannah State
6/96	James Larranaga	Providence
7/113	Steve Kelly	Brigham Young

8/130	Wayne Jones	Niagara
9/146	Paul Botts	Central Michigan
10/162	Steve Butcher	Pikeville
11/177	Larry Saunders	Duke
12/190	Bob Horn	Drake
13/202	Willie Roberson	Wyoming
14/212	Art Davis	J.C. Smith
15/221	James Fleming	Alcorn A&M
16/228	Fred Smiley	Detroit College
17/232	Leroy Jenkins	Detroit College
18/235	Ike Bundy	Detroit Tech
19/237	Ed Jenkins	Shaw College

1972

1/4	Traded pick to Phoenix	
1/9	Bob Nash	Hawaii
2/17	Chris Ford	Villanova
3/34	Traded pick to Phoenix	
4/51	Ernie Fleming	Jacksonville
5/67	Ernest Pettis	Western Michigan
6/84	Terry Benton	Wichita State
7/101	Bruce Anderson	Arizona
8/116	Ben Kelso	Central Michigan
9/132	Jessie Mangham	Ferris State
10/145	Kent Hollenbeck	Kentucky

1973, April 23

1/9	Traded pick to Atlanta	
2/27	Traded pick to Atlanta	
3/44	Dwight Lamar	SW Louisiana
4/61	Ken Brady	Michigan
5/78	Henry Wilmore	Michigan
6/95	Dennis Johnson	Ferris State
7/112	Fred Smiley	Northwood Institute
8/129	Ben Kelso	Central Michigan
9/145	Bill Kilgore	Michigan State
10/159	Bob Solomon	Wayne State
11/171	Len Paul	Akron
12/180	Clarence Carlisle	Ferris State

1974, May 28

1/15	Al Eberhard	Missouri
2/33	Eric Money	Arizona
3/51	Roland Grant	New Mexico State
4/69	Mickey Martin	Pittsburgh
5/87	Joe Newman	Temple
6/105	Mike Sylvester	Dayton
7/123	Sammy High	Tulsa
8/141	Greg Newman	Drexel
9/158	Gary Deitelhoff	Millikin
10/175	Bill Ligon	Vanderbilt

1975, May 29

1/10	Traded pick to N.Y. Knicks	
2/27	Walter Luckett	Ohio
3/44	Pete Trgovich	UCLA
4/64	Lindsay Hairston	Michigan State
5/81	Clifford Pratt	Shaw College (Mich.)
6/98	Allen Spruill	N. Carolina A&T
7/118	Ike Williams	Armstrong (Ga.)
8/135	John Kelley	Dillard (La.)
9/151	Terry Thomas	Detroit
10/169	Mickey Fox	St. Mary's (Nova Scotia)

1976, June 8

1/4	Leon Douglas	Alabama
2/21	Traded pick to Phoenix	
3/38	Phil Sellers	Rutgers
4/55	Scott Thompson	Iowa
5/72	Jim Hearns	Marymount
6/90	Russell Davis	Virginia Tech
7/108	Curt Peterson	Puget Sound
8/126	Randy Henry	Illinois State

9/144	Bill Martin	Hartwick College
10/162	Bob Johnson	Wisconsin

1976 ABA DISPERSAL

1/4	Marvin Barnes	St. Louis Spirits

1977, June 10

1/14	Traded pick to Washington	
2/36	Ben Poquette	Central Michigan
3/58	John Irving	Hofstra
4/80	Bruce King	Iowa
5/102	Jim Kennedy	Missouri
6/124	Herb Nobles	Kansas
7/144	Robert Lewis	J.C. Smith
8/163	Tim Appleton	Kenyon College

1978, June 9

1/7	Traded pick to Seattle	
2/23	Terry Tyler	Detroit
2/29	John Long	Detroit
3/51	Traded pick to Buffalo	
4/73	Traded pick to Buffalo	
5/95	Dave Caligaris	Northeastern
6/117	Audie Matthews	Illinois
7/139	Herb Entzminger	J.C. Smith
8/158	Earl Evans	UNLV
9/175	Ulice Payne	Marquette
10/190	Dave Grauzer	Central Michigan

1979, June 25

1/4	Gregory Kelser	Michigan State
1/5	Traded pick to Milwaukee	
1/10	Roy Hamilton	UCLA
1/15	Phil Hubbard	Michigan
2/25	Traded pick to Denver	
2/29	Tony Price	Penn
3/48	Terry Duerod	Detroit
4/69	Traded pick to Milwaukee	
5/92	Flintie Ray Williams	UNLV
6/113	Truman Clayton	Kentucky
7/136	Ken Jones	St. Mary's (Calif.)
8/157	Rodney Lee	Memphis State
9/180	Val Bracey	Central Michigan
10/201	Willie Polk	Grand Canyon (Ariz.)

1980, June 10

1/1	Traded pick to Boston	
1/17	Larry Drew	Missouri
2/24	Compensation to Utah	
2/45	Brad Branson	Southern Methodist
3/47	Traded pick to Denver	
3/64	Jonathan Moore	Furman
4/70	Darwin Cook	Portland
5/93	Tony Fuller	Pepperdine
6/116	Tony Turner	Alaska-Anchorage
7/139	Carl Pierce	Gonzaga
8/162	Leroy Loggins	Fairmont (W.Va.)
9/185	Terry Dupris	Huron (S.D.)

1981, June 9

1/2	Isiah Thomas	Indiana
1/12	Kelly Tripucka	Notre Dame
2/25	Traded pick to Boston	
3/48	Compensation to Washington	
4/71	John May	South Alabama
4/89	Donnie Koonce	UNC-Charlotte
5/94	George DeVone	UNC-Charlotte
6/117	Vince Brookins	Iowa
7/140	Greg Nance	West Virginia
8/163	Joe Schoen	St. Francis (Pa.)
9/186	Ed Baker	Alcorn State
10/209	Melvin Maxwell	Western Michigan

1982, June 29

1/9	Cliff Levingston	Wichita State
1/18	Ricky Pierce	Rice
2/32	Traded pick to Houston	
3/55	Traded pick to Utah	
4/78	Walker D. Russell	Western Michigan
5/101	John Ebeling	Florida Southern
6/124	Gary Holmes	Minnesota
7/147	Dean Marquardt	Marquette
8/170	Brian Nyenhuis	Marquette
9/193	Kevin Smith	Michigan State
10/214	Dave Coulthard	York (Ontario)

1983, June 28

1/8	Antoine Carr	Wichita State
2/32	Compensation to Washington	
3/55	Erich Santifer	Syracuse
4/78	Steve Bouchie	Indiana
5/101	Ken Austin	Rice
6/124	Derek Perry	Michigan State
7/147	Rob Gonzalez	Colorado
8/170	George Wenzal	Augustana
9/193	Marlow McClain	Eastern Michigan
10/216	Issac Person	Michigan

1984, June 19

1/20	Tony Campbell	Ohio State
2/32	Eric Turner	Michigan
2/43	Traded pick to Indiana	
3/66	Kevin Springman	St. Joseph's
4/89	Philip Smith	New Mexico
5/112	Rick Doyle	Texas-San Antonio
6/135	Rennie Bailey	Louisiana Tech
7/158	Barry Francisco	Bloomsburg State
8/181	Dale Roberts	Appalachian State
9/203	Ben Tower	Michigan State
10/225	Dan Pelekoudas	Michigan

1985, June 18

1/18	Joe Dumars	McNeese State
2/41	Traded pick to Atlanta	
3/60	Andre Goode	Northwestern
3/64	Richie Johnson	Evansville
4/87	Spud Webb	N. Carolina State
5/110	Mike Lahm	Murray State
6/133	Vince Giles	Eastern Michigan
7/156	Frank James	UNLV

1986, June 17

1/11	John Salley	Georgia Tech
2/27	Dennis Rodman	SE Oklahoma State
2/40	Traded pick to Cleveland	
3/63	Traded pick to Utah	
4/86	Chauncey Robinson	Miss. State
5/109	Clarence Hanley	Old Dominion
6/132	Greg Grant	Utah State
7/155	Larry Polec	Michigan State

1987, June 22

1/19	Traded pick to L.A. Clippers	
2/24	Freddie Banks	UNLV
2/42	Traded pick to Atlanta	
3/65	Eric White	Pepperdine
4/88	Dave Popson	North Carolina
5/111	Gerry Wright	Iowa
6/134	Antoine Joubert	Michigan
7/157	Mark Gottfried	Alabama

1988, June 28

1/22	Traded pick to Phoenix	
2/30	Fennis Dembo	Wyoming
2/48	Micheal Willams	Baylor
3/72	Lee Johnson	Norfolk State

1989, June 27
1/27   Kenny Battle   Illinois
2/54   Traded pick to Philadelphia

1990, June 27
1/26   Lance Blanks   Texas
2/52   Traded pick to Philadelphia

1991, June 26
1/19   Traded pick to Dallas
2/40   Doug Overton   LaSalle
2/46   Traded pick to Phoenix

1992, June 24
1/19   Don MacLean   UCLA
2/46   Traded pick to Denver

1993, June 30
1/10   Lindsey Hunter   Jackson State
1/11   Allan Houston   Tennessee
2/38   Traded pick to Washington

1994, June 29
1/3   Grant Hill   Duke
2/29   Traded pick to Phoenix
2/48   Jevon Crudup   Missouri

1995, June 28
1/8   Traded pick to Portland
1/18   Theo Ratliff   Wyoming
1/19   Randolph Childress   Wake Forest
2/30   Lou Roe   Massachusetts
2/37   Traded pick to Washington
2/58   Don Reid   Georgetown

1996, June 26
1/18   Traded pick to San Antonio
1/26   Jerome Williams   Georgetown
2/48   Traded pick to Philadelphia

1997, June 25
1/19   Scot Pollard   Kansas
2/32   Charles O'Bannon   UCLA
2/50   Traded pick to Atlanta

PISTONS CHOSEN IN EXPANSION DRAFT

1961 — Archie Dees to Chicago Packers
1966 — Don Kojis and John Barnhill to Chicago Bulls
1967 — Charles Vaughn to San Diego Conquistadors; Ron Reed and Dorie Murrey to Seattle SuperSonics
1968 — Len Chappell and George Patterson to Milwaukee Bucks; Paul Long to Phoenix Suns
1970 — Paul Long to Buffalo Braves; McCoy McLemore to Cleveland Cavaliers
1974 — Stu Lantz to New Orleans Jazz
1980 — Terry Duerod to Dallas Mavericks
1988 — Ralph Lewis to Charlotte Hornets
1989 — Rick Mahorn to Minnesota TimberWolves

· APPENDIX M ·

PISTONS TRANSACTIONS AND KEY DATES

1957-58
April 3, 1957 — Obtained Harry Gallatin, Dick McGuire, Dick Atha and Nat "Sweetwater" Clifton from New York Knicks for Mel Hutchins, rights to Pistons' 1957 first-round draft pick Charlie Tyra and Pistons' 1958 first-round pick.
May 14, 1957 — Obtained El Kalafat from Minneapolis Lakers for Walt "Corky" Devlin.
Sept. 12, 1957 — Obtained Walter Dukes from Minneapolis Lakers for Larry Foust.
Dec. 10, 1957 — Purchased Phil Jordon from New York Knicks and Tom Marshall from Cincinnati Royals.
Dec. 19, 1957 — Coach Charlie Eckman fired, Red Rocha hired.
Dec. 28, 1957 — Purchased Joe Holup from Syracuse Nationals.

1958-59
June 10, 1958 — Purchased Earl Lloyd and Dick Farley from Syracuse Nationals.
Feb. 12, 1959 — Obtained Ed Conlin from Syracuse Nationals for George Yardley.

1959-60
March 31, 1959 — Obtained Archie Dees and 1959 second-round pick from Cincinnati Royals for Phil Jordon.
Nov. 10, 1959 — Sold Barney Cable to Syracuse Nationals.
Dec. 28, 1959 — Coach Red Rocha fired, Dick McGuire hired.

1960-61
April 16, 1960 — Obtained Bob Ferry from St. Louis Hawks for Ed Conlin; purchased rights to Don Ohl from Philadelphia Warriors.

1961-62
Dec. 1, 1961 — Sold Shellie McMillon to St. Louis Hawks.

1962-63
Aug. 29, 1962 — Obtained Darrall Imhoff and cash from New York Knicks for Gene Shue.
Sept. 19, 1962 — Sold George Lee to San Francisco Warriors.

1963-64
May 1, 1963 — Coach Dick McGuire resigns, Charley Wolf hired.
Oct. 9, 1963 — Walter Dukes waived.
Oct. 29, 1963 — Obtained Larry Staverman from Baltimore Bullets for Kevin Loughery.
Dec. 16, 1963 — Obtained Donnis Butcher and Bob Duffy from New York Knicks for Johnny Egan; traded Larry Staverman to Cincinnati Royals for Hub Reed.

1964-65
April 16, 1964 — Sold Darrell Imhoff to Los Angeles Lakers.
June 18, 1964 — Obtained Terry Dischinger, Rod Thorn and Don Kojis from Baltimore Bullets for Bailey Howell, Don Ohl, Bob Ferry and rights to draft picks Les Hunter (second round) and Wali Jones (third round).
Nov. 8, 1964 — Don Wattrick named general manager.
Nov. 9, 1964 — Coach Charley Wolf fired, Dave DeBusschere named player-coach.
Dec. 31, 1964 — Willie Jones waived.

1965-66
May 8, 1965 — Obtained rights to Bill Chmielewski from Cincinnati Royals.
Dec. 24, 1965 — Obtained Charles Vaughn and John Tresvant from St. Louis Hawks for Rod Thorn.
Dec. 28, 1965 — Obtained John Barnhill from St. Louis Hawks for Joe Caldwell.

1966-67
Jan. 16, 1967 — Traded Ray Scott to Baltimore Bullets in three-team deal that was to have brought Rudy LaRusso to Pistons from Los Angeles Lakers. When LaRusso failed to report, Pistons were awarded Lakers' 1967 first-round draft pick.
March 7, 1967 — Dave DeBusschere relinquishes coaching duties, assistant Donnis Butcher elevated to head coach.

1967-68
Oct. 2, 1967 — Traded Reggie Harding to the Chicago Bulls for future draft pick and cash.
Nov. 27, 1967 — Obtained Len Chappell from Cincinnati Royals for 1968 third-round draft pick.
Feb. 1, 1968 — Obtained Happy Hairston and Jim Fox from Cincinnati Royals for John Tresvant and Tom Van Arsdale.

1968-69
Dec. 2, 1968 — Coach Donnis Butcher fired, assistant Paul Seymour elevated to head coach.
Dec. 8, 1968 — Acquired Bud Olsen on waivers from Boston Celtics.
Dec. 17, 1968 — Obtained McCoy McLemore from Phoenix Suns for Jim Fox and Pistons' 1969 third-round draft pick.
Dec. 19, 1968 — Obtained Walt Bellamy and Howie Komives from New York Knicks for Dave DeBusschere.
Jan. 1, 1969 — Obtained Dave Gambee from Milwaukee Bucks for Rich Niemann.

...l "Butch" van Breda Kolff hired.

...ed Erwin Mueller from Seattle SuperSonics for 1970 second-round

— Obtained Bill Hewitt and 1970 third-round draft pick from Los Angeles ...s for Happy Hairston.

Feb. 1, 1970 — Obtained Bob Quick and 1970 second-round draft pick from Baltimore Bullets for Eddie Miles; received John Arthurs from Milwaukee Bucks in three-team trade that sent Walt Bellamy to Atlanta Hawks.

1971-72

April 2, 1971 — Obtained 1972 first-round draft pick from Phoenix Suns for Otto Moore.

Nov. 1, 1971 — Coach Bill van Breda Kolff resigns, Terry Dischinger named acting coach.

Nov. 8, 1971 — Earl Lloyd named head coach.

Dec. 10, 1971 — Obtained Jim Davis from Houston Rockets for Pistons' 1972 first-round draft pick.

1972-73

July 31, 1972 — Obtained Fred Foster from Philadelphia 76ers in three-team trade in which Terry Dischinger is sent to the Portland Trail Blazers and Portland sends draft choice to Philadelphia.

Aug. 1, 1972 — Obtained Stu Lantz from Houston Rockets for Jimmy Walker.

Sept. 30, 1972 — Obtained 1973 second-round draft pick from Buffalo Braves for Howie Komives.

Oct. 28, 1972 — Coach Earl Lloyd fired, assistant Ray Scott elevated to head coach.

Oct. 31, 1972 — Obtained Don Adams from Atlanta Hawks for Pistons' 1973 second-round draft pick.

Nov. 10, 1972 — Obtained John Mengelt from Kansas City-Omaha Kings for Buffalo's 1973 second-round pick obtained in Howie Komives trade.

1973-74

April 15, 1973 — Obtained George Trapp from Atlanta Hawks for Pistons' 1973 first-round draft pick.

1974-75

July 29, 1974 — Team sold by Fred Zollner to group headed by glass magnate William Davidson.

Dec. 26, 1974 — Obtained Howard Porter from New York Knicks for Pistons' 1975 first-round draft pick.

Feb. 18, 1975 — Don Adams waived.

1975-76

May 28, 1975 — Obtained Earl Williams from Phoenix Suns for 1976 second-round draft pick.

Aug. 28, 1975 — Obtained Kevin Porter from Washington Bullets for Dave Bing and Pistons' 1977 first-round draft pick.

Sept. 24, 1975 — Obtained Archie Clark from Seattle SuperSonics for Pistons' 1978 first-round draft pick.

Jan. 26, 1976 — Coach Ray Scott fired, assistant Herb Brown elevated to head coach.

1976-77

Oct. 20, 1976 — Obtained Ralph Simpson from the Denver Nuggets in three-team trade which sent Pistons' Curtis Rowe to Boston Celtics and Celtics' Paul Silas to Denver.

Nov. 18, 1976 — Sold John Mengelt to Chicago Bulls.

1977-78

Nov. 7, 1977 — Obtained Al Skinner and second-draft draft picks in 1978 and 1979 from New Jersey Nets for Kevin Porter and Howard Porter.

Nov. 23, 1977 — Obtained John Shumate, Gus Gerard and Milwaukee's first-round draft pick in 1979 or 1980 from Buffalo Braves for Marvin Barnes and Pistons' 1978 third- and fourth-round draft picks.

Dec. 15, 1977 — Coach Herb Brown fired, general manager Bob Kauffman becomes interim coach.

Feb. 1, 1978 — Obtained Jim Price and 1979 first-round draft pick from Denver Nuggets for Ralph Simpson.

1978-79

May 1, 1978 — Dick Vitale hired as coach.

Sept. 8, 1978 — Obtained Kevin Porter from New Jersey Nets for Eric Money.

Oct. 10, 1978 — Obtained Rickey Green from Golden State Warriors for future considerations and cash.

Oct. 19, 1978 — Obtained Earl Tatum from Boston Celtics for Chris Ford and Pistons' 1981 second-round draft pick.

Oct. 23, 1978 — Obtained Otis Howard from Milwaukee Bucks for Pistons' 1979 fourth-round draft pick.

Feb. 15, 1979 — Obtained Jim Brewer from Cleveland Cavaliers for future considerations.

1979-80

April 12, 1979 — Sent Earl Tatum to Cleveland Cavaliers to complete Feb. 15 acquisition of Jim Brewer.

June 25, 1979 — Obtained 1979 first-round draft pick (fourth overall) from Milwaukee Bucks for Pistons' 1979 first-round draft pick (fifth overall) and cash.

July 12, 1979 — Received Washington Bullets' first-round draft picks in 1980 and 1982 as compensation for Washington signing free agent Kevin Porter.

Aug. 27, 1979 — Obtained 1981 fourth-round draft pick from Phoenix Suns for Andre Wakefield.

Sept. 6, 1979 — Obtained Bob McAdoo from Boston Celtics for Pistons' 1980 first-round draft pick and Washington Bullets' 1980 first-round draft pick received in Porter compensation.

Sept. 18, 1979 — Obtained 1981 second-round draft pick from Portland Trail Blazers for Jim Brewer.

Oct. 30, 1979 — John Shumate waived.

Nov. 1, 1979 — Sent 1980 second-round draft pick and cash to Utah Jazz as compensation for Detroit's signing veteran free agents Ben Poquette and James McElroy.

Nov. 8, 1979 — Coach Dick Vitale resigns, assistant Richie Adubato elevated to interim head coach.

Dec. 11, 1979 — Jack McCloskey named general manager.

Jan. 25, 1980 — Obtained Ron Lee and 1980 second- and third-round draft picks from Atlanta Hawks for James McElroy.

Feb. 4, 1980 — Obtained Kent Benson and 1980 first-round draft pick from Milwaukee Bucks for Bob Lanier.

1980-81

June 5, 1980 — Scotty Robertson named head coach.

Oct. 1, 1980 — Obtained Wayne Robinson from Los Angeles Lakers for Portland's 1981 second-round draft pick received in Jim Brewer trade.

Oct. 7, 1980 — Obtained Paul Mokeski from Houston Rockets for Pistons' 1982 second-round draft pick.

Nov. 13, 1980 — Signed veteran free agent Larry Wright and compensated Washington Bullets with Pistons' 1981 third-round draft pick and 1983 second-round draft pick.

Dec. 16, 1980 — Trade Greg Kelser to Seattle SuperSonics for 1983 first-round draft choice, but trade is nullified next day when he fails his physical.

March 21, 1981 — Bob McAdoo waived.

1981-82

June 9, 1981 — Isiah Thomas drafted with second overall draft pick and Kelly Tripucka drafted 12th overall.

June 11, 1981 — Obtained Edgar Jones from New Jersey Nets for cash.

July 31, 1981 — Signed Isiah Thomas to multiyear contract.

Aug. 26, 1981 — Obtained second-round draft picks in 1982 and 1984 from Kansas City Kings for Larry Drew.

Sept. 25, 1981 — Traded negotiating rights to 1980 draft pick Brad Branson to Dallas Mavericks for future considerations.

Oct. 1, 1981 — Obtained Jeff Judkins from Utah Jazz for Pistons' 1982 third-round draft pick and future considerations.

Nov. 21, 1981 — Obtained Vinnie Johnson from Seattle SuperSonics for Greg Kelser.

Feb. 16, 1982 — Obtained Bill Laimbeer and Kenny Carr from Cleveland Cavaliers for Phil Hubbard, Paul Mokeski and Pistons' 1982 first- and second-round draft picks.

April 9, 1982 — Announced Pistons' All-Time team: Dave Bing, Dave DeBusschere, Bailey Howell, Bob Lanier, Gene Shue and George Yardley.

1982-83

June 23, 1982 — Obtained 1982 first-round draft pick from Portland Trail Blazers for Kenny Carr.

Aug. 2, 1982 — Received 1984 third-round draft pick from Portland Trail Blazers for waiving right of first refusal after Portland's signing of free agent Jeff Judkins.

Sept. 23, 1982 — Obtained Tom Owens from Indiana Pacers for Pistons' 1984 second-round draft pick.

Oct. 6, 1982 — Obtained 1986 second-round draft pick from Cleveland Cavaliers for Steve Hayes.

Feb. 10, 1983 — Obtained 1984 second-round draft pick and 1985 third-round draft pick from San Antonio Spurs for Edgar Jones.

Feb. 13, 1983 — Obtained Ray Tolbert from Atlanta Hawks for second-round draft picks in 1984 and 1985.

March 18, 1983 — Dave Bing's No. 21 retired.

April 18, 1983 — Coach Scotty Robertson fired.

1983-84

May 17, 1983 — Chuck Daly hired as coach.

Aug. 18, 1983 — Obtained Petur Gudmundsson from Portland Trail Blazers for 1984 third-round draft pick (originally Portland's).

Oct. 17, 1983 — Traded Ricky Pierce to San Diego Clippers for second-round draft picks in 1985 and 1986, then traded those picks to Phoenix Suns for David Thirdkill.

Nov. 12, 1983 — Signed free agent Earl Cureton and traded second-round draft picks in 1989 and 1990 to Philadelphia 76ers for waiving their right of first refusal.

1984-85

June 18, 1984 — Obtained Dan Roundfield from Atlanta Hawks for Cliff Levington, draft rights to Pistons' No. 1 pick Antoine Carr and second-round picks in 1986 and 1987.

1985-86

June 17, 1985 — Obtained Rick Mahorn and Mike Gibson from Washington Bullets for Dan Roundfield.

Nov. 20, 1985 — Accepted exchange of 1986 first-round draft slots as compensation for Sacramento Kings' signing of free agent Terry Tyler.

Nov. 29, 1985 — Signed free agent Chuck Nevitt.

1986-87

Aug. 21, 1986 — Obtained Adrian Dantley and second-round draft picks in 1987 and 1990 from Utah Jazz for Kelly Tripucka and Kent Benson.

Aug. 22, 1986 — Obtained Sidney Green from Chicago Bulls for Earl Cureton and 1987 second-round draft pick.

Sept. 30, 1986 — Obtained two second-round draft picks from Seattle SuperSonics for John Long.

Jan. 29, 1987 — Obtained Kurt Nimphius from Los Angeles Clippers for Pistons' 1987 first-round draft pick and an acquired 1987 second-round pick.

1987-88

June 22, 1987 — Obtained William Bedford from Phoenix Suns for Pistons' 1988 first-round draft pick.

Oct. 28, 1987 — Obtained Ron Moore and 1988 second-round draft pick from New York Knicks for Sidney Green.

Nov. 26, 1987 — Obtained Darryl Dawkins from Utah Jazz for 1988 second-round draft pick.

Feb. 24, 1988 — Obtained James Edwards from Phoenix Suns for Ron Moore and 1991 second-round draft pick.

April 24, 1988 — Signed free agent Walker D. Russell.

1988-89

Feb. 15, 1989 — Obtained Mark Aguirre from Dallas Mavericks for Adrian Dantley and Pistons' 1991 first-round draft pick.

Feb. 23, 1989 — Signed free agent John Long.

1989-90

June 27, 1989 — Obtained draft rights to Anthony Cook from Phoenix Suns for Micheal Williams and draft rights to Kenny Battle.

July 17, 1989 — Signed free agent Scott Hastings.

Oct. 4, 1989 — Signed free agent David Greenwood.

Dec. 6, 1989 — Signed free agent Gerald Henderson.

1990-91

Sept. 28, 1990 — Obtained 1992 second-round draft choice from Denver Nuggets for Anthony Cook.

Jan. 24, 1991 — Signed free agent John Long.

1991-92

Aug. 13, 1991 — Obtained Orlando Woolridge from Denver Nuggets for Scott Hastings and Pistons' 1992 second-round draft pick; obtained Jeff Martin and 1995 second-round draft pick from Los Angeles Clippers for James Edwards.

Sept. 4, 1991 — Vinnie Johnson waived.

Sept. 4, 1991 — Obtained Darrell Walker from Washington Bullets for second-round draft picks in 1993 and 1995.

May 5, 1992 — Coach Chuck Daly resigns.

1992-93

May 18, 1992 — Tom Wilson named team president.

May 21, 1992 — Ron Rothstein hired as head coach.

May 29, 1992 — General manager Jack McCloskey resigns.

June 23, 1992 — Billy McKinney named director of player personnel.

June 24, 1992 — Obtained Olden Polynice from Los Angeles Clippers for William Bedford and draft rights to Pistons' first-round draft pick Don MacLean.

Sept. 8, 1992 — Obtained 1993 first-round draft pick, conditional second-round pick and Isaiah Morris from Miami Heat for John Salley.

Sept. 30, 1992 — Signed restricted free agent Terry Mills.

Nov. 15, 1992 — Obtained Gerald Glass and Mark Randall from Minnesota TimberWolves for Lance Blanks and Brad Sellers.

Nov. 25, 1992 — Darrell Walker waived.

Jan. 9, 1993 — Bob Lanier's No. 16 retired.

Feb. 25, 1993 — Obtained Alvin Robertson from Milwaukee Bucks for Orlando Woolridge.

1993-94

May 3, 1993 — Coach Ron Rothstein fired, assistant Don Chaney elevated to head coach.

Sept. 8, 1993 — Signed unrestricted free agent Greg "Cadillac" Anderson.

Oct. 1, 1993 — Obtained Sean Elliott and David Wood from San Antonio Spurs for Dennis Rodman and draft considerations.

Oct. 7, 1993 — Mark Aguirre waived.

Nov. 1, 1993 — Signed Tracy Moore and Dan O'Sullivan.

Nov. 19, 1993 — Obtained Mark Macon and Marcus Liberty from Denver Nuggets for Alvin Robertson.

Dec. 1, 1993 — Bill Laimbeer retires.

Dec. 14, 1993 — Signed unrestricted free agent Todd Murphy.

Jan. 5, 1994 — Todd Murphy waived.

Feb. 5, 1994 — Vinnie Johnson's No. 15 retired.

Feb. 10, 1994 — Signed unrestricted free agent Charles Jones.

Feb. 20, 1994 — Obtained Pete Chilcutt and draft considerations from Sacramento Kings for Olden Polynice.

May 11, 1994 — Isiah Thomas retires.

1994-95

July 19, 1994 — Obtained draft rights to Bill Curley and 1997 second-round draft pick from San Antonio Spurs for Sean Elliott.

July 25, 1994 — Obtained Eric Leckner from Philadelphia 76ers for 1996 second-round draft pick.

July 29, 1994 — Signed unrestricted free agent Rafael Addison.

Aug. 1, 1994 — Obtained Mark West from Phoenix Suns for 1996 second-round draft pick.

Sept. 6, 1994 — Signed restricted free agent Oliver Miller.

Oct. 10, 1994 — Signed unrestricted free agent Johnny Dawkins.

Feb. 4, 1995 — Bill Laimbeer's No. 40 retired.

April 19, 1995 — Rafael Addison waived.

April 25, 1995 — Coach Don Chaney fired.

April 26, 1995 — Billy McKinney fired as director of player personnel.

1995-96

April 29, 1995 — Doug Collins hired as head coach.

June 27, 1995 — Obtained two 1995 first-round draft picks (18th and 19th overall) and second-round draft pick from Portland Trail Blazers for Pistons' 1995 first-round draft pick (eighth overall).

Sept. 20, 1995 — Obtained Otis Thorpe from Portland Trail Blazers for Bill Curley and draft rights to Randolph Childress.

Jan. 5, 1996 — Stephen Bardo and Rodney Zimmerman waived.

Jan. 31, 1996 — Signed Michael Curry.

Feb. 17, 1996 — Isiah Thomas' No. 11 retired.

April 11, 1996 — Mark Macon waived.

1996-97

June 29, 1996 — Obtained Ron Riley from Seattle SuperSonics for 1997 second-round draft pick.

July 15, 1996 — Re-signed free agents Michael Curry and Don Reid.

July 15, 1996 — Obtained Grant Long and Stacey Augmon from Atlanta Hawks for two conditional first-round draft choices and two second-round draft choices.

Aug. 7, 1996 — Re-signed free agent Otis Thorpe.

Sept. 17, 1996 — Signed unrestricted free agent Kenny Smith.

Nov. 23, 1996 — Kenny Smith waived.

Jan. 24, 1997 — Obtained Aaron McKie, Randolph Childress and Reggie Jordan from Portland Trail Blazers for Stacey Augmon.

Jan. 25, 1997 — Chuck Daly's No. 2 retired.

1997-98

July 30, 1997 — Re-signed free agent Joe Dumars.

Aug. 7, 1997 — Traded Otis Thorpe to Vancouver Grizzlies for conditional first-round draft pick in 1998-2003 span.

Aug. 8, 1997 — Re-signed free agent Lindsey Hunter.

Aug. 16, 1997 — Signed free agent Brian Williams.

Aug. 25, 1997 — Signed free agent Malik Sealy.

PISTONS INDIVIDUAL RECORDS

REGULAR SEASON RECORDS

SEASON

STAT	RECORD	PLAYER	SEASON
Points	2,213	Dave Bing	1970-71
Scoring Average	27.8	George Yardley	1957-58
Field Goals	836	Dave Bing	1967-68
Field Goals Attempted	1,903	Dave Bing	1967-68
Field Goal Percentage	.595	Dennis Rodman	1988-89
Free Throws	655	George Yardley	1957-58
Free Throws Attempted	808	George Yardley	1957-58
Free Throw Percentage	.900	Joe Dumars	1989-90
3-Point Goals	191	Allan Houston	1995-96
3-Point Attempts	468	Lindsey Hunter	1996-97
3-Point Percentage	.432	Joe Dumars	1996-97
Rebounds	1,530	Dennis Rodman	1991-92
Offensive Rebounds	523	Dennis Rodman	1991-92
Defensive Rebounds	1,007	Dennis Rodman	1991-92
Assists	1,123	Isiah Thomas	1984-85
Steals	204	Isiah Thomas	1983-84
Personal Fouls	344	Joe Strawder	1966-67
Disqualifications	22	Walter Dukes	1958-59
Turnovers	343	Isiah Thomas	1986-87
Blocked Shots	247	Bob Lanier	1973-74
Minutes	3,361	Gene Shue	1960-61
		Dave Bing	1972-73

GAME (OR PORTION)

STAT	RECORD	PLAYER	DATE	OPPONENT
Points				
Game	56	Kelly Tripucka	Jan. 29, 1983	vs. Chicago
Half-1st	28	Kelly Tripucka	Jan. 29, 1983	vs. Chicago
		Kelly Tripucka	March 12, 1982	vs. Golden State
Half-2nd	37	Dave Bing	April 1, 1968	vs. Boston
Quarter-1st	20	Kelly Tripucka	Nov. 12, 1983	vs. Kansas City
Quarter-2nd	23	Joe Dumars	Jan. 19, 1990	vs. Golden State
Quarter-3rd	24	Isiah Thomas	Feb. 26, 1984	vs. Cleveland
		Joe Dumars	April 12, 1989	at Cleveland
Quarter-4th	24	Isiah Thomas	March 12, 1983	vs. Atlanta
		Isiah Thomas	March 11, 1989	at Philadelphia
Field Goals				
Game	22	Dave Bing	Feb. 21, 1971	vs. Chicago
Half	14	Terry Dischinger	Nov. 14, 1967	vs. St. Louis
Quarter	11	Isiah Thomas	Feb. 26, 1984	vs. Cleveland
Field Goals Attempted				
Game	41	Bob Lanier	Feb. 21, 1971	vs. Chicago
Half	24	Bob Lanier	Feb. 21, 1971	vs. Chicago
Quarter	15	George Yardley	Jan. 3, 1959	vs. New York
Free Throws				
Game	20	George Yardley	Dec. 26, 1957	at St. Louis
		Walter Dukes	Jan. 19, 1961	at L.A. Lakers
		Kelly Tripucka	Jan. 29, 1983	vs. Chicago
Half	17	Adrian Dantley	Dec. 10, 1986	vs. Sacramento
Quarter	14	Adrian Dantley	Dec. 10, 1986	vs. Sacramento
Free Throws Attempted				
Game	24	George Yardley	Dec. 26, 1957	at St. Louis
		Walter Dukes	Jan. 19, 1961	at L.A. Lakers
		Bob Lanier	Oct. 13, 1978	vs. New Jersey

Half	20	Isiah Thomas	Oct. 26, 1985	at Chicago
Quarter	15	George Yardley	Dec. 25, 1957	vs. Minneapolis
3-Point Goals				
Game	10	Joe Dumars	Nov. 8, 1994	vs. Minnesota
Half	7	Allan Houston	Feb. 17, 1995	at Chicago
		Joe Dumars	April 5, 1995	at Orlando
Quarter	6	Allan Houston	March 10, 1995	vs. Denver
3-Point Goals Attempted				
Game	18	Joe Dumars	Nov. 8, 1994	vs. Minnesota
Half	11	Allan Houston	Feb. 17, 1995	at Chicago
Quarter	6	Joe Dumars	Feb. 26, 1993	vs. New York
		Isiah Thomas	Jan. 13, 1994	vs New York
		Joe Dumars	Jan. 24, 1994	vs. Chicago
		Marcus Liberty	April 24, 1994	at Philadelphia
Rebounds				
Game	34	Dennis Rodman	March 4, 1992	vs. Indiana (OT)
Half	21	Bailey Howell	Nov. 25, 1960	vs. L.A. Lakers
Quarter	14	Ray Scott	Dec. 20, 1961	vs. Philadelphia
Offensive Rebounds				
Game	18	Dennis Rodman	March 4, 1992	vs. Indiana (OT)
Half	8	Dennis Rodman	March 4, 1992	vs. Indiana (OT)
Quarter	6	Willie Norwood	Dec. 12, 1973	vs. L.A. Lakers
		Lindsay Hairston	Dec. 17, 1975	vs. Golden State
		Earl Cureton	Feb. 22, 1984	vs. New York
		Dennis Rodman	March 4, 1992	vs. Indiana (OT)
Defensive Rebounds				
Game	22	Dennis Rodman	March 14, 1992	at Sacramento
Half	16	Bill Laimbeer	Nov. 15, 1988	at Dallas
Quarter	9	Bill Laimbeer	April 6, 1989	vs. Chicago
Assists				
Game	25	Kevin Porter	March 9, 1979	vs. Boston
		Kevin Porter	April 1, 1979	vs. Phoenix
		Isiah Thomas	Feb. 13, 1985	vs. Dallas
Half	16	Isiah Thomas	Feb. 13, 1985	vs. Dallas
Quarter	11	Isiah Thomas	Jan. 24, 1985	vs. Golden State
		Isiah Thomas	Nov. 24, 1989	vs. Cleveland
Steals				
Game	9	Earl Tatum	Nov. 28, 1978	at L.A. Lakers
		Ron Lee	March 16, 1980	vs. Houston
Half	6	Chris Ford	March 26, 1976	at Chicago
		Isiah Thomas	Nov. 25, 1983	vs. Washington
Quarter	5	Chris Ford	March 25, 1975	vs. Golden State
		Ron Lee	Nov. 19, 1981	vs. Washington
		John Long	Dec. 3, 1983	vs. Indiana
Personal Fouls				
Quarter	6	Roger Brown	March 25, 1977	vs. Golden State
		Paul Mokeski	Jan. 24, 1981	vs. Cleveland
		Joe Dumars	Feb. 28, 1986	vs. Atlanta
Half	6	Terry Dischinger	Dec. 12, 1969	at Philadelphia
Turnovers				
Game	12	Kevin Porter	Feb. 7, 1979	at Philadelphia
Half	8	Isiah Thomas	April 19, 1985	vs. Indiana

Blocked Shots

Game	10	Edgar Jones	Dec. 17, 1981	vs. Indiana
Half	7	Edgar Jones	Dec. 17, 1981	vs. Indiana
		Terry Tyler	Nov. 3, 1982	vs. Chicago
Quarter	5	Terry Tyler	Nov. 10, 1978	vs. Chicago
		Terry Tyler	Feb. 7, 1980	vs. Seattle
		Terry Tyler	Feb. 15, 1980	vs. Philadelphia
		John Salley	Feb. 21, 1990	vs. Orlando

PLAYOFF RECORDS

CAREER

STAT	RECORD	PLAYER
Points	2,261	Isiah Thomas
Scoring Average	25.6	Bob Lanier
Field Goals	825	Isiah Thomas
Field Goals Attempted	1,869	Isiah Thomas
Free Throws	530	Isiah Thomas
Free Throws Attempted	689	Isiah Thomas
Rebounds	1,097	Bill Laimbeer
Offensive Rebounds	277	Dennis Rodman
Defensive Rebounds	840	Bill Laimbeer
Assists	987	Isiah Thomas
Steals	234	Isiah Thomas
Personal Fouls	408	Bill Laimbeer
Disqualifications	13	Bill Laimbeer
Blocked Shots	146	John Salley
Games Played	113	Bill Laimbeer

GAME (OR PORTION)

STAT	RECORD	PLAYER	DATE	OPPONENT
Points				
Game	44	Dave Bing	April 1, 1968	vs. Boston
Half	37	Dave Bing (2nd)	April 1, 1968	vs. Boston
Quarter	25	Isiah Thomas (3rd)	May 8, 1987	vs. Atlanta
		Isiah Thomas (3rd)	June 19, 1988	at L.A. Lakers
Field Goals				
Game	19	Dave Bing	April 1, 1968	vs. Boston
Half	16	Dave Bing (2nd)	April 1, 1968	vs. Boston
Quarter	11	Isiah Thomas	June 19, 1988	at L.A. Lakers
Field Goals Attempted				
Game	38	Dave Bing	April 1, 1968	vs. Boston
Half	28	Dave Bing (2nd)	April 1, 1968	vs. Boston
Quarter	17	Dave Bing (4th)	April 1, 1968	vs. Boston
Free Throws				
Game	14	Isiah Thomas	May 3, 1992	at New York
		Bob Ferry	March 18, 1961	vs. L.A. Lakers
Half	12	Bill Laimbeer (1st)	April 19, 1984	vs. New York
Quarter	10	Bill Laimbeer (1st)	April 19, 1984	vs. New York
Free Throws Attempted				
Game	17	Isiah Thomas	May 3, 1992	at New York
		Joe Dumars	June 13, 1989	at L.A. Lakers
Half	14	Joe Dumars (1st)	June 13, 1989	at L.A. Lakers
Quarter	10	Bill Laimbeer (1st)	April 19, 1984	vs. New York

Rebounds

Game	26	Dave DeBusschere	March 24, 1963	vs. St. Louis
Half	17	Dave DeBusschere (1st)	March 24, 1963	vs. St. Louis
Quarter	10	Bob Lanier (1st)	April 24, 1976	vs. Golden State
		Dennis Rodman (1st)	May 31, 1989	at Chicago

Offensive Rebounds

Game	10	John Salley	April 30, 1988	vs. Washington
Half	7	John Salley (2nd)	April 30, 1988	vs. Washington
Quarter	6	Dennis Rodman (1st)	April 28, 1991	vs. Atlanta

Defensive Rebounds

Game	16	Bill Laimbeer	May 21, 1987	at Boston
		Bill Laimbeer	June 14, 1990	at Portland
Half	11	Bob Lanier (2nd)	April 9, 1974	at Chicago
		Bill Laimbeer (2nd)	June 14, 1990	at Portland
Quarter	8	Dennis Rodman (4th)	May 31, 1989	at Chicago
		Bill Laimbeer (3rd)	June 14, 1990	at Portland

Assists

Game	16	Isiah Thomas	April 17, 1986	at Atlanta
		Isiah Thomas	April 24, 1984	at New York
Half	11	Isiah Thomas (1st)	April 17, 1986	at Atlanta
Quarter	8	Isiah Thomas (1st)	April 17, 1986	at Atlanta

Steals

Game	6	Isiah Thomas	April 22, 1984	at New York
Half	5	Dave Bing (2nd)	April 10, 1975	vs. Seattle
		Isiah Thomas (2nd)	April 22, 1984	at New York
Quarter	3	Six occasions		

Blocked Shots

Game	7	Bob Lanier	April 30, 1976	vs. Golden State
Half	6	Bob Lanier (2nd)	April 30, 1976	vs. Golden State
Quarter	5	Bob Lanier (3rd)	April 30, 1976	vs. Golden State

CONSECUTIVES

REGULAR SEASON RECORDS

Season

Free Throws	62	Joe Dumars (13 games)	March 9 - April 5, 1991
Games	574	Terry Tyler	Oct. 13, 1978 - April 14, 1985

GAME (OR PORTION)

Field Goals	13	Isiah Thomas	Feb. 26, 1984	vs. Cleveland
Free Throws	16	George Yardley	Feb. 4, 1958	vs. Syracuse
		Gene Shue	Nov. 10, 1961	at New York
		Isiah Thomas	Feb. 28, 1986	vs. Atlanta

PISTONS RECORD AGAINST ALL NBA TEAMS SINCE 1957

(Regular Season Only)

Detroit Pistons vs.	GP	HOME	ROAD	NEUT.	TOTAL
Atlanta Hawks (a)	269	66-56	47-77	10-13	123-146
Boston Celtics	235	39-71	22-74	4-25	65-170
Charlotte Hornets	38	12-7	8-11	—	20-18
Chicago Bulls	175	55-30	29-57	2-2	86-89
Cleveland Cavaliers	131	48-18	32-33	—	80-51
Dallas Mavericks	34	13-4	12-5	—	25-9
Denver Nuggets	48	15-9	11-13	—	26-22
Golden State Warriors (b)	196	52-34	28-57	5-20	85-111
Houston Rockets (c)	99	35-12	14-33	4-1	53-46
Indiana Pacers	108	39-15	20-34	—	59-49
Los Angeles Clippers (d)	76	30-8	20-18	—	50-26
Los Angeles Lakers (e)	213	33-59	29-65	15-12	77-136
Miami Heat	34	9-8	6-11	—	15-19
Milwaukee Bucks	158	43-36	22-55	0-2	65-93
Minnesota TimberWolves	16	7-1	5-3	—	12-4
New Jersey Nets (f)	100	34-16	25-25	—	59-41
New York Knicks	238	58-51	33-72	12-12	103-135
Orlando Magic	31	13-3	6-9	—	19-12
Philadelphia 76ers (g)	237	55-49	27-72	14-20	96-141
Phoenix Suns	93	26-21	17-28	1-0	44-49
Portland Trail Blazers	77	27-12	12-26	—	39-38
Sacramento Kings (h)	214	66-24	32-52	16-24	114-100
San Antonio Spurs	50	11-14	9-16	—	20-30
Seattle SuperSonics	95	29-17	12-32	5-0	46-49
Toronto Raptors	8	3-1	4-0	—	7-1
Utah Jazz (i)	56	17-11	8-20	—	25-31
Vancouver Grizzlies	4	2-0	2-0	—	4-0
Washington Wizards (j)	206	60-31	33-59	14-9	107-99
TOTALS	**3239**	**897-618**	**525-957**	**102-140**	**1524-1715**

(a) includes St. Louis Hawks 1957-68
(b) includes Philadelphia Warriors 1957-62 and San Francisco Warriors 1962-79
(c) includes San Diego Rockets 1967-71
(d) includes Buffalo Braves 1970-78 and San Diego Clippers 1978-84
(e) includes Minneapolis Lakers 1957-60
(f) includes New York Nets 1976-77
(g) includes Syracuse Nationals 1957-63
(h) includes Cincinnati Royals 1957-72 and Kansas City Kings 1972-85
(i) includes New Orleans Jazz 1974-79
(j) includes Chicago Bullets 1961-63, Baltimore Bullets 1963-74 and Washington Bullets 1974-97

ALL-TIME WINNING PERCENTAGES

Site	GP	W	L	PCT
Home	1515	897	618	.592
Road	1482	525	957	.354
Neutral	242	102	140	.421
TOTALS	**3239**	**1524**	**1715**	**.471**

PISTONS ATTENDANCE

ANNUAL ATTENDANCE

OLYMPIA STADIUM	GM	TOTAL	AVG
1957-58	28	134,411	4,789
1958-59	30	119,351	3,978
1959-60	31	178,007	5,742
1960-61	31	164,230	5,298

COBO ARENA	GM	TOTAL	AVG
1961-62	30	143,081	4,769
1962-63	30	144,150	3,806
1963-64	30	100,386	3,346
1964-65	30	121,239	4,011
1965-66	30	120,013	4,000
1966-67	30	193,782	6,459
1967-68	32	224,164	7,005
1968-69	38	201,433	5,301
1969-70	38	167,648	4,412
1970-71	41	283,913	6,925
1971-72	41	188,763	4,604
1972-73	41	212,094	5,190
1973-74	41	300,565	7,331
1974-75	41	307,180	7,492
1975-76	41	251,352	6,130
1976-77	41	303,792	7,410
1977-78	41	223,382	5,448

PONTIAC SILVERDOME	GM	TOTAL	AVG
1978-79	41	389,936	9,510
1979-80	41	333,233	8,128
1980-81	41	228,349	5,569
1981-82	41	406,317	9,910
1982-83	41	522,063	12,733
x-1983-84	41	652,865	15,923
x-1984-85	41	691,540	16,867
x-1985-86	41	695,239	16,957
x-1986-87	41	908,240	22,152
x-1987-88	41	1,066,505	26,012

THE PALACE	GM	TOTAL	AVG
1988-89	41	879,614	21,454
1989-90	41	879,614	21,454
1990-91	41	879,614	21,454
1991-92	41	879,614	21,454
1992-93	41	879,614	21,454
1993-94	41	785,187	19,151
1994-95	41	719,090	17,538
1995-96	41	730,573	17,819
1996-97	41	820,585	20,014

x-led league

LARGEST HOME CROWDS

(All at Silverdome)

DATE	ATT.	OPPONENT
x-Jan. 29, 1988	61,983	Boston
Feb. 14, 1987	52,745	Philadelphia
March 30, 1988	47,692	Atlanta
Feb. 21, 1987	44,970	Atlanta
Feb. 15, 1986	44,180	Philadelphia
Feb. 16, 1985	43,816	Philadelphia
yz-June 16, 1988	41,732	L.A. Lakers
March 14, 1987	41,311	Philadelphia
Feb. 13, 1988	40,369	Chicago
Jan. 8, 1988	40,278	L.A. Lakers
y-June 12, 1988	39,188	L.A. Lakers
y-June 3, 1988	38,912	Boston
Feb. 1, 1987	38,873	Chicago
April 5, 1987	37,712	Milwaukee
Feb. 28, 1988	37,462	Boston
Jan. 10, 1987	37,279	Boston
Feb. 12, 1988	35,884	Atlanta
March 31, 1984	35,407	Milwaukee
Feb. 11, 1984	35,364	San Antonio

x-NBA record

y-playoff game

z-final game at Silverdome